Project Management

Ninth Edition

DENNIS LOCK

GOWER

Published by
Gower Publishing Limited
Gower House
Croft Road
Aldershot
Hampshire GU11 3HR
England

Gower Publishing Company
Suite 420
101 Cherry Street
Burlington,
VT 05401-4405
USA

Dennis Lock has asserted his moral right under the Copyright, Designs and Patents Act, 1988, to be identified as the author of this work.

British Library Cataloguing in Publication Data
Lock, Dennis
  Project management. – 9th ed.
  1. Project management
  I. Title
  658.4'04

  ISBN-13: 978-0-566-08772-1 (pbk)
          978-0-566-08769-1 (hardback)

Library of Congress Cataloging-in-Publication Data
Lock, Dennis.
  Project management / by Dennis Lock. -- 9th ed.
    p.cm.
  Includes bibiliographical references and index.
  ISBN 978-0-566-08769-1 (hardback) -- ISBN 978-0-566-08772-1 (pbk) 1. Project management. I. Title.
  T56.8.L6 2007
  658.4'04--dc22
                                                              2006037664

Printed and bound in Great Britain by MPG Books Ltd, Bodmin, Cornwall

Project Management

Project and Programme Management Resources for Students

Gower have teamed up with a major provider of project management training, **ESI International**, to bring you a range of project and programme resources to support your learning.

Visit www.projectmanagement9.com and:

- **Download** white papers on topics as diverse as the project communication, project leadership, risk management and project troubleshooting.
- **View** professional project webinars from some of the leading presenters on project management covering topics such as: risk management, troubled project recovery, portfolio management, business requirements, earned value management, performance-based service contracting.
- **Learn** about the qualifications and development available from the PMI, Project Management Institute, the world's largest non-profit professional association in project management.
- **Link to** further resources, professional bodies, news sites and more.

These resources are designed to help you develop your learning on project management and start you on the road to professional qualifications or further development, once you have finished your degree or your current qualification.

Visit
www.projectmanagement9.com

Contents

List of Figures		*xiii*
Acknowledgments		*xix*
Preface to Ninth Edition		*xxi*

Chapter 1   **Introduction to Project Management**   **1**

Brief history of project management   1

Different types of projects   5

Project life cycles and life histories   7

Customers, clients, contractors and end users   12

Associations representing the profession of project management   13

References and further reading   15

Chapter 2   **Factors for Project Success or Failure**   **17**

Success or failure factors in relation to the initial project definition   17

Factors for success or failure during the project fulfilment (execution) period   19

Triangle of objectives and trade-offs between cost, performance and time   21

Perceptions of project success or failure beyond the three primary objectives   24

Identifying and ranking the stakeholders   25

Benefits realization   26

References and further reading   27

Chapter 3   **Defining the Project Task**   **29**

Importance of initial project definition   29

Projects which are difficult or impossible to define   29

Feasibility studies to improve early project definition   32

Checklists   32

Enquiries and proposals for new projects   34

Defining the project scope   37

Contractor's strategy and design specification   39

Specifications for internally funded projects   41

Developing and documenting the project specification   46

Chapter 4	**Estimating the Project Costs**	**49**
	Introduction to cost estimating	49
	Classification of costs as direct or indirect	51
	Estimating accuracy	51
	Classification of estimates according to confidence	52
	Estimating accuracy in relation to prices and profits	53
	Version control of project cost estimates	54
	Top-down or bottom-up?	55
	Compiling the task list	55
	Level of detail in project cost estimating	57
	Estimating formats	57
	Estimating manufacturing costs	61
	Estimating project labour costs	63
	Personal estimating characteristics	66
	Estimates for material and equipment costs	67
	Reviewing the cost estimates	68
	References and further reading	69
Chapter 5	**First Steps in Planning the Timescale**	**71**
	General introduction to project planning	71
	What makes an ideal project plan?	75
	Museum project: a case example	75
	Distinction between planning and scheduling	81
	References and further reading	81
Chapter 6	**Financial Appraisal and the Business Plan**	**83**
	Project feasibility analysis	83
	Different viewing platforms for the project investor and the project contractor	84
	Introduction to project financial appraisal methods	86
	Simple payback method	87
	Discounted cash flow	89
	How much confidence can we place in the data?	92
	Project funding	95
	References and further reading	97
Chapter 7	**Risk**	**99**
	Introduction to project risk management	99
	Identifying the possible risks	100
	Risk appraisal and analysis	100
	Risk register	104

	Methods for dealing with risks	105
	Insurance	107
	Planning for a crisis	112
	References and further reading	113
Chapter 8	**Project Authorization**	**115**
	Introduction to project authorization	115
	Project authorization criteria for the project owner	116
	Authorization documents issued by the project owner	118
	Project registration and numbering	120
	Project authorization in a contracting organization	121
	Authorizing work without a contract or customer's order	123
	References and further reading	125
Chapter 9	**Project Organization Structures**	**127**
	Effective organization and communications	127
	Organization charts	127
	Emergence of project management in a developing company	129
	Project matrix organizations	133
	Project teams and task forces	137
	Organization of central administration functions	139
	Which type of project organization is best?	140
	Organizations with more than one project manager	144
	References and further reading	148
Chapter 10	**Organization of Management Change and IT Projects**	**149**
	Special characteristics of management change projects	149
	Case example: the Coverite plc office relocation project	150
	PRINCE2™	154
	References and further reading	154
Chapter 11	**Key People in the Organization**	**155**
	Project manager	155
	Director of projects or programme manager	159
	Project engineer	159
	Project support office	161
	References and further reading	162
Chapter 12	**Work Breakdown and Coding**	**165**
	WBS concept	165
	Coding systems	170
	Benefits of a logical coding system	173

Choosing a coding system ... 175

What happens when the customer says 'You shall use my coding system!'? ... 176

References and further reading ... 177

Chapter 13 Completing the Breakdown Structures 179

Developing a project organization breakdown structure ... 180

Relationship between the project WBS and OBS ... 183

Introducing the cost breakdown structure ... 185

References and further reading ... 186

Chapter 14 Detailed Planning: An Introduction to Critical Path Networks 187

Gantt charts: their advantages and limitations ... 187

Background to critical path analysis ... 188

Different network notation systems ... 188

Critical path analysis using arrow diagrams ... 190

Critical path analysis using precedence notation ... 196

Case example: furniture project ... 199

More complex network notation ... 203

References and further reading ... 207

Chapter 15 Detailed Planning: Critical Path Networks in Practice 209

Developing the network logic ... 209

Level of detail in network planning ... 212

Interface events and activities ... 215

Milestones ... 215

Estimating task durations ... 216

Is the predicted timescale too long? ... 218

Case example: the museum project ... 218

A case for drawing networks from right to left ... 226

Network analysis as a management tool ... 227

References and further reading ... 228

Chapter 16 Principles of Resource Scheduling 229

What are resources and which of them can be scheduled? ... 229

Role of network analysis in resource scheduling ... 231

Resource scheduling case example: the garage project ... 231

Float (or slack) ... 240

Two fundamental priority rules for resource scheduling ... 245

Summary: the elements of a practicable schedule ... 247

References and further reading ... 248

Chapter 17 Scheduling People (and Other Reusable Resources)   **249**

Choosing which resources to schedule   249

Choice of resource units   251

Rate-constant and non rate-constant usage of resources   252

Specifying resource availability levels   253

Using different calendars for resource scheduling   254

Seven logical steps of project resource scheduling   256

References and further reading   257

Chapter 18 Scheduling Materials   **259**

Manufactured parts and materials scheduling compared with general
project scheduling   259

Identifying and quantifying common parts for manufacturing projects   260

Case example: a filing cabinet project   261

Line of balance   264

Computer solutions for scheduling manufacturing materials   272

Using purchase control schedules to schedule equipment for capital projects   272

References and further reading   274

Chapter 19 Scheduling Cash Flows   **275**

Cash flow scheduling in general   275

Scheduling cash flows in different kinds of projects   276

Using project management software to schedule cash outflows   281

Using the computer to schedule cash inflows   283

Conclusion   283

Chapter 20 Computer Applications   **285**

Choosing suitable software   285

Special network logic required for computer applications   291

Preparing for the first computer schedule   292

Case example: the garage project   299

Data entry errors   303

Network plotting   306

Time analysis of the garage project network   306

Resource scheduling for the garage project   308

Standard and customized output reports   313

Updating the schedules and reports   316

Chapter 21 Managing Project Start-up   **317**

Preliminary organization of the project   317

Correspondence and other documents   318

Engineering standards and procedures 322

Physical preparations and organization 323

Getting work started 325

Issuing detailed planning and work instructions 327

Chapter 22   Aspects of Commercial Management   331

Contracts 331

Purchase orders 334

Terms of trade used in international business (Incoterms 2000) 337

Pricing a contact proposal 338

Contract payment structures 340

Timing of payments 343

Financial viability of participating organizations 344

References and further reading 344

Chapter 23   Managing Procurement   345

Purchasing cycle 345

Roles in the purchasing organization for a large international project 346

Purchase specification: defining what has to be bought 349

Supplier selection 357

Purchase requisition and order 361

Expediting 364

Special timing of orders and deliveries 364

Purchase quantities 366

Purchase order amendments 367

Correlation between specification, enquiry, requisition and order numbers 367

Project or stock purchasing? 368

Marking and labelling goods before transit 369

Goods receipt 369

Stores administration 370

Vendors' documents 372

Materials management as a shared or common service 373

References and further reading 374

Chapter 24   Managing Progress   375

Progress management as a closed-loop control system 376

'Management by' styles 376

Updating schedules and records 379

Collecting progress information 380

Statistical checks 383

Managing the progress and quality of bought-in materials and equipment 383

Managing subcontractors and agency employees   387

Routine priority allocation in manufacturing projects   389

When the news is bad   390

Corrective measures   391

Immediate action orders   392

Construction site organization and management   395

Project meetings   396

Progress reports   401

References and further reading   402

Chapter 25   **Managing Changes**   **403**

Impact of changes in relation to the project life cycle 403

Origin and classification of changes   403

Authorization arrangements   406

General administration   408

Estimating the true cost of a change   411

Forms and procedures   414

Version control for modified drawings and specifications 422

Emergency modifications   424

Chapter 26   **Managing Project Costs**   **429**

Principles of cost control   429

Controlling variable costs   430

Controlling fixed costs and overhead cost recovery   431

Additional cost control factors   433

Total cost approach   434

Checklist of cost management factors   436

Setting and resetting cost budgets   437

Cost collection methods   438

Audits and fraud prevention measures   442

Comparing actual costs against planned costs   443

References and further reading   443

Chapter 27   **Earned-Value Analysis and Cost Reporting**   **445**

Milestone analysis   445

Earned-value analysis   450

Earned-value analysis prediction reliability and implications 455

Evaluating cost performance for materials and bought-in equipment 457

Effect of project changes on earned-value analysis   458

Project ledger concept   459

Predicting profitability for a whole project   459

Post mortem 464

References and further reading 464

Chapter 28   Managing Multiple Projects, Programmes and Portfolios   465

Project management or programme management? 465

Managing a portfolio of management change and IT projects 466

Multi-project resource scheduling 467

Project resource scheduling in the corporate context 473

References and further reading 474

Chapter 29   More Advanced or Less Frequently Used Techniques   475

Line of balance charts in construction projects 475

Dealing with network plans for large projects 477

PERT 478

Standard networks 480

Templates (standard network modules) 482

Chapter 30   Managing Project Closure   491

Reasons for closing a project 491

Formal project closure 492

Final project cost records 494

Disposal of surplus material stocks 494

Final project definition: the end of a continuous process 494

As-built condition of a manufacturing or capital engineering project 495

As-built condition of a multiple manufacturing project 497

As-built condition of a project that is interrupted before completion 498

Managing files and archives 500

Bibliography 503

Contents Comparison Between the Eighth and Ninth Editions 507

Index 511

List of Figures

1.1	Whistle-stop journey through project management history	2
1.2	Four project types	5
1.3	Project life cycle	8
1.4	More comprehensive example of a project life history	9
1.5	Demonstration of how the chapters in this book broadly follow a project life history	12
1.6	Examples of project relationships	13
2.1	Perceptions of success or failure during a project life history	18
2.2	Barnes's original triangle of objectives and some derivatives	21
2.3	Matrix of stakeholders' objectives	26
3.1	Definition of a large project from initial concept to completion	30
3.2	Part of a project definition checklist	33–4
3.3	Initial task checklist for a management change project	35–6
3.4	An action plan for screening and progressing sales enquiries	38
4.1	Typical summary layout of a project cost estimate	50
4.2	Project cost estimate arranged by the work breakdown structure	58
4.3	Useful format for general cost estimating	59
4.4	Format for estimating the costs of materials and bought-out equipment on larger projects	60
4.5	General purpose format for indicating the price of a small project	61
5.1	Project planning environment	72
5.2	Checklist for an ideal plan (shown checked early in the project life cycle)	76
5.3	Museum project: Gantt chart	78
5.4	Museum project: linked Gantt chart with date cursor set at week 15	79
5.5	Museum project: checklist comparing diary and linked Gantt chart plans	80
6.1	Luxury service apartments project: cost/benefit patterns	85
6.2	Boiler replacement project: payback calculation	88
6.3	Boiler replacement project: payback graphs	88
6.4	Table of discount factors for calculating net present values	89
6.5	Boiler replacement project: net present value calculation	90
6.6	Tollbridge project: net present value calculation	92
6.7	Histogram and probability curve from Monte Carlo Analysis	94
6.8	Chart comparing project cost and benefits after Monte Carlo analysis	95
7.1	Ishikawa fishbone diagram	101

7.2	Part of a failure, mode and effect matrix (FMEA)	102
7.3	Matrix for qualitative risk classification	102
7.4	Qualitative risk assessment matrix	103
7.5	Part of a failure, mode effect and criticality analysis matrix (FMECA)	104
7.6	Format of a risk register (or risk log)	105
7.7	Risk and insurance in project management	107
8.1	Example contents of a project initiation document (PID)	119
8.2	Project register	120
8.3	Works order example for a manufacturing project	122
8.4	Project authorization form used by a mining engineering company	123
8.5	Typical project engineering cost/time relationship	124
9.1	Organigram conventions	128
9.2	Example of a manufacturing organization	132
9.3	Project cycle	133
9.4	Functional matrix for a single project in a manufacturing company	134
9.5	Matrix organization for several simultaneous manufacturing projects	135
9.6	Matrix organization for mining, petrochemical or construction projects	136
9.7	Project team organization	138
9.8	Project team v balanced matrix	144
9.9	Hybrid organization	145
9.10	Project with more than one project manager	146
9.11	Joint venture organization	147
10.1	Coverite plc: development of the relocation project organization	151
11.1	Possible management roles in a matrix organization	161
11.2	Possible management roles in a multi-team organization	162
12.1	Simplified WBS for an automobile project	166
12.2	WBS for a national charity fundraising week	167
12.3	Part of the first three WBS levels for a very large mining project	168
12.4	Work breakdown for a project to build a new railway	169
12.5	Two alternative WBS patterns for a large wedding project	170
12.6	WBS and coding structure for a radiocommunications project	172
12.7	Detail from the work breakdown for the radiocommunications project	172
12.8	Project coding system used by a heavy engineering company	174
12.9	Project coding system used by a mining engineering company	175
13.1	Organigram of Cuttit Ltd	182
13.2	Lawnmower project: OBS	182
13.3	Lawnmower project: upper WBS levels	183
13.4	Lawnmower project: WBS in relation to the OBS (with cost account examples)	184
13.5	Lawnmower project: analysis of a cost account code (chosen at random)	185
13.6	WBS meets OBS and CBS	186
14.1	Main elements of arrow logic	191
14.2	Tree project using arrow notation	192
14.3	Example of arrow network time analysis	193
14.4	Three different methods for showing times on arrow networks	195
14.5	An activity in precedence notation	196
14.6	Tree project using precedence notation	198
14.7	Example of precedence time analysis	199

14.8	Furniture project: task list	200
14.9	Furniture project: activity-on-arrow network diagram	201
14.10	Furniture project: precedence network diagram	202
14.11	Furniture project: time analysis	203
14.12	Overlapping activities in arrow and precedence networks	204
14.13	Constraint options in precedence networks	206
14.14	Using dummies to clarify cluttered logic	206
15.1	Common error in arrow networks	211
15.2	Level of detail in a purchasing sequence	214
15.3	Network interfaces	215
15.4	Museum project: first precedence diagram	219
15.5	Museum project: time analysis of the initial network diagram	220
15.6	Museum project: network with crashed times	222
15.7	Museum project: time analysis after crash actions	223
15.8	Museum project: network crashed and fast-tracked	225
15.9	Museum project: time analysis after crashing and fast-tracking	226
16.1	Garage project: network diagram	234–35
16.2	Garage project: task list and time analysis	236
16.3	Garage project: bar chart and resource histogram – aggregation	237
16.4	Garage project: bar chart and resource histogram – resource-limited	239
16.5	Garage project: bar chart and resource histogram – time-limited	241
16.6	Garage project: float analysis of activity G1016 (10–16)	242
16.7	Time-limited versus resource-limited rules for resource scheduling	245
17.1	Rate constant and variable resource usage for a project task	253
17.2	The complexity of project resource scheduling	256
17.3	Seven logical steps to a practical project resource schedule	257
18.1	Filing cabinet project: exploded view of the product	261
18.2	Filing cabinet project: simple parts list	262
18.3	Filing cabinet project: family tree	264
18.4	Filing cabinet project: parts list arranged in subassemblies	265
18.5	Filing cabinet project: delivery data	265
18.6	Filing cabinet project: family tree redrawn for line of balance	266
18.7	Filing cabinet project: calculation of lead times for parts	267
18.8	Filing cabinet project: delivery commitment graph	268
18.9	Filing cabinet project: calculation for line of balance at day 4	269
18.10	Filing cabinet project: line of balance at day 4	270
18.11	Filing cabinet project: line of balance completed for day 4	271
18.12	Front page headings for a purchase control schedule	272
18.13	Complete purchase control schedule	274
19.1	Essential elements of a project cash outflow schedule	276
19.2	Project cash flow schedule for an outdoor concert	277
19.3	Essential elements of a project net cash flow schedule	278
19.4	Cash outflow schedule for a construction project	279
19.5	Net cash flow schedule for a construction project	280
19.6	Network detail needed to schedule purchase commitments and cash outflows	282
20.1	Suggested procedure for buying project management software	287
20.2	Checklist for choosing project management software	288–89

20.3	Suggested procedure for implementing new project management software	293
20.4	Garage project: precedence network diagram	300
20.5	Garage project: cost estimates	302
20.6	Garage project: data errors	305
20.7	Garage project: summary network plotted by *4c*	307
20.8	Garage project: time analysis using *Microsoft Project 2000*	309
20.9	Garage project: time-limited resource histograms using *Primavera*	311
20.10	Garage project: resource-limited resource histograms using *Primavera*	312
20.11	Garage project: cost report using *Primavera*	314
20.12	Garage project: useful cost and resource summary	315
21.1	Linear responsibility matrix	319
21.2	Document distribution matrix	320
21.3	Standard project start-up network	326
21.4	Possible column headings for a drawing schedule	329
22.1	Elements of a typical purchase order	335
22.2	Relationship between payment terms and the control needed	341
23.1	Value of purchasing in project management	346
23.2	Purchasing cycle	346
23.3	Elements of a purchasing organization for a large international project	347
23.4	Stages in the purchase of equipment for a large international project	350–52
23.5	Purchase specification: front sheet	354
23.6	Purchase specification: second sheet	355
23.7	Purchase specification: continuation sheet	356
23.8	Purchase enquiry request	358
23.9	Common arrangement for inviting and considering bids	360
23.10	Bid summary example	362
23.11	Purchase requisition	363
24.1	A familiar sign: but will this project start and finish on time?	375
24.2	Control loop	376
24.3	Materials shortage list format	378
24.4	Combined work-to list and progress questionnaire	381
24.5	Inspection and expediting report	385
24.6	Immediate action order	393
24.7	Construction site organization	396
24.8	Combined meeting agenda and action sheet	399
25.1	Cost of a given change in relation to project life cycle phases	404
25.2	Some origins of project changes	405
25.3	Decision tree for change requests	408
25.4	General-purpose change register	410
25.5	Car project: estimated modification cost	412
25.6	Project variation order	416
25.7	Engineering change request	418
25.8	Production permit or concession	419
25.9	Engineering query note	421
25.10	Inspection report	423
26.1	Project cost elements in the context of cost control	430
26.2	Typical project cost/time patterns and the impact of fixed costs	432

26.3	Three ways of recording the cost of project materials	439
26.4	Weekly timesheet	441
27.1	Comparison of actual costs against a time-scaled budget	446
27.2	Project cost and achievement comparison using milestones	448
27.3	Data for a milestone chart	449
27.4	Earned-value analysis for an engineering department	454
27.5	Cost/profit prediction graph	461
27.6	Tabulated project cost report	463
28.1	Programme of projects in a large contracting company	466
28.2	Managing a multi-project model	470
29.1	Five-house project: Gantt chart	476
29.2	Five-house project: line of balance chart	476
29.3	Eighty-house project: line of balance chart	477
29.4	Rolling wave planning	478
29.5	Breaking down a large project plan into subnetworks	479
29.6	Transfer line project: early example of standard network module (template)	483
29.7	Transfer line project: procurement and machining template	484
29.8	Templating case example: template library principle	485
29.9	Templating case example: standard start template TCSAA and template B	486
29.10	Templating case example: template D and standard finish template TCSFF	487
29.11	Templating case example: template library browser	488
29.12	Templating case example: network diagram	488
29.13	Templating case example: network fragment	488
29.14	Templating case example: Gantt chart produced by *4c*	489
30.1	Project closure notice with checklist	493
30.2	Build schedule sheet	499

Acknowledgements

I am grateful to the following people and organizations who have helped in different but valuable ways in the preparation of this edition and its immediate predecessor:

4c Systems Limited
Dr Martin Barnes
Professor Sally Brailsford
Association for Project Management
Alan Fowler
Primavera
Robert Pow
Welcom Software

Artemis Views is a registered trademark. *Deltek Open Plan™* is a registered trademark of Deltek. *Primavera Project Planner* is a registered trademark. *PRINCE2* is a trademark of the Office of Government Commerce. *Windows* and *PowerPoint* are trademarks of Microsoft Corporation. *4c* is a trademark of 4c Systems Limited.

Preface to Ninth Edition

The changes for each new edition of *Project Management* are fuelled largely by my continued learning and experience. This knowledge originated from my experiences as a manager working in a number of quite different industries, augmented by a number of successful and fulfilling consultancy assignments. I have enjoyed the *schadenfreude* frisson of learning from the mistakes of others, and equally from the humiliating embarrassments of my own errors. A rich source in more recent years has come from the challenge of teaching well over 1000 post-graduate management students from all parts of the world, an experience that (apart from one unpleasant encounter with a cohort of ten surly English MBA aspirants) has proved wholly and mutually challenging and very rewarding.

Somewhere embedded in all this learning experience is the advice that I receive from time to time from reviewers, almost all of whom have been encouraging and supportive. A few have even been so kind as to offer free advice. One kind reviewer of the eighth edition suggested that my chapter sequence should be changed to observe more strictly the life cycle pattern of a typical project. This book has always vaguely been modelled on the start-to-finish progress path of a project, but I am very grateful to that reviewer for his good advice. As a direct result I have taken this book apart and rebuilt it so that it now sticks far more faithfully to the project life cycle phases from initial project idea to final closure. This closer adherence to the project life cycle has allowed the chapters to follow in a continuous, almost seamless flow and for that reason it was no longer necessary to divide the book into the separate parts used in earlier editions.

Every new edition seems to grow in size. That has never been my direct intention, but it still happens every time. I perform my own brand of liposuction to remove surplus fat, and I excise material that no longer enjoys being flavour of the month. This time, for instance, I have saved considerable space by consolidating the two former cost estimating chapters into one, by merging three computing chapters into one, and by condensing the three previous purchasing chapters into one. Nothing of any substance has been lost through these consolidations which, together, should have reduced the number of chapters from the former 25 to 20. Yet the book has instead grown to 30 chapters, and the number of illustrations has increased from 164 to very nearly 200. These statistics indicate the extensive scope of this revision.

Work breakdown structure and coding is now given more prominence as a separate chapter and the new chapters subjects include:

- factors for project success or failure;
- first steps in planning the timescale;
- financial appraisal and the business plan;
- organization of business change and IT projects;
- key people in the organization;

- combining the work-, organization- and cost-breakdown structures;
- scheduling cash flows;
- advanced or less frequently used project management methods.

All the former case studies have been reviewed and augmented. Some of these are fairly detailed, whilst others are simply vignettes drawn from my past experiences. To be consistent these are now all referred to as case examples.

The general balance of the book has changed slightly to include more on management change and IT projects, against which there is now slightly less emphasis on manufacturing projects and production operations.

I feel moved to mention one old favourite that is missing from this new edition. I have used the gantry project as a case example in all previous editions of this book and in countless lectures to illustrate critical path network logic and time analysis. I realized some time ago that building a stand-alone gantry on a remote hillside was a particularly useless endeavour, and I am astonished that no one has ever questioned the motives or provenance of that futile project. Now it's dead and buried (probably on the same remote hillside) and will soon be forgotten. I doubt whether it will find any mourners, but it left a gap that needed a replacement and for that I have introduced a more realistic refurbishment project for a museum and art gallery.

As ever, I always have the reader in my mind's eye as I write, and I have particular sympathy with the many students attending our universities whose first language is not English. Thus I try to avoid unnecessary jargon or management-speak. I attempt to write in English that is readily understandable, and which does not require the reader to have a dictionary constantly on hand.

Every diagram has been reviewed or is new for this edition, and I have taken great care taken to ensure that each supports the text and is legible and accurate.

Most chapters end with a 'References and further reading' section. The few do that not deal with subjects that are very poorly represented in the literature. There is, once again, a general bibliography and that has been updated as far as possible.

I want to acknowledge the assistance of Robert Pow who, once again, has reviewed and corrected the insurance section in Chapter 7. I am very grateful to Alan Fowler who, as well as being managing director of Isochron Ltd, is a person of tremendous ability, imagination and forward thinking. My synergistic collaboration with him on another Gower book taught me a great deal in a very short time about huge management change and IT projects, and I have drawn on that experience for this ninth edition. I have almost come to take for granted the expert and highly professional team at Gower, every member of which has been magnificent and supportive throughout.

Dennis Lock

1 *Introduction to Project Management*

Project management has evolved to plan, coordinate and control the complex and diverse activities of modern industrial, commercial and management change and IT projects. All projects share one common characteristic – the projection of ideas and activities into new endeavours. The ever-present element of risk and uncertainty means that the events and tasks leading to completion can never be foretold with absolute accuracy. Examples abound of projects that have exceeded their costs by enormous amounts, finishing late or even being abandoned before completion. Such failures are far too common, seen in all kinds of projects in industry, commerce and (especially, it seems) the public sector.

The purpose of project management is to foresee or predict as many of the dangers and problems as possible and to plan, organize and control activities so that projects are completed successfully in spite of all the risks. This process should start well before any resource is committed, and must continue until all work is finished. The primary aim of the project manager is for the result to satisfy the project sponsor or purchaser and all the other principal stakeholders, within the promised timescale and without using more money and other resources than those that were originally set aside or budgeted.

BRIEF HISTORY OF PROJECT MANAGEMENT

Clearly, man-made projects are not new: monuments surviving from the earliest civilizations testify to the incredible achievements of our forebears and still evoke our wonder and admiration. Modern projects, for all their technological sophistication, are not necessarily greater in scale than some of those early mammoth works. But economic pressures of the industrialized world, competition between rival companies, and greater regard for the value, well-being and hence the employment costs of working people have all contributed to the development of new project management ideas and techniques. Figure 1.1 is a cursory, rather light-hearted romp through the history of project management. It makes generalizations and the dates are approximate, but the story is interesting and an appropriate introduction to the fascinating subject of project management. Those with the time available to study an authoritative and comprehensive account of project management history should read Morris (1994).

Projects from prehistory to Victorian times (before 1900)

Projects from ancient times have left impressive legacies on our architectural and industrial culture. We wonder how some of those early masters managed without the technology that is readily and cheaply available today. However, with the exception of a few notable philanthropic employers,

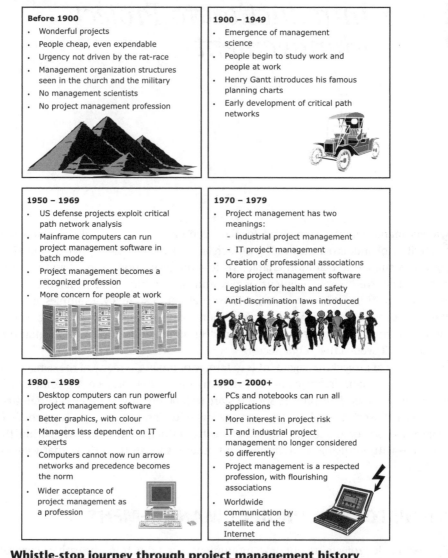

Before 1900
- Wonderful projects
- People cheap, even expendable
- Urgency not driven by the rat-race
- Management organization structures seen in the church and the military
- No management scientists
- No project management profession

1900 – 1949
- Emergence of management science
- People begin to study work and people at work
- Henry Gantt introduces his famous planning charts
- Early development of critical path networks

1950 – 1969
- US defense projects exploit critical path network analysis
- Mainframe computers can run project management software in batch mode
- Project management becomes a recognized profession
- More concern for people at work

1970 – 1979
- Project management has two meanings:
  - industrial project management
  - IT project management
- Creation of professional associations
- More project management software
- Legislation for health and safety
- Anti-discrimination laws introduced

1980 – 1989
- Desktop computers can run powerful project management software
- Better graphics, with colour
- Managers less dependent on IT experts
- Computers cannot now run arrow networks and precedence becomes the norm
- Wider acceptance of project management as a profession

1990 – 2000+
- PCs and notebooks can run all applications
- More interest in project risk
- IT and industrial project management no longer considered so differently
- Project management is a respected profession, with flourishing associations
- Worldwide communication by satellite and the Internet

Figure 1.1   Whistle-stop journey through project management history

concern for the welfare and safety of workers was generally lacking and many early project workers actually lost their lives through injuries, disease and sheer physical exhaustion. People were often regarded as a cheap and expendable resource.

Formal management organization structures have existed from early times, but these flourished in military, church and civil administrations rather than in industry. Industrial organization came much later. I have an organization chart showing a Chinese bridge-building team that is reputed to date back to the Ming dynasty (1368–1644) but that was an army team.

Projects before 1900 were generally managed by the creative architects and engineers themselves. Many of us are familiar with stories of the giants who flourished in the latter part of this historical period; people such as Sir Christopher Wren (1632–1723), Thomas Telford (1757–1834) and Isambard Kingdom Brunel (1806–59). You can read about Brunel in Vaughan (1991). There was no separately recognized profession of project management. Commonsense, determination, hard work (sometimes at the expense of neglecting personal health) usually got the job done. The time had not yet come for the industrial engineers and behavioural scientists who would eventually study working practices, organization theory and people at work.

1900 to 1949

Rapid industrialization and the demands of munitions production in World War 1 saw the emergence of management scientists and industrial engineers such as Elton Mayo and Frederick Winslow Taylor, who studied people and productivity in factories (Kanigel, 1997). Henry Ford made production-line manufacture famous with his Model T automobile and, especially important for project managers, Henry Gantt (1861-1919), who worked for Taylor, developed his now-famous charts which are still popular and used universally today.

It is not generally appreciated that early examples of critical path networks were developed before 1950, although their value was not widely appreciated at the time. Without the existence of computers, they were inflexible to change, tedious to translate into working schedules and thus impracticable and difficult to use. Gantt's bar charts were generally preferred, often set up on proprietary charts that allowed rescheduling using movable magnetic or plug-in strips or cards. Everything from the allocation of work to people and machines to holiday schedules was controlled by charts, usually prominently displayed on office walls.

1950 to 1969

The emergence of mainframe digital computers made the processing and updating of critical path networks faster and easier. The American defence industry and Du Pont were among the organizations quick to exploit this powerful planning and scheduling tool in the 1950s. The manufacturing and construction industries soon came to recognize the benefits of these new methods.

Computers were large, extremely expensive, and required their own dedicated air-conditioned clean rooms. Their capital and operating costs were beyond the budgets of all but the biggest organizations, so that many planners in smaller companies bought their computing time from bureaux, where project schedules were processed in batch mode. These bureau facilities were provided both by computer manufacturers and by large companies whose computers had free time. It was at this time that I cut my project management teeth, and I have fond memories of being able to plan and control projects and programmes of multiple projects very successfully, although processing time was measured in days rather than in today's nanoseconds.

Project management became a recognized job description, if not yet a respected profession. Companies were showing more concern for the welfare of people at work, although discrimination because of race, sex and age was still too common. The year 1968 saw publication of the first edition of this book, at a time when most other publications dealt with planning and scheduling as separate techniques rather than treating project management holistically as a management discipline.

1970 to 1979

This period saw rapid growth in information technology, or 'IT' (as it soon became known). Industrial project management continued as before, but with more project management software available and wider recognition of the role. However, the spread of IT brought another, different kind of project manager on the scene. These were the IT project managers: people who had no project planning or scheduling experience and no interest or desire to learn those methods. They possessed instead the technical and mental skills needed to lead teams developing IT projects. These IT project managers were usually senior systems analysts, and one of their characteristics was their scarcity. High demand for their services led them to make frequent career jumps, moving rapidly up a generous salary scale.

Development of the professional project management associations grew during this period, which also saw the development of legislation to protect workers' health and safety. Other new laws were intended to discourage unfair discrimination of people because of their race, religious beliefs or sex.

Although project management software became more widely available, processing continued to be carried out on big expensive mainframe computers in batch mode. Graphics were primitive compared with modern equipment. Data input was still accomplished by copying data from network diagrams on to coding sheets from which cards had to be punched and verified, sometimes needing two cards for every network activity. After sorting, these punched cards had to be taken to trained computer operators, who worked in clean air-conditioned rooms where entry was usually forbidden to project managers. The first process results always seemed to produce a large pile of print-out listing a crop of errors that needed considerable detective work before the faults could be identified, and then corrected by punching several new cards before the computer could produce its practical working schedules.

All the output reports in those early computing days came as text from line printers, so that graphics such as bar charts were crudely formed from patterns of alphanumeric characters. Yet the process was stimulating, exciting and fun. We had our mishaps, for example when over 2000 pre-sorted punched cards were accidentally scattered over the floor of the London taxicab that was transporting them to the computer bureau. But we got our schedules calculated, managed our projects and enjoyed ourselves in the process.

1980 to 1989

During this decade project managers became far less dependent upon IT experts. They now had their own desktop computers that could run most project management software. Graphics were greatly improved, with smaller printers available locally in the office that could produce complex charts in many colours. However, productivity did not match this growth in technology as quickly as one might have expected because managers became more interested in the technology itself than in the work that it was intended to manage. People were frequently seen grouped round each other's screens asking questions such as 'What happens if you do this?' and 'Have you tried that?' or 'Why has it crashed and lost all my data?' In other words, managers had to learn to become 'computer literate' and be far less dependent on IT experts.

Software that could run activity-on-arrow networks became obsolete. All planners have since had to use activity-on-node (precedence) networks in their computers and adapt to the relatively small areas of network visible on the small screen. However, processing times were cut dramatically, so that schedules could be up and running much faster for new projects. Schedules could now be updated almost immediately from the planner's own keyboard to cope with progress information and project changes.

1990 to the present day

Practically all software suppliers recognized the need to make their products compatible with Microsoft Windows. Microsoft themselves introduced Microsoft Project into their Office suite of programs. One or two operating and plotting faults in very early versions of Microsoft Project were eliminated in later versions, and the program is now by far the most widely used, especially among students who appreciate its user-friendly features (www.microsoft.com/office/project). However, many professionals continue to use programs at the high end of the software market, preferring their greater power, versatility and adaptability for particular project applications.

Project risk is taken seriously and people pay more attention to predicting risk events so that contingencies and risk mitigation strategies can be planned.

Of immense importance is the power of communication made possible by satellites and the Internet, effectively shrinking the world and making it possible to transmit drawings, reports and other documents almost instantaneously to almost anywhere.

Project management is no longer considered as two separate branches (one for industrial projects and another for IT projects). There is wider and welcome acceptance that managing company changes as projects can bring faster and better results.

Many good books dealing comprehensively with all aspects of project management (except purchasing) are now available in most languages, and there is no shortage of training courses. Well-regarded professional qualifications awarded by universities, management schools and the professional organizations can be gained by those who follow the appropriate training and can demonstrate competence. With this wealth of knowledge and experience we might ask why so many modern projects fail so dramatically. Eurotunnel, for example, operates at the time of writing with an unmanageable debt burden exceeding £6.5 billion. The new Wembley Stadium project finished late and cost twice its original budget. Government IT projects are not exempt from spectacular failure. We hear of projects that suffer 'soaring costs', yet the UK annual cost inflation is at the very low rate of around 2 per cent.

In spite of the failures, we should be proud of the many successful modern projects, in aviation, aerospace, construction, medicine and all other branches of human industry. Apart from the threat of hostilities and terrorism, it seems certain that climate change and the exhaustion of natural fossil fuel resources will provide the biggest challenges in the future. We shall need effective project managers to deal with these challenges if humankind is to survive.

DIFFERENT TYPES OF PROJECTS

The principal identifying characteristic of a project is its novelty. It is a step into the unknown, fraught with risk and uncertainty. No two projects are ever exactly alike: even a repeated project will differ from its predecessor in one or more commercial, administrative or physical aspects. However, I have found it possible and convenient to classify projects as four different general types. These are shown in Figure 1.2.

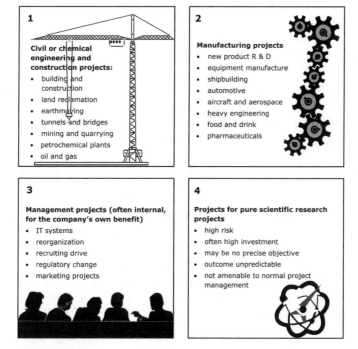

Figure 1.2   Four project types

Type 1 projects: civil engineering, construction, petrochemical, mining and quarrying

Projects in this category are those which spring most readily to mind whenever industrial projects are mentioned. One common feature is that the actual work (the fulfilment phase) must be conducted on a site that is exposed to the elements, and usually remote from the contractor's head office. As such they are often open to the public gaze.

These projects incur special risks and problems of organization. They may require massive capital investment, and they deserve (but do not always get) rigorous management of progress, finance and quality. Operations are often hazardous so that health and safety aspects demand special attention, particularly in heavy work such as construction, tunnelling and mining.

For very large industrial projects the funding and resources needed can be too great for one contractor to risk or even find. The organization and communications are therefore likely to be complicated by the participation of many different specialists and contractors, possibly with the main players acting together through a consortium or joint venture company established specifically for the project.

Type 2 projects: manufacturing

Manufacturing projects result in the production of a piece of mechanical or electronic equipment, a machine, ship, aircraft, land vehicle, or some other product or item of specially designed hardware. The finished product might be purpose-built for a single customer but internal research and development projects for products to be sold in all market sectors also fall into this manufacturing category.

Manufacturing projects are usually conducted in a laboratory, factory or other home-based environment, where the company should easily be able to exercise on-the-spot management and provide an optimum environment in which to do and manage the work. Of course, these ideal conditions do not always apply. Some manufacturing projects involve work away from the home base, for example in installing and commissioning a machine or equipment on a customer's premises, customer training and post-project service and maintenance.

More difficult is the case of a complex product that is developed and manufactured by a consortium of companies, sometimes with members based in different countries. A common example is aircraft production, where the engines might be developed and manufactured in one country, the wings in another and the final assembly taking place in a third country. Such international manufacturing projects are prone to higher risk and difficulties in control and coordination arising through organizational complexity, national rivalries, contracts, long-distance communications, multiple languages and conflicting technical standards.

Type 3 projects: IT projects and projects associated with management change

This class of project proves the point that every company, whatever its size, can expect to need project management expertise at least once in its lifetime. These are the projects that arise when companies relocate their headquarters, develop and introduce a new computer system, launch a marketing campaign, prepare for a trade exhibition, produce a feasibility or other study report, restructure the organization, mount a stage show, or generally engage in any operation that involves the management and coordination of activities to produce an end result that is not identifiable principally as an item of hardware or construction.

Not all projects are conducted commercially or for profit. Most not-for-profit organizations, including national and local government departments, professional associations, charities and disaster relief agencies conduct projects that fall into this category of management projects.

Although management projects do not usually result in a visible, tangible creation such as a piece of hardware, much often depends on their successful outcome and they can require enormous investment. There are several well-known cases where, for instance, failure to implement a new computer system correctly has caused serious operational breakdown, exposing the managers responsible to public discredit. Effective project management is at least as important for these projects as it is for the largest construction or manufacturing project.

Type 3 projects may be associated with or even depend upon Type 1 or Type 2 projects. For example, if a company decides to relocate to a new, purpose-built office, the overall relocation project is itself a Type 3 management project but its success will depend also on the Type 1 project needed to construct the new building. Thus projects of different types may be associated with each other in a company's project programme or project portfolio.

Type 4 projects: projects for pure scientific research

Pure scientific research projects (not to be confused with research and development projects) are truly a special case. They occasionally result in dramatically profitable discoveries. On the other hand, they can consume vast amounts of money over many years, yet yield no practical or economic result. Research projects carry the highest risk because they attempt to extend the boundaries of current human knowledge. The project objectives are usually difficult or impossible to define and there may be no awareness of the possible outcome. Therefore, pure research projects are not usually amenable to the project management methods that can be applied to industrial, manufacturing or management projects.

Some form of control over pure research projects must, however, be attempted. Money and other resources cannot be spent without any form of monitoring or restraint. Budgets have to be set in line with available funding.

A sensible method for controlling a pure scientific research project is to conduct regular management reviews and reassessments of the potential value of the project. At each of these reviews, a decision can be taken to stop the project (known colloquially as pulling the plug) or release new funding to allow it to continue at least until the next review. Although this can be unsettling for the scientists involved, the project sponsor is not expected to pour money for ever into a vast hole. This procedure, where continued project funding is dependent upon the outcome of regular reviews, is known as *stage-gate control*.

Although the research activities might themselves lie outside the scope of familiar project management methods, the provision of accommodation, communications, equipment and research materials might well constitute Type 1, 2 or 3 capital investment projects to which proper project management can and must be applied.

PROJECT LIFE CYCLES AND LIFE HISTORIES

Some projects come into being gradually, and others fade out slowly, so that their precise beginning and end dates can be difficult to recognize. However, most projects have not only actual beginning and end dates but also one or more significant dates between these can be identified as key events or 'milestones'.

The period between the beginning and end of a project is usually referred to as the project life cycle. It is convenient and necessary here to introduce three key players in the project life cycle:

- *The customer* (in some projects known as the client) is the person or organization that wants to buy the project and put the end product to use in its own business or sell (or lease) it on to a third party.
- *The contractor* is the organization principally responsible to the customer for carrying out the project work.
- *The project manager* is a person employed by the contractor (or occasionally by the customer) to plan and manage all the project activities so that the project is finished on time, within budget and within its specification.

These definitions do not apply strictly to all projects, but they are adequate for the purposes of this introductory chapter. In a Type 3 management project, the customer and the contractor might reside within the same company, so that the company's executives (who represent the customer in this case) instruct a departmental manager (the contractor) to carry out a project for the company's own use. However, such complexities can be disregarded for the moment: organization patterns and roles will be discussed more exhaustively in Chapters 9, 10 and 11.

Life cycle of small projects

Consider, first, the typical life cycle of small projects: projects that have relatively short duration, do not involve large amounts of capital expenditure and are relatively straightforward to manage. Most authorities and writers, when they talk about the life cycle of a project, refer to the period that begins with the authorization of work on the project (or signing of a customer-contractor contract) up to the handover of the desired product to the customer. This can be a view that is too simplistic, but it is the part of projects that is of most concern to their project managers. Figure 1.3 shows that the activities which take place during this period do form a true cycle, because they begin and end with the customer.

Travelling clockwise round the cycle reveals a number of steps or *phases*, each of which is represented by a circle in the diagram. The boundaries between these phases are usually blurred in

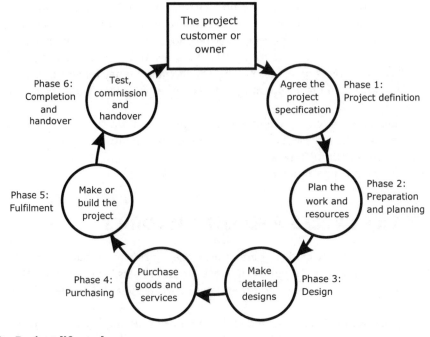

Figure 1.3   Project life cycle

practice, because the phases tend to overlap. For example, some project purchasing and fulfilment work can usually start before well before design is complete.

This view of a project life cycle is, in very many cases, too simplistic because it ignores everything that happens before the start of actual work, and also takes no account of what happens to the project after its delivery to the customer. For a more complete picture, we really have to consider not only the project life cycle as seen by the project manager, but also the entire life history of the project from its conception to death and disposal.

More comprehensive view of the project life cycle or history

The simple life cycle shown in Figure 1.3 holds good for small, relatively simple projects but for most capital projects many more phases can usually be identified. For example, the six phases of Figure 1.3 have grown to 15 separately identifiable phases in Figure 1.4, which represents the life history of a fairly large capital project. Projects differ so greatly that there is no such thing as a typical life history pattern but the sequence in Figure 1.4 is broadly applicable to capital projects that involve many stakeholders and public interests (stakeholders are discussed in Chapter 2).

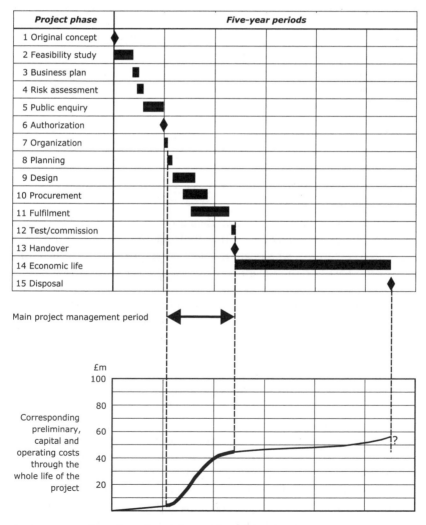

Figure 1.4   More comprehensive view of a project life history

Explanation of the life history phases

The upper portion of Figure 1.4 is a Gantt chart setting out the phases of a large capital project against the total life history timescale (for more on Gantt charts see Chapter 14). In this case, the total period spanned by the project is about 27.5 years, but remember that this is only an example: actual cases might be anything from one or two years to several decades.

All projects begin as a concept, a gleam in the eye of their progenitor. An entrepreneur or organization recognizes the need for a project and forms an initial idea that justifies further investigation. Phases 1 to 4 comprise this formative period, which should end in proposals and a business plan that describes the project, sets out the financial requirements, the intended benefits and the principal milestones. Taken together, these early phases form the initial project definition.

Projects in the public eye, or which have significant potential environmental or social impact, might have to be subjected to one or more public enquiries and prolonged planning applications (Phase 5), which can seriously delay or even prevent the start of the actual project.

Once everyone has agreed the project definition, all permissions have been granted, and the funds are available, the project can be authorized (Phase 6). Authorization should really be almost an instantaneous event or milestone rather that a time-consuming phase, but some organizations are very cautious about this process and can drag their feet for several months before agreeing to release the funds and other resources required for the project to start.

When the project has been authorized, the organization has to be put in place. This is Phase 7 in our example and, together with Phase 8, constitutes the project start-up period. Phase 7 includes the appointment of the project manager and the setting aside or provision of office space and other accommodation. Only then can real work on the project start, which is signalled by the project manager arranging for detailed planning and mobilization of the workforce (Phase 8).

Phases 9, 10 and 11 cover the overlapping periods of design, procurement and manufacture or construction (or, for Type 3 projects, management change). The project is finished when it is handed over to the customer to be put into operational use (Phase 13) but this cannot usually be done before the contractor has carried out commissioning and tests or trials (Phase 12) to ensure that the project will be fit for its intended purpose.

Many project management publications limit their account of the project life cycle or life history to Phases 6 through 13. The reason for this is that these are the phases that most directly involve the control of the project manager, who might not actually come on to the scene until Phase 6 or 7. They constitute the most active or fulfilment period of the project life history and can be compared loosely with the life cycle in Figure 1.3.

Another glance at Figure 1.4 shows that our version of the project life history not only begins much earlier than some published versions, but also does not finish until very much later, when the outcome of the original project has come to the end of its useful economic life and is scrapped or otherwise disposed of.

Expenditure in relation to the project life history

The graph in the lower portion of Figure 1.4 sets out a pattern of expenditure that might be expected throughout the life history of a project. It is drawn on the same timescale as the Gantt chart above and indicates general patterns of expenditure rather than actual monetary levels (since total costs obviously vary enormously between different projects).

Some expenditure must be made by the project owner or sponsor during the formative, definition phases. In our example I have shown this expenditure to be at a modest level but some projects require considerable investigation before they can actually start. A feasibility study costing many millions of pounds might have to be commissioned to explore the risks, benefits and best strategy for the proposed project. Public enquiries and wrangling over the specification can delay the project start and soak up yet more money. The new Wembley Stadium project, for example, underwent a prolonged definition period that consumed some of the time and money that had originally been set aside for the actual construction. Some large projects might even be preceded by pilot projects that themselves demand substantial investment.

The portion of the expenditure curve drawn with a bold line corresponds to the project fulfilment period when the project manager is actively involved. Almost all the money spent during this time should be built into the real project, to add value as well as cost. This is one area of the life history where we can be reasonably confident that the pattern will be similar from one project to the next. Expenditure usually builds up very slowly as people are gradually assigned to work on the project, with only a relatively few staff involved in the early stages to carry out initial design and planning. Later, as working drawings or specifications begin to emerge from the designers or technologists, money has to be committed in buying materials and equipment so that the main workforce can be engaged to use these purchases to fulfil the project. Nearer the end of the fulfilment phase (Phase 11 in our example) most purchasing costs are over, and people begin to leave the workforce, so that the rate of expenditure falls. This expenditure pattern (although not the vertical scale) can be claimed as typical of most projects and is commonly known as the S-curve. It is the time when the project manager has most direct influence over control of the project's capital costs.

Phase 14 marks the end of expenditure on the project's capital cost and the project moves into a completely different mode. This is the useful operating life of the project, when all the expenditure involved is incurred by the project customer (the project owner) in operating, maintenance, repairs and consumable materials. This is the period, for example, during which a building can be occupied, an IT system remains accurate and efficient, a special machine continues to perform its designed task, a mine or quarry produces minerals on an economic scale or a drug continues to be dispensed to patients before a new, improved drug is developed by the pharmaceutical industry.

When the project nears the end of its economic life, either the owner has no further use for it or the costs of operating, maintenance and repair begin to rise to uneconomic proportions. So the time comes to dispose of the project. In the case of a building this might be centuries after it was originally built, with ownership having been transferred many times as different occupants come and go. On the other hand, a modern high technology project might be rendered obsolete after only a few years of successful operation. In some cases the redundant project can be sold on to a third party for scrap, yielding a small cash inflow. At the other extreme, disposal costs for a nuclear power generating station can rival or even exceed the original capital costs, owing to difficulties in handling and storing materials that are dangerously radioactive. For that reason, I have shown a question mark at the end of the project life history costs, because the disposal costs (or cash returns) are so very different from one project to the next.

Chapters of this book in relation to the project life history

Figure 1.5 sets out the life history of a large project again, but this time it is presented as a flow chart instead of the Gantt chart seen in Figure 1.4. A flow chart such as this is an elementary form of the activity-on-node network planning method described in Chapter 15. In practice the sequence can be slightly more complicated because some tasks have to be repeated at different stages in the life of the project as more detailed information becomes available. For example, cost estimating (Chapter 4) requires a simple version of the coded work breakdown structures that must be developed later in the project (described in Chapters 12 and 13). However, Figure 1.5 shows that the chapters in this book have been arranged as far as possible in line with the life history phases of a large project.

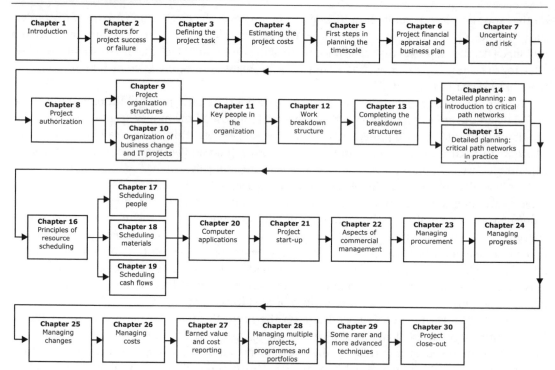

Figure 1.5 Demonstration of how the chapters in this book broadly follow a project life history

CUSTOMERS, CLIENTS, CONTRACTORS AND END USERS

Throughout this book I have used the following expressions to represent the three principal parties in a project contract:

- *Customer* – the person or organization for which the project is being conducted. I have also used the terms *client* and *project owner* in this context, although these are not always true synonyms. The project customer is traditionally a person or organization that pays another organization money in return for a project. However, in many management change projects the company is, in effect, both customer and contractor, with the board or senior management of the company acting as the customer, whilst the manager or department instructed to carry out the project assumes the role of contractor.

- *Contractor* – the organization that is principally responsible for executing the project work to the customer's requirements. I have not restricted this term to its more common use (in the contracting industry for construction projects). So, again purely for convenience, I use the term contractor in my text to describe any organization or group that carries out a project, whether or not the project is carried out against a formal sales contract. I use this term, for example, in the context of manufacturing projects, for projects in the not-for-profit sector and for management change projects.

- *End user* – the individual or organization that will ultimately own and operate the project. This is not always the same person or organization that paid for the original project. Consider, for example, a research and development project carried out by the Whitewash Company PLC to develop washing machines for sale in the retail sector. The customer for this project would be Whitewash PLC, the main contractor would be the design engineering department of Whitewash PLC, and members of the public who bought the machines would be the end users.

Project Type	Project example	Project customer	Principal 'contractor'	End user	Operated and maintained by:
1 Civil engineering, construction, petrochemical, mining and quarrying	Local authority housing development	Local authority	Wimply	Housing tenants	Local authority
	Private toll road	Landowner	Tarpack	Road users	Landowner's agent
	Copper mine	Cupric Ltd	Cupric Ltd (head office engineering)	Cupric (Zambia) Ltd	Cupric (Zambia) Ltd
2 Manufacturing	New passenger aircraft	Going Ltd	Going Ltd	Various airlines	Various airlines
	Automatic rifle	Ministry of Defence	Small Arms Ltd	Military units	Military units
	Washing machine development	Hotwash Ltd	Hotwash R&D dept	Domestic users	Domestic users
3 Management	Design and implement new sales procedures	ABC Ltd	ABC Ltd (with external consultant)	ABC staff	ABC Ltd
	Office relocation	Greens of London	Greens' (internal task force)	Greens of Exeter	Greens of Exeter
4 Research	Speculative research for new plastic materials	Chemikl Ltd	Chemikl Ltd (laboratory)	Unknown	Not applicable

Figure 1.6 Examples of project relationships

A few simplified examples to illustrate that project relationships can extend well beyond the boundaries of customer and contractor.

Projects are very diverse in their natures and the common notion that every project is carried out by one organization or contractor for one customer is really too simplistic. Figure 1.6 gives a taste of this diversity, with examples given for each of the four project types identified earlier in this chapter. For convenience and simplicity, however, I have confined most of the illustrations and case studies throughout this book to the simple customer-contractor relationship.

ASSOCIATIONS REPRESENTING THE PROFESSION OF PROJECT MANAGEMENT

International Project Management Association (IPMA)

The profession of project management is represented by the International Project Management Association. Originally known by the initials INTERNET, the Association was eventually forced to switch to the abbreviation IPMA, for very obvious reasons.

Association for Project Management (APM)

The corporate member of the IPMA in the UK is the Association for Project Management (APM) and further information is available from their secretariat at:

Association for Project Management
150 West Wycombe Road
High Wycombe
Buckinghamshire, HP12 3AE
Telephone: 0845 458 1944; Email: info@apm.org.uk; Website: www.apm.org.uk

APM arranges seminars and meetings through a network of local branches and, ten times year, publishes the journal *Project*. It also produces other publications, foremost among which is its *APM Body of Knowledge*. Personal or corporate membership of APM is an excellent way for project managers and all others involved in project management to meet and to maintain current awareness of all aspects of project management.

Membership starts at student level and rises through various grades to full member (MAPM) and fellow (FAPM). APM's basic professional qualification, which depends on suitable experience and written examinations, is APMP. This qualification recognizes an individual's baseline knowledge and experience in project management. It is regarded by APM as the benchmark qualification in the project management profession and is the first step towards certification.

APM has a well-established certification procedure for project managers, who must already be full members. To quote from APM's own literature, 'the certificated project manager is at the pinnacle of the profession, possessing extensive knowledge and having carried responsibility for the delivery of at least one significant project'. As evidence of competence, certification has obvious advantages for the project manager, and will increasingly be demanded as mandatory by some project purchasers. Certification provides employers with a useful measure when recruiting or assessing staff and the company that can claim to employ certificated project managers will benefit from an enhanced professional image. Certification has relevance also for project clients. It helps them to assess a project manager's competence by providing clear proof that the individual concerned has gained peer recognition of their ability to manage projects.

Project Management Institute (PMI)

Founded in the US in 1969, PMI is the world's leading not-for-profit organization for individuals around the globe who work in, or are interested in, project management. PMI develops recognized standards, not least of which is the widely respected project management body of knowledge guide, commonly known by its abbreviated title the *PMBOK Guide*.

PMI publications include the monthly professional magazine *PM Network*, the monthly newsletter *PMI Today* and the quarterly *Project Management Journal*. In addition to its many research and education activities, PMI is dedicated to developing and maintaining a rigorous, examination-based professional certification program to advance the project management profession and recognize the achievements of individual professionals. PMI claims that its Project Management Professional (PMP) certification is the world's most recognized professional credential for project management practitioners and others in the profession. For more information, contact PMI at:

PMI Headquarters
Four Campus Boulevard
Newtown Square
PA 19073-3299, USA
Telephone: +610-356-4600; Email: pmihq@pmi.org; Website: www.pmi.org

REFERENCES AND FURTHER READING

APM (2006), *APM Body of Knowledge*, 5th Edition (High Wycombe: Association for Project Management) (also available on CD-ROM).

Barnes, M. (2002), *A Long Term View of Project Management – Its Past and its Likely Future*, Keynote speech to the IPMA 16th World Congress on Project Management, Berlin.

Kanigel, R. (1997), *The One Best Way: Frederick Winslow Taylor and the Enigma of Efficiency* (London: Little, Brown and Company).

Morris, P. (1994), *The Management of Projects* (London, Thomas Telford).

PMI (2004), *A Guide to the Project Management Body of Knowledge*, 3rd Edition (Newtown Square, PA: Project Management Institute).

Vaughan, A. (1991), *Isambard Kingdom Brunel: Engineering Knight-Errant* (Cambridge: Cambridge University Press).

2 *Factors for Project Success or Failure*

T he manager of a typical project would consider the task well done if the project finished on time, according to its specified performance and within its budgeted cost. These three objectives (time, performance and cost) are traditionally the basic parameters for measuring project success or failure and they will be discussed later in this chapter. However, although important, they relate principally to the execution or fulfilment stage of a project, which is the period of most direct interest to the project manager and the principal contractor. Other people (not least the customer) might have quite different views about the ultimate success or failure of a project. A project that is delivered on time, within budget and in line with its specification might provide the contractor with a good profit, beneficial publicity and a warm glow of satisfaction. However, a customer who subsequently discovers that the project fails to live up to its initial promise and does not deliver its expected return on investment will perceive the result as a failure. Other stakeholders might have their own, quite different, parameters for measuring success.

The upper portion of Figure 2.1 repeats the Gantt chart view of a project life history first seen in Figure 1.4. However, the project life is now compared not with rates of expenditure, but with some of the factors that determine actual or perceived success or failure as the project life history unfolds.

SUCCESS OR FAILURE FACTORS IN RELATION TO THE INITIAL PROJECT DEFINITION

Initial project definition leads to the business case on which the decision to authorize or disallow the project start will principally depend. This initial definition takes during Phases 1 to 6 in the Gantt chart of Figure 2.1. This is clearly too early for anyone to measure the success or failure of the project but it is the time in the project's life history when the foundations for success or failure are laid.

Any of the following shortcomings during this early period can condemn a project to almost certain failure:

- The project scope (the extent of work required) is not clearly stated and understood.
- The technical requirements are vague.
- Estimates of cost, timescale or benefits are too optimistic.
- Risk assessment is incomplete or flawed.
- The intended project strategy is inappropriate.
- Insufficient regard is paid to cash flows and the provision of funds.
- The interests and concerns of stakeholders are not taken into account.

- Undue regard is paid to the motivation and behaviour of people who will execute the project.
- Particularly in management change projects, insufficient thought is given to how all the managers and workpeople affected by the project will be motivated to adapt to the changes expected of them.
- Approval to proceed with the project is given for political, personal or intuitive reasons without due consideration to the business plan.

These are some of the things that can predetermine failure before any actual work begins. These early tasks, analyses and decisions are clearly important, and the following six chapters all deal with various aspects of project definition.

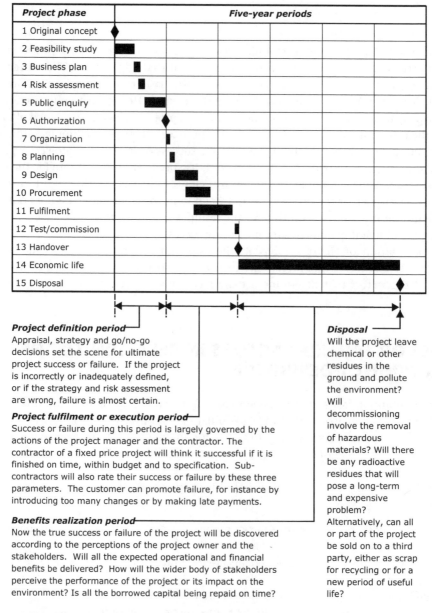

Project phase	Five-year periods
1 Original concept	
2 Feasibility study	
3 Business plan	
4 Risk assessment	
5 Public enquiry	
6 Authorization	
7 Organization	
8 Planning	
9 Design	
10 Procurement	
11 Fulfilment	
12 Test/commission	
13 Handover	
14 Economic life	
15 Disposal	

Project definition period
Appraisal, strategy and go/no-go decisions set the scene for ultimate project success or failure. If the project is incorrectly or inadequately defined, or if the strategy and risk assessment are wrong, failure is almost certain.

Project fulfilment or execution period
Success or failure during this period is largely governed by the actions of the project manager and the contractor. The contractor of a fixed price project will think it successful if it is finished on time, within budget and to specification. Sub-contractors will also rate their success or failure by these three parameters. The customer can promote failure, for instance by introducing too many changes or by making late payments.

Benefits realization period
Now the true success or failure of the project will be discovered according to the perceptions of the project owner and the stakeholders. Will all the expected operational and financial benefits be delivered? How will the wider body of stakeholders perceive the performance of the project or its impact on the environment? Is all the borrowed capital being repaid on time?

Disposal
Will the project leave chemical or other residues in the ground and pollute the environment? Will decommissioning involve the removal of hazardous materials? Will there be any radioactive residues that will pose a long-term and expensive problem? Alternatively, can all or part of the project be sold on to a third party, either as scrap for recycling or for a new period of useful life?

Figure 2.1   Perceptions of success or failure during a project life history

FACTORS FOR SUCCESS OR FAILURE DURING THE PROJECT FULFILMENT (EXECUTION) PERIOD

When authorization has been given for the project to start, it is the contractor (or the main contractor, if there are several subcontractors) and the project manager who take over most of the responsibility for success or failure. Remember that the term 'contractor' is used here to mean not only a company that manages or undertakes a project for an external customer, but it also applies equally to an internal manager or team responsible for a management change, IT or similar in-house project. Similarly, the term 'customer' can mean not only an external client or customer, but also the executive management of a company carrying out its own internal project.

The success of the contractor and the project manager will usually be judged according to how well they achieve the three primary objectives of cost, performance and time. Many things need to be in place and many actions taken during the project execution period to help ensure success. Among other things, these include:

- good project definition and a sound business case
- appropriate choice of project strategy
- strong support for the project and its manager from higher management
- availability of sufficient funds and other resources
- firm control of changes to the authorized project
- technical competence
- a sound quality culture throughout the organization
- a suitable organization structure
- appropriate regard for the health and safety of everyone connected with the project
- good project communications
- well-motivated staff
- quick and fair resolution of conflict.

These issues are all important for good project management.

The primary objectives of cost, performance and time are clear benchmarks against which to judge success or failure when (or soon after) a project is finished and handed over to the customer. The project manager needs to understand what each of these objectives implies and how the three can interrelate with each other.

Cost objective

Every project should be controlled against detailed cost budgets to ensure that the expenditure authorized in its contract or charter is not exceeded. Failure to complete work within the authorized budget will reduce profits and the return on the capital invested, with risk of a more serious (even terminal) financial outcome in extreme cases.

Most projects are undertaken with the expectation of benefits, either on completion or later in their life history. However, there are many projects where there is no initial profit motive. Here are some examples:

- pure scientific research programmes;
- fieldwork and other projects carried out by charitable organizations (with the exception of fundraising projects);
- local or national government projects that are paid for from public funds;
- other work carried out by organizations in the not-for-profit sector.

However, even with no profit motive, strict attention to cost budgets and financial management is usually vital. A project might have to be abandoned altogether if funds run out before completion, in which case the money and effort already invested become forfeit and must be written off. In extreme circumstances over-expenditure could cause the end of the organization responsible.

Performance (or quality) objective

Quality has often been used as an alternative (but less satisfactory) name for the performance project objective. General understanding of project or product quality conjures up several things in our imagination. Perceived quality characteristics will depend on the nature of the project or product, but here are a few general examples:

- performance at least equal to the specification;
- reliability and freedom from malfunction;
- long useful and economic life;
- safe: posing no unintentional threat of harm to living creatures (the adjective 'unintentional' is used here to accommodate, for example, projects carried out by arms manufacturers, pesticide companies and mouse trap manufacturers);
- low operating and maintenance costs;
- comfort and a pleasant impact on the human senses (sight, smell, taste, touch, hearing);
- environmentally friendly.

A copper refinery that was intended and designed to process 200 000 tonnes of cathode copper per annum must be able to do so, and it must produce that copper at the specified level of purity. The plant must function reliably, efficiently and safely. There will be trouble for all concerned if the plant causes environmental pollution.

Development projects for consumer goods must produce articles that satisfy the market requirements and conform to relevant legislation. The design concept and manufacture have to result in a product that is safe, reliable and appealing to the customer.

If a project is undertaken to reorganize a company, relocate its headquarters and install new IT systems, the IT must perform as expected, and the accommodation and all other conditions must be conducive to staff satisfaction and productivity.

At one time quality in manufacturing and other industrial projects was seen primarily as the responsibility of a quality control department. Great reliance was placed on inspection and testing to discover faults (called non-conformances in quality management jargon), and then arranging for these faults to be rectified. In more recent years organizations, in all market sectors, have embraced the concept of total quality management (TQM). In TQM a 'quality culture' is created throughout the organization, with quality built in to all design and work processes, and with responsibility for quality shared by all the staff and workforce from top management downwards. Quality considerations extend well beyond industrial projects and are regarded as equally important in the service industries and other businesses. The ISO 9000 series of standards is widely accepted as the base from which to design, implement and operate an effective quality management system, with the ultimate objective of creating a quality culture throughout the organization. The International Organization for Standards (ISO) publishes the ISO 9000 series and a full range of other international standards (www.iso.org).

Time objective

Actual progress has to match or beat planned progress. All significant stages of the project must take place no later than their specified dates, to result in total completion on or before the planned finish date.

Late completion of a project will not please the project purchaser or sponsor, to say the least. Consistently failing to keep delivery promises cannot enhance the contractor's market reputation. Further, any project that continues to use resources beyond its planned finish date can have a knock-on effect and disrupt other projects that are either in progress or waiting to follow.

A common risk to projects is failure to start work on time. Very long delays can be caused by procrastination, legal or planning difficulties, shortage of information, lack of funds or other resources, and a host of other reasons. All of these factors can place a project manager in a difficult or impossible position.

A project not started on time can hardly be expected to finish on time.

TRIANGLE OF OBJECTIVES AND TRADE-OFFS BETWEEN COST, PERFORMANCE AND TIME

Of course, the aim of a project manager must be to achieve success in all aspects of the project. But it is occasionally necessary to identify one of the three primary objectives as being of special importance. This emphasis can affect the priority given to the allocation of scarce resources and the way in which management attention is concentrated. It can also influence the choice of project organization structure (which is discussed in Chapters 9 and 10).

In the mid 1980s Dr Martin Barnes introduced the first version of his triangle of objectives (shown in the top left-hand quadrant of Figure 2.2). The purpose of this triangle was to illustrate that the three primary objectives of cost, time and quality are interrelated. A management decision to place greater emphasis on achieving one or two of these objectives must sometimes be made at the expense of the remaining objectives. Thus project sponsors or managers sometimes have to decide on giving priority to one or more of the three objectives in a trade-off decision.

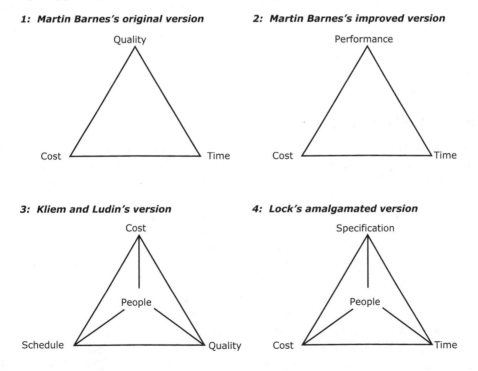

Figure 2.2 Barnes's original triangle of project objectives and some derivatives

Shortly after his triangle's initial introduction Dr Barnes changed 'quality' to 'performance' because, in his own words:

'Quality' implied little more than compliance with spec., but 'performance' I intended to mean 'the project, on completion, does what it is supposed to do'. (quoted from private correspondence)

Thus the triangle, shown in the top right-hand quadrant of Figure 2.2, is the more widely known version of the Barnes triangle.

Whenever someone has a good, clearly stated original idea, be certain that others will come along later to complicate the concept needlessly. There are many such examples in the techniques and practice of project management. Thus the Barnes triangle has even been converted to a complex three-dimensional vector diagram in one book. However, two derivatives of the Barnes triangle are worthy of mention, not least because one of them is my own.

The good management, organization and motivation of all who contribute to a project cannot be taken for granted and this must be acknowledged from the start. With this in mind, Kliem and Ludin (1992) set out a modified triangle of objectives with people shown at its centre. The Kliem and Ludin triangle is shown in the bottom left-hand quadrant of Figure 2.2.

Like Dr Barnes, I was not content with the word 'quality' and searched for an alternative. For reasons explained in the following section, I prefer to use 'level of specification' instead of 'quality'. The triangle in the bottom right-hand quadrant of Figure 2.2 combines my preference with those of Barnes, Kliem and Ludin.

The outcome of a trade-off decision can be indicated by placing a spot or blob within the triangle boundaries. For example, if cost is the greatest consideration, the blob will be placed in the cost corner. If all the objectives are regarded as equal (balanced), the blob will be put in the middle of the triangle.

A project for a charitable organization with very limited funds would have to be controlled very much with budgets in mind, so that costs must be the project manager's chief concern. Industries such as aerospace and nuclear power generation have to place high emphasis on safety and reliability, so performance becomes their most important objective. A project to set up and stock a stand at a trade exhibition, for which the date has been announced and the venue booked, is so dependent on meeting the time objective that it might be necessary to accept overspent budgets if that is the only way to avoid missing the date.

Quality/cost relationship

It is a mistake to believe that there can be a simple and acceptable trade-off between quality and cost. Those who promote total quality management argue, quite rightly, that quality can be achieved without extra cost (see, for example, Crosby, 1979). However, there is an even more fundamental reason why quality is not an objective that can be downgraded or compromised. This becomes clear if we accept Juran's definition of quality as a service or product that is 'fit for the purpose for which it was intended' (Juran and Godfrey, 1999). No contractor or project manager should contemplate a result that is not 'fit for purpose'. Therefore quality is *not* negotiable. Downgrading quality is not an option. That is why 'performance' or 'level of specification' are more appropriate names for this objective because, in many cases, they *are* negotiable.

Suppose that the initial estimates for a new building are too high and that construction costs must be reduced. One option might be to build on relatively simple foundations instead of using deep sunk piles, which could save thousands of pounds. But if the ground conditions demand piling for the building to be safe, that cost-saving option is ruled out on the grounds of reliability and safety. It would compromise quality and is not a true option. The building would not be fit for its intended purpose.

Now suppose that the same developer reviews the specification for interior finishes and finds that marble-finished floors could be replaced with carpeted floors at a substantial cost saving. The floors would still be serviceable, safe, reliable and fit for purpose. Carpeting would, therefore, be an option that would not compromise quality. Quality has not been changed, but the level of specification has.

The developer might also review the performance specifications for services such as lighting and air conditioning. It is possible that the performance parameters could be downgraded slightly for a significant saving in capital and operating costs. Again, this should not affect the safety and reliability of the building and, provided that lighting and ventilation are adequate and within legislative requirements, would not render the building unfit for its intended purpose.

Time/cost relationship

Remember that TIME IS MONEY!

(Benjamin Franklin, in *Advice to a Young Tradesman*, 1748).

There is usually a direct and very important relationship between time and money. If the planned timescale is exceeded, the original cost estimates are almost certain to be overspent. A project costs money during every day of its existence, working or non-working, weekday or weekend, from day one of the programme right through until the last payment has exchanged hands. These costs arise for a variety of reasons, some of which will now be explained.

Effect of project delays on direct costs

The *variable* or *direct* project costs of materials and workforce man-hours are time-related in several ways. Cost inflation is one factor, so that a job started and finished later than planned can be expected to cost more because of intervening materials price rises and increases in wages, salaries and other costs.

There are other, less easily quantifiable, causes where late working implies inefficient working, perhaps through lost time or waiting time (often the result of materials shortages, missing information, or poor planning, communications and organization). If any project task takes longer to perform than its planned duration, it is probable that the budgeted man-hours will also be exceeded. This is true not only for a single task, but also for the project as a whole.

Effect of project delays on indirect (overhead) costs

The *fixed* or *overhead* costs of management, administration, accommodation, services and general facilities will be incurred day by day, every day, regardless of work done, until the project is finished. If the project runs late, these costs will have to be borne for a longer period than planned. They will then exceed their budget.

Effect of project delays on the costs of financing

Another important time-related cost is financing. Where the contractor has an overdraft at the bank or relies on other loan financing, interest has to be paid on the loan. Even if the contractor can finance the project from internal funds, there is still a notional cost of financing, equivalent to the interest or dividends that the same funds could have earned had the contractor invested the money elsewhere (such as in a bank deposit account). If a project runs late, the financing period is extended, and the total amount of interest or notional interest payable must increase correspondingly.

Much of the finance raised for a large project is likely to be invested in work in progress as the project proceeds through the execution stage of its life history. This work in progress includes not only the tangible results of a project such as construction or manufacture, but also the intangible elements such as planning and engineering or design. In many projects the contractor can only charge the customer for work that can be demonstrated as finished. For example, in construction and manufacturing projects the amount of work completed usually has to be inspected and certified by an independent quality surveyor or engineer before it can be charged out to the customer. The customer will not pay without the receipt of certified invoices. Certified invoices are often linked to planned events or *milestones*. If the planned amount of work has not been done, or if a milestone has not been reached, a certified invoice cannot be issued. The contractor's revenue is then delayed, which means that the contractor must continue to finance the mounting costs of the project. The contractor could suffer severe cash flow problems as a result, even leading to bankruptcy in the worst case.

Cost penalties

Late completion can invoke the ignominy of contract cost penalties. Some contracts contain a penalty clause which provides the customer with the sanction of a cost penalty against the contractor for each day or week by which the contractor fails to meet the contracted delivery obligation.

Total cost effect of project delays

All these time/cost considerations mean that delays on a large project can easily cause additional costs amounting to thousands of pounds per day. It is clear, therefore, that if work can be carefully monitored and managed so that it proceeds without disruption against a sensible, achievable plan, much of the battle to control costs will already have been won.

PERCEPTIONS OF PROJECT SUCCESS OR FAILURE BEYOND THE THREE PRIMARY OBJECTIVES

Most project managers are expected to complete their projects so that they satisfy the three primary objectives of time, performance and cost. These are usually the most important factors that drive the project contractor and they should align with the foremost expectations of the project owner. Most project management procedures (and this book) are directed towards achieving these goals, which could be summarized as delighting the customer while creating a commercial success for the contractor. In this context the contracting organization and the customer are both primary stakeholders in the project.

It must be recognized, however, that many projects have to satisfy more than two primary stakeholders. For example, a bank that has provided loan finance for a project will have a keen interest in whether the project succeeds or fails.

There will always be people and organizations who, while not being principal stakeholders, nonetheless have an interest in how the outcome of a project might affect them. Subcontractors and suppliers are an obvious example. Staff working on a project have a stake in the outcome because project success or failure can (apart from contributing to job satisfaction) have profound implications for their future employment and careers.

Perceptions of success or failure will differ between the various stakeholders. The residents of houses lying in the path of a proposed new motorway would take a very different view from that of the potential motorway users. A project to build a transport system that runs out of cash and ruins its main contractor would be an undoubted failure from the point of view of the shareholders, project staff and unpaid creditors. But road users would not regard that project as a failure if a replacement contractor and fresh cash injections allowed the new road to be opened as planned.

Some environmental groups might be dismayed by new project proposals. Many project managers have learned to their cost that work can be seriously delayed by determined protesters, who may be able to publicize a good case, attract a great deal of public support and even trespass on the owner's site or premises.

It is clear, then, that the true measure of project success or failure depends on how the project outcome is perceived by all the stakeholders. Hartman (2000) declares that a 'project is successful if all the stakeholders are happy'. Although that ideal may not always be achievable, it is best project management practice to try to identify all the stakeholders and satisfy their aspirations as far as possible.

IDENTIFYING AND RANKING THE STAKEHOLDERS

The range and nature of stakeholders will vary very greatly from one project to another but the principle of stakeholder identification can be illustrated by an example. Suppose that a project has been proposed to redevelop a derelict urban area. This ambitious project will provide a shopping mall, offices, cinema and live entertainments, other leisure facilities, new connecting roads and so on. The primary stakeholders for this project will certainly include the main project contractor and the project owner. The banks or other organizations financing the project will also have a considerable primary interest in the project's success or failure.

Not least of the stakeholders are all those who hold shares or have otherwise invested in participating companies that, by accepting an element of risk, stand to make a profit or loss as a result of the project.

Subcontractors, suppliers, staff, artisans and labourers can all be considered stakeholders too, although perhaps these could be placed in the second rank. Intended occupiers of the shops, offices and other premises also have a large stake in the project.

There are others who will be dependent on the secondary stakeholders. These are the wholesale suppliers of merchandise to be sold in the new shops, service staff such as car park attendants, shop and office workers, companies expecting to provide security, cleaning and maintenance services, and so on.

Public transport organizations must consider how the development will affect passenger numbers: some of their existing services might need to be changed to suit the new travel patterns (and take advantage of the new business generated).

Then there are the various regulatory authorities, such as the local building inspectors, planning office and many other official organizations. These are all stakeholders whose decisions and actions can affect the project.

People living near the proposed development will benefit from the new shopping and leisure facilities but might resent the inconvenience of construction works and the prospect of increased traffic and noise when the new premises start to function. Parents might be concerned that their schoolchildren will have to cross streets that are busier and more hazardous. Motorists and other road users will be interested in how the new road layouts will affect their journeys. The new entertainments facilities will provide wider opportunities for live artistes.

This discussion could be carried on at length to identify still more stakeholders. Some will have the power to influence the project, while others will be able only to voice opinions. All stakeholders might be ranked (primary, secondary, tertiary and so on) according to the power that they can wield and the impact that the project will have on them.

Stakeholders	Objectives		
	Time	Cost	Specification
Project owner			
Project manager			
Bank			
Guarantor			
Statutory bodies			
Main contractor			
Subcontractors			
Suppliers			
Project workers			
General public			
Local residents			
Environmental groups			
and so on			

Figure 2.3   Matrix of stakeholders' objectives

This extends the concept of the triangle of objectives and allows the perceived priorities of all project stakeholders to be considered.

Consideration of the stakeholders' interests

Once all the stakeholders have been identified, the means of communicating and dealing with them will have to be considered. Regulations and local byelaws will determine how local government and other official bodies must be consulted. There might have to be meetings with some stakeholders' groups or associations. Publicity can include, for example, announcements in the local press and advance public display of architects' plans and models. Consultation is always better than confrontation.

When the preliminary investigation of stakeholders' interests is finished, the triangle of objectives could, in theory at least, be supplemented by a more complex matrix of stakeholders' perceptions. Figure 2.3 above shows a theoretical format.

BENEFITS REALIZATION

In most industrial and manufacturing projects the project owner should start to realize the expected benefits immediately or shortly after the project is successfully finished and handed over (Phase 13 in Figure 2.1). A chemical plant, once successfully commissioned, will be capable of producing saleable product. A new office building might require attention to the occupier's snagging list during the first few weeks of occupation but should nonetheless provide a pleasant working environment that can immediately improve staff satisfaction (and thus productivity). However, business change and IT projects can be quite different because their most significant benefits tend to be realized later in the project life history, during the first months (or even years) of the period shown as Phase 14 in Figure 2.1.

Consider, for example, a large-scale project that is intended to replace and standardize the customer service and invoicing systems of all the companies in an international group. The execution phase of the project is finished when the IT designers have developed, documented and tested the software. If the IT was contracted out, the IT specialist contractor might have had a successful project outcome, with all three primary objectives of cost, performance and time satisfied at the time of handover to the user company.

However, the proof of the pudding is in the eating. There is much more to the success of a management change project than the technical excellence and performance of the IT. It is only when the new system is up, running and accepted by the managers and staff of all the companies in the group that the project owner can begin to regard the project as a success. That implementation process can be long and difficult.

There may be a requirement for one or more special mobile implementation teams to be set up. A team will visit each of the different companies, and stay with that company until the staff are trained to use the new system, the initial problems are solved and benefits begin to become apparent.

Introducing new systems and procedures can be very difficult in any organization where the staff resist change, have understandable concerns about possible redundancies, come from a rich mix of different cultures, or resent having to cope with all the initial teething problems that significant changes create. Such difficulties are made worse by the spread of rumours (true or false) through the unofficial communication grapevine.

In recent years all these difficulties have led to new ways of assessing and managing the benefits realization of management change and IT projects. It is now recognized that the benefits realization process should start during early project definition by establishing benchmarks that can be put in place in the business plan. These benchmarks have some similarity with the milestones set in the project execution plans of all projects, but for management change and IT projects there are two important differences:

- The most important benchmarks often occur some time after initial handover and commissioning of the project from the contractor to the customer (remembering yet once again that the contractor and owner can be in the same company).
- Each benchmark must be *directly* associated with a cash inflow, cost saving or other real benefit that can be tracked to a favourable entry in the company's accounts or management reports.

Benefits realization is appreciated among the more enlightened management fraternity as the most important driver in managing a management change or IT project, so that the intended long-term benefits are kept in the minds of the project manager and the other project stakeholders.

There are management consultant companies that specialize in helping organizations to achieve their project implementation benefits, and some have proprietary methods and software programs for the purpose. An Internet search for 'benefits realization' is a good pathway to these companies and their methods. One specialist company is Isochron Limited, and that organization uses the terms 'recognition events' and 'value flashpoints' to identify milestones and financial benchmarks respectively. Isochron's methods are explained in Fowler and Lock (2006).

Although triggered by difficulties peculiar to management change and IT projects, there is no reason why some of these new and specialized benefits realization management processes should not be applied or adapted for use in industrial and management projects.

REFERENCES AND FURTHER READING

Bradley, G. (2006), *Benefit Realisation Management: A Practical Guide to Achieving Benefits Through Change* (Aldershot: Gower).

Capper, R. (1997), *A Project-by-Project Approach to Quality: A Practical Handbook for Individuals, Teams and Organizations* (Aldershot: Gower).

Crosby, P. B., (1979), *Quality is Free: the Art of Making Quality Certain* (New York: McGraw-Hill).

Fowler, A. and Lock, D., (2006), *Accelerating Business and IT Change: Transforming Project Delivery* (Aldershot: Gower).

Hartman, F.T. (2000), *Don't Park Your Brain Outside* (Newtown Square, PA., Project Management Institute).

Juran, J. and Godfrey, A.B. (eds) (1999), *Juran's Quality Handbook*, 5th Edition (New York: McGraw-Hill).

Kliem, R. L. and Ludin, I. S. (1992), *The People Side of Project Management* (Gower: Aldershot).

Oakland, John S. (2004), *Oakland on Quality Management: 3rd Edition of Total Quality Management: The Management of Change Through Process Improvement* (Oxford: Butterworth Heinemann).

Seaver, M. (ed.) (2003), *Gower Handbook of Quality Management*, 3rd Edition (Aldershot: Gower).

3 *Defining the Project Task*

Project definition starts when the idea of a project is first conceived, at the very beginning of the project life history. Strictly, it does not end until the last piece of information has been filed to describe the project in its finished or 'as-built' condition. Figure 3.1 illustrates the complete definition process for a very large project. It shows how information and changes accumulate with time, so that the project definition becomes more complete and accurate as the project progresses from concept to completion. These general principles apply to almost any kind of civil engineering, construction, manufacturing project or other industrial project. For some very large and complex projects, and for many IT and management change projects, the definition process extends beyond the handover from the contractor to the customer owing to the late discovery of design errors or the need for changes revealed during implementation.

This chapter deals with the early stages of definition. These are the foundation stages that should result in a specification written in sufficient detail to define the requirements and scope of the proposed project, list the principal tasks and outline the intended strategy for designing and executing the work.

IMPORTANCE OF INITIAL PROJECT DEFINITION

Before any person or organization considers investment in a new project, before a contractor can begin to prepare a tender for undertaking work for a customer, or before a company executive can be asked to accept responsibility for managing an internal IT or management change project, the project requirements must be clearly established, documented and understood. The project has to be defined as accurately and fully as possible before it is allowed to start. The investor must know how the money will be spent and what benefits can be expected in return. The contracting organization needs to know for what it is bidding and what its commitments would be in the event of signing the contract. The manager of an internal IT or management change project cannot be expected to carry it out successfully if the requirements are not adequately defined in a project charter or specification.

PROJECTS WHICH ARE DIFFICULT OR IMPOSSIBLE TO DEFINE

This book generally takes a deterministic approach, which begins with the assumption that project objectives can be agreed early in the life history, well before the project enters its execution stages. Of course changes will occur during the course of most projects that can modify the original objectives.

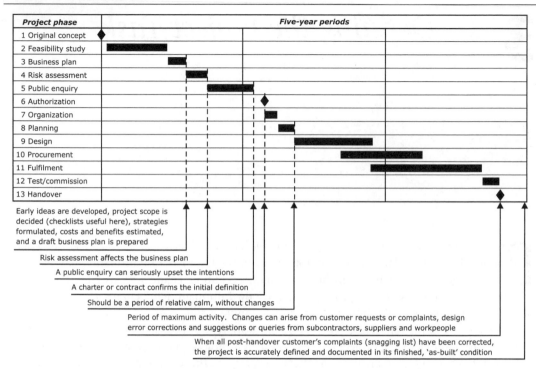

Project phase	Five-year periods		
1 Original concept			
2 Feasibility study			
3 Business plan			
4 Risk assessment			
5 Public enquiry			
6 Authorization			
7 Organization			
8 Planning			
9 Design			
10 Procurement			
11 Fulfilment			
12 Test/commission			
13 Handover			

Early ideas are developed, project scope is decided (checklists useful here), strategies formulated, costs and benefits estimated, and a draft business plan is prepared

Risk assessment affects the business plan

A public enquiry can seriously upset the intentions

A charter or contract confirms the initial definition

Should be a period of relative calm, without changes

Period of maximum activity. Changes can arise from customer requests or complaints, design error corrections and suggestions or queries from subcontractors, suppliers and workpeople

When all post-handover customer's complaints (snagging list) have been corrected, the project is accurately defined and documented in its finished, 'as-built' condition

Figure 3.1   Definition of a large project from initial concept to completion

But the essence of successful project management is a positive and determined attitude towards setting, maintaining and eventually achieving firmly set objectives, with action taken wherever necessary to keep the project on its planned course.

Most of the procedures and project cases described in this book are written from the point of view of the project manager. They assume that the customer's or investor's project objectives and the contractor's commitments have been well defined and documented in advance, enabling all stages of the project and its expenditure to be managed effectively against clear benchmarks.

Methods for dealing with uncertainty and risks are described in Chapter 7 but there are projects that are so complex, or are otherwise surrounded by so much uncertainty, that they simply cannot be defined adequately before work starts. A few project concepts cannot even be defined beyond vague outlined intentions, so that the money invested is something of a gamble, and might either be completely wasted or result in huge benefits. In other words, there are projects for which a proposal or business plan simply cannot be compiled with the data and forecasts that businesspeople would normally expect to see before making their investment decision.

Safeguards for ill-defined projects

When a project cannot be adequately defined, special measures must be taken to limit the risks if the idea of the project is not to be abandoned altogether.

Stage-gating

Projects for pure scientific research are an extreme case of initial uncertainty, even to the extent that their outcomes are often completely unpredictable. Chapter 1 mentioned how a step-by-step or 'stage-gating' approach can be used to authorize such projects, releasing resources in controlled amounts (*tranches*) so that the risks can be kept within defined bounds. Each new tranche of investment depends on the satisfactory outcome of a periodical review and reassessment of the project. If the outlook is completely bleak, the plug can be pulled on the project and all further expenditure denied.

Stage-gating is a valuable tool for the sponsor of any kind of project that cannot be defined with certainty in its early days. However, people working in a stage-gated project are unlikely to be well motivated because they work under the constant threat of sudden project closure. If the employer cannot guarantee equivalent alternative employment on other projects, some staff might feel so insecure that they decide to end the uncertainty by seeking safer employment elsewhere. However, most project managers are not faced with such extreme uncertainty and can adopt other measures to limit their company's exposure to risk.

Avoidance of fixed-price contracts

A commercial contractor asked to embark upon a project in which its expected role is not adequately defined can of course accept the order with some confidence if the payment arrangements guarantee reimbursement of all the contractor's costs plus reasonable fees or profit mark-ups. That method will ensure that the customer or investor bears the financial risk. However, even with the promise of full cost reimbursement, poor project definition can still be difficult for the contactor. It is always inconvenient for a contractor to muster and commit resources to a project whose duration is unknown and which is liable to be cancelled at short notice.

Provisional cost items in fixed-price contracts

Customers generally prefer to sign contracts against fixed price quotations, so that they know their commitments and can set their investment budgets with some degree of confidence. Contractors will, understandably, be less enthusiastic about quoting a firm, fixed price when there are significant elements of the project that cannot be well defined. Contractors (particularly for construction projects) deal with this difficulty by identifying and listing separately all parts of the project that cannot adequately be defined and which are beyond the contractor's control. Those features will be listed separately in the contractor's tender, outside the scope of work covered by the quoted fixed price, and they are known as provisional cost items (or pc sums).

Consider, for example, a proposed project to refurbish a building where part of the structure is hidden from view and is in uncertain condition. The fixed-price proposal might be conditional upon no structural defects being found when work starts. A provisional cost item would be inserted in the proposal to estimate the extra costs to be charged to the customer should additional work be necessary when work begins and the true extent of structural decay or damage is revealed.

Another example is occasionally seen in tenders for the demolition of a building and its replacement with a new construction. Customers sometimes ask that specified items, such wood panelling, carved figures, doors and partition panels should be saved from the demolition process and used in the new building. The customers' motives might be to save money or to preserve some fond memories of the old building. The customer expects a firm price to be quoted for the project but the contractor will be concerned that some or all of the items specified for salvage either cannot be saved when demolition starts, or they will be found to be unsuitable for use in the new building. The contractor would cover those contingencies by adding provisional cost items to the fixed-price tender to cover the possibility of having to purchase new materials in place of the unsuitable salvaged items.

FEASIBILITY STUDIES TO IMPROVE EARLY PROJECT DEFINITION

The investor faced with a very uncertain prognosis for a project might start by commissioning a feasibility study from a consultant or professionally orientated contracting company to obtain more facts and expert advice. This approach is frequently used to examine and appraise the technical, logistical, environmental, commercial and financial aspects of all kinds of projects that require a high level of investment. Banks and other institutions asked to finance or otherwise sponsor ill-defined projects may require a satisfactory feasibility study report before committing funds. Government departments often demand or commission study reports for projects which are of significant public or international importance.

A feasibility study for a large capital project can be quite an undertaking in itself, perhaps taking years to prepare and costing many millions of pounds. But a good feasibility study report can do much to point a project in the right direction, recommend the most effective strategy and define the risks and achievable objectives.

CHECKLISTS

Checklists are a very useful way of ensuring that no important task or cost item is forgotten when a new project is being evaluated. Contractors who have amassed a great deal of experience in their particular field of project operation will learn the type of questions that must be asked to fill most of the information gaps and they can develop comprehensive checklists for use in project cost estimates and proposals.

Familiar checklist examples

One very simple application of a project definition checklist is seen when a sales engineer takes a customer's order for equipment that is standard, but which can be ordered with a range of options. The sales engineer might use a standard proforma (either on a pad or a computer screen), entering data in boxes and ticking off the options that the customer requires.

People selling replacement windows with double glazing use such methods. So do salespeople in automobile showrooms. Standard forms are convenient and help to ensure that no important detail is forgotten when the order is taken and passed back to the factory or warehouse for action.

Construction project checklists

Companies about to tender for large civil engineering, construction, petrochemical or mining projects can make good use of checklists. One such list might be concerned with ensuring that all aspects of the building and performance of a new chemical plant are considered. Another case would be to ensure that the accommodation space and standards in a new building can be properly specified. Local climatic and geological data at an intended project construction site may have to be defined.

The designer or contractor of a construction project may not be aware of potential physical hazards such as high winds, earth tremors or flooding. It is also necessary to check whether or not any special statutory regulations apply in the region, particularly when it is overseas in unfamiliar territory. Other data might cover national working practices and the influence of local trade unions, the availability of suitable local labour, facilities to be provided for the contractor's expatriate staff and so on. Many, many questions should be asked and answered. Checklists are ideal in these circumstances. The example in Figure 3.2 includes some of the items that might feature in a complete list for an overseas project that involves civil engineering or construction at a foreign site.

Project site and other local conditions

Availability of utilities
- Electrical power
- Potable water
- Other water
- Sewerage
- Other services
Transport
- Existing roads: Access difficulties (low bridges, weight limits, etc.)
- Nearest railpoint
- Nearest suitable seaport
- Nearest commercial airport
- Local airstrip
- Local transport and insurance arrangements
Physical conditions
- Seismic situation
- Temperature range
- Rainfall or other precipitation
- Humidity
- Wind force and direction
- Dust
- Barometric pressure
- Site plans and survey
- Soil investigation and foundation requirements
Local workshop and manufacturing facilities
Local sources of bulk materials
Local plant hire
Site safety and security
Local human resources available
- Professional
- Skilled
- Unskilled
Site accommodation arrangements for:
- Offices
- Secure stores
Site living accommodation for:
- Expatriate managers and engineers
- Artisans
- Short-stay visitors
- Married quarters (see separate checklist if these are required)

Other site facilities
- First aid, medical and hospital facilities
- Catering and messing arrangements
- Hotels or other accommodation for VIPs
- Local banking arrangements
Communications
- General mail and airmail service
- Special mail or courier service
- Telephone over public network
- Telephone over dedicated terrestrial or satellite link
- Fax
- E-mail
- Other

Contractual and commercial conditions

How firm are the proposals?
What are the client's relative priorities for:
- Time?
- Cost?
- Quality?
What are the client's delivery requirements?
Do we know the client's budget levels?
Scope of work envisaged:
- Basic design only?
- Fully detailed design?
- Procurement responsibility: (ourselves, the client, or someone else?)
- Construction responsibility: (ourselves, the client or a managing contractor?)
- Commissioning, customer training, operating and maintenance manuals, etc. (these must be specified)
How accurate are the existing cost estimates:
- Ball park?
- Comparative?
- Have all estimates been checked against the estimating manual checklist?
How is the project to be financed?
Is there to be a financial guarantor?
What do we know about the client's financial status and invoice payment record?
Are contract penalty clauses expected?
Is the pricing to be firm or other?
What are the likely arrangements for stage or progress payments?
What retention payment will be imposed?
What insurances must we arrange?
What guarantees or warranties will the client expect?

Figure 3.2 Part of a project definition checklist

The first pages of a checklist used by an international mining company for initial project definition. Any experienced contracting company should be able to develop its own list.

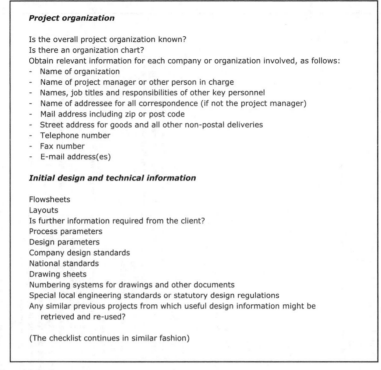

Project organization

Is the overall project organization known?
Is there an organization chart?
Obtain relevant information for each company or organization involved, as follows:
- Name of organization
- Name of project manager or other person in charge
- Names, job titles and responsibilities of other key personnel
- Name of addressee for all correspondence (if not the project manager)
- Mail address including zip or post code
- Street address for goods and all other non-postal deliveries
- Telephone number
- Fax number
- E-mail address(es)

Initial design and technical information

Flowsheets
Layouts
Is further information required from the client?
Process parameters
Design parameters
Company design standards
National standards
Drawing sheets
Numbering systems for drawings and other documents
Special local engineering standards or statutory design regulations
Any similar previous projects from which useful design information might be
    retrieved and re-used?

(The checklist continues in similar fashion)

Figure 3.2 *Concluded*

Checklists for management change and IT projects

It is not generally appreciated that internal management change projects can consume prodigious amounts of time, money and other resources but cause considerable harm within and sometimes outside the organization if they fail. Inadequate project definition can be the root cause of such disasters and, here again, checklists are invaluable.

There is a difficulty in compiling checklists for management change projects when compared with other projects. Organizations that embark on very large internal change projects will probably do so very infrequently, perhaps only once in ten years or longer. Whereas the contractors of multiple, repetitive industrial and commercial projects learn from their past experience (and mistakes), companies intending to make big changes to their internal organization, procedures and IT do not have the experience of past projects that is essential for compiling checklists. However, some consultancy companies do build up such experience because they work with many different clients and are accustomed to giving advice and helping to define this kind of project. A checklist compiled by one such company (Isochron) is shown in Figure 3.3.

ENQUIRIES AND PROPOSALS FOR NEW PROJECTS

Enquiries and subsequent orders for commercial projects generally enter contracting companies through their sales engineering or marketing organization. Even when enquiries bypass the sales organization and are received by other members of staff, sensible company rules should operate to ensure referral to the sales or marketing department so that all enquiries can be 'entered into the system' for effective handling and response. This will ensure that every enquiry received from a potential external customer can be subjected to a formal screening process that will assess its potential project scope, risk and value.

Code Category/sub-category/cost element

010000 — Business analysis
010100 — Business redesign
010101 — Major process procedures design
010102 — IS procedures design
010103 — Data model design (logical)
010104 — Report and management information design
010105 — Develop procedures documentation
010200 — Current state assessment
010201 — Information systems review
010202 — Use organization assessment
010203 — Process assessment
010204 — Reporting and MI assessment
020000 — Business change
020100 — Business user training
020101 — Identify communities to be trained
020102 — Conduct training needs analysis
020103 — Develop training plan
020104 — Develop training course material
020105 — Schedule training events
020106 — Administer training events
020107 — Deliver training courses
020108 — Monitor training feedback
020200 — Communications
020201 — Identify communication audiences
020202 — Develop communication strategy
020203 — Select communication media
020204 — Develop communication plan
020205 — Implement communication plan
020206 — Assess audience understanding of key message
020207 — Update communication plan
020300 — Project contract development
020301 — Identify objectives
020302 — Identify event milestones
020303 — Identify business values
020304 — Match flashpoints to value drivers
020305 — Quantify values
020306 — Determine project cost
020307 — Balance value against cost
020308 — Develop project contract
020309 — Obtain approval

Code Category/sub-category/cost element

020400 — Stakeholder management
020401 — Develop stakeholder management plan
020402 — Implement stakeholder management plan
020403 — Stakeholder analysis
020404 — Develo stakeholder role transformation plan
020405 — Implement stakeholder role transformation plan
020406 — Manage stakeholder issues
020407 — Integrate stakeholder management and communication plans
030000 — Project running costs
030100 — Facilities
030101 — Accommodation charges
030102 — IT charges
030103 — Room hire
030104 — Food and refreshments
030105 — Printing and stationery
030200 — Overhead allocations
030201 — Other contributions to central funds
030300 — Project administration
030301 — Project accounting
030302 — Resource management
030303 — Project facilities management
030304 — General administration
030400 — Project management
030401 — Project structuring
030402 — Project planning
030403 — Project control
030404 — Project monitoring
030405 — Issue management
030406 — Change management
030407 — Project reporting
030408 — Travel
030409 — Hotel
030410 — Subsistence
040000 — Technology solution
040100 — Applications support
040101 — Design support model
040102 — User environment design
040103 — IS environment design
040104 — Procedures design
040105 — Training design
040106 — Implement support model
040107 — Monitor support services

Figure 3.3   Initial task checklist for a management change project

By kind permission of Isochron Ltd.

```
Code Category/sub-category/cost element

040200 --- Custom development
040201 --- Application infrastructure development
040202 --- Business system design
040203 --- Testing design
040204 --- Data conversion application development
040205 --- Application software development
040206 --- System testing
040207 --- Implementation planning
040300 --- Hardware
040301 --- Servers
040302 --- Clients
040303 --- Connectivity
040304 --- Peripherals
040400 --- Implementation
040401 --- Data conversion
040402 --- Acceptance testing
040203 --- Installation of production system
040204 --- Refine production system
040205 --- Evolution planning
040300 --- Package integration and testing
040301 --- Installation and environment set-up
040302 --- Package integration design and pilot
040303 --- Package business system design
040304 --- Package application development
040304 --- Package integration testing design
040305 --- Data conversion application development
040306 --- System testing
040307 --- Implementation planning
040400 --- Package selection
040401 --- Package requirements analysis
040402 --- Vendor and package screening
040403 --- Package shortlist evaluation
040404 --- Final evaluation and selection
040405 --- Contracts and technology acquisition
040406 --- Development planning
040407 --- Licences
```

Figure 3.3 *Concluded*

Enquiries for management change and IT projects usually start from a source within the company's own organization, so that the sales or marketing department is not initially involved. Although there is no external customer, in a large group of companies requests for projects received at the head office can sometimes seem as if they come from external customers. The important project definition actions described here and in the following chapters have the same importance for all projects, whether they are for external customers or are to be funded from within as management projects. However, when a project proposal is prepared for a management change project or other internal project, it is documented in a business plan for consideration by the company's own board. Chapter 6 deals with business plans.

Receipt and registration of project enquiries

Every enquiry must be registered and given a reference name or number that identifies it uniquely. There is no point in spending time and money in defining a project at the enquiry stage unless it is going to be possible at all subsequent times to know without ambiguity to which enquiry – and, just as important, to which *version* of that enquiry – a particular definition refers. The procedure can be quite simple; the register can be similar to the project register described in Chapter 21.

A company whose work involves a large number of small projects can receive a proportionately large number of customer enquiries, often as telephone calls. A useful and common practice is to provide the sales engineers or other relevant members of staff in such companies with preprinted pads or a computer-based system, designed with two purposes in mind:

- The first purpose is to provide a checklist of information requirements, arranged so that the person receiving an enquiry is prompted to ask all the necessary questions. The form or computer screen will have space in which the name and address of the potential customer can be written, together with the name and job title of the person calling. There must also be space for a summary of the work required. A company specializing in a particular technology will be able to devise tick-squares or boxes in which commonly used design and performance parameters can be entered.

- The other purpose of using preprinted forms is that, when well designed and properly used, they can save a great deal of time in taking down the initial enquiry details.

Screening enquiries from external customers and clients

The work involved in responding to an enquiry and preparing a tender can constitute a small project in itself, sometimes needing significant preliminary engineering design work plus sales and office effort that must be properly authorized and budgeted. The contractor will need to assess every new enquiry to decide how to respond. Enquiries from potential customers with a poor reputation for paying their bills or who are not financially sound are likely to be viewed with some disfavour. Other enquiries might be outside the contractor's capability or be inconvenient and unwanted for other reasons.

It is customary, therefore, for companies to subject enquiries for new projects to a rigorous screening process to determine the appropriate response and either authorize or refuse to commit the time and costs needed to prepare a formal tender. Screening decisions are usually made at fairly senior management level, often at regular meetings held for the purpose. Some companies record their screening decisions and manage appropriate follow-up action using a form for every enquiry such as that shown in Figure 3.4.

The potential customer will almost certainly set a date by which all competitive tenders for a project must be submitted, so the time available for preparation of a formal project proposal is usually limited. Everything must be properly planned, coordinated and controlled if a tender of adequate quality is to be delivered on time. What often happens is that tender preparation starts at a slack pace, with inadequate control, so that insufficient time is left for the end activities of typing, checking, correcting, printing, binding, signing and dispatch. Then there is a frantic last minute rush, with people working all night to produce the final version and special messengers or couriers given the almost impossible task of delivering the tender by the customer's deadline.

Customer's project specification

Initial enquiries from customers can take many different forms. Perhaps a set of plans or drawings, or a written description of the project objectives will be provided. Ensuing communications between the customer and contractor, whether written or spoken, can be long and protracted, often resulting in subsequent qualifications, changes or additions to the original request.

All of these elements, when taken together and documented, constitute the 'customer specification', to which all aspects of any tender and subsequent project authorization must relate. As with all other types of specification, the customer's project specification must be identifiable at all times by means of a unique reference number, date, and the issue or revision number.

DEFINING THE PROJECT SCOPE

If a project contract is eventually agreed, the contractor will have to ensure that the customer's specification is satisfied in every respect. The contractor's commitments will not be confined to the technical details but must also encompass the fulfilment of all specified commercial conditions. The terms of the order might lay down specific rules governing methods for invoicing and certification

ACTION PLAN

Project title:		Enquiry number	Rev. or case

Client's name and address:

Client's reference:
Enquiry date:
Telephone:
Fax:
E-mail

Name and title of contact:

Outline project description:

Screening committee authorization: Comments and special instructions

We will bid, inform client: ☐

We will not bid, inform client: ☐

Clarify with client and
screen again: ☐   Signed:

Action	For action by	Authorized budgets			Date wanted
		Labour	Travel	Other	
Define the task					
Review task definition with client					
Develop possible solutions					
Evaluate client's operating costs					
Review outline solutions with client					
Estimate our project costs					
Write proposal and draw artwork					
Print and bind the proposal					
Time/costs of proposal delivery					
Presentation meeting					
Total budgets					
Name of engineer in charge:					

Figure 3.4   An action plan for screening and progressing sales enquiries

of work done for payment. Inspection and quality standards may be spelled out in the contract and one would certainly expect to find a well-defined statement of delivery requirements. There might even be provision for penalties to be paid by the contractor should the agreed project completion date not be met.

Any failure by the contractor to meet the contractual obligations could obviously be very damaging for the contractor's reputation. Bad news travels fast, and the contractor's competitors will, to put it mildly, not attempt to slow the process. The contractor may suffer financial loss if the programme cannot be met or if they have otherwise miscalculated the size of the task undertaken. It is therefore extremely important for the contractor to *determine in advance* exactly what the customer expects to receive for the project price or budget.

The customer's specification should set out all the requirements in unambiguous terms, so that they can be understood and similarly interpreted by customer and contractor alike. Of particular importance is the way in which responsibility for the work is to be shared between the contractor, the customer and others. In more precise terms, the scope of work required from the contractor (that is, the size of the contractor's contribution to the project) must be made clear.

At its simplest, the scope of work required might be limited to making and delivering a piece of hardware in accordance with drawings supplied by the customer. At the other extreme, the scope of a large construction or process plant project could be defined so that the contractor handles the project entirely, and is responsible for all work until the purchaser is able to accept delivery or handover of a fully completed and proven project (known as a 'turnkey operation').

Whether the scope of work lies at one of these extremes or the other, there is almost always a range of ancillary items that have to be considered. Will the contractor be responsible for any training of the customer's staff and, if so, how much (if any) of this training is to be included in the project contract and price? What about commissioning, or support during the first few weeks or months of the project's working life? What sort of warranty or guarantee is going to be expected? Are any operating or maintenance instructions to be provided? If so, how many and in what language?

Answers to all of these questions must be provided, as part of the project task definition before cost estimates, tenders and binding contracts can be considered.

CONTRACTOR'S STRATEGY AND DESIGN SPECIFICATION

Suppose that, after serious consideration of the customer's enquiry specification, a contractor decides to prepare a tender. The contractor must obviously develop and record an intended design strategy, possibly after performing some preliminary technical investigation. Without having a good understanding of the project requirements and the intended strategy for meeting them, cost estimating, budgeting and pricing would be very uncertain processes.

It is usually necessary to translate the customer's technical requirements into a form compatible with the contractor's own normal practice, quality standards, technical capabilities and chosen design strategy.

Methods for estimating project costs are considered in Chapter 4. However, it can be appreciated that the outline technical strategy, for both hardware and software, must be established before serious attempts at cost estimating can start. Those estimating the project costs need to know the intended design and work strategy so that they can assess the scale of work and its costs.

Without a documented internal project specification for design and strategy, there would be a danger that a project could be costed, priced and sold against one design and strategic intention but executed using a different, more costly, approach. This risk increases when there is a long delay between submitting the tender to the potential customer and actually receiving the order.

All this emphasizes the importance to the contractor of compiling an internal design specification when a project tender is prepared. It is part of project task definition.

A specification is intended to do what its name implies: to specify that which shall be done. Managers who allow those reporting to them to depart without good cause from a design specification are guilty of incompetence, or weakness, or both.

Not invented here

It sometimes happens that engineers prefer to create a new design even though a perfectly adequate design already exists. They feel that they could do better themselves, or find fault unreasonably with the designs of others (even though those other engineers might enjoy a good reputation and their designs have been proven in successful earlier projects). This state of affairs is sometimes called the 'not invented here' syndrome. The results can be ugly. Two (of many) examples from my own experience follow; names have been omitted to avoid any risk of subsequent unpleasantness.

Case 1

A British company won an important export order to design, supply and install expensive electronic medical equipment to the teaching hospital of a famous European university.

Following an internal reorganization, the project's chief engineer resigned. His successor had different ideas and caused all design work completed or in progress to be scrapped and restarted. The design costs alone of that project eventually reached the same figure as the fixed price for which the whole project had originally been sold. That meant that the company had to write off the original design costs and bear all the considerable manufacturing and installation costs of the project itself.

The university professor was, quite understandably, making regular use of the telephone to ask, with commendable politeness, what were these 'unforeseen circumstances' that were preventing him from receiving his desperately needed equipment. Not only did the British contractor make a huge loss, but also the university had to wait for more than a year past the originally promised delivery date.

Case 2

An American company with a very high reputation for product excellence sent a set of engineering and manufacturing drawings to its new British subsidiary. This was a complete, finished design package for a large heavy engineering project. The intention was that it would provide the brand new machining and assembly shops with work during the start-up period when the local British design team was becoming established.

However, the drawings produced in America required Anglicizing. The intention was that the British engineers should check through all the drawings and, with help from the new purchasing department, ensure that the standards specifications and lists of bought-out components would be suitable for purchase from British suppliers.

What actually happened was that the UK team poured scorn on the American design, and the whole project was re-engineered from scratch at a cost of several million pounds.

Production methods for manufacturing projects

Similar arguments to those discussed above for specifying engineering design strategy apply to the need to associate the production methods actually used in manufacturing projects with those assumed in the cost estimates and subsequent budgets.

It can happen that certain rather bright individuals come up with suggestions during the proposal stage for cutting corners and saving expected costs – all aimed at securing a lower and more competitive tender price. That is, of course, laudable. Provided that these ideas are recorded with the estimates, all should be well and the cost savings can be achieved when the project goes ahead.

Now imagine what could happen if, for instance, a project proposal were to be submitted by one branch of the organization, but that for strategic reasons the company's managers decide to switch the work to a production facility at another, far-away location in the organization. If all the original ideas for saving production costs had not been recorded, the cost consequences could prove to be disastrous.

Unfortunately, it is not necessary to transfer work between different locations for mistakes of this kind to arise. Even the resignation of one production engineer from a manufacturing company could produce such consequences if his or her intentions and bright ideas had not been adequately recorded.

The golden rule, once again, is to define and document the project in all essential respects before the estimates are made and translated into budgets and price.

Construction specification

Construction projects offer another example of work that has to be defined by specification. All building contractors of any repute work from detailed specifications. The requirement to satisfy the statutory authorities is just one reason for documenting specifications of building location, layout, intended use, means of escape in case of fire, appearance and many other factors.

There are, of course, many design aspects of a building which can greatly affect its costs, including for instance the style of interior decoration, the quality of the fittings and installed equipment, lighting and air-conditioning standards.

Disputes can be minimized, if not prevented altogether, when a contractor produces a detailed project specification and asks the customer to accept it before the contract is signed. Any changes subsequently requested by the customer can then be identified easily as changes from the agreed specification and charged as variations to the original order.

SPECIFICATIONS FOR INTERNALLY FUNDED DEVELOPMENT PROJECTS

Development programmes aimed at introducing additions or changes to a company's product range are prone to overspending on cost budgets and late completion. One cause of this phenomenon is that chronic engineer's disease which I call 'creeping improvement sickness'. Management change and IT projects are also prone to unauthorized departures from the original intentions. Here are two case studies to illustrate these points. Case 1 is fiction and Case 2 happened in real life.

Case 1

The project

Bikes 'n Skates plc, a company producing bicycles and other wheeled devices, decided to add a children's motorized scooter to its product range. The aim was to produce a colourful two-wheeled affair with a foot platform and simple front column steering. That is the traditional scooter design with which we are all familiar from our childhood days, but with the important addition of a small petrol motor to drive the rear wheel. A simple brake on the front wheel would also be needed, to help prevent accidents to the riders, pedestrians and property.

Fierce competition from cheap foreign imports did not allow Bikes 'n Skates to set high prices, although the company commanded a small price premium because of its established name and reputation for making attractive, reliable, safe and high-quality products.

The scooter project was started in January, at the start of a new year, with the intention of having scooters in the warehouse for distribution and sale during the next Christmas season. The product was to be advertised in the run up to Christmas (which in the UK begins in July or August). In addition, models were to be exhibited and demonstrated at an autumn toy trade fair.

Management confidence was high. They had commissioned market research and the reports were favourable. The company had the necessary resource and manufacturing skills. By any standards this was a simple, small project. Its management required only straightforward budgeting and a modest degree of project control: it was certainly not dependent for its success on state-of-the-art project management techniques. Everything should have been straightforward. There was nothing that could go wrong. Or was there?

The kick-off meeting

The launch of the new product design can be visualized, starting with a meeting in the chief engineer's office. In addition to the chief engineer the meeting included representatives from other interested departments, such as sales and production. The other member needed to establish the necessary quorum was, of course, the design engineer (George) assigned to carry out the development and drawing work.

Discussion was focused on setting George on the right track to create the scooter envisaged by the company's directors. Thus George was given a set task with a number of objectives. However, these objectives were fairly broadly based and they were not written into a formal specification.

George can be imagined emerging from the meeting, full of ideas arising from the discussion and carrying his own rough notes and sketches. He would undoubtedly have been given some idea of target production costs, styling, performance, the preferred selling price and a date for stocks to be available in the warehouse for distribution and release to the market. He looked forward with excitement to testing the prototype himself, in the company car park.

Initial design

George was bubbling over with enthusiasm. Most competent engineers become keen when given responsibility for a new project on which their creative abilities can be unleashed. After few weeks' activity involving George and the company's prototype model workshop, George was able to wheel out the first experimental model of the new scooter. This model was subjected to test rides, reliability and safety tests, and the critical attention of various experts. Among these witnesses were marketing staff, an industrial styling designer and production engineers from the factory departments that were going to manufacture the scooter.

Preproduction stage

Following successful evaluation of the prototype and incorporation of recommendations from the experts, the next stage in the project was the preparation of production drawings, parts lists and specifications from which a small pilot preproduction batch of scooters could be manufactured. As one might reasonably expect, this preproduction phase of the project took considerably longer than the few weeks needed to build the first trial model. The production department decided to go ahead with some limited tooling, and the production engineers and others began to plan for full-scale manufacture.

Second thoughts

Apart from having to answer occasional production or purchasing queries, George had to endure a period of waiting. He became bored. His active mind was starved of work. This caused him to reflect on his design and led him to some second thoughts. On thumbing through the engine supplier's catalogue he found that he could have specified a better petrol engine, capable of propelling a heavier, older rider and giving more power in reserve. An informal telephone call to the supplier revealed that the order for engines could be changed without cancellation charges. So George, not a faint-hearted person afraid to make decisions, told the supplier to change the order. Then, almost as an afterthought, George asked Bikes 'n Skates's astonished purchasing manager to issue a purchase order amendment for the new engines, mentioning that the new engines would cost 15 per cent more than the first choice and take three weeks longer to deliver.

Early modifications

George then had to redesign the scooter chassis to provide stronger fixings for the new engine at a stage when the trial production batch had just started. Only simple changes were needed, but the trial batch (work-in-progress) had to be scrapped. Modified drawings and parts lists had to be prepared and issued to the production and purchasing departments. The change caused a three-week hold-up in the programme.

Unforeseen problems

At length, and in spite of the delays and additional expense, the prototype batch was completed and passed back to George and others for evaluation. George was dismayed to find that, because the enhanced engine power has increased the maximum speed from five to eight miles per hour, the braking system was no longer adequate. It was unsafe. That left George with the following two choices:

1.   Revert to the initial design, using the original engine and chassis.
2.   Modify the brake design.

George, a man of high ideals, could not contemplate the first choice because the idea of degrading the performance did not appeal to him. George considered redesign and changes to the brake manufacture a small price to pay in return for the improved performance. Accordingly George made and issued new drawings for the brake components and assembly.

Once again the manufacturing department had to be told to stop work and cancel a batch of components. George had produced the new drawings as quickly as he could, but the project was delayed by four more weeks. However, the modified prototypes eventually passed all their tests, so that tooling and planning for full-scale production could begin. All design and performance characteristics of the scooter were now excellent, exceeding those envisaged by the marketing department.

A good result?

The resulting scooter was unquestionably very good. When the production line started, the Bikes 'n Skates staff knew that they were making high-performance scooters. George was well pleased with the results of his labours and congratulated himself on a job well done.

The company's management was not so well pleased. The oft-repeated phrase 'time is money' is as true in project management as anywhere, and it is usually fairly safe to assume that if the planned timescale has been exceeded, so have the budgeted costs. It is apparent that development costs for this small scooter project rocketed over budget. Not only did it cost more to design the scooter than intended, but also the manufacturing costs had become so high that the intended profit margin was severely reduced. The first batch of scooters was produced so late that only a preproduction model could be exhibited at the autumn trade fair, and there were no warehouse stocks from which to supply the Christmas orders.

This disaster could have been prevented if George had carried out his original instructions. But what exactly were those original instructions? Where was the documentary proof? George was given only vague guidelines at the start of this project and it was easy for him to choose and change his own course of action. This simple example serves to show some of the pitfalls that can happen in a project that is not controlled from an adequate project specification.

George did, in fact, design a very good product, but not the product that management expected. He allowed his own ideas to intrude and he lost sight of the original objectives. George fell into a common trap by allowing the *best* to become the enemy of the *good*.

The Bikes 'n Skates project revisited: how it should have been done

It might be as well to take a second look at the scooter project and see how the course of events would have run under a regime employing some of the essential elements of project control.

Written specification

The project should have been launched with a written specification. In a well-conducted project each specification would define clearly all the design objectives from the start. The scooter project specification would also have included an account of the expected performance, with quantified data, quality and reliability standards, styling guidelines, size and weight limits, intended production costs and so on.

There is also the important question of timescale. The target date for project completion has to be decided carefully. It must be an objective that can be achieved. Product release target dates are often chosen to allow the product launch announcement to be made at an important trade exhibition.

Planning and control

A more effective check could have been kept on progress in our example if a simple programme schedule (such as a bar chart) had been included as part of the project specification. Provided that this identified all the important project events (milestones), regular management checks would have indicated the danger of late running soon enough for corrective action to be taken.

Change control

Now suppose that George had reached the stage in the project where previously he was allowed to introduce his first design change (the large engine). Under conditions of effective control he would not have been allowed to introduce any change after the issue of production drawings without prior discussion with other departments likely to be affected.

It is usual for changes of this nature to be brought up for approval before a representative 'change committee', 'change board' or at the least, a fairly senior manager. The committee will assess all the possible effects of any proposed change on stocks and work in progress, reliability, costs, timescale and so on before giving their consent or other instructions. We can be sure that at least some of the adverse effects of George's first change idea would have been foreseen. Apart from any technical reasons, this change would have been nipped in the bud because of the threat it posed to costs and the timescale.

Procedures for controlling changes are given in Chapter 25. It is enough at this stage to note that any other unnecessary changes proposed for the scooter project would also have met with an early demise under a sound administration.

George would have been kept on the right lines by the provision of a formal product specification and development programme, by the sensible control of modifications and, of course, by the day-to-day supervision of his superiors.

Case 2

Almost all projects in a large London engineering company were carried out for associated companies within the same group under cost-plus terms. Project pricing and charging methods are explained more fully in Chapter 22 but cost-plus arrangement meant that, instead of being charging fixed project prices, each client received a monthly bill for labour (the cost of time worked by the technological and scientific staff), the cost of materials and equipment used in construction, plus a small mark-up for profit. Considerable sums were involved for some of these projects.

To assess the labour charges each person filled in a weekly timesheet. There were up to 500 such timesheets to collect and check each week. Accounts clerks allocated the hours entered on the timesheets to their relevant projects, converted the hours to money using agreed rates, and billed the client companies accordingly. Managers received reports each month to show how the people in their departments had divided their working time between different clients' projects. All timesheet entries and analyses were subject to approval and independent audit to help prevent incorrect billings.

A separate clerical system was used to compare the number of drawings released for construction against the total number of drawings needed for the project. That system gave a crude form of progress measurement for inclusion in the monthly cost and progress reports sent to each client.

Timesheet analysis took approximately three weeks, so that clients with cost-plus contracts could not be billed immediately the revenues became due. Both the timesheet and the progress systems were slow, labour intensive and prone to clerical mistakes. Departmental managers complained that their attempts at cost control were hampered by the delays in getting feedback from the accounts department.

The project and its kick-off meeting

Senior management recognized that an internal IT system could be devised to improve the timesheet and progress analysis and reporting systems. In a one-to-one meeting with no witnesses present and no minutes taken, the general manager asked the computing manager to produce a program that would carry out timesheet analysis and produce cost and progress analyses for clients and the company's own managers. This was intended to be the beginning of a more comprehensive management information system and it was, indeed, called the MIS from the start.

The computing manager was asked to make the system modular, so that it could be extended later with add-on modules to include additional database functions. Another important requirement was that the system should be flexible to change.

Design and initial implementation

The computing manager gave the work priority within his IT department and the new timesheet analysis and reporting system was ready within a few weeks. First trial results were promising and timesheet data were processed within one week instead of the previous three.

The system for drawing progress reports was less successful, but that difficulty resulted from the problem (common in many companies) that engineering managers either submitted their progress inputs late or even failed to provide any input at all.

Everyone was pleased with the improvement in cash flow. Departmental managers appreciated the improved speed and accuracy of internal project cost reports. For these reasons, the MIS project was considered to be a success.

Unforeseen problems

A management consultancy firm was engaged to study the company's organization and recommend any changes thought to be desirable. They were conducting their investigation at the same time as the IT department was designing the new MIS project, but the consultants were working in comparative secrecy and neither they nor the IT department knew what the other was doing. As a result of the consultants' recommendations the senior company management agreed a fundamental reorganization of the company's project engineering departments.

I was present in the boardroom when the intention to change the organization was announced at a meeting of all the departmental managers. The computing manager was not present at this meeting. He was enjoying an extended 'fact-finding tour' of overseas companies in the group, all of which happened to be in the Southern hemisphere whilst those of us in London were enduring the English winter. No one had warned him that anyone whose job is insecure should never go on holiday, fall ill, or otherwise be away for more than a few days. (I've known several occasions when a manager returned from an extended absence to find their job and office chair occupied by another person.)

Thus, in the absence of his superior, it was the deputy computing manager who had to face questions on how long it would take to change the MIS to cope with the new organization structure. He replied that it would require a completely new program, written almost entirely from scratch, taking several weeks and costing a great deal of money. The existing system was neither modular nor flexible, as intended and, incidentally, the deputy manager had never been told of these requirements.

At this point another manager went bright scarlet in the face, and using language never before heard in that hallowed boardroom and strong enough to strip wallpaper, gave his critical opinion of the computing manager's competence before storming out of the room. When everyone had recovered from the shock, the deputy computing manager was given full responsibility for overseeing a new project to redesign the revised MIS software.

After several more weeks and additional expense, a good MIS system emerged that served the company well, but only after a good deal of time and money had been wasted. This case provides another example of a project that was flawed from the outset because it was not properly defined and there was no project specification. Another important contributing factor to this project failure was lack of communication between the senior management, the external management consultants and the IT department.

DEVELOPING AND DOCUMENTING THE PROJECT SPECIFICATION

Given the importance of specifying project requirements as accurately as possible, it is appropriate to end this chapter with some thoughts on the preparation of a specification document.

Producing the project specification

Although customers might be clear from the very first about their needs, it is usual for dialogue to take place between a customer and one of more potential contractors before a contract for any project of significant size is signed. During these discussions, each contractor can be expected to make various preliminary proposals to the customer for executing the project. Some of those proposals might suggest changes to the customer's initial enquiry specification – changes intended to improve the project deliverables or otherwise work to the mutual benefit of customer and contractor.

In some engineering companies this pre-project phase is aptly known as 'solution engineering'. Each contractor's sales engineering group works to produce and recommend an engineering solution which they consider would best suit the customer (and win the order). Solution engineering might last a few days, several months or even years. It can be an expensive undertaking, especially when the resulting tender fails to win the contract.

Although it is tempting to imagine the chosen contractor's sales engineers settling down contentedly to write a single, definitive project specification, the practice is likely to be quite different. The first draft descriptive text, written fairly early in the proceedings, will probably undergo various additions and amendments as the outline solution develops. It is likely to be revised and reissued more than once. The text will typically be associated with a pile of drawings, artists' impressions, flowsheets, schedules or other documents appropriate to the type of project. Those documents, too, might suffer several changes and re-issues before the agreed solution is reached.

Projects of all types can undergo a process similar to the solution engineering process just described. For example, the requirements for a management change or IT project are likely to evolve as the various stakeholders make their views known, until a final consensus definition of the project task is reached.

A fundamental requirement when a contract is eventually signed, or a charter is approved for a management change project, is to be able to refer without ambiguity to the correct revision of the project specification. The correct version is that which defines the project according to the finally agreed intentions. Remember that the *latest* issue of any document might not be the *correct* issue.

The only safe way to identify any document is to label it with a unique serial or identifying number, and augment that with a revision number every time the document is re-issued with changes.

Format and content

The format described here is typical for a well-prepared project specification:

1. *Binder* – The specification for a large project is going to be around for some time and receive considerable handling. It deserves the protection of an adequate binder. The binder should be loose-leaf, or otherwise allow the addition or substitution of amended pages.

2. *Specification identifier* – The binder should carry the specification serial (identification) number, the project number (if different) and the project title. All of these should be prominently displayed.

3. *Control schedule of specification documents* – This vital part of the specification complements the specification identifier by denoting the revision status of the complete document. Ideally it should be bound in the folder along with the main text (either in the front or at the back). The control schedule must list every document which forms part of the complete specification. This includes drawings too large to be conveniently bound with the main text and other external documents that are relevant to adequate project definition (for example, engineering standards specifications or statutory regulations).

   Minimum data required for each document are its title, serial number and correct revision number. Should any associated document itself be complex, it too should have its own inbuilt control schedule.

   The control schedule should be given the same serial and amendment number as the document that it controls. If the specification is numbered XYZ123 and is at revision 6, then the control schedule itself should also be numbered XYZ123, revision 6. Thus the amendment state of the entire project specification (including all its attachments and associated documents) can always be identified accurately simply by giving one amendment number.

4.   *Descriptive text* – The narrative describing the project should be written clearly and concisely. The text should be preceded by a contents list, and be divided logically into sections, with all pages numbered.

Every amendment must be given an identifying serial number or letter, and the overall amendment (or revision) number for the entire specification must be raised each time the text is changed. Amended paragraphs or additional pages should be highlighted, for example by placing the relevant amendment number alongside the change (possibly within an inverted triangle in the manner often used for engineering drawings).

5.   *Supporting documents* – Most project specifications need a number of supporting technical and other documents that cannot conveniently be contained within the binder. These effectively form part of the specification and they must all be listed in the control schedule.

6.   *Distribution list* – A responsible person must keep a list of all those who received the initial issue of the specification. This can be used as a control document to ensure that all holders of the specification receive subsequent amendments. The safest form of control is to bind the distribution list in with all copies of the specification, although this can occasionally be politically undesirable.

4   *Estimating the Project Costs*

Reliable cost estimates are necessary for all projects, whether or not they are to be sold for a fixed price to an external customer. Without a cost estimate it would be impossible to carry out financial appraisal, prepare a business plan, establish detailed budgets, control spending, assess manpower requirements or perform many other management procedures.

INTRODUCTION TO COST ESTIMATING

Figure 4.1, shows a cost estimate summary as it might be set out for a typical project. It is generally understood in accounting circles that the word 'cost' should never be used alone, without a qualifying adjective. Some cost accounting terms that occur frequently in project management are shown in Figure 4.1, and in the following section.

Terms commonly used in project cost accounting

Absorption costing – a method that attempts to recover indirect costs (overheads) by apportioning them over all the company's direct costs.

    Below-the-line costs – a collective name for the various allowances that are added once a total basic cost estimate has been made. Below-the-line costs typically include allowances for cost escalation, exchange rate fluctuations, contingencies and provisional cost items.

    Cost escalation – increases in all costs above their original estimates owing to national cost inflation and increases in wages and salaries. Usually expressed as a rate per cent and only significant in times of high inflation, or for projects planned to last for several years.

    Direct costs – costs that can be directly attributed to project work. These are also 'variable costs', because their rate of expenditure depends on the intensity of project activity. When no work is being done on the project, there are no direct costs.

    Cost of sales – equivalent to the sum of all the above-the-line costs shown in Figure 4.1.

    General and administrative costs – a general cost burden, added as a proportion per cent of the above-the-line costs by some companies to recover selling and other expenses (for instance head office costs) that are not included in the overhead costs.

    Indirect costs – costs that must be incurred by the organization to provide heat, light, accommodation, insurances, maintenance, accountants, secretaries, welfare, management salaries, and other general running costs of the business that cannot be attributed as costs to be charged to a specific project. Because these costs do not vary from day to day they are also 'fixed costs'. Also known as 'overhead costs'. However, the administration and accommodation costs of a construction

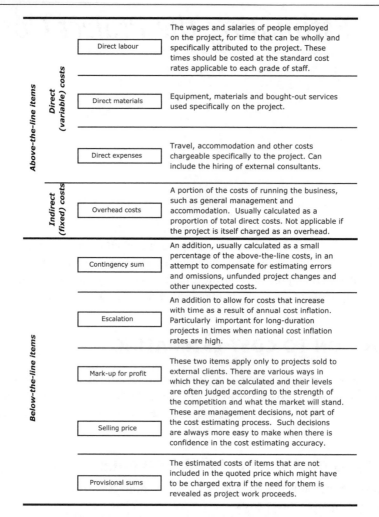

Above-the-line items	**Direct (variable) costs**	Direct labour	The wages and salaries of people employed on the project, for time that can be wholly and specifically attributed to the project. These times should be costed at the standard cost rates applicable to each grade of staff.
		Direct materials	Equipment, materials and bought-out services used specifically on the project.
		Direct expenses	Travel, accommodation and other costs chargeable specifically to the project. Can include the hiring of external consultants.
	Indirect (fixed) costs	Overhead costs	A portion of the costs of running the business, such as general management and accommodation. Usually calculated as a proportion of total direct costs. Not applicable if the project is itself charged as an overhead.
Below-the-line items		Contingency sum	An addition, usually calculated as a small percentage of the above-the-line costs, in an attempt to compensate for estimating errors and omissions, unfunded project changes and other unexpected costs.
		Escalation	An addition to allow for costs that increase with time as a result of annual cost inflation. Particularly important for long-duration projects in times when national cost inflation rates are high.
		Mark-up for profit	These two items apply only to projects sold to external clients. There are various ways in which they can be calculated and their levels are often judged according to the strength of the competition and what the market will stand. These are management decisions, not part of the cost estimating process. Such decisions are always more easy to make when there is confidence in the cost estimating accuracy.
		Selling price	
		Provisional sums	The estimated costs of items that are not included in the quoted price which might have to be charged extra if the need for them is revealed as project work proceeds.

Figure 4.1   Typical summary layout of a project cost estimate

site are a special exception because they *can* be directly attributed to the particular construction project and can therefore be treated as direct costs.

Labour burden – an amount, usually a percentage of wages or salaries, that is added to the basic hourly or weekly rate for employees to allow for non-working time and various additional expenses such as the cost of paid holidays and per capita amounts payable by the employer as employee benefits, either voluntarily or as a requirement of the national legislation. In the UK, for example, these would include employers' National Insurance contributions. For project estimating and control, it is best if this burden is included in standard labour cost rates.

Materials burden – an amount added by some contractors to the actual cost of bought out materials to recover their purchasing administration costs. This might be charged at 10 per cent or less for very high-cost but at (say) 25 per cent on small low-cost items that have relatively high handling and administration costs. A common all-round rate used for the materials burden is 15 per cent.

Overhead rate – more properly called the overhead absorption rate, this is a rate calculated by accountants that expresses the company's total expected overhead costs for a given period (usually a year) as a proportion of the expected direct costs over the same period. It is used to calculate the overhead recovery amount included in prices (see Figure 4.1). There are differences between companies in the treatment of overhead costs, but a common method in projects is to apportion the overhead costs as a percentage of direct labour costs. Overhead rates vary considerably from one company to another, perhaps from as low as 50 to as high as 200 per cent or even more. In a few cases contractors will even apply different overhead rates to different projects. The rate used will depend on many factors that include, for example, the ratio of direct to indirect staff, the amount of internally funded research and development being done, local authority and public utility charges, and so on. High overhead rates increase prices and reduce competitive advantage. There is more on overhead costs in Chapter 26.

Prime cost – the sum of all the direct costs needed to fulfil a particular job or project (direct labour plus direct materials plus direct expenses).

Standard costing – an important and common accounting system in which cost estimates and actual project expenditure are calculated using average or 'standard costs' for direct labour and materials. These standards are calculated by cost accountants as expected averages for each grade of labour and for materials that are commonly held in stores and issued from general stock. Standard costs for materials are particularly relevant to manufacturing projects. Standard labour costs are important for most projects and they greatly simplify cost estimating. From time to time the accountants check the current standard labour cost rates against actual expenditure and they will issue revised standard rates whenever the variances become significant (usually as a result of cost inflation).

Variance – a term commonly used by accountants to describe the difference between actual costs and standard costs in a standard costing system. More widely, it is the amount by which any actual cost differs from its corresponding estimate or budget. Also used less commonly for the difference in time between an actual event and its planned time. Variances concentrate management attention on departures from budget or plan and are a good example of 'management by exception'.

CLASSIFICATION OF COSTS AS DIRECT OR INDIRECT

There are considerable differences between companies in the interpretation of direct and indirect costs. Some firms charge to projects the costs of printing drawings, for example, and recover those costs directly by billing them to the client or customer. Other firms would regard such costs as indirect, and charge them to overheads. Sometimes the classification of costs as direct or indirect can vary even from project to project within the same company, depending on what each customer has agreed and contracted to pay for as a direct charge. To a large extent, the type of projects usually undertaken by a company and the industry in which the company operates will determine how the split between direct and indirect costs is made. Solicitors, for example, often charge their clients for the costs of correspondence and telephone calls that many other companies would regard as indirect costs to be included in the general overheads.

Cost estimators and project managers must be clear about the distinction between direct and indirect costs in their particular company. They must also be made aware of any exceptions to the rule caused by special terms in a project contract that allow the contractor to bill items that would otherwise be covered in overheads.

ESTIMATING ACCURACY

Estimating must start from a task list or some form of project specification, the preparation of which was described in Chapter 3. It is clear that the better the project can be defined at the outset, the less chance there should be of making estimating errors. However, the possibility of error can never be reduced to zero. No sensible person could ever declare the initial cost estimates for a total project to be entirely free from error and completely accurate. Estimating always involves an element of personal judgement. A project, because it is a new venture, must contain some surprises. If the final project costs did happen to equal the initial estimates, that would be a matter for some congratulation and celebration but it would also be a matter of chance. In some cases it might not even be possible to declare with confidence what the true costs actually are at the end of a project, owing to the complexities of cost collection, cost apportionment and accounting methods.

There are clearly many reasons beyond the estimator's control why the final project costs might differ from the best possible estimates. It is, therefore, inappropriate to label early estimates as 'accurate' or 'inaccurate' because the outcome can never be foretold with certainty and one can only determine the true accuracy of any estimate after the work has been done and the true costs become known. Perhaps 'reliability' or 'degree of confidence' would be better measures of an estimate's quality.

Steps can, of course, be taken to remove some sources of estimating errors. Several methods are discussed in this chapter and elsewhere in this book. Cost estimators should be aware of the problems, but must not allow these to deflect them from their primary task, which must always be to use all the data and time available to produce the best estimate possible – in other words a calculated judgement of what the project *should* cost if all goes according to plan.

Estimates made with a high degree of confidence will greatly assist those responsible for any competitive pricing decision, and good estimates improve the effectiveness of cost budgets and resource schedules.

CLASSIFICATION OF ESTIMATES ACCORDING TO CONFIDENCE

Some companies find it convenient to classify project cost estimates according to the degree of confidence that their estimators can express in their ultimate accuracy. These classifications depend on the quality of information available to the estimators, the time allowed for preparing the estimates and the stage reached in the project life history. Different organizations have their own ideas, but here is one example of a classification set.

- *Ballpark estimates* are those made when only vague outline information exists and when practically all details of the work have yet to be decided. Ballpark estimates are also made in emergencies, when all the detailed information necessary for a more detailed estimate is available but there is insufficient time allowed for its proper consideration. An example of such a ballpark estimate is seen when a manager is presented with a set of manufacturing drawings and, when asked to answer the question 'What will this lot cost to make?', weighs the pile of drawings thoughtfully in his/her hands and declares 'About fifty thousand pounds'.

  Ballpark estimates are widely used in many industries. They are particularly valuable for carrying out preliminary checks on possible resource requirements, for screening enquiries for tenders and for other early decisions. Ballpark estimates are unlikely to provide sufficient accuracy for other purposes and should clearly not be used as a basis for fixed price-tendering. A well-reasoned ballpark estimate might achieve an accuracy of ±25 per cent, given a very generous amount of luck and good judgement but far wider divergence can be expected.

- *Comparative estimates*, as their name implies, are made by comparing work to be done on the new project or one of its tasks with similar work done on previous projects. They can be attempted before detailed design work takes place, when there are no reliable materials lists or work schedules. They depend on a good outline project definition, which must enable the estimator to identify all the principal elements and assess their degree of size and complexity. The other main requirement is access to cost and technical archives of past projects which contain comparable (they need not be identical) elements. Apart from commercial risks outside the estimator's control (foreign exchange rate fluctuations, for example), accuracy will depend very much on the degree of confidence that can be placed in the proposed design solutions, on the working methods eventually chosen and on the closeness with which the new project elements can be matched with those of previous projects. It might not be possible to achieve better than ±15 per cent accuracy.

Comparative estimates are commonly used as the basis for tenders in manufacturing and other engineering projects. When the time available for tendering is very short, contractors for construction projects may also be obliged to rely on comparative estimates, but they should then build in as many allowances for contingencies as competitive pricing will permit.

- *Feasibility estimates* can be derived only after a significant amount of preliminary project design has been carried out. In construction projects, for example, the building specification, site data, provisional layouts and outline drawings for services are all necessary. Quotations must be obtained from potential suppliers of expensive project equipment or subcontracts, and material take-offs or other schedules should be available to assist with estimating the costs of materials. The accuracy 'confidence factor' for feasibility estimates should be better than ±10 per cent. This class of estimate is often used for construction tenders.
- *Definitive estimates* cannot be made until most design work has been finished, all significant purchase orders have been placed at known prices and work on the project is well advanced or nearing completion. Definitive estimates can be produced from scratch, but the best practice is to arrive at them by updating the original comparative or feasibility estimates routinely as part of the project cost reporting and control procedure. Barring shocks or disasters during project execution, the accuracy of the total project estimate should improve as work proceeds and the estimated costs are, one by one, replaced by their corresponding actual costs. Estimates can be labelled as 'definitive' when the time is reached where their accuracy is regarded as ±5 per cent or better. Unless the accounting and cost control systems are flawed the figures for actual project costs and the definitive project estimate should converge when all work on the project is finished.

The degrees of accuracy quoted in these examples are about as good as could ever be expected. It is very likely that many organizations will assign wider limits. It is also common to find asymmetric limits, slewed about zero. A company might, for example, work on the assumption that its ballpark estimates are accurate to within +50 or –10 per cent.

All those using estimates for pricing decisions, setting budgets, financial planning or any other purpose need to be aware of how much confidence can be placed in the figures put before them. If the organization's estimating procedures recognize and define different categories, such as ballpark, comparative, feasibility, definitive or whatever, then managers can make their decisions accordingly, and to better effect.

ESTIMATING ACCURACY IN RELATION TO PRICES AND PROFITS

It is difficult to lay down rules on the degree of estimating accuracy needed for setting fixed prices. Different companies will undoubtedly have their own rules or traditions. For pricing purposes much depends on the size of the intended profit margin, since a large margin will cushion the effects of small estimating errors. Margins vary greatly, depending on market conditions and, particularly, on accepted practice in the relevant industry. Reliable estimates are a valuable asset to managers faced with the difficult task of trying to price a project in the teeth of keen competition, where there is no scope for the luxury of safety factors such as a high mark-up on costs or the inclusion of substantial contingency allowances.

Vulnerability of profit margins to estimating errors and cost variances

The vulnerability of profits to erosion from costs which exceed their budgets is not always appreciated. A simple example will illustrate this point.

Consider a project which was sold for a fixed price of £1million against a total cost estimate of £850 000. The budgeted gross profit was therefore £150 000, which is 15 per cent of the selling price.

Now suppose that the project actually cost £910 000 instead of the estimated £850 000. This £60 000 cost variance represents an estimating error of about 7 per cent. Some might think this a small error, and the managers of several recent projects in the public eye that have cost over double their estimates would be delighted by such a result. However, a cost estimating error of 7 per cent would cause a significant reduction in gross profit. In this case it has been slashed from a planned £150 000 to only £90 000, a reduction of not 7 per cent but 40 per cent. The expected profit has been almost halved. That is how this outcome would be viewed by the company's management and other stakeholders.

Planned profits can fall victim to many risks. Some of these can be predicted but others often come as unpleasant surprises. The aim must be to reduce the number of unknown variables or risks as far as possible, and then provide a sensible allowance to cover those that remain.

Profits are vulnerable and deserve the protection of good estimates and budgets. Managing a project which has been underestimated can be a soul-destroying experience, with everything running late, everyone demoralized and all remaining cost predictions made only for the purpose of assessing the size of the impending loss. Project managers who have presided over this depressing state of affairs would not wish to repeat the experience. If they were in any way responsible they may not be given the chance.

VERSION CONTROL OF PROJECT COST ESTIMATES

It is not unusual, especially for large capital projects, for protracted technical and feasibility discussions to take place between the contractor and the potential client before agreement and authorization of a final version of the project specification and its associated cost estimate. The client's ideas on project scope might change during these discussions, and some versions could envisage different roles for the contractor. Proposed engineering solutions often change, particularly when the contractor's engineers are able to suggest alternative technical solutions that would bring mutual benefit to both the client and the contractor.

Project feasibility studies are another case where several versions of a project might be specified. Quite often a number of rather different project strategies are thoroughly investigated, each with its own project specification, cost estimate and financial appraisal report.

Each different version of a proposed project is certain to require its own, unique, cost estimate. It is therefore important to be able to relate every one of these different cost estimates to the relevant version of the project specification. Enormous risks could face a contractor if a fixed-price tender based on the wrong cost estimate were to be offered and accepted.

The solution is usually straightforward. Each different version of the project specification must be given a unique case number. For example, suppose that a project specification were to be developed and given the serial number X1234. As different strategies and solutions are investigated, the relevant versions of the project specification would be numbered X1234 case A, X1234 case B, X1234 case C and so on. Each cost estimate can then carry the same serial and case number as its corresponding project specification.

Further refinement might be needed if any or all of these cost estimates should be re-issued with corrections or small changes, in which case revision numbers would also have to be added. Thus, if an error resulted in the re-issue of a cost estimate for project X1234 case B, the corresponding estimate would be labelled X1234 case B, revision 1 (the original would be issued at revision 0).

These considerations are often considered tedious and boring, not challenging for the creative mind, but version control is important for all significant project documents, not least their cost estimates.

TOP-DOWN OR BOTTOM-UP?

There are two fundamentally opposite ways of approaching cost estimating for a large project. The approach taken depends upon the time available, the degree of accuracy expected and, above all, the level of project definition.

Top-down

Very early in the project life history, there will be outline proposals for the nature and scope of the project, but certainly no detailed task list or comprehensive work breakdown. Thus cost estimates can be made only on a global comparative basis. That means trying to assess the cost of the whole project by comparing it with similar projects that have been completed in the recent past and for which their actual cost records can be accessed.

If the project can be divided into a few major parts at this early stage, it should be possible to distribute the total estimate over those parts, remembering to leave something in reserve in the form of a separate contingency item. Thus all estimates originate from the whole, or top of the project, which is why this approach is called top-down.

It is apparent that top-down estimates must usually be ballpark. They have the disadvantage of not being based on a detailed project specification. They cannot take into account many factors that will not become known until much later in the project life history and their inherent accuracy will not be high. However, because top-down estimates are often based on comparisons with completed projects, there is less risk (when compared to bottom-up estimating) of forgetting to include items and thus arriving at dangerously low estimates.

Bottom-up estimating

The opposite extreme to the top-down approach is bottom-up estimating. This method can only take place when a good project specification exists and a fairly complete task list has been compiled. Bottom-up estimating begins at the lowest level of detail, and is gradually extended up through the hierarchical structure of the project until the total estimated project cost is reached at the top of the tree (work breakdown structures are explained in Chapter 12). Because bottom-up estimates are made later in the project life history, when more is known about the project, they should be more accurate than top-down estimates. However, bottom-up estimates can be more prone to errors of omission than top-down estimates. The methods that follow in this chapter are all based on bottom-up estimating.

COMPILING THE TASK LIST

The first stage in the bottom-up cost estimating process is to compile a complete list of every known item that is going to cost money. This can prove difficult. But any item inadvertently left out of the cost estimates will result in an underestimate for the project as a whole. That could jeopardize planning and scheduling and (if not realized in time) lead to serious problems and red faces when the time comes to hand the project over to the customer. And, of course, if the project has been sold for a fixed price, any items forgotten by the estimator must be paid for not out of the budgeted project funds, but from the contractor's expected profits.

Work breakdown structure as a starting point

Preparation of a work breakdown structure (which is a project family tree or 'goes into chart'), complete with cost codes, is a logical way of considering the total project and should reduce the risk of errors of omission in cost estimates. Coded work breakdowns are described in Chapter 12 and an outline example is given later in this chapter as Figure 4.2. However, cost estimates are usually required during the early project definition stages, before a contract exists. Many of the smaller cost items will be unknown or ill-defined at this estimating stage and it would be difficult or impossible to compile a work breakdown structure in sufficient detail for bottom-up estimating. Thus, whilst a detailed work breakdown structure is the ideal framework for a project cost estimate, in practice the earliest estimates will have to be compiled from a simple task list or, at best, a rudimentary form of the work breakdown structure. A fair degree of skill and judgement is, therefore, necessary in listing all the items that should be included in the early project cost estimates and there is plenty of scope for errors. Yet many important decisions usually depend on these estimates, including fixed-price quotations and project approval or rejection.

Using checklists

One very useful way of helping to prevent forgotten tasks is to use checklists, such as those used for early project definition (described in Chapter 3). Every company with sufficient experience can develop these. A full checklist would include all possible factors – technical, commercial, statutory, environmental, social and so on – that might eventually have a bearing on the work and its costs.

Some checklists can be long and detailed documents. Typically they will list as many possibilities as the compiler can think up, so that they must inevitably include some irrelevancies and seem tedious to use. It is, however, in this very wealth of detail that the importance and strength of checklists lie.

Software tasks

The task list must include not only all the obvious items of project hardware, but also every associated software job. Software is a familiar term in the context of computers and IT projects, but most projects quite remote from computer work have their own software content. Schedules for production inspection and testing, instruction and maintenance manuals, lists of recommended spares and consumable items may have to be specially written. These, together with any other documentation specified in the proposal or contract, are software tasks which must usually be allowed for in the estimated costs.

Forgotten tasks

Activities often forgotten during the estimating phase of manufacturing projects, only to be remembered too late for inclusion in the project budgets (and prices), include incidental processes such as paint spraying, heat treatments, inspection and testing. In some firms these may be covered by the general overhead rate, but in many others they will not and must be listed among the direct cost estimates. Protective plating, silk-screen printing, engraving and so on are frequently omitted from estimates. A more serious omission during project cost estimating is the work entailed in final commissioning, handover and customer acceptance of the completed project.

Contracts often require the project contractor to provide training facilities for some of the customer's staff. The manufacturer of a complex and special machine might be expected, for example, to install the machine and supervise its start-up by training the customer's operatives and maintenance technicians. Training sessions can involve the contractor's senior engineers in much hard work, both in the actual training and in preparing the training manuals beforehand. Incidental expenses may also arise for accommodation and meals, depending on where the training is to be carried out.

Whether the proposal is for a manufacturing project, a large capital construction project, management change or an IT project, the business of filling as many gaps as possible in the task list is a continuous aspect of project definition. Indeed, the project specification might have to be revised and reissued more than once as the task list is developed.

LEVEL OF DETAIL IN PROJECT COST ESTIMATING

Some difficulty might be experienced in deciding how much detail to show in the task list. What is a 'task' for this purpose?

Consider, for instance, the problem of estimating the total cost of a manufacturing project, as part of the process of preparing a fixed-price proposal. The cost estimate must be made before any detailed design has taken place, and therefore without the benefit of any drawings. It will not be possible to list all the manufacturing operations or the raw materials needed for each separate part. It will not even be known at this early stage what or how many parts are going to be needed. Therefore this initial cost estimate, even though it might lead to a fixed-price commitment, can only be carried out on a much broader scale than estimates for run-of-the-mill production.

Each task should be selected so that it is small enough to be visualized easily for estimating purposes. On the other hand, the task must be large enough to represent a measurable and significant part of the whole project. The design and manufacture of each subassembly from a main piece of equipment might rank as a task, while the final assembly of all these subassemblies could be regarded as another.

An example that applies to many kinds of projects is the writing, editing and printing of an instruction manual or an operating and maintenance manual. These are items that should be set out as discrete tasks. Separately identifiable purchases of expensive bought-out components and equipment should also be listed, where these are not already included in other tasks. Any special requirement for packing and despatch of the final project might have to be listed as a task, particularly if the project has to be delivered to a customer overseas.

Every one of the examples just given is an identifiable and specific part of the project, chosen at a level intended to make the job of estimating easier and more reliable. Careful identification of all significant tasks at this stage, in addition to the importance for cost estimating, will provide a basis for budgeting, scheduling and subsequent control.

ESTIMATING FORMATS

Completion of a task list has established the basis for project cost estimating. When the estimates have been collected they will contain a large amount of data. These data should be presented in a format that will allow easy reference, detailed analysis and extension into total amounts – whether for departmental costs or for packages at any level of the project work breakdown.

A certain amount of procedural discipline has to be imposed on the estimating function throughout the organization, and from one project to another. Estimates should be tabulated according to a standard company procedure, itemized where possible by cost codes within the work breakdown structure (see Chapter 12). This will help to ensure that comparisons can readily be made later in the project life history between the estimates and the cost accountant's records of the actual costs eventually incurred, on a strict item-for-item basis. This is essential as part of the cost control function. As experience builds up over a few years and more data are collected it will also contribute to the accuracy of comparative estimates for new projects.

If no work breakdown structure exists, and the initial cost estimate is simply set out like a shopping list, it should be reorganized into a hierarchical work breakdown format as soon as the project's work breakdown structure becomes known.

Some cost estimates, especially those for defence and other national government projects, may be liable to investigation by external auditors at one or more stages. These investigations can be exhaustive and taken into considerable detail. Paying careful attention to logic and detail in presenting the cost estimates can help to establish the good relations necessary for reaching a fair agreement.

Observance of company policy on cost rates and costing methods, as well as the need to determine working budgets, imposes an obligation on the project manager to ensure that the estimates are set down in a standard and logical manner. Calculations performed in odd corners of notebooks, on scraps of paper and on the backs (or fronts) of envelopes are prone to error and premature loss. They will be unlikely to fulfil any of the conditions already mentioned. In other words, standardized estimating formats are needed (either as hard copy or as forms on a computer).

All estimating forms are spreadsheets. A large project will need many of these, and they should be compiled in sets and subsets that reflect the anatomy of the whole project. The work breakdown structure (WBS) is the ideal model, where such exists. The WBS principle is shown in Figure 4.2 and explained more thoroughly in Chapter 12. Each item should have a cost code, allocated according

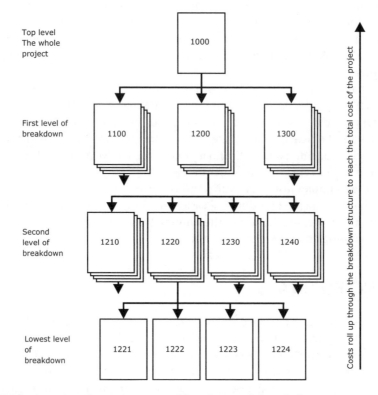

Figure 4.2   Project cost estimate arranged by the work breakdown structure

to a hierarchical system. These codes (also described in Chapter 12) are essential for sorting and retrieving not only the estimates, but also their corresponding actual costs in a computer database. That system will allow the cost estimate for any item to be estimated and filed in a place from which it can easily be retrieved later. It will also facilitate any calculations that require various permutations and combinations of the cost estimates.

General purpose cost estimating format

An example of a general purpose estimating tabulation is given in Figure 4.3. This design is based on a form used for projects ranging from small electronics units to prefabricated hospital operating theatres. All these projects, although very different in design and work content, shared the typical project characteristic of requiring special engineering design, followed by project purchasing, leading to manufacture, testing and completion in single or small batch quantities.

The general purpose format in Figure 4.3 allows for six labour grades to be shown and assumes that all hours will be costed at standard cost rates. Six grades should be adequate, provided that the standard costing system has been designed sensibly and has not been complicated by interference from the 'wouldn't it be nice if ...' brigade. The standard grade code and cost rate used should be entered in the space at the head of each column to show the rates that were current at the time of estimating.

There is no need to complicate a general purpose estimating form by adding columns for such things as special tooling. Such items can easily be accommodated by considering each as a separate task in its own right. Each can be entered on a row, and the costs added up along the row in the same way as for any other task.

The inclusion of a column headed 'Longest delivery' in the materials section might appear unusual in a form intended primarily for cost estimating. However, the people who estimate material costs are also the people most probably able to predict delivery times. It is convenient and more efficient to collect both sets of data from them as early as possible and on the same occasion. This extends the usefulness of these forms by enabling their use as a valuable information source for subsequent timescale planning.

COST ESTIMATE									Project number or sales reference:				Estimate number: Case: Date:			
Estimate for:									Compiled by:				Page of			
1	2	3	4	5	6	7	8	9	10	11	12	13	14	15		
Code	Item description	Qty	Labour times and costs by standard grade						Total direct labour cost	Overhead cost	Materials			Total cost 10+11 +12+13		
			Grade 1	Grade 2	Grade 3	Grade 4	Grade 5	Grade 6			Standard or net cost	Burden	Longest delivery			
			Hrs	£	Hrs	£	Hrs	£	Hrs	£	Hrs	£	Hrs	£		%	cost	%	(weeks)	

Figure 4.3   Useful format for general cost estimating

Additional columns could be provided on the estimating form to allow mark-ups and selling prices to be shown. These were omitted from the example in Figure 4.3, partly through lack of space but particularly because the relationship between cost estimates and project pricing is not usually simple and is often decided by senior management according to the circumstances surrounding each project.

Estimating format for materials purchases on larger projects

In larger projects, general all-purpose forms are inadequate for listing all the cost estimate considerations for the purchases of materials, components and equipment.

Estimates for many of the bulk materials used in construction projects are often made on very detailed schedules or material 'take-offs' which are specially designed for each of the particular engineering disciplines involved (such as piping take-offs compiled by fluids engineers and steel take-offs worked out by the civil and structural engineers).

However, the form shown in Figure 4.4 can be used for listing the cost estimates for significant items of equipment or other high-cost purchases required for a project. Provision is made on this form for including freight and duty costs, which are of course especially relevant when the delivery site is distant or overseas from the source of supply. Totals or convenient subtotals from materials take-offs and other materials schedules can be transferred to this type of form to allow the complete project materials costs to be summarized and totalled.

General purpose project cost and price summary format

The format in Figure 4.5 can be used in many cases to summarize project cost estimates and assist in pricing. This has been designed for flexibility, for use over a wide range of different projects and companies. Although spaces for various rates, allowances and mark-ups are provided, the way in which these are used can be chosen to fit in with a particular company's management and accounting

COST ESTIMATE FOR MATERIALS AND PURCHASED EQUIPMENT					Project number or sales reference:					Estimate number: Case: Date:			
Estimate for:						Compiled by:				Page	of		
Cost code	Description	Spec. No (If known)	Proposed supplier	Unit	Unit cost F.O.B.	Quoted currency	Exchange rate used	Converted FOB cost	Qty	Project FOB cost	Ship mode	Freight Cost	Taxes/ duties	Delivered cost
					Total delivered materials and equipment costs this				→					

Figure 4.4 Format for estimating the costs of materials and bought-out equipment on larger projects

PROJECT COST AND PRICE SUMMARY   Estimate ref:

Project title:Case number:

Client/customer:ˋDate:

                                                                £

Labour costs by standard grade

1 hours at £ _____   = £ _____ _____

2 hours at £ _____   = £ _____ _____

3 hours at £ _____   = £ _____ _____

4 hours at £ _____   = £ _____ _____

5 hours at £ _____   = £ _____ _____

6 hours at £ _____   = £ _____ _____

Total labour cost   ⟶

Materials, equipment and bought-out services   ⟶

Other expenses(professional fees, licensing, etc.) ⟶   _____

Prime cost   ⟶

Overhead costs at _____% of total labour cost   ⟶

Materials burden at _____% (if any)   ⟶

Overseas costs and handling charges (if any)   ⟶   _____

Basic estimated project cost   ⟶

                          Allowances

Escalation at _____% per annum for_____years   ⟶

Contingency _____%   ⟶

Other allowances (if any)   ⟶   _____

Total estimated project cost   ⟶

Mark-up_____%   ⟶

Indicated selling price   ⟶ [   ]

Notes, provisional items, etc.

Figure 4.5   General purpose format for indicating the price of a small project

requirements. The form allows the actual figures and formula used in the cost/price relationship to be recorded but it does not dictate the pricing mechanism too rigidly, because the price must usually be considered by senior management according to the merits of each case.

ESTIMATING MANUFACTURING COSTS

Manufacturing organizations prefer to use drawings and parts lists or bills of material as the basis for making cost estimates. Those documents allow accurate estimation of the raw materials and components needed, and production engineers can work out the operations needed to make the parts and estimate labour times from those. Several common key factors can be identified in the use of routine methods. Work is always broken down into small elements before estimates are applied. The estimates themselves can usually be described as 'standard' or 'known' quantities, and any need for guesswork is either eliminated or reduced to a minimum. Reliance is placed not on personal opinions of how long each job should take, but on the results of long experience, detailed analysis and scientific work measurement.

Estimating manufacturing costs without detailed drawings

Project cost estimating is usually quite different from routine manufacturing estimating because the estimates must be made long before detailed drawings exist. Suppose that an estimate is to be prepared for a control unit. This is a box that will be filled with instrumentation. However, detailed design has yet to take place and manufacturing drawings do not exist. Only one box of this special type is to be made, for use on the particular project. The only information on which a cost estimate can be based is an engineer's written design specification. This specification includes little or no information about dimensions, materials or the contents of the box. It simply states the functional performance expected of the completed product in terms of its input and output parameters and its planned operating environment. If the estimator is very lucky, there might be a rough outline sketch of the box.

Standard estimating tables will be of little help here. Build-up of time and cost standards depends upon the establishment of production continuity, which demands in turn that a certain minimum volume of production must take place. Such standards cannot be applied to one-off production, where unknown variables dominate the picture. In any case, there are no drawings from which to break the work down into its constituent operations, so there is no hope of using standard estimates.

A stage in the project preparation and planning process has now been reached where many professional estimators, production engineers and work study devotees find themselves floundering well out of their normal depth. Their trusted records of standard times, with which they have worked for many years, and much of their professional training will be virtually useless when they are faced with the problem of estimating for work where no drawings exist. Drawings and parts lists are the customary means of expression and communication for these people. Without such aids they are rendered helpless. They feel deprived and will be unwilling to commit themselves to forecasts that they might be called upon to justify later.

Project cost estimating is not made any easier by the short time usually available. All too often a tender has to be prepared within a few days if it is to meet the deadline set by a prospective customer. Failure to meet the closing date could mean that the proposal is automatically disqualified, with the order irrevocably lost to a competitor. Within the short time available, cost estimates might have to be made for a large number of items. The project might need, for example, hundreds of control units, all different and all to be manufactured singly. Even if drawings could be found, there would be insufficient time to analyse these for detailed cost estimating.

The job of cost estimating can itself be expensive. It is easy to spend a great deal of time and money in the process, especially where there is no pressure to produce the estimates quickly. Low probability of obtaining a project order might not justify much expenditure on estimating and tender preparation.

Project estimating, as has already been seen, is carried out on a much broader scale than run-of-the-mill production work. In the absence of detailed information, larger work packages must be visualized. The only people capable of taking this broader view are likely to be the more senior members of the organization. Departmental managers often become involved, if not in making the estimates at least in approving them. For project manufacturing estimates, therefore, input will probably be needed from production management.

There is no simple solution to all these problems, but it is possible to outline an approach that can yield acceptable results. Fortunately the lack of drawings and the need for making estimates in a short space of time are both conditions that demand a similar estimating technique.

Within the context of our simple example of a control unit (a small metal box filled with instrumentation) the estimating method might proceed along the following lines. First, a description of the proposed box is needed, with some idea of its likely contents. The design engineers must provide this information, because they are the only people at this early stage who can possibly have any real idea what the final, assembled box will be like.

Once a description of the box has been set down it is usually possible to scan the archives to find a previous piece of work which bears some resemblance to the new job. Classification and coding of past work and cost records can be a great help when it comes to making such a search. Once again it is only the design engineers who can be asked to draw useful comparisons at this early stage. It might well be found that no direct parallel exists but that a previous similar job was carried out which was somewhat simpler than the present object of concern. 'How much simpler?' is the question that must now be asked. The engineer might say that about 10 per cent more components will be needed this time, giving a basis on which the production department can make a comparative estimate.

When the records of actual expenditure on the previous box have been looked up, the production supervisor or production manager can reasonably be expected to make an estimate for the new work, given the information that about 10 per cent more components will have to be accommodated and assembled. If the old box took one man-week to fabricate, this might be considered a good enough estimate for the new sheet metal operations. Only a couple more holes are going to be needed to fix the extra components. Wiring and piping must take longer, however, since the 10 per cent increase in the number of components must result in a corresponding increase in the number of connections to be made. A previously recorded assembly time of two man-weeks might therefore be extended to give an estimate of two and a half man-weeks for the slightly more complex box.

These comparative estimates can never, of course, be considered or expressed in fine units of time. Man-weeks or man-hours are the usual choices. Using anything less (man-minutes, for example) would expose the cost estimator to the same trap as the scientist who carries out research using data and measurements accurate to no better than 1 or 2 per cent, but then has the temerity to express the final results using long strings of decimal places.

Once the idea has been accepted that production time estimates have to be seen in broad terms, on a scale that equates with packages in the work breakdown, they can be collected and collated in exactly the same way as estimates for design engineering and other non-manufacturing project activities. The estimating system can therefore be standardized, with all cost predictions collected according to the same set of rules and using a common estimating form.

ESTIMATING PROJECT LABOUR COSTS

Application of standard costing to labour cost estimates

Standard costs make the life of the cost estimator relatively easy, because there is no need to consider differences in wages or salaries paid to different people of equivalent staff grade. The cost estimator cannot possibly name the individuals who will be engaged on jobs that might not be started for months, even years after the estimates are made. Also, the use of standard labour cost rates means that the wages and salaries paid to individuals can be kept confidential.

For a standard costing system, the first step in determining standard labour cost rates is to classify people according to some convenient rules (usually based on a combination of the work that they do and their general level in the salary structure). Categories which one international company found suitable for its home office engineering and clerical staff are listed below. These six grades were found to be sufficient even for large capital projects involving engineering, purchasing and construction:

- *Grade 1* – company directors, divisional managers and professional staff of consultant rank
- *Grade 2* – departmental managers and the chief engineers of specialist engineering groups

- *Grade 3* – project engineers and senior engineers in all the specialist engineering disciplines
- *Grade 4* – engineers in all the specialist disciplines
- *Grade 5* – drawing office group leaders and checkers
- *Grade 6* – draughtsmen and women plus all clerical and general administrative staff except managers.

It is best if the number of standard grades can be kept to a minimum (not more than ten). The accountants work out an average salary cost (the standard cost) for those in each grade. All estimates and actual jobs are then costed using these grades and standard rates.

Because the standards are calculated within the confines of the accounts department, the method has the advantage of preserving the confidentiality of individuals' earnings: cost estimators and project administration staff need only be told the current standard rates. However, these standard rates should still be treated as confidential proprietary information because they might be of use to competitors.

Using and archiving labour times rather than labour costs

Generally speaking, while wages and their related standard cost rates change from year to year, the time needed to carry out any particular job by a given method should not. Work-time is therefore regarded as the fundamental basis for labour cost estimates. Conversion from man-hours to money can only be regarded as a derivative, secondary process which is dependent on factors and other influences that change costs with the passage of time. Comparative estimates for labour should be made by comparing man-hours or other time units, not costs, from records of past projects.

Responsibility for estimating labour times

In project work there is a shift of emphasis compared with routine manufacturing cost estimating, where detailed estimates could safely be entrusted to an individual or a group specializing only in cost estimating or production engineering. Wherever possible, estimates for project labour times should be obtained from managers or senior individuals of the departments that are going to be responsible for carrying out the project tasks later. It would be reasonable, for example, to expect the chief design engineer to provide the design engineering estimates.

Decentralizing the estimating function in this way reflects the change in scale when progressing from production estimating to project work. It is not done simply to gain a more accurate estimate of project costs, although that is usually the prime reason. When a large project is being planned, the labour time estimates can have a profound influence on the staffing budgets for years to come. Any departmental budget, whatever the type of work involved, should be more realistic and achievable if the departmental manager has either produced or fully agreed the cost estimates on which the budget (and the manager's future commitments) is based.

Collecting estimates for labour times

If the labour estimates for a project are to be obtained from a number of different departmental managers or their senior representatives, it follows that the set of project estimating forms must be circulated among all the participating departments. This can be done in several ways, with varying degrees of effectiveness.

The first proposition is that one master set of forms could be assembled, attached to a circulation list and sent to the department that is first on the list. That department would be expected to enter its estimates and pass the set of forms on to the next-listed department until, all the estimates having been completed, the bundle should arrive back on the project manager's or proposals manager's desk. Everyone knows how long a library copy of a magazine takes to complete its circulation and of the risks that it faces on its journey – it might never be returned to the library at all. For the same reasons the circulation method can be dismissed as impracticable for collecting project estimates.

A second possibility is to prepare a set of pre-headed estimating forms for each department and send them all out simultaneously, either as hard copy or over a computer network. This has the advantage of cutting out the serial delays of the first proposition but it still relies on the wholehearted cooperation of all the departmental heads. Late input can be expected, while it is known from bitter experience that some hard copy sets might even be lost altogether.

Estimating is often regarded as an unpleasant task, a chore to be avoided at all costs if other priorities can be found as an excuse. Therefore no one can expect to rely solely upon polite requests for data to be provided on blank estimating forms. A more direct approach is sometimes needed.

Another way in which to collect the estimates would be to ask for them during early project planning meetings and complete a set of estimating sheets on the spot. This occasion provides the opportunity, since all key project members should be on hand. This approach might be considered for very small projects but there are at least four snags:

1. Network planning estimates are always made principally for individual task durations (for total elapsed time) rather than for their work content in man-hours. However, some form of work content estimates are made at planning meetings in addition to the task duration estimates if the plans are to be the basis of subsequent resource scheduling.

2. Project planning meetings can involve much effort and take considerable time – perhaps needing more than one session of several hours. Protracted meetings do not produce the best results and it is wise to avoid asking too much of the members. The law of diminishing returns can apply when any meeting exceeds about two hours. Members will start to fidget, want to get back to their departments to sort out more pressing problems or go home.

3. Material costs are not usually considered at project planning meetings. A separate estimate collection exercise for material costs would therefore be needed in most cases.

4. Perhaps the most important problem of all is that detailed project planning and scheduling sessions are likely to take place far later than the time when the cost estimates are needed for the project proposal or tender.

Short of applying legal compulsion or threat of physical violence, personal canvassing is the best way to get quick and dependable results. The process starts by preparing a complete set of estimating sheets for the project, on which every known task is listed and cost coded. If a work breakdown structure exists, the sheets should be arranged in logical subsets as illustrated in Figure 4.2. The project manager (or delegate) can then embark on a tour of all the departments involved, arriving purposefully at each manager's desk in turn. This applies even if the estimating forms have been set up in a computer. The aim is to remain firmly rooted in each department until all the desired data have been entered on the forms or in the computer system. The person performing this task may become unpopular in the process, but becoming well-liked is not the most important aspect of a project manager's job.

Canvassing affords the project manager or proposals manager an opportunity to assess the estimating capabilities of all the individuals concerned. Any estimate which appears unrealistic or outrageous can be questioned on the spot, and many other details can be sorted out with the least possible fuss and delay. One type of question which must frequently be asked of the estimator takes the form: 'Here is a job said to require four man-weeks; can four people do it in one week, or must the job be spread over four weeks of elapsed time with only one person able to work on it?' The answers to such questions are of obvious importance in scheduling time and resources, of which more will be said in later chapters.

Production staff often need help in their project estimating task. If engineers collect the estimates, they can often supply this help by explaining the design specification in terms that production people can understand. Similarities with past projects can be suggested and any artists' impressions or other sketches that might be available can be shown and amplified by verbal description.

PERSONAL ESTIMATING CHARACTERISTICS

Project cost estimating is never an exact science. Much of the process, particularly when estimating labour times, has to rely on the subjective judgement of individuals. If any ten people were to be asked separately to judge the time needed for a particular project task, it is hardly conceivable that ten identical answers would be received. Ask these same ten people to estimate the times for a large number of different project tasks, and a pattern should emerge when the results are analysed. Some people will tend always to estimate on the low side. Others might give answers that are consistently high. The person collecting project cost estimates needs to be aware of this problem. In fact, just as it is possible to classify estimates according to confidence in their accuracy, so it is possible to classify the estimators themselves.

Optimistic estimators

As a general rule it can be taken that estimates for any work will more frequently be understated than overstated. Many people seem to be blessed with an unquenchable spirit of optimism when asked to predict completion times for any specific task. 'I can polish off that little job in three days,' it is often claimed, but three weeks later the only things produced are excuses. Without such optimism the world might be a much duller place in which to live and work, but the project manager's lot would be far easier.

An interesting feature of optimistic estimators is the way in which they allow their cloud-cuckoo-land dreams to persist, even after seeing several jobs completed in double the times that they originally forecast. They continue to churn out estimates which are every bit as hopeful as the last, and appear quite unable to learn from their previous experience. Fortunately the 'ill wind' proverb holds good here, with the wind in this case blowing to the good of the project manager. The source of consolation in analysing such estimates lies in the fact that they are at least consistent in their trend. Shrewd project managers will come to learn by experience just how pronounced the trend is in their own particular company. Better still, they will be able to apportion error factors to particular individuals. A typical multiplication factor is 1.5; in other words it is often necessary to add about 50 per cent to the original estimates.

Pessimistic estimators

Occasionally another kind of individual is encountered who, unlike the optimist of more customary experience, can be relied upon to overestimate most tasks. This characteristic is not particularly common and, when seen, it might pay to investigate the underlying cause. Possibly the estimator lacks experience or is incompetent. These explanations are unlikely, since the typical symptom of estimating incompetence is random behaviour and not a consistent error trend.

The picture becomes clearer, if more unsavoury, when it is remembered that project estimates play a large part in determining total departmental budgets. Higher project estimates mean (if they are accepted) bigger budgets for costs and manpower, and thus expanding departments. This in turn adds to the power and status of the departmental heads. In these cases, therefore, 'E' stands not only for 'estimator' but also for 'empire builder'. Correction factors are possible, but action is more effective when it is aimed not at the estimates but at their originators.

Inconsistent estimators

The inconsistent estimator is the universal bane of the project manager's existence. Here we find a person who is seemingly incapable of estimating any job at all, giving answers that range over the whole spectrum from ridiculous pessimism to ludicrous optimism. The only characteristic reliably displayed is inconsistency. Incompetence or inexperience suggest themselves as the most likely causes. Complacency could be another. People looking forward to retirement rather than promotion, and staff who were overlooked during the last round of promotions can display these symptoms.

Unfortunately this category can manifest itself at departmental head level – precisely the people most frequently asked to provide estimates. Only time can solve this problem.

Accurate estimators

It has to be allowed that there is a possibility, however remote, of finding a manager capable of providing estimates that are proved to be consistently accurate when the work actually takes place. This contingency is so remote that it can almost be discounted. When this rare phenomenon does occur it is apt to produce a very unsettling effect on the work-hardened project manager who has, through long experience, learned that it pays always to question every report received and never to take any forecast at its face value.

Making allowances

Why should we not try to educate the estimators? Prevention, after all, is better than cure. But the results of such a re-education programme must be unpredictable, with the effects varying from person to person, upsetting the previous equilibrium. In any case, all of the estimators could be expected to slip back into their old ways eventually and, during the process, their estimating bias could lie anywhere on the scale between extreme optimism and pessimism. Arguing wastes time if nothing is achieved. Accept the situation as it exists and be grateful that it is at least predictable.

Here, then, is a picture of a project manager or proposals manager obtaining a set of estimates for a project, sitting down with a list of all the estimators who were involved, complete with the correction factor deemed appropriate for each individual, and then factoring the original estimates accordingly. Far fetched? The value of this procedure has been proved in practice.

ESTIMATES FOR MATERIAL AND EQUIPMENT COSTS

Materials always need two types of estimate. For each purchase these are as follows:

1. *total expected cost*, including all charges and taxes payable in transporting the materials to the project location;
2. *total lead time*, which is the time expected to elapse between issuing the purchase order and receiving the consignment (failure to get materials on time is a common cause of delays and late project completion).

It might also be necessary to make estimates of other factors for operational purposes; for example the volume or weight of materials (information needed for storage and handling).

If detailed design has yet to be carried out, no parts lists, bills of materials or other schedules will exist from which to start the estimating process. Therefore the next best approach is to ask the engineers to prepare provisional lists of materials for each task. This may be impossible to carry out in detail, but the problem is not as difficult as it would first seem. In most work the engineers have a very good idea of the more significant and most expensive items that will have to be purchased. There might be special components, instruments, control gear, bearings, heavy weldments or castings, all depending of course on the type of project. Items such as these can account for a high proportion of the costs and are frequently those which take the longest time to obtain. In construction projects outline assumptions can be made for the types and quantities of bulk materials needed.

Foreknowledge of these main, most expensive items of expense reduces the unknown area of estimating and therefore improves the forecasting accuracy. If all the important items can be listed and priced, the remaining miscellaneous purchases can be estimated by intelligent guesswork. Records of past projects can be consulted to help assess the probable magnitude of the unknown element. If, for example, the known main components are going to account for 50 per cent of the total material costs, an error of 10 per cent in estimating the cost of the other materials would amount only to 5 per cent of the total. It is most important, however, to prepare the list of known items very carefully, ensuring that the job is done conscientiously and without serious omissions.

The purchasing department or purchasing agent should be involved, and estimates for prices and delivery times must be obtained through their efforts whenever possible. If the purchasing organization is not allowed to partake in preparing the detailed estimates, a danger exists that when the time eventually comes to order the goods these will be obtained from the wrong suppliers at the wrong prices. It is far better if the big items of expense can be priced by quotations from the anticipated suppliers. The buyer can file all such quotations away in readiness for the time when the project becomes live. If the purchasing department is to be held down to a project materials budget, then it is only reasonable that they should play the leading role in producing the material estimates.

The responsibility for estimating materials, therefore, lies in two areas. The engineers or other design representatives must specify what materials are going to be used. The purchasing department should be expected to find out how much those materials will cost and how long they will take to obtain.

Any estimate for materials is not complete unless all the costs of packing, transport, insurance, port duties, taxes and handling have been taken into account (see, for example, the reference to Incoterms in Chapter 23). The intending purchaser must be clear on what the price includes, and allowances must be made to take care of any services that are needed but not included in the quoted price.

Another cautionary word concerns the period of validity for quotations received from potential suppliers. Project cost estimates are often made many months – even years – before a contract is eventually awarded. Suppliers' quotations are typically valid for only 90 days or even less, so that there could be a problem with the materials cost budget or the availability of goods when the time eventually arrives for the purchase orders to be placed.

REVIEWING THE COST ESTIMATES

When all the detailed estimates have been made it should, theoretically, be possible to add them all up and produce a bottom-up forecast of the whole project cost. When this stage has been reached, however, it is never a bad plan to stand well back for a while and view the picture from a wider angle. Perhaps a top-down estimate of the project might be made for comparison. Or, as a particularly valuable exercise, try converting the figures for labour times from hours into man-years.

Suppose that the engineering design work needed for a project appears to need 8225 man-hours or 235 man-weeks (according to which units were used). Assume that 1645 man-hours or 47 man-weeks are roughly equivalent to one net man-year (after allowing for holidays and other non-productive absences). Dividing the 8225 man-hours estimate by 1645 shows that five man-years must be spent to complete the project design. Now assume that all the design is scheduled to be finished in the first six months of the programme. This could be viewed (simplistically) as a project requirement of ten engineers for six months.

The manager starting this project might receive a rude awakening if he/she makes a top-down estimate for the project or refer to records of past projects. These might well show that projects of similar size and complexity took not ten engineers for six months, but the equivalent of ten engineers for a whole year. An apparent error of five man-years exists somewhere. This is, in any language, a king-sized problem. Part of its cause could be the failure of estimators to allow for that part of engineering design which is sometimes called 'after-issue' work, which means making corrections, incorporating unfunded modifications, answering engineering queries from the workforce or the customer, writing reports and putting records to bed.

It goes without saying that cost estimates for a project are extremely important. Any serious error could prove disastrous for a fixed-price contractor – and for the customer too if it leads the contractor into financial difficulties. A competent person who is independent of the estimate compiler should, therefore, always check estimates as far as possible. Comparisons with actual cost totals experienced on past projects (for all materials and labour, not just engineering design) are valuable in checking that the new cost estimate at least appears to be in the right league.

Because the project cost estimate will be used for many important commercial and management decisions, it is sensible to arrange for an authorizing signature from a responsible senior person who is satisfied that all reasonable care has been taken.

REFERENCES AND FURTHER READING

CIMA (2000), *Management Accounting Official Terminology* (London: Chartered Institute of Management Accountants).

Drury, Colin (2004), *Management and Cost Accounting*, 6th Edition (London: Thomson Learning).

Ostwald, P. F. and McLaren, T. S., (2003), *Cost Analysis for Engineers and Management* (Hemel Hempstead: Prentice Hall).

Rad, P. F. (2001), *Project Estimating and Cost Management* (Vienna, VA: Management Concepts).

Smith, N. J. (1995), *Project Cost Estimating* (London: Thomas Telford).

Spon's pricing books and estimating cost guides (updated annually). A comprehensive range of pricing and estimating books and CD-ROMs for architects and the construction industry trades (London: Spon).

Stutzke, R. (2005), *Software Project Estimation: Projects, Products and Processes* (Boston, MA: Addison Wesley).

Taylor, J. C. (2005), *Project Cost Estimating Tools, Techniques and Perspectives* (Boco Raton, FL: St Lucie Press).

5 First Steps in Planning the Timescale

Whenever any job has to be accomplished according to a time or date deadline, it is advisable to have at least some idea of the relationship between the time allowed and the time needed. This is true for any project, whether a dinner is being prepared or a motorway constructed. In the first case one would be ill-advised to tell guests 'Dinner is at seven – but the potatoes will not be ready until 7.30'. Similarly, there would be little point in having an eminent personage arrive to open a new motorway if, by cutting the tape, the eager and unsuspecting traffic stream were to be released towards a bridge that still consisted of a few girders over a yawning chasm, complete with rushing torrent below. So it is a safe assumption that a plan of some sort is always advisable if a project is to be finished on time. In our culinary example planning is simple and informal, conducted solely within the brain of the cook. Projects such as motorways are more complicated and have to be planned with more formal techniques.

After introducing the subject of project planning in general, this chapter deals particularly with simple charting methods. Simple charts can sometimes be adequate without further elaboration for planning and progressing very tiny projects through to completion. However, they are introduced here, relatively early in these 30 chapters, because they are particularly useful during the early life cycle phases of even very large projects. Well-presented charts are especially relevant as plans before project authorization for two principal reasons:

1. In the very early days of most projects there is little or no detailed information available about the project tasks that lie ahead. Therefore planning cannot be done in great detail. More sophisticated methods (such as those described in Chapters 14 and 15) must usually wait until the project has been authorized and senior members of the project organization have been appointed. Often it is not until that later stage has been reached that a professional planner is brought on to the scene.

2. Charts are likely to feature in business plans and project proposals that will have to be seen, understood and approved by senior managers who are untrained in the project management arts. Such people often like to have their time saved by having facts summarized and presented to them in simple tables and diagrams (preferably printed in attractive colours in picture book style).

GENERAL INTRODUCTION TO PROJECT PLANNING

This section introduces the subject of project planning and sets out some of the principles and problems that planners have to bear in mind. These considerations apply at all stages in the project life cycle.

Planning and scheduling environment

Anyone planning a project of significant size will soon find that there are a number of factors, both inside and outside the project organization, which can have a profound effect on the project. Also, the quality of the plans and schedules that are produced will greatly influence the benefits that can be expected for the company and everyone else concerned in carrying out the project. Figure 5.1 is a graphical representation of these ideas.

External factors

External factors are events and conditions that lie outside the control of the project management organization. Some of these factors can affect or completely wreck attempts at project planning. They can even result in project cancellation. The following paragraphs list a few examples from the many possibilities.

Acts of God – all projects are subject to risk, and many of those risks can have an enormous impact on plans. The following are just four from a long catalogue of happenings that can be classified as Acts of God:

- An earthquake devastates a project organization's headquarters.
- A hurricane and flood put a project site under a metre of water and delay the start or ruin the work in progress.
- An influenza epidemic puts half the project workforce out of action.
- The project manager (a keen golfer) is struck by lightning.

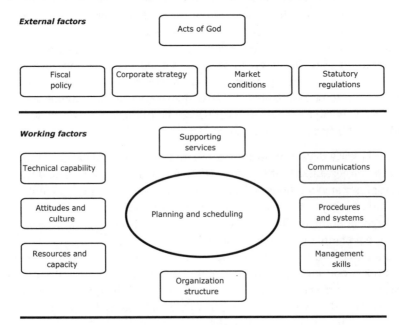

Figure 5.1   Project planning environment

Fiscal policy – the actions of a national government in respect of taxation and other financial measures can have a profound effect on projects and their planning. One extreme manifestation of this is seen when a government-funded project is cancelled or abandoned through a political decision. Less immediate, but of general concern, are the wider and longer-term economic consequences of government fiscal policies, such as (for example) the diversion of funds or special taxation relief to or from different national regions. Such policy decisions can lead to project downscaling, delays and cancellations in all sectors of industry.

Corporate strategy – strategic decisions made by managers outside and above the project organization can affect many aspects of planning. Here are just a few examples:

- A decision is made at the top management level of a group of companies to conduct a project in a different company within the group from that originally intended.
- A decision is made to delay the start of an internal project owing to diversion of funds for other purposes.
- A strategic decision is made to halt all new staff recruitment or even to downsize, so reducing the resources previously expected to be available for projects.
- Directives are received from a senior manager to change previously agreed project priorities. Project managers often regard such instructions as unwelcome and unwarranted interference.
- The top managers of a company are replaced following a takeover by another company, and the new managers fail to appreciate the nature or purpose of project management and close the project management function down altogether in a mistaken effort to save overhead costs. Kerzner (2000) includes such a case.

Statutory regulations – legislation by national and regional governments can impose extra burdens on project designers, staff and participating organizations that have to be taken into account at the planning stage. This can be a particularly important feature of projects carried out in foreign countries, where the project manager would need to research the local employment, welfare, technical and commercial regulations before committing resources to a plan.

Working factors

The items labelled 'working factors' in Figure 5.1 are those that are most likely to affect the project manager and the project on a day-by-day basis. The factors shown in the figure should be self-explanatory. They can apply to all kinds of projects and project organizations. Although these working factors can have a profound effect on the project outcomes, the project manager will often find that some or all of them are determined by managers or circumstances over which the project manager has no authority or power. Project managers have to learn what the organizational difficulties are for their particular project. They must then plan and act according to the amount of power or influence that they can command through their own personality, drive and strength of character, by their status in the organizational hierarchy and by the amount of support that can they can draw down from higher management.

Contribution of good planning to results

As one of the foundations of project management, planning should promote efficient working when it has been done sensibly and logically. Project workers who are spared the frustration of constantly trying to overcome crises caused by bad planning can devote more of their time to achieving the quality standards expected. Thus a well-planned project stands a far greater chance of being completed within time and budget. That should contribute greatly to cost effectiveness and profitability.

Planning time frame

Planning (and scheduling) can be considered from two opposite viewpoints:

- A task list and set of duration estimates could be obtained and used to produce a plan that predicts a project completion date. This is *bottom-up* or task-led planning, because the duration is decided by considering the all the tasks in detail, from the ground up.
- The alternative to bottom-up planning is to set a target completion date for the project, and then plan to meet that date. This is *top-down* or target-led planning.

Each of these approaches has its merits and disadvantages.

Bottom-up (task-led) planning

Plans produced entirely with well-considered task duration estimates, with no external pressure to compress the timescale within preset target completion dates, should allow the planner to develop a working schedule that is capable of being achieved with confidence and a great deal of certainty. There is no need to overstretch any person or resource in the project organization because the plans have been made with due and careful consideration for their availability, skills and performance capabilities. Some might regard this as an ideal state of affairs, with risks of failure reduced to a minimum. However, a new project plan made with no external pressure whatsoever is likely to predict an end date that is way beyond the project sponsor's or customer's requirements.

Bottom-up planning therefore has its dangers. Pressure to force project completion reasonably quickly is not such a bad thing remembering that, because *time is money*, projects that are allowed to drag their feet will attract higher costs from fixed overheads and other causes. Giving planners complete freedom to dictate the project timescale might, therefore, not be so advisable as it at first seems.

Top-down (target-led) planning

If a plan has to be suited to a predetermined target delivery requirement, all the estimates must be fitted into the available time frame as best they can. Projects to meet publicly announced completion dates fall into this category. Here are a few examples:

- preparations for trade exhibitions such as motor shows
- productions of stage plays, musicals or operas
- pop festivals, steam rallies and other open air events
- a spectacular municipal fireworks display for Guy Fawkes night on 5 November
- society weddings
- summit conferences of international leaders, including all administrative, timetable, security, protocol and media arrangements.

One temptation that must be strongly resisted by the project manager is to allow task duration estimates to be shortened for no better reason than that the time available is too short. Projects planned with such artificial gestures can have little practical possibility of achieving their accelerated targets. Another danger is of removing all possible reserves (for example by planning to work constant overtime or seven-day weeks) so that the plan is too tight, leaves no room for error, and would drive all the participants to the point of exhaustion or worse.

Of course it is sometimes possible to reduce times by allocating more resources or by running jobs concurrently instead of consecutively, but never must the project manager be persuaded or coerced into trying to expedite a plan simply by 'marking down' the estimates without any justification. Such optimistic plans can gain a temporary advantage by serving to pacify higher management or by deceiving a trusting customer into placing an order. However, the unfortunate truth is bound to emerge sooner or later, bringing much grief, gnashing of teeth and consequent discredit to the project organization and its manager. Valid methods for squeezing a project into a short or reduced time frame include crashing and fast tracking, both of which are explained in Chapter 15. At least one company (Isochron Ltd) recommends target-led plans for all management change and IT projects, with the plans worked backwards from target dates and maximum use of concurrency (Fowler and Lock 2006). That approach brings risks, but projects given the incentives of challenging target dates, and which are led with deterministic enthusiasm, can often be fulfilled very successfully in all respects.

Consider, on the other hand, what might happen when the target time for a new project is set months later than strictly necessary, so that the project plan is relaxed and stripped of all urgency. Such cases are unusual but not impossible. Relaxed schedules are an ideal breeding ground for budgetary excesses according to Professor Parkinson's best-known law, where 'Work expands so as to fill the time available for its completion' (Parkinson 1958). Give people an inch, and they will take a mile (a proverb that seems to lose its force when metric units are substituted).

WHAT MAKES AN IDEAL PROJECT PLAN?

Given the foregoing explanations (plus a little imagination and new thought) it is possible to set out the attributes of an ideal plan. These are shown in Figure 5.2, which can be used by project managers as a checklist to decide how effective their particular planning method will be likely to prove.

During the earliest phases of a project's life history, most planning will have to be top-down and target-led because not enough will be known about the detailed tasks to come. Early plans are typically made in outline, often using simple charts such as those introduced later in this chapter. The ticks and crosses in Figure 5.2 have been placed to show how a plan made with such limited information might stand up to comparison against the checklist. Attempts to produce a plan that is perfect in every detail must usually wait until after project authorization, when senior members of the project organization have been appointed and more detailed information can be gathered.

MUSEUM PROJECT: A CASE EXAMPLE

The museum project is introduced here to demonstrate ways of planning a project during its conceptual stages. This project will be revisited in Chapter 15 to show how more sophisticated planning methods can be used later in the life cycle, even to the extent that most of the checklist parameters in Figure 5.2 can be ticked.

Early definition of the museum project

The museum project is set in Liverchester, which (you are invited to believe) is a busy port and tourist centre in the North of England. There are two well-managed museums within the city boundaries, both managed by the entertainments department of the city council.

One of these museums, the FitzDennis Gallery of Fine Art, is crammed to overflowing with paintings and small sculptures, including some masterpieces by well-known artists. The other establishment, the Liverchester Museum, contain items of local social and industrial history and artefacts of Roman or earlier origin.

The city council has long been concerned that the FitzDennis gallery is overcrowded, with many paintings having to be locked away in its vaults.

PLAN CHECKLIST

1	Does the plan include all known major project tasks?	✓
2	Is the plan drawn in enough detail to generate work-to lists?	✗
3	Are all tasks placed in their logical chronological sequence?	✓
4	Have task interdependencies been respected? (no cart placed before a horse)	✓
5	Is the plan easy to understand and is it visually effective?	✓
6	Is the plan flexible and easy to adapt to take account of changes to project requirements or strategy?	✓
7	Are the project milestones shown?	✓
8	Are all the duration estimates feasible and achievable?	✗
9	Are urgent and high priority tasks clearly highlighted?	✗
10	Have key managers and supervisors participated in the plan and accepted it as their commitment?	✗
11	Can the plan be used to check day-to-day project progress?	✗
12	Has the plan been made to take account of our resources?	✗
13	Have the resource needs of other projects been considered?	✗
14	Will the plan satisfy all stakeholders' expectations?	✓

Figure 5.2   Checklist for an ideal plan (shown checked early in the project life cycle)

The Liverchester Museum, on the other hand, has fine large rooms with space to spare for additional exhibits. But these museum rooms do not have the benefit of climate control, and the security systems are not of a very high standard.

A project to build an extension to relieve overcrowding at the FitzDennis Gallery was rejected unanimously by the council as been too expensive at an estimated total cost of £15 million. An alternative project proposal is now under discussion, in which the roles of the two museums would be reversed, with the two collections swapped between them. That approach would remove the need to extend the FitzDennis Gallery of Fine Art. This museum project, if approved, would involve the following principal tasks:

1. Close the Liverchester Museum temporarily and remove all the historical exhibits to a place of temporary but secure storage.
2. Install climate control systems in the empty Liverchester Museum, refurbish the rooms, place new public signs and rename the building as the Liverchester Gallery of Fine Art.
3. Close the FitzDennis Gallery of Fine Art and move all its exhibits, staff and equipment to the 'new' more spacious Liverchester Gallery of Fine Art.
4. Publicize the new Liverchester Gallery of Fine Art and reopen it under its new name.
5. Refurbish the closed FitzDennis Gallery and rename it the FitzDennis Museum of Local History.
6. Complete the project by moving the historical artefacts from their temporary store into the refurbished FitzDennis Museum of Local History.

All museum staff would be retained throughout the project, either to help with the project or with other temporary council duties. Thus no staff redundancies or recruitments are envisaged.

Our discussion of this project will be concentrated on its early planning and strategy, without considering cost estimates, detailed budgets and the various subcontractors. We do need to bear in mind that the total estimated costs of the museum project are £500 000, which is far less than the £15 million estimated for the original proposal to build a new art gallery extension. However, the combined intrinsic value of both museum collections is at least £100 million, so safety and security are important requirements.

As projects go, this one is small. However, it will have a high public profile, use public funds, and has the potential for disaster if it is not planned well and managed effectively.

Mention of public funds signals that this public sector project will be subject to the European Public Procurement Directives. These rules are intended to give equal opportunities for contractors throughout Europe to bid for project works and service contracts in the public sector. The rules apply only to contracts that exceed certain threshold values, which will change from time to time. Although ignored for simplicity in this case example, in practice there would be a requirement to advertise certain contract opportunities in *The European Journal*, and the whole process could be expected to add months to the project duration. There is a wealth of information on the Internet about these European rules; for example at www.publictender.co.uk/eu-procurement.html.

Diary planning

Most project plans begin by defining the project and its strategy and then producing an initial task list. The strategy and an outline task list already exist for this museum project, as explained in the above introduction. The next phase in the life cycle is to seek approval for the project and its funding, for which a business plan must be prepared. An important feature of any business plan must be a summary time plan for the project. At this early stage, no project manager has been appointed, little is known about the detailed tasks needed, and there is no planning expert on hand. So, the planning method must be simple and the results must be visually attractive to the senior executives who will have to consider the business plan.

Imagine an early meeting called by the entertainments director to discuss this project, with a view to preparing its business plan. High on the agenda must be the outline timescale for the project. Those present at the meeting will include the entertainments director, the directors of both museums, and possibly some other senior members of the museum staffs. Everyone present agrees that it would be sensible to begin the project in the winter season, when tourist levels are low. The aim should be to have both museums open again before the following autumn season, when attendance figures at these museums have traditionally been at their peak.

Now is the moment when the meeting must start to assign target dates to the individual tasks. After some discussion, based closely on the simple task list that we have already seen, the following schedule becomes the early outline plan for the museum project:

	Task	Start	Finish
1	Close the Liverchester Museum and store the exhibits.	5 Jan 09	20 Feb 09
2	Carry out all changes in the old, empty Liverchester Museum	23 Feb 09	29 May 09
3	Move the paintings and fine art into their new home	1 Jun 09	19 Jun 09
4	Publicize and open the new Liverchester Gallery of Fine Art	1 Jun 09	22 Jun 09
5	Convert the old art gallery to the local history museum	22 Jun 09	21 Aug 09
6	Move the stored historical artefacts into their new home	24 Aug 09	11 Sep 09
7	Publicize and open the FitzDennis Museum of Local History	24 Aug 09	14 Sep 09

This is an example of simple diary planning – a method that is fine for keeping personal appointments with hairdressers and dentists but which cannot be recommended for controlling the project after it has been authorized. Try comparing this plan with the checklist in Figure 5.2. The museum diary plan *does* include all *known* tasks but in this case some important tasks have been forgotten (for example finding a secure place of temporary storage).

This diary plan does, however, provide a list of provisional target dates (which subsequent detailed planning might show as either being easy to achieve or completely impossible).

Diary plans are inadequate for project control when work actually begins because the intervals between the dates are too great to provide benchmarks against which to measure day-to-day progress. But, even with this limited information, a diary plan can be used to support the business plan provided that the targets have been set by people who have researched (or who have direct experience of) similar past projects. However, the presentation of a diary plan will usually be improved by converting it into a Gantt chart.

Chart methods for planning the museum project

Simple Gantt chart

Figure 5.3 shows how the diary plan for the museum project converts into a simple Gantt chart. Now, all the tasks have been set out clearly on a time scale. The task list here is slightly more detailed, to redress some of the more serious omissions of the diary plan. For example, the task to find a suitable temporary store is now included. However, because the project is not yet authorized, its actual start date is not yet known and all times have to be shown as week numbers.

Linked Gantt chart

Simple Gantt charts do not clearly indicate how the start of one task is dependent upon the completion of one or more other tasks. Provided that there are not too many tasks and the plan is relatively simple, these task interdependencies can be indicated by drawing links on the chart. The chart will then be known as a linked Gantt chart. The linked Gantt chart for the museum project is shown in Figure 5.4.

All good project management software can convert plans into reader-friendly linked Gantt charts, no matter how sophisticated and complex the underlying planning method might be. However, the

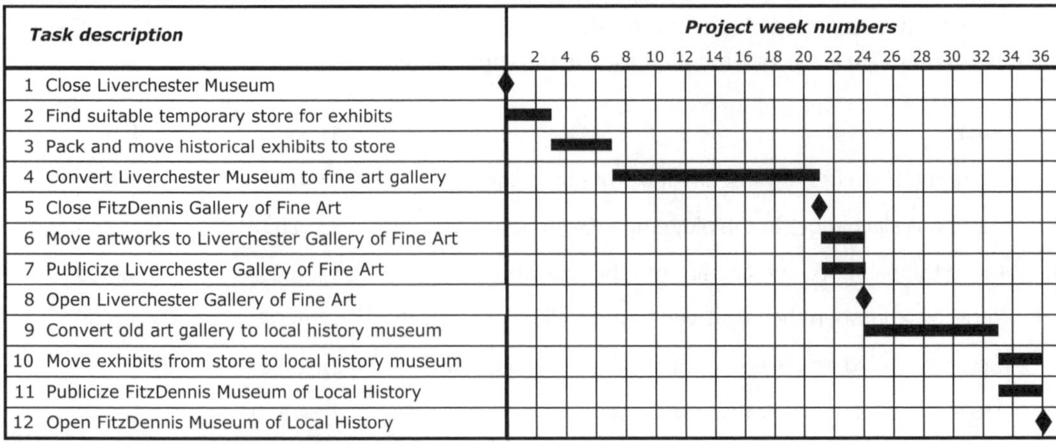

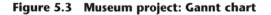

Figure 5.3 Museum project: Gantt chart

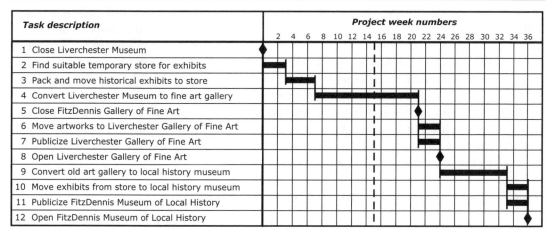

Task description	Project week numbers
	2 4 6 8 10 12 14 16 18 20 22 24 26 28 30 32 34 36
1 Close Liverchester Museum	
2 Find suitable temporary store for exhibits	
3 Pack and move historical exhibits to store	
4 Convert Liverchester Museum to fine art gallery	
5 Close FitzDennis Gallery of Fine Art	
6 Move artworks to Liverchester Gallery of Fine Art	
7 Publicize Liverchester Gallery of Fine Art	
8 Open Liverchester Gallery of Fine Art	
9 Convert old art gallery to local history museum	
10 Move exhibits from store to local history museum	
11 Publicize FitzDennis Museum of Local History	
12 Open FitzDennis Museum of Local History	

Figure 5.4   Museum project: linked Gantt chart with date cursor at week 15

links on such charts can be difficult to follow, particularly when the plan contains more than a few linked tasks. The planning logic or sequence is usually easier to follow when the plan is seen as a network diagram (See Chapters 14 and 15).

Addition of a date cursor

Gantt charts are often used for the day-to-day control of small projects. In those cases a 'today's date' cursor can be a useful aid for progress control. The vertical dotted line in Figure 5.4 represents such a date cursor. When this line is placed at the current date it becomes a basic aid to progress measurement because everything to the left of the line should be completed, whilst tasks immediately to the right of the line should be just starting.

Date cursors have their origins in early Gantt charts constructed as wall charts, before the days of computer scheduling. In those days the cursor was usually made from a vertical red cord or tape that could be placed on 'today's date' or 'time-now' by moving it along the chart.

Where the date cursor intersects a task that is scheduled to be in progress, the project manager can see the proportion of a task that should have been completed at the measurement date. In Figure 5.4 the cursor crosses task 4, which is the conversion of the Liverchester Museum. Ideally this long task should be shown in greater detail (thus breaking it up into shorter periods) but the date cursor in Figure 5.4 enables the project manager to see that this task should be about 60 per cent completed when it is reviewed at the end of week 15.

Week numbers and calendar dates

Very early in the project life cycle, the precise calendar date when the project will be given approval to start (if, indeed it is to be given approval at all) cannot be predicted precisely. With no agreed starting calendar date from which to calculate the start and finish times of all subsequent tasks, tasks have to be timed using day or week numbers. Week numbers were used in Figures 5.3 and 5.4.

If a project does eventually receive approval to start (which might be much later in the life cycle than during the provisional planning phase described in this chapter) it is highly probable that the project will be replanned bottom-up, in much greater detail, by a professional planner using critical path network analysis (Chapters 14 and 15). Day or week numbers will be used again for such detailed plans when they are first sketched and calculated manually. However, conversion to calendar dates is a simple process when the network plan is subsequently processed by a computer and the actual start date for the project is known.

Some project managers continue to use week numbers throughout the active fulfilment phases of their projects, but that practice can cause inconvenience to subcontractors, suppliers and others outside the internal project organization. Imagine the difficulties that a subcontractor would face when working on several projects for different customers if the managers of those projects each used a different set of project week numbers. Calendar dates, on the other hand, are internationally recognized and should not cause confusion. However, different countries have their own ways of writing down calendar dates so that 2/9/10 would mean 2 September 2010 in Britain but 9 February 2010 in the US. This difficulty, which could prove very embarrassing in an international project, is easily overcome by writing all dates in the form 02Sep10. This has the added advantage of compressing the column space taken up by dates in tables and charts.

Effectiveness of the museum project Gantt chart

Try comparing the linked Gantt chart in Figure 5.4 against the Figure 5.2 checklist for an ideal plan and you will find that the Gantt chart has some advantages over the original diary plan. Figure 5.5 repeats the checklist, annotated to show these new advantages. Remember that the Gantt charts shown here are early plans, made without critical path network analysis or detailed resource scheduling and they were never intended for controlling the project after authorization.

Even with the linked Gantt chart, there are still far too many crosses in the checklist this plan to be considered as effective for project control. Remember, however, that these plans have been made

PLAN CHECKLIST	Diary plan	Linked Gantt chart with date cursor
1 Does the plan include all known major project tasks?	✓	✓
2 Is the plan drawn in enough detail to generate work-to lists?	✗	✗
3 Are all tasks placed in their logical chronological sequence?	✓	✓
4 Have task interdependencies been respected? (no cart placed before a horse)	✓	✓
5 Is the plan easy to understand and is it visually effective?	✗	✓
6 Is the plan flexible and easy to adapt to take account of changes to project requirements or strategy?	✓	✓
7 Are the project milestones shown?	✗	✓
8 Are all the duration estimates feasible and achievable?	✗	✗
9 Are urgent and high priority tasks clearly highlighted?	✗	✗
10 Have key managers and supervisors participated in the plan and accepted it as their commitment?	✗	✗
11 Can the plan be used to check day-to-day project progress?	✗	✓
12 Has the plan been made to take account of our resources?	✗	✗
13 Have the resource needs of other projects been considered?	✗	✗
14 Will the plan satisfy all stakeholders' expectations?	✓	✓

Figure 5.5   Museum project: checklist comparing diary and linked Gantt chart plans

during early project days, before authorization and will probably be adequate for inclusion in the proposal or business plan.

Later, when the project is approved and the organization is established, the project manager will be able to arrange for key participants to meet and make a detailed plan for the project – a plan that can be used as a day-to-day document for issuing work and controlling the project. The detailed planning and scheduling process should be based on a critical path network, must take into account the availability of resources, and should be undertaken or supervised by a professional planner.

DISTINCTION BETWEEN PLANNING AND SCHEDULING

In project management terminology, the words 'plan' and 'schedule' can have different meanings. I have found it convenient to observe the following distinction.

A plan can be considered as the listing or visual display that results when all project activities have been subjected to estimating, logical sequencing, target timing and the determination of priorities. For projects of any significant size, some form of network analysis (Chapters 14 and 15) is usually the preferred method for preparing a plan. However, some charting methods provide better visual aids, can be more effective for communicating plans to project personnel and are often quite adequate for small projects.

A schedule is obtained by doing additional work on the initial plan, so that resources needed to carry out all the project activities are taken into account (see Chapters 16, 17 and 18). In other words, a schedule is the practicable working document that results by matching the organization's available resources to the initial plan.

When a suitable computer application is used to process planning and scheduling, and to filter and sort all the resulting data, all the project planning and scheduling requirements can be satisfied (and all the items in the checklist in Figure 5.2 can be ticked).

REFERENCES AND FURTHER READING

Fowler, A. and Lock, D. (2006), *Accelerating Business and IT Change: Transforming Project Delivery* (Aldershot: Gower).

Kerzner, H. (2000), *Applied Project Management: Best Practices on Implementation* (New York: Wiley).

Parkinson, C. Northcote (1958), *Parkinson's Law or the Pursuit of Progress* (London: John Murray).

6   *Financial Appraisal and the Business Plan*

The methods and procedures described in previous chapters have not advanced us very far through the project life cycle, and there will be more data to analyse and more decisions to be made before any actual project work can be authorized. But at least we can now have an outline definition of the project, together with an estimate of what it should cost and how long it will take to complete. This chapter advances the process of project consideration a little farther by comparing the estimated time and costs with the benefits that the project investor or owner wants. Those data and comparisons will form the basis of the business plan or project proposal.

PROJECT FEASIBILITY ANALYSIS

Managers frequently have to make decisions on whether or not to authorize investment in a project, or they might be asked to decide between two or more different project options. Depending on the type of project under consideration, their final decision will depend on many factors, including answers to questions like the following:

- Is the project feasible technically?
- Are we confident that the claims of the engineers, designers, consultants or architects are valid?
- What are the environmental implications?
- What are the implications, if any, for our staff?
- For a new consumer product development, can we produce it, will people like it, how many can we sell and at what price?
- Is the project likely to be finished on time?
- How much will it all cost?
- For machinery or process plant, what are the expected operating costs?
- Will the proposed new plant produce as much output as the experts claim?
- What is the expected operational life of the new machinery?
- Is there no better project strategy than the one proposed?
- What are the technical risks?
- What are the commercial risks?
- Is the return on our investment going to be adequate?
- For a management change project, have the intangible benefits been evaluated as well as the tangibles?
- How can we raise the investment money?

It is sometimes necessary to commission one or more feasibility studies from independent experts to answer many of these questions. A feasibility study might examine more than one possible project strategy in depth.

For example, a project to develop a copper mine in an undeveloped region can be approached from a number of strategic standpoints. Many geological, environmental, political and economic factors must be considered for each of a number of different case options. Should the ore be mined, given some treatment to concentrate the copper, and then be shipped a great distance to an existing smelter and refinery? Or should a smelter and refinery be built at the new mine location? A feasibility study for any new project could, therefore, examine several different strategic options in considerable depth.

Experts' reports can be open to doubt or give rise to further questions but a feasibility report will usually be required as part of the business case to be considered by the potential owner or fund provider for a very large project. Whatever the circumstances, a careful appraisal of the expected financial outcome is likely to have great influence on most project authorization decisions.

DIFFERENT VIEWING PLATFORMS FOR THE PROJECT INVESTOR AND THE PROJECT CONTRACTOR

Most projects involve as least two different principal organizations, each on one side of a contract. On the one hand there is the organization that perceives a need for the project and then finds the motivation and the money that allows it to happen. On the other side of the contract is the organization hired to undertake the work (the contractor). These two principal participants can be found in almost every project, although their identities are often shrouded in organizational complexities. For example, in IT and management change projects the customer and main contractor often reside within the same company or group of companies. Also, many projects have several small contractors rather than one main contractor.

This chapter, therefore, examines the comparisons of expenditure and resulting benefits as they might be viewed by the customer and the contractor. The relationships between the timing of payments and the resulting revenues or benefits are quite different for these two parties.

In a typical project the project owner must find all the funds and cannot usually expect any benefits until after the project has been completed. The project contractor, on the other hand, can expect to receive interim payments (known as progress payments or stage payments) from the project owner, in accordance with the amount of work that can be certified as being successfully completed. Thus the project contractor does not usually have to fund the whole cost of the project up to completion and handover. The following case example illustrates these points.

Case example: the luxury service apartments project

A property development company, APDC plc, has identified a site upon which to construct a building that will contain 10 luxury apartments. APDC estimates the total project construction cost to be £5 million. The location is attractive and all apartments should be let as soon as they are built and ready for occupation. The company intends to let these to tenants as service flats, which means that maintenance and other services will be included in the rentals. The life cycle and cost/benefit patterns for this project are presented in Figure 6.1.

Construction projects have one or two unique characteristics. Unlike many other projects, much of the initial design must be done early in the life cycle, because plans will have to be approved by the local authority before any work can be done on the construction site. Another important aspect of construction projects, especially when compared with management change projects, is that the

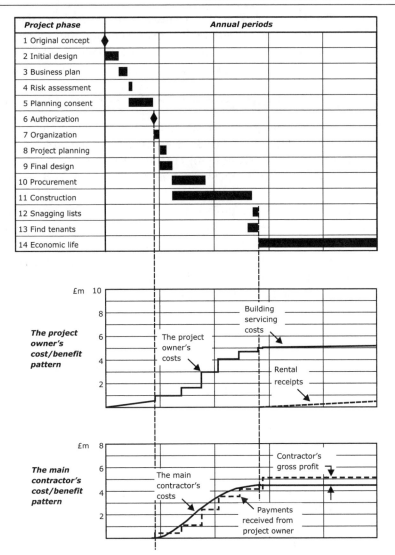

Figure 6.1   Luxury service apartments project: cost/benefit patterns

money invested in the project should be recoverable by the investor because it is embodied in a building that will almost certainly appreciate in value and can be resold later at a profit.

Thus, for an outlay of £5 million, APDC will finish up owning a building with an appreciating resale value of at least £5 million. In addition to capital appreciation of the property, the periodical benefits resulting from this project will comprise the rent and service charges to be paid each month by the tenants. These have been set at an average of £3000 per calendar month per apartment. Provided all the apartments can be let without delay, this will produce a gross annual income of £360 000, which is a gross annual return on investment of 7.2 per cent.

The financial calculations for the main contractor are also straightforward. The cost estimate before allowance for contingencies was £4 million, so that a fixed price of £5 million should theoretically net the contractor a gross mark up on costs of 25 per cent (which is a gross profit of 20 per cent of sales). In practice, many things can happen on a construction site to increase costs and erode profit, but a competent contractor should feel reasonably confident of achieving the target profit.

It is apparent that a construction project of this nature need not be subjected to further financial appraisal. The owner can regard it as a secure capital investment and the contractor can expect to be repaid with a fair profit. Of course there would be some risk of failure, but that risk is very small when compared with many other kinds of projects.

Relevance of project financial appraisal to the potential investor

Most projects requiring considerable financial investment will involve more uncertainty and risk than the luxury service apartments project just described. In many such projects, some or all of the capital invested might be lost in the event of project failure. This increased project risk must often be compensated for in higher expected benefits, and most projects will need an in-depth financial appraisal before they can be authorized.

Management change and IT systems projects are particularly prone to failure and the costs of such failures can be considerable. There are many examples of high profile public projects that have, to say the least, not provided their expected benefits on time and within budget. Statistics show that past management change and (especially) public sector IT projects have included more failures than successes. Think what a project of this kind (involving high capital expenditure in IT systems and in massive staff reorganization and retraining) would mean for the project investor if it failed. Here are some points to ponder:

- None of the money invested in the failed IT software and systems design will be recoverable.
- IT hardware is not best known as an investment proposition, and depreciates so rapidly that it becomes obsolete and worthless in a matter of a year or two, if not worse.
- Staff who have been affected by the failed project, some of whom might have resisted the proposed changes, will be demotivated, demoralized.
- Far from achieving the expected benefits, the failed project will have damaged the organization's performance, prestige and prospects.
- Customers will suffer reduced or interrupted service.

Competent financial appraisal can go a long way towards preventing project failure. Several methods are available to the prospective project investor and case examples follow to demonstrate some of these financial appraisal methods. These will be viewed through the eyes of the project investor, but the viewpoint of the project contractor will be revisited in the last sections of this chapter.

INTRODUCTION TO PROJECT FINANCIAL APPRAISAL METHODS

There are two common approaches to financial appraisal. One is the simple payback method and the other uses one of a range of techniques based on discounting the forecast cash flows. Whichever of these methods is chosen, the appraiser needs to have a good estimate of the amount and timing of each significant item of expenditure (the cash outflows) and of the revenue or savings expected (the cash inflows).

The main cash outflow elements of a project can include items such as the following:

- the initial acquisition cost of software, plant or equipment needed for the project (this might be a single purchase payment, a series of phased payments, or payments scheduled against a leasing or rental plan; the differences between these options are important not only for the timing of payments, but also for the tax implications);

- interest payable on financing loans;
- if the project is for new machinery or plant, the costs of operating and maintenance;
- commissioning, debugging and other implementation costs;
- staff or operator training costs;
- all other expenses and fees payable as a result of the new project.

Against these items of expenditure must be balanced all the savings and revenues (the project benefits) that the new project is expected to generate. The following items are just a few of the many possibilities:

- savings in operating and maintenance costs achieved by replacing old methods with the new project (for example, although a stainless steel tower bought to replace an old steel tower might be expensive initially it would have a longer life and would not need regular repainting);
- revenue from the sale of products or services made possible by the new project;
- proceeds from the sale of assets no longer required as a result of the new project;
- proceeds from the eventual sale of the new project hardware, some time in the future, after the new project has reached the end of its economic life.

Fiscal measures can have a significant effect on the outcome. Many cash inflows will attract taxes, while some expenditure might be offset by allowances against taxation. Some capital investment projects might generate cash inflows in the form of government grants or special tax incentives and allowances. These circumstances vary considerably from place to place and from one country to another. They can complicate financial appraisal calculations considerably and are best handled by experts. The examples in this chapter illustrate general methods and have been kept relatively simple by excluding these fiscal elements.

SIMPLE PAYBACK METHOD

Simple payback is the appraisal method familiar to most managers. It seeks to answer the blunt question 'How long would this project take to pay for itself?' The method compares the predicted cash outflows and inflows relating to a new investment option against those of an alternative option (which in many cases means comparing the relative merits of proceeding with a project against the option of doing nothing). Costs and income or savings are analysed over consecutive periods (typically years) until a point is reached where the forecast cumulative costs of the new project are balanced (paid back) by the cash inflows that the project is expected to generate.

Case example: payback analysis of a boiler replacement project

A project is under consideration for the installation of new, more efficient central heating boilers for a group of industrial buildings situated in a cold region. Also included within the scope of this project are an electronic optimizer control unit and heat insulation for the buildings (all measures that should improve fuel economy). Total installed cost of the project is estimated at £60 000, and the work could be carried out over a week or so in mid-2009.

Benefits claimed for the new system include a reduction in fuel costs from the current £90 000 to £80 000 in each calendar year, although only £5000 savings could be expected in the year 2009 because the project would not come on stream until July. Maintenance of the new plant is free for the remainder of the year 2009, under the terms of a guarantee. After that, maintenance costs are expected to be £6000 for the second year, rising to £8000 for the third year as the plant begins to age, finally reaching £10 000 per annum (which is the same maintenance rate as the old system).

The forecasts for each calendar year can be tabulated, as shown in Figure 6.2. In this case, it is seen that the project seems set to break even before the end of 2013, so that the payback period is between four and five years.

The payback period can be pinpointed with greater accuracy by drawing a graph. There are two ways in which this can be done and both methods are shown in Figure 6.3.

The curve labelled *A* is the expenditure to be expected if the existing plant is retained and the proposed new project is not authorized. Curve *B* is the alternative expenditure pattern expected if the project proposal is accepted and the new plant is installed during June 2009 for start up on 1 July 2009. Curves *A* and *B* intersect at *C*, which is the breakeven point, where the additional costs of the new project have just been balanced by the resulting savings. A vertical line *D* has been drawn to highlight the breakeven date, which is seen to be about two-thirds through 2013.

Curve *E* shows another way of drawing the graph. In this case only one curve has to be drawn. This is the cumulative net cash flow, plotted with data from the table in Figure 6.2. The point at which this changes from an outflow to an inflow is marked at *F*, the point where the curve crosses

Year	2009	2010	2011	2012	2013	2014
Existing system:						
Fuel	90	90	90	90	90	90
Maintenance	10	10	10	10	10	10
Annual cash outflows	100	100	100	100	100	100
Cumulative outflow	100	200	300	400	500	600
New proposal:						
New plant investment	60					
Fuel	85	80	80	80	80	80
Maintenance		6	8	10	10	10
Annual cash outflows	145	86	88	90	90	90
Cumulative outflow	145	231	319	409	499	589
Saving (loss) if new plant starts up on 1 July 2009						
Annual cash saving (loss)	(45)	14	12	10	10	10
Cumulative cash saving (loss)	(45)	(31)	(19)	(9)	1	11

Note: All figures are £'000s

Figure 6.2 Boiler replacement project: payback calculation

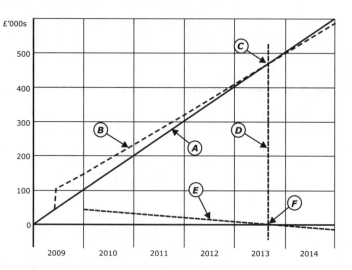

Figure 6.3 Boiler replacement project: payback graphs

zero. This should, and does, give the same breakeven result as the two-curve method described above. It would, however, allow more sensitive vertical scaling, giving a greater crossing angle at the intersection and, therefore, a more accurate result.

DISCOUNTED CASH FLOW

The simple payback method is adequate provided that the total payback period is one or, at the most, two years. It is less satisfactory when looking ahead for longer periods, especially when high rates of return on investment are required. The reason for this is that any given sum of money earned or spent in the future has less real value than the same amount of money earned or spent today. The main cause lies in the notional earning power of today's money. If £100 is received today and invested for an annual net return of 10 per cent, that £100 should be worth £110 after one year. Put another way, £110 received or spent in one year's time is equivalent to receiving or spending only £100 today. Today's £100 is called the discounted or 'net present value' (npv) of the future £110.

Although cost inflation can also have a significant effect, it is usually ignored for the purposes of appraisal calculations (partly because the amounts arising from inflation usually occur on both sides of the inflow/outflow equation and therefore tend to cancel out).

Tables can be obtained which list discount factors over a wide range of percentage discounting rates and periods. Project life periods are usually broken down into years for discounting, but shorter periods are sometimes chosen, especially where very large sums are involved. A short but useful table of discount factors is given in Figure 6.4.

The discounting rate used for a particular project is a matter for management judgement, subject to the following influences:

- prevailing interest rates
- the rate of return on capital invested expected in corporate financial objectives (the dominant factor)
- advice from the company's financial director or senior accountants.

Year	1%	2%	3%	4%	5%	6%	7%	8%	9%	10%	11%	12%	13%	14%	15%	16%	17%	18%	19%	20%
0	1.000	1.000	1.000	1.000	1.000	1.000	1.000	1.000	1.000	1.000	1.000	1.000	1.000	1.000	1.000	1.000	1.000	1.000	1.000	1.000
1	0.990	0.980	0.971	0.962	0.952	0.943	0.935	0.926	0.917	0.909	0.901	0.983	0.885	0.877	0.870	0.862	0.855	0.848	0.840	0.833
2	0.980	0.961	0.943	0.925	0.907	0.890	0.873	0.857	0.842	0.826	0.812	0.797	0.783	0.770	0.756	0.743	0.731	0.718	0.706	0.694
3	0.971	0.942	0.915	0.889	0.864	0.840	0.816	0.794	0.772	0.751	0.731	0.712	0.693	0.675	0.658	0.641	0.624	0.609	0.593	0.579
4	0.961	0.924	0.889	0.855	0.823	0.792	0.763	0.735	0.708	0.683	0.659	0.636	0.613	0.592	0.572	0.552	0.534	0.516	0.499	0.482
5	0.952	0.906	0.863	0.822	0.784	0.747	0.713	0.681	0.650	0.621	0.594	0.567	0.543	0.519	0.497	0.476	0.456	0.437	0.419	0.402
6	0.942	0.888	0.838	0.790	0.746	0.705	0.666	0.630	0.596	0.565	0.535	0.507	0.480	0.456	0.432	0.410	0.390	0.370	0.352	0.225
7	0.933	0.871	0.813	0.760	0.711	0.665	0.623	0.584	0.547	0.513	0.482	0.452	0.425	0.400	0.376	0.354	0.333	0.314	0.296	0.279
8	0.923	0.854	0.789	0.731	0.677	0.627	0.582	0.540	0.502	0.467	0.434	0.404	0.376	0.351	0.327	0.305	0.284	0.266	0.249	0.233
9	0.914	0.837	0.766	0.703	0.645	0.592	0.544	0.500	0.460	0.424	0.391	0.361	0.333	0.308	0.284	0.263	0.243	0.226	0.209	0.194
10	0.905	0.820	0.744	0.676	0.614	0.558	0.508	0.463	0.422	0.386	0.352	0.322	0.295	0.270	0.247	0.227	0.208	0.191	0.176	0.162
11	0.896	0.804	0.722	0.650	0.585	0.527	0.475	0.429	0.388	0.351	0.317	0.288	0.261	0.237	0.215	0.195	0.178	0.162	0.148	0.135
12	0.887	0.789	0.701	0.625	0.557	0.497	0.444	0.397	0.356	0.319	0.286	0.257	0.231	0.208	0.187	0.169	0.152	0.137	0.124	0.112
13	0.879	0.773	0.681	0.601	0.530	0.469	0.415	0.368	0.326	0.290	0.258	0.229	0.204	0.182	0.163	0.145	0.130	0.116	0.104	0.094
14	0.870	0.758	0.661	0.578	0.505	0.442	0.388	0.341	0.299	0.263	0.232	0.205	0.181	0.160	0.141	0.125	0.111	0.099	0.088	0.078
15	0.861	0.743	0.642	0.555	0.481	0.417	0.362	0.315	0.275	0.239	0.209	0.183	0.160	0.140	0.123	0.108	0.095	0.084	0.074	0.065
16	0.853	0.728	0.623	0.534	0.458	0.394	0.339	0.292	0.252	0.218	0.188	0.163	0.142	0.123	0.107	0.093	0.082	0.071	0.062	0.054
17	0.844	0.714	0.605	0.513	0.436	0.371	0.317	0.270	0.231	0.198	0.170	0.146	0.125	0.108	0.093	0.080	0.069	0.060	0.052	0.045
18	0.836	0.700	0.587	0.494	0.412	0.350	0.296	0.250	0.212	0.180	0.153	0.130	0.111	0.095	0.081	0.069	0.059	0.051	0.044	0.038
19	0.828	0.686	0.570	0.475	0.396	0.331	0.277	0.232	0.195	0.164	0.138	0.116	0.098	0.083	0.070	0.060	0.051	0.043	0.037	0.031
20	0.820	0.673	0.554	0.456	0.377	0.312	0.258	0.215	0.178	0.149	0.124	0.104	0.087	0.073	0.061	0.051	0.043	0.037	0.030	0.026

Figure 6.4   Table of discount factors for calculating net present values

Case example: net present value of the boiler replacement project

The boiler replacement project described earlier in this chapter can be used to demonstrate the net present value concept. The example has been kept simple and does not include all the possible cash flow items. Taxation has not been taken into account: in practice benefits would have a corresponding tax charge against them, whilst many outflow items would be set against tax as allowable expenses.

A five-year total period has been chosen in this case, because the company's management has considered this to be a reasonable life expectancy for the new boiler without further change. In many other financial appraisal cases, some event forecast or planned for a fixed date in the future will place a finite limit on the project life and determine the appraisal period. Examples of such events are the expiry of a lease on a building, the planned discontinuance of a product, or the date forecast for a mineral deposit to become exhausted to the point where it is no longer economic for mining.

Net present value calculations can seem a little strange at first but they are really quite simple if the correct procedure is followed. The secret lies in careful tabulation of all the financial elements, setting each item of cash inflow and outflow in its appropriate time period on a sensibly designed layout.

In the boiler project example, the tabulation and calculation of net flows before discounting has already been performed (Figure 6.2). The discounting calculations are illustrated in Figure 6.5. Using a discount rate of 10 per cent, it is seen that this project has a net present value of *minus* £1812 after five years. In fact it would not break even (the npv would not become positive) until the year 2019. That result depends on the boiler working well without major overhaul for more than its expected trouble-free life of five years. This is a more pessimistic (but more realistic) result than that obtained from simple payback analysis. It suggests that the project cannot be justified on purely financial grounds (although there might, of course, be environmental, staff welfare or other good reasons for going ahead).

Calculating the expected rate of return on investment for the boiler project

Suppose that management want to know the expected rate of return on their company's investment in the boiler project over the five-year period. The rate of return is equivalent to the percentage discounting rate that would give a forecast net present value of zero. This rate can be found by

Year	Cash inflows £	Cash outflows £	Net cash flows £	Discount factor at 10% rate	Discounted cash flows £
0 (2009)		45 000	(45 000)	1.000	(45 000)
1 (2010)	14 000		14 000	0.909	12 726
2 (2011)	12 000		12 000	0.826	9 912
3 (2012)	10 000		10 000	0.751	7 510
4 (2013)	10 000		10 000	0.683	6 830
5 (2014)	10 000		10 000	0.621	6 210
Net present value					(1 812)

Figure 6.5   Boiler replacement project: net present value calculation

An annual discounting rate of 10 per cent has been used in this example. The factors were taken from Figure 6.4.

repeating the calculation shown in Figure 6.5 with different percentage discounting rates until one is found that yields the required zero npv. There are three possible ways in which this can be done:

1. One of the test calculations might, with good fortune, yield zero npv or a value which is sufficiently close to zero to be accepted.
2. It is more likely that no calculation using a whole-number percentage rate will give zero npv. The calculation will probably have to be performed several times (called reiterations), changing the discounting rate in small steps until the rate is found that gives zero npv.
3. A graphical method can be used instead of reiterations by trial and error, calculations can be made using a few whole-number discounting rates that give a range of fairly small positive and negative npv values. These npv values must be plotted on a graph against the discounting rates that produced them. The point at which the line crosses zero npv will allow the forecast percentage return on investment to be read off.

Although many computer programs are capable of carrying out discounted cash flow calculations, the process can be followed quickly and easily using an ordinary pocket calculator. It is not even necessary to use tables of discount factors, since the calculator will provide these on demand. If, for example, the discount rate to be tested is 7.5 per cent per annum, it is only necessary to divide 1 by 1.075 to find the discount rate for year 1 (0.9302). On most calculators, repetitive use of the = button will immediately give the discount factors for as many subsequent years as are needed.

Case example: financial appraisal of a tollbridge project using discounted cash flows

Here is a slightly more complicated case. Mrs Goldbags, a lady of considerable wealth, owns land that includes a long section of a river valley. Two fairly busy highways run alongside both banks of the river for many miles and Mrs Goldbags wishes to profit by linking these highways with a short road bridge that would cut road journeys and save road users much time and inconvenience. She plans to recover her initial investment and thenceforth make a profit by charging a toll for each road user who crosses the bridge in either direction. Here are the parameters for the proposed tollbridge project:

- Project start, 1 July 2010
- Forecast road opening date, 1 July 2012
- Total costs of designing and building, £20 million, spread evenly over the two-year construction period. For simplicity, this includes start-up costs of recruiting and training staff just before the road opens
- Toll revenues, based on traffic predictions, £3 million per annum, with no allowance made for growth
- Maintenance costs free for the first full year of operation (1 July 2012 to 30 June 2013)
- Subsequent maintenance costs £1 million per annum, starting 1 July 2013
- Management and administration costs (insurances and staff salaries) £100 000 in each full year of operation
- All funding is from existing cash reserves, so that there are no loan interest charges to be incurred
- Rate of return on investment required is 7.5 per cent over an appraisal period ending on 31 December 2025.

The discounted cash flow schedule in Figure 6.6 indicates a net present value of *minus* £3.612 million for the tollbridge project. So, this project cannot yield the required 7.5 per cent return on capital invested according to the parameters given. Recalculations tested with different discount

Year	Item	Cash outflows £'000s	Cash inflows £'000s	Net cash flows £'000s	Discount factor at 7.5%	Discounted cash flows £'000s
0 (2010)	Design and building costs	5 000		(5 000)	1.0000	(5 000)
1 (2011)	Building costs	10 000		(10 000)	0.9302	(9 302)
2 (2012)	Building costs	5 000				
	Administration expenses	50		(3 550)	0.8653	(3 072)
	Revenue from tolls		1 500			
3 (2013)	Administration expenses	100				
	Maintenance costs	500		2 400	0.8050	1 932
	Revenue from tolls		3 000			
4 (2014)	Administration expenses	100				
	Maintenance costs	1 000		1 900	0.7489	1 423
	Revenue from tolls		3 000			
5 (2015)	As for year 4	1 100	3 000	1 900	0.6966	1 324
6 (2016)	As for year 4	1 100	3 000	1 900	0.6480	1 231
7 (2017)	As for year 4	1 100	3 000	1 900	0.6028	1 145
8 (2018)	As for year 4	1 100	3 000	1 900	0.5607	1 065
9 (2019)	As for year 4	1 100	3 000	1 900	0.5216	991
10 (2020)	As for year 4	1 100	3 000	1 900	0.4852	922
11 (2021)	As for year 4	1 100	3 000	1 900	0.4513	857
12 (2022)	As for year 4	1 100	3 000	1 900	0.4199	798
13 (2023)	As for year 4	1 100	3 000	1 900	0.3906	742
14 (2024)	As for year 4	1 100	3 000	1 900	0.3633	690
15 (2025)	As for year 4	1 100	3 000	1 900	0.3380	642
Net present value						(3 612)

Figure 6.6　Tollbridge project: net present value calculation

factors (not illustrated here) show that the net present value becomes positive when the discount factor (and the required rate of return on capital invested) is reduced to 5 per cent.

Other ways of viewing this project give different but misleading results. A full year's operating profit and loss account would, before taxation, show total costs of £1.1 million against sales revenue of £3 million, which is a handsome gross annual operating profit of 63.33 per cent. But that ignores the sunk costs (the invested capital) of £20 million. Using a simple payback calculation (again not illustrated here) this project would give the falsely optimistic impression that this project would break even during the year 2022 (after about 12 years).

What the discounted cash flow method shows in this case is that Mrs Goldbags might be better advised to abandon the idea of this project (with all its attendant risks) and place her £20 million in bonds or deposit accounts with a guaranteed yield of 5 per cent or more per annum.

HOW MUCH CONFIDENCE CAN WE PLACE IN THE DATA?

The results of project financial appraisal can be the prime factor in deciding whether or not to commit vast sums of money in launching a new project. Senior managers who are presented with a business case will, if they are good at their jobs, ask searching questions. In particular, they should be asking how much confidence can be placed in the data used in the appraisal. Most estimators and analysts tend to be too optimistic in their predictions. A financial appraisal that predicts a good, very positive net present value at the end of several pages of tables and arguments can be very persuasive. However, many of the estimates of costs and time used to build up the business case are only estimates, made as judgements by fallible human beings. They are not facts set in tablets of stone. Quite often, the estimators get it wrong and the project fails to produce all the expected benefits.

We need to make some sense out of such uncertainty. Two commonly used methods are sensitivity analysis and Monte Carlo analysis. Both of these methods deal with the possibility that the data are flawed. They deal with uncertainty, but not with risk events that might change the intended course of the project (risk is the subject of Chapter 7).

Sensitivity analysis

Sensitivity analysis is one way to gain more confidence in the reliability of an appraisal. The process consists of repeating the discounted cash flow calculations with a changed value for one or more of the parameters to test the effect (sensitivity) on the predicted net present value.

Still considering the tollbridge project described in the previous section, the estimated cost of maintenance and repairs might be arrived at with some degree of confidence by obtaining an advance quotation for a service contract to carry out this work. The annual costs of managing the operation should be relatively simple to estimate, because the number of staff needed and the salaries to be paid can be assessed fairly well. Two factors in the tollbridge project cannot be so reliably predicted however. These are as follows:

1. Unforeseen problems during construction that, although not affecting the fixed price agreed, could delay the completion date, thus putting back the start of operations and cash inflows. A few examples from similar projects in the past include exceptionally bad weather, actions by environmental groups, discovery of archaeological remains, disturbance of rare fauna or flora, stoppages through industrial action, unexpected geological conditions and so forth.
2. The forecast for traffic flows and consequent toll revenues might prove to be very inaccurate when the bridge opens, possibly resulting in revenues well below the target levels.

Using sensitivity analysis, each or both of these factors could be changed, either independently or in combination. The changes might, for argument's sake, be made in steps of ±5 per cent. After each change, net present value must be recalculated to assess the impact of the changed parameter. The sensitivity of net present value to these changes will help to indicate the reliability of the financial appraisal.

Monte Carlo analysis

Monte Carlo analysis is a statistical method, associated with some very impressive (but to most of us not very helpful) mathematics. Fortunately, the process is made simple for project managers and financial analysts by the number of off-the-shelf software applications now available. Development of this software in the project management context was originally focused on attempts to predict the probability of finishing a project on time. However, the same principles and a very similar process can be used to predict the probability of cost estimates being under- or overspent.

Monte Carlo analysis of time and cost estimates are both relevant to uncertainty in financial project appraisal because time and costs are greatly interdependent. The illustration in this chapter is for a Monte Carlo analysis of a project's cost estimates. An example of the time analysis application will be found in Chapter 29.

An example of Monte Carlo analysis of cost estimates

In Monte Carlo cost analysis, the estimator or some independent authority must first review each cost estimate and from it produce two further estimates. Thus, for every original cost item estimated, three new estimates must be tabled. These are as follows:

1. the original estimate, which should be the most likely cost expected for the cost item;
2. a higher estimate, set at the highest possible or most pessimistic estimate for the item;
3. a lower value, which is the lowest possible, or most optimistic estimate for the item.

Thus every item on the original task list will now have three estimates attached to it, the most likely, the most pessimistic and the most optimistic. Monte Carlo analysis makes use of these different estimates by substituting them at random in many reiterations of the total project cost estimate. At one extreme the computer calculation might contain all the improbably low estimates. At the other extreme all the highest, most pessimistic estimates would be included. Between these least likely calculations, the computer can be made to carry out a great number of project cost calculations in which any of the three possible estimates for each cost item is used at random.

Figure 6.7 shows the kind of result that Monte Carlo analysis can produce after many hundreds or even thousands of repeat calculations. The height of each vertical bar in the histogram indicates the frequency, which is the statistical term for the number of calculations that produce a particular estimated total project cost. The envelope containing these bars is seen to follow an approximately normal distribution curve about a mean figure of about £3.4 million.

In practice, the curve might be skewed towards a higher or lower probable total project cost but in this case the highest probability is that the project will cost £3.4 million. If the curve is slewed towards the right (that is, towards the higher cost end of the graph) that implies a higher risk of the project overrunning its budgets or even failing.

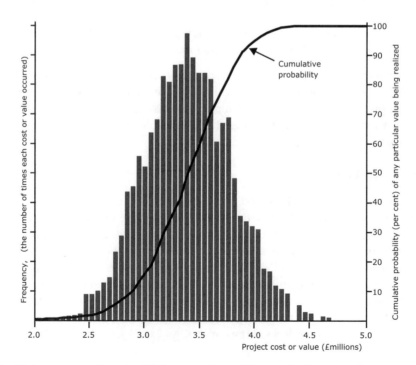

Figure 6.7 Histogram and probability curve from Monte Carlo analysis

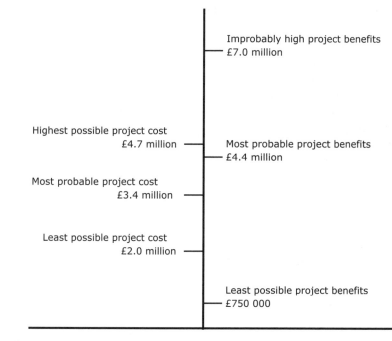

Improbably high project benefits
£7.0 million

Highest possible project cost
£4.7 million

Most probable project benefits
£4.4 million

Most probable project cost
£3.4 million

Least possible project cost
£2.0 million

Least possible project benefits
£750 000

Figure 6.8   Chart comparing project cost and benefits after Monte Carlo analysis

Uncertainty in project benefit estimates

Just as cost estimates can be subjected to Monte Carlo analysis, the same three-estimate approach can be used to assess the probability of achieving the desired project benefits. Provided there are enough data, Monte Carlo analysis will produce another graph of the same form as that shown in Figure 6.7, but the distribution curve might have a quite different shape.

At least one company (Isochron Ltd) displays the results of Monte Carlo cost and benefit analyses in a chart which they call the 'Monte Carlo Box'. Figure 6.8 shows a similar chart based on that concept. This chart demonstrates how project financial analysts might summarize and compare results from cost and benefit analyses in a business plan, using a format that senior managers can readily understand.

PROJECT FUNDING

Project owner's viewpoint

Project funding may not be of direct concern to every project manager – unless shortage of funds puts the future of the project (and its manager) in question. However, here is a list of possible sources from which an organization may be able to find the capital needed for investment in a project:

- cash reserves (money held in the bank or in short-term investments, including profits not distributed as dividends to shareholders);
- sale of assets (for example, the owner of a stately home sells a valuable work of art to raise capital for a building restoration project, or a company realizes cash on its real estate in a sale and leaseback deal);
- mortgaging property;

- borrowing from a bank or other financial institution, either as an overdraft or as a fixed-term loan;
- borrowing through a lease purchase agreement;
- renting or leasing (in which case the project will be owned by the financing institution and not by the project user);
- issuing debentures or loan stock;
- raising share capital, either in a private or public company (the company may be specially set up for the project);
- collaborating with other companies to set up a consortium or a joint venture company in which skills, resources and risk are all shared;
- government sources at international, national or local level, through direct grants or fiscal incentives;
- for export projects it might be possible to borrow from a bank against security provided by a government's export credit guarantee scheme.

Project funding from the contractor's viewpoint

Project funding considerations are not the sole concern of the purchaser. Contractors often need to take a serious interest in the financing of projects for several reasons:

- In some cases the contractor might offer to help or advise the customer to arrange finance. Financing proposals may even feature in the contractor's project tender.
- The contractor must be assured that the customer is financially viable, and has access to sufficient funds to meet all project costs. Will the customer be able to pay the bills? Financial viability is considered further in Chapter 22.
- The contractor may need finance to invest in new plant or to expand other facilities in order to be able to carry out the project.
- If the project size is significant compared to the contractor's other work, cash flow will have to be considered. The contractor may have to fund costly work-in-progress until payment is eventually received from the customer. This difficulty can be made worse if invoices are disputed, delaying revenue receipts. Some customers pay late, not just through innocent tardiness but because of a deliberate policy to delay payment of every bill for as long as possible. The experienced contractor will attempt to minimize these effects by insisting on a contract that allows for progress payments, and by efficient invoicing and credit control methods.
- Money due from overseas customers can be particularly difficult to collect, with risk of serious delays or non-payment. It is easy for the inexperienced contractor to cause delay in payment through any failure (however trivial) to observe the complex documentation formalities imposed by some governments. The big banks are excellent sources of advice for those new to exporting.

A contracting company will be able to reduce its borrowing requirement if it can improve its cash flow. The following are some of the methods that might be considered:

- reducing inventory (stocks and work-in-progress);
- using trade creditors to advantage, negotiating longest possible credit terms for the payment of suppliers' and subcontractors' invoices;
- keeping trade debtors to a minimum through prompt and accurate invoicing, asking for progress payments where appropriate, and applying rigorous credit control.

REFERENCES AND FURTHER READING

Dayananda, D. et al. (2002), *Capital Budgeting: Financial Appraisal of Investment Projects* (Cambridge: Cambridge University Press).

Lumby, S. and Jones, C. (1991), *Investment Appraisal and Financial Decisions*, 6th Edition (London: Thomson Learning).

Lumby, S. and Jones, C. (2003), *Corporate Finance: Theory and Practice*, 7th Edition (London: Thomson Learning).

Turner, J. R. and Simister, S. J. (eds) (2000), *Gower Handbook of Project Management*, 3rd Edition (Aldershot: Gower).

7 Risk

Everything we do from getting out of bed in the morning to returning there at night carries risk. Come to think of it, even lying in bed can be risky. It is not surprising that projects, which metaphorically (and sometimes literally) break new ground, attract many risks. Project risks can be predictable or completely unforeseeable. They might be caused by the physical elements or they could be political, economic, commercial, technical or operational in origin. Freak events have been known to disrupt projects, such as the unexpected discovery of important archaeological remains or the decision by a few members of a rare protected species to establish their family home on what should have been the site of a new project.

The potential effects of risks range from trivial inconvenience to project disaster. Project risk management (and much of mainstream project management) is concerned with attempting to identify all the foreseeable risks, assessing the chance and severity of those risks, and then deciding what might be done to reduce their possible impact on the project or avoid them altogether.

INTRODUCTION TO PROJECT RISK MANAGEMENT

Risks can occur at any stage in a project. Some are associated with particular tasks and others originate from outside the project and can manifest themselves without warning. Generally speaking, a risk event that occurs late in a project can be more costly in terms of time and money than a similar event nearer the start of the project. That is because as time passes there will be a greater value of work in progress and higher sunk costs at risk of loss or damage.

Some projects, because they are small or similar to projects that the contractor has undertaken in the past, might not need special attention to risk management other than considering some of the insurance issues discussed later in this chapter. However, for any project that breaks new ground or is complex and large, a risk management strategy must be developed, first to identify as many potential risks as possible and then to decide how to deal with them.

For very large projects it might be necessary to appoint a risk manager, who can devote all or most of his or her time to ensuring that a comprehensive risk strategy is put in place and then reviewed from time to time throughout the project to ensure that it remains valid. If a project support office exists (see Chapter 11) that is a logical place for the risk management function to reside.

Project risk management is a complex subject. Even the classification of risks is not straightforward and can be approached in different ways. There are several techniques for assessing and dealing with project risks, some of which are shared with other management disciplines (particularly with quality management and reliability engineering). This chapter will outline a few of the methods commonly used.

IDENTIFYING THE POSSIBLE RISKS

It is almost certain that some tasks will not be completed in line with their duration estimates and budgets. Some might exceed their estimates, whilst others could be finished early and cost less than expected. As explained in the previous chapter, statistical tools such as Monte Carlo analysis can be used to attempt an assessment of the probability of the project finishing by its target completion date or of the intended return on investment being realized. However, those measures deal with uncertainty rather than with risk. Risks are unforeseen (and often unforeseeable) events that can result in a change of project plans or even total project failure.

Risks events can occur in any kind of project and they can range from the 'accident waiting to happen' variety to the most unexpected and bizarre. In a lifetime spent with projects I have known risk events ranging in scale from a tragic underground mining disaster to an exploding hearing aid. They can even occur late in the project life history, after the project is finished and handed over (design modifications needed for the Millennium Bridge project in London, for example). I was once responsible for a design error that resulted in a worldwide product recall from distributors and customers. Management change and IT projects seem to be particularly prone to risk of failure, with huge losses of money. With this vast breeding ground for possible risk events it is apparent that the risk manager's first problem is to identify the risks that might affect his or her project.

Checklists, which grow in size and value as companies gain more project experience, are a good starting point for listing the foreseeable risks. Studying the history of similar projects can also highlight possible problems and help the project manager to learn from the mistakes and experiences of others.

Brainstorming is an effective technique for considering many aspects of risks. A brainstorming meeting of key staff is a particularly productive method for identifying all the possible risks along with many of the improbable ones. Much depends on how the brainstorming session is conducted. The leader or chairperson should encourage an atmosphere of 'anything goes', so that participants feel free to propose even the most bizarre risks without fear of ridicule. All suggestions, without exception, should be recorded for subsequent assessment and analysis.

RISK APPRAISAL AND ANALYSIS

Once identified and listed, risks can be ranked according to the probability of their occurrence and the severity of the impact if they should occur. This process will eliminate the most improbable risks arising from brainstorming, but it should bring to the fore those risk events that are most likely to happen or which would have the greatest impact on the project. For this analysis it is necessary to consider the possible causes and effects of every risk. Risk analysis can be qualitative or quantitative.

Qualitative risk analysis involves considering each risk in a purely descriptive way, to imagine various characteristics of the risk and the effect that it might have on the project.

Qualitative risk analysis goes at least one stage further than qualitative analysis by attempting to quantify the outcome of a risk event or to attach a numerical score to the risk according to its perceived claim for preventive or mitigating action.

Qualitative cause and effect analysis

Fault-trees and fishbones

Fault-tree analysis (not described here) and Ishikawa fishbone diagrams are methods commonly used by reliability and safety engineers to analyse faults in design and construction. Figure 7.1, for instance, shows how an Ishikawa fishbone diagram might be compiled to analyse the numerous

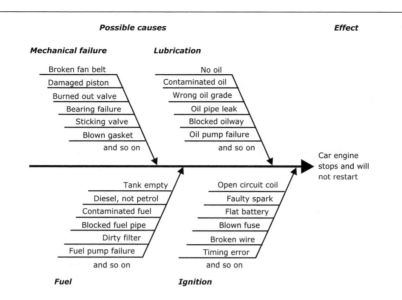

Figure 7.1 Ishikawa fishbone diagram

This cause and effect diagram examines the possible causes of a risk event. Project risk management is more often concerned with the possible outcomes of a risk event, for which failure mode effect analysis is a more appropriate method (see Figure 7.2).

reasons why a car engine fails to start. Many items in this car engine example could be expanded into greater detail, leading to quite a complex diagram, with many branches to the 'fish skeleton'.

Fishbone diagrams can easily be used without adaptation to examine failures or poor performance in organizations. The process generally starts by thinking about the effect, and then looking for the possible causes. However, project risk management is more often conducted from the opposite viewpoint, which means first listing all the possible causes (risks) first and then assessing their probable effects.

Failure mode and effect analysis (FMEA)

Failure mode and effect analysis has also been imported into project risk management from reliability and quality engineering, but this method is possibly more helpful because it starts by considering possible risk events (failure modes) and then proceeds to predict all their possible effects. Figure 7.2 shows a simple FMEA chart. Item 1 in this example is related to the car engine problem in the fishbone diagram (Figure 7.1) but now we look beyond the simple fact of engine failure to consider the possible consequential effects of the engine failing to start. A final column allows space for pre-emptive actions to be recommended that might mitigate or prevent damage from the risk.

Only three items are shown in Figure 7.2 but there might be hundreds of items in a large, complex project. Another column is sometimes added to show when in the project life cycle the risk is most likely to occur. The chart illustrates a qualitative process because the characteristics of each risk are considered, but there is no attempt to give each risk a priority ranking number or to quantify the effects if the risk should occur.

Risk classification matrices

Figure 7.3 shows a risk classification matrix chart. This matrix comprises nine sections. Although this is a simple classification method, an even simpler four-section matrix is often used, containing the following quadrants:

- high chance – high impact

- high chance – low impact
- low chance – high impact
- low chance – low impact

As with failure mode and effect analysis, this again is a qualitative method, in which no attempt is made to evaluate any risk numerically. Each risk item is considered for its likelihood of occurrence (chance) and for the relative scale of the impact on the project should it occur.

Suppose, for instance, that a project is being planned to move a large company headquarters from a central city location to a purpose-built office building on the outskirts of a country town (let's think of Swindon). The following are a few of the many risk events that might be visualized and assessed:

- Some office equipment could be damaged or stolen in transit. The risk of that happening might be high, but the impact could be considered medium because equipment is replaceable.

	Item	Failure mode	Cause of failure	Effect	Remedy: recommended action
1	Project manager's car	Engine refuses to start	Poor maintenance	Project manager marooned at remote site with no other means of transport	Ensure good vehicle maintenance and keep back-up car at project site
2	Main building	Building collapses during installation of heavy machinery	Errors in floor loading calculations	Personal injuries Project delays Loss of reputation	Triple check key structural calculations
3		Building collapses during installation of heavy machinery	Floor slabs incorrectly poured	Personal injuries Project delays Loss of reputation	Ensure operatives get good training and instruction. Employ competent site engineering manager.

Figure 7.2   Part of a failure mode and effect matrix (FMEA)

Potential impact	Chance of occurrence		
High	Severe impact risk with low chance of occurrence	Severe impact risk with medium chance of occurrence	Severe impact risk with high chance of occurrence
	Medium impact risk with low chance of occurrence	Medium impact risk with medium chance of occurrence	Medium impact risk with high chance of occurrence
Low	Low impact risk with low chance of occurrence	Low impact risk with medium chance of occurrence	Low impact risk with high chance of occurrence
	Low		High

Figure 7.3   Matrix for qualitative risk classification

- Some key staff might decide not to relocate with the company. That could be thought to have a medium chance, and the effect would have a medium impact on the company's performance when starting up in the new location.
- The collapse of the new premises just before occupation date through an earthquake in Swindon would be very low chance, but the impact would unquestionably be devastatingly high.
- The chance of moving day being made thoroughly miserable for all concerned through rain would be high, but with low practical impact.

Figure 7.4 shows a simple qualitative risk assessment matrix showing how the principles illustrated in Figure 7.3 might be applied in practice. This exercise is not complete, because as yet no thought has been given about what to do should any risk event occur.

Quantitative analysis

Quantitative analysis methods attempt to assign numerical values to risks and their possible effects. They often examine the probable impact on project time and costs. Alternatively, the evaluation process can produce a ranking number for every identified risk. Ranking numbers denote the priority that a risk should claim for management attention and expenditure on preventative measures.

Although all quantitative methods produce actual numbers they can give a false sense of precision. It has to be remembered that the results are based on estimates, assumptions and human judgement. Those contributing assessments might be fundamentally flawed, mistaken or simply too difficult for any person to make with any degree of certainty.

Failure mode effect criticality analysis (FMECA)

The qualitative failure, mode and effect analysis method illustrated in Figure 7.2 can be adapted and extended to attempt risk quantification. The method then becomes failure mode effect and

Risk event	Chance of happening	Potential severity	Difficulty of detection	Comment
Action by environmentalists	High	High	Low	We shall be building in a nature reserve.
Strikes or other industrial action	Low	High	Low	Loyal workforce with no previous problems.
Project manager struck by lightning	Low	High	Low	But she is a keen golfer.
Hairline cracks in structural steel	Low	High	High	Suppliers have high quality reputation.
Software bugs	Medium	High	High	Process safety depends on computer controls.
Exchange rate changes	Medium	Medium	Low	Not difficult to detect but impossible to predict.
Materials shortages	Medium	Medium	Low	

Figure 7.4   Qualitative risk assessment matrix

criticality analysis (FMECA). Figure 7.5 shows one version. In this example three assessment columns are provided, in each of which the risk analyst is expected to enter a number expressing the degree of significance. Every item is ranked on a scale of one to five, with the highest numbers indicating the greatest degree of significance. The entries might be those of the risk analyst or, preferably, the collective opinions of a risk committee or brainstorming group. In some procedures the column headed 'Detection difficulty' is replaced by one headed 'Prediction difficulty'.

Item 2 in Figure 7.5, for example, considers the possibility and potential seriousness of a building collapse. This is for a building created as part of the project, and the collapse in question might happen during the installation of heavy machinery on upper level floors. If the floors have been incorrectly designed, they might not be sufficiently strong to carry the weight of the machinery. The assessor clearly thinks this is unlikely to happen because she has ranked 'Chance' at the bottom end of the 1–5 scale. There is no doubt, however, that if this event did occur it would be extremely serious, so 'Severity' has been marked as 5.

'Detection difficulty' means the perceived difficulty of noticing the cause of this risk (design error in this case) in time to prevent the risk event. Here there is a considerable element of judgement, but the assessor thinks that although the chance of a design error is very low, the difficulty of spotting a mistake if it did occur would be higher (3 on the scale of 1–5).

The product of these three parameters, $1 \times 5 \times 3$ gives a total ranking number of 15. Theoretically, when this exercise has been performed on every item in the list, the list can be sorted in descending sequence of these ranking numbers, so that risks with the highest priority for management attention come at the top of the list.

Some assessors use weighted parameters. For example, it might be considered that the severity of the risk should play a higher part in deciding ranking priority. So the severity column could be marked on a higher scale, say from 1–10. Item 2 in Figure 7.5 might then be marked 9 on this extended scale, which would increase the ranking factor for this item from 15 to 27.

Although not usual practice, a case might be argued for allowing zero scores in the 'Chance' and 'Severity' columns. That could, of course, result in a total ranking factor of zero. That would be one way in which to dispose of some of the more outlandish risk events identified during an anything-goes brainstorming session.

RISK REGISTER

When all the known risks have been listed, assessed and ranked it is time to consider what might be done about them. That process requires that all potential risks be listed in a risk register (or risk

Item	Failure mode	Cause of failure	Effect	Chance	Severity	Detection difficulty	Total ranking
1 Project manager's car	Engine refuses to start	Poor maintenance	Project manager marooned at remote site with no other means of transport	2	1	3	6
2 Main building	Building collapses during installation of heavy machinery	Errors in floor loading calculations	Personal injuries Project delays Loss of reputation	1	5	3	15
3	Building collapses during installation of heavy machinery	Floor slabs incorrectly poured	Personal injuries Project delays Loss of reputation	1	5	2	10

Figure 7.5 Part of a failure mode effect and criticality analysis matrix

log). A fairly typical example of a risk register page is shown in Figure 7.6, and it should be apparent that this is modelled closely upon the FMECA method demonstrated in Figure 7.5. However, the risk register has the following noticeable additions:

- an ID number for each risk listed;
- space for writing in the proposed action that would be taken should the risk event materialize;
- a column headed 'Action by' in which the name of the person or manager responsible for taking action for each risk can be entered.

The risk register should be reviewed and updated regularly throughout the life of the project. It is advisable to use the computer to sort the risks according to their ranking, with the highest ranked risks placed at the top.

METHODS FOR DEALING WITH RISKS

When all the known risks have been identified, assessed, ranked and registered it is time to consider what might be done about them. These are the decisions that must be entered in the two columns at the right hand of the risk register. The project manager usually has a range of options:

1. *Avoid the risk* – The only way to avoid a risk is to abandon the possible causes, which could even mean deciding not to undertake a project at all.
2. *Take precautions to prevent or mitigate risk impact* – This is a most important part of risk management, requiring the active participation of all managers and staff. It needs high-level risk prevention strategy combined with executive determination to ensure that

Risk ID	Date registered	Risk description and consequences	Probability P = 1-3	Impact (severity) S = 1- 3	Detection difficulty D = 1-3	Ranking P x S x D	Mitigating or avoiding action	Action by:

Figure 7.6 Format of a risk register (or risk log)

all preventive measures are always followed throughout all parts of the organization. It requires the creation of a risk prevention culture, covering all aspects of project tasks, health and safety, and consideration for the environment. Here are a few examples of the many possible practical measures, listed in random sequence:

- high security fencing to reduce the chance of gatecrashers at an open air pop festival;
- provision of marquees at a garden party in case of rain;
- regular inspection and testing of electrical equipment to ensure safe operation;
- double-checking to detect errors in design calculations for vital project components or structures;
- provision of back-up electrical power supplies for vital operations, essential services and computers;
- frequent back up and secure offline storage of business data;
- avoidance of trailing electric cables in offices;
- ensuring that means of escape routes in buildings are always clear of obstructions and that smoke screen doors are kept closed;
- regular fire drills, testing of fire alarms and emergency lighting;
- on-the-job training of back-up staff to understudy key roles in the organization;
- regular inspection and maintenance of lifts and hoists;
- provision of safety clothing and equipment to protect workers, and enforcement of their use;
- restricted access to hazardous areas;
- provision of secure handrails to all stairways;
- choosing the time of year most likely to provide fair weather for outdoor projects;
- adequate training of all those operating potentially hazardous machinery;
- regular financial audits and the installation of procedures to identify or deter fraud;

and so on, and so on: this list could be very long.

3. *Accept the risk* – Rain might make the day chosen for office relocation miserable for all concerned but the risk would have to be accepted. There are numerous small things that can go wrong during the course of any project, and most of these risks can be accepted in the knowledge that their effect is not likely to be serious, and that they can be overcome by corrective measures or replanning.

4. *Share the risk* – If a project, or a substantial part of it, appears to carry very high risk, the contractor might seek one or more partners to undertake the work as a joint venture. Then the impact of any failure would be shared among the partners. Sharing a risk big enough to ruin one company might reduce its impact to little more than a temporary inconvenience.

5. *Limit the risk* – There are occasions when project risks should only be accepted with safeguards in place to limit their potential effect. A good example is an internal project, perhaps for pure research, that cannot be adequately defined at the outset. No one can tell how much the project will eventually cost or what its outcome might be. Yet the opportunities are too great to consider avoiding the risk altogether.

The usual solution to starting an ill-defined project is to limit the risk by authorizing work step by step. It may be possible to divide the project into a number of stages for this purpose: indeed the process is sometimes called stage gating. The stages might be determined by:

- the occurrence of significant events in the project that can easily be recognized when they happen;

- the imposition of a time limit for each stage;
- a budgetary limit for each stage; or
- a combination of any two or all of these.

Funding or authorization of expenditure on each new stage of the project would depend on a critical review of the work carried out up to the review date, coupled with a fresh appraisal of the value of continuing with the project. This approach has the advantage of limiting the committed risk. Although it is not possible to define the entire project in advance, it should be possible to look the short way ahead necessary to define each new step. Each limited step so defined may then be amenable to the project management procedures that cannot be used for the whole project.

In the step-by-step or stage-gated approach it always has to be borne in mind that it might become necessary to abandon the project at any stage and write off the expenditure already incurred.

6. *Transfer the risk* – Some risks, or substantial parts of them, can be transferred to another party on payment of a fee or premium. This leads to the important subject of insurance, which is discussed in the next section.

INSURANCE

The financial impact of many risks can be offset by insuring against them. The client pays the insurance company a premium for this service, and the insurer might itself choose to spread the risk by sharing it with one or more other insurance companies. Figure 7.7 shows that managers do not enjoy complete freedom of choice when deciding which risks should be included in their insurance portfolio.

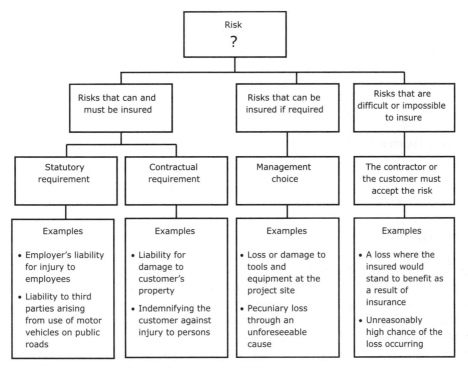

Figure 7.7   Risk and insurance in project management

Since January 2005 the insurance market has been regulated by the Financial Services Authority (FSA). This has led to some changes in the way in which insurance customers are defined, and the information supplied to customers before making a contract of insurance. Customers are either 'retail' or 'commercial'.

A retail customer is a 'natural person' (policyholder or potential policyholder) acting outside their normal trade or profession. A commercial insurance customer is someone acting within their normal profession.

An example of a retail customer would be an individual (a 'natural person') who is not connected with the construction trade and who project-manages the construction of their own house on their own plot of ground. Greater protection and more information are provided to a retail customer than to a commercial customer because the commercial customer is deemed to have greater knowledge or to have access to a professional insurance intermediary.

The policyholder (or potential policyholder) should be given all the necessary information before the inception of insurance cover, to assist them to arrive at an informed decision. In addition, the actual policy wording, terms and conditions must be available and agreed before inception to achieve 'contract certainty'. In plain English, that means that the intending policyholder must know exactly what will or will not be covered by the insurance, together with details of the cost.

The FSA regulates and authorizes all insurance providers (insurance companies) and insurance intermediaries (brokers). It is illegal for someone or a firm to deal in insurance unless they are regulated and authorized by the FSA.

Categories of insurance

There are four main classes of insurance:

1. legal liabilities (payments to others as a result of statutory, contractual or professional commitments, compensation awarded by the courts, legal expenses, but not fines imposed by the courts);
2. protection against loss or damage to property, including temporary works and work in progress, owned construction plant, hired-in plant and employees' effects;
3. cover relating to personnel;
4. pecuniary loss.

A policy may combine cover for two or more of the above classes of risk.

Obligatory insurances

Legal requirements oblige companies to obtain adequate insurance cover against some risks. These obligations arise either from various government laws and regulations or from conditions contained in a binding commercial contract.

Statutory requirements

At the top of the insurance shopping list are those items which must be insured in order to comply with laws and regulations. Third-party insurance for motor vehicles used on public roads is a familiar example. Employers are obliged to insure their employees against injury or illness arising from their employment (Employers' Liability Insurance) and every employer has to display a valid certificate on its notice boards to show that such insurance exists.

Statutory regulations of particular interest to the manager of construction and engineering projects cover the periodic inspection and certification of lifting equipment, pressure systems and local-exhaust ventilation plant. No project which includes the installation of such equipment should be handed over to a client without the relevant written (or other) scheme of examination and the accompanying inspection certificates. If the correct documentation is not supplied, the client will not legally be able to operate the equipment. In the UK these regulations form part of the Health and Safety at Work Act 1974. Much of this legislation resulted from European Directives and similar legislation has been enacted in other EU member countries. The principal regulations are:

- Lifting Operations and Lifting Equipment Regulations 1998 (LOLER)
- Provision and Use of Work Equipment 1998 (PUWER)
- The Management of Health and Safety at Work Regulations 1999
- The Pressure Systems Safety Regulations 2000 (PSSR)
- Control of Substances Hazardous to Health Regulations 1998 (COSHH)
- Electricity at Work Act 1988 (E@W).

Regulation of the relevant inspection services is carried out by the Health and Safety Executive for and on behalf of the Crown. All inspection bodies must be accredited by the United Kingdom Accreditation Society (UKAS) to in accordance with (at the time of writing) ISO/IWC 17010.

Inspection work is usually performed by engineer-surveyors employed by an engineering insurance company. The insurance company is sometimes engaged by the contract principal, but more usually by the main contractor. The larger of these insurance companies, with many years' experience of such work, are able to advise on compliance with national and local legislation covering equipment and construction materials.

The project or site manager must check that inspection certificates required by the regulations are current and valid for plant hired for use on a construction site. This will help to protect the project manager's organization from any liability that might arise from the use of a plant hire fleet that has been poorly managed by the plant hire company.

Failure to comply with these, and other, regulations may have an adverse effect on the insurance cover. In addition, non-compliance could render the parties liable to prosecution by the Health and Safety Executive.

Contractual requirements and other legal liabilities

In commercial and industrial projects, whether for construction or manufacturing, it is certain that some onus will be placed upon the parties (usually the contractor) to insure against several risks. All the model terms of contract for engineering, civil and construction contracts embody such requirements. The project contractor will also wish to make certain that subcontractors are bound, in turn, by similar conditions.

Liability insurances are most likely to feature prominently in project contracts. The project purchaser will want to know, for example, that the contractor has adequate cover for legal liability in the event of personal injury, illness or death caused to anyone as a result of the project.

In summary, liability insurances may be required for:

- compensation to persons for bodily harm (employees of either party, others working on site, visitors and members of the public
- property loss or damage, including work in progress
- financial loss
- infringement of property rights
- accidents
- product liability (arising from use of a product)
- professional negligence
- nuisance caused by the works
- environmental damage.

Every organization or professional person with project responsibility (including architects, consultants, surveyors, designers and project management organizations) must make certain that they have adequate professional liability insurance to cover any liability that they might incur in the course of their work.

Other risks that can be covered by insurance

In addition to the statutory and contractual requirements, there is a range of other risks against which a contractor might be required to insure, or for which a contractor might decide that insurance is prudent. Some of these are listed below.

Contractors' all risks insurance for construction and engineering projects

All risks insurance cover provides protection during the works, until the project is complete and handed over to the customer. Thereafter, insurance becomes the customer's responsibility.

All risks policies typically protect work-in-progress and temporary works against fire, storm damage, theft and malicious damage but any new policy proposal should be studied with care, as it is likely to list exceptions. In addition to work-in-progress, the cover should include loss or damage to:

- construction plant and machinery
- hired plant
- construction materials in transit to site
- temporary buildings and site huts
- employees' tools and effects.

In addition there will be other, minor, extensions of cover built into the policy for little or no extra cost.

Reinstatement costs after an accident will also be covered, including the costs of removing debris and the fees of architects, surveyors and consulting engineers. The insurer might also agree to pay additional expenses (such as overtime costs and express carriage rates) incurred as a result of expediting reinstatement work.

Contract all risks (CAR) policies usually apply to civil engineering and construction projects, while the less common engineering all risks (EAR) policies are for contracts that relate specifically to the construction and installation of machinery.

Exclusions and conditions in the policy, and in the policy schedule, should be examined carefully and understood before the insurance is entered into.

Decennial (latent defects) insurance

Decennial insurance, which can cover a period of up to ten years, is designed to insure against damage to premises caused specifically by an inherent defect in the design, materials or construction of a project. In the event of a successful claim, decennial insurance removes the need for the project owner to suffer the expense of taking legal action for recompense against the contractor.

Accident and sickness insurance

Provisions for personal accident, sickness and medical expenses insurance will need particular consideration when employees are required to travel, whether at home or abroad. Those working on projects in foreign countries will expect to be adequately covered for the higher risks involved, and such cover will have to be extended to spouses and children if they are also allowed to travel.

Key person insurance

Key person insurance offers various kinds of protection to an employer against expenses or loss of profits which result when illness, injury or death prevents one or more named key persons from performing the duties expected of them. Arrangements are flexible and policies can be tailored to suit particular circumstances.

Pecuniary insurance

Pecuniary insurances are designed to protect a company against financial losses from a variety of causes. Risks that can be covered include embezzlement, loss through interruption of business, and legal expenses. Advance profits insurance may be possible in some limited circumstances to provide cover for delay in receiving planned return on project investment caused by late completion of the project.

Of particular interest to contractors where business with foreign customers is involved is export credit insurance. In the UK, the Government's Export Credits Guarantee Department (ECGD) provides guarantees that can provide security against bank loans for large capital goods and long-term projects. Most industrialized companies have similar schemes. The contractor will be expected to bear some of the risk, although its proportion will usually be small. The security offered by credit insurance can be an important factor in obtaining finance for a project.

Risks which cannot be covered by insurance

There are risks which an underwriter will either refuse to insure, or for which the premium demanded would be prohibitive. Such cases arise in the following circumstances:

- where the chances against a loss occurring are too high or, in other words, where the risk is seen as more of a certainty than reasonable chance. Examples are losses made through speculative trading or because of disadvantageous changes in foreign exchange rates;
- where the insurer is not able to spread its risk over a sufficient number of similar risks;
- where the insurer does not have access to sufficient data from the past to be able quantify the future risk;
- where the insured would stand to gain as a result of a claim. Except in some forms of personal insurance, the principle of insurance is to attempt to reinstate the insured's position to that which existed before the loss event. A person cannot, for example, expect to benefit personally from a claim for loss or damage to property not belonging to them (property in which they have no *insurable interest*).

These items must, therefore, be excluded from the insurance portfolio. In some cases other commercial remedies might exist for offsetting the risks.

Obtaining insurance

Insurance can be sought directly from an underwriter, or through a broker; preferably one with a good reputation and experienced in the insured's type of project activity. The insurer will need to be supplied with sufficient information for the risk to be adequately defined, and the contractor will be expected to inform the insurer of any change of circumstances likely to affect the risks insured. The insurer may wish to make investigations or even follow up the project work using its own experts.

Professional advice from insurers can often be of great benefit in reducing risks, especially in the areas of health and safety and crime prevention.

Two events in 2001 had a severe impact on insurers and will affect reinsurance and capacity for many years to come. One of these events was the insolvency and collapse of Independent Insurance plc, a company that insured a large number of contractors and construction trade clients for very low premiums. This caused every insurance company and broker to conduct internal audits, critically re-examining the risks to their own businesses. The other 2001 event was, of course, the 11 September terrorist atrocities in the US, which highlighted to insurance and reinsurance companies the potential for such enormous claims to be repeated in the future, whether from terrorist attacks or other causes. Insurers have since sought to limit their exposure to such risks and they have instituted a regime of stricter underwriting controls and lower risk acceptance thresholds.

Liability insurance is becoming expensive. Employer's liability cover, even though a legal requirement, is becoming difficult to obtain. Some insurance companies have had to close because they are unable to effect such insurance.

It is, therefore, now more important than ever for a project manager to involve an insurance specialist at a very early planning stage, lest they should find that no insurance cover is available at short notice.

PLANNING FOR A CRISIS

Some risk events can have such a potential impact on a project that special crisis management contingency plans must be made. Such contingency plans can extend to projects that would need to be set up specially and rapidly to deal with the sudden crisis, for example in areas that are particularly liable to epidemic diseases, famine, flooding, hurricanes, earthquakes or other natural disasters. Crisis contingency plans should also be put in place by process industries and other companies that carry out operations which, if they should go wrong, could be hazardous for people and the environment beyond the factory gates. One cannot always say when or where a disaster will strike, but at least plans can be put in reserve to be implemented immediately when the need arises.

Organization

Once the possibility of a crisis has been established, the first step in devising a contingency plan is to identify the key people who will take charge of the crisis management project. These people will constitute a sleeping organization, ready to awake at a moment's notice in case of need. The core organization might include senior representatives of local and national government, the emergency services, particular charities and relief organizations, and so on. Each person should have the authority to instruct others within their home organization and the permission to identify the relevant resources that could be made available should the crisis happen. A team leader or steering committee must be appointed that will manage the project should it become live. This group of key people might be called the crisis action committee.

Contingency planning

Once the key people have been elected or selected to serve on the action committee, they must meet to design appropriate contingency plans, and then meet again at regular intervals to ensure that the plans are kept up to date. The committee might have to arrange for emergency funds, stores and special equipment to be stockpiled or at least located against the time when they might suddenly be needed. Lists of secondary organizations and other helpers must be established, which although not part of the action committee could be called upon to give urgent and immediate assistance. These secondary associations might include, for example, specialist engineering or chemical contractors, explosives or decontamination experts, building and demolition contractors, caterers, and a wide range of charitable organizations that could offer relief services. There might also be a need to plan for immediate advertising in the appropriate media to make public appeals for funds.

Tabletop and other exercises

One thing that the action committee will need to do as early as possible is to assess what might happen should the crisis arise. The committee will need to use their collective imagination to consider and be prepared in advance for as many of the problems as possible.

A tabletop exercise can contribute to this process, where the members of the action committee carry out a role-playing exercise to consider as exactly as possible what might happen and what they themselves and their subordinates might do should the crisis happen.

Many crisis contingency plans can be tested by field exercises, in which some or all of the services act out their parts as if the crisis had actually happened. Field exercises can reveal shortcomings in the contingency plans and test vital aspects such as mobility, response speeds, and how to communicate and coordinate the various participants under emergency conditions, when power, water and telephones might all be out of action.

When the plans have been made and tested they must be documented, incorporating all the lessons learned from tabletop and field exercises so that they are ready to put into action effectively and with minimum delay. This is, in effect, creating a project handbook or project manual for a project that might never happen. When a crisis does cross from imagination to reality, however, contingency planning can save time and many lives.

REFERENCES AND FURTHER READING

Association for Project Management, (2004), *Project Risk Analysis and Management Guide*, 2nd Edition (High Wycombe: APM Publishing).
Chapman, C.B. and Ward, S.A. (2003), *Project Risk Management: Processes, Techniques and Insights*, 2nd Edition (Chichester: Wiley).
Hillson, D. and Murray-Webster, R. (2005), *Understanding and Managing Risk Attitude* (Aldershot: Gower).
Kluwer's Insurance Buyer's Guide 2005/2006 (Kingston upon Thames: Croner); this title is updated annually.
Ould, M. (1999), *Managing Software Quality and Business Risk* (Chichester: Wiley).
Sadgrove, K., (2005), *The Complete Guide to Business Risk Management*, 2nd Edition (Aldershot: Gower).
Webb, A. (2003), *The Project Manager's Guide to Handling Risk* (Aldershot: Gower).

8   *Project Authorization*

Most lecturers will, perhaps once in their lifetime, meet an audience with whom they cannot establish the rapport essential to teaching and learning. My own worst experience by far in that respect was with a small group of part-time MBA students. During one drizzly, dreary Saturday morning, when every one of us would far rather have been somewhere else, we reached the subject of project authorization. Each person was asked to outline the project authorization procedures used by their company. Astonishingly, it seemed that in no company where these people worked was there any formal procedure for approving expenditure on a new project. Worse, no student could even see the point of the question. Thus this chapter has to begin by explaining the reasons for having a formal project authorization procedure.

INTRODUCTION TO PROJECT AUTHORIZATION

Previous chapters have described processes that should take place early in the life history of most kinds of project. Those processes should define the project to the point where a business plan or project proposal will allow the project owner to decide whether or not to authorize the project and thus commit expenditure and other valuable resources. That decision is an important project milestone because it defines the boundary between the preparatory, theoretical stages of the project and its practical fulfilment.

Purposes of a project authorization procedure

Company directors have a prime responsibility to shareholders and other stakeholders to ensure that the capital invested in the company is used prudently. Directors are expected to maximize the return on investment for the ultimate benefit of the company and its shareholders. Thus, the principal reason for having a project authorization procedure is to ensure that money will only be invested in projects that directly (or indirectly through subsequent projects) have an acceptably high probability of achieving a return on investment that is at least in line with corporate objectives.

If there were no filter to block expenditure on inappropriate projects, one could imagine that individuals within the company might embark willy-nilly on their own high-risk schemes, perhaps relying only on their intuition, on flawed personal opinions or even on pressure from peers, without adequate financial appraisal. That would lead to a serious drain on capital that might not be discovered until too late. It could also open easy paths for fraud.

Thus the need to control capital expenditure on new projects and to strive for maximum possible return on investment must top the following list of reasons why companies need formal project authorization procedures. Project authorization procedures are also necessary for administrative reasons. The prime reasons for having a formal project authorization procedure are as follows:

- to control the use of capital expenditure in the best interests of shareholders and other stakeholders;
- to announce that approval has been given for the project to start;
- to communicate details of the project nature and scope throughout the organization;
- to announce the project's name and number as it will appear in all accounts and reports;
- to announce key project milestones and financial targets;
- to announce the name of the project manager and confirm his or her authority to manage the project;
- to define any restrictions or limits on expenditure, in cases of provisional authorizations.

Project authorization as a chain reaction

Great fleas have little fleas upon their backs to bite 'em,
And little fleas have lesser fleas, and so ad infinitum.

Augustus de Morgan (1806–71) in *A Budget of Paradoxes* (after Jonathan Swift).

Once a project of any significant size has been fully authorized by its owner it is common for many other companies to become involved as contractors, subcontractors, suppliers, consultants and so on. Thus project authorization usually triggers a chain reaction. It begins with the project owner making the initial decision to invest money in the project, usually against the expectation of valuable benefits later in the project life history.

When contractors or other external companies are engaged by the owner to work on the project, they too will apply project authorization procedures within their own organizations before they allow their staff to begin work or place external purchase orders and subcontracts. However, the authorization criteria for those contractors and external companies will usually depend not on predicted longer-term post-project benefits, but on the more immediate revenues and profits to be realized at or before project completion.

Figure 6.1, for the luxury service apartments project case in Chapter 6, was a very simple example that illustrated these differences between the cost/benefit expectations for a project owner and the main external contractor. So, just as the project owner and the project contractor approach project *appraisal* from different viewing platforms, so there are some differences between the criteria that the owner and the contractors have to apply to project *authorization*.

PROJECT AUTHORIZATION CRITERIA FOR THE PROJECT OWNER

The processes of project authorization used by project owners are particularly relevant to change management and IT projects, and they often involve difficult decisions. This section will therefore take a glimpse at the process of project authorization from the viewing platform of the project owner. For a fuller account see Chapter 5 in Fowler and Lock (2006).

Authorization of minor works and very small projects

Clearly, every company will want to authorize internal projects of a minor nature from time to time when the full force of a formal authorization procedure would be inappropriate.

A prudent board of directors will often allow discretionary power to named more junior managers that allow them to authorize projects on their own authority, without need for further reference to the board. There are two ways in which this can be done:

- by specifying a maximum project size that a named manager can authorize, that size being defined by the estimated total project cost;
- by treating minor projects and small works as operational expenses within the annual budget allocated to and controlled by a departmental manager.

The second of these options is easier to control, given an adequate company accounting system and good cost reporting.

However, whenever any manager is given independent authority to initiate expenditure, fraud prevention demands that a different manager should approve all resulting invoices for payment of significant sums to external suppliers and contractors. To explain the reason for such precautions, consider the extreme (but not unknown) case of a manager who could authorize a project for work on a private residence, fraudulently using company funds. Unless an independent manager sees the incoming invoices for approval, the fraud might go unnoticed.

Authorization criteria for a single management change or IT project

Imagine that you have prepared a business plan for a new project, and that you have the task of presenting the plan to your board of directors in the expectation of receiving authorization for the project to go ahead. No doubt you will have prepared an impressive PowerPoint® presentation that sets out the costs and benefits of your project, and you will hand out fact sheets to all those present at the meeting. Which of the criteria in your presentation do you think would most influence the directors' decision?

Supposing, for the moment, that this is the only new project under consideration, the directors will probably want to know the answers to several important questions, such as:

- Do all the cost/benefit predictions point to a positive net present value that would yield at least the return on investment expected in the corporate objectives? If not, what are the alternative justifications for this project?
- How certain can we be that the cost estimates are safe and include all known items?
- Are there any special risks associated with the project that might prevent its success?
- Are the predicted benefits achievable or over-optimistic?
- Do we have, or can we get, the resources needed for the project?
- Will the project be difficult to implement: will it disrupt our current operations and what impact will it have on our staff?
- Have other companies attempted similar projects, and what were their experiences?

If the answers to these questions are favourable, you should expect that the board will approve your project and the authorization process can be put in motion.

Authorizing projects that have no immediate or apparent benefits

There are projects that must sometimes be undertaken where there are no immediately obvious tangible benefits. There are many examples, including projects in not-for-profit organizations, projects carried out in accordance with statutory instructions, and feasibility study projects.

Suppose, for instance, that the owner of a large hotel has been served notice to carry out specified works costing £500 000 before a Fire Certificate can be issued. At first glance, this project has no measurable tangible benefits, the npv would be a huge negative value, and there would appear to be no reason for going ahead with the project on purely financial grounds. But, if the owner failed to do that project, no Fire Certificate could be issued and the hotel would have to close down.

Feasibility projects have no *direct* benefit for their owners. One feasibility project for developing a new copper mining complex took two years and cost the owner many millions of pounds in engaging external consultants. Of course the consultants made money (as consultants usually do). But the owner had to authorize the project as an essential and prudent precursor to the much larger mining development project to follow, and pay the whole cost from reserve capital.

There are countless other examples of such feasibility projects, many in the public eye. The new Wembley Stadium project, for instance, underwent considerable preliminary studies and debate before the actual construction project was authorized (and even then the outcome did not immediately produce the expected benefits).

Authorization criteria for additional management change or IT projects

The authorization decision for a new project will be complicated if other management change or IT projects are already in progress in the organization, or if the application for the project is one of several such applications. This takes us into the territory of 'portfolio management'. Managing a number of simultaneous projects within a company or group of companies is called 'programme management'.

Now a new set of decision parameters must be added to the seven decision criteria listed above. Not only must the board of directors consider the implications of each new project application on its own merits, but they must also decide whether the organization will have enough resources to add the new project to its portfolio. Very often, companies have to make a choice between different projects, any one of which might appear to be justifiable but for which resources cannot be made available.

Standardizing multiple business plan presentations

The authorization decision process is often made more difficult for the directors of a large organization or group of companies because business plans for proposed projects can be prepared in a variety of different formats. Imagine keen managers in different companies within the group, all potential initiators of new management projects, and all having their own individual ideas of how to prepare a business plan. That difficulty can be eased by appointing a coordinator or portfolio manager who will make certain that all proposals for new projects are accompanied by well-reasoned business plans, all presented in a common standard format.

The board of directors must always be clear that the portfolio of authorized projects represents the projects that fully deserve highest priority, that is, the highest claim on the group's finite resources.

AUTHORIZATION DOCUMENTS ISSUED BY THE PROJECT OWNER

The complexity of the project authorization procedure must depend to a large extent upon the estimated cost of the project and the size of the impact that it would have on the business. Management change projects of any significant size will usually require a 'charter and contract', 'project initiation document' or 'works order' procedure.

Authorization by charter and contract

Some organizations invoke a lengthy authorization procedure that consists of a project charter, followed by a contract.

The charter is a form of specification that sets out the principal objectives and is prepared for consideration and approval by the company's senior management. It reflects the business plan, item for item. Once the charter has been approved, a separate and subsequent exercise is undertaken to translate the charter into a contract.

The contract is a working document that establishes the project in the organization under the nominated project manager. The contract is internal, between the project manager and the board of directors.

My own view is that the charter and contract method is somewhat cumbersome, expensive to administer and can delay the start of work unnecessarily for many months.

Authorization using a product initiation document

Although still fully comprehensive, a project initiation document (PID) of a form similar to that shown in Figure 8.1 is a concise and more practical alternative to the charter and contract arrangement. The PID can fulfil both the role of the charter and of the contract.

PROJECT INITIATION DOCUMENT

Project name:
Project number:

Contents

Authorization
       For the investment: (signed by a company director)
       For benefits realization: (signed by the project manager)
Document control
       Version control and issue date
       Distribution
Key project personnel
Purpose of this document
       Application
       Focus and closure
       Change and return on investment
       References and links
Contract summary
       Baseline state
       Details of subsequent changes
Objectives and scope
Deliverables (including the recognition events)
Benefits (including the value flashpoints)
Costs
Overall cost/benefit analysis
Sponsorship and stakeholders
Project team
Business team
Governance (project management methods)
Reporting requirements

Figure 8.1   Example contents of a project initiation document (PID)

By kind permission of Isochron Ltd

Authorization by internal memorandum

Small in-house projects are often authorized by an internal memorandum issued by a senior manager to the department or project manager responsible. For example, a company may decide to refurbish a small area of its office premises, perhaps finding temporary occupation for the staff for two or three weeks while the refurbishment takes place. That work must certainly be managed as a project, but it hardly needs an elaborate authorization procedure. A memorandum from the managing director to the facilities manager specifying the requirements and the budget is all that is needed.

An internal memorandum that authorizes a small project constitutes a contract between the project owner (represented by the board of directors or senior management in this case) and the contractor (which, for an internal project, is the departmental manager to whom the memorandum is issued).

PROJECT REGISTRATION AND NUMBERING

Once a new project of any kind has entered an organization it has to be formally 'entered into the system' so that all the necessary accounting, planning, progressing and other administrative procedures can be put in place.

One of the first steps is to allocate an identification number to the new project which, depending on the procedures of the particular company, will be used henceforth as a basis for drawing numbers, cost codes and other important project documentation. Project numbers are usually derived serially from a register, which might be a loose-leaf book or a computer file. A typical project register page is shown in Figure 8.2. Project numbering systems are discussed in Chapter 12.

The purpose of a project register is, of course, not only to allocate numbers. The register of current projects lists all authorized work within the organization against which time may legitimately be booked by staff on timesheets and against which the costs of project materials and expenses may be charged.

PROJECT REGISTER					Date of last revision	
Project number	Project title	Project manager	Customer	Date opened	Comments Special restrictions	Date closed

Figure 8.2   Project register

Whenever it is necessary to retrieve information about a project, current or long past, the project register is usually the best, often the only, starting place to begin the search. In most management information systems or archives, the project number is the essential element leading to the various document files and project data. But the project number might not be known or remembered. Very often historical searches start with only a vague recollection of the project description, or the name of the customer, or the approximate dates. Each project entry in the register should therefore record the following data:

- project title
- start date and (eventually) closure date
- project manager responsible
- project number
- the customer
- the customer's order number or letter reference.

A well-kept register will enable any project to be identified even when only one or two of the associated data items listed above are known. When projects are closed, the register information should be kept in a secure but accessible archive.

PROJECT AUTHORIZATION IN A CONTRACTING ORGANIZATION

Project authorization by a contractor usually means that the contractor has been instructed by the owner, customer or client to proceed with the project on terms that have previously been negotiated and agreed. This instruction might be received in the form of a contract, a purchase order or (less desirably) a letter of intent.

The resulting authorization document issued within the contracting company might be entitled 'project authorization' or perhaps 'works order'. This document carries essential data that define the levels of expenditure authorized (the departmental and purchasing cost budgets), planned start and finish dates, details of the customer's order, pricing information, invoicing and delivery instructions and so on.

One vital item on a project authorization is the signature of a member of the contractor's senior management. That is the signal that the project is properly authorized, that work can begin and that costs can be incurred or committed.

Format and general content of a project authorization

The data in project authorizations are usually summarized, often to the extent that all the information can be printed on one side of an A4 page. This can be true even for large capital projects. Precise project definition is achieved by listing the relevant technical and commercial documents on the authorization form. If, for example, the project has been won after in-depth negotiation of a detailed contract, coupled with the discussion of technical and commercial sales specifications, the project authorization must identify those documents without ambiguity by giving their serial numbers and all approved amendments or revision numbers.

Figure 8.3 shows a works order form of a type that has been used for many years in manufacturing companies handling special projects. The information given on budgets and schedules is necessarily brief, and is provided on the form only to allow outline planning and to place overall limits on the amount of expenditure authorized. Detailed budgets and work-to lists usually take some time to prepare and may be delayed by several weeks after the project is authorized.

WORKS ORDER		Project number	

Customer   **Delivery address (if different)**

Project title

Drawings, specifications and other documents defining this project	Number	Rev

Budget summary	Hours	Schedule summary	Project start and finish dates are firm. Others subject to detailed planning.		
Engineering design				Start	finish
Design after issue		Design and drawing			
Works		Purchasing			
Assembly		Manufacturing			
Final testing		Assembly			
Installation		Final test			
Commissioning		Install and commission			
Materials, services and expenses	£	Overall project dates			

Commercial summary   **Contract type and total price**

Sales engineer:

Sales reference:

Customer's order No.

Notes/limitations

Authorization   (subject to any limitations listed above)

Project manager assigned: Authorized by:

Distribution

Chief engineer ☐	Project manager ☐	Works director ☐	Materials manager ☐	Quality manager ☐	Accounts manager ☐	Office manager ☐

Figure 8.3   Works order example for a manufacturing project

Figure 8.4 shows a project authorization form used by a mining engineering company to initiate and authorize projects ranging from small feasibility studies and minor plant extensions to very large capital projects. Again, the form summarizes the essential points (although this company did tabulate more detailed budgets on the reverse side of the form). A fairly comprehensive management information system was in use and the form was designed to provide the basic input data to the system (as well as informing departmental managers about the new project).

Distribution of project authorization documents

Project authorizations are distributed to all company departments for general information, but the full supporting technical and commercial documents are handed over only to the project manager. It becomes the project manager's responsibility thereafter to ensure that all other managers in the organization are made aware of their particular project requirements in detail, and sufficiently in advance to enable them to make any necessary preparations.

```
┌─────────────────────────────────────────────────────────────┐
│ PROJECT AUTHORIZATION                                         │
│                                                               │
│ Client _____       │
│ Scope of work _____       │
│        _____       │
│        _____       │
│        _____       │
│        _____       │
│        _____       │
│                                                               │
│ Source documents _____       │
│        _____       │
│        _____       │
│                                                               │
│ Project number (to be entered by accounts department) ▯▯▯▯▯▯ │
│                                                               │
│ Project title (for computer reports) ▯▯▯▯▯▯▯▯▯▯▯▯▯▯▯▯▯▯▯▯    │
│                                                               │
│ Project manager (name) _____  Staff number ▯▯▯▯      │
│                                                               │
│ Project engineer (name) _____  Staff number ▯▯▯▯      │
│                                                               │
│ Project start date (enter as 01-JAN-03)     ▯▯-▯▯-▯▯         │
│                                                               │
│ Target finish date (enter as 01-JAN-03)     ▯▯-▯▯-▯▯         │
│                                                               │
│ Contract type:                                                │
│                       Lump         Other                      │
│ Reimbursable ▯        sum ▯        (Specify) _____      │
│                                                               │
│ Estimate of man-hours                                         │
│ ┌──────────────────┬──┬──┬──┬──┬──┬──┬──┬──┐                 │
│ │Standard cost grade│1 │2 │3 │4 │5 │6 │7 │8 │                 │
│ ├──────────────────┼──┼──┼──┼──┼──┼──┼──┼──┤                 │
│ │Man-hour totals   │  │  │  │  │  │  │  │  │                 │
│ └──────────────────┴──┴──┴──┴──┴──┴──┴──┴──┘                 │
│                                                               │
│ Notes:                                                        │
│                                                               │
│                                                               │
│ - - - - - - - - - - - - - -     - - - - - - - - - - - - - -  │
│ Authorization (1)               Authorization (2)            │
│ ┌────────────┬──┬──────────────┬──┬─────────────┬──┬────────┐│
│ │Project manager│ │Marketing   │  │Contracts dept.│ │Purchasing││
│ ├────────────┼──┼──────────────┼──┼─────────────┼──┼────────┤│
│ │Project engr.│ │Central registry│ │Cost/planning│  │Accounts dept.││
│ └────────────┴──┴──────────────┴──┴─────────────┴──┴────────┘│
└─────────────────────────────────────────────────────────────┘
```

Figure 8.4   Project authorization form used by a mining engineering company

AUTHORIZING WORK WITHOUT A CONTRACT OR CUSTOMER'S ORDER

The golden rule

One of the things that all managers are taught is that no expense shall be committed on any project unless the customer's written authority to proceed (and promise to pay) has first been obtained. The risks for disobeying this rule are obvious. Once the customer knows that the contractor has already become committed to actual costs, the contractor's bargaining position in contract negotiations has been weakened. Worse still, if the customer decides not to go ahead with the project or give the work to another company, all the contractor's committed costs will be forfeit.

For these good reasons, an internal project authorization document will not normally be issued unless the customer's written authority to proceed has been obtained.

Breaking the rule

In spite of convention, there might be occasions when a very limited amount of work can be authorized before receipt of a firm order from the customer. This poses risks. Indeed, to many work-hardened managers it will sound like heresy. Nevertheless, provided the risks can be quantified and contained within controlled limits it is often possible to gain several weeks' progress in the project calendar for the expenditure of only a tiny fraction of the total project cost. Of course, no orders for materials can be placed, but it might be possible to carry out activities from a preliminary project start-up checklist without committing more than one or two people over the limited period concerned.

Naturally, such advance work in the absence of a customer order will only be authorized where this strategy has advantages for the contractor. These advantages might include the avoidance of possible trouble later on, if the overall project timescale is seen to be particularly tight.

If the contractor foresees a trough in the organization's total workload, it could suit the contractor to carry out a little preliminary work, to enable full-scale work on the new project to start as soon as the order is received.

By these methods, progress on a new project might be pulled forward by a month or two. Conversely, doing absolutely nothing and waiting until the official order is received from the customer could mean that the main project workload will be delayed until it interferes with work for other projects.

Graphs of project expenditure plotted against time display a characteristic S shape (see Figure 8.5). The rate of expenditure usually starts very slowly, increases greatly during the middle part of the project life cycle, and then falls off as the project nears completion. Any talk of authorizing advance expenditure must be limited to the first few weeks, when the rate of expenditure is very low and confined to preliminary engineering or administrative tasks. Steps must be taken to ensure that the expenditure rate remains low. Any decision to allow advance work is always risky, and this must be reflected in the conditions listed in the authorizing document. A preliminary issue of the project authorization can be used but only with the following provisos:

- Authorization must be limited to allow only one or two named individuals to do the work.
- The project accounting system should be programmed to reject time booked by people who are not on the authorized list.
- No materials or equipment must be ordered.

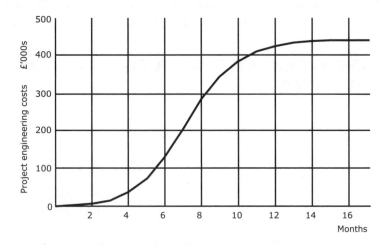

Figure 8.5   Typical project engineering cost/time relationship

- There must be a total budget allocation for this work, regarded as the 'write-off' value of the risk.
- The work to be done should be defined and confined by a checklist or schedule.
- Progress and costs must be monitored and reported to senior management so that work can be stopped immediately at any time.

REFERENCES AND FURTHER READING

Fowler, A. and Lock, D. (2006), *Accelerating Business and IT Change: Transforming Project Delivery* (Aldershot: Gower).

Rosenau, M. D. jnr and Githens, G. D. (2005), *Successful Project Management: a Step-by-Step Approach with Practical examples*, 4th Edition (New York: Wiley); one of few texts to give practical advice on project authorization.

9   *Project Organization Structures*

It should be obvious that, if all the project objectives are to be achieved, the people, communications, jobs and resources must be properly organized. But the form which that organization should take might not be so obvious.

Every company has its own ideas about how to organize itself and its work. It is highly probable that if three companies doing similar work could be compared, three different organization structures would be found. Further, all three companies might be equally successful (or equally unsuccessful), implying that it is not always possible to say with any degree of confidence that there is one best organization solution.

This chapter (together with Chapter 10) cannot, therefore, declare exactly how every project should have its organization structured. Instead, it starts by setting out some of the properties that are essential for efficient organization. It then describes possible organization options, together with their advantages and disadvantages.

EFFECTIVE ORGANIZATION AND COMMUNICATIONS

An effective organization will have clear lines of authority and every member of the project will know what he or she is expected to do to make the project a success. This is part of the management communication framework needed to motivate all the staff employed. A well-motivated group can be a joy to work with. A badly informed group, with vague responsibilities and ambiguous levels of status and authority, is likely to be poorly motivated, slow to achieve results, costly to run and extremely frustrating to work with.

The complement of good management communications is the provision of adequate feedback paths through and across the organization. These facilitate cooperation and coordination. They allow progress to be monitored and difficulties to be reported back to executive management. They should also give all participants access to the relevant experts for advice or instruction on technical and commercial difficulties.

ORGANIZATION CHARTS

It is not possible to discuss organizational structures in any depth of detail without the aid of charts (or 'organigrams' as they are often unfortunately known). No organigram can adequately depict all the nuances and politics of a particular organization, but we all need to understand, as far as possible, the meanings of the charts that we encounter during our working lives. The chart in Figure 9.1,

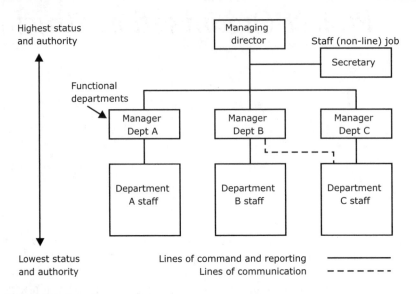

Figure 9.1 Organigram conventions

although very simple, contains all the essential conventional notational elements. The standard conventions are as follows:

- Each box represents an organizational role or job.
- The convention is to write job titles in the boxes in preference to the jobholders' personal names (although both job title and name are often given). The thinking behind this rule is that the organization structure is regarded as a fairly stable pattern of roles, but as people are promoted, demoted or given different appointments the names of people fulfilling those roles are more likely to change
- The authority and status of each role reduces from top to bottom of the chart in hierarchical fashion. So the most powerful role in the organization is placed at the top of the chart
- Solid lines indicate lines of command, down which commands are given, and up which corresponding reporting is expected
- Dotted or broken rules indicate specifically designated lines of communication. For example the manager of Department B in Figure 9.1 has a specific need to communicate regularly with staff who report directly to the manager of Department C
- The various departments depicted on the chart are usually grouped by their specialist functions (such as electrical engineering or accounting) so that these charts are often called line and function charts
- Roles lying outside the line reporting structure and are called staff roles. People in staff roles have no direct line authority, but can enjoy status and indirect power through the support of their line manager. Thus the secretary in Figure 9.1 is in a staff role without power, but others in the organization who treated that secretary without due respect would probably incur the wrath of the managing director.

Shortcomings of organigrams

The principles listed above might seem logical and unambiguous. However, in practice organizations can be far more complex. For example, in all except the most outdated, authoritarian, militaristic style of company there will always be informal lines of communication and feedback up, down, sideways and diagonally across the organization. That's no problem and is usually to be encouraged.

Organizations thrive on fast and effective communications, whether electronic or face to face. The only difficulty is that organigrams cannot possibly show every communication channel, and they are certainly incapable of defining every subtle influence that one person might be able to exert over another.

Whenever an organization changes, or when a new project is opened, it is wise and customary to produce a new organization chart and distribute it. But that simple process, however innocently intended, can provoke strong and unexpected reactions.

There will be employees who feel aggrieved when they find that their names are not included on the chart, which they perceive as a personal insult. Those people will believe that they have been overlooked and that their roles and are not appreciated as being sufficiently important.

The issue of a new organization chart can also give rise to feelings of envy or injustice when individuals feel that their particular box should have been placed higher up in the hierarchical pecking order. At least one company has attempted to solve this problem by issuing circular charts, but that is a not a complete solution because those nearest the outer rim of the circle might feel that they should be nearer the centre.

However, organigrams with all their deficiencies and potential for causing individual discontent are the best, indeed the only, practicable way of depicting an organizational structure. They are, in themselves, a form of communication. Thus you will find organigrams sprinkled liberally throughout this chapter and the next.

EMERGENCE OF PROJECT MANAGEMENT IN A DEVELOPING COMPANY

The subject of project management organization can be introduced conveniently by considering the historical development of a small company. The organization invented for this example happens to be a manufacturing company, but many of the principles and arguments apply equally to all kinds of other projects.

Case study: Street Components Ltd

The company

Street Components Ltd had its origins, many years ago, as a manufacturer of street lamps and other associated items of 'street furniture'. Later, the company's expertise and activities were developed to include components for automatic traffic signals (traffic lights). In more recent times, the company's expertise and range of products have been extended to many other aspects of traffic control equipment and systems, which it sells to local government authorities, developers and other large companies.

Routine manufacture

The time is sixty years ago.

Street Components Ltd employs 200 people, and is making and selling small street lamps and other associated products. Manufacture takes place in batches or in continuous assembly lines, depending on the product. All operations are managed by a production manager, who relies on a production controller to schedule all the work.

In normal conditions the backlog of work awaiting issue to the workshops might run, at most, into a few weeks. Loading of production departments and their machines must be arranged to ensure a reasonably smooth flow of work without bottlenecks and without too much idle time, but planning methods are straightforward and within the capability of the competent production controller. Exceptional work peaks or bottlenecks are resolved by rearranging the existing schedules, overtime working or by the short-term employment of subcontractors.

Estimators, job planners and production engineers analyse all new manufacturing drawings and specifications. The time required for every manufacturing operation can therefore be assessed with reasonable accuracy, based on past experience of similar operations. There is no need for any specialized planning or scheduling technique other than the application of well-proven production control methods, such as daily loading wall charts.

Job costing is carried out in arrears by recording the man-hours and materials used. The time from start to finish of each operation is fairly short, and the total cost of each unit produced usually becomes evident fairly soon after the work has been done, using normal cost accounting procedures.

Transition from high-volume/low-cost to low-volume/high-cost manufacture

The time is thirty years ago.

Street Components Ltd has grown, and has extended its product range. It now offers a standard range of traffic control products, which include relatively simple sets of traffic lights (each set comprising a standard controller, three or more signal lamp assemblies, vehicle sensors and cabling). Most of the manufacture still takes place in batches, or as continuous production for stock. Routine production management and production control procedures still apply, now assisted in some areas by computer systems.

One complication is that customers occasionally ask for non-standard items which do not form part of the customary catalogued range. Many of these special items are trivial variations on the normal production theme, but other requested changes are more radical and complex. These special requests are regarded by the production management team as a nuisance, and they also create difficulties and additional work for the company's engineering design department.

As the company's expertise and size expand, the increased level of sales includes more orders for sets of traffic signals that differ in some respect from the standard catalogue description and have to be custom-built. Some of these products have become so specialized that no market could be found for them outside the needs of the customers who have ordered them. The company that once mass-produced simple street lights as standard catalogue items is now supplying some of its customers with traffic signal sets that are becoming more complex and more costly. Street Components Ltd is experiencing a change from high-volume/low-cost to high-cost/low-volume production.

Some of the equipment included on the customers' orders is becoming so specialized that usual production control and work scheduling methods are proving difficult to apply, with risk of late delivery or worse. There are now many more components to be designed, manufactured or specially purchased and assembled into each new customer order. The company's cost estimators are having difficulty in evaluating new work, for which there is often no precedent and (at the cost estimating stage) no detailed drawings. The time from receipt of order to delivery has grown from one or two weeks to several months.

In these circumstances, Street Components Ltd is experiencing some difficulty in coordinating all the requirements. The company must start to question whether or not special management methods are needed to handle these special orders.

Transition from product manufacturer to project contractor

The time is the present.

As road traffic demands have become heavier, many traffic control systems must be planned on a larger scale. Instead of considering just one crossroad or junction individually, whole road systems have to be taken into account. For each of these systems, traffic volumes must be recorded and analysed at key points throughout the area before a control system can be designed. Then the sequence and timing of signals at all the road junctions have to be calculated and coordinated to ensure optimum traffic flow. Street Components Ltd has been forced to expand its design, engineering and manufacturing capabilities accordingly.

Now, when an order is placed for a town traffic control system, Street Components Ltd is involved in much more than the supply and installation of a single set of traffic lights. The company might be called upon to provide automatic diversion signs, remote-controlled television cameras, automatic car park routeing and status signs, several sets of traffic lights and other highly sophisticated paraphernalia, all linked to one or more controlling computers.

The company is no longer concerned with the sale of equipment or 'hardware' alone. It now has to support its sales with a high proportion of customer consultation, systems engineering and other services or 'software'. Instead of being able to satisfy each customer order by supplying direct from a finished stocks warehouse, it has to design, manufacture, install and commission complex systems to highly specialized customer requirements. Customer orders that could once be delivered within a few days or weeks have been supplanted by orders for projects that can take many months, if not years, to complete.

Work scheduling and control must take into account all the activities needed to bring the project to a successful conclusion (including all the software tasks, such as writing computer programs and preparing operating and maintenance instructions). Some of the items purchased by the company as part of the project must themselves be considered as special, and they too will have to be brought into the control function. Some of those purchased items might be sufficiently complex for their suppliers to manage their design and manufacture as projects in their own right.

Cost control (a basic factor in achieving profitability) has become more complex. Cost and management accountants are not the only contributors to this process; they must be helped by specialists who can define the total work content in detail and then report on achievement and cost implications as the project proceeds.

When this stage has been reached, where simple jobs have given way to complex projects, the answer to the question of whether or not new management methods are needed becomes very clear. Customary procedures for work planning and control will no longer be just difficult to apply: they will fail altogether if they are not brought into a wider framework of management. A total *project management* system is required.

Work management in a conventional manufacturing organization

A clearer picture of some of the problems encountered in project handling can be seen by studying the management organization structure of a manufacturing company. A small engineering company like Street Components Ltd might have been organized in its earlier days as outlined in Figure 9.2.

Organizations of this type are known as 'line and function', because they are set up to manage work within departmental (functional) boundaries or specialist disciplines. Thus the chief engineer is responsible for design and development but very little else. The works manager concentrates on the production aspects of the business. Managers concentrate on those reporting directly to them in the line and they generally have no direct responsibilities outside their own functions. Of course, no company could ever exist on such a rigid basis and there must be some cooperation and interaction

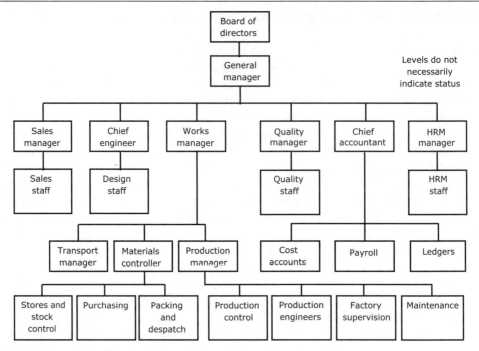

Figure 9.2   Example of a manufacturing organization

This is a line and function organization. It may be ideal for the continuous or batch manufacture of standard products but no provision is made to coordinate the activities of special projects.

between different managers. Nevertheless, any cross-functional relationships that do exist are regarded as secondary to the main line structure. They are not defined, no special provision is made for them and they are not brought under any form of control. Such communication weaknesses are potentially damaging to any company, but they become particularly serious when a firm undertakes a multidisciplinary project.

One might ask whether general managers should not play a significant part in coordinating all the various project functions. To some extent they might, of course, but they cannot be expected to deal efficiently or effectively with the level of detail involved in the day-to-day running of projects. The company's general management should be left free to make higher level decisions about the business, implement policies decided by the board of directors and carry out administration at high level.

Even if the general manager or other senior executive is held to be ultimately responsible for the success of projects, they must be able to delegate the tasks of planning, coordination and day-to-day management. But delegate to whom? In the organization structure depicted in Figure 9.2 there is no obvious person who can logically be charged with the direct responsibility for following any complex project through all its stages. The positions of line responsibility are clearly shown for each function, but the coordination between them, necessary for effective project control, is missing.

Communications throughout the project cycle and the need for a project manager

Engineering projects, in common with most other customer-funded projects, are partly cyclical in nature. This is illustrated in Figure 9.3, which shows some of the key fulfilment stages for a typical project. Each project is conceived when the customer and the contractor's sales engineering department first make contact. The project is given life when the customer issues a purchase order

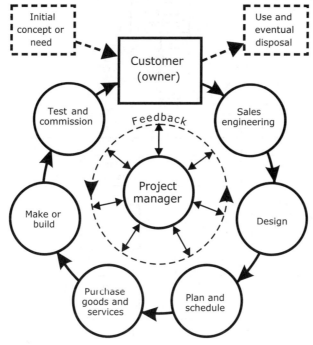

Figure 9.3 Project cycle

The role of the project manager as coordinator and communicator is emphasized here.

or when some other contract document is signed. Thereafter many other stages must be passed through in turn, until the work finally arrives back at the customer as a completed project. Clockwise rotation around the cycle only reveals the main stream. Within this flow many small tributaries, cross-currents and even whirlpools are generated before the project is finished.

As instructions are issued within departments and from one department to another, information must be fed back along the communication channels to signal the results obtained as each instruction is carried out. These feedback data are used to correct any errors discovered in the design drawings and for the essential task of controlling the general progress of the project.

Much project information will not flow along the defined lines of authority, but will cross them in complex and changing patterns. In fact, when a manufacturing project is compared with routine production, the emphasis has shifted from looking principally at the line relationships to consideration of the functional connections. This will have to be reflected in the formal organization structure if the project is to be coordinated and managed satisfactorily. Someone must be made responsible for managing the project as an entity, rather than having this responsibility spread vaguely over a number of managers in the line structure. What is needed is a kind of project champion, a person who can ensure that all the activities are planned, coordinated and directed towards the clear aim of achieving the project objectives. Thus, at the hub of the project cycle, a new figure has emerged – the *project manager*.

PROJECT MATRIX ORGANIZATIONS

Matrix organization for a single project

Figure 9.4 shows how a project manager might be introduced into a company that is undertaking a special, complex project alongside its more routine manufacturing activities. It could apply, for

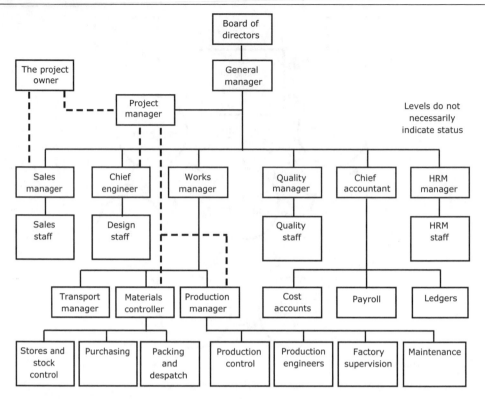

Figure 9.4 Functional matrix for a single project in a manufacturing company

In addition to its standard production range, the company depicted in Figure 9.2 has now undertaken a special project for a customer. A project manager has been introduced to plan and progress the special project work through the organization. The project manager has no direct line authority and acts as a coordinator.

instance, to one of the first projects undertaken by Street Components Ltd. This arrangement is fairly common. It allows the general line organization of the company and its departmental management structure to continue normally, but the project manager is asked to give undivided attention to the 'intruding' project. Here the project manager acts principally as a coordinator, and has no direct line authority over any other manager or their staff. The names given to this organizational arrangement are a 'functional matrix' or a 'coordination matrix'.

When conflict arises or when people refuse to cooperate with the project manager or with each other, lack of authority can make the project manager's job very difficult, causing great demands on his or her skills in dealing with people. If all else fails, the project manager must be able to call on the support of the company's senior management so that they can exert their authority or take other action to resolve the problem.

Matrix organization for multiple projects

The case described above for the functional matrix becomes a little more complicated when a company is handling several projects at the same time.

Figure 9.5 is an organization chart for a manufacturing company which customarily handles several projects simultaneously. In this example, each project is either big enough to justify its own full-time project manager or it can be coupled with one or more other suitable projects to allow sharing (so that one project manager looks after two or more projects). This matrix is the multiple-project variant

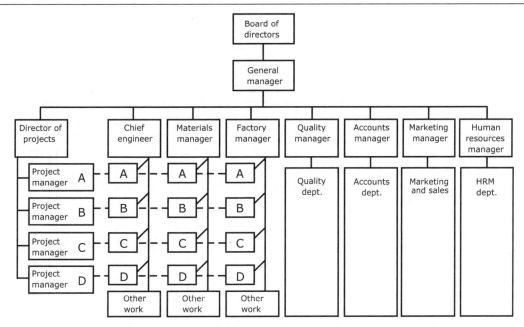

Figure 9.5 Matrix organization for several simultaneous manufacturing projects

Several projects are being handled by this manufacturing company (Projects A, B, C and D are shown here). All projects share the company's design and manufacturing resources but each has its own project manager. The degree of authority given to these project managers by comparison with the departmental managers varies between companies.

of the single-project functional matrix described in the previous section and illustrated in Figure 9.4. Street Components Ltd, the company described earlier, might benefit from this kind of structure.

Figure 9.6 shows a similar organization structure, but suitable for the head office of a company that specializes in the design and fulfilment of capital projects, such as those in the construction, mining or petro-chemical industries.

Both of these examples are matrix organizations. Permanently established groups of people are organized according to their special skills or functional disciplines. The people in these functional groups are responsible to their own departmental line managers, but also have to take account of the project managers' directions to a lesser or greater degree.

Different matrix strengths

The question now arises of how the degree of authority given to a project manager in a matrix compares with that enjoyed by the departmental or functional managers. That balance of power must be decided mainly by more senior management and can vary enormously from one matrix organization to another. The personal qualities of individual managers will also have influence on this power-sharing balance.

Charts such as those shown in Figures 9.5 and 9.6 cannot usually indicate the balance of authority between project and departmental or functional managers. The organigrams used conventionally to depict matrix organizations therefore remain valid whether project managers have weak authority or are given supreme power. Thus a matrix organigram is a case of 'one size fits all', and it is not possible or necessary to provide a different organigram for each of the matrix variants described below.

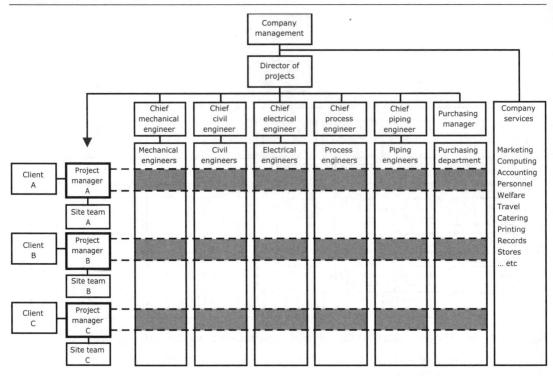

Figure 9.6 Matrix organization for mining, petrochemical or construction projects

This chart shows a company that is organized functionally for engineering several large simultaneous projects. There are dual lines of command, so that a person in a functional group might have to take instruction from both their own departmental manager and a project manager. Note that general company services lie outside the matrix. Many companies will also exclude the purchasing department from the matrix.

Weak matrix

In a 'weak matrix', each project manager's degree of authority and control is less than that enjoyed by the managers of the functional departments. Each project manager is expected to plan and coordinate the project work, but is not empowered to issue direct commands through the line organization. Thus every project manager in a weak matrix is entirely dependent on the departmental managers for the provision of people and equipment for project tasks. The project managers, although key people, have to be content with a coordinating role.

The weak matrix can encourage conflicts. For example, different project managers might compete with each other in claiming attention and resources for their own projects, and they can also come into conflict with the departmental managers over the allocation of people, machines and other facilities to project tasks. An additional complication is that functional departments usually have work, both routine and occasional, that is not connected with any current project. The departmental managers might decide, without agreement from the project managers, to give non-project work priority over project tasks.

These arguments are not intended to condemn the weak matrix. But, as with the case of the single-project functional matrix, the project managers must depend on their motivational and persuasive skills to achieve their aims, and they must be able to call upon higher-level management support to resolve any dispute that cannot be settled at the project and departmental management level.

Balanced matrix

The 'balanced matrix' (or overlay matrix) is very similar to a weak matrix and is sometimes described as such. In the balanced matrix, there is a declared balance of power and authority between the project managers and the functional department managers. Project and functional managers are expected to collaborate constructively and allocate personnel and other resources to tasks according to genuine priorities to ensure the successful outcome of all projects. This is perhaps the most common form of matrix. It is elegant in theory and has many advantages over other forms of organization. It is not however, as some have claimed, a universal solution for all projects. All organization forms have their advantages and disadvantages (discussed later in this chapter).

Like the weak matrix, the balanced matrix can also give rise to conflict between project managers and departmental managers. There can also be motivational difficulties for people working within functional groups, who find themselves with a dual reporting line that violates the principle of *unity of command*. Suppose that you are an electrical engineer, and that you are told by your boss, the chief electrical engineer, to do one thing but the project manager wants you to do something different. Which boss should you obey?

Stronger forms of the matrix

In a 'project matrix' the authority of each project manager takes precedence over the authority of the functional managers, at least as far as the allocation and progressing of work is concerned.

In a 'secondment matrix', which is the strongest form of the matrix, the functional managers must nominate and assign members of their departments to work full-time for the project managers. The people assigned report principally to their respective project managers for as long as each project manager needs them (although they might have to remain physically located in their home departments).

PROJECT TEAMS AND TASK FORCES

Pure project team organization

It is, of course, possible to arrange things differently from the matrix options described above. A complete workgroup or team can be created for each project as a self-contained unit with the project manager placed at its head. The project manager is given direct line authority over the team and is responsible not only for planning, progress and work allocation but also for all technical aspects of the project.

A project team is depicted in Figure 9.7. This example shows a team that should be able to devise the processes and reagent flows, specify and purchase the plant and equipment, design, build and commission all the buildings and other facilities for a chemical processing plant or a mining complex. The project manager is in direct and supreme command, with complete authority for directing the participants so that the project meets all the objectives.

Communications across the various technical and professional disciplines are easier when the project manager is in total command. All members of the team identify with the project and can (at least in the short term) be strongly motivated towards achieving the project goals.

It is best if the key members of the team can be located near each other in the same building but this is not always practicable. If possible, an office should be set aside for use as a 'project war room', where some or all of the team's senior members can meet formally or informally whenever

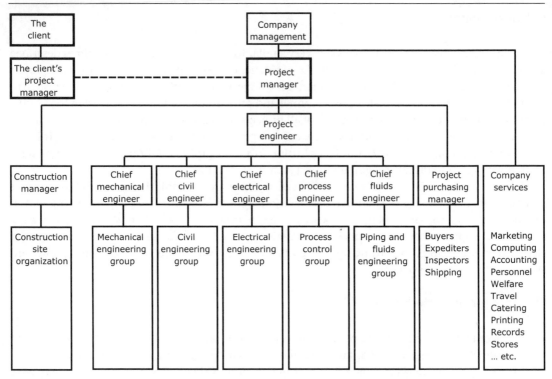

Figure 9.7 Project team organization

This example shows the organization of a project team brought together for the design, procurement, construction and commissioning of a chemical processing plant. The project manager has complete responsibility for all aspects of the project, backed by the clear authority of direct command.

they wish, and where drawings, charts and plans can be displayed on tables and walls. War rooms should include computers and other electronic communications equipment.

Task force organization

A task force is a form of pure project team, but its name implies a particular urgency and common sense of purpose. Task forces are particularly useful in management change projects, an argument that will be expanded in the next chapter. However, a task force can be used in any kind of project, whether it is to deal with a natural disaster or a particularly urgent industrial project.

Use of a task force to rescue a late-running manufacturing project

A complete, all embracing, self-contained project team can be impracticable to organize in a manufacturing company owing to the nature of the facilities and machinery required. Many of those facilities represent considerable capital investment and, together with their human operators, cannot be allocated full-time to a single project team. These facilities must be shared among all the projects and other work being undertaken by the company. Project managers cannot be given direct line authority over any of those shared manufacturing functions and a matrix organization of some sort is indicated rather than a pure team.

Now suppose that a project is running extremely late and is in dire need of a rescue operation. In other words, there is an existing or impending crisis. In those circumstances, the company's management would be well advised to consider setting up a task force to finish the remainder of that project in the shortest possible time. But the problem remains of how to deal with common manufacturing facilities that must continue to carry out other work.

In this example a practicable task force solution is possible. It starts by seconding managers (or their senior deputies) from all the relevant departments to form a task force dedicated to executing the project work remaining in the shortest possible time. A leader for this task force must be found, preferably from within the company. This person must possess determination and a positive outlook. He or she should also be experienced in the project management arts: if not, it might be prudent to engage an external consultant to provide urgent on-the-job training and guidance. The task force members will communicate more effectively and make better and faster decisions if they can be located together, away from their usual offices or workplaces. Better still, they should be provided with a dedicated office that can be used as their project war room.

The resulting task force should be a powerful and effective management team, with all the expertise and authority needed to give the project the best chance of success. Although the project might still depend on the use of resources and facilities shared with other work, the seniority of the task force members will ensure that all critical project tasks get top priority. Suppose, for instance, that the machine shop is represented on the task force by its manager or a deputy. Then, when a critical project task requires the use of a machine that is used heavily for other work, the project task force leader is provided with a direct line of authority over the use of that machine through the senior machine shop delegate who is serving on the task force.

Construction site organizations

Team organization is the customary arrangement where a project construction site manager and all those working on the project have been assembled at a site that is some distance away from the company's home office. It is then usually more sensible to place all site staff under the direct command of the most senior manager located at the site, rather than depend on multiple lines of command back to the home office.

Unless the project is so large that the company must set up local semi-permanent design and administration offices, the site team will probably operate as a sub-organization within a matrix or larger project team. Figures 9.6 and 9.7 both indicate site teams set up in this way, with the site team managers reporting to the overall project managers back at the home office.

There is more on construction site organization and management in Chapter 24.

ORGANIZATION OF CENTRAL ADMINISTRATION FUNCTIONS

A mistake sometimes made is to show all company functions, whatever their purpose, as part of the project team or lying within the project boundaries in a matrix. This error is seen even in well-respected textbooks. Functions such as accounting, marketing, human resources, facilities management and general administration, although they might provide essential support to projects, are not usually involved directly in performing scheduled project tasks.

There are exceptions, especially for management projects. For example, the HR department would be directly involved in a project set up to recruit staff or relocate a company. Marketing staff would be the principal players in a market research or new product promotion campaign. But, for most industrial projects the project manager must regard these other company functions as general supporting services rather than resources under their control. So it is important to draw the boundaries of the project manager's authority with care.

WHICH TYPE OF PROJECT ORGANIZATION IS BEST?

Consider a company which is about to embark upon a project for the first time. A competent project manager is available, but this firm has never had to handle a complex project before and now has to set up the most suitable organization. If asked to advise, the project manager might immediately be faced with the question that often causes much controversy:

- Should the company take all the key people destined to work on the project and place them under the direct management of the project manager, so that a purpose-built team will carry out the project?

Or, at the other extreme:

- Would it be better to have a weak or balanced functional matrix in which the project manager, although held responsible for the whole project, has no direct line authority over the workforce. The project manager must then rely on the goodwill and cooperation of all the line managers for the success of the project.

It must be said that project managers do not always enjoy the luxury of being able to organize their own workforce. They are more likely to be appointed to an organization that either exists already or has been established by more senior managers. In both cases the project manager has to accept the organization as a fait accompli. For some management and IT projects carried out for UK Government departments, even the senior management may have to suffer the restriction of being forced to work under PRINCE2™ principles (see the following chapter). However, in most cases senior managers will have to determine the organization structure so, if only for their benefit, the arguments for and against the principal options are presented below.

The first point to note is that the most successful organization will make the best use of the people working within it. Those faced with the task of designing a new or changed project organization would do well to imagine themselves working as a person within the proposed organization and ask themselves the following questions:

- Would they have a clear sense of purpose and direction?
- How strongly motivated would they feel towards contributing to the project objectives?
- How easy would it be to communicate with other members of the organization?
- Would they have ready access to expert help or advice on technical matters within their own professional discipline?
- How would they perceive their short- and long-term career prospects?

The case for a dedicated project team

Project teams have the advantage that they can each be directed to a single purpose: the successful completion of one project. A team can be completely autonomous. It is provided with and relies upon its own resources. There is no clash of priorities resulting from a clamour of different projects in competition for common (shared) resources.

Short-term leadership and motivation

Much is rightly said and written about the importance of motivating people who work on projects. An important aspect of motivation is the generation of a team spirit, in which everyone feels part of the team and strives to meet the common team goals. It is clearly easier to establish a team spirit when a project team actually exists, as opposed to the case where the people are dispersed over a matrix organization which is handling more than one project.

A person working within a project team is made responsible to one manager (who is either the project manager or a manager who reports directly to the project manager). The line of authority is unambiguous. There is unity of command. Team members know exactly where they stand and there should be little chance of their being given conflicting instructions from more than one superior.

Good cross-functional communications

Most projects require people from many different skills or professional disciplines to work together. In a project team organization, the project manager can ensure that strong and fast communication links exist up, down and across the project organization. There should be no delays while information has to cross departmental boundaries. Decisions can be made more easily and with greater speed. Action can follow decisions with little or no delay.

Security and confidentiality

If work is being conducted for a government defence contract, or for any commercial project that requires a secret or confidential environment, the establishment of a project team greatly helps the organizers to contain all the work and its information within closed, secure boundaries.

The case against the team

Inflexibility and inefficiency in the use of resources

Unless a project is very big, the individual specialist subgroups set up to perform all the varied activities within the project team will be too small to allow sufficient flexibility of labour and other resources.

Where, for example, a design department of 100 people is coping with several projects in a matrix organization, the absence of a few people through sickness would cause temporary difficulties, but these could probably be overcome to a great extent by rescheduling work within the department. If, on the other hand, a project team had been set up to include its own small independent design group, perhaps needing only five people, the absence of two or three of these for any reason could pose a more serious problem.

An item of manufacturing plant purchased specially for use by a project team will undoubtedly spend much of its time idle. The same item of plant installed in a common production facility would, on the other hand, be available for general work and it could probably be used far more efficiently, with less idle time for the machine and its operator. Then, the return on the capital invested in that plant should be greater. The same argument might be applied to any expensive facility set up for the sole use of a project team.

Now consider the example of a chemical plant construction project, the team organization of which is like that shown in Figure 9.7. Suppose that the team includes four electrical engineers. The project manager might face one or both of the following problems:

- difficulty in finding enough tasks to keep all four electrical engineers gainfully occupied all the time;
- severe problems if two or more of the engineers fall ill at the same time or are otherwise unavailable for work at times of peak project activity.

If, instead of a project team, the company operated a matrix organization (like that shown in Figure 9.6), those same engineers would be part of a larger electrical engineering group. They would be found working alongside engineers allocated to all the other projects. The larger group would offer far more flexibility, and the chief electrical engineer should be able to reallocate work among the remaining engineers to minimize the effect of a temporarily depleted workforce or the peak demands of a single project.

Inflexibility associated with small groups can also be expected in some of the specialist administrative functions, where it is often more difficult, if not impossible, to rectify matters at short notice using temporary employees. In the manufacturing case, for example, it is quite possible that only one or two people would be responsible for all project purchasing, or for project production control. Indeed it is not unknown for one person to be responsible for both of these activities on a small project team. In such circumstances, the fate of the project may depend on the capabilities and health of just one individual, who becomes virtually indispensable and almost impossible to replace at short notice.

Isolation of specialists

Specialist engineers and other experts located in small project teams are deprived of the benefits of working in a department with colleagues of their own specialist discipline. They are less able to discuss technical problems with their peers or to have access to the valuable fund of general historic technical and professional data plus current awareness that permanently organized specialist departments accumulate.

Administrative difficulties

Even if a project is of sufficient size to justify its own exclusive team, not all the problems of project coordination will necessarily be overcome. Very often it might be found impossible to house all the participants under one roof, or even in the same locality. Although team organization might be logical and ideal for the project, it could be physically impossible to achieve in practice.

Life after the project

When the project is completed, the team and its project manager have no further purpose. As various aspects of the project are finished, so the team will gradually be reduced in size until it is finally disbanded. Think of Haydn's Farewell Symphony where, as the music draws to its conclusion, the orchestral players depart one by one, extinguishing the candles on their desks as they go, so that the stage is finally left in darkness and silence. People working on a project team know that something similar will happen to them. That knowledge can be a powerful demotivator.

Another possible danger is that something could go seriously wrong with the project after its supposed completion, with expert attention required from the team's engineers to satisfy the client and put matters right. If the team no longer exists, and the engineers who designed the project have been dispersed, events could take an embarrassing, even ugly, turn for the company.

The project customer or client will expect the provision of post-project services from the project contractor. These services can include advice on difficulties experienced by the customer in operating plant and equipment, recommendations for routine care and maintenance, and prompt action to rectify any hardware or software malfunction. The project contractor should also be able to carry out possible future orders from the customer to adapt, modify, expand, augment or replace plant or equipment supplied with the original project. Temporary project teams do not survive for long enough to provide continuity of service to the customer and the company must make alternative, more permanent arrangements.

The case for the matrix

The matrix option allows the establishment of specialist functional groups which, in theory, have 'eternal life', independent of the duration of individual projects. Each member of every specialist group should be able to enjoy a reasonably stable basis for employment (provided that the order book remains full). An environment is created that facilitates the building of long-term trust and loyalty. Pooling specialist skills gives greater flexibility in allocating resources to projects. Concentration of specialist skills enhances the organization's collective technical ability and quality. Organizational continuity promotes the accumulation of knowledge, expertise and experience with the passage of time, both for individuals and for the group as a whole.

There is usually a clear promotion path within each group, and any person with sufficient drive and ambition should be able to compete fairly against their colleagues for more senior positions as vacancies arise, with chief engineer or department manager and beyond being seen as achievable longer-term goals.

Performance assessments of each individual, and recommendations for promotion, improved salary or other benefits, are carried out by a manager of the same professional skill within the stable group. This is more likely to result in a fair assessment and employee satisfaction. These possibilities are not readily available to the specialist engineer or other professional person working alone in a multi-disciplined project team.

The case against the matrix

The matrix organization has its own characteristic disadvantages. Not least of these is the split responsibility which each group member faces between their line manager and the project manager.

Too much reliance can be placed on the supposed eternal life of the matrix organization in modern times, when many businesses face sudden devastating changes as a result of mergers, takeovers, corporate re-engineering, downsizing or even failure.

Most of the advantages connected with a project team (listed above) are denied to the project manager in a weak matrix, but this situation is improved when the matrix is made stronger (with more authority given to the project manager).

Comparison of team and matrix

The arguments will no doubt continue as to which is the better of the two organizations. Some of the pros and cons are summarized in Figure 9.8. As a general rule (but it is dangerous to generalize in this subject) large projects of long duration will probably benefit from the formation of project teams. The same applies to projects that are, by their nature, self-contained, such as work on a remote construction site. Matrix organizations are indicated for companies which handle a number of relatively small simultaneous projects in the same premises.

Hybrid option

Sometimes companies adopt the solution of a hybrid organization, operating a matrix organization in general, but with teams set up for certain projects when the need arises. An example of such an organization is shown in Figure 9.9. It is arranged principally as a matrix, with specialist groups under their respective highly qualified and experienced chief engineers. The project management group contains project managers and project engineers who draw on the resources of the specialist groups for the skilled engineering and expert advice needed for most projects.

If, however, a project should arise which is predominantly within one of the specialist skills, the company might decide to appoint a project manager from within the relevant specialist group,

Characteristic	Organization indicated	
	Team	Matrix
Maximum authority for the project manager	✓	
Freedom from duplicated or ambiguous lines of command	✓	
Maximum motivation of staff to meet difficult targets	✓	
High security of information: by enclosing work in secure areas	✓	
High security of information: by restricting the number of staff who need to know about the work	✓	
Most flexible deployment of resources		✓
Most effective use across the company of those with rare specialist skills or knowledge		✓
Large project, employing many people for a long duration	✓	
Several small simultaneous projects, each needing a few people for a short time		✓
Career motivation of individuals: opportunities for promotion within a person's specialist discipline		✓
Career motivation of individuals: through long-term continuity and relative stability of the organization		✓
Post-design support to construction or commissioning staff		✓
Efficient post-project services to the customer		✓
Establishment of `retained engineering' information banks from which future projects can benefit		✓

Figure 9.8   Project team *v* balanced matrix

managing a team contained within the group. For example, a project to install a large new electrical transformer in an existing plant might be regarded as a project that could be handled entirely by a team within the electrical department. Similarly, a land reclamation project might be assigned solely to the civil engineering group, who would set up their own internal team to deal with it under a civil engineer as project manager.

Another type of hybrid organization occurs when a company operates generally as a project matrix organization but sets up a separate, autonomous, team whenever the size and scope of a project justifies that arrangement, even though the separate project is multi-disciplined.

ORGANIZATIONS WITH MORE THAN ONE PROJECT MANAGER

Any project of significant size will probably have more than one project manager. These can usually be found spread throughout the overall project organization on the staffs of the customer, important subcontractors and the manufacturers of some specially purchased goods and equipment.

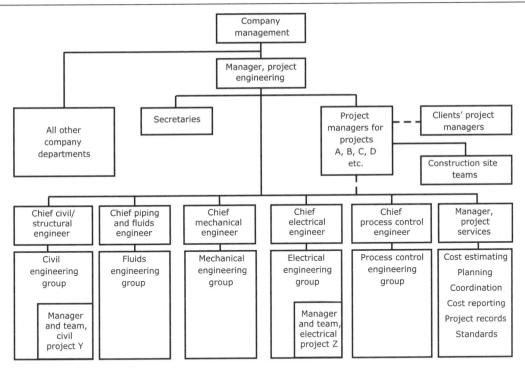

Figure 9.9 Hybrid organization

This international mining company is organized as a matrix. However, a team will be set up within the relevant depart-ment for any project that is confined to a specialist function. For example, project Y is wholly confined to civil engineer-ing tasks and project Z is for the replacement of a large electrical transformer.

Customer's project manager

Whenever a company sells a project to a customer, that customer will probably wish to monitor progress in order to be assured that there is every chance of the work being completed in accordance with the contract. For simple manufacturing contracts this role might be performed by the customer's purchasing department, using its own expediting and inspecting personnel. But, except in this very simple case, the customer might want to appoint an internal project manager to oversee the contract and manage the customer's own activities for accepting and taking over the completed project. The appointment of a customer's project manager would be expected, for example, where the customer is involved in planning to accommodate, install and start up plant supplied under the project.

Sometimes the customer will seek the services of an independent professional project manager, to oversee the project in return for a management fee. This role is often undertaken by specialist companies or by professional partnerships and individuals (such as consulting engineers or architects).

Project managers in customer/supplier chains

There is often more than one project contractor, especially in projects involving construction work. In multi-contractor projects it is probable that one contractor would be nominated by the project customer (the project owner) as the main or the managing contractor, with overall project responsibility to the owner for managing or coordinating all the other contractors and subcontractors.

The managing contractor, in addition to serving the project customer, will itself be a significant purchaser (that is customer) for all the expensive equipment and other goods or services to be provided by suppliers and subcontractors. For large projects some of these subcontracts could amount to significant projects in their own right, each needing planning and project management procedures similar to those used by the managing contractor. Some equipment manufacturers and construction subcontractors would therefore need to assign project managers to manage their own internal subprojects. Indeed, the managing contractor might even insist that such project managers are appointed, and could wish to question and approve the project management methods to be used, possibly as a precondition to awarding the purchase orders or contracts.

There is thus a chain of suppliers and customers in the project organization hierarchy. Such chains can be complex, extending to several levels, with project managers found scattered all over the organization in the offices of key participating companies. Those project managers are important not only for the purposes of planning and control, but they also provide unambiguous and safe points of contact in the network of project communications.

Contract matrix organizations

In large projects the customer/supplier chains are found in a type of organization which is sometimes called a contract matrix. A contract matrix is illustrated in Figure 9.10. In the example shown, the project owner (the customer or client) has engaged a managing contractor to design the project,

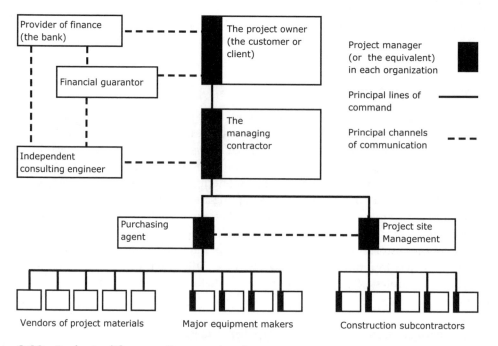

Figure 9.10   Project with more than one project manager

Most big projects will have at least two project managers, one employed by the organization with principal responsibility for carrying out the work and the other representing the client or project owner. The construction project organization shown here is sometimes called a contract matrix. It includes several people who must practise project management skills. Every special equipment manufacturer, for example, needs a project manager to plan and control its share of the project. Many of the practices and principles described in this book apply to all these 'satellite' project managers as well as to the principals.

carry out purchasing, hire subcontractors and generally manage all the activities at a construction site.

The organization chart shows that many of the companies involved in the project will have their own project managers, in addition to the principal project manager employed by the main contractor.

This project is being funded initially by a bank. The bank in this case has lent the funds on condition that the project owner finds a guarantor who is willing to underwrite a substantial part of the lending risk. In the UK, for example, the Export Credits Guarantee Department (ECGD) acts as guarantor for some projects carried out for overseas clients. Visit <www.ecgd.gov.uk> for more information about ECGD.

Both the bank and the guarantor are in need of expert independent advice. This has been provided in the example of Figure 9.10 by a professional engineering organization. This organization, sometime known simply as 'the engineer', can inspect progress and certify all significant claims for payments so that monies are only paid against work that has actually been performed correctly and in the quantities listed on the contractor's invoices.

Joint venture projects and other large organizations

For very large projects several companies might agree to combine their resources and share the technical problems, expense and risk by forming a consortium or joint venture company. This approach will add yet another complication to the organization and at least one more project manager. An example of a joint venture organization is given in Figure 9.11.

For any complex project, apart from the obvious need to define responsibilities and all the contractual details, it is vital that the lines of communication between all the parties are clearly established and specified. It is not unusual to find projects where the participants are separated by international borders and thousands of miles. The volume of information for a large project, whether in the form of drawings, other technical documents, commercial correspondence, queries, and even hotel and travel arrangements can be mind-boggling.

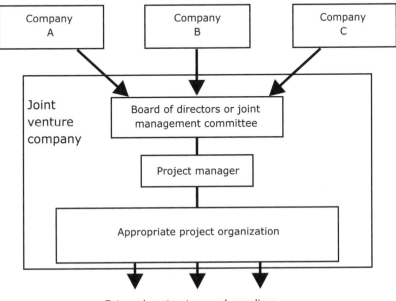

Figure 9.11 Joint venture organization

In any project organization that is complicated by the number of different participating companies, it makes sense to nominate one individual in each suborganization (including the customer) as the principal local information and communications coordinator. Each suborganization within the overall project organization is likely to have its own project manager and they will often be able to nominate and supervise an appropriate information coordinator. These coordinators can ensure that all significant incoming documents and other communications are directed to the responsible recipients for action, followed up where necessary, and recorded for safekeeping and subsequent retrieval. E-mail and other electronic messages are a little more difficult to control and can bypass official communication channels but provision should be made in procedures for all material with contractual or significant technical content to be seen by the coordinator.

REFERENCES AND FURTHER READING

Belbin, R. M. (2003), *Management Teams: Why They Succeed or Fail*, 2nd Edition (Oxford: Elsevier Butterworth-Heinemann).

Buchanan, D.A. and Huczyinski, A. (2003), *Organizational Behaviour: An Introductory Text*, 5th Edition (Hemel Hempstead: FT Prentice-Hall).

Capon, C. and Didsbury, A. (2003), *Understanding Organisational Context: Inside and Outside Organisations*, 2nd Edition (London: Financial Times Management).

Meredith, J. R. and Mantel, S. J. jnr (2003), *Project Management: a Managerial Approach*, 5th Edition (international edition) (New York: Wiley).

10   *Organization of Management Change and IT Projects*

The previous chapter described project organization structures that can be applied to projects in general. This relatively short supplementary chapter adds a few observations on the organization of management change and IT projects.

SPECIAL CHARACTERISTICS OF MANAGEMENT CHANGE PROJECTS

Although management change projects and IT projects range from small internal ventures to multi-million pound projects, they all share common characteristics:

- They are usually high-risk projects, often with the potential to bring either valuable benefits or disaster to the project owner.
- When one of these projects fails it can disrupt or even destroy the service provided to the project owner's customers.
- When one of these projects fails for a public sector owner the consequences will attract widespread adverse media attention and can even damage the ruling political party.
- The project owner has ultimate responsibility for managing the project and can be regarded as both owner and main contractor – in other words the core of the project is internal to the organization.
- The successful outcome of a management change project depends particularly on the cooperation of staff in accepting changes that can sometimes profoundly affect their jobs.
- Research leading to project definition and a business plan must often be conducted in secrecy to prevent premature leakage of information that could spread damaging rumours and staff unrest throughout the project owner's organization and, in some cases, to the shareholders and business world at large.

Given a sound business plan, management change and IT projects will stand the greatest chance of success if project execution is entrusted to a task force that is staffed with people who understand the business and are given sufficient seniority to be able to make executive decisions. A task force organization is best able to generate the team spirit and rapid inter-functional communications that are essential for driving these projects towards their intended goals.

Many organizations, such as those in the service and financial industries, carry out routine work every day, perhaps on a large scale, but have to cope only rarely with special projects. Thus when such organizations do need to carry out a management change project they might have to look outside the organization to find a competent project manager.

Some of the points made here can be illustrated by the following case example.

CASE EXAMPLE: THE COVERITE PLC OFFICE RELOCATION PROJECT

Introduction to Coverite plc

Imagine that Coverite plc is a long-established company that specializes in motor insurance for private and fleet vehicle owners. All operations and administration are carried out by the 250 people who work in its London headquarters. The company stresses its dedication to providing a personal, prompt, ethical and efficient customer service and states specifically in its publicity that clients will never be directed to an offshore call centre.

The company is organized in a line and function structure, as shown in the top section of Figure 10.1. This organization chart cannot show every department, job role and small detail and is not claimed to be typical of a motor insurance company but it is adequate for the purposes of this case example.

Birth of the project

Coverite plc's London offices are almost full, and the company must plan to increase its office capacity. Advisors believe that the company will need at least 25 per cent more office space over the next ten years. All options are open for consideration, including the following:

- build an extension to the existing building on adjacent land (the company must ensure it can include car park spaces for the additional staff); or
- relocate the offices.

If the company should choose to relocate, a further range of options would become available:

- remain in London, but on a larger site (all the current staff might then be retained); or
- relocate to another town or city.

There are then at least two further options to consider:

- buy land and construct a new purpose-designed office building; or
- find a suitable building that either exists or is about to become available.

Make the wrong choice, and the company's performance could suffer. Make the right choice, and there will be valuable benefits, such as reduced operating costs and increased employee satisfaction.

Company organization during project definition

Coverite plc recognizes that it needs expert advice. Therefore the company has decided to engage an external consultant, in the shape of an organization that specializes in advising companies and guiding them through management change projects. The initial brief for the consultant is the consideration of all the options outlined above, and the conduct of research leading to one or more business plan proposals.

The external consultant will need to have regular and close contact with senior members of Coverite plc's management team. The managing director of Coverite plc has, therefore asked each of the six departmental directors or managers to serve on a specially convened steering committee. This steering committee will report to the managing director and it will exist until the project has

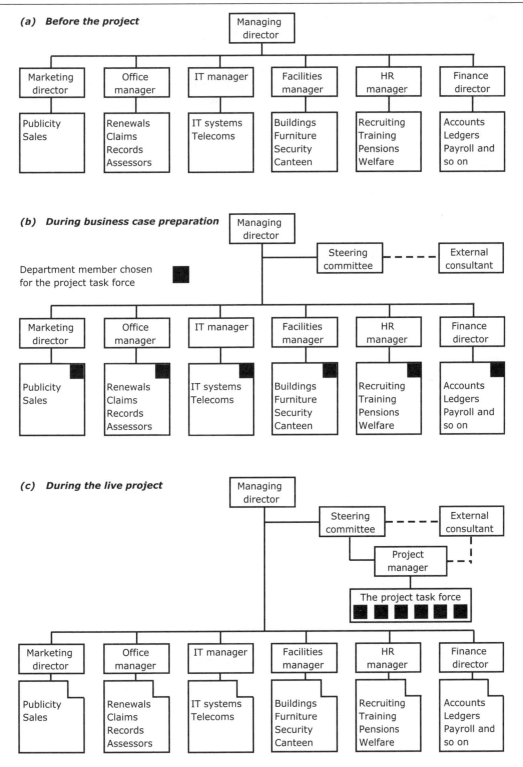

(a) *Before the project*

Managing director

Marketing director	Office manager	IT manager	Facilities manager	HR manager	Finance director
Publicity Sales	Renewals Claims Records Assessors	IT systems Telecoms	Buildings Furniture Security Canteen	Recruiting Training Pensions Welfare	Accounts Ledgers Payroll and so on

(b) *During business case preparation*

Managing director

Steering committee — — — External consultant

Department member chosen for the project task force ■

Marketing director	Office manager	IT manager	Facilities manager	HR manager	Finance director
Publicity Sales	Renewals Claims Records Assessors	IT systems Telecoms	Buildings Furniture Security Canteen	Recruiting Training Pensions Welfare	Accounts Ledgers Payroll and so on

(c) *During the live project*

Managing director

Steering committee — — — External consultant

Project manager

The project task force ■ ■ ■ ■ ■ ■

Marketing director	Office manager	IT manager	Facilities manager	HR manager	Finance director
Publicity Sales	Renewals Claims Records Assessors	IT systems Telecoms	Buildings Furniture Security Canteen	Recruiting Training Pensions Welfare	Accounts Ledgers Payroll and so on

Figure 10.1   Coverite plc: development of the relocation project organization

been successfully concluded. All day-to-day communications between the external consultant and Coverite plc will be dealt with by the steering committee chairperson or an appropriate member.

This project has now entered the definition phase in its life history. This phase in a project of this kind will probably end with the preparation of more than one business plan, each of which will be based on a different possible solution. The investigative period might last for many months, and could involve considerable research, including visits to possible relocation areas. The organization of Coverite plc during this investigative phase is shown in the middle section of Figure 10.1.

One duty of the steering committee will be to identify in advance suitable individuals from the various departments who will eventually be capable of joining a project task force if the relocation project is approved. Each of these nominees is represented in Figure 10.1 by a solid black square. These nominees will not be told that they have been preselected for the task force at this stage, in order to preserve confidentiality and keep the number of people who need to know about the project to a minimum.

Confidentiality during project definition

During the investigative stages in the project the research must be conducted with a degree of secrecy. No information about the proposed office relocation should be allowed to leak out before a firm decision has been made, because such leaks can spread false information and cause unnecessary alarm and despondency. For example, I remember witnessing staff interrupting their daily tasks to discuss questions and rumours of the following kind when a London company was considering building new offices in Newbury:

- Who are those strangers wandering around our offices and why are they using tape measures?
- We are being moved to Exeter late next year, I know its true because one of the cleaners told me.
- I heard it's to be Warwick.
- It will probably be St Albans, because most of our directors live there.
- Which of us will be asked to move and how many of us will be made redundant?
- What compensation shall we get for moving or leaving?

In the event, this company (which had indeed looked at Exeter and Warwick in addition to Newbury) chose not to move. So all the unnecessary staff unrest could have been prevented if confidentiality had been maintained.

Of course consultation with staff will be needed, followed by the provision of support and advice both to those who will be moving and to those forced to leave the company. But the time for those consultation processes to begin is after the company knows what it intends to do and the business plan has been approved. That should still allow time for all the staff issues to be resolved.

Organization of Coverite plc during the actual relocation project

Once the company has chosen a relocation strategy, the active project organization must be set up. The project strategy need not be amplified here but in practice it could be shown and communicated by means of the logic diagram of a critical path network.

Coverite plc has decided to relocate to an existing empty office building in Peterborough. So the chosen few will be now be briefed on the project and asked to leave their routine departmental tasks and take up their temporary duties on the project task force. The bottom section of Figure 10.1 shows the task force in position.

The most important addition to this organization is the project manager, who will be responsible (through the steering committee) to Coverite plc's board of directors. But where is this project manager to come from? Most service companies (such as Coverite plc) do not routinely employ any person who is expert in project management. The recruitment obvious options include the following:

1. Engage a professional project manager on a short-term contract. A professional organization such as the Association for Project Management might be able to assist in recruiting someone suitable.
2. Pick a likely member of the existing staff and arrange for him or her to have a crash course on project management.
3. Ask the external consulting company that helped with the investigation to manage the project.
4. Ask the external consultant company to lend a member of its staff on secondment to manage the task force (and the project).

Each of these options is associated with a delay between starting the search and installing a fully competent project manager. The fourth option can work very well, especially if the chosen project manager has already worked on the project definition and is thus familiar with the project requirements and the company.

Responsibilities within the Coverite plc project task force

Fowler (Fowler and Lock 2006) believes that only experts should be employed on management change and IT projects and that trainees, apprentices and others without sufficient experience should learn their craft elsewhere, where they will not delay the project or cause other harm. All members of the Coverite plc task force have been chosen for their detailed knowledge of the department from which they have been temporarily removed.

Further, these people are sufficiently senior to be entrusted to make decisions on day-to-day operational issues without having to make frequent reference back to their departmental managers. Thus, in that respect, they can all deputize for their departmental managers. However, any change in project scope, or any other change that would significantly increase the project cost or extend its time, will need to be approved by the steering committee.

Each person on the task force should know in detail the IT, accommodation and telecommunication requirements of their departments and will be able to contribute to planning for a seamless changeover from the old offices to the new. With a company such as Coverite plc it is vital that clients should suffer no interruption or deterioration of service during the physical removal operations. A driver who has just seen a car written off in an accident does not want his or her troubles to be increased by being told that the insurance claim must wait for two weeks until the new offices and IT are up and running.

Frequency of meetings

The steering committee in this case will meet once a week in full session to review progress, consider change requests, and endorse decisions made by the project manager and the task force. The average duration of a weekly session will probably not need to exceed one or two hours.

Unlike the steering committee, the task force will be in almost constant session. It will in effect become a separate, self-contained, multi-disciplined functional department of Coverite plc for the duration of the project. However, not every member of the task force will need to serve full time on the project, and some might be able to split their working hours between the task force and their home departments. Any such time-sharing between task force and home department must be approved by the project manager and the task force commitment must always take priority.

Limitations of the organigram

All organigrams are limited in what they can show and Figure 10.1 is no exception. For example, Figure 10.1(c) shows the internal core organization of Coverite plc during the relocation project but in practice many suppliers and subcontractors will join the project organization from time to time. Each of these will be asked to report to the project manager or to appropriate members of the task force.

The organigram does not reveal that members of the steering committee are, in this Coverite plc project, the same managers and directors who head up the functional departments on a routine basis. The chart is also unable to show that some task force members may be able to spend part of their time back with their home departments.

In practice people learn to tolerate the inadequacies of organigrams. The chart can be drawn to a larger scale to allow greater detail to be shown but, even then, charts seldom tell the full story.

PRINCE2™

PRINCE (**P**rojects **in** **C**ontrolled **E**nvironments) is a UK Government initiative that recommends a project organizational structure template, defines the roles of senior members of the organization, and sets out a recommended approach to the management of projects. Originally intended for use on IT projects, the methodology has since been further developed as PRINCE2 and is now claimed to be effective for any kind of project. Some companies working on projects for the UK Government might find themselves under some pressure to adopt this project management system.

The PRINCE2 methodology has many advocates and is well supported by a number of training establishments. I have always had some personal reservations about the methodology and will not describe it further here. However, I can unreservedly recommend a visit to the splendid website at www.ogc.gov.uk/prince2. There readers will able to learn about the technology and gain access to the latest training information, news and publications. You will also find a number of case studies and very useful project management forms that can be downloaded as templates for immediate use in your own organization.

REFERENCES AND FURTHER READING

Bartlett, J. (2000), *Managing Programmes of Business Change*, 3rd Edition (Hook, Hampshire: Project Manager Today).

Bradley, G. (2006), *Benefit Realisation Management: A Practical Guide to Achieving Benefits Through Change* (Aldershot: Gower).

Fowler, A. and Lock, D. (2006), *Accelerating Business and IT Change: Transforming Project Delivery* (Aldershot: Gower).

Office of Government Commerce (2005), *Managing Successful Projects with PRINCE2* (London: OGC).

11 *Key People in the Organization*

Chapters 9 and 10 outlined some of the organization structures that are peculiar to projects. Hundreds, even thousands of people might work directly on a project and it is clearly not possible to describe all those job roles within the space of this chapter or even this book. For example, the project organization and its manager will often be heavily dependent on other managers' functions in other departments such as sales engineering, purchasing, accounting and HR management. Some construction projects have large organizations employing many people at the construction site, and that subject is covered briefly in the context of progress management (Chapter 24). This chapter will, therefore, concentrate on just a few of the key roles that are closest to the project manager within the core project organization. Inevitably, we must start with the project manager.

PROJECT MANAGER

Job title and role in the organization

It can happen that, when a company organization is searched to find a project manager, the first results are fruitless because no one with that job title can be found. The project manager's identity is often hidden behind some other organizational title. For example, a person with the title 'facilities manager' might temporarily become a project manager during a reorganization of accommodation or the installation of some new air conditioning plant or other machinery. Another example is where a person styled 'senior engineer' is made responsible for managing a costly new product design and development project.

Even where project management is accredited with the importance of a full-time appointment, the situation can be made less clear by the variety of titles used to describe the job. Contract manager, scheduling and estimating manager, project coordinator, project coordination engineer, programme engineer, project leader and project manager are a few of the titles which have been used. Previous editions of this book have recommended the adoption of 'project manager' as a standard title (which has long been the usual practice in the construction industry). The trend in recent years has been encouraging, and project management is now widely recognized as a profession that deserves reasonable status and rewards, with its own professional associations (the Association for Project Management in the UK) and with far less confusion over the job title.

The organization structures described in Chapters 9 and 10 demonstrate that the levels of responsibility and authority given to project managers vary considerably from one organization to another. In some cases project managers act only as planners and coordinators, with minimal power and authority. In other businesses the project manager will have complete authority over all those responsible for achieving the project objectives.

Among many possibilities, the career of a project manager might have started as an IT specialist, a contracts manager or a qualified engineer. One of the more common routes to project management lies through the engineering design department. Frequently the engineer in command of a particular project design is charged with some degree of overall responsibility for seeing the entire project through to completion. When this happens, the engineer has a dual organizational position, exercising direct line authority and supervision over the engineering design staff, while acting only in a functional role when trying to influence all the other departments engaged on the project.

The project management function in a small company might be conducted entirely on a part-time basis by one of the existing department heads, or by some other individual as in the case of the engineer just described. Other companies could be forced to recognize the need for a full-time project manager, the incumbent being held responsible for either one individual project or for handling several projects simultaneously.

Seniority

The questions 'How senior is the project manager?' and 'To whom should the project manager report?' now arise.

The person appointed will be expected to provide the company's general management with relevant facts whenever it becomes necessary for them to exert their senior authority or take other executive action to maintain the project on its specified financial, technical and delivery course. The project manager should therefore have reasonable access to general management.

Much of the project manager's time will be spent in coordination – steering and integrating the activities of some departments and relying on others for information or supporting services. This demands cooperation with and from the managers of most departments in the company, whether these departments are directly engaged in project fulfilment (such as engineering and production) or are service departments (like accounts and personnel). Ideally, therefore, the project manager should not be handicapped by being placed in an organizationally inferior position to any departmental manager in particular or to departmental managers in general.

Thus the desirable organizational status for the project manager appears to be indicated on a level at least equivalent to the company's departmental managers. This view is reinforced when it is realized that the person appointed will probably be called upon to supervise subcontractors. For industrial and commercial projects, when the project enters its fulfilment phase it is the project manager who most often takes over from the marketing or sales department to represent the company to the customer. Thus the project manager is often a significant part of the corporate image that the company presents to the outside world.

Personality

What is the ideal personality specification for a project manager? One project manager might operate successfully by inducing fear and trepidation in their subordinates, so that every word is seen as a command to be instantly obeyed. Another might achieve the same results through gentle but firm persuasion. The essential element here is the ability to motivate people, by whatever means: the seasoned expert will be able to vary their management style according to the response of the individual being managed.

The average project participant will appreciate being led by a project manager who displays competence, makes clear decisions, gives precise, achievable instructions, delegates well, listens to and accepts sound advice, is enthusiastic and confident, and thus generally commands respect by example and qualities of leadership.

Perceptiveness and the use of project information

Other essential characteristics of the project manager can be grouped under the heading of perceptiveness. Project managers must be able to spot the salient facts from a set of data or a particular arrangement of circumstances. They must then be able to use these facts to best effect by taking action or reporting important exceptions to executive management, whilst filtering out the unimportant and irrelevant material.

Most project managers will become accustomed to being presented with information that is incomplete, unduly optimistic, inaccurate or deliberately misleading. Therefore it is important that project managers should not be gullible. They will learn to check much of the information which they receive, particularly by knowing what questions to ask in order to probe its validity. As they gain experience they should become capable of assessing the reliability of individuals, departments and external organizations, so that they can apply 'confidence factors' to the data and stories that they provide.

Project managers of any merit will know the frustration caused, not only by receiving inaccurate information, but also by receiving no information at all. Data deficiencies can take the form of delayed instructions or approvals from the customer, late information from subcontractors and vendors, and tardy release of design and other information within the project manager's own company. It can be difficult to obtain reliable and regular reports of cost and progress from far-flung project outposts, particularly where the individuals responsible feel themselves to be remote and out of range from the project manager's authority or are educated to standards below those of the more developed nations.

The ability to gather, assess and act upon relevant data is, therefore, another essential property for project managers. It is no good expecting to obtain the complete picture and manage a project simply by sitting behind a desk for the duration of the project. Project managers must take (and be seen to take) an active interest. They should visit personally and regularly those parts of the organization on which the project is dependent (a process sometimes known as 'management by walking about'). It might be necessary for the project manager to visit vendors, subcontractors, the customer and a remote construction site at suitable intervals to gather facts, resolve local disputes, generate enthusiasm, or simply to witness progress at first hand.

General knowledge and current awareness

Project managers in the age of technology could be described as specialists. Their background may be in one of the specialist engineering or other professional disciplines and they will certainly need to be trained in one or more of the current special project management techniques if they are to operate effectively. Nevertheless the term 'specialist' can be misleading, since much of the project manager's time will be taken up with coordinating the activities of project participants from a wide variety of administrative, professional, technical and craft backgrounds. This work, far from requiring specialization, demands a sufficient general understanding of the work carried out by those participants for the project manager to be able to discuss the work sensibly, understand all the commercial and technical data received, and appreciate (or question) any reported problem.

Project managers should have a general understanding of administrative procedures as they will be applied throughout the project organization. If managers are asked to handle a flow of project data between different departments, they should be able to use their understanding of the administration and its procedures to arrange for the information to be presented in the form most likely to be helpful to the various recipients. In the jargon of computer technology, the project manager may be asked to solve interface problems, the solutions to which need some understanding of how the peripheral units operate.

There is no doubt that project management tools, techniques and philosophy will continue to undergo development and change. The project manager must be prepared to keep abreast of this development, undergoing training or retraining whenever necessary, and passing this training on to other members of the organization where appropriate. Some new developments will advance the practice of project management in general and others will not. Some practices and techniques will be more useful to a particular project than others and the project manager must be able to choose, use or adapt the most appropriate management methods for the particular project. The temptation to impose unsuitable methods on an organization for the sole reason that they represent the height of current fashion must be resisted.

Support, cooperation and training for the project manager

No matter how experienced, competent, enthusiastic and intelligent the person chosen for the job of project manager, he or she cannot expect to operate effectively alone, without adequate support and cooperation. This includes the willing cooperation of all staff engaged on the project, whether or not they report to the project manager in the line organization. It also includes support from higher management in the organization, who must at least ensure the provision of finance, accommodation, facilities, equipment, manpower and other resources when they are needed and the availability of suitable clerical or other supporting staff. Just as those working on the project need to be properly motivated, so does the project manager, and supportive higher management who show constructive and helpful interest in the project can go a long way to achieve this. They can also help in the longer term by providing opportunities for training as new techniques or management systems are developed.

A person who is responsible for the overall allocation and progressing of project tasks will inevitably be called upon to decide priorities or criticize progress. Project managers, especially in a matrix organization, must often arrange for the issue of work instructions knowing that they have no direct authority over all the departments involved. In a weak matrix, the functional or departmental managers alone are responsible for the performance, day-to-day management and work allocation within their own departments. I have even known cases where departmental managers have told project managers to keep out of their departments. In such circumstances the project manager's influence can only be exerted as reflected authority from higher management, without whose full backing the project manager must be ineffective.

Whatever the organization structure, the main show of authority that project managers can wield stems from their own personality and ability to persuade or motivate others. In these enlightened times discipline no longer implies the imposition of rigid authoritarian regimes or management by fear through the constant threat of dismissal or other punitive action. Mutual cooperation and established job satisfaction are the more likely elements of an effective approach, especially in the long term. There will, however, be occasions when firm discipline has to be exercised; when, in the last resort, the full backing and support of higher management must be available as a reserve force which the project manager can call upon in any hour of need.

Sometimes it would be apt to include project managers in that group of individuals described as 'human dynamos'. There will be times when the apathy or inertia of some project participants has to be overcome by an electrifying injection of enthusiasm. The output of any dynamo, however, may be weakened if it is switched into an inefficient or wrongly connected circuit. The astute project manager will soon recognize any wasteful shortcomings in the project organization. If this happens, and an alteration in the organization can be proven as necessary, the project manager should be able to rely on senior management to authorize and implement the change. Higher management, after installing the project manager, must provide continuous support and encouragement and work with him or her to create an ideal project management environment.

To maintain the company's competitive edge, the project manager should keep abreast of new developments in project control and management techniques and thinking. Senior management must recognize that much training is a continuous process and not simply a question of sending a person away for a one- or two-day course. Various training authorities arrange project management seminars where, in addition to the formal training given, delegates from different companies are able to meet and discuss mutual problems and solutions, and exchange views and experiences generally. The effectiveness of these individuals and of the profession as a whole must benefit from this type of exchange. It should also be remembered that the most effective form of learning is achieved from on-the-job training, which might need help from an external training consultant so that the training can be purpose-designed.

Just as important as the project manager's own training is the creation of an enlightened and informed attitude to modern project management methods among all those in the project organization. Ideally, when the objectives of a particular project are outlined the project manager should ensure that participating managers, engineers and line supervisors have at least been given an elementary grounding in the appreciation of network analysis, scheduling, principles of cost and progress control, and the interpretation of associated computer reports. This should all be with specific relevance to the procedures chosen for use on the actual project. Training or instructions should be given in the use of the various forms and other documents to be used and (where appropriate) in the active use of relevant computer systems. There is a serious danger that people who are suddenly asked to work with unfamiliar techniques and procedures, without sufficient training or explanation, will fail to cooperate. People neglected in this respect cannot be expected to provide the necessary feedback and other responses. If participating staff understand the procedures and the reasons for them, their cooperation is far more likely to be forthcoming and effective.

Women as project managers

Women can be excellent project managers, at least the equal of men. But there are far too few women project managers. Fewer than ten per cent of the Association for Project Management's members are women. That Association even has a specific interest group (SIG) called 'Women in Project Management'. Why? We don't have a specific interest group for 'Men in Project Management'. It seems that women are sufficiently rare in this profession to be treated as a special case. We have to hope that this disappointing imbalance will eventually disappear.

DIRECTOR OF PROJECTS OR PROGRAMME MANAGER

A company that engages continuously in the performance of projects, and always has several projects running simultaneously might choose to appoint a projects director to oversee all managers of individual projects. This projects director will ensure standardization of the best aspects of project management procedures across the whole company and will arbitrate in disputes. If the organization is a matrix, the managers of all the technical functions and the drawing office would most probably report to the projects director rather than to the managing director or to the general manager. If the organization is set up as one or more teams, then only the project managers would report to the project director

PROJECT ENGINEER

The term 'project engineer' has two quite different meanings. In both cases the role demands someone who is highly proficient in the dominant project technology. In one case the project engineer is internal to the company and reports directly to the project manager. The other kind of project engineer works as an independent adviser from outside the core project organization, typically as the engineer in a contract matrix (as shown in Figure 9.10).

The project engineer as a senior member of a project team

Although most project managers will be sufficiently qualified to understand both the technical and the administrative details of their projects, it is possible for a non-technical person to manage a technical project *provided that they have the inherent management skills*. This principle is proved and exploited, for example, during 'action learning' programmes. Action learning is a management development method developed by the late Professor Reg Revans (Casey and Pearce 1977). In an action learning programme, managers from different professions are switched between jobs for a few months under the supervision of a professional trainer. Transfers can even be made between companies operating in completely different industries so that, for instance, a manager from a bank and an executive from an oil company might swap their jobs for a few months. Each knows little or nothing about the technology of their temporary job. However, the individuals gain personally from their experiences and have their horizons extended, whilst the participating companies gain from fresh ideas that the temporary jobholders bring in.

There are two principal reasons why a project manager might not be able to exercise fully all the necessary technical skills necessary to direct and approve the project design:

*   The project manager, although a good administrator, does not have the relevant technical training and qualifications to understand every detail of the project design.
*   The project manager, although technically proficient, has so many management and administrative duties that they have insufficient time left to spend on detailed supervision of the project design.

In both of these cases the project manager needs continual and reliable expert technical support and advice. That role might be performed collectively by the various functional managers, each of whom will be expert in a particular engineering discipline. But the project manager still needs a single source of technical support, someone who can oversee the design and reliability aspects of the project and resolve any technical conflict between the different engineering disciplines. That role is often performed by a project engineer.

Whereas a good non-technical administrator might be able to act as project manager, the role of the project engineer is unequivocally technological. The project engineer *must* be highly proficient in the main technology of the project. In many cases it is the project engineer who will approve all designs and specifications and oversee the quality and reliability aspects of the project. Thus the project engineer fulfils a very senior role in the project organization, usually second in command to the project manager.

Contractual context

Some conditions of contract require that an independent, external project engineer be engaged to monitor design and progress. A bank that has advanced money to a project owner, a financial guarantor or insurance company, or the project owner itself, will often require that someone with relevant technical experience protects their interests by acting as an independent adviser. This role was explained briefly in the contracts matrix section of Chapter 9.

In construction projects an independent quantity surveyor is employed to protect the owner's interests by certifying contractors' invoices for progress payments. The engineer's role has some similarities but is wider, and the engineer will be expected to visit the project design offices from time to time to review the contractor's design progress and performance. The engineer will often have to certify the contractor's invoices to the owner (or a funding bank) for design stage payments. The role of the engineer is explained more fully in Marsh (2001).

PROJECT SUPPORT OFFICE

Unless the organization is too small to support the additional expense, it makes sense to support the project management function by setting up a central project management services group or project support office (PSO). This group is staffed with people (not too many!) who are capable of taking on the day-to-day chores, which can include the following functions:

- project registration
- planning
- resource scheduling
- cost estimating
- cost reporting and cost control
- issue of work-to lists
- progress reporting
- change coordination
- earned value management
- supervision of the company's project management computer systems
- programme and portfolio management.

A project support office can be used in most kinds of project organization from medium size upwards. The group can be a functional department within a pure project team, where it will serve and report directly to the project manager. If the organization is a multi-project matrix or a hybrid organization, the project support office can be established as one of the departmental functions (an arrangement which is shown in Figure 11.1). A company that operates a number of separate project teams simultaneously can establish a central project support office to serve all those project managers (Figure 11.2).

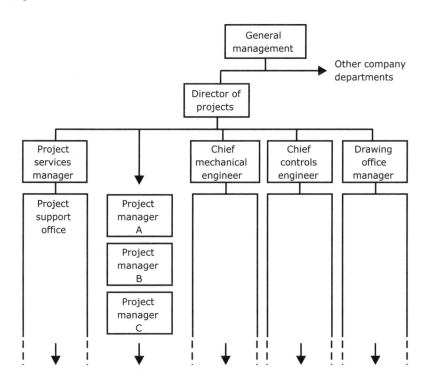

Figure 11.1   Possible management roles in a matrix organization

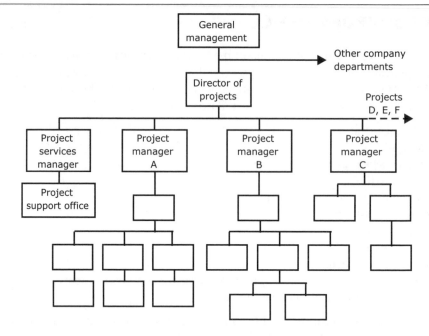

Figure 11.2 Possible management roles in a multi-team organization

For a company that handles a relatively large number of small projects, none of which is big enough to justify its own full-time project manager, the project support office can actually play a project management role, acting like the project coordinator in a coordination matrix. When the project support office has this coordinating role, its manager must be given sufficient seniority in the organization for the coordination and control to be effective.

A project support office concentrates a company's expertise in the techniques of project management just as any other functional grouping can enhance a particular professional discipline. Centralization helps to standardize project administration procedures across all projects in a company. A project support group can be the logical place in the organization from which to coordinate all parts of the project cycle, from authorization to closedown. It can perform procedures such as cost estimating, project registration, risk logging, planning, resource scheduling and change control. It is also a logical home for the tedious but vital function of contract administration.

A well-motivated and expertly staffed project support office can spearhead the development and effective implementation of advanced project management procedures, so that the organization can benefit by exploiting methods such as standard networks, templating and other methods (described in Chapter 29).

Some powerful project management computer systems, especially those handling multiproject scheduling, are best placed under the supervision of specially trained experts. Those experts must have a good working knowledge of all the organization's projects and combine that with special training in using the system and safeguarding the integrity of its database and back-up files. A project support office is an excellent place in which to place that responsibility.

REFERENCES AND FURTHER READING

Casey, D. and Pearce. D. (eds) (1977), *More than Management Development: Action Learning at GEC* (Farnborough: Gower); in spite of its age, still a relevant book on action learning experiences.

Marsh, D. E. (2000), *The Project and Programme Support Office*, Vol. 1 Foundation (Hook: Project Manager Today).

Marsh, D. E. (2000), *The Project and Programme Support Office*, Vol. 2 Advanced (Hook: Project Manager Today).

Marsh, P. D. V. (2001), *Contracting for Engineering and Construction Projects*, 5th Edition (Aldershot: Gower).

Pedler, M. (1997), *Action Learning in Practice*, 3rd Edition (Aldershot: Gower).

Weinstein, K. (1998), *Action Learning*, 2nd Edition (Aldershot: Gower).

12 *Work Breakdown and Coding*

I magine yourself as a project manager, having to start a very simple project. You might begin with a task list (a kind of shopping list of what has to be done) and simply work down the list until the project is finished. That approach is fine when the task list contains only 10 or 20 entries. But most projects contain hundreds of tasks and some will progress through many thousands of different tasks before they are done. Therefore, after familiarizing yourself with the project definition, your first job as project manager is to organize all these tasks in some logical way that will allow them to be planned in time and allocated to all the various people and managers across the project organization. Put another way, the previous three chapters have described the ways in which people might be organized to carry out the project, and now we have reached the stage in the project life history when we must consider how the work itself can be organized. So, this chapter describes the work breakdown structure (WBS) process, which means breaking the project down into manageable chunks from which work can be allocated to departmental managers and other members of the project organization.

WBS CONCEPT

No one makes the case for developing a project work breakdown structure more eloquently than Stephen Devaux (1999), who wrote:

> *If I could wish but one thing for every project, it would be a comprehensive and detailed WBS. The lack of a good WBS probably results in more inefficiency, schedule slippages, and cost overruns on projects than any other single cause. When a consultant is brought in to perform in the role of 'project doctor', invariably there has been no WBS developed. No one knows what work has been done, nor what work remains to be done. The first thing to do is assemble the planning team and teach them how to create a WBS.*

A work breakdown structure is a logical, hierarchical tree of all the tasks needed to complete a project. The top of the tree is the project itself. The next layer or level down contains the main 'work packages'. Levels below that progressively get more and more detailed until the bottom level is reached that shows all the smallest day-to-day tasks or project components. Anyone familiar with the arrangement of folders and files in a computer memory, or who has researched their ancestral family tree, should be familiar with this idea.

The work breakdown concept is also seen in the 'goes-into charts' that engineers and designers use when organizing their drawings, bills of materials and parts lists into a logical pattern. So, the first example of a WBS in this chapter is for a manufacturing project. Figure 12.1 is a summarized version of the top WBS levels for an imaginary project to design and develop a prototype automobile.

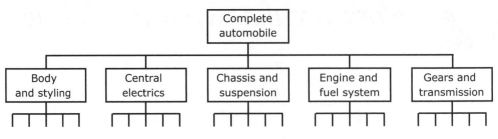

The work breakdown continues for as many further levels as necessary

Figure 12.1   Simplified WBS for an automobile project

All engineers will recognize how this WBS arrangement corresponds closely to a goes-into chart. Apart from its obvious relationship to the major components of the vehicle, one can see how this breakdown might also dictate the allocation of various senior engineers or design managers to different parts of this design and development project.

Logical interfacing and completeness

In addition to regarding the work breakdown as a family tree, it is also possible to visualize it as a jigsaw puzzle, with every piece put in its right place and with no piece missing. This concept is useful on two counts:

*   It is important that when the work breakdown is produced every piece of the puzzle is included, with no piece missing to spoil the total picture. This objective is sometimes difficult to achieve, but the risks of omission can be reduced by the use of suitable checklists. Brainstorming can be useful for projects with no similar predecessors.
*   A method must be found that clearly and simply identifies each piece of the puzzle and denotes its position in relation to all the other pieces. This objective can be achieved by giving each piece an identification number which, through the use of a carefully devised, logical coding system, acts as a locator or address. Coding systems are introduced later in this chapter.

WBS examples

A few people find difficulty in constructing work breakdown charts and I have seen students' coursework in which work breakdown charts have been confused with organigrams. Thus this chapter contains a liberal sprinkling of WBS examples, representing various kinds of projects.

Project for a national charity fundraising week

Much of the work carried out by any charity must be devoted to collecting as much money as possible. Without such mercenary efforts a charity would not be able to render its humanitarian service. Thus the (fictitious) Society for Impoverished Writers has decided to organize an annual national fundraising week. Being sensible people, the charity managers have decided to treat this as a project, and one of the first things that they must do is to draw a WBS. The result is shown in Figure 12.2.

This WBS is seen to have four main elements or principal work packages, and one can easily imagine that a different senior manager should be made responsible for each of these.

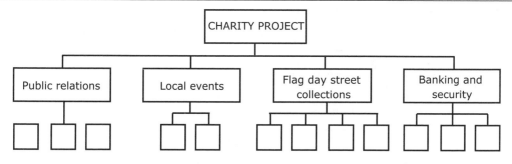

Figure 12.2   WBS for a national charity fundraising week

One manager will organize all public relations activities nationwide that tell the public about this special week. Thus the second level WBS breakdown for this public relations work package might include newspaper advertising, television commercials, posters, billboards, mailshots and so on.

Someone else can be put in charge of local events. These will be arranged through a network of volunteers, and might include coffee mornings, students' rags, village fetes, sponsored walks and so on.

No fundraising week would be complete without its flag day, in which volunteers make their presence felt in the streets of towns and cities throughout the land, carrying tin cans with slots in their tops for the receipt of donations. Optimists might even be seen carrying buckets for this work. Someone must organize the production of cans and their labels, find the volunteers, and make sure that all the cans are eventually returned to headquarters.

If the fundraising week is successful, hundreds of thousands of pounds might be collected. In all events where money is concerned there is scope for fraud and theft, so the charity has been wise enough to appoint a manager to oversee the handling of all the money collected, to try to ensure that it ends up in the charity's bank.

Copper mining project

One of the world's largest mining organizations has discovered deposits of copper ore in the middle of a large uninhabited area of scrub and desert. The area is utterly devoid of any sign of civilization. Figure 12.3, which is based on just such a real project, shows a small part of the large work breakdown chart that would be needed for this project.

Each of the main work packages at level 1 is concerned with a significant part of the whole mining community, complete with a brand new township containing facilities for the mine's construction and operating staff, their families and visitors. There is nothing at all at the site when this project begins except a few drill rigs and lots of hope. Thus everything has to be provided as part of this enormous project, including all the infrastructure of the new town in the desert.

Level 2 of this WBS expands each of the work packages from level 1. Just one of these is shown in Figure 12.3, which is for the mining complex itself. This mining complex includes all the buildings and plant necessary for extracting the ore from deep underground and then processing it to produce bars of almost pure copper.

One part of the mining complex is the concentrator plant, which crushes the rock to a powder and removes much of the non-copper bearing material. This has its own place in level 3 of the WBS.

And so this work breakdown structure must be continued until, eventually, the lowest levels are reached in which all the tiniest components of the new mine town and plant are listed. Thus this

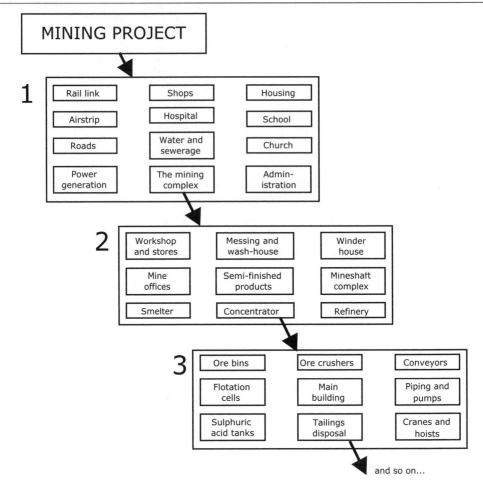

Figure 12.3   Part of the first three WBS levels for a very large mining project

This chart is based on an actual project. It shows how the work breakdown expands in steps of increasing detail. The complete breakdown would continue down to the level of all the individual tasks and small purchases.

WBS can only be drawn at the upper levels when the project starts, and the lowest levels will not be known until much of the design has been completed.

Railway project

A railway company has been formed and, by Act of Parliament, given the authority to construct a new passenger railway line that will connect several rural communities and two towns. The WBS for this project is seen in Figure 12.4. Really one could see no better way in which this breakdown might have been arranged. It mirrors the physical pattern of all the necessary works and also suggests the organization of managers to perform different functions in the project team. It is entirely logical and largely self-explanatory. Thus, for instance, a legal and finance department is responsible for all contracts, for negotiating land deals, and for local authority planning applications. Looking at the 'buildings' work package, a construction manager might be placed in charge of all the buildings, and the detailed management of each bridge, workshop, lineside building, office, and passenger station would be entrusted to its own nominated manager or overseer.

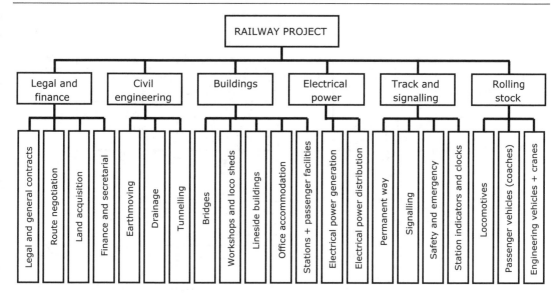

Figure 12.4   Work breakdown for a project to build a new railway

This logical work breakdown of the total project is very closely related to the management structure needed to execute the work

Large wedding project

This is an example of a 'management project'. When the project is finished there is no tangible result and nothing visible to hand over to a project owner – except perhaps a marriage certificate and a photograph album. When judged against the scale of many modern projects, organizing a wedding might seem a relatively trivial venture. However, suppose that *you* have been asked to manage a large, society wedding. There are going to be thousands of guests coming from many parts of the world, lavish displays or flowers, music and entertainment, sightseers, media representatives and many other things to plan for and manage. You would need a lot of management help, and that would involve delegating parts of the project to experts. How would you go about breaking that project down into manageable chunks?

The WBS solution for this management project is not quite as straightforward as might first be thought. In fact, there is more than one solution, any of which might be workable. Two of these solutions are shown in part in Figure 12.5. In both cases only the first level of breakdown is shown, and some work packages have been left out through lack of space (for example, preparation of invitations and the gift request list). However, the diagrams in Figure 12.5 are more than adequate for the purposes of illustration.

Remember that the aim of the WBS is to break the project down into bits that can be assigned to different managers or people in a logical way.

In the upper WBS it is assumed that a different manager will be engaged for each specialist function. For example, a music and entertainments organizer will be expected to choose the music for the wedding ceremony in the cathedral and engage performers for the reception event. The person organizing the floral displays will be expected to provide these inside the cathedral, at possible external locations, and at the reception. One important role is the security manager and he or she will have ultimate responsibility for security at all venues connected with this wedding.

Now consider the lower of the two WBS patterns given in Figure 12.5. Here the major work packages have been determined primarily by the location of the tasks involved. Thus the person responsible for airport arrangements will organize meeting guests at the airport and possibly also

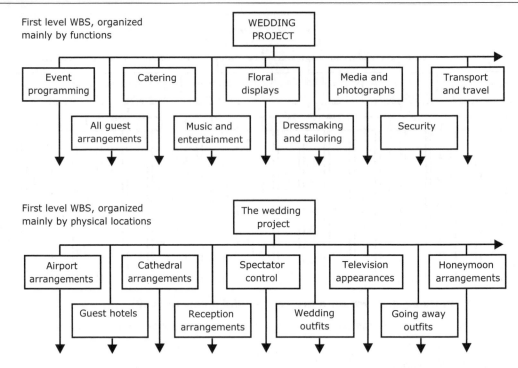

First level WBS, organized mainly by functions

WEDDING PROJECT

Event programming | Catering | Floral displays | Media and photographs | Transport and travel

All guest arrangements | Music and entertainment | Dressmaking and tailoring | Security

First level WBS, organized mainly by physical locations

The wedding project

Airport arrangements | Cathedral arrangements | Spectator control | Television appearances | Honeymoon arrangements

Guest hotels | Reception arrangements | Wedding outfits | Going away outfits

Figure 12.5   Two alternative WBS patterns for a large wedding project

transporting them to their hotels, but a different manager will book the guests' hotel accommodation. One manager is responsible for all the cathedral arrangements, including the order of service, music, flower arrangements, seating plan and even security.

My own preference is, at first glance, for the functional solution shown in the upper Figure 12.5 diagram. This is probably more cost effective and tends to place top level tasks in the hands of fewer managers and, moreover, managers who should have the essential technical or operational skills. Even if there are better solutions, this case proves the point that there are some projects where more than one acceptable pattern of the WBS can be found

CODING SYSTEMS

General

Every project task will need to be given a name or descriptive title, but such names must always be augmented by a specific code. Names usually describe the nature of the task (for example, dig hole, paint door, install and test new server, and so on) but they do not usually indicate where the task lies with respect to the work breakdown or, indeed, within the physical breakdown of the finished project. Moreover, names are often abbreviated in schedules, so that 'test customer billing system' might be reduced to 'test cust bill' where column space is limited in a schedule or report. It is essential that every task be given some tag that identifies it uniquely and, at the same time, indicates its exact position in the WBS hierarchy.

A code may be a sequence of alphabetic characters, a set of numerical digits, or some mix of these two (an alpha-numeric code). Coding systems should be designed so that the maximum amount of information about each item is conveyed by the minimum possible number of characters.

The designer of a project management coding system must always bear in mind that it should not be treated in isolation from other management and engineering information systems in the same organization. There are many advantages to applying a common coding system over all a company's projects, and across other areas of the company's activities in addition to cost estimating, accounting and budgetary control. Some of these benefits are listed later in this section.

Functions of code

A code is a shorthand and precise method for conveying essential data about an item. For project management purposes an item might be anything from the whole project to the smallest part of it, physical or abstract. It could be a component, a drawing, a job, a manufacturing operation, a piece of construction work, an engineering design activity, part of a computer program – anything, in fact, which is necessary for the project. One thing that most of these items have in common is that they are associated with cost. Each item (either by itself or grouped with others) has costs that must be estimated, budgeted, spent, measured, reported, assessed and (where appropriate) recovered.

There are many reasons for allocating codes to items, rather than simply describing them in words. For example, codes can be designed to be precise and unambiguous. They also have the advantage, essential in computer systems, of facilitating filing, analysis, editing and sorting for reporting and control.

The code for a particular item will perform the first or both of the following functions:

- A code must act as a unique name that *identifies* the item to which it refers.
- The identifying code, either by itself or by the addition of subcodes, can be arranged so that it categorizes, qualifies, or in some other way *describes* the item to which it relates.

The best coding systems are those which manage to combine both these functions as simply as possible in numbers that can be used throughout a company's management information systems.

Typical examples of coding systems

Listed below is the kind of information that can be contained within the code for any item. The systems used as examples here and illustrated in Figures 12.6, 12.7, 12.8 and 12.9 are taken from light and heavy engineering and from mining, but the general principles are interchangeable between these and all other types of projects.

- *Project identifier* – The project identification number for the breakdown shown in Figure 12.6 is 110-0000. This number is sufficient to identify the project for all accounting, engineering and manufacturing purposes. Such project numbers are typically allocated from a register (see Chapter 8). Some companies might call them contract numbers or works order numbers instead. It is possible to design the project numbering method in a way that allows each number to signify certain key information about its project, in addition to acting as a simple identifier. Examples of this occur in Figures 12.8 and 12.9.
- *Item identifier* – Each number, provided it is unique within the system, is an unambiguous way of naming any item. It is easy, however, to transpose digits or make other errors when entering numbers on forms or keyboards. It is wise, therefore, to bracket a concise description with the number whenever possible as a simple precaution against undiscovered numerical errors. Thus it is usually better to refer to an item as 'Transformer 110-2210' in documents such as purchase requisitions rather than just '110-2210'.
- *Relationship within the project* – Further examination of Figure 12.6 shows that the code numbers have been designed to correspond with the work breakdown (or family tree) hierarchy. Examples are given for components of the Transformer 110-2210 and set out

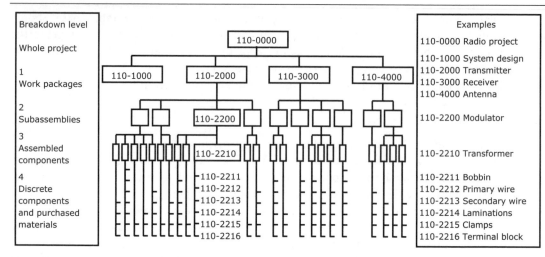

Figures 12.6 WBS and coding structure for a small radiocommunications project

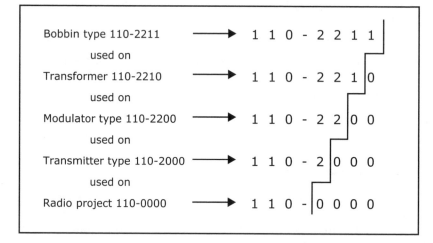

Figure 12.7 Detail from the work breakdown for the radiocommunications project

This small extract from the WBS in Figure 12.6 (drawn upside-down here) shows how the coding system can be used to denote the position of any component within a project. This arrangement works well for individual items but needs adaption for parts that are used on more than one place in the project (common parts)

more clearly in Figure 12.7. The numbers denote that all numbers starting with the string 110 are used on Project 110-0000 and, further that numbers starting 110-221 are used on Transformer 110-2210.

- *Operation identifier* – The task of winding the purpose-built transformer 110-2210 might be given a related cost code, such as 110-2210C, where the C suffix denotes the coil winding operation. A two-digit suffix is more likely to be used than a single letter, allowing greater scope for detailed breakdown into several individual operations.

- *Identifiers for department, discipline or trade and labour grade* – A one- or two-digit subcode is often incorporated to show which department is responsible for a particular task or cost item. More digits can be added to denote the trade or engineering discipline involved. Consider, for instance, the activity of designing Transformer 110-2210. The cost code might be 110-2210-153 with the three-digit subcode 153 in this case showing that the engineering department (1) is responsible for the task, the engineering discipline is electrical (coded 5), and the last digit (3) indicates the standard cost grade of person (for example senior engineer, engineer or designer) normally expected to carry out the task of designing this transformer.

- *Family identifier* – Many items to be considered for coding can be classified into families. Such families extend across all projects and can apply to huge capital projects or to the smallest engineering and manufacturing projects. The convenience of grouping items into families of items with common or similar characteristics is important for many comparative purposes. Family grouping and identification can be built into item codes using suitable digits as subcodes.

  A family might comprise, for example, all pumps specified by a mining or petrochemical company. Another example might be that the subcode digits 01 appearing in a particular place in the item code for a piece of manufactured equipment would always indicate the mainframe assembly. Another type of family is encountered in machined objects that have similar shapes or other physical characteristics which call for similar machining operations – an application of family coding vital to the manufacture of components in group technology cells.

BENEFITS OF A LOGICAL CODING SYSTEM

Although the primary purpose of a coding system might be to identify parts or to allocate costs, there are many benefits available to the company which is able to maintain a logical coding system in which all the codes and subcodes have common significance throughout the company's management information systems. These benefits increase with time and the accrual of records, provided that the system is used consistently without unauthorized adaptations or additions.

The benefits depend on being able to retrieve and process the data effectively, which invariably requires the use of a computer system. If a coding system is designed logically (taking account of hierarchical structure and families) and is well managed, some or all of the following benefits can be expected:

- Easy retrieval of items from records of past projects which correspond to or are similar to items expected in new projects, essential as a basis for making comparative cost estimates.
- Easy search and retrieval of design information (especially flowsheets, calculations and drawings) for processes, assemblies or components used on past projects which are relevant to a current project. This 'retained engineering' can save considerable engineering design work, time and costs if all or part of the previous design can be re-used or adapted. Not only does such design retrieval avoid the unnecessary costs of designing everything afresh, but it also allows the new project to incorporate designs that have already been proven or debugged, so that the scope for errors is reduced.
- Rapid identification of purchase requisitions and specifications from previous projects for equipment which corresponds to new equipment requirements. One application of this is to speed the preparation of new purchase specifications, particularly when much or all of the previous text can be used again.
- Grouping of components into families according to their basic shapes and sizes. This is particularly necessary for manufacturing operations where the plant is arranged in cells for group technology.
- If it is possible to use a common system, cost estimates, budgets, recorded costs, drawing schedules, many other documents, and tasks on the project plan can all be related in a database for project administration, management reports and control.

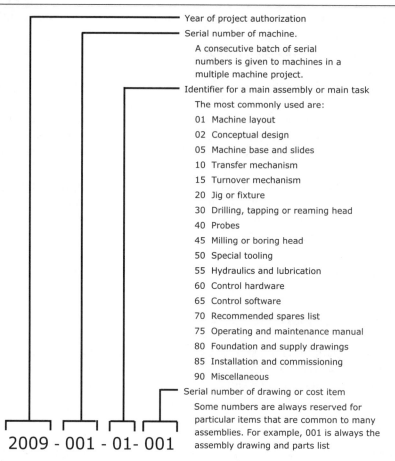

Figure 12.8 Project coding system used by a heavy engineering company

This company designs and manufactures heavy special-purpose machine tool systems

- The ability to carry out statistical analyses on cost records and other documents from past projects for a variety of reasons, including monitoring performance trends.

The following examples from my experience had great practical use in a heavy engineering company, and illustrate only two of the many possibilities for exploiting properly coded records:

- The averaging of recorded costs for commonly recurring work packages in a range of categories from many past projects. This led to the preparation of project estimating tables (expressed in man-hours and updated materials costs). These tables proved very useful for planning and resource scheduling new projects and for making global checks on detailed estimates for new project proposals.
- Analysis in detail of past shipping records enabled a table to be compiled that listed all the main components commonly produced in the company's very heavy engineering projects. For each item it was possible to forecast the most likely average and the maximum weight of each part of the project after it had been broken down into parts of 20 tonnes or less for shipping. Cost estimates were added with the help of a shipping company. The result was given to the materials control manager as a 'ready-reckoner'. With occasional updating, this table was used successfully for estimating future project shipping weights and costs to all parts of the world.

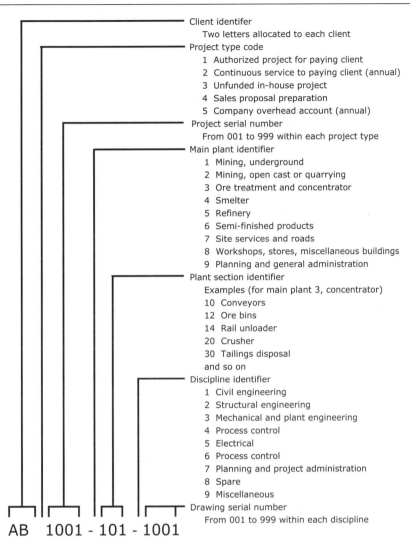

Figure 12.9 Project coding system used by a mining engineering company

CHOOSING A CODING SYSTEM

Once a coding system has become well established it is difficult and unwise to make any fundamental change. Any comprehensive system has, therefore, to be designed with a great deal of care, so that it will serve the organization well into the future. Suppose that a company has been operating for many years with a comprehensive arrangement of codes that are recognized by all its management information systems. Suppose, further, that this arrangement of codes is common to many applications and procedures. As an example, the number for the drawing of a manufactured component would also be used as (or would be a recognizable constituent of) related manufacturing job numbers, job cost records and the stock and part number of the component itself. If this company were to make a change to the numbering system, so that numbers which previously had one meaning would denote something entirely different in the future, some of the following problems might arise:

- drawings filed under two different systems;

- similar inconvenience caused to long-standing customers who maintain their own files of project drawings;
- no easy way of identifying similar previous jobs for the purpose of comparative cost estimating;
- difficulty in retrieving earlier designs – the opportunity to use retained engineering from past work to reduce future design effort might be lost;
- staff must live with two different systems instead of one universal set of numbers;
- problems for storekeepers and stock controllers, with more than one part numbering method – parts common to earlier projects may have to be renumbered for newer projects, so that there is a possibility of having identical common parts stored in two places with different part numbers;
- mayhem created in any attempt to use a relational database that relies on code numbering.

Need for simplicity

This is the place to insert another word of warning. It is tempting to be too ambitious and try to make numbers include too much information. The result can be codes that contain 14, 15 or more characters. It is easy to fall into such a trap, especially when the system is designed by a committee, each of whose members contributes their own idea of what the numbers might be expected to denote. Beware of phrases such as 'Wouldn't it be nice if ...'.

The designer of a system that depends on exceptionally long codes may feel very proud of the system's capability. Computer systems are well able to accept and process huge numbers, but please remember the human element – the 'people interface'. People will have to work with these numbers, entering them in written or electronic records. I remember an attempt to introduce a very complex coding system on a mine development project in a remote area of Australia. The system designer was a highly qualified and well-respected member of the London head office management staff. Supervisors, professional people and artisans at the mine were all expected to read and write 18-digit job codes on documents without making mistakes while exposed to unpleasant and hazardous conditions both above and below ground. The people at the mine never even attempted to use the codes. Even if they had used them, the depth of information that the codes contained was far in excess of that needed for management information. Simple codes use less effort and result in fewer errors. Remember the sensible slogan KISS: **K**eep **I**t **S**imple, **S**tupid.

WHAT HAPPENS WHEN THE CUSTOMER SAYS 'YOU SHALL USE MY CODING SYSTEM!'?

Not infrequently, an irritating problem arises when customers insist that their own numbering system be used, rather than the project contractor's own long-established and proven arrangement. This happens, for example, when a project owner is to be presented with a complete set of project drawings as part of the contract and wants to be able to file these along with all the other drawings in the owner's head office system. This, unfortunately, is a case where 'the customer is always right'.

This problem of having to use customers' codes is not always restricted to drawings. In some projects it can apply to equipment numbers or part numbers. It also occurs, and is a great nuisance, in the cost codes used for work packages or large purchases for major projects. The customer and contractor sometimes work together to plan, authorize and arrange the release of funds (either from the customer's own resources or from an external financing organization). In such cases the customer might insist that all estimates, budgets and subsequent cost reports for the project are broken down against the customer's own capital appropriation or other cost codes.

Three options

There are three possible options when the customer asks the contractor to use a 'foreign' coding system.

Option 1: Say No! to the customer

The person who adopts this course takes is either courageous or foolhardy. It might even be impossible under the terms of contract. In any case, it would be a short cut to achieving bad customer relations or losing the customer altogether.

Option 2: Change over completely to the customer's system

With this option, the contractor calls the project a 'special case', abandons the in-house system, asks the customer for a set of its procedures, and uses those for the project. This option cannot be recommended for the following reasons:

- The information management benefits of the in-house system would be lost for all data for the project.
- It will soon be discovered that every project is a 'special case'. The contractor might soon find have to deal with as many coding systems as there are customers.

Option 3: Use both systems simultaneously

This option, the sensible compromise course, offers the only proper solution. Every drawing and other affected item must be numbered twice, once for each system.

Everything must, of course, be diligently cross-referenced between the two systems. This is tedious, time consuming and means that staff have to learn more than one system. Some time ago it would have caused enough extra work to provide a weak argument for trying to obtain extra reimbursement from the customer. Fortunately, computer systems greatly reduce the effort needed for cross-referencing, sorting and retrieving data numbered under duplicate systems.

REFERENCES AND FURTHER READING

Devaux, S. A. (1999), *Total Project Control: a Manager's Guide to Integrated Planning, Measuring and Tracking* (New York: Wiley).

13 *Completing the Breakdown Structures*

A typical project has many dimensions. Chief among these are the following:

- *the organization dimension* – which means how different people and functions are grouped and distributed. Chapters 9 and 10 (in particular) described basic organizational patterns and explained how these can be represented by organigrams;
- *the work dimension* – the understanding of which begins with project definition, then proceeds through listing the tasks and is finally defined by the work breakdown structure (Chapter 12);
- *the cost dimension* – which means the estimated and real costs of all the work, both by individual tasks and collectively. This dimension was introduced in Chapter 4 but will be developed slightly further in this chapter;
- *the time dimension* – which was visited briefly in Chapter 5 but will be dealt with more exhaustively in Chapters 14 and 15;
- *the resources dimension* – which is a more detailed view of personal skills and material resources (including money) without which no project can be completed. Chapters 16, 17, 18, 19 and 23 are all devoted to this important (but sometimes neglected) dimension.

None of these dimensions exists by itself, and all are interrelated in various ways, both within the project and with the company's general management and accounting procedures. They overlay each other or are interlaced, often in mind-boggling complexity. Yet the project manager must be able to see across and into all these complex patterns in detail and make sense of them if the project is to be managed successfully. This would seem to be an impossible task for the average human mind and, indeed, these dimensional relationships are not easy to describe in words and pictures. Fortunately, however, all this complexity can be reduced to sensible and manageable proportions by taking the following relatively straightforward steps:

1. Prepare a work breakdown structure (WBS) for the project and code it hierarchically.
2. Prepare an organizational breakdown structure (OBS) and code that hierarchically too.
3. Using competent project management software, arrange for a computer to process, sort, filter and report data according to the WBS and OBS codes so that each manager gets schedule, progress and cost data that are specific to his or her responsibilities (that is, on a need-to-know basis).

Chapter 12 described the first of the above steps (WBS preparation), so now it is time to consider the OBS.

DEVELOPING A PROJECT ORGANIZATION BREAKDOWN STRUCTURE

Some people tend to confuse company organization structures with project OBSs. Although the two are very closely related, an organigram is not quite the same as an OBS. This is best explained by a case example.

Case example: lawnmower project

Cuttit Ltd is a company that produces garden machinery. The company has launched a project for the design and development of a cordless electric rotary lawnmower, to which it has allocated the project number LM15.

Project definition for the lawnmower project

This lawnmower will have a 45cm one-blade cutter mounted on the vertical shaft of a battery-driven electric motor. For safety the shaft must have an automatic brake that stops the blade within one second when power is switched off or lost for any reason. Another safety feature is that the mower will have a switch on each of its two shaft handles, so that the motor will not run unless both the gardener's hands are on the mower handles. The machine frame will be mounted on four non-driven wheels, and a grass collection box and on-board battery charger must be provided.

The project deliverable is to be a fully tested working prototype batch of ten machines and a set of manufacturing drawings and specifications. The manufacturing cost of these machines when produced in production batch quantities must not exceed £60 each, but this case example description does not include cost estimating and budgeting.

General organization of Cuttit Ltd

Cuttit Ltd. has a line and function structure, the organigram for which is shown in Figure 13.1. In project management terms this organization is a coordination matrix, because the project management function is entrusted to a project coordinator who has no line authority and is embedded in the design department. This arrangement is quite common and can work well for small projects. The lawnmower project should fit quite nicely into the Cuttit Ltd organization.

Note that the organigram is partly cost coded, so that each departmental manager has his or her own two-digit cost code. This coding arrangement has been made to fit the requirements of the company's management information system (MIS), which is administered by the accounts department. These departmental codes enable the computer to filter and sort costing data to produce separate monthly budget and cost statements for each departmental manager. Cuttit Ltd has found this organigram and its coding system to be fine for the MIS and for general cost and management accounting.

However, although the coded organigram is fine for *company* accounting and budgetary control, it is not designed for *project* cost and progress control. The codes do not drill down far enough into the organization for the MIS computer to produce project cost reports in sufficient detail for the chief engineer and the project coordinator. On the other hand, the company organigram includes departments that have no direct involvement with projects and whose costs and budgets are of no concern to the chief engineer or the project coordinator. So, the organigram in Figure 13.1 is not an OBS for the lawnmower project (or for any other project), but it does contain all the elements from which an OBS can be developed.

OBS for the lawnmower project

Unlike a general company organigram, a project OBS is concerned principally with those departments and work groups that will carry out project tasks. In other words, it contains only those departments over which the project manager needs to exert control or coordination. However, for all those organizational elements that belong in the project OBS, more attention to coding will be needed if the computer is to process, filter and sort all the project cost data.

A company that routinely carries out projects should always develop an OBS. Once a company has done that, the OBS and its coding should be applicable to most or all of its projects. The management of Cuttit Ltd developed the OBS shown in Figure 13.2, and it can easily be seen how this has been derived from the company organigram in Figure 13.1. The OBS contains only those departments that work directly on projects. For example, the chief engineer and the project coordinator are not directly interested in the costs, budgets and performances of the accounts department or HRM. Note particularly that the OBS cost codes are extended from the company's departmental cost codes as used in the MIS, a course that Cuttit Ltd's management was wise to adopt.

Unlike the organigram from which it is derived, the OBS focus is not based on people and their individual names and job titles but is instead directed to the project functions that they perform or represent. This is apparent in Figure 13.2, where the names in the boxes now describe more what people *do* than what they *are*. For example, the managing director's box in the organigram becomes the company in the OBS.

Some companies regard project management or project coordination as an overhead cost, but many others (including Cuttit Ltd) decide that they wish to collect and monitor the costs of this function separately and so it has been given a code.

Levels of breakdown required for an OBS

Cuttit Ltd is not a very large company and it has decided that it needs only three OBS levels which, as seen in Figure 13.2, are company, department and functional group.

Large projects, projects of any size carried out in large companies, and projects that spread over more than one company will all need more OBS levels than the relatively simple case of Cuttit Ltd and its lawnmower project. The situation will be further complicated where a large group of companies is carrying out a number of related projects (called a programme of projects). Even where multiple projects in an organization are not directly related to each other by their objectives, they will usually be connected by their claim on common resources. The following OBS levels might therefore be needed for some of these more complex cases:

- *Level 1* – the global organization, including all the companies directly involved in projects, allowing for complex multiproject programmes that contain projects of different types (for example a mix of IT and construction projects);
- *Level 2* – the global organization, including all the companies directly involved in one large project or in several projects of the same type;
- *Level 3* – companies within the global organization;
- *Level 4* – divisions within companies;
- *Level 5* – departments within divisions;
- *Level 6* – functional groups within departments.

It can be argued that even more levels are needed, for example breaking the functional groups down to the individual skills or people contained in them. Fortunately, few project managers will need all these levels and most can manage nicely using only levels 5 and 6.

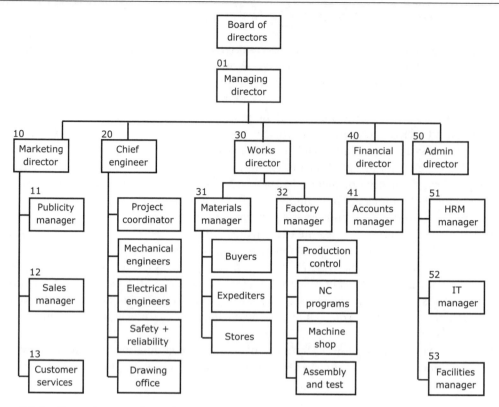

Figure 13.1   Organigram of Cuttit Ltd

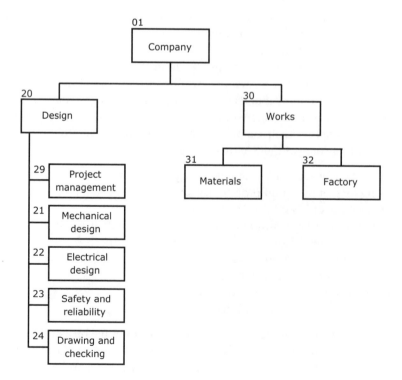

Figure 13.2   Lawnmower project: OBS

RELATIONSHIP BETWEEN THE PROJECT WBS AND OBS

The lawnmower project provides a suitable case for examining how a project OBS and WBS relate. Before that can be considered further we shall need the lawnmower project's WBS.

WBS for the lawnmower project

Figure 13.3 shows the uppermost levels of the WBS for the lawnmower project. It can be seen that task codes have been added to this WBS in typical hierarchical fashion, so that each code indicates the place occupied by each component or task in the project build. The work breakdown structure for this project follows very closely the physical build of the lawnmower and indeed the WBS codes will eventually be built into the parts numbering system when the machine goes into full production.

Marrying the WBS and the OBS

The lawnmower project's WBS and OBS have been brought together as a matrix chart in Figure 13.4. At each intersection of the matrix there is a possible cost account that relates the work required from the WBS with the organizational group that will carry out the work and incur the cost. Although the WBS and the OBS shown here are both simplified, it is apparent that even for this tiny project this is a complex pattern in which it is hardly possible to detail every possible cost account. If this were a very large project, a diagram showing every possible cost account might need a sheet of paper as large as a football pitch. However, here are two items of good news:

- Even though Figure 13.4 is greatly simplified, it is adequate for demonstrating the principles of the WBS/OBS/cost account relationships.
- In practice project managers need only produce the WBS and OBS separately, and never have to draw the complex relationship diagram. Providing that the coding systems are logically designed, the relational database in the computer will take care of the complexity. So that enormous sheet of paper will never be needed.

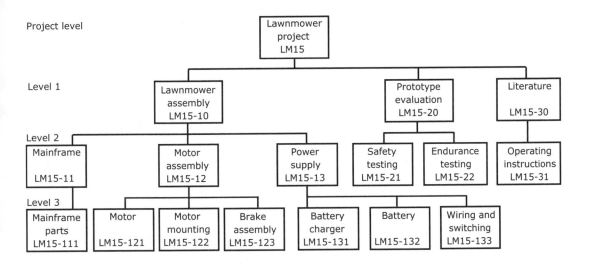

Figure 13.3   Lawnmower project: upper WBS levels

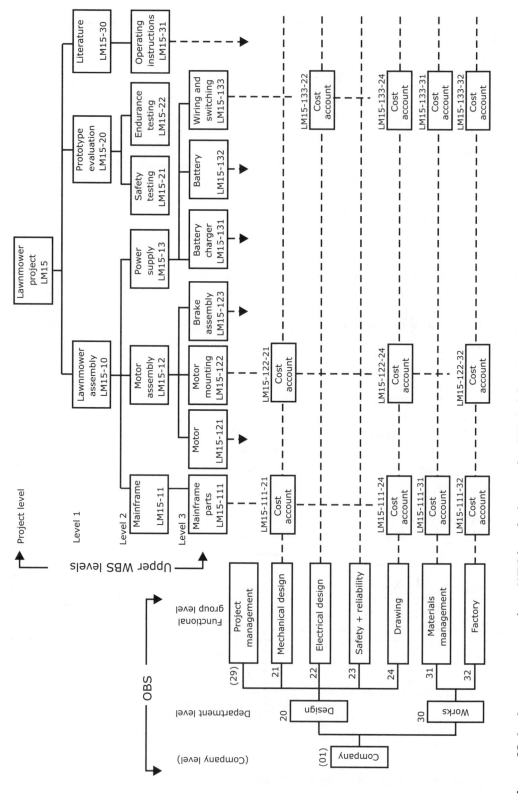

Figure 13.4   Lawnmower project: WBS in relation to the OBS (with cost account examples)

To understand in greater detail how the WBS and OBS relate, look for instance at task LM15-133, wiring and switching, as it is depicted in Figure 13.4. This task covers:

- design
- drawing and checking
- purchasing (as part of materials management in this case)
- assembly of all parts needed for the lawnmower's wiring harness, including the switches.

Each one of these actions for the wiring and switching task has its own cost account. For example, the WBS code LM15-133 identifies the task as wiring and switching, and the two-digit suffix –22 narrows this down to the work done within the electrical design group, which itself is part of the design department. Figure 13.5 analyses the constituents of this LM15-133-22 code and demonstrates its hierarchical structure.

Now, therefore, there is a system for allocating the costs of time and materials not only to each task, but also to the group or department that does the work. All of these results will depend on having systems for collecting the actual costs as they are incurred, and that subject is dealt with in Chapter 26. Those cost collection systems will need yet more codes (not discussed here) which include the following:

- *staff codes* – that identify individual people within HRM and accounts records;
- *standard cost codes* – codes that identify different bands within the direct labour cost structure (a subject that was introduced very briefly in Chapter 4).

With the OBS, WBS and all these coding systems in place, we can now contemplate one further related system, which is the cost breakdown structure.

INTRODUCING THE COST BREAKDOWN STRUCTURE

So far it is apparent that, using a combination of the WBS, OBS and the resulting cost accounts, it is possible for a computer to compile cost reports that break costs down into tasks and the organizational elements involved in carrying out those tasks. However, project managers, cost engineers and some senior managers will be interested in another dimension, which is how the project costs can be grouped by categories such as total labour, total bought-out materials and total expenses. That introduces the dimension of the cost breakdown structure (CBS). The elements of the CBS will depend to a large extent on the type of project, so that (for example) a construction project

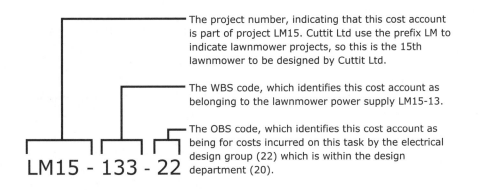

The project number, indicating that this cost account is part of project LM15. Cuttit Ltd use the prefix LM to indicate lawnmower projects, so this is the 15th lawnmower to be designed by Cuttit Ltd.

The WBS code, which identifies this cost account as belonging to the lawnmower power supply LM15-13.

The OBS code, which identifies this cost account as being for costs incurred on this task by the electrical design group (22) which is within the design department (20).

LM15 - 133 - 22

Figure 13.5 Lawnmower project: analysis of a cost account code (chosen at random)

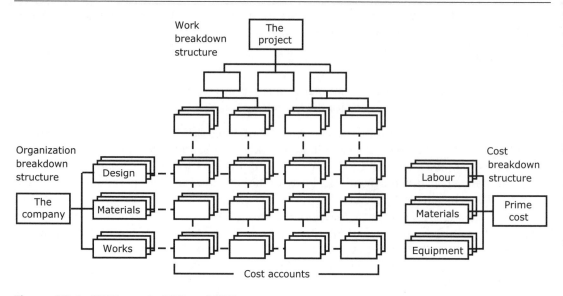

Figure 13.6   WBS meets OBS and CBS

CBS will usually contain a high subcontracts cost, and a mining project will have some expensive individual items of equipment (such as cranes and locomotives).

As with the OBS/WBS/cost accounts matrix, any attempt to chart every possible element leading to the cost breakdown structure detail would need a sheet of paper of enormous and impracticable size. However, once again this is a very complex system that is greatly simplified by the use of a relational database which can filter, sort, process and report permutations and combinations of cost elements based on logical coding systems.

These principles are summarized in Figure 13.6 above. The top-level components of the CBS shown here are for the prime cost (all direct costs) and do not include overheads and other general administration expenses. This is usual. The CBS will, however, contain all costs for which the project manager can reasonably be held responsible.

REFERENCES AND FURTHER READING

Devaux, S.A. (1999), *Total Project Control: a Manager's Guide to Integrated Planning, Measuring and Tracking* (New York: Wiley).

Gray, B., Gray, C. F. and Larson, E.W. (2005), *Project Management: the Managerial Process*, 3rd Edition (Singapore: McGraw-Hill).

Harrison, F. and Lock, D. (2004), *Advanced Project Management: A Structured Approach*, 4th Edition (Aldershot: Gower).

Kerzner, H. (2006), *Project Management: A Systems Approach to Planning, Scheduling and Controlling*, 9th Edition (New York: Wiley); particularly good, but expensive.

14 *Detailed Planning: An Introduction to Critical Path Networks*

After a brief revisit to the Gantt charts that were introduced in earlier chapters, this chapter introduces the more powerful planning systems that use critical path network analysis.

GANTT CHARTS: THEIR ADVANTAGES AND THEIR LIMITATIONS

Gantt charts need little explanation and no training because anyone who can understand a holiday wall chart or even a calendar should be able to understand a project Gantt chart. It was explained in Chapter 1 that Gantt charts are named after the American industrial engineer Henry Gantt (1861–1919). They are also known widely as bar charts. The upper half of Figure 1.4 showed a typical Gantt chart and Figure 5.3 was a preliminary Gantt chart for the museum project (to be developed further in Chapter 15).

Gantt charts are always drawn to a linear timescale. They are excellent visual aids and their effectiveness can be enhanced by the use of different colours. Gantt charts are useful for very simple resource scheduling because the amount of any particular kind of resource needed in a given time period can be calculated by adding the number of times that tasks needing that resource appear in each period column. Before the advent of computers this was the only resource scheduling method possible, and we used to plan using Gantt charts set up on wall-mounted pegboards that allowed the tasks to be represented by coloured plastic strips. These strips could be plugged in and moved around to achieve the best possible resource usage pattern. Another version of these charts used Lego bricks, and yet another idea was based on magnetic strips stuck to a steel back plate, rather in the manner of fridge magnets.

Senior executives and others unskilled in the project management arts often prefer to be given Gantt charts in reports because the more powerful network planning diagrams need some training before they can be interpreted. However, as explained in Chapter 5, Gantt charts are not able clearly to show all the complex interdependencies that exist between the different tasks in most projects.

All competent project management computer programs can convert critical path network diagrams into Gantt charts, optionally showing all the complex inter-task dependencies. However, except in the very simplest cases, such as the example given earlier in Figure 5.4, a project Gantt chart can become very cluttered and difficult to follow when the inter-task links are added and it is usually best to hide them. Critical path network diagrams provide the notational methods needed to overcome these difficulties.

BACKGROUND TO CRITICAL PATH ANALYSIS

Network analysis is a generic term for several project planning methods that originated in Europe and elsewhere before 1950, but their full exploitation was not seen until the late 1950s, when they were used with great success and much publicity for the planning and control of US defence projects. The striking improvements demonstrated over earlier planning methods have since led to their widespread adoption in many industries far removed from either America or defence.

Whereas Gantt charts are usually very good visual aids that can be understood on sight, networks can appear strange and unfamiliar when people are first confronted with them. Proficiency in both the use and understanding of network diagrams requires some initial learning and practice. Those who compile network diagrams must have some skill in reasoning and the application of logical argument. Those who play chess, or do well at intelligence tests will probably make good network planners.

Network diagrams, unlike Gantt charts, are not usually drawn to scale. They simply show all the project tasks in their logical sequence and juxtaposition. Some computer programs can plot networks to a timescale, but the results tend to occupy large areas of paper and, if a timescale is required, it is better to convert the network to its Gantt chart equivalent. Time-scaled network diagrams are not in common use, and will henceforth be ignored in this book.

Although network diagrams are weak in their ability to display tasks on a timescale, they have other very significant compensating strengths. When compared with Gantt charts (including linked Gantt charts), critical path networks provide the more powerful notation needed to show all the logical interdependencies between different jobs. The planner can ensure, for example, that bricklaying will not be scheduled to start before its supporting foundations are ready or that a company department is not expected to move to its new offices before all the essential facilities are in place and tested. Such logical mistakes are relatively easy to make with Gantt charts, especially where their size and complexity prevents all the logical links from being shown. Even when a Gantt chart can be drawn to conform with all logical inter-task constraints, errors will probably be introduced during updating unless the chart is plotted by a computer running critical path based project management software.

Another great strength of networks is that they allow priorities to be quantified, based on an analysis of all the task duration estimates. Those tasks that cannot be delayed without endangering project completion on time are identified as critical, and all other tasks can be ranked according to their degree of criticality.

Networks cannot, by themselves, be used for resource scheduling. In this respect Gantt charts are superior and easier to understand, provided that the number of activities is very small. However, networks (because they quantify priorities and highlight critical jobs) make a vital contribution to the resource scheduling process. When a suitable computer program is used, very powerful resource scheduling capabilities result.

DIFFERENT NETWORK NOTATION SYSTEMS

Several network systems emerged during the second half of the twentieth century, but these all fit within one or other of two principal groups, determined by the method of notation:

- *Activity-on-arrow networks* (often simply called arrow networks) – the names used within this group include:
  - ADM (arrow diagram method), CPM (critical path method) or CPA (critical path analysis). These three names are now synonymous for all practical purposes;

- PERT (programme evaluation and review technique), which uses ADM notation but with probabilistic forecasts for task durations (best, worst and most likely times). This method is explained in Chapter 29.
- *Activity-on-node networks* – these include:
  - PDM (precedence diagram method), which is by far the most commonly used today;
  - Roy method (named after its inventor), otherwise known as the method of potentials (MOM or MPM). This is an early activity-on-node system, very similar to precedence notation, now rarely (if ever) used;
  - some very early, no longer used, arrow networks, which placed the activities on the circular nodes instead of on the linking arrows.

There are also systems used in production and materials control that are really networking methods. These are generally outside the scope of this book but one (line of balance) is described in Chapter 29.

Inevitably, with the passage of time, the distinction between PERT, CPA, and CPM has become clouded and the terms are often wrongly interchanged (which is no great cause for concern).

The terms 'activity' and 'task', although occasionally used by some authorities with different meanings, are treated as interchangeable synonyms throughout this text.

Which system should be used?

Network analysis, and particularly the use of arrow diagrams, gave planners a valuable new tool with which they could express the logic of a proposed work plan for their projects. Coupled with the concept of the critical path and the use of float (discussed later in this chapter) to determine priorities, these were big steps forward. But arrow diagrams still had their drawbacks. Not least of these was the difficulty experienced by early network analysts in trying to persuade their managers and others to accept the new and unfamiliar notation. Gantt charts were still preferred (they still are in many places).

The precedence system has become far more popular and is in widespread use. One reason for this is that precedence diagrams appear more user friendly to people with no planning experience because they bear a close resemblance to engineering flow charts. Moreover, although arrow diagrams could show many complex relationships between different activities and events, there were limitations – particularly where it was desired to show activities whose starts and finishes could be allowed to overlap. Precedence networks allow a range of more complex constraints to be shown and planned.

A very strong reason for the use of precedence networks is that modern computer software will only accept precedence notation.

Why, then, does arrow notation survive and why describe it in this book? Proficiency in arrow notation remains a very useful skill for the planning professional, and I use both arrow and precedence networks, each for a particular purpose. Arrow networks are often better for initial planning because they are very much faster and easier to sketch freehand. This speed saves valuable time at project planning meetings (which are invariably attended by managers and other senior people whose time is expensive). The sketching speed and flexibility of arrow diagrams makes them particularly useful in brainstorming sessions when logic is being discussed and hammered into shape. Later, when the networks are being tidied up, checked and redrawn before input to the computer, it is a fairly simple matter to convert to precedence notation.

Precedence logic is particularly easy to draw and edit on the computer screen but the small screen size compared with large sheets or rolls of drawing paper limits the size of network that can be seen as a complete 'map'. Each computer screen image is more like a page in an atlas, so that the complete journey from project start to finish through all possible paths cannot be seen without much tedious scrolling up, down and sideways.

The principal reason why arrow networks are easier to sketch freehand is that the event circles can be scribbled quickly, whereas the activity boxes in precedence networks take longer to draw. I have been told that this difficulty can be overcome in team brainstorming sessions if Post-it notes are used for the activity boxes. These can be stuck on a flip chart or roll of paper as the ideas emerge from the collective planning brainpower. No doubt the Post-it notes could be preprinted or rubber-stamped with blank activity boxes, complete with all their lines.

Which system would you prefer to read about?

The serious student or professional planner should be aware of both arrow and precedence diagrams and both are described in this book.

Some people might wish always to use computers for their networks, perhaps even drawing the logic directly on the screen. For those people, arrow networks can have little interest and they will probably want to skip the next main section of this chapter. For that reason, I have set out the text describing arrow diagrams and precedence networks as two separate self-contained sections. This has, inevitably, meant duplicating some of the explanations in the following pages.

CRITICAL PATH ANALYSIS USING ARROW DIAGRAMS

Arrow logic diagrams

The heart of any activity-on-arrow system is the arrow diagram or 'network', itself. This differs from the more familiar Gantt chart in several important respects. Arrow diagrams, in common with all other network methods, are not drawn to scale. Every network is, however, constructed with careful thought to show as accurately as possible the logical relationships and interdependence of each activity or task with all the other activities in the project. Indeed, it is for this reason that networks are sometimes called 'logic diagrams'.

Activities and events in arrow diagrams

Figure 14.1 shows a very simple arrow diagram. Each circle represents an event in the project. An event might be the start of a project, the start of an activity (or task), the completion of a task or the end of a project. The arrow joining any two events represents the activity, task or time delay that must take place before the second event can be declared as achieved. Events are usually shared between tasks, so that a single event might signal the completion of one or more tasks and the start of one or several more tasks. In Figure 14.1 it can be seen that that 10 events are linked by 11 activities.

Jargon

I prefer to avoid technical jargon as much as possible but readers may meet other terms that describe the network event circles and activity arrows. These strange terms have their origins in the mathematical theory of networks. In this alternative language, the circles are termed 'nodes' and the arrows become 'arcs'. The event at the tail of the arrow (the activity's preceding event) is called the *I* node for that activity, and the event at the arrowhead (the succeeding event) is called its *J* node. Arrow networks are occasionally referred to, therefore, as '*IJ* networks'. This jargon is not necessary for practical project network analysis, but the terms might be found in the literature.

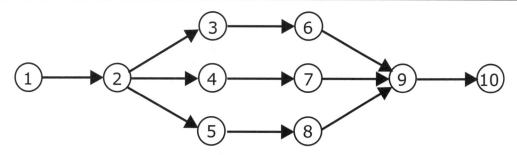

Figure 14.1   Main elements of arrow logic

Direction

By convention, activity arrows are always drawn from left to right. This means that the arrowheads are not strictly necessary and could be omitted. However, when a network is altered or when space is limited it might be impossible to avoid drawing an arrow vertically or even from right to left. In those exceptional cases the arrowheads *must* be shown so that there can be no ambiguity about the direction of any arrow.

Scale

Unlike Gantt charts, network diagrams are not usually drawn to any scale. The length of the arrows and size of the event circles have no significance whatsoever.

Identification numbers in arrow diagrams

The numbers written in the event circles are identifier codes that label the events: they allow the events and their associated activities to be referred to without ambiguity. In Figure 14.1 the arrow from event 1 to event 2, for example, can be described as activity 1,2 or 1–2. This labelling is convenient for all arrow networks and is essential for anyone who still has software capable of processing arrow networks.

Logical activity dependencies and constraints in arrow diagrams

In any arrow diagram, no event can be considered as achieved until all the activities leading into it have been finished. Activities leading out of an event must wait for that event to be achieved before they can start. This can be demonstrated by reference to Figure 14.1. Event 9 cannot be considered as being reached or achieved until all three activities leading into it from the left have been achieved. Only when event 9 has been achieved, and not before, can activity 9–10 start. Similarly, activities 2–3, 2–4 and 2–5 must all wait until activity 1–2 has been finished before they can start.

Now, applying the arrow diagram method to an everyday project, suppose you want to plant a tree. If you were misguided enough to consider an arrow diagram necessary for this simple project, the result would look something like the sequence shown in Figure 14.2. The interdependence of activities is clear in this case, and only one sequence is possible. The tree cannot be placed in the hole before the hole has been dug, and there would be little point in filling in the hole before putting the tree into it.

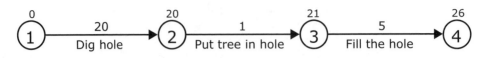

Figure 14.2 Tree project using arrow notation

Activity duration estimates and descriptions

One of the most important tasks in any planning operation is to estimate how long each task will take. This is an estimate in units of elapsed time, not necessarily connected with man-hours or other units of work. Estimates for the duration of each activity have been made for the simple tree project, as follows:

Activity	Description	Estimated duration
1–2	Dig the hole	20 minutes
2–3	Position the tree	1 minute
3–4	Fill the hole	5 minutes

No one needs network analysis to realize that this project is going to take a minimum of 26 minutes to complete. Notice, however, that the estimated duration for each arrow is written above its arrow.

The description of each activity (or task) is written below its arrow. Space is limited in all network diagrams and in subsequent computer reports, so planners must become adept at describing tasks in the least possible number of words.

The estimated achievement time for each event (written above the event circle) is calculated by adding up the estimated durations of all the preceding activities from left to right along the arrow path. These event times are the earliest possible times by which the events can be achieved.

Dummy activities

The network in Figure 14.3 represents a slightly more complex project (shown here without its activity descriptions). Now the configuration is actually seen to be a network of activities, and not just a simple straight-line sequence. As in all project networks, there is more than one path through the arrows from project start to finish. In this example there are three possible routes to the final event 6, one of which flows through the dummy activity arrow linking event 4 to event 3.

Dummy activities (called dummies for short) do not represent actual work and almost always have zero duration. Rather, they denote a constraint or line of dependence between different activities. In Figure 14.3, therefore, the start of activity 3–6 is dependent not only upon completion of activity 2–3, but it must also await completion of activity 1–4. Alternatively expressed, activity 3–6 cannot start until events 3 and 4 have both been achieved.

The arrows for dummy activities are always drawn with dotted or broken lines.

Time analysis with arrow networks

Time units for activity durations

In Figure 14.3 (as in the simple tree project) numbers have been written above the activity arrows to show their estimated durations. Planners should always choose these time units according to

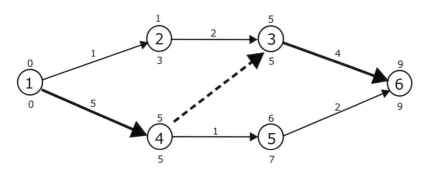

Figure 14.3   Example of arrow network time analysis

The number above each event circle is its earliest possible completion time and the number below is the latest permissible completion time (see text for more details). The longest path through the network is the critical path, shown here in bold arrows. Some networks have more than one equal critical path.

their suitability for the project. In the tree project, minutes were the most appropriate unit of time. Days or weeks are most often used in practice for project plans, and weeks have been chosen for this example. The best computer programs will accept any unit of time from minutes to years.

Some computer programs allow different units of time to be mixed in the same project network but I cannot recommend this practice. Mixing time units in the same network can lead to some very peculiar results and messy tabulations when the computer prints out the results. Best practice has always been that the planner chooses a suitable unit and uses it consistently throughout the network.

Forward pass through the network

In the project network of Figure 14.3, the earliest possible time for each event and the earliest possible time for project completion at event 6 have been calculated by adding activity duration estimates along the arrows from left to right. This is always the first step in the full time analysis of any network and is known as the *forward pass*.

The forward pass process is more complicated in this case than it was in the simple tree project because there is more than one possible path through the network. The earliest time indicated for each event might appear to depend on which path is followed, but only the longest preceding path will give the correct result. The earliest possible completion time for event 3, for instance, might seem to be 1 + 2 = 3, if the path through events 1, 2 and 3 is taken. Event 3 cannot really be achieved, however, until the end of week 5 because of the longer path through the dummy. This also means that the earliest possible start time for activity 3–6 is the end of week 5 (or, for more practical purposes, the beginning of week 6).

Thus the earliest possible time for any event is found by adding the estimated durations of all preceding activities along the path that produces the greatest time. By following this procedure through the network to the end of the project at event 6 it emerges that the earliest possible project completion time is estimated as nine weeks.

Backward pass through the network

Now consider event 5 in Figure 14.3. Its earliest possible achievement time is the end of week 6, three weeks before the earliest possible time for finishing the project at event 6. It is clear that activity 5–6, which is only expected to last for two weeks, could be delayed for up to one week without upsetting the overall timescale. In other words, although the earliest possible achievement time for event 5 is week 6, its latest permissible achievement time is the end of week 7. This result can be indicated on the arrow diagram by writing the latest permissible time underneath the event circle. The result is found this time, not by addition from left to right along the arrows, but in exactly the opposite way by subtracting the estimated durations of activities from right to left (9 − 2 = 7 for event 5).

This subtraction exercise can be repeated throughout the network, writing the latest permissible times below all the event circles. Where more than one path exists, the longest must always be chosen so that the result after subtraction gives the smallest remainder. This is illustrated at event 4 in Figure 14.3, where the correct subtraction route lies through the dummy.

Float or slack

The term 'slack' indicates the amount of leeway available for achieving an event (the difference between its earliest possible and latest permissible times) without jeopardizing the earliest possible completion time for the whole project. The amount of slack at an event also determines the leeway available for starting and finishing activities that pass through the event. Strictly speaking, 'float' is the correct word for the leeway of activities (as opposed to slack for events). However, 'slack' and 'float' are now used synonymously and 'float' is the term used throughout this book. There are various categories of float. These are explained in Chapter 16 but can be ignored for the examples in this chapter.

Critical path

When all the earliest possible and latest permissible times have been added to the diagram there will be at least one chain of events from the start of the network to the end where the earliest and latest event times are the same, indicating zero float. These events are critical to the successful achievement of the whole project within its earliest possible time. The route joining these events is not surprisingly termed the 'critical path'. Although all activities may be important, it is those that lie on the critical path that must claim priority for management attention and the supply of scarce resources.

It is always possible that two or more different paths through a network will have the same total duration, so that there might be more than one critical path.

Three ways of showing times on arrow networks

The times written on arrow networks usually refer to the *events* rather than directly to the *activities*. Project managers, however, need to know the times when each activity should start and finish. Although these times are easily derived from an arrow network, they cannot easily be shown owing to lack of space on the arrow diagram. This is demonstrated in Figure 14.4, using a fragment from a larger network. All the estimates are in days.

Refer to version A in Figure 14.4. This shows arrow network notation according to the early British Standard BS 4335:1987. This notation, although favoured by some writers, is not well suited to freehand sketching (the principal remaining role for arrow networks) because:

- Relatively large diameter event circles are required, which reduce the amount of network detail that can be drawn on a sheet of paper.
- Each event must be drawn very carefully, taking time that is not usually available in a brainstorming planning session.

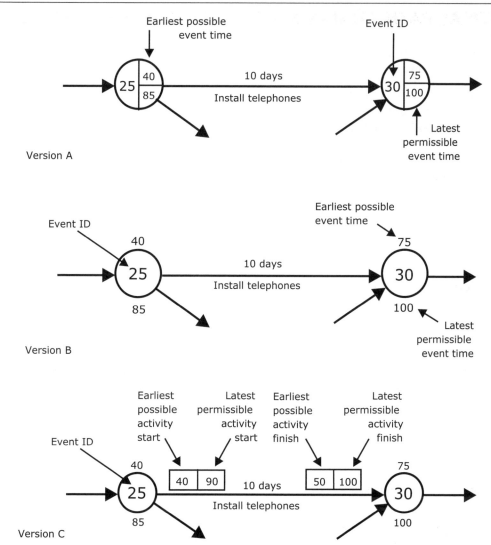

Figure 14.4 Three different methods for showing times on arrow networks

Version B in Figure 14.4 is a form of notation used in many countries and generally throughout this book. It allows rapid freehand sketching, is economical of space on a sheet or roll of paper and is my own preferred choice.

Now consider activity 25–30 in Figure 14.4 (using either version A or B). The time analysis data for this activity are not all immediately apparent from the network. Certainly its earliest possible start is day 40, the earliest completion time for event 25. The latest permissible start for this activity is the latest permissible time for event 30 minus the activity duration, which is 100 minus 10, giving day 90 (not the day 85 shown as the latest permissible completion for event 25). This arises because other activities entering and leaving events 25 and 30 affect the times for those events independently of activity 25–30.

The 'missing' time analysis data for any activity can be added if desired (and if space and drafting time allow) using version C.

These difficulties do not arise with precedence notation.

CRITICAL PATH ANALYSIS USING PRECEDENCE NOTATION

The precedence system of notation is preferred by many and has emerged as the dominant method for the following reasons:

- Precedence logic diagrams more closely resemble engineering flow diagrams or block schematic diagrams than arrow diagrams and are therefore more easily understood by people with no network training.
- Precedence notation allows clear illustration of activities whose starts and finishes do not coincide directly with the starts and finishes of their immediate predecessors and successors. In other words, precedence networks can show activities that can be allowed to overlap each other or which, conversely, must be separated by a time delay.
- Precedence networks are widely supported by computer software. Arrow diagrams are not.

As with arrow diagrams, precedence networks cannot be used to schedule resources without either conversion into Gantt chart form (for tiny projects) or the use of a computer.

Precedence logic diagrams

Activities in precedence diagrams

Figure 14.5 shows the convention for an activity in precedence notation. Although this must be the preferred pattern when networks are drawn by hand, it is an ideal not achieved when networks are plotted by computer because the software will limit the amount of data that can be included in each activity box. Without such limitation, networks would take up far too much screen space and be difficult to plot.

Direction

The flow of work in a precedence diagram is (as for arrow diagrams) always from left to right.

Scale

Precedence diagrams are not drawn to scale. The lengths of the links or the sizes of activity boxes have no significance whatsoever.

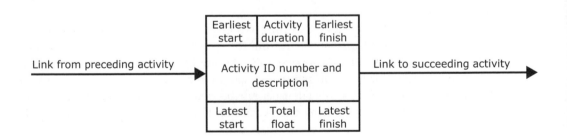

Figure 14.5   An activity in precedence notation

Activity identifiers

Every activity is given a unique identification number, usually referred to as its 'ID code'. These codes are necessary for computer processing. Activity identification is a little simpler in precedence networks because, unlike their arrow network counterparts, it is not necessary to specify a preceding event code and a succeeding event code. A single code for each activity is all that is required. These ID codes can range from small serial numbers to complex alphanumeric codes, depending on the size and complexity of the networks and the capacity of the computer software for accommodating long ID numbers.

Logical dependencies and constraints

All the activities comprising a project are linked by lines which, unlike the arrows in arrow diagrams, almost always have zero duration.

Precedence notation allows more freedom to express complex inter-activity relationships than the arrow diagram method. Activities can, for example, be shown to overlap rather than follow each other in strict sequence. Complex links are described later in this chapter (see Figure 14.13). Their use can be valuable, but is far less common than simple finish–start links. Although most project management computer programs allow complex links, they usually assume finish–start relationships by default.

Activity duration estimates and descriptions

The tree project, which was shown as three sequential arrow activities in Figure 14.2, translates easily into the precedence diagram shown in Figure 14.6. The activity duration estimates for this very simple project are repeated below:

Activity	Description	Estimated duration
1	Dig the hole	20 minutes
2	Position tree	1 minute
3	Fill in the hole	5 minutes

The earliest estimated start and finish times for these activities, found by adding up the estimated durations from left to right, have been written in the activity boxes. Although minutes were used in this simple case, days or weeks are the more customarily used project time units.

Dummy activities

A dummy activity is an activity requiring no work and signifying no actual activity or duration. Therefore all the links in precedence networks can be regarded as dummies, because they incur no effort or expense and (almost always) no time. But these links are never called dummies. The name 'dummy' is only used in precedence networks for an activity box that has zero duration. Such dummy activities are usually unnecessary in precedence networks, but they are useful as start and finish activities (see Figure 14.7, for instance). They can also be inserted in networks at points where there are interfaces with other networks (interface activities that are common to two or more different project networks are explained in Chapter 15). Dummies can also be useful occasionally in

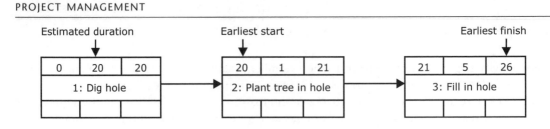

Figure 14.6 Tree project using precedence notation

precedence networks to make the logic easier to follow by eye (as demonstrated later in this chapter, in Figure 14.14).

Time analysis with precedence networks

Figure 14.7 is a very simple precedence network (the equivalent of the arrow network in Figure 14.3). The identifier codes placed in brackets show how these precedence activities correspond with those in the arrow network version. All duration estimates are in weeks for this example.

The start and finish activities are not strictly necessary, and have no corresponding activities in the arrow diagram equivalent. They have been introduced here because it is always desirable to start and finish a network at single nodes. When networks are processed by computer it is best to expect only one start and one finish activity in all output reports, including error log reports. A report of more than one start or finish will then clearly indicate an error in the input data (a point that is explained more fully in the error detection section of Chapter 20).

Forward pass

In the project network of Figure 14.7, the earliest overall project duration possible has been calculated by adding activity duration estimates through the links, passing from left to right. There is more than one possible path through the network and the path with the longest duration will determine the earliest possible finish time for this project.

The earliest possible start time for activity 4 might seem to be 0 + 1 + 2 = 3 (the end of week 3) if the path through activities 1, 2 and 3 is taken. However activity 4 cannot start until the end of week 5 (which in practice, means the beginning of week 6) because it is constrained by the longer path through activities 1 and 5.

By following this procedure through the network to the end of the project at activity 8 it emerges that the earliest possible estimated project duration is nine weeks (with completion at the end of the week 9).

Backward pass

Now consider activity 7 in Figure 14.7. Its earliest possible finish time is the end of week 8, one week before the earliest possible time for finishing the project at the end of week 9 (activity 8). It is clear that activity 7 could be delayed for up to one week without upsetting the overall timescale and delaying the project. This possible delay can be expressed as a total float of one week, entered in the centre bottom box of the activity. This result is also indicated on the activity box by writing the latest permissible finish time in its bottom right hand corner. The result is found this time, not by addition from left to right through the network, but in exactly the opposite way of subtraction from right to left. So the latest permissible start for activity 7 is seen to be (9 − 2) = 7 (meaning the end of week 7 or the beginning of week 8).

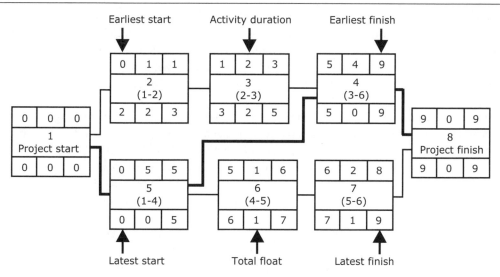

Figure 14.7   Example of precedence network time analysis

The critical path is shown by the bold links. Activity ID numbers in brackets denote the corresponding activities in the arrow version of this network, shown in Figure 14.3.

This subtraction exercise must be repeated throughout the network, working backwards from right to left, writing the latest permissible times and floats along the bottom rows of all the activity boxes. Where more than one path exists, the longest must always be chosen so that the result after subtraction gives the smallest remainder (earliest time). This is illustrated in Figure 14.7 at activity 5, for instance, where the correct subtraction route lies through the activities 8 and 4.

Float or slack

The term 'float' indicates the amount of leeway available for starting and finishing an activity. The subtle differences between the terms 'float' and 'slack' have been lost over the years and the two terms are now synonymous, although there appears to be a preference for slack in the US and float in the UK. There are various categories of float. These are explained in Chapter 16, in the context of deciding priorities during resource scheduling, but they can be ignored for the purposes of this simple example.

Critical path

When all the earliest possible and latest permissible times have been added to the diagram, there will always be at least one chain of activities where the earliest and latest times coincide, indicating zero float. These activities are critical to the successful achievement of the whole project within its earliest possible time and the route following these activities through the network is called the 'critical path'.

Although all activities may be important to successful project conclusion, it is the critical activities that must claim priority for scarce resources and for management attention.

CASE EXAMPLE: FURNITURE PROJECT

The Eaton Sitright company is conducting a development project to design and build a prototype matching chair and desk set for assessment before possibly putting this furniture into full-scale production. This is a small project but, even so, when the company attempted to plan this work using a Gantt chart, it found that the chart was not able clearly to show all the different task interdependencies. For example, neither the chair frame nor the desk frame can be painted until the paint colour has been decided and the paint has been bought but when these constraints were added as links to the Gantt chart the picture became congested and confused. The project has therefore been replanned using network analysis.

Network diagrams can be drawn using the collective minds at a brainstorming session, but for this small project the company was able to produce a complete project task list (which is the simplest form of work breakdown structure). The task list for this furniture project is given in Figure 14.8. Note that this has a column that lists all the activities that must *immediately* precede each activity. In other words, the list states, for each activity, the ID numbers of all activities that must be finished just before the new activity can start. All time estimates are in working days, so that five days are equivalent to one calendar week.

The resulting network diagram for the furniture project is given in Figure 14.9 as an arrow diagram and in Figure 14.10 as the equivalent precedence diagram.

Figure 14.9 clearly illustrates the use of dummies in arrow networks. However, although it is of little consequence now (when computer programs for arrow networks are practically extinct) there is a drafting error because Figure 14.9 has two activities with the same ID numbers 6–14. Had this network been intended for input to a computer, it would have been necessary to add a dummy activity in the path of one of these two parallel activities to create different identifying events.

Time analysis has been completed on both diagrams and, as should be expected, the data are identical. Figure 14.11 tabulates these data in a widely used and practicable format. The tasks have

Activity	Activity description	Duration (days)	Preceding activities
	Chair		
A	Anatomical study for chair	15	None
B	Design chair	5	A
C	Buy materials for chair seat	6	B
D	Make chair seat	3	C
E	Buy chair castors	5	B
F	Buy steel for chair frame	10	B
G	Make chair frame	3	F
H	Paint chair frame	2	G+U
I	Assemble chair	1	D+E+H
J	Apply final finishes to chair	2	I
	Desk		
K	Design desk	10	None
L	Buy steel for desk frame	10	K
M	Make desk frame	5	L+O
N	Paint desk frame	2	M+U
O	Buy wood and fittings for desk	5	K
P	Make desk drawer	6	O
Q	Make desk top	1	O
R	Assemble desk	1	N+P+Q
S	Apply final finishes to desk	2	R
	General activities		
T	Decide paint colours	10	None
U	Buy paint and varnish	8	T
V	Final project evaluation	5	J+S

Figure 14.8 Furniture project: task list

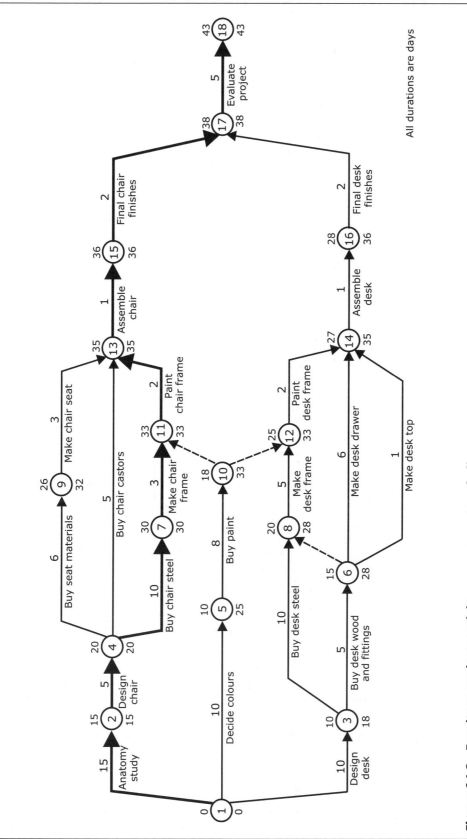

All durations are days

Figure 14.9 Furniture project: activity-on-arrow network diagram

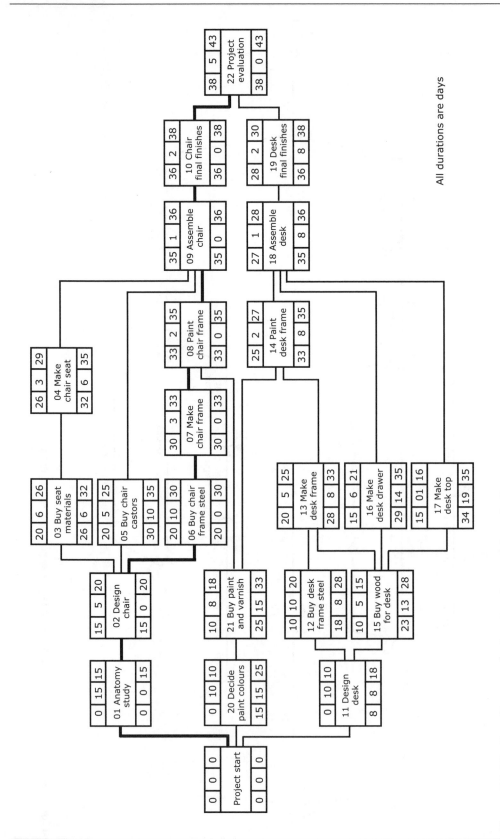

All durations are days

Figure 14.10 Furniture project: precedence network diagram

ADM only		PDM only	Activity	Duration	Earliest	Latest	Earliest	Latest	Total
Prec. Event	Succ. event	Task ID	description	(days)	start	start	finish	finish	float
1	2	01	Anatomical study for chair	15	0	0	15	15	0
2	4	02	Design chair	5	15	15	20	20	0
4	9	03	Buy materials for chair seat	6	20	26	26	32	6
9	13	04	Make chair seat	3	26	32	29	35	6
4	13	05	Buy chair castors	5	20	30	25	35	10
4	7	06	Buy steel for chair frame	10	20	20	30	30	0
7	11	07	Make chair frame	3	30	30	33	33	0
11	13	08	Paint chair frame	2	33	33	35	35	0
13	15	09	Assemble chair	1	35	35	36	36	0
15	17	10	Apply final finishes to chair	2	36	36	38	38	0
1	3	11	Design desk	10	0	8	10	18	8
3	8	12	Buy steel for desk frame	10	10	18	20	28	8
8	12	13	Make desk frame	5	20	28	25	33	8
12	14	14	Paint desk frame	2	25	33	27	35	8
3	6	15	Buy wood and fittings for desk	5	10	23	15	28	13
6	14	16	Make desk drawer	6	15	29	21	35	14
6	14	17	Make desk top	1	15	34	16	35	19
14	16	18	Assemble desk	1	27	35	28	36	8
16	17	19	Apply final finishes to desk	2	28	36	30	38	8
1	5	20	Decide paint colours	10	0	15	10	25	15
5	10	21	Buy paint and varnish	8	10	25	18	33	15
17	18	22	Final project evaluation	5	38	38	43	43	0

Figure 14.11   Furniture project: time analysis

been sorted in this table in ascending order of their precedence ID numbers. Another, more practical, sort sequence would have been in ascending order of earliest start times.

All times are given here are as day numbers. This is typical of a plan where the project start date is not known. As soon as authority is given for a project to start, the start time of the first activity can be converted to the appropriate calendar date, and then all subsequent start and finish times can be given as calendar dates instead of day numbers. A practical working plan would ensure that only working days would be valid for inclusion, so that no task would be scheduled to start, continue or be finished over a weekend or public holiday shutdown. This conversion from numbers to dates is awkward as a mental exercise, especially when weekends and holidays have to be taken into account, but this becomes painless when a computer is used.

The network diagrams in Figures 14.9 and 14.10 both show clearly all the activity interdependencies that a linked Gantt chart could not. Time analysis has indicated all the critical tasks. They are the tasks with zero total float. All these critical tasks must be started and finished at their earliest possible times if this project is to be finished as soon as possible.

MORE COMPLEX NETWORK NOTATION

Overlapping activities in arrow networks

In Figure 14.12 several versions of a small extract from a larger network are shown. Three activities are shown: design engineering, drawing and the procurement of components and materials, a sequence that is common in projects for design and new product development.

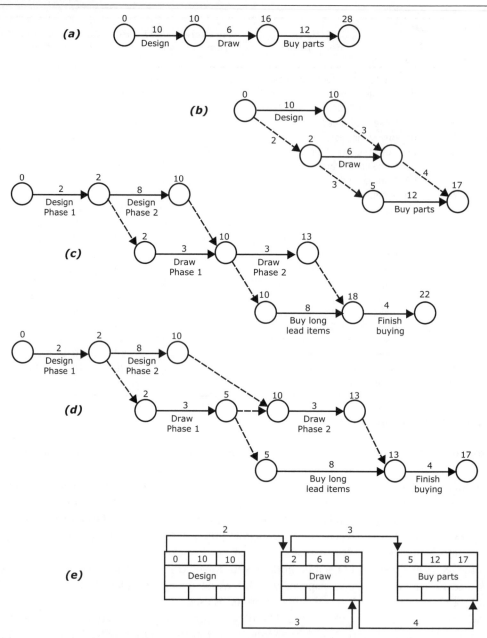

Figure 14.12 Overlapping activities in arrow and precedence networks

Figure 14.12(a) shows the network fragment as it was originally drawn, with the three activities following each other in sequence and bound by rigid finish-to-start constraints. What this network tells us is that each of these activities cannot begin until its immediate predecessor has been completely finished. The combined duration of these activities is 28 weeks.

Re-examination of the network uncovers a fundamental but commonly made flaw in the logic. Does all the engineering design have to be finished before detailed drawing can start? Of course not. These activities can be allowed to overlap to some extent. Similarly, some of the long-lead purchase items can be ordered in advance, as soon as the designers can specify them; it is not necessary to wait for the final parts lists.

In Figure 14.12(b) an attempt has been made to indicate the permissible overlap of activities by redrawing the network fragment. The start and finish constraints have now been relaxed by inserting dummies, each of which has been given a duration value. Drawing can start two weeks after the start of engineering, but cannot be finished until three weeks after the completion of engineering. Purchasing can begin three weeks after the start of drawing, at which time it is estimated that the long-lead items can be specified. Some purchased items cannot be ordered, however, until the parts list is issued along with the general assembly drawing, and delivery of these late-purchased items is not expected until four weeks after the completion of drawing.

By these means the timescale for this small part of the main network has been reduced from 28 to 17 weeks – almost halved. The product can start to come off the production line 11 weeks earlier than if the activity boundaries had been adhered to rigidly.

In arrow notation, overlapped activities drawn as in Figure 14.12(b) are called 'ladder networks' or 'ladder activities'. Although it is drawn to the correct ladder network convention, the logic of Figure 14.12(b) does not stand up to close scrutiny. It might be assumed that drawing could start two weeks after week 0 even if no engineering had been carried out, and that procurement could start at week 5, whatever the state of engineering or drawing. Clearly this was not the planner's intention when the network was drawn, and alternative networks might be suggested.

In Figure 14.12(c) the same sequence of activities has been depicted but, by splitting engineering into two phases and doing something similar with drawing, the true relationships and constraints are more clearly defined. But a different, and wrong, answer has been obtained this time. The mistake lies in the start restriction imposed on buying, which is in fact dependent not on the completion of engineering but only upon phase 1 of the drawing.

The true picture is obtained by drawing the network in Figure 14.12(d), where all the dummies are correctly placed.

It is apparent from this example that ladder networks are not a very elegant solution and other methods for dealing with complex conditions at the boundaries between two activities have exercised the minds of the planning professionals. Some fairly early project management software allowed lags and overlaps to be specified between activities when the data were input. Another useful instruction was to specify two activities as 'tied', meaning that the succeeding activity must start as soon as its predecessor had been finished.

However, most of these problems can now be overcome using the more versatile precedence system. The precedence solution for the arrow network fragment is shown at (e) in Figure 14.12.

Complex constraints using precedence notation

Overlapping activities and other more complex constraints are best served by precedence notation. Complex, in this sense, means any link between two activities that differs from the usual finish-start constraint (which says that an activity can be started as soon as its predecessor has finished, but not before).

Figure 14.13 shows the four types of precedence links that can be used. Even a normal finish-start relationship, shown in Figure 14.13(a), can be made more complex if required by placing a time value on the link. This would force a delay between the finish of one activity and the start of the next. This type of lag relationship is useful for activities such as waiting for concrete to cure or watching paint dry.

Devaux (1999) gives some particularly useful examples of complex constraint applications.

An interesting comparison between arrow and precedence logic

One apparent disadvantage of the precedence system is illustrated in Figure 14.14. Whenever a significant number of activities have to be linked independently to several following activities, the

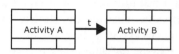

(a) Finish-to-start. Activity B cannot start until t network time units after the finish of Activity A. Most constraints are of this type, but t is usually zero.

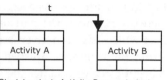

(b) Start-to-start. Activity B cannot start until t network time units after the start of Activity A.

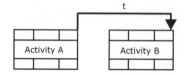

(c) Finish-to-finish. Activity B cannot be finished until t network time units after the finish of Activity A.

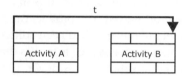

(d) Start-to-finish. Activity B cannot be finished until t network time units after the start of Activity A.

Figure 14.13   Constraint options in precedence networks

The different kinds of links that can be used in a precedence network.

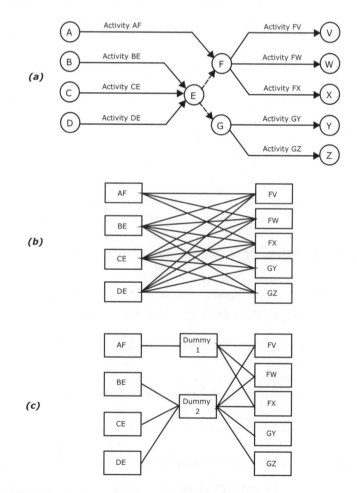

Figure 14.14   Using dummies to clarify cluttered logic

use of dummies in an arrow diagram can seem to produce a clearer diagram than in its precedence counterpart. This can be seen by comparing the arrow network shown at (a) in Figure 14.14 with its precedence equivalent at (b). All parts of Figure 14.14 show the same actual logic.

Although precedence networks do not normally have dummies, these can be introduced artificially as a convenient method for clarifying the logic. The two dummies introduced at Figure 14.14(c) have produced a dramatic improvement in network clarity without changing the actual logic meaning.

REFERENCES AND FURTHER READING

Devaux, S.A. (1999), *Total Project Control: a Manager's Guide to Integrated Planning, Measuring and Tracking* (New York: Wiley).

Gordon, J. and Lockyer, K. (2005), *Project Management and Project Planning*, 7th Edition (London: Financial Times Prentice Hall).

Gray, B., Gray, C. F. and Larson, E.W. (2005), *Project Management: the Managerial Process*, 3rd Edition (Singapore: McGraw-Hill).

15 *Detailed Planning: Critical Path Networks in Practice*

T he previous chapter introduced project network analysis by explaining the diagramming methods and demonstrating the principles of time analysis. This chapter describes procedures and methods needed to implement project network analysis successfully in practice. Several of the steps described anticipate the use of a computer for time analysis, resource scheduling and reporting.

DEVELOPING THE NETWORK LOGIC

Network diagrams provide the notation that enables planners to document the processes for executing a project, clearly, in great detail and in the preferred sequence. This is a valuable tool that should always be fully exploited. Brainstorming is probably the best approach for any new project because it can extract and combine the thoughts of the best available minds.

Arranging a brainstorming meeting

The number of people involved in drawing a network clearly depends to some extent on the size of the project and its organization. It is customary, and desirable, to have at least one responsible person on hand who can speak for each department or suborganization involved. The participants should be of sufficient seniority to enable them to commit their departments to the resulting plan, and to any intended work processes or strategies upon which the agreed plan and its time estimates are based.

The network should be drawn rapidly, as large as possible and in full view of all those who are contributing information. Nowadays it is easy to draw a network directly with a computer and the use of a projector means that everyone present at the meeting can follow the process. Unfortunately the computer is not capable of displaying an entire network of any significant size on a single screen, which means that it is necessary to scroll up, down and across the screen to see the whole picture. Ideally everyone at the meeting should be able to see the whole logic pattern as it develops and be able to follow every path through from start to finish. A large sheet or roll of paper laid out on a long table or fixed to a wall is still the method that I prefer.

Arrow notation is best suited to this brainstorming purpose, because it can be sketched far more quickly than a precedence diagram. It is always easy to convert an arrow diagram to precedence later, after the meeting, thus saving the precious and costly time of all those attending the meeting. However, as explained in the previous chapter, if a precedence diagram is to be sketched the process can be helped by the use of a Post-it note for each activity.

A useful time-saving kit for sketching arrow networks comprises:

- A large sheet or roll of paper, arranged so that it can be seen by all those taking part in the meeting
- A supply of sharpened soft pencils
- A soft eraser
- A long ruler
- A template for drawing event circles (which can be a hole carefully drilled in the aforementioned ruler).

Initial networks can, of course, be drawn freehand but a ruler and circle template will help to keep the initial sketch neat and relatively small without adding significantly to the time needed. A sprawling sketch can prove awkward if it causes the network to overflow the sheet when the later stages are reached. Whilst an initial network sketch can be redrawn more tidily after the meeting, if it is not produced with a little care in the first place it will soon become unreadable and vague because of the inevitable erasures, corrections and additions made during the meeting.

Contribution of the planning expert

It has to be assumed that the person who wields the pencil and commits all the working proposals to paper is competent to do so. The person entrusted with this task should be as skilled and experienced a network analyst as possible.

The task of the expert will be made easier if everyone present has received some prior training and is able easily to follow the meaning of the network as it grows. Although complete mastery of the art of network logic takes time and practice, the essential elements are not difficult and can be learned in a few hours.

There are several pitfalls that can rob a potential expert of accuracy and success. Although all network logic is built from only a few simple basic symbols, it is not always easy to assemble those symbols in a way that avoids mistakes. To a great extent the degree of success depends on the aptitude of the individual. Getting the logic right can be compared to solving a recreational puzzle. Some people see the challenge of drawing networks in that light. Networking can, indeed, be fun.

Give three different project planners the same data for a project, and they would probably produce three different networks, each signifying a different personal vision of how the work should logically proceed. This does not necessarily mean that any of the networks is wrong. Each proposed method of working could be valid, and lead to a satisfactory result.

A skilled analyst should be allowed to control the brainstorming meeting effectively (regardless of seniority). He or she will ensure that the logic develops along the right lines, asking check questions from time to time in order to prove the logic and avoid errors. Check questions can take the following forms:

- 'We've shown work starting on site immediately but should we deliver some machinery first, or set up a site hut, or deliver some materials?'
- 'Won't it be necessary to check these drawings before they can be issued?'
- 'Is customer approval needed before work can start on this activity?'
- 'Does this steelwork need priming or any other protective treatment before erection?'
- 'Can this tower really be erected as soon as the concrete base has been poured, or will it ooze slowly downwards into wet cement?
- 'This method failed us badly on the last project. Isn't there a better way?'
- 'Does the start of this activity really depend on all these incoming activities?'
- 'OK, you've told me to add this activity marked "transfer all data from old system" but can this be done safely after "install computer" or should we insert an activity for debugging and testing the system?'

A diagram that emerges from the initial meeting bearing the scars of many erasures and changes shows that a great deal of active and careful thought has gone into the logic. The network analyst must never be too lazy or too reluctant to erase and redraw parts of the network as the combined brainpower of the meeting develops and agrees the preferred logic.

Common error trap in arrow logic

It is possible to introduce logical errors unwittingly as the plan builds up. An example is shown in Figure 15.1, which is a classic trap well known to all experts who use arrow logic during planning sessions.

Imagine that a construction firm is drawing up a network for the planning and control of a new building project. Figure 15.1(a) shows a fragment of this network at an early stage during the planning meeting. Notice that the roof frame cannot be started until the brick walls have been erected because, obviously, it has to be built on top of the walls. The roof frame will be built by a carpenter from wood, and so the roof frame also depends on the timber being purchased. All of this is recognized in the network logic at event 30. So far, so good.

Pointing of the brickwork can start as soon as the walls have been built, after event 30. The trap is to draw the logic as shown in Figure 15.1(a), simply by adding the activity for pointing the brickwork as emerging from event 30. This logic is wrong because it is not necessary to buy the roof timbers before the brick walls can be pointed. The planner has corrected this mistake by introducing the dummy 21–30, shown in Figure 15.1(b).

The planner who uses arrow notation must always question the logic when there are multiple input activities and output activities at an event, as in the general pattern of Figure 15.1(c). The correct precedence equivalent of this logic is shown at Figure 15.1(d). It is more difficult to make this

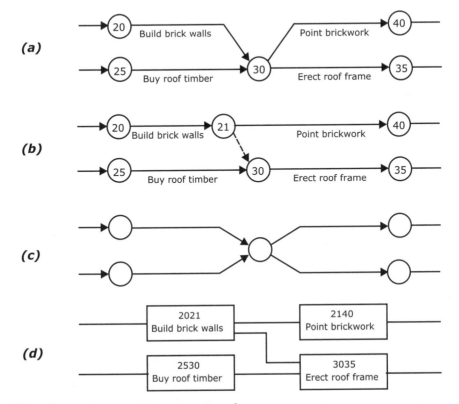

Figure 15.1   Common error in arrow networks

particular kind of mistake using precedence. However, it is still good practice, whatever the notation used, to check the logic wherever multiple links enter and leave a node.

LEVEL OF DETAIL IN NETWORK PLANNING

A question often facing planners new to the art is 'How much detail should we show in the network?' In other words which activities should be included in the network and which should be left out or combined with others? To some extent this depends on the size and duration of the project, the duration units chosen, the amount of detailed knowledge available and the purpose of the network.

Guidelines

There are several guidelines and hints that can help to decide the level of detail which should be shown in project network diagrams.

Activities with relatively very short durations

It is probably well to avoid showing jobs as separate activities if their durations amount only to a very small fraction of the expected overall timescale, especially if they do not require resources. Of course these activities cannot be ignored, but they can often be included in the network as parts of other activities. An example is the preparation of a set of drawings for a single component or small subassembly. There might be 20 drawings in such a set, each of which has to be drawn and checked. If each of these drawings were to be shown separately on the network, that would add 40 activities (20 for all the drawing tasks and a further 20 for the checking). But the planner knows that this set of drawings will be produced as one lot in the same department, all under the control of one manager or supervisor, so that they can be lumped together on the plan. So, instead of 40 activities, the plan will have just two, namely:

- Draw sub-assembly X
- Check sub-assembly X.

In a project lasting only a few weeks (for example, the overhaul and maintenance of an electricity generating station during a planned shutdown period) it would be reasonable to use network planning units of days or fractions of days, and to include activities lasting only half a day or less. For projects lasting several years, the planning units might be weeks, with very few activities included that have less than one week's duration.

As with all rules, however, there are exceptions. Some activities with very short durations might be so important that they must be included. One example is an activity for obtaining authorization or approval before subsequent work can proceed. That activity might have a duration of only one day, but it could also be a milestone.

Level of detail in relation to task responsibility

A network path should be interrupted whenever the action moves from one department or organization to another – in other words where the immediate management responsibility for executing the work changes. In the days when practically everyone used arrow networks this concept was easy to define: a new event should be created whenever responsibility progressed from one manager to another (or from one department to another). In precedence networks this rule can be expressed by saying that if a single activity covers consecutive tasks by two different departments, it should be split into two activities, so that each task has only one manager responsible for it.

A useful guide is to remember that the ultimate purpose of the network is going to be to allow the project work to be scheduled and controlled. In due course, work-to-do lists for different managers will be generated from the network. The network must, therefore, contain all the jobs needed for these lists. This means that:

- No network activity should be so large that it cannot be assigned for the principal control of one and only one department or manager.
- An activity that is long compared to the project timescale should probably be broken into two or more activities. This will ensure that the plan provides frequent progress monitoring checkpoints.

A network that is sufficiently detailed will enable project stages such as those in the following examples to be identified, planned and progressed:

1. work authorization, either as an internal works order or as the receipt of a customer order or contract;
2. drawing and design approvals from the customer (especially where the absence of these might hold up work during the course of the project);
3. financial authorizations from the customer where the contract requires that these be obtained before expenditure can be committed to significant purchases or new phases of the project;
4. local authority planning application and consent;
5. the start and finish of design for any manufactured subassembly, construction work area or significant part of a management change project. If the planned duration of a design task is longer than two or three weeks it might be advisable to break the design task down into shorter activities, corresponding to identifiable design phases;
6. release of completed drawings for production or construction (probably for specific sets of drawings rather than for individual sheets);
7. the start of purchasing activity for each subassembly or work package, signified by the engineering issue of a bill of material, purchase specification or advance release of information for items which are known to have long delivery times;
8. issue of invitations to tender or purchase enquiries;
9. receipt and analysis of suppliers' or subcontractors' bids;
10. following on from 7, 8 and 9, the issue of a purchase order to a supplier or subcontractor (again at the level of work packages and subassemblies rather than small individual purchases);
11. delivery of materials to the point of usage – this might be the most significant or last-expected item needed for a subsequent project activity: for international projects, this delivery point may be to a ship or to an aircraft, with subsequent transit time shown as a separate, consecutive activity (when responsibility transfers from the supplier to the carrier or freight forwarding agent);
12. the starts and completions of manufacturing stages (in large projects usually only looking at the entries into, and exits from, production control responsibility and again considering work packages or subassemblies rather than individual small parts);
13. the starts and finishes of construction subcontracts, and important intermediate events in such subcontracts (see the section on milestones later in this chapter);
14. handover events for completed work packages – this would include handing over the finished project (or substantial parts of it) to the customer, but would also ensure that associated items such as the compilation of maintenance and operating manuals were itemized in the network plan.

These are, of course, only guidelines. The list is neither mandatory nor complete.

Level of detail in relation to activity costs

Cost control methods are described later in this book but certain aspects of cost reporting and control will be impossible if sufficient attention to certain activities is not given when the network diagram is prepared.

It is possible to assign a cost to an activity, such as the purchase of materials. If an activity is included on the network for the planned issue of every significant purchase order, then the purchase order value can be assigned to these activities. This makes possible the preparation of reports from the computer which will list these costs at the times when the orders are placed, thus giving a schedule of purchase cost commitments.

If another activity is added for the receipt of goods against each of these purchase orders, the same order value can be assigned to these later activities. Using suitable computer techniques, cost schedules can be derived that relate to the time when invoices will become due. The timing of these schedules will indicate actual cash flow requirements, rather than purchase commitments.

None of this would be possible with insufficient detail on the network. Figure 15.2 illustrates this case.

The small upper network shows the entire purchasing process for a large piece of equipment as one activity. That might be adequate in an enormous project where it is necessary to restrict the total number of activities and where the project manager can delegate the purchasing activity to the purchasing department with complete confidence. The expanded version of the network, in the lower part of Figure 15.2, lies towards the other extreme. It gives the project manager far more assistance in the preparation of working schedules and allows more detailed supervision of the purchase process.

Is size important? Should a large network be broken down into smaller networks?

Networks containing thousands of activities might sound impressive, but they become unwieldy, difficult to follow and subject to errors. Although, in the distant past, I have successfully used networks drawn on paper showing over 1000 activities, this is not possible using today's computer screens. This problem can be overcome to some extent by choosing the level of network detail carefully, as explained in the previous section.

Some companies draw outline networks of their projects, perhaps containing only 100 or 150 activities in fairly coarse detail. These are used as higher-level management controls. Every summary

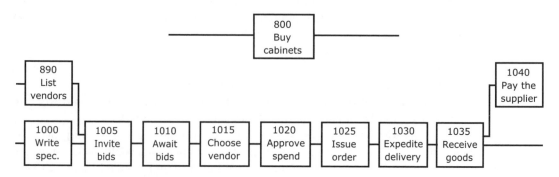

Figure 15.2   Level of detail in a purchasing sequence

project network must then be backed up by a set of detailed networks, each of which is produced by or for the project department whose activities it covers. All these constituent networks must be tied together and to the summary plan so that their corresponding events or activities are scheduled on the same dates and have the same degree of float or slack.

This correlation can be achieved by designating all the detailed networks as subnetworks of the main control network and by identifying shared events or activities as interface events or activities (see the following section).

INTERFACE EVENTS AND ACTIVITIES

There are several circumstances in which an activity or event in one network can have a logical link with, or impose a constraint on, an activity or event in another network. The need to identify interface activities or events arises most frequently in projects where the total project network has been broken down into a number of smaller, more manageable subnetworks. This might be the result of a work breakdown or organizational breakdown decision. It could also be that several small network modules or templates have to be merged to constitute the whole network (a technique described in Chapter 29). There are occasions when a common interface appears in more than two subnetworks, for example when several subnetworks share the same start or finish.

Interfaces should only be allowed for true logical links. They should not be used in an attempt to depict operational problems such as attempting to delay the start of an activity until resources come free from an activity in another project. Such competition for scarce resources requires a different approach, for which more appropriate methods will be described in the following chapters.

Each interface in a precedence logic diagram should be identified by encasing the activity box with double ruled lines, as shown in Figure 15.3. Interface events in arrow diagrams are similarly identified by using two concentric circles instead of a single circle, but this use is now rare because the complexity of interfacing several networks needs the use of a computer, and no modern software of which I am aware can process arrow networks.

MILESTONES

An important purpose of any plan is to produce a schedule from which project progress can be managed. Progress checkpoints must be provided at suitable intervals throughout every network and any schedules that are derived from it. Events or activities that have particular significance can each be designated as milestones. A milestone is achieved when the relevant milestone activity is finished in a precedence network or when a milestone event is achieved in an arrow network.

Figure 15.3   Network interfaces

An interface is a node that is common to two or more different network diagrams. Each interface is given the same ID number and description wherever it appears, so that the computer will identify it as the same event or activity. Interfaces thus link the different networks together. Interfaces are usually drawn with a double-ruled border.

Computer programs for project scheduling allow reports to be filtered and printed so that they contain only milestones. These greatly help the assessment of progress against time and costs and are of value in reporting to higher management and (when the contract demands) to the customer. Some milestones can be associated with stage or progress payments, according to contractual agreements between clients and contractors.

Milestones are described in more detail in Chapter 27, in the context of measuring progress and value achieved.

ESTIMATING TASK DURATIONS

Either when the network is drawn, or as soon after as possible, it is necessary for all the task durations to be estimated. These estimates are for the time that will pass from the start of each task to its finish (the elapsed time). Duration estimates do not necessarily relate directly to cost estimates or work content.

Units of duration

What units of duration should be used? This will often depend on the duration of the project. Days are very often used and are suggested as the default units in most computer software, with weekends assumed as non-working days so that five units are equivalent to one calendar week. For projects that are expected to last for a very long time it might be more convenient to estimate using weeks. However, even when the project duration extends to several years, the use of day units is no problem when a computer is used for the subsequent calculations and calendar date conversions.

If the chosen software allows, or when doing all the calculations mentally, a very useful unit for general purposes is the half-day, since many projects are conducted on a five-day week basis and a week then becomes 10 units. Resolution of estimates to better than half-day duration is not usually required, but some computer programs can even accept minutes.

Once a unit of duration has been decided, the same unit should be used consistently throughout the network. Some computer programs (including Microsoft Project) will allow different units of time to be mixed in the same network but that practice can result in messy and horrible printouts.

The choice of duration units will, of course, ultimately determine how the numbers on a network will be converted into the more practicable calendars dates. This raises the questions of public holidays and shift working. Specification of working calendars and the conversion of network times into calendar dates are subjects that are explored further in the context of resource scheduling and computer applications, particularly in Chapters 17 and 20.

Procedure for estimating activity durations

The usual procedure is for the estimates to be added as the network is drawn, during a planning meeting. That occasion has the advantage that all of the key managers and supervisors should be present. Another approach is for the network sketch to be carried from one department to another, each responsible manager adding estimates to the activities for which they are responsible.

Some people recommend that activities should be estimated at random rather than in a continuous left-to-right sequence. They argue that estimating sequentially along network paths could lead to early awareness of possible critical activities or programme overruns. In other words, the impartiality of the estimators might become impaired, the estimates being influenced by project demands rather than by the true nature of each job and the time properly required to complete it.

Overtime

Convention and commonsense demand that any temptation to assume that overtime will be worked should be avoided. Thus estimated durations should not be made with overtime working in view. Whilst overtime can often be used to shorten the elapsed time of an activity, it should always be regarded as a reserve resource, to be held back for use as a corrective action against unforeseen (but inevitable) contingencies.

Early consideration of resource constraints and their effects upon activity durations

Nothing has been said so far about possible scarcity of resources and the additional constraints that such shortages of people, cash or materials might impose on the network logic or estimated activity durations.

Consider, for example, the simplest case of a resource constraint, where one particular individual is going to have to perform several network activities single-handed. Assume that this person cannot perform two activities at the same time. The planner, knowing this, might be tempted to add dummies or links to the network to indicate this resource constraint and prevent any two of these activities from being planned as simultaneous tasks. But if all these activities lie on different paths in a complex network, where should the linking constraints be placed to avoid double-booking the resource? Before time analysis has been completed the planner cannot possibly know (and should not assume) in which order and at what times all these jobs should be performed.

Similar worries about resources might attach to other activities where the resource requirements are more complex, when several tasks can be allowed to run in parallel or overlap provided that the total resources needed do not exceed the total available.

Fortunately there is a simple solution to the problem of all such resource constraints. IGNORE THEM! No, this is not a question of opting out from responsibility. The purpose of drawing the initial network is to establish the logic of the most desirable work pattern (assuming no resource constraints). Time analysis follows to establish the amount of float available, which effectively allots priority values to all activities. All of this information provides a sound basis for *subsequent* resource scheduling, which is a quite *separate* procedure (described in following chapters). Planning and scheduling have to be carried forward step by logical step, and consideration of resource constraints is a step that is not usually taken when the first network is drawn.

However, the planner must use common sense in this respect. Suppose that an activity requiring skilled fitters has been estimated to require 150 man-hours, and that several people could work on the task if required (without getting in each other's way). The duration for this activity would therefore depend on the number of people assigned. Suppose that the resource/time relationship for this activity is as follows:

- 1 fitter for twenty days

or

- 2 fitters for ten days

or

- 3 fitters for seven days

or

- 4 fitters for 5 days

and so on.

The correct approach in these circumstances is for the planner is to ask the manager (or delegate) of the department responsible to say how many fitters would be best for this task, and write the corresponding duration on the network. The possible demands of other activities on these fitters are disregarded at this stage. However, if the company only employs two suitable fitters in total, the planner would be stupid to schedule more than two for this or any other activity. This is where common sense comes in.

IS THE PREDICTED TIMESCALE TOO LONG?

A new network diagram should always be checked to ensure that it reflects the most practicable and efficient way of working. More often than not, however, the first forward pass through an expertly drawn network will predict a completion date that is far too late. The planner will then be under pressure to come up with an alternative shorter plan (which might have to satisfy a delivery promise already made to a customer).

The planner might be tempted to cut estimates arbitrarily, perhaps on the ill-considered advice of other managers, until the work fits neatly into the timescale. That must, of course, never be considered as a valid option unless good reasons can be given to show how the shorter times can be achieved.

To examine common methods that can help to solve these problems, we can revisit the museum project that was introduced in Chapter 5. Remember that Chapter 5 dealt with initial, provisional planning early in the stages of the project life cycle. Those were outline plans intended to support the business case. Now the time has been reached in the project cycle where the project has been authorized, or is about to be authorized. Now it is necessary to plan with the care and attention to detail that will produce practicable working schedules from which to issue and control work.

CASE EXAMPLE: MUSEUM PROJECT

The museum project was first described in Chapter 5 and its provisional plan is illustrated in the Gantt charts of Figures 5.3 and 5.4. Those charts indicated a total project time of 36 weeks which, allowing five working days per week and ignoring holidays, amounts to a target project duration of 180 days. For simplicity, I shall use days as duration units in this section, and I shall continue to ignore calendar dates and holidays. (In practice, with the use of a computer, holiday allowances and calendar conversions would be easy and automatic, and would take account of all specified holidays and other non-working days.)

We pick this project up at a point when all design is complete and approved, the contractors have been appointed, and the Liverchester council is just about to give permission for actual work on the project sites to begin.

First network diagram for the museum project

Being a sensible person, the director of the Liverchester entertainments department, as soon as he heard that the museum project had been approved, decided to hire the services of a professional project manager (Helen) to oversee the project. Helen's first actions were to familiarize herself with the project design, the business plan and the intended project strategy. She also studied the departmental organization in order to identify the key personnel and to gain some idea of the resources available internally.

From the earlier Gantt chart (Figure 5.3) and the business plan Helen noted that the expected completion time for this project was 36 weeks, equivalent to 180 working days. Deciding immediately and wisely that a more detailed plan would be needed to control this project, Helen organized a planning meeting with relevant senior council staff and, using brainstorming methods, she

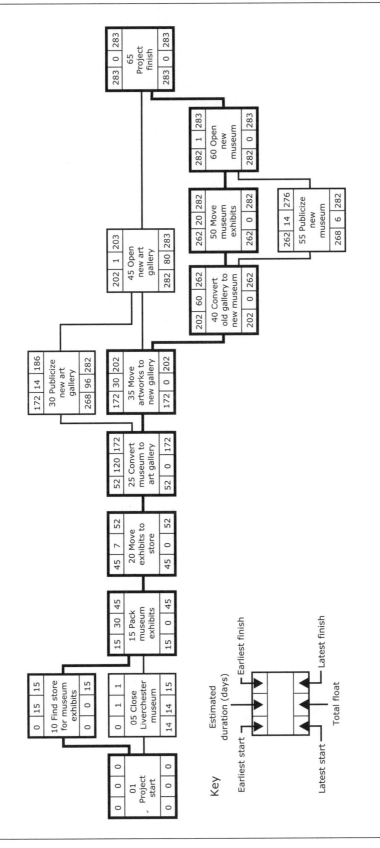

Figure 15.4 Museum project: first precedence diagram

produced the draft network diagram shown in Figure 15.4. The associated time analysis results are tabulated in Figure 15.5.

Some of the larger tasks in this museum project must be entrusted to various subcontractors, and each of those will be expected to plan their contribution to the project in greater detail. So, the network in Figure 15.4 is, to some extent, a summary plan.

As drawn, the network plan and its time analysis indicates that the opening of the new art gallery might be delayed until day 283 whereas, in fact, the Liverchester council would probably want to open it as soon as possible, which appears to be day 202. However, we can ignore this anomaly for the present and, in practice, the gallery would of course be opened without waiting for the end of the entire project.

This initial network plan is based on sound logical reasoning. Although its strategy still follows broadly the original intentions expressed in the Gantt chart of Figure 5.4, Helen has asked everyone involved in the planning process to review and confirm the task duration estimates, and this has resulted in a few changes from their earlier thoughts, partly as a result of talking to the appointed sub-contractors.

So, now we have a network plan for the authorized museum project. But see what has happened to the planned duration! Where the Gantt chart for the business plan predicted a project lasting 36 weeks, the revised estimates in this better-considered plan now forecast an earliest possible project completion at day 283, which is 57 weeks after the project start. That, clearly, is not acceptable and something will have to be done about it.

This shock result from the first network time analysis is very common in project planning, and several methods have evolved over the past 60 years or so for reducing the overlong project durations. Methods that might now be listed include the following:

- Shorten the estimates arbitrarily until the plan is reduced back to 180 days. That recipe for disaster should be explored no further, because it relies on wishful thinking and unfounded optimism.

Task ID	Task description	Duration (days)	Earliest start	Latest start	Earliest finish	Latest finish	Total float
01	Project start	0	0	0	0	0	0
05	Close Liverchester museum	1	0	14	1	15	14
10	Find store for museum exhibits	15	0	0	15	15	0
15	Pack museum exhibits	30	15	15	45	45	0
20	Move museum exhibits to store	7	45	45	52	52	0
25	Convert museum to art gallery	120	52	52	172	172	0
30	Publicize new art gallery	14	172	268	186	282	96
35	Move artworks to new art gallery	30	172	172	202	202	0
40	Convert old art gallery to new museum	60	202	202	262	262	0
45	Open new art gallery	1	202	282	203	283	80
50	Move exhibits from store to new museum	20	262	262	282	282	0
55	Publicize new museum	14	262	268	276	282	6
60	Open new museum	1	282	282	283	283	0
65	Project finish	0	283	283	283	283	0

Figure 15.5 Museum project: time analysis of the initial network diagram

- Shorten the estimates for some or all of the tasks on the critical path by injecting more resources, or by changing the proposed working methods. This is the basis of a method known as 'crashing' or, in its more sophisticated form, 'cost/time optimization'.
- Re-examine the network logic, and ask whether every finish-start constraint is strictly necessary. Are there some tasks that could be started earlier? Overlapping tasks or running them concurrently instead of serially is the basis of a process that is called 'fast-tracking'.
- Combine crashing and fast-tracking to obtain the benefits of both methods.

Crashing the museum project

To shorten the planned duration of the museum project, Helen's first approach was to attempt some crash actions. Attention must be focused on critical activities because there is no point in spending extra effort and money in trying to speed up a task that has plenty of float, and thus is not critical.

During a series of hastily convened meetings with council officers and sub-contractors, the following possible steps were discussed.

1. **Task 15** – reduce the time needed to pack the museum exhibits from 30 days to 15 days by hiring temporary staff from an external agency. The additional cost was estimated at £1200 (which works out at an additional cost of £80 for each of the 15 day's time saved).
2. **Task 25** – after discussion with all the subcontractors, it was agreed that work would start earlier each day, and run late into each evening, with each day divided into two working shifts. Night shifts were considered but ruled out on the grounds of expected opposition from nearby residents. It was agreed that the time required for this task could be reduced from 120 days to 80 days, thus saving 40 days. The subcontractors would be involved in some additional overtime costs and the payment of shift working premiums, which they must pass on to the council. The 40 days saved on this task would therefore add £24 000, which equates to £600 for every day's time saved.
3. **Task 35** – this task, moving the artworks from the gallery to their new home, requires special care involving scarce, highly skilled labour. Helen was able to negotiate possible new subcontract terms for this work and reduce the time required from 30 to 20 days. However the specialist contractor involved was demanding an additional price of £15 000, a cost of £1500 for each day saved. Helen considered that this contractor was taking unfair advantage of the situation and that the rate was unacceptable (she actually used far stronger language to express her disapproval). Thus this possible crash action was rejected.
4. **Task 40** – the conversion of the old art gallery to the new museum would be relatively easy, because the premises were already secure and air-conditioned. It was agreed with the subcontractors involved that the total time required could be reduced from 60 to 40 days by working overtime and weekends. This saving of 20 days could be accomplished by spending an additional £10 000, which worked out at £500 for each day saved.
5. **Task 50** – Drafting in extra hands from other council departments for this relatively unskilled task would reduce the time needed to move the museum exhibits from their temporary store to the new museum building from 20 days to 15 days at no additional cost to the project. That action was agreed.

The revised network plan is shown in Figure 15.6 and the resulting time analysis is given in Figure 15.7. The 80 days total time saved by crash actions 1, 2, 4 and 5 have reduced the planned time for the museum project from 283 days to 203 days, against the original business plan requirement of 180 days. This considerable improvement will, however, add a total of £35 200 to the £500 000 original project cost estimate.

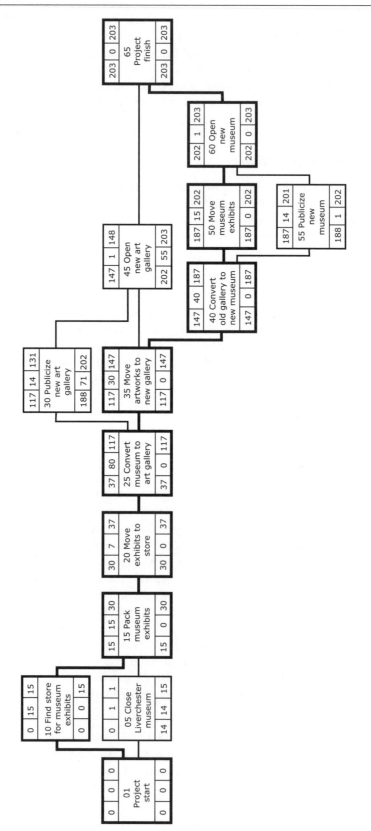

Figure 15.6   Museum project: network with crashed times

Task ID	Task description	Duration (days)	Earliest start	Latest start	Earliest finish	Latest finish	Total float
01	Project start	0	0	0	0	0	0
05	Close Liverchester museum	1	0	14	1	15	14
10	Find store for museum exhibits	15	0	0	15	15	0
15	Pack museum exhibits	15	15	15	30	30	0
20	Move museum exhibits to store	7	30	30	37	37	0
25	Convert museum to art gallery	80	37	37	117	117	0
30	Publicize new art gallery	14	117	188	131	202	71
35	Move artworks to new art gallery	30	117	117	147	147	0
40	Convert old art gallery to new museum	40	147	147	187	187	0
45	Open new art gallery	1	147	202	148	203	55
50	Move exhibits from store to new museum	15	187	187	202	202	0
55	Publicize new museum	14	187	188	201	202	1
60	Open new museum	1	202	202	203	203	0
65	Project finish	0	203	203	203	203	0

Figure 15.7   Museum project: time analysis after crash actions

Crashing for time/cost optimization

In a larger project than this museum project, the network diagram would have many more branches and a greater number of critical or near-critical tasks. When the project manager or planner attempts to crash such a network, they must bear in mind the cost per day's time saved. We have already seen that in the museum project the cost per day saved could vary from zero for task 50 to £1500 per day for task 35.

In the case of a larger network diagram, the planner might not need to crash all the critical activities to achieve the required earlier project completion. In that case it would be wise to choose first those tasks that cost least money per day's time saved.

When one or more critical tasks are crashed, it is possible that the original critical path is no longer the longest path through the network, and other tasks become critical. So, to shorten the project duration still further, tasks on the new critical path have to be crashed. That, in turn, can cause yet another path or paths to become critical. In fact it is possible to imagine this process of crashing to be continued, critical task by critical task, until nearly all tasks in the shortened project have become critical.

The optimum cost-to-project-time saved is achieved by always choosing first the activities that are cheapest to crash. When taken to its limit, the process will produce a network in which the project can be completed for the shortest possible time (according to the revised network logic) for the least possible additional cost.

This concept of an optimum cost to crashed time relationship is fine in theory but must be regarded with some circumspection in practice. Remember that every task duration in a network diagram is only an estimate – the best judgement that people can make. When work actually takes place, the time/cost relationships are almost bound to change as the project progresses and problems occur. Nevertheless, the principle of cost/time optimization is a good one to follow when time is paramount.

Concurrency or fast-tracking for the museum project

The position with the museum project so far is that by spending an additional £35 200 the planned project duration can be crashed from 283 days to 203 days. However, this is still 23 days more than the 180 days required in the business plan. Helen could always change her mind and agree to pay the extra £15 000 to crash task 35, but that would be unacceptable. So what else might be done?

Network logic should always be questioned to ensure that the constraints shown are really necessary. Does the start of every task really depend upon all its predecessors being completely finished? Well, sometimes that is not the case. It is usually possible to find tasks in a network that can be allowed to overlap other tasks or even run concurrently with them.

In the museum project, the following options become apparent when re-examining the network logic.

1. **Tasks 10 and 15** – why not begin to pack the museum exhibits as soon as the museum is closed? There is no need to wait until a suitable store is found. That could save 15 days.
2. **Tasks 15 and 20** – the first batch of goods could be packed and ready for removal 3 days after the start of task 15 and a start-start link has been included to show that fact. However, the beginning of removals cannot actually begin until the storage facility is ready, at the end of task 10. Packing and removals can be allowed to take place simultaneously to some extent, but Helen has estimated that all packing must be finished 6 days before removals can end, and this has been indicated by the finish-finish link between tasks 15 and 20.
3. **Tasks 25 and 35** – some rooms in the new art gallery will be ready before completion of task 25 and it would physically be possible to move some of the paintings earlier. However, this action has been ruled out on security grounds because of the risk of theft or damage to the valuable artworks.
4. **Tasks 40 and 50** – most of the museum exhibits have far less intrinsic value than the artworks and it would be feasible to begin moving them as soon as rooms in the new museum become available. Tasks 40 and 50 could, therefore, be overlapped by 5 days. The times allocated to the start-to-start and finish-to-finish links between tasks 40 and 50 have been calculated to provide this overlap.

Following options 1, 2 and 4 above has shaved 20 more days off the planned project duration, bringing the total estimate down to 183 days. This is considered to be close enough to the original 180-day target. The final network diagram is shown in Figure 15.8 and its resulting time analysis is given in Figure 15.9.

This case example has shown that when the project duration cannot be shortened sufficiently either by fast-tracking or by crashing alone, the two methods can be combined.

Crashing versus fast-tracking: which is the better approach?

Most networks only use simple finish-start relationships but the experienced planner will always bear in mind the availability of complex precedence constraints and use them in those cases where the project might benefit from the potential time saving.

One clear advantage of fast-tracking by overlapping tasks or allowing jobs to run concurrently is that, unlike crashing, it adds no cost to a project. It can, however, add risk. When one task is started before another is completely finished, especially in design engineering and drawing, there is always a risk that some work will have to be scrapped and done again.

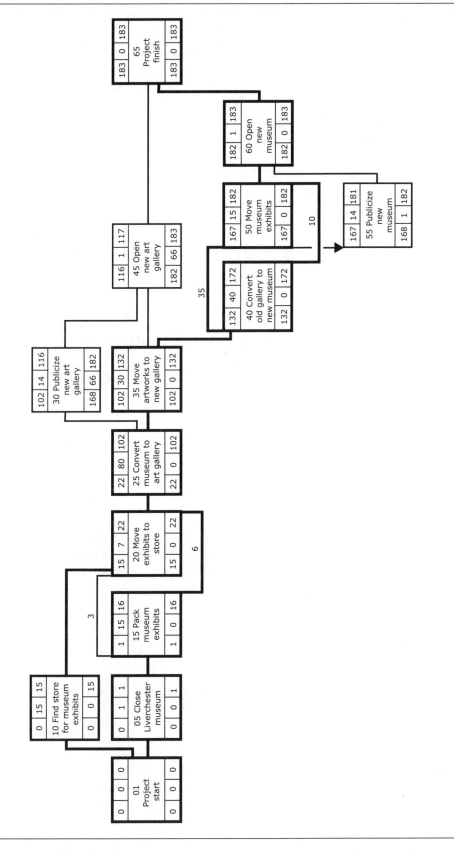

Figure 15.8   Museum project: network crashed and fast-tracked

Task ID	Task description	Duration (days)	Earliest start	Latest start	Earliest finish	Latest finish	Total float
01	Project start	0	0	0	0	0	0
05	Close Liverchester museum	1	0	0	1	1	0
10	Find store for museum exhibits	15	0	0	15	15	0
15	Pack museum exhibits	15	1	1	16	16	0
20	Move museum exhibits to store	7	15	15	22	22	0
25	Convert museum to art gallery	80	22	22	102	102	0
30	Publicize new art gallery	14	102	168	116	182	66
35	Move artworks to new art gallery	30	117	117	147	147	0
40	Convert old art gallery to new museum	40	132	132	172	172	0
45	Open new art gallery	1	116	182	117	183	66
50	Move exhibits from store to new museum	15	167	167	182	182	0
55	Publicize new museum	14	167	168	181	182	1
60	Open new museum	1	182	182	183	183	0
65	Project finish	0	183	183	183	183	0

Figure 15.9   Museum project: time analysis after crashing and fast-tracking

A CASE FOR DRAWING NETWORKS FROM RIGHT TO LEFT

The following case illustrates how a skilled and experienced network planner can control and lead a brainstorming meeting to extract a workable plan from a seemingly hopeless situation. The example also points to a circumstance where it can be better to draw the network from right to left, from finish to start. This is based on a true story, which had a happy ending.

Medical trade exhibition case example

A project had been in progress for several months. Its purpose was to provide prototypes or production models from four related development streams and assemble them on a stand at a national trade exhibition. The product designs came from different geographical locations in the company but all were the responsibility of one production management organization and included the following items:

- prefabricated modular hospital operating theatres
- a range of electronic patient monitoring devices for intensive-care purposes
- heart-lung machines and associated equipment
- large steam and gas sterilizers.

The target end date for this project was fixed by the opening date of the exhibition and was fast approaching. Planning had been neglected, and there was a problem caused by poor coordination between different parts of the company. The situation had been allowed to drift out of control. The divisional manager therefore called in an experienced network planner, arranged a meeting of all the managers responsible for the various products, and put the planner in charge.

The planner (let's call her Dorothy) found that no one could say what the current state of progress was. There were so many loose ends that no one knew where to start making a plan. Dorothy asked everyone to concentrate on the end event, with the exhibition stand ready for the opening day. This final event was then drawn at the right-hand end of the network sheet (as a circle in arrow notation). 'I want you to picture the stand just before the exhibition is opened and the visitors pour in', said Dorothy. 'What is the last thing to be done to make the stand ready and presentable?' Slowly the answer came, 'Vacuum the carpets and generally clean up.' This activity arrow was drawn in front of the final event.

And so the questioning continued, going into more and more detail. The confidence of the members at the meeting grew, and so did the network – from right to left. Duration estimates were added as it went along.

The network continued to expand in a series of logical steps, working through each product to be exhibited in turn, until the diagram finally terminated at the left-hand side in a number of straggling start events. Each of the start events related to either:

- a particular aspect of the current state of progress;

or

- an activity that had not previously been thought of. (Indeed, if this network had not been drawn backwards, these forgotten activities would have been remembered too late or not at all.)

Now everyone knew exactly:

- the current state of progress;
- the tasks remaining and their logical sequence;
- the time needed and which jobs were most critical.

There was now a detailed plan from which to issue and progress the remaining work. By adapting the planning tactics to suit the particular project case, order had been retrieved from chaos. The exhibition did open on time, with all the new products displayed on the stand.

NETWORK ANALYSIS AS A MANAGEMENT TOOL

Network analysis demands the application of sound common sense and very little else. When the techniques were first introduced they were regarded with suspicion by many, and tended to be protected by an elitist mystique. That was unfortunate and unnecessary. The elements of network notation are simple. Although a project network can contain thousands of activities, all the basic notation is demonstrated by the simple examples that were shown in Chapter 14.

Anyone with a fair share of mental aptitude could be expected to acquire at least a working knowledge of logic diagram preparation in just one day. However, the method of teaching is important. Premature introduction of all but the basic bones of the system must be avoided. It is also sensible to start by practising, to gain competence in using the notation, getting the logic right, and time analysing small networks mentally. All of this should take place before going on to use a computer and more advanced procedures such as cost and resource scheduling.

Those who choose to go through project life in ignorance of the finer points of networking language may find themselves at some disadvantage if called upon to discuss network problems with their more erudite colleagues. Every profession has its own technical language, and without it communication must suffer. Nevertheless, critical path techniques can be applied very effectively by anybody with a grasp of the logical concepts involved. Basic network analysis is a simple but valuable management tool, which should never be regarded as a complicated and advanced technique reserved for the specialist.

There is always a danger of trying to be too clever by dotting every 'i' and crossing every 't'. Planning is not a precise technique and networks will be more effective if they can be kept as simple as possible, although incorporating all the essential activities and constraints. It is very probable that attempts to improve existing techniques arise not because the techniques themselves are inadequate, but because the planners are not able to exploit them properly.

The benefits to be derived from drawing a network are in themselves often worthwhile, even if no duration estimates are made, no time analysis takes place and the network is not used to control subsequent progress. Networking encourages logical thinking and planning. A network meeting can be regarded as a very productive form of brainstorming. Not only does the notation allow expression of all inter-activity dependencies and relationships, but there is also the important possibility that activities may be brought to light that might otherwise have been excluded from schedules, estimates and (most important) project pricing.

It would be unreasonable and unrealistic to expect the project manager to carry out network planning (or any other kind of planning) in isolation. The project manager must be able to count on the support and cooperation of members from every department in the organization. This applies not only to the initial planning session, but also to all subsequent discussions and progress monitoring and network updating. This support will only be possible if suitable training has been provided. Most important of all, encouragement and support must come from the top – from the company's senior management. Once the idea of project planning and control by networks has been accepted throughout the organization, the battle will largely have been won.

REFERENCES AND FURTHER READING

Devaux, S.A. (1999), *Total Project Control: a Manager's Guide to Integrated Planning, Measuring and Tracking* (New York: Wiley).

Fowler, A. and Lock, D. (2006), *Accelerating Business and IT Change: Transforming Project Delivery* (Aldershot: Gower).

Gordon, J. and Lockyer, K. (2005), *Project Management and Project Planning*, 7th Edition (London: Financial Times Prentice Hall).

Kerzner, H. (2006), *Project Management: A Systems Approach to Planning, Scheduling and Controlling*, 9th Edition (New York: Wiley).

Meredith, J. R. and Mantel, S. J. jnr (2003), *Project Management: a Managerial Approach*, 5th Edition, international edition (New York: Wiley).

16 *Principles of Resource Scheduling*

Resource scheduling is a complex subject that can be viewed from a number of different standpoints. At the strategic level it can be seen as an important element in formulating the long-range plans of companies. In this book, the subject is treated from the point of view of the project manager, who is more likely to be concerned with the shorter-term operations of the business. However, the techniques described here for project resource management cannot be regarded in isolation from the longer-term strategy, since project and other working schedules contribute vital information to the higher-level strategic planning process.

There are arguments (not discussed here in detail) concerning the attitude of company management to the stability of its workforce. In an organization that cherishes a stable labour force, with job security and long-term career development high on the list of its perceived staff motivators, resource scheduling can be seen as the process of identifying the resources available to the project organization and then attempting to deploy those resources as efficiently as possible to achieve the business objectives. The number of organizations which take that approach seems to have become fewer in recent years. More companies now start by examining or re-examining the needs of the organization, and then match their staff numbers accordingly (which can mean ruthless downsizing).

Resource management can also be looked at in other ways, depending on the nature of the business and on management attitudes. In those industries with a high proportion of casual labour, or which subcontract large elements of their work, detailed in-house resource scheduling can usually be confined to the relatively few permanent headquarters staff. Even in those industries, however, some knowledge of future resource requirements is desirable, so that subcontractors can be forewarned for instance.

An organization that handles projects using its own permanent engineering and manufacturing or construction workforce will need to take resource scheduling very seriously. It will have to calculate detailed working schedules that satisfy not only needs of each individual project, but also the combined effect of all work on the organization's total resource pool. The possible effects of predicted new work must be tested, preferably using 'what-if?' modelling. Information must be gathered on the longer-term work requirements of the organization, so that facilities can be planned and provided for the future expected workload.

WHAT ARE RESOURCES AND WHICH OF THEM CAN BE SCHEDULED?

A project resource is any person, object, tool, machine or sum of money needed for work on a project. Resources can be categorized in several ways and it is interesting to start by identifying three main classes (the definitions are my own).

Exhaustible resources

Once an exhaustible resource has been used, it is no longer available for use on a project. Replenishment is physically impossible.

Time is the most important exhaustible resource. Time is truly exhaustible. Once spent, it has gone for ever and can never be renewed. Time is a very special resource, needing its own techniques for planning and scheduling. These range from the simple day-to-day diary to the methods described in the preceding chapters.

Fossil fuels (such as coal, oil and natural gas) and mineral deposits (like the ores used in mining) are exhaustible resources. Once the deposits in a particular region have been used up, they cannot be replaced and the life cycle of the project that exploited them must end.

Exhaustible resources feature in project feasibility and strategic studies and in total life cycle analysis but (with the exception of time) they do not generally feature in project resource scheduling and are not considered further in this book.

Replenishable resources

Materials and components obtained through purchasing are replenishable resources. Although stocks of these resources might become exhausted when they are built into a project, they can usually be replenished by buying fresh supplies. The principal methods for scheduling materials come within the realm of stock control and purchasing, but information from project planning provides the control framework for purchasers and stock controllers by stating how much will be needed and when.

Although not considered specifically in this chapter, agricultural crops and their products are replenishable resources. However, they may not all be replenishable in the short term (timber, for example).

Some project management programs can schedule replenishable resources directly if required. This scheduling might include, for instance, the phasing of materials deliveries to a construction site so that the quantities on site match the rate of progress expected from the project critical path network.

Money, especially when it is scarce, might be regarded by some as an exhaustible resource. Strictly, however, it *is* replenishable. There are many examples of projects where the sponsors have been persuaded to provide more money for an ailing project rather than see it and their initial investment sink into oblivion. As with materials, project management data can determine how much cash will be needed and when. Cash flow predictions are a form of project resource scheduling and all competent project management software can be used to generate cash flow schedules. Cash flow scheduling is discussed further in Chapter 19.

Reusable resources

Reusable resources are assets that are required for use on project work but which remain available for reuse after each task has been performed. They can be compared to catalysts in a chemical reaction: they are necessary to promote the reaction but at the end they emerge unchanged. Levels of reusable resources tend to remain fairly stable over the longer term. They might, however, be scarce, in which case their use requires careful planning and scheduling.

People, with their particular skills and aptitudes, are the most common type of reusable resource. Some might claim that people do not emerge from a project unchanged, but (ageing apart) they should be available for work on consecutive projects. Chapter 17 is concerned particularly with scheduling people as a resource.

Industrial plant and machinery, other manufacturing facilities, test centres and so on can also be considered and treated as reusable resources. Although people and machines are very different resources, the same techniques and computer programs can be used to schedule them, provided that their use can be categorized by a simple code and their quantity can be specified in straightforward units.

Factory or office space is, of course, a reusable resource. One usually has to consider not only the number of space units (square metres or square feet) but also the shape of the space and, sometimes, also its volume. In heavy machine tool design and manufacturing projects, for example, machines set up for pre-shipment testing might have to be positioned in the assembly and test bay according to their height and foundation requirements, and it might be necessary to save space by allowing for machines from different projects to overhang each other. Project management software is not capable of dealing with these aspects of scheduling. In practice the solutions are best left to production engineers (for factory space) or facilities managers (for office space). They would use floor plans or three-dimensional models, either with or without the aid of a computer. However, the project manager still has a vital role to play, because it is principally he or she who can tell the production engineer or facilities manager when the space will be needed for each project.

ROLE OF NETWORK ANALYSIS IN RESOURCE SCHEDULING

A network cannot be used by itself to demonstrate the volume of resources needed at any given point in project time. In fact, when the network is drawn no considered account can be taken of the resources, which will be available. The start of each task is usually assumed to be dependent only upon the completion of its preceding tasks, and not on the availability of resources at the right time.

Naturally if a planning team knows that, for the sake of argument, a total of four pipefitters are employed in the project organization, they would not estimate the duration of any pipefitting task at a level which demands the employment of more than four pipefitters on that task. However, the chance of other pipefitting tasks occurring elsewhere in the network at the same time is impossible to deal with when the network is being drawn because the timing of those other tasks cannot be known before the network has been completely drawn and time analysis has been carried out.

In general, therefore, network logic shows only those constraints between tasks that are related to the logical, preferred sequence of working. Thus, although a network should be fine in logical theory, it is not always possible in practice to start all tasks at their earliest possible times. In fact, if too many tasks clamour for too few resources it might be impossible to carry out the project in the time indicated by the critical path.

This is far from saying that work spent in preparing a critical path network has been wasted. The network diagram and its time analysis must be seen as the first essential step in the wider process of scheduling project resources. The results of critical path network time analysis play a key role in resource scheduling, but the practicable allocation of project resources to tasks requires at least one more stage of calculation after determining the amount of float available for each task and locating the critical path.

Allocating priorities according to float

The results of network time analysis determine task priorities. When different tasks compete simultaneously for the same limited resources, priority rules can be applied so that the resources are allocated where they are most urgently needed. Usually tasks with least float are given the highest priority.

RESOURCE SCHEDULING CASE EXAMPLE: THE GARAGE PROJECT

The principles and some of the problems of resource scheduling can be introduced by considering a small construction project. Manual methods (as opposed to the use of a computer) are described here, because these demonstrate the underlying processes. In practice, one of the many commercially available computer programs could be used (see Chapter 20).

Garage project definition

A small firm of builders has been commissioned to erect a detached garage. The building is to be constructed of brick, with a corrugated sheet roof. This roof will incorporate some transparent sheets as roof lights instead of windows. The doors are to be timber-framed and hung on strap hinges. No heavy lifting is involved in this project and no task needs more than two people.

Resources available

The building firm engaged on the garage project is a very tiny outfit, comprising the not unusual father-and-son team. The father, no longer capable of sustained heavy work, is nevertheless a good all-round craftsman with long experience. The son, on the other hand, can best be described as a strong, willing lad, sound in wind and limb but lacking any special experience or skill. This firm's resource availability can therefore be listed as follows:

- skilled persons – 1
- labourers – 1.

Critical path network diagram for the garage project

Figure 16.1 shows the network diagram for this project. For comparison, this is given in both arrow and precedence versions. The number of tasks that can be shown clearly on a book page is limited so, for clarity of illustration, activities such as allowing time for paint to dry or for concrete to cure have not been included in these networks and it is assumed that all materials and hire plant needed are already available on site.

All the task durations have been estimated in days, and they assume that only the small labour force already described (one skilled all-round craftsman and one labourer) will be available to this project.

When the network was drawn, no consideration was given to any competition for these very limited resources that might be caused by the possibility of two or more tasks requiring them at the same time. The planner, correctly, followed this course knowing that any such problems would be resolved in a subsequent, quite separate, resource scheduling calculation.

Time analysis and the calendar

The results of time analysis for the garage project network are given in Figure 16.2, which also provides the task list. If unlimited resources could be used, so that all the earliest possible dates could be achieved, the whole project should take 24 working days. But there is no direct indication from the network or its time analysis of how many craftsmen and labourers would be needed to achieve this result.

All times refer to *close of work* on the given days. Thus a task scheduled to finish on (for example) day 8, means that it should be finished at close of work on day 8. A job scheduled to start on day 8 means that it could start at the *end* of day 8 which, in practice, really means the *beginning* of day 9.

This rule can be explained best by reference to the arrow diagram in upper section of Figure 16.1. A network event (as opposed to a task) occupies no time itself and its achievement takes place at the instant when all its preceding tasks have been completed. Subsequent tasks can start at the same instant. Task 01– 02 (dig foundations) for instance, starts at time 0, which is the end of an imaginary day 0 or, in reality, the *beginning* of day 1. The intervening night hours are simply not recognized as time available for work by the computer and are thus completely ignored. The estimated duration of task 01– 02 is four working days, which means that its earliest possible completion is at the *end* of day 4. Event 02, therefore, can be achieved at close of work on day 4. The following task, 02–05 (concrete foundations) can therefore start on day 4, but that means the *end* of day 4. In practice, therefore, task 02– 05 would not start until the *beginning* of day 5.

This convention can give rise to an interesting anomaly for zero duration tasks that are processed by some computer programs. Suppose that a zero duration task is shown as starting on 1 May. That really means start of work on 1 May, typically at 9.00 a.m. Because computers ignore non-working night hours, the finish of this same task might be shown as 31 March, because to the computer, 5 p.m. on 31 March is the same instant in time as 9.00 a.m. on 1 May. So apparently we have a task finishing one day before it starts! However, most modern programs overcome this problem.

Gantt chart (bar chart) for the garage project

Because we are not using a computer in this introductory case, the first step in determining the labour requirements is to convert the network diagram into a Gantt chart (most workmen would call this a bar chart because they have would never have heard of Henry Gantt). Figure 16.3 shows the initial bar chart for this project, with every task placed at its earliest possible time.

Please imagine the bar chart in Figure 16.3 as having been set up on a wallboard, using strips that plug into holes on a grid pattern, or are otherwise attached so that they can be moved sideways to adjust the schedule as required. Each bar represents a task on the network, with its length scaled according to the task's estimated duration.

The bars are coded according to the type of resource needed, black indicating a skilled person and grey for a labourer. No task in this project needs more than one skilled person or more than one labourer. Some tasks need both one skilled person and one labourer, and for those tasks black and grey bars have been drawn side by side.

Calendar and timescale details

The garage project timescale starts at the beginning of 13 May and network day numbers have been converted into calendar dates for the working schedule. These conversions are valid for the year 2013. The project calendar has been arranged with no weekend working so that only weekday dates are valid for scheduling. Because Saturdays and Sundays are non-working days, their dates are excluded from the schedule. In practice, public holidays would similarly be excluded as working days, but they have been ignored for this case example.

The schedule in Figure 16.3 shows that the earliest possible completion date for this project is 13 June. Saturday mornings (not shown on the chart) could be considered as time to be held in reserve against unforeseen contingencies. Evening overtime is another possible reserve resource. However, these possible additional working hours are hidden reserves and the project planner was quite right not to build them into the initial plan.

Resource scheduling for the garage project

Simple resource aggregation

Each task on the bar chart in Figure 16.3 is shown starting at its earliest possible time. No thought has yet been given to the resources needed and it is now time to start putting that right. The resources needed each day to carry out this simple plan are easy to calculate. It is only necessary to add up the number of times a strip of each code (grey or black) occurs in each day's column.

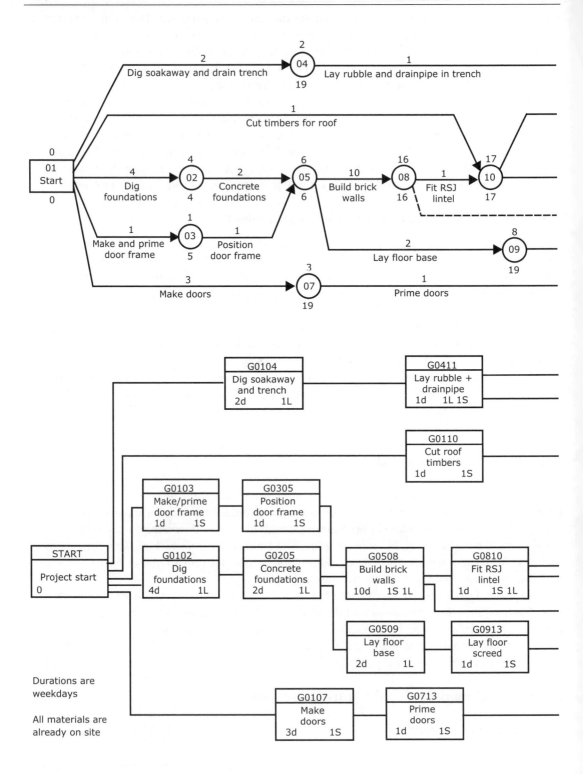

Figure 16.1   Garage project: network diagram

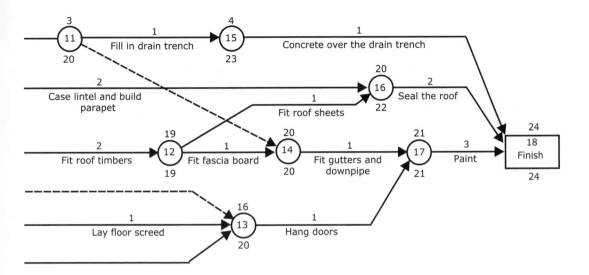

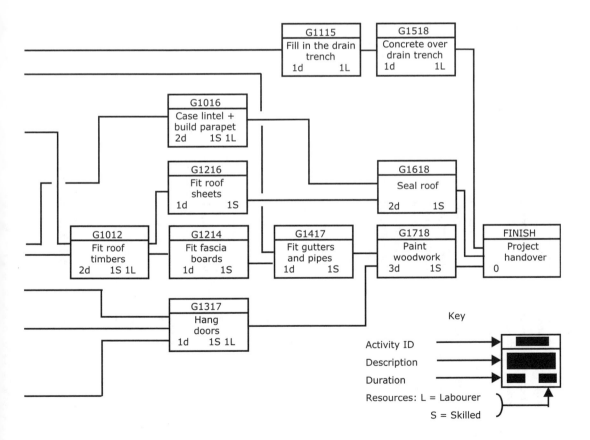

Figure 16.1 *Continued*

ADM only Prec. event	Succ. event	PDM only Activity identifier	Activity description	Duration (days)	Earliest start	Latest start	Earliest finish	Latest finish	Total float	Resources
		START	Project start	0	0	0	0	0	0	
01	02	G0102	Dig foundations	4	0	0	4	4	0	1L
02	05	G0205	Concrete foundations	2	4	4	6	6	0	1L
01	03	G0103	Make and prime door frame	1	0	4	1	5	4	1S
03	05	G0305	Position door frame	1	1	5	2	6	4	1S
05	08	G0508	Build brick walls	10	6	6	16	16	0	1S 1L
08	10	G0810	Fit RSJ lintel over doors	1	16	16	17	17	0	1S 1L
01	10	G0110	Cut roof support timbers	1	0	16	1	17	16	1S
10	16	G1016	Case the lintel and build parapet	2	17	20	19	22	3	1S 1L
10	12	G1012	Fit the roof support timbers	2	17	17	19	19	0	1S 1L
12	14	G1214	Fit fascia boards for gutters	1	19	19	20	20	0	1S
12	16	G1216	Fit roof sheets	1	19	21	20	22	2	1S
01	04	G0104	Dig soakaway and trench for pipe	2	0	17	2	19	17	1L
04	11	G0411	Lay rubble and drainpipe to soakaway	1	2	19	3	20	17	1S 1L
11	15	G1115	Fill in the drain trench	1	3	22	4	23	19	1L
15	18	G1518	Concrete over the drain trench	1	4	23	5	24	19	1L
05	09	G0509	Lay concrete floor base	2	6	17	8	19	11	1L
09	13	G0913	Lay floor screed	1	8	19	9	20	11	1S
01	07	G0107	Make the doors	3	0	16	3	19	16	1S
07	13	G0713	Prime the doors	1	3	19	4	20	16	1S
13	17	G1317	Hang the doors and fit locks	1	16	20	17	21	4	1S 1L
17	18	G1718	Paint all woodwork	3	21	21	24	24	0	1S
14	17	G1417	Fit gutters and downpipe	1	20	20	21	21	0	1S
16	18	G1618	Seal the roof	2	20	22	22	24	2	1S
		FINISH	Hand project over to customer	0	24	24	24	24	0	1S

Figure 16.2 Garage project: task list and time analysis

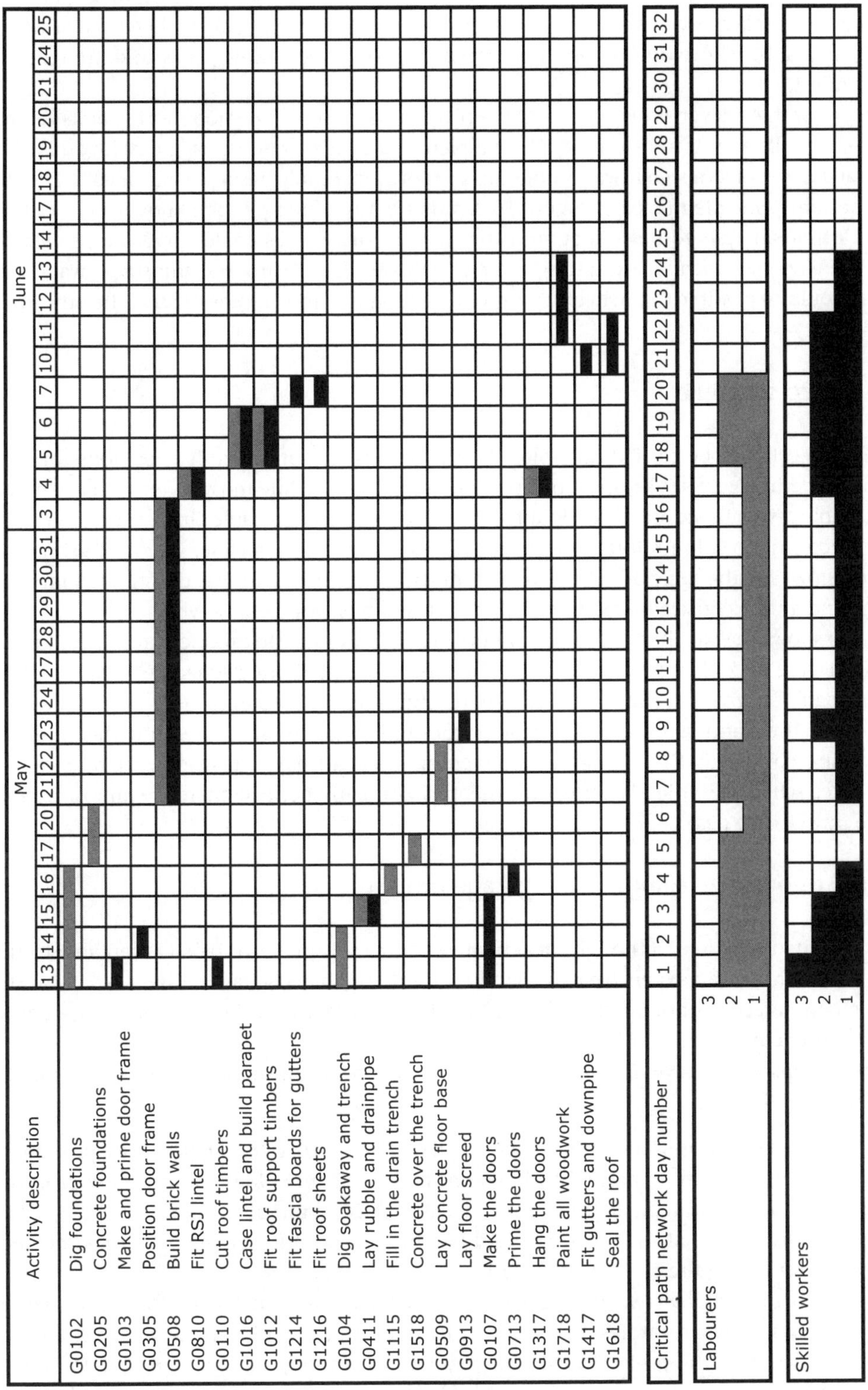

Figure 16.3 Garage project: bar chart and resource histogram – aggregation

The planned total daily resource requirements are entered at the foot of the chart. This has been done in the form of a histogram in our example. The result is, to say the least, unsatisfactory. On some days the workers are expected to be idle; on other days three people will be needed where only one is available. The workload is unbalanced, showing too many peaks and troughs for profitable comfort.

The reason for this uneven schedule is that the planner has shown every job starting at its earliest possible date, regardless of need or priority. Such a plan is known as 'resource-aggregated' and it has little practical use except as a step towards obtaining a more practicable 'resource-allocated' schedule.

The important principle missed in Figure 16.3 is that many of the jobs are known from critical path network time analysis to have float, and the starts of these tasks could therefore be delayed to smooth the workload without extending the project's end date. Using the adjustable wallchart, therefore, it should be possible to reschedule non-critical tasks to remove some or all of the unwanted workload peaks.

Resource-limited schedule

If the garage project is to be carried out solely by the father-and-son team, it is obvious that the schedule displayed in Figure 16.3 cannot be implemented. The schedule must be rearranged so that the modest resources available are never double-booked. Using the adjustable chart, the tasks can be shuffled around until no column total exceeds the number of people available. When this shuffling is carried out, however, the logic of the network from which the bar chart was constructed must be remembered and all the constraints between different tasks must still be observed.

Figure 16.4 shows the bar chart for the garage project after levelling to produce a resource-limited schedule (see Figure 16.7 for an explanation of the term resource-limited schedule). The resulting workload histogram is given at the foot of the chart. Imposing the resource-limited constraint has therefore delayed the planned finish of this project from 13 June to 26 June, extending the timescale by nine working days (plus the additional intervening weekend days). However, there is now a smooth resource schedule, which is perfect for this tiny company because there are almost no idle days and no unwelcome peaks.

Time-limited resource levelling for the garage project

The resource-limited schedule, although ideal for the contractor, may not be so acceptable to the customer. She has ordered an expensive new car and wants to be able to garage it safely as soon as she gets it. If the new garage cannot be promised in time the customer may decide, not unreasonably, to look for another contractor.

In these circumstances, several courses of action are open to the small builder. These include the following:

1. Work to the resource-limited timescale of 33 days (Figure 16.4), but make a false promise to the customer that the garage will still be finished on 13 June. Making such false promises can never be recommended, for commercial as well as for moral reasons.
2. Tell the customer that the project cannot be finished by 13 June – and lose the order as a penalty for telling the unvarnished truth.
3. Revert to the original resource-aggregated schedule shown in Figure 16.3 and take on additional workers, regardless of cost, in order to finish the project in 24 working days.
4. Plan to complete the project within the required 24 working days, accept that additional workers will be needed, but review and adjust the resource-aggregated schedule in an attempt to smooth the workload into a more cost-effective pattern.

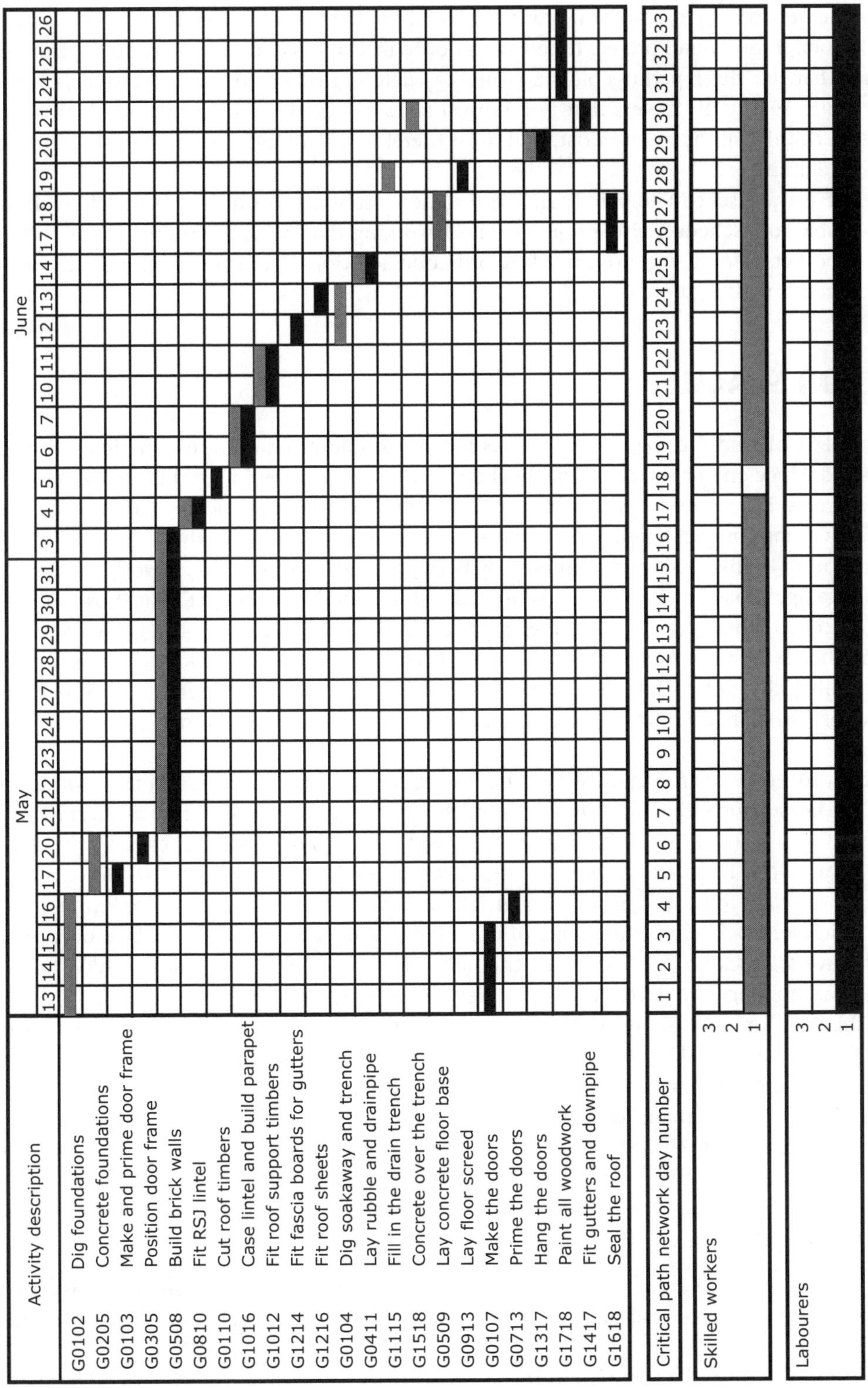

Figure 16.4 Garage project: bar chart and resource histogram – resource-limited

Activity description

G0102	Dig foundations
G0205	Concrete foundations
G0103	Make and prime door frame
G0305	Position door frame
G0508	Build brick walls
G0810	Fit RSJ lintel
G0110	Cut roof timbers
G1016	Case lintel and build parapet
G1012	Fit roof support timbers
G1214	Fit fascia boards for gutters
G1216	Fit roof sheets
G0104	Dig soakaway and trench
G0411	Lay rubble and drainpipe
G1115	Fill in the drain trench
G1518	Concrete over the trench
G0509	Lay concrete floor base
G0913	Lay floor screed
G0107	Make the doors
G0713	Prime the doors
G1317	Hang the doors
G1718	Paint all woodwork
G1417	Fit gutters and downpipe
G1618	Seal the roof

Critical path network day number

Skilled workers

Labourers

Option 4 is one that is commonly taken in project scheduling, and it will work well for the garage project. Remember that this rescheduling of tasks can only take place within the constraints imposed by the network logic, so that no task may be started before all its predecessors have been achieved. Further, if the overall project timescale is not to be extended, no task may be rescheduled to start later than its latest permissible start time, as determined by the network time analysis (shown in Figure 16.2). This means that non-critical tasks can be delayed within the float which they possess. Critical tasks have zero float, and must therefore always be scheduled to start at their earliest possible times.

Figure 16.5 is the rescheduled bar chart. The resource histogram at the foot of the chart shows that it is possible to reschedule this project over 24 working days with a resource usage pattern that is far smoother than aggregation, needing only one additional person of each skill category. Compare this result with Figure 16.3.

FLOAT (OR SLACK)

The concept of 'float' and the specific definitions for its possible variations are sometimes difficult to comprehend. Since one of the more practical applications of float is found during the resource scheduling process, it is convenient to illustrate and define float in some detail at this point. The network for the garage project (Figure 16.1) will provide a suitable case for study.

The illustration in this section is supported by both precedence and arrow network references.

Consider garage project task G1016 (10–16), 'Case lintel and build parapet'. For those with no experience of construction projects, this means encasing the steel lintel over the garage doors in concrete and then building a brick parapet on top of it. The duration of this task has been estimated (perhaps optimistically) at two days. For clarity, this task has been extracted from the main network and is shown as a separate detail in Figure 16.6. All the data relevant to calculating float are included in this extract.

A glance at this network fragment shows that the earliest possible start for this task is (the end of) day 17. The latest permissible finish is day 22. Allowing for the two-day duration of this task, it is easy to see that its start (and its finish) could be delayed by up to 3 days without causing any delay to the tasks that follow. This three days is the total float possessed by task G1016 (10–16).

If, because of delays in the project or through intentional resource scheduling, the lintel cannot be encased in its earliest possible time, some (if not all) of the float for this task will be eroded. This will usually have a knock-on effect through the network, robbing float from tasks which follow, because they can no longer be started at their earliest possible times.

In fact the float for any task must always be seen in relation to how it is likely to affect, or be affected by, the float possessed by other tasks in the network. Consideration of these effects gives rise to definitions for various types of float. These definitions will now be given, but it is not necessary to be conversant with all of them. Before the start of a project, planners and project managers are generally most concerned with 'total float'. From the time when resource scheduling starts, and throughout the active life of the project, the focus is on 'remaining float'.

Total float

'Total float' is defined as the amount by which a task can be delayed if all its preceding tasks take place at their earliest possible times and following tasks can be allowed to wait until their latest permissible times.

The early and late times for event 10 in the arrow network are both 17. Because these times are equal, event 10 is fixed in time and thus has zero float. However, that applies only to the *event*, and not to all the *tasks* passing through it. Although event 10 lies on the critical path, the path

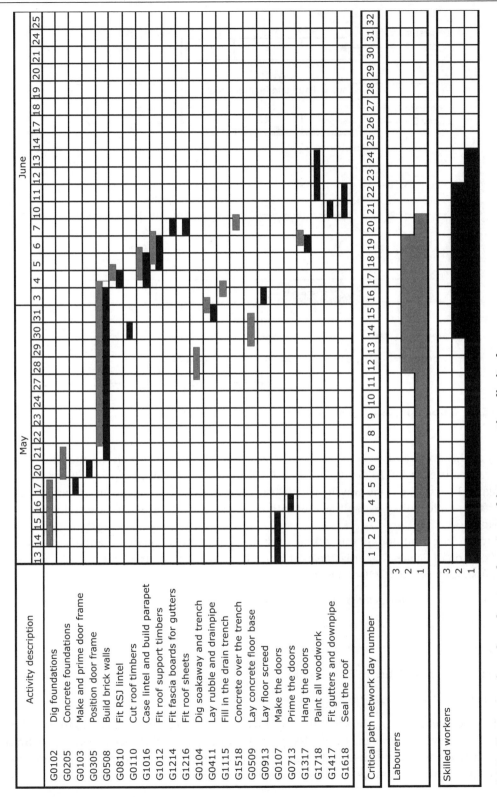

Figure 16.5 Garage project: bar chart and resource histogram – time-limited

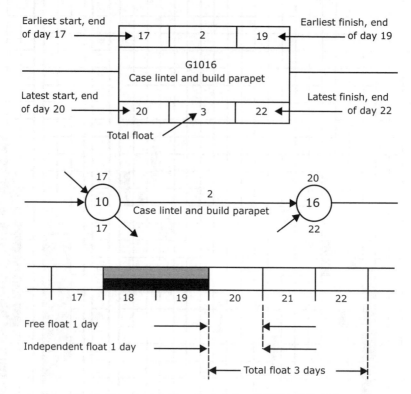

Figure 16.6 Garage project: float analysis of activity G1016 (10–16)

branches at this event and a glance at the whole network in Figure 16.1 shows that the critical path actually misses task G1016 (10–16). Task G1016 (10–16) does indeed possess float. Version (c) in Figure 14.4 showed one way in which this difficulty can be avoided in arrow networks. However, the problem disappears altogether with precedence notation, as can be seen in the upper half of Figure 16.6.

The actual float conditions of this task are illustrated best in the segment of Gantt chart included in lower portion of Figure 16.6. It is apparent from this diagram that, using the formal definition, the total float for task G1016 (10–16) is three days.

Total float =   *latest permissible task finish time*

 minus   *the earliest possible task start time*

 minus   *the estimated task duration*

Applying the data from Figure 16.6 to this formula:

Total float of task G1016 (10–16) = (22 – 17 – 2) = 3 days

In the precedence version, shown in the upper part of Figure 16.6, the calculation for total float can be made simply by subtracting the earliest possible finish time from the latest permissible finish time, which gives the same result (22 – 19) = 3 days. Subtracting the earliest possible start time from the latest permissible start time gives the same result (20 – 17) = 3.

Free float

'Free float' is defined as the amount of float available to a task when all its preceding tasks take place at their earliest possible times and following tasks can still take place at their earliest possible times.

In the arrow network, free float is found as follows:

Free float =	earliest possible end event time
minus	the earliest possible start event time
minus	the estimated task duration

Applying the arrow network data from Figure 16.6 to this formula:

Free float of activity G1016(10–16) = (20 – 17 – 2) = 1 day

In the precedence network the calculation for free float is different, and it is necessary to refer back to the full diagram in Figure 16.1 and its time analysis in Figure 16.2. The calculation of free float using precedence notation is as follows:

Free float =	earliest start of the immediately following activity or activities
minus	the earliest finish of the task under consideration

From the precedence network diagram in Figure 16.1 can be seen that the task immediately following task G1016 is task G1618. The time analysis data tabulated in Figure 16.2 show that G1016 has an earliest possible finish of day 19, and G1618 has an earliest possible start time at day 20. Thus the free float of task G1016 is (20 – 19) = 1 day.

Independent float

Now consider task G1016 (10–16) once again (as shown in Figure 16.6). Notice that it is possible to shuffle this task around over a one-day period, whatever happens to the schedule for all other network tasks. It matters not whether the preceding events are allowed to run up to their latest permissible times, or whether the following events must start at their earliest possible times. This task can be moved backwards and forwards within one day before any other task is affected. This small amount of float, because it is entirely independent of all surrounding tasks, is called 'independent float'.

Defined formally, independent float is the amount of float available to a task when all its preceding tasks take place at their latest permissible times and all following tasks can still take place at their earliest possible times. Independent float is easiest to observe in arrow networks, from which the mathematical expression for independent float is as follows:

Independent float =	the earliest possible end-event time
minus	the latest permissible start-event time
minus	the task duration

Task G1016 (10–16) in Figure 16.6 does happen to possess some independent float, as illustrated in the Gantt chart fragment and as calculated by using the task data in the above mathematical expression:

Independent float of task G1016 (10–16) = (20 – 17 – 2) = 1 day

It is purely coincidental that the free float and independent float have the same value in this case.

Independent float is almost always zero and is generally ignored.

Remaining float

The total float possessed by any task is at risk of erosion from the moment that project resource scheduling starts right up to the time when the task is actually completed. Total float can be reduced, for example, as a result of a conscious decision to delay the planned start of a task as part of the resource scheduling process (in order to achieve a smoother workload plan). There is also the risk that preceding tasks will run late, absorbing some or all of the total float previously possessed by the current task.

For practical purposes, once a project is started the project manager is not interested in the total float that a task had in the beginning of the project, when the network was first drawn. It is the residue of the total float still possessed by each uncompleted task that should concern the project manager. This is the remaining float.

Tasks with zero remaining float

Tasks which have zero remaining float have become critical tasks. They should claim priority for resources and for management attention to ensure that they are finished without delay. Otherwise the project completion must itself be delayed.

Tasks with negative float

Suppose that the critical path through a network has a total estimated duration of 100 weeks. The end task will therefore have an earliest possible completion time of 100 weeks. Barring other considerations, the latest permissible completion time for the project will also be at the end of the 100th week. Time analysis will, in the usual way, produce one or more critical paths back through to the start of the network in which all the critical tasks have zero total float. Suppose, however, that those 'other considerations' include a promise to the customer that the project will be completed in only 90 weeks. The latest *permissible* project end date is therefore 10 weeks before its earliest *possible* date. If 90 weeks is substituted as the latest permissible date for completion of the final task, the backward pass through the network will now reduce the float of all those activities on the critical path from zero to minus 10 weeks.

Negative float can be caused whenever impossible scheduled target dates are imposed on the end task, or indeed on any other task in a project network. Negative float will appear in any schedule (including those computer printouts produced by software which has the capability of reporting it) where it is impossible to achieve scheduled target dates for the following reasons:

- The shortest possible duration of the relevant path through the network to a task bearing an imposed target date is longer than the time allowed by the target date (that is, an impossible target has been set).
- Delayed progress prevents one or more tasks being finished by their latest permissible finish dates.
- Tasks have to be delayed beyond their latest permissible dates because resources are inadequate.

Needless to say, tasks with negative float have become hypercritical. Prompt management action is essential in attempting to expedite them and rescue the project.

TWO FUNDAMENTAL PRIORITY RULES FOR RESOURCE SCHEDULING

The approach to resource scheduling must usually be governed by the choice between two planning options or priority rules, namely whether the schedule should be resource-limited or time-limited. These options occurred in the garage project earlier in this chapter, but they require further explanation. The choice between these two rules must be made whenever there is a clash between meeting a project completion date and finding the necessary resources.

Figure 16.7 is a graphical illustration of the resource- and time-limited concepts. The balloon represents a project, which should be imagined as an incompressible fluid of constant volume being squeezed between the two main constraints of time and resources.

Resource-limited scheduling

Resource-limited scheduling results in a plan that never exceeds the declared levels of available resources. This often means accepting a project end date that is later than the earliest possible date

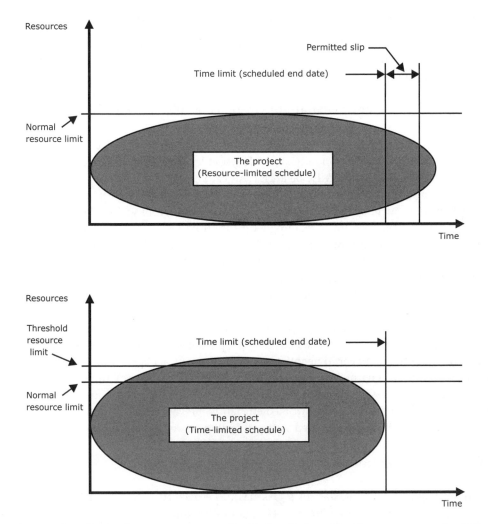

Figure 16.7   Time-limited versus resource-limited priority rules for resource scheduling

predicted from network time analysis. In other words, working within available resource levels is seen as the first scheduling objective, with secondary priority for completing the project in the shortest possible time. This condition is shown in the upper diagram in Figure 16.7.

Time-limited scheduling

If the completion time is the paramount objective, the planning procedure must be time-limited. The overriding objective in this case is to ensure that the project can be scheduled for completion by a specified date. This date is often the earliest possible completion date indicated by network time analysis (the duration of the critical path) but it might be some slightly later target date.

Time-limited scheduling means that any predicted resource overloads must be accepted, probably on the assumption that these can be made good by hiring subcontract labour or by making other suitable short-term resource arrangements. Even though resource constraints are seen as having secondary priority in a time-limited schedule, the planner should still aim at a smooth resource usage pattern, avoiding unnecessary interruptions, peaks and troughs in the workload patterns of all the project resources. The time-limited condition is depicted in the lower half of Figure 16.7.

Methods for easing the resource and time restrictions

If neither strict resource limitation nor time limitation fail to produce an acceptable schedule, it might be necessary either to breach the limits or, alternatively, attempt to ease them to allow a compromise solution.

Using threshold resources to extend the resource availability limit

Sometimes it is possible to consider a second tier, or 'threshold' level of a particular resource, to be used in schedules only when all the normally available resources have been allocated to tasks, and when the project timescale would otherwise be at risk. An example would be an engineering department with a declared resource strength of 75 permanent staff employees, where the engineering manager knows that an additional 30 engineers could be made available from various subcontract agencies.

When a computer is used for scheduling with threshold resources available, it first attempts to generate a schedule that only uses the normally available resources. The additional resources are only brought into play when the computer is unable to schedule a task without exceeding the stated amount or threshold of normally available resources. The schedule might still exceed the target completion date, but at least the use of threshold resources can take some of the strain, as shown in the lower part of Figure 16.7.

In the case of the engineering department, the engineering manager would receive a computer report showing how many of the 30 subcontract people are expected to be needed, with the dates. This should enable the manager to negotiate with the subcontract agencies well in advance for the supply of the additional engineering staff. It would also give the company time in which to arrange for the hire of any necessary accommodation and equipment for them. This is another example taken from real life, where the system worked efficiently, prevented last minute panics and allowed plenty of time for seeking subcontracted staff and facilities from the most cost-effective sources.

Specifying alternative resources

It sometimes happens that the start of a task has to be delayed because the specified resource is not free, although there exists in the project organization another type of resource that could be substituted. This state of affairs could occur, for example, in an engineering office. It might be that a specialist in electronic engineering also has skills in control and lubrication design. Some computer programs allow the planner to specify such alternative resources in the initial plan, so that the computer can take advantage of their availability in time of need.

Allowing project end-slip

Some computer software allows the planner to declare an element of acceptable project slip, beyond the preferred target completion date. The computer is then able to make use of this extra time if, but *only* if, resource limits would otherwise be exceeded in a time-limited scheduling calculation. Such end slip is not counted during time analysis, and float is still calculated from the normal end of the project. Thus if, for instance, a slip period of eight weeks is allowed after the last project task, the calculated critical path length will exclude this eight weeks: otherwise eight weeks of artificial float would be created to give everyone involved on the project a false sense of security.

In the top part of Figure 16.7 the computer has not been able to contain the project within the permitted slip, and the project is scheduled to end late because of the resource limitations.

This kind of facility does not exist in all the popularly available software.

SUMMARY: THE ELEMENTS OF A PRACTICABLE SCHEDULE

An example of how not to schedule

An engineering director I once knew called for a departmental plan, drawn on a sheet of paper covering a long reference table, which was supposed to allocate 30 engineers (identified by their names) to jobs from several projects (actual project orders and expected future orders) at weekly intervals covering a period of no less than two years ahead. This elaborate chart therefore needed about 3000 pencilled entries. It cost about ten days of a highly paid chief engineer's time and involved detailed discussions with the engineering director and other senior people.

The schedule did look quite impressive when it was finished, but it was completely inflexible and virtually impossible to update. Not surprisingly, it became outdated and totally useless after only a few weeks. Even if the work plans had been soundly based (which they were not) it is always ludicrous to expect to be able to allocate named individuals to specific jobs on precise dates so far into the future. Even if all expected orders for new projects had been received (they were not), and all the jobs did by some chance happen to materialize in the particular weeks shown on the plan, there would still be a large question mark regarding how many of the 30 named engineers would continue to be employed by the company. In fact, that particular firm was wound up with big debts before the two years covered by the plan had expired.

How it should be done

Chapter 5 included a checklist for an ideal project plan (Figure 5.2). The points listed in that checklist are repeated below for convenience:

1. Does the plan include all known major tasks?
2. Is the plan drawing in enough detail to generate work-to lists?
3. Are all tasks placed in their logical chronological sequence?
4. Have task interdependencies been respected?
5. Is the plan easy to understand and is it visually effective?
6. Is the plan flexible and easy to adapt to take account of changes to project requirements or strategy?
7. Are the project milestones shown?

8. Are all the duration estimates feasible and achievable?
9. Are urgent and high priority tasks clearly highlighted?
10. Have key managers and supervisors participated in the plan and accepted it as their commitment?
11. Can the plan be used to check day-to-day progress?
12. Has the plan been made to take account of resources?
13. Have the resource needs of other projects been considered?
14. Will it satisfy all the stakeholders' expectations?

A point has now been reached in this text where most of the methods necessary to meet the above conditions have been described. Manual scheduling methods will not provide the flexibility needed to meet all the above conditions, but once a computer is introduced all the above conditions can be satisfied.

The following chapter continues this subject of planning and resource scheduling and is based on the assumption that a computer, loaded with capable project management software, will be used. Chapter 20 is concerned more specifically with such computer applications.

REFERENCES AND FURTHER READING

Devaux, S. A. (1999), *Total Project Control: a Manager's Guide to Integrated Planning, Measuring and Tracking* (New York: Wiley); this text is practical throughout and is far better than most in its definitions of float and examples of complex precedence relationships.

Kerzner, H. (2006), *Project Management: A Systems Approach to Planning, Scheduling and Controlling*, 9th Edition (New York: Wiley).

Meredith, J. R. and Mantel, S. J. Jnr (2003), *Project Management: a Managerial Approach*, 5th Edition, international edition (New York: Wiley).

17 *Scheduling People (and Other Reusable Resources)*

T he previous chapter introduced some of the principles on which project resource scheduling should be based, particularly with regard to the relationship between critical path network logic, float-determined priorities and the availability of resources. The examples used were, necessarily, very simple. When resources are to be scheduled on a more realistic scale, the use of a computer is essential. Every project manager or planner will be faced with questions that either raise problems or force decisions when data are being assembled for the computer. This chapter answers some of those questions, concentrating on reusable resources, by far the most important of which are the people who will design and execute the project.

CHOOSING WHICH RESOURCES TO SCHEDULE

In a typical organization it is the direct workers rather than the indirect staff (management infrastructure) who have to be scheduled. For example, suppose that there are 20 people capable of mechanical engineering design in a company's engineering department. It is obviously desirable to schedule the issue of mechanical design tasks to those people at a rate that never requires more than 20 of them at the same time. However, the time of the engineering manager will be spread very widely over all the tasks in their department, and will probably be treated as an overhead (indirect) expense. The main definition of indirect workers is that their time cannot easily be attributed to direct tasks, and it is thus not sensible to attempt scheduling them.

Most project management software will allow hundreds of different resource categories to be specified and processed but the planner who makes too much use of this facility will regret it. Network diagrams, schedules and reports will become very complicated and difficult to manage if every possible type of resource in the organization is entered in the scheduling process. The computer will struggle but fail to produce workload levels that are really smooth and satisfy everyone. Processing time and the risk of errors will increase beyond acceptable levels.

My approach has always been first to analyse the organization and its working patterns, pick out the mainstream resources on which project work is heavily dependent (certainly no more than ten categories), and then schedule those as well as possible. Provided that the available capacities for all resources throughout the organization exist in the appropriate proportions, other tasks will most probably be scheduled at a rate commensurate with their undeclared resources. This is, of course, empirical and a view which is based on my own experience.

Some readers might not agree with this approach but it always pays to start implementing any new scheduling system as simply as possible. Think big, start small. Other resource types can be added to the database later, if that proves to be necessary.

Engineers and designers

Petrochemical and construction projects

In the engineering design for large petrochemical or construction projects it would usually be necessary to schedule work and headquarters manpower resources for each of the main engineering disciplines (civil, structural, mechanical, electrical, piping and so on). This scheduling might be further broken down into engineering, drawing and checking (although computer-aided design can blur these boundaries and reduce the need for such breakdowns). The size of tasks for this purpose would not usually go down to the level of individual detail drawings, but would probably encompass groups of drawings for plant or building areas, or for other suitable small work packages.

Design tasks for manufacturing projects

In the engineering design for manufacturing projects, again confining the scheduling detail to subassemblies and groups of drawings rather than to individual drawings, it can be sufficient to consider only three resource types during scheduling, designated as follows:

- layout (senior engineers)
- detailers
- checkers or group leaders.

Clearly this will not cover every grade of engineering and drawing office staff. For example, many mechanical engineering design activities might also attract a proportion of lubrication and process control design. The common sense approach here (remembering the warnings in the introduction to this section) is to avoid getting into too much detail. If the company knows, from experience, that process control engineering always takes place alongside mechanical design, but typically requires only 10 per cent of the level for mechanical design, then there might well be no need to include process control design specifically in the resource scheduling process. It is then only necessary to schedule the mechanical design engineers.

In such circumstances, process control design activities would not even have to be shown on the network diagram, unless they had particular individual significance. The process control manager can be left to schedule his or her department's work in line with the mainstream mechanical design schedule, and the process control engineering manpower requirements can be assumed as being 10 per cent of those calculated for the mechanical engineers. This approach may not appeal to the fastidious expert or the timid planner, but it saves considerable planning and scheduling effort and has been proved to be perfectly effective in practice.

Manufacturing

For scheduling projects through a factory, it might again be possible to choose only two or three essential key resource types. I have very successfully used the following crude selection:

- light machining
- heavy machining
- assembly.

The selections will of course, depend on the organization and its processes. If this degree of simplification sounds surprising, remember that the project planner and project manager are not usually concerned with the day-to-day detail of job scheduling in the manufacturing plant, which is the separate function of production control. The purpose of the project work-to lists that derive from resource scheduling is simply to ensure that work packages are loaded to the factory at a rate consistent with its available capacity.

For similar reasons, it is not usually necessary to be concerned about the workload fluctuations that would normally occur when manufacturing a group of components that might be represented on the network and its resulting schedules by a single task. It is usually only necessary to specify an average rate of usage for each production resource, spread evenly over the duration of each production activity on the project network diagram.

The justification for this approach is that each network activity, although perhaps representing several manufacturing operations, is likely to be very small in relation to the total workload of hundreds or even thousands of other manufacturing activities in the total project or multi-project calculations. Workload peaks and troughs of individual activities are so small in relation to the whole that they tend to even out, especially since the activities have been scheduled so as not to exceed the total stated production capacities.

Project resource allocation can therefore ensure that work is fed to the factory at a pace that will not overload the total resource capacities. The production control department and the production engineers should then be able to expand the resulting project work-to lists into the far more detailed schedules necessary for day-to-day manufacturing control.

These arguments concerning summarized manufacturing activities, because they rely on statistical probability, need a large sample. They are justified when the total manufacturing workload for all projects is represented by at least several hundred activities. This usually depends on the use of multi-project scheduling, in which all the organization's projects and resources are scheduled together in one comprehensive multi-project model, as described later in Chapter 28.

CHOICE OF RESOURCE UNITS

Whenever resources are scheduled, it is necessary to choose suitable numerical units to define the quantities. Simple numbers can usually be used to quantify people within a special skills group or from a particular department. If 50 labourers are available for allocation to the project, then 50 resource units are entered in the system as the available strength. If eight of those labourers are required to work on a single activity, this might be indicated on the network, computer input, and subsequent schedules as 8LAB (where 'LAB' or some other suitable code identifies the resource as labourers).

An activity might have two, three or many more different types of resource assigned to it. This was seen even in the tiny garage project in Chapter 16, where some activities required both a skilled person and a labourer.

Decimal resource quantities

There are occasions when one or more people working on a project might have to spread their time over several activities simultaneously. Buyers in a purchasing department are a good example. An average purchasing activity might only involve each buyer intermittently, because most buyers handle several enquiries and orders at the same time. Large projects can impose a heavy and uneven workload on purchasing departments, and the planner might decide that some way must be found to allocate buyers part-time to activities so that project purchasing can take place in the correct sequence of priorities without causing health-threatening overloads.

A group of five buyers might be dealing with 50 enquiries and purchase orders in various stages of preparation at any one time. The planner could overcome this scheduling problem by reasoning that the average buyer only spends 10 per cent of his or her available time on one task, so that a usage rate of 0.1BUY might be used to show the resource requirement for a typical purchasing activity. A purchase ordering activity with an estimated duration of two weeks and a resource requirement of 0.1BUY would then mean that ten per cent of a buyer's time must be spread over two weeks for the purchase order to be raised and issued.

Factored units

Some computer programs might not be able to accept resource quantities that are not integers. If the software cannot accept decimal quantities, it is necessary to resort to tricks. Factoring is one solution that I have found effective. This approach can be explained by referring once again to a buying department.

In the case of the buyers quoted above, the units could be factored by ten. Then 10 resource units (10BUY) would represent not ten, but just one buyer. The declared number of *available* buyers must then also be multiplied by 10. Thus a group of five buyers would be declared as a resource availability of 50BUY. Now when 1BUY is written against a two-week's purchase order activity on the network, this actually signifies one buyer spending 10 per cent of their time over the two-week activity duration.

If factored units are used, any cost rate specified for the resource must be divided by the same factor so that cost reports will be corrected to counteract the large quantities created artificially by the factoring trick. Once again quoting the buyers, suppose that the standard cost rate for one buyer is £150 per day and that days have been used as the standard duration units on the network. Because the units have been factored by ten, the standard daily cost rate for 1BUY unit must be specified as £15.

Competent software will accept decimal quantities and will not demand the use of factoring or similar tricks.

Use of man-hours

Some programs will allow resources to be specified in terms of man-hours, both as the daily requirement and as the availability. This is allowed even when the activity durations are estimated in days. Thus, taking a seven-hour day as an example, when an activity duration of one day is specified on the network this will be interpreted as a resource-usage time of seven hours. Seven units of any resource on that activity (when rate constant) means seven hours per day (one person per day). A resource usage of one in this case means only one hour per day, or one seventh of a person's time throughout the activity.

Use of man-hour units in this way means that decimal resources and factored resources should not be necessary.

My own preference, however, is to keep everything as simple as possible and not to allow numbers to become unnecessarily large. For all projects except those lasting only a few weeks this means using days throughout, both for task durations and for resource usage times.

RATE-CONSTANT AND NON RATE-CONSTANT USAGE OF RESOURCES

The easiest, and usually acceptable method is to assume that a resource will be used at a constant rate over the life of an activity. Thus if an activity is shown with an estimated duration of five days, needing 1BKL and 1LAB (where 'BKL' is a code for bricklayers and 'LAB' signifies labourers) this means that the job requires one bricklayer and one labourer each working full time for five days. This is known in scheduling terms as a rate-constant use of resources.

Planning for uneven resource usage within one activity is possible with some computer systems. For example, the activity just described might have needed no bricklayer or labourer for two days in the middle of its period, but two bricklayers and two labourers for the last two days. The total resource cost and requirement for the task is the same, but the usage pattern is no longer rate-constant. This is illustrated, for the bricklayers, in Figure 17.1.

In practice, it is seldom necessary to be concerned with such fine detail in project scheduling, especially in large networks where the numbers of activities being scheduled should tend to smooth out any small ripples. The use of most, if not all, resources in a project schedule can usually be considered as rate-constant.

SPECIFYING RESOURCE AVAILABILITY LEVELS

Efficiency and the sludge factor

If there are 100 people of one resource type in a department, it might seem reasonable to declare that 100 units of that resource are available to the project. There are, of course, complications. Some of these people will probably be needed for other projects. That problem can be overcome by scheduling all projects together in a multi-project system, which is described in Chapter 28.

No department or group of workers ever achieves 100 per cent efficiency. People take time off or work at reduced efficiency for a variety of reasons (illness, annual holidays, dentist, brief visits to the cloakroom, longer visits to the cloakroom, time waiting for work to be allocated, machine or computer failures, training and so on). Some of these people will also be working on unscheduled jobs, including rectification work and the like.

The answer here is to estimate the level of efficiency for each department or resource type, and to declare a correspondingly reduced level of that resource as being available to the project. If in doubt, start by assuming a relatively low efficiency of 80 per cent, and amend this as experience builds up. So, although there might be 100 people of a particular resource category on the permanent strength of a department, 80 would be the total strength of this resource declared as available for scheduling across all projects. That leaves a 20 per cent sludge factor to cover unplanned absences and down time, and also to allow for work that is impossible or impracticable to schedule. I have used 85 per

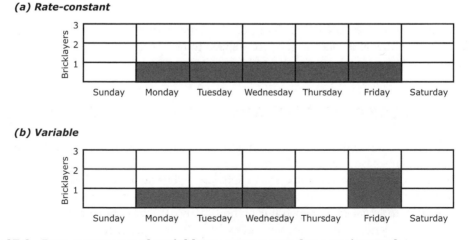

Figure 17.1   Rate constant and variable resource usage for a project task

cent successfully as the general availability level, leaving a sludge element of 15 per cent dispersed over activities and absences that cannot be scheduled.

Overtime as a resource availability

Projects should not generally be scheduled with the intention of using resources during overtime. This point was made in Chapter 15 in the context of estimating task durations. It applies with equal force and for the same reasons when the time comes to set up the resource files in the computer. Declared availability levels should be limited to the capacities present during normal working hours.

Planning for changes in availability levels

The availability level for any manpower resource can change during the life of a project, possibly increasing as a result of recruitment or decreasing if redundancy measures have to be taken. The extent and timing of such planned changes should be available from the organization's long-term budgets and manpower plans. These plans will themselves be influenced by the results of project scheduling, so the process is one of cross-fertilization.

Clearly the resources declared as available for project scheduling need to be kept in step with the forward manpower planning levels. Computer scheduling programs usually allow such changes to be specified well in advance. Typically, the planner is prompted to specify the planned availability level of each resource for a given period. Several such periods can be specified for each resource type to allow for planned staff changes. The following table is typical of the input that might be given to a project management software package in a company with a gradually expanding workforce. These data are for design engineers, who have been given the identifying resource code DE. The numbers indicate that this successful company expects to recruit two additional design engineers during June 2010, a further two at the end of 2010, two more in the middle of 2011, and then remaining constant until the foreseeable future (which in this case is the end of 2015).

Code	Period start	Period end	Amount
DE	01Jan2010	30Jun2010	48
DE	01Jul2010	31Dec2010	50
DE	01Jan2011	30Jun2011	52
DE	01Jul2011	31Dec2015	54

The pattern for the declared availability of a resource can thus be specified for very many years in advance, either at a constant level, or stepped to take account of planned recruitments (or departures).

USING DIFFERENT CALENDARS FOR RESOURCE SCHEDULING

Readers will know that computers have an inbuilt calendar that recognizes calendar dates over a very wide time-span – past, present and future.

The computer and its project management software will undoubtedly offer the project planner a default calendar for general project scheduling. This is the calendar that will convert day numbers from time analysis to actual dates, depending on how many days are to be worked in each week. The most usual default calendar is a working week of five days. Many specify the time of day too, and the default condition in those cases might be from 09.00 to 17.00 daily. That means that no activities can be scheduled to take place during nights or weekends. No dates that fall during weekends will be valid and they will not appear in any calculated schedules or work-to lists.

The planner will be able to modify the default calendar, for example by specifying forthcoming public holiday dates. Whenever a new task is entered into the computer, the default calendar will be assumed but the planner will have the option to specify an alternative, special calendar for application to that task and all its resources.

All competent project management software allows the planner to set as many special calendars as the project requires. Some software will also allow the planner to specify calendars that apply by default not to tasks, but instead to each resource category.

Weekend and shift working

It sometimes happens that a schedule must allow for a mix of single-shift (normal) working with two- or three-shift working. Perhaps all the office staff, including design engineers, work five days in a week and the factory staff work two or three shifts within each 24-hour period. This will complicate scheduling somewhat. Matters will be even more complicated if some, but not all, people normally work over weekends.

These problems can be overcome by setting up and using special calendars. Any task that requires resources during times not allowed for in the 5-day week default calendar can then be assigned to its appropriate calendar, specially created for the purpose.

One calendar might, for example, allow two-shift working per day from Monday to Saturday (inclusive). Another might allow three-shift working for seven days each week.

A special calendar that ignores holidays and weekends, allowing scheduling for seven days of every week, is useful not only for special resource scheduling, but also for tasks such as allowing concrete to cure or paint to dry.

If weekend working is not involved in the mix, the problem of shift working can be overcome simply by multiplying the number of resource units declared as available for an average shift by the number of shifts to be worked each day. If three fitters are to work on each of two shifts, then six fitters are the total available resource within each working day. That method avoids the use of special calendars but can lead to errors.

Holidays

There are two fundamentally different kinds of holidays to cater for in project scheduling. The definitions are my own, as follows:

- **Personal holidays** – absences of individual people for days taken from their personal holiday entitlement, for compassionate leave, for training or for any other special reason.
- **Organizational holidays** – times during which no work on the project can take place. These include public holidays and annual plant shut-downs.

Scheduling personal holidays

Unless the individual concerned is alone in their own resource category (which would be very unusual) the simplest, most convenient, and acceptable way of dealing with individual absences for any reason is to include personal absence times in the sludge factor that was mentioned earlier in this chapter. In other words, the general availability of the resource category is purposely understated to take account of the fact that, at any given time, a certain percentage of the workforce will be absent or otherwise unavailable for project work.

Of course every departmental manager will need to plan for individual staff absences, but the familiar holiday chart will probably be the most appropriate method in most cases.

At least one computer program (from 4c Systems Ltd) allows a staff file to be associated with the resource pool. Various employment details of each staff member can be held on file, including planned vacation dates, so that individual holidays and other planned absences can be specified and taken out of the resource availability pool. However, that degree of sophistication is rarely necessary and there might be a risk of conflict with the more confidential files maintained by the HRM department.

Scheduling organizational holidays

General public holidays, and annual plant shut-downs (known as wakes weeks in some regions of Britain) are dealt with by removing the relevant days from the default calendar.

In international projects, where project tasks are spread over a number of different countries, each country will have its own set of public holidays. Some countries will even have different workings days in each week. This apparent difficulty is easily overcome by creating a special calendar for each different country and it is then only necessary to assign tasks carried out overseas to their relevant calendars.

SEVEN LOGICAL STEPS OF PROJECT RESOURCE SCHEDULING

Many factors may have to be taken into account before a workable resource schedule can be produced for a project. Some of these factors are depicted in Figure 17.2.

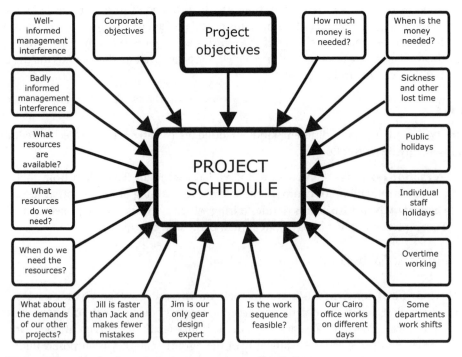

Figure 17.2 The complexity of project resource scheduling

So many factors affect the final project working schedule that scheduling is often regarded as very difficult or as requiring an intuitive gift. But no magic is needed. The mystery is removed when the process is carried out in a logical sequence.

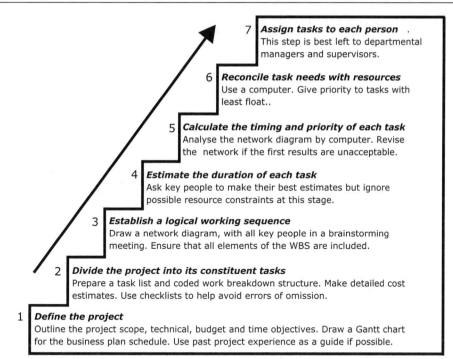

7 **Assign tasks to each person** .
   This step is best left to departmental managers and supervisors.

6 **Reconcile task needs with resources**
   Use a computer. Give priority to tasks with least float..

5 **Calculate the timing and priority of each task**
   Analyse the network diagram by computer. Revise the network if the first results are unacceptable.

4 **Estimate the duration of each task**
   Ask key people to make their best estimates but ignore possible resource constraints at this stage.

3 **Establish a logical working sequence**
   Draw a network diagram, with all key people in a brainstorming meeting. Ensure that all elements of the WBS are included.

2 **Divide the project into its constituent tasks**
   Prepare a task list and coded work breakdown structure. Make detailed cost estimates. Use checklists to help avoid errors of omission.

1 **Define the project**
   Outline the project scope, technical, budget and time objectives. Draw a Gantt chart for the business plan schedule. Use past project experience as a guide if possible.

Figure 17.3   Seven logical steps to a practical project resource schedule

A mathematician faced with a problem containing a number of unknown quantities would adopt a logical approach, and attempt to evaluate the unknowns by solving them one at a time. Project scheduling benefits from this approach, and there are seven recognizable stages leading from potential chaos to a practicable solution. The seven steps are listed in Figure 17.3.

The methods for undertaking each of these seven steps have all been described in this text, with one very important exception. No project can have its resources scheduled in isolation from the demands of other projects being conducted in the same organization. Except in the case of an isolated pure project team, resources usually exist as a common pool, and wherever there is more than one project being worked in an organization, resource scheduling must be global and multi-project. Chapter 28 deals with these wider and more advanced aspects of scheduling multiple projects as one model across a company or group.

REFERENCES AND FURTHER READING

Most project management writers do not give resource scheduling sufficient prominence or explanation but the following are among the better works in this respect.

Devaux, S. A. (1999), *Total Project Control: a Manager's Guide to Integrated Planning, Measuring and Tracking* (New York: Wiley).

Gray, B., Gray, C. F. and Larson, E. W. (2005), *Project Management: the Managerial Process*, 3rd Edition (Singapore: McGraw-Hill).

Meredith, J. R., and Mantel, S. J. jnr (2003), *Project Management: a Managerial Approach*, 5th Edition, international edition (New York: Wiley).

Shtub, A., Bard, J. F. and Globerson, S. (1994), *Project Management: Engineering, Technology and Implementation* (Englewood Cliffs: Prentice Hall).

18 *Scheduling Materials*

Materials and parts are just as much part of the resources for projects as money and labour. Although the examples given in Chapters 16 and 17 demonstrated the scheduling of human resources, the same methods can be used for project materials. Most project management computer packages can carry out this function, provided that the materials requirements for any network task can be specified in amounts defined by simple units of quantity (for example, tonnes of sand). Project management packages can also be used to schedule the overall loading of manufacturing facilities. But there are at least two aspects of project materials scheduling that need their own specialized procedures. These, which are outlined in this chapter, are the following:

- scheduling parts and components for operations in manufacturing projects;
- scheduling the purchases of equipment for capital projects such as mining, civil engineering, petrochemical projects and other large construction projects.

MANUFACTURED PARTS AND MATERIALS SCHEDULING COMPARED WITH GENERAL PROJECT RESOURCE SCHEDULING

Manufactured and purchased parts for manufacturing projects attract different scheduling problems from those associated with the purchase of bulk materials. A great deal more detail is required in manufacturing schedules than can easily or feasibly be included on the main project schedule. Solving the problems of parts scheduling falls more properly within the ambit of operations management than project management (see, for example, Slack, Chambers and Johnston 2003). This chapter can, however, provide a glimpse into this subject.

Parts scheduling requires close analysis of drawings, meticulous attention to detail, and specialized techniques. At one time the only practicable approach depended on manual methods, often using elaborate compilations of index cards. The amount of work required could be prodigious, especially when attempting to identify and coordinate the usage of parts common to more than one part of the project or, worse still, common also to other projects and routine manufacturing. The methods were cumbersome, prone to error, and could not easily cope with changes. Those methods can be consigned to history and earlier editions of this book. Now the problems of complexity, inflexibility and errors can be solved more easily using computers.

Any system of parts scheduling demands the assembly of data structured on bills of materials or parts lists. Since these documents are products of design engineering, it follows that project parts scheduling cannot take place until design is substantially complete, considerably later in the project life cycle than when the main project schedules are made. The methods described here assume that the project manager already has the main project plans and schedules, and knows when each significant assembly or subassembly will be required for the project. That information must be derived from the overall project plan (using critical path networks or bar charts). Then, provided all the human resources and overall manufacturing facilities are scheduled sensibly (at departmental or group levels), production managers are given a time framework into which the manufacture and procurement of parts and smaller subassemblies can be fitted.

Activities in overall project schedules cannot usually be chosen to show a depth of detail much smaller than main assemblies, or at least fairly large subassemblies. Factory schedules will even have to include all the separate manufacturing operations needed to make each part. Scheduling at the much greater level of detail needed for individual parts must be carried out by the manufacturing organization using their own specialized methods. These manufacturing schedules might contain a mix of specially purchased components, items manufactured within the company's own factory and other parts which are usually held in store as general stock.

IDENTIFYING AND QUANTIFYING COMMON PARTS FOR MANUFACTURING PROJECTS

The parts scheduling task is usually complicated because some of the parts for one assembly are also used on other assemblies or even other projects, so that provisioning must take all these different uses into account. Suppose that a project needs 100 cam-operated electrical switching subassemblies, all slightly different in design but each containing a particular type of microswitch in varying quantities. Thus there might be 100 sets of detail and assembly drawings for these switching subassemblies, each with its own parts list or bill of materials. Someone has to discover how many of these switches are needed in total for the project, make sure that the requirements are collated, and that 100 separate purchase orders for microswitches are not placed. The same switching subassemblies might easily have other components that must be investigated to discover their total requirements as common items (cams and servo motors, for example).

Batch differences

Another complication arises if a project has to result in more than one similar output batch, produced at different times. Consider, for instance, a defence contractor who is working to produce a state-of-the-art weapons guidance system. The initial contract might be for the design and manufacture of six identical Mark 1 prototype units, to be delivered at two-monthly intervals. An improved version (Mark 2) could be under development before all the prototypes have been delivered, so that Mark 1 and Mark 2 systems are both in different stages of production in the factory at the same time, with some parts common to both batches. While all this is going on, engineering changes can of course be expected to affect one or both batches, or even individual units within a batch.

When parts scheduling becomes particularly complex, the project planner or project support office can provide help to the materials manager and production managers by collating all the known parts requirements, listing the assemblies and subassemblies on which the parts are to be used, and relating this information to the dates on the project plan. That information can provide the input to a manufacturing requirements package (MRP II).

CASE EXAMPLE: A FILING CABINET PROJECT

Some aspects of parts scheduling for a manufacturing project can be demonstrated using a simple example. For clarity in these pages this study will not be taken down to the level of individual manufacturing operations and excludes finishing processes such as plating and painting.

A company has designed a steel two-drawer filing cabinet, an exploded view of which is shown in Figure 18.1. In the first instance, only one cabinet is to be made.

Simple parts list for a filing cabinet

All the parts needed for the filing cabinet can be seen in the exploded view (Figure 18.1), and these could easily be listed on a parts list or bill of materials. This might be compiled using a computer-aided design (CAD) system, or manually on a form such as that shown in Figure 18.2. The item numbers on this parts list correspond with those in the circles on the exploded view. It shows total quantities without regard for breakdown into production subassemblies.

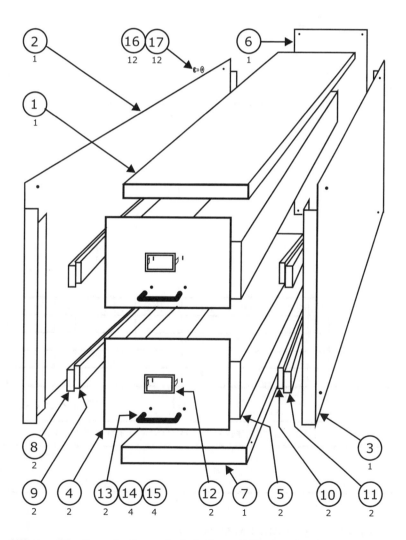

Figure 18.1 Filing cabinet project: exploded view of the product

| Item No. | Our part number | Description | Quantity | | Remarks |
			Unit	No	
01	FC1001	Top panel	Each	1	MF Panel shop
02	FC1002L	Side panel, left	Each	1	MF Panel shop
03	FC1002R	Side panel, right	Each	1	MF Panel shop
04	FC1003	Drawer chassis	Each	2	MF Panel shop
06	FC1005	Rear panel	Each	1	MF Panel shop
07	FC1006	Plinth	Each	1	MF Panel shop
08	A502-A	Runner, outer, left	Each	2	SP Smiths plc
09	A502-B	Runner, inner, left	Each	2	SP Smiths plc
10	A503-A	Runner, outer, right	Each	2	SP Smiths plc
11	A503-B	Runner, inner, right	Each	2	SP Smiths plc
12	A209	Title card holder	Each	2	CS Carter
13	A350	Handle	Each	2	CS Epsom and Salt
14	S217	Screw	Each	4	CS Acme Screws
15	W180	Washer,shakeproof	Each	4	CS Acme Screws
16	S527	Screw, self tapping	Each	12	CS Acme Screws
17	W180	Washer,shakeproof	Each	12	CS Acme Screws

MF = Make
SP = Special purchase
CS = Common stock

Iss	Mod No	Date	Iss	Mod No	Date	Iss	Mod No	Date	Iss	Mod No	Date
A	Prot	4Jun10									
1	-	3Aug10									
2	1	17Nov10									

Drawn by: EFP	Checked by: TQM	Approved *David Woodford*

Heath Robinson Furniture Plc   Birmingham   England

Title: Filing cabinet: Elite series Two drawer Without locks	Sheet 1 of 1 sheets	Assembly number: FC 1000

Figure 18.2   Filing cabinet project: simple parts list

Armed with the simple parts list, the company's purchasing and production control departments would be able to provision all the materials by drawing available items from existing stocks, and either buying or making the remainder. There is no ambiguity about the total required quantity of any item and no complicated calculations are needed. Everything is detailed on one simple parts list.

Given a target completion date for the single cabinet, it would also be fairly simple to decide when each item must be ordered. Priorities must be given to those parts having the longest purchase or manufacturing lead times.

Structured parts list for a filing cabinet

The best sequence of manufacture for the filing cabinet would be as follows:

1. Make individual components and obtain bought-out items.
2. Assemble the parts into subassemblies.
3. Carry out the final, main assembly.

The simple parts list arrangement shown in Figure 18.2 is not very convenient for the production department because, ideally, they need a separate parts list from which to issue the manufacturing kit for each subassembly.

In order to produce these separate parts lists, it is usual for the designer to start by drawing a family tree or goes-into chart showing how all the subassemblies and individual parts come together for the final assembly. The family tree for the filing cabinet is shown in Figure 18.3. This is a hierarchical structure not unlike the larger-scale work breakdown structure for a project, but the level of detail here goes down to the very lowest level, including every nut, bolt and washer. Further, the tree must show the quantity of each part needed (the circled numbers in the figure show the quantities needed for each subassembly or main assembly on the next higher level of the tree). Coding (part numbering) is essential.

The example in Figure 18.3 reveals that four separate subassemblies have to be made before final assembly of one filing cabinet can take place. So, the simple parts list of Figure 18.2 has to be structured as five separate lists, one for each subassembly and one for the final main assembly. This arrangement is summarized in Figure 18.4.

While the arrangement of parts lists in the filing cabinet family tree grouping (Figure 18.3) is ideal for manufacturing purposes, it is not so convenient for the purchasing of parts, or for the scheduling of manufacture for parts common to more than one subassembly.

For example, the washer, part number W180, is common to two assemblies. It appears twice on the simple parts list of Figure 18.2, where it is an easy matter to add up the quantities to find the total number of washers needed to make one filing cabinet (4 + 12 = 16). On the family tree in Figure 18.3 and on the manufacturing parts lists derived from it in Figure 18.4, this result is not quite so obvious. Anyone glancing at either the family tree or at the five separate parts lists might be forgiven for assuming that only 14 washers type W180 were needed (12 on the final assembly and two on the drawer assembly). On each of the separate parts lists the washer (and every other item) only appears in the quantities needed to make one particular subassembly, regardless of how many subassemblies are needed. The catch is, of course, that two drawer assemblies are needed for one filing cabinet, so that the total number of washers needed for one cabinet is 12 + (2 x 2) = 16.

To find out how many of any item must be bought or made in total, therefore, it is necessary to work up through the family tree, multiplying the quantities as necessary. That gives the result for one filing cabinet, which must be multiplied again by the batch size to find the total quantity for each component. So, if the production batch comprised 10 filing cabinets, at least 160 washers type W180 must be obtained.

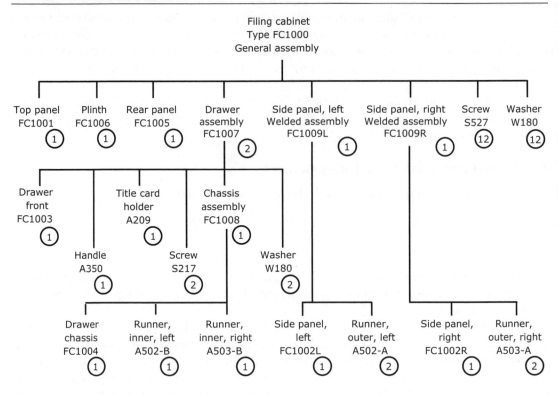

Figure 18.3   Filing cabinet project: family tree

LINE OF BALANCE

An extension of the parts scheduling and collation problem occurs when more than one project is being undertaken at the same time, especially when parts or assemblies used on one project are also required for some or all of the others. The line of balance case study which follows demonstrates some of the principles of complex parts scheduling.

The subject of this case study is the same filing cabinet that was illustrated in Figures 18.1 to 18.4. This time, however, this is a limited edition filing cabinet to be made in a total quantity of 50, and the orders for the delivery of these have been received according to the first two columns in Figure 18.5. Although this is a small quantity by any manufacturing standards, suppose for the sake of this study that these cabinets must be manufactured in small batches, each batch being initiated by a separate customer order. In all the following calculations calendar dates have been converted into numbers, with the promised delivery time for the first batch taken as the datum (time zero). All other customer delivery dates are related to this datum, shown in the column headed 'Delivery day No.' in Figure 18.5.

Calculating the quantities and lead times

Simple parts collation takes no account of the different lead times needed to make or buy all the various parts. To create a manufacturing schedule for all batches it is necessary to reconcile the quantities of all the parts needed with the complex delivery schedule.

The first step in a line of balance calculation is to obtain a family tree for the parts needed to build one complete product. A family tree already exists for the filing cabinet (Figure 18.3) but for

FC1000 Filing cabinet: final assembly			Revision 2
	Parts list		
Part number	Description	Quantity	Remarks
FC1007	Drawer assembly	2	
FC1009L	Side panel, left, welded assembly	1	
FC1009R	Side panel, right, welded assembly	1	
Fc1001	Top panel	1	
FC1006	Plinth	1	
FC1005	Rear panel	1	
S257	Screw, self-tapping	12	Acme Screws
W180	Washer	12	Acme Screws

FC1007 Drawer assembly		Used on filing cabinet FC1000	
	Parts list		
FC1008	Drawer chassis subassembly	1	
FC1003	Drawer front panel	1	
A209	Title card holder	1	Carter
A350	Handle	1	Epsom and Salt
S217	Screw	2	Acme Screws
W180	Washer	2	Acme Screws

FC1008 Drawer chassis subassembly		Used on drawer FC1007	
	Parts list		
FC1004	Drawer chassis	1	
A502B	Runner, inner, left hand	1	Smiths plc
A503B	Runner, inner, right hand	1	Smiths plc

FC1009L Side panel, left, welded assembly		Used on filing cabinet FC1000	
	Parts list		
FC1002L	Side panel, left hand	1	
A502A	Runner, outer, left hand	2	Smiths plc

FC1009R Side panel, right, welded assembly		Used on filing cabinet FC1000	
	Parts list		
FC1002R	Side panel, right hand	1	
A5032A	Runner, outer, right hand	2	Smiths plc

Figure 18.4 Filing cabinet project: parts list arranged in subassemblies

Customer	Date promised	Delivery day No.	Lead time day No.	Quantity ordered	Cumulative quantity
Jones	7 Oct	0	-32	5	5
Jenkins	11 Oct	4	-28	5	10
Griffiths	29 Oct	16	-16	10	20
Morgan	4 Nov	20	-12	10	30
Edwards	14 Nov	28	- 4	10	40
Williams	26 Nov	36	4	5	45
Evans	2 Dec	40	8	5	50

Figure 18.5 Filing cabinet project: delivery data

line of balance purposes it is more convenient to redraw this tree laterally, so that the sequence flows with time from left to right. The redrawn family tree is shown in Figure 18.6.

Quantities

The number written in the small circle alongside each part number in Figure 18.6 shows, as before in Figure 18.3, the quantity of that part which must be provided to construct one of the subassemblies on which it is used.

Lead times

Figure 18.7 shows the next step in the scheduling process shown. Squares have been added at every intersection and at the ends of the tree branches, rather in the fashion of the event nodes in an arrow network diagram. Indeed, the following steps bear a very close resemblance to network time analysis.

For each item, the elapsed time between placing an order (either a purchase order or a factory manufacturing order) for each item and the day when that part will be needed must be estimated. These are total duration estimates, which means that all activities such as the preparation and issue of orders, machine setting times, suppliers' lead times, shipping times and stores kitting times have to be allowed for in the times. Each estimate has been written directly below the branch to which it refers. Estimates are in working days, with all figures rounded up to the nearest whole day.

Now the total project lead time for any part can be found. This is done by adding up the individual lead times backwards through the tree, working through every path from right to left. The results are shown inside the 'event' squares in Figure 18.7.

The family tree, set up and annotated as in Figure 18.7, now tells us all we need to know about the provision of parts for one filing cabinet. Taking part A503B as a random example, we know that two of these must be provided, and that they have to be *ordered* at least 32 days before the

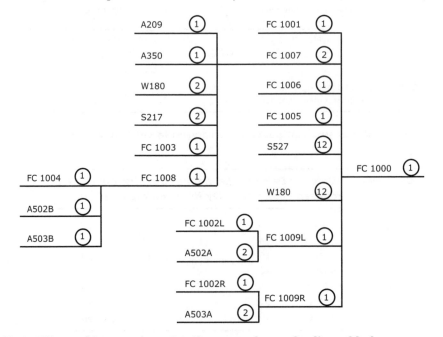

Figure 18.6 Filing cabinet project: family tree redrawn for line of balance

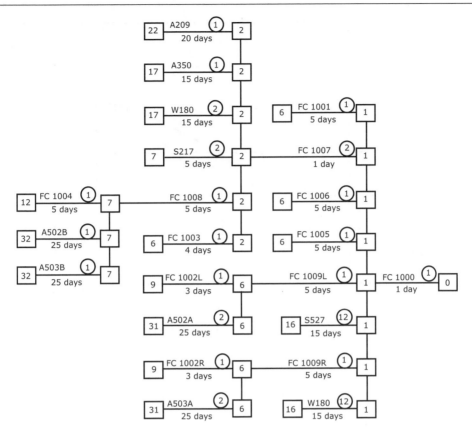

Figure 18.7 Filing cabinet project: calculations of lead times for parts

filing cabinet is wanted. If they are not *received* by the seventh day before completion is due, the programme is bound to run late. Notice that, unlike an arrow network diagram, everything on this family tree is critical. All times are latest times. No float exists anywhere. A column has been included in Figure 18.5 to show these lead times as project day numbers, all with respect to the day zero datum.

All of these quantities for a single cabinet must obviously be multiplied by the batch quantity to complete the total quantities needed for each production batch.

Time/quantity relationships for multiple manufactured batches

Before a series of repetitive batches can be considered, it is necessary to draw a graph showing the cumulative quantities to be delivered against time. Figure 18.8 shows the graph for the filing project, drawn according to the cumulative quantities given in Figure 18.5. The time axis is scaled in working days, starting from day zero, which is the first day of the delivery schedule.

Now suppose that day 4 of the programme has been reached and that the current status of production has to be checked against the delivery commitments. Again taking the drawer runner, part number A503B as an example, the lead time for ordering this part is known to be 32 days (from the data in Figure 18.7). Two of these runners are needed for each cabinet. By projecting forward along the delivery graph from day 4 by the lead time of 32 days, day 36 is reached. The graph shows that 45 cabinets should be delivered by day 36. This means that at day 4 all the runners needed to make these 45 cabinets should either be issued, available or on order. In other words a total of 90 parts number A503B must have been ordered at or before day 4.

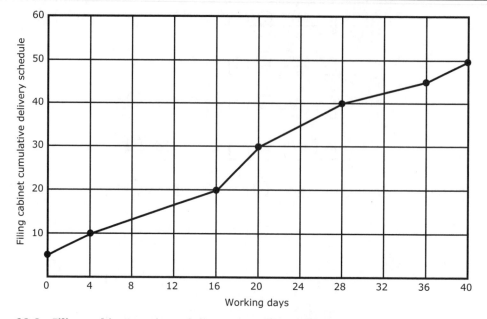

Figure 18.8 Filing cabinet project: delivery commitment graph

Not only is it possible to calculate how many parts should have been ordered, but also it is possible to work out how many parts from those orders must actually be available in stock or already used. This is done by considering the end 'event' for the relevant part or subassembly in each case instead of its start 'event'. For part A503B at day 4, the result would be based on a lead time of seven days, which takes the projection on the delivery graph up to day 11. Reading off the graph at day 11 shows that a sufficient quantity of this part must therefore be in stock or issued by day 4 to make 16 cabinets (32 parts).

In the table of Figure 18.9 similar calculations have been performed for all the filing cabinet parts. The quantities all relate to day 4 of the programme. The start events have been used in this example, so that the total quantities shown include the totals of parts which should be on order, in progress, in stock or already dispatched in completed cabinets.

Drawing the line of balance chart

Now refer to Figure 18.10, where the data from Figure 18.9 have been converted into chart form. Each separate item has been allocated a column to itself, and the total minimum quantity required is shown as a horizontal line drawn at the appropriate scale height across the relevant column. These quantities are the necessary balance quantities for the programme, and the stepped graph which they form is known as the line of balance. Remember that this whole chart has been calculated with respect to day 4, and is only valid for that single day of the manufacturing programme.

The last step is to find out what the actual progress is and plot these results on the same line of balance chart. The chart should take on an appearance similar to that shown in Figure 18.11, where some imaginary progress results have been assumed and plotted. The fruits of all the calculations and planning labours should now become obvious, since it is clearly seen that any achievement which falls below the line of balance indicates that the delivery schedule has slipped and customers will not receive their cabinets on time.

Data for one complete filing cabinet				Project quantities to be finished or in progress at day 4	
Part number	Used on	Total lead time in days	Quantity	For how many cabinets?	Total number of parts
FC1000		1	1	11	11
FC1001	FC1000	6	1	15	15
FC1002L	FC1009L	9	1	18	18
FC1002R	FC1009R	9	1	18	18
FC1003	FC1007	6	2	12	24
FC1004	FC1008	12	2	20	40
FC1005	FC1000	6	1	15	15
FC1006	FC1000	6	1	15	15
FC1007	FC1000	2	2	12	24
FC1008	FC1007	7	2	16	32
FC1009L	FC1000	6	1	15	15
FC1009R	FC1000	6	1	15	15
A350	FC1007	17	2	31	62
A502A	FC1009L	31	2	45	90
A502B	FC1008	31	2	45	90
A503A	FC1009R	31	2	45	90
A503B	FC1008	31	2	45	90
A 209	FC1007	22	2	38	76
S217	FC1007	7	4	16	64
S527	FC1000	16	12	30	360
W180*	FC1007	17	4	31	124 $\Big\}$ =484
W180*	FC1000	16	12	30	360

*Common part

Figure 18.9   Filing cabinet project: calculation for line of balance at day 4

Using the line of balance chart

In the filing cabinets example, parts W180, S527 and S217 have been purchased in total quantities from the start, because these are inexpensive items and they take up little storage space. Part A350 is seen to be below the line of balance, indicating that more should have been ordered by day 4.

Everything illustrated here relates to day 4 of the delivery programme, and the chart is valid for only for that day. A separate chart would have to be calculated for any other day on this project, which could be from day –32 up to day 40.

The vertical scale can prove troublesome because of the wide range of quantities that might have to be accommodated. This was true to some extent in the filing cabinet example. If the problem is particularly acute, a logarithmic scale can be considered.

Although line of balance charts cannot, of course, show the reason for any shortages, they are effective visual displays and particularly good at highlighting deficiencies. As such they are useful for showing to higher executives at project meetings, where they save time by satisfying the principle of management by exception.

In practice it is necessary, although even more laborious, to split up the family tree and all the charts into more detail, not just into parts and subassemblies but also into the manufacturing operations needed to make the individual parts. All of these operations would then be allotted columns on the line of balance chart. This might seem a high price to pay for a chart, which is only valid for one day, but the line of balance principle becomes far more useful when the results are used not to draw charts but to plan and initiate work from computer-generated schedules.

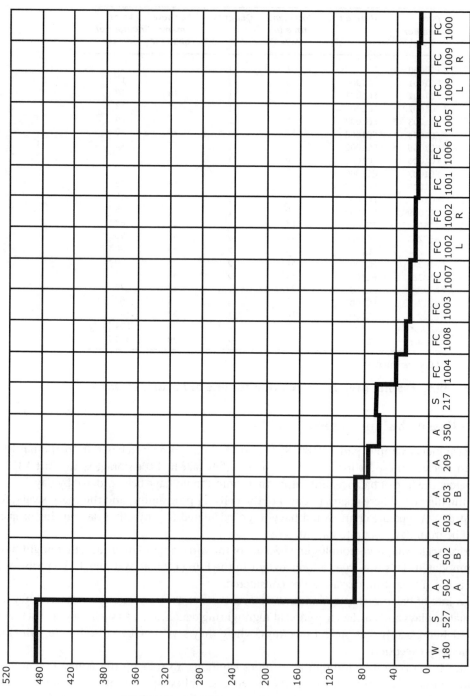

Figure 18.10 Filing cabinet project: line of balance at day 4

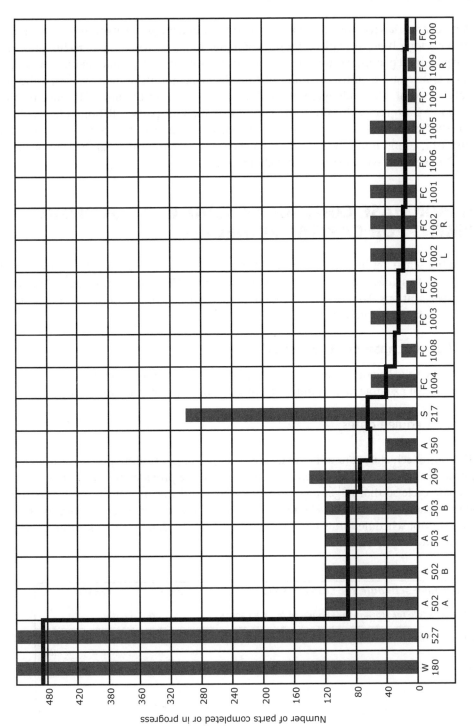

Figure 18.11 Filing cabinet project: line of balance completed for day 4

COMPUTER SOLUTIONS FOR SCHEDULING MANUFACTURING MATERIALS

The problems of materials records, collation from parts lists, and timescale planning of manufacturing operations have long been recognized by the computer industry, resulting in techniques such as materials requirement planning (MRP) and its successor manufacturing requirements planning (MRP II). Any such system still requires the input of considerable amounts of data. Accuracy and proper administration is vital. The underlying methods are very similar to the line of balance technique, described above. However, with MRPII, the family tree analysis, parts collation and scheduling is automated. The system is therefore dynamic and responsive to change. Also, with a computer system that can list, edit, count, multiply and report on each item, careful watch can be kept on stocks to minimize shortages or prevent excessive stockholdings.

USING PURCHASE CONTROL SCHEDULES TO SCHEDULE EQUIPMENT FOR CAPITAL PROJECTS

Purchase control schedules list all the significant items of equipment required for a project and are used by the project engineers as registers from which to control the serial numbering and preparation of purchase specifications. They are to the capital project what the parts list or bill of materials is to the smaller manufacturing project.

Format of a purchase control schedule

Figure 18.12 shows the layout of main and column headings for a typical purchase control schedule page. This particular example has columns allowing for the entry of both timescale and cost data.

Inclusion of scheduled dates

If purchase control schedules are to be used subsequently for controlling progress throughout the purchase cycle for each item listed, a separate column must be provided for every significant event in the purchase cycle so that target dates can be shown. This means using a format considerably more complex than that shown in Figure 18.12 and the amount of schedule data to be entered on purchase control schedule forms becomes considerable. The data must be kept up to date with changes in the project schedule.

Purchase schedule for Loxylene Plant (Huddersfield)					Page	of		
Subschedule for storage tankhouse code LX 5150-450					Issue date:			
Spec. no.	Rev no.	Description	Qty	Supplier	Order no.	Amdt no.	Date needed	Cost on-site

Figure 18.12   Front page headings for a purchase control schedule

At one time it was necessary to use entirely manual methods for compiling purchase control schedules, so that the entry of planned target dates was a tedious and expensive chore. Updating a large schedule in line with progress became a prodigious undertaking.

Even with computer-controlled scheduling, difficulties remain. It is not likely that every item of equipment or supplies shown on the purchase control schedule will be represented by a separate chain of activities on the project network diagram. Even where that is the case, the degree of detail allowed on the network might not depict and date all parts of the purchase life cycle.

There are several possible remedies for reducing the amount of clerical work needed or, indeed, of eliminating it altogether. All of these require that the degree of planning detail on the critical path network is adequate and chosen with common sense.

One approach would be to represent every item of equipment by a separate activity chain on the network. Then every date needed for control could come off a computer-generated work-to list that acts as the purchase control schedule. The arrangement would be dynamic and flexible to change. The big snag with this method is that the degree of detail needed would be difficult to achieve and manage. The network would probably become huge and unmanageable.

A more practicable approach is to plan all items of equipment on the network in groups according to the areas in the finished project where they are going to be needed. For example, all the pumps for a particular plant area might be represented on the network simply as 'pumps for bay 3', even though there might be many of these pumps, occupying one or more sheets of the complete purchase control schedule. The equipment on the purchase control schedule sheets can be listed in a separate block for each plant area group. The schedules can then:

- simply refer to the relevant activity ID code for each group of equipment items;

or

- show all the dates in detail, derived and printed from the project management database (with identical dates shown for each item of equipment within the same group);

or

- a combination of both of these.

Preparing purchase control schedules

An effective arrangement for the preparation of purchase control schedules is to ask each project engineering discipline group (civil, structural, mechanical, piping and fluids, electrical, process control and so on) to prepare a separate schedule of the equipment for which it is responsible. Apart from the obvious common sense technical advantages of this approach, it can greatly simplify the allocation of purchase specification serial numbers.

If the project is of any significant size, or if the company procedures so demand, the schedules can be broken further broken down into subsets according to the various project plant sections. Thus the total set of purchase control schedules for a project could be arranged as shown in Figure 18.13 (which also shows how serial numbers might be allocated).

Distribution of purchase schedules

During the project execution, it is usual to merge all parts of the purchase control schedule into the complete purchasing schedule for the project. This complete version is then made available to all the engineering discipline groups (along with the drawing schedules), to the buyer or purchasing agent, and possibly to the client. Once the site management team has been set up, it too should receive the schedules to allow pre-planning of storage facilities and to assist in the planning of work on site.

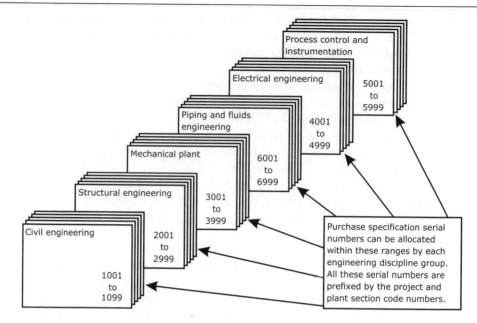

Figure 18.13   Complete purchase control schedule

REFERENCES AND FURTHER READING

Slack, N., Chambers, S. and Johnston, R. (2003) *Operations Management*, 4th Edition (London: Financial Times Prentice Hall).

19 *Scheduling Cash Flows*

Cash is the lifeblood of projects. Without money to pay the people, suppliers and subcontractors, all work will stop and then even the most promising project will fail.

Cash flow forecasting was introduced in Chapter 6 in the context of financial project appraisal. That was very early in the project life cycle, when project investments and possible cash returns were being considered to support (or condemn) the business case. This chapter revisits cash flow scheduling much later in the project life cycle. Now the project scope and deliverables are well established. There is a coded work breakdown structure, a detailed critical path diagram and a computer system all ready to go. Detailed resource scheduling and the issue of work-to lists can take place as soon as the project start date is authorized and announced. Actual work (and serious spending) can then begin. Now is the time to take a much closer look at project cash flows, to ensure that enough money will always be in the bank to pay the bills.

CASH FLOW SCHEDULING IN GENERAL

Project managers tend to occupy their minds with day-to-day matters such as technical difficulties, design errors, the allocation of work, progress against the schedule, performance of subcontractors and expenditure against the cost budgets. The vital subject of project cash flow might be appreciated by a few of the senior staff who work in project organizations, but it is more often completely misunderstood. Two very common mistakes are:

- confusing cash *outflow* schedules with *net* cash flow schedules;
- regarding a predicted final project profit and loss statement as being completely satisfactory if it forecasts a good end result, but without giving any thought to the cash flows that must take place before the project can be finished.

Main contractors and other managers of large capital projects may be asked to predict cash flows as a service to their clients. Customers need to know when to expect claims for payment from the contractor. In some projects customers buy equipment for the project themselves, or at least pay the suppliers' invoices directly and, again, they need to be advised in advance of the likely amounts and timings of these commitments. So project cash flow schedules can serve a dual purpose, helping both the contractor and the customer to make the necessary funds available to keep the project afloat and financially viable.

SCHEDULING CASH FLOWS IN DIFFERENT KINDS OF PROJECTS

Scheduling cash outflows for internally funded projects

Cash flow patterns depend, among other things, upon the nature of the project. Business change and IT projects usually require considerable expenditure during the fulfilment phases of their life cycles, but will not earn any financial return until some time after their completion. The same applies to projects for the design and development of new products, which must wait for successful sales of the new product before investment in the development project can be repaid. The common factor among all these projects is that they are internally funded, which means that no external customer or client is there to pay for the project work while it is actually taking place.

Thus the cash flows for internally funded projects are principally *outflows*, which means that all expenditure must come from cash in hand, financial reserves, loans or some other source. The cash *inflows* or project benefits (if any) will not usually happen until some time after the initial project has been finished. Thus, whilst managing day-to-day work during the active part of the project life cycle, the project manager usually needs only to schedule the cash outflows for these projects.

In order to produce a schedule of cash outflows, it is necessary to have a set of budgets or cost estimates, together with a schedule of work that will allow all the outgoing costs to be set in their respective time periods. That requirement is illustrated in Figure 19.1.

Given detailed cost estimates and a practicable project plan, the scheduling of project cash outflows becomes fairly straightforward arithmetic. However, it is very important to set each item of expected expenditure in the period when the payment will actually become due. For example, the cash outflow for purchasing an item of equipment or a bulk supply of materials takes place not when the purchase order is placed (the time of cost commitment) but at the time when the invoice will actually be paid. Of course the act of committing the project to any new cost is important, but that comes within the context of *cost* control (described in Chapter 26) and not *cash* control.

Every item in any cash flow schedule, whether for outflows or inflows, is the best estimate of two different things, which are:

- the amount of cash involved;
- the date when that amount of money will actually change hands.

Scheduling cash flows for a simple commercial project

Suppose that you, as an impresario or entrepreneur, decide to stage a musical event on a summer's evening in a park or field. You want to attract well-known performers who will occupy a sound stage for the evening, delighting family audiences, and the whole affair will be rounded off with a magnificent fireworks display.

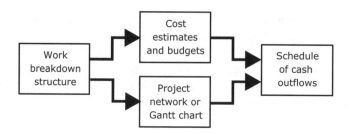

Figure 19.1   Essential elements of a project cash flow schedule

Scheduling the cash flows for such an event requires a lot of business sense and common sense, but no project management training. Simple diary plans and straightforward cost estimates are all that are needed. The resulting cash flow schedule might look something like the one presented in Figure 19.2.

This example tells the organizers that they will need to invest £2000 of their own money at the very beginning, but by March they will expect to recoup £1000, leaving a debt of £1000. Thereafter, all the estimated inflows exceed the outflows until August, by which time there should be a considerable bank balance from which to make the bulk of payments due to the artistes and other contributors.

Of course, this is a high-risk venture. If ticket sales are too low, or if the expected sponsorship does not materialize, you will find yourself in considerable debt and be unable to make all the payments. This kind of failure is by no means unknown, and has led to artistes (including one known to me) being unpaid. The advance cash flow schedule is important because it sets out clearly the figures that must be achieved to avoid bankruptcy and ensure project success.

Net cash flow schedules for larger and more complex commercial projects

A typical large project that is carried out by a contractor for a commercial client will involve a very complex pattern of cash flows.

The inflows will come mainly as progress or stage payments made by the client to the contractor when particular project milestones have been achieved or when an independent engineer or chartered surveyor certifies to the supplier that a measured amount of work has been done. Outflows will take place when wages are paid, when subcontractors submit their bills, and when materials are purchased (again talking about the times when invoices are actually paid and money changes hands rather than dates when orders are placed).

There may be thousands of tasks and purchases to be taken into account when preparing such a cash flow schedule, and evaluating all the costs and putting them into their appropriate time slots

Net cash flow forecast for the 2010 Loxville music festival									
							All figures are £'000s		
Item	*Feb*	*Mar*	*Apr*	*May*	*Jun*	*Jul*	*Aug*	*Sep*	*Item totals*
Cash inflows									
Sponsors		5	10	20	5	5			45
Ticket sales			5	10	180	180			375
Advertising							5		5
Total inflows (i)		5	15	30	185	185	5		425
Cash outflows									
Contractors					10	15	5	3	33
Artistes					1	20	150	48	219
Fireworks						20			20
Administration	2	4	6	10	10	15	40	2	89
Total outflows (o)	2	4	6	10	21	70	195	53	361
Net cash flows (i -o)									
Each month	(2)	1	9	20	164	115	(190)	(53)	
Cumulative	(2)	(1)	8	28	192	307	117	64	64

Figure 19.2 Project cash flow schedule for an outdoor concert

can be a very large task, covering many pages of calculations. Fortunately, much of the effort can be saved if the project has had its resources scheduled by a computer, because it is possible to schedule cash outflows as part of the resource scheduling process. This process will be explained later in this chapter.

The information needed to produce a *net* cash flow schedule, which balances inflows against outflows, is depicted in Figure 19.3.

First consider the cash outflows. Everything starts from the work breakdown structure or detailed task list that specifies what has to be done. Then, a combination of the project work schedules and detailed cost estimates enables each cash outflow item to be placed in its appropriate period. An example of a cash outflow schedule is given in Figure 19.4. This is fairly typical of a large construction project, which in this case is to build a plant for the manufacture of the imaginary chemical Loxylene (at least, an Internet search proved that it *was* imaginary at the time of writing).

Figure 19.4 shows the summary or 'cost roll up' sheet for the Loxylene project, which in practice would be backed up by many other sheets, each of which would detail the cash flows of items lower down in the work breakdown structure. The timescale in this example is arranged in three-monthly (quarterly) periods.

The cash outflow schedule is only the first part of the story. The financial director for the main contracting company will need to know how these predicted cash outflows compare with expected inflows, so that he or she can be assured that the bank balance will always be satisfactory, and sufficient to fund each month's work.

Returning to Figure 19.3, it can be seen that knowing both the prices to be charged to the client (as progress payments for this construction project) and the project schedule will enable a schedule of cash inflows to be made. When that has been done, the forecast cash inflows and outflows can be compared to assess how much cash will flow in or out of the contractor's bank each month (the *net* flows). That, in turn, will enable the project manager to report the effect that these cash movements will have on balances at the bank.

The net cash flow scheduling process is exactly the same (but on a far larger scale) as the calculations that most of us have to perform each month to ensure that our expenditure does not exceed our personal income. We know the amount of our salaries or other income and when to expect payment, and we know when certain expenses such as Council Tax, energy bills, credit card statements and so on will fall due for payment. If we do not manage all these inflows and outflows successfully, our accounts might become overdrawn, causing our bank managers to send us polite but unpleasant letters containing phrases such as 'unarranged borrowing' or 'in view of the figures that I see before me'. (Yes, I'm writing from early experience.)

Hundreds of sheets of calculations would be needed to calculate the net cash flow schedule for the Loxylene plant project, but it is the summary sheet, shown in Figure 19.5, that is most important to the financial director and the contractor's other senior management.

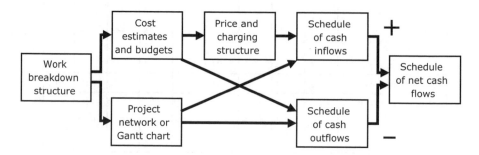

Figure 19.3   Essential elements of a project net cash flow schedule

PROJECTS UNLIMITED LTD — Loxylene Chemical Plant for Lox Chemical Company — Project number P21900, Issue date March 2008

Quarterly periods — all figures £'000s

Cost item	Cost code	2009 1	2	3	4	2010 1	2	3	4	2011 1	2	3	4	2012 1	2	3	4	Total budget
ENGINEERING	A																	
Design	A105	10	20	50	70	75	50	30	10	5	5	3	2					315
Support	A110									5	5	3	2	2	2	2	2	44
Commission	A200													2	6	10	10	28
Project management	A500	4	5	7	8	8	8	8	8	7	6	6	4	3	2	2	2	88
PURCHASES	B																	
Main plant	B110					400		500		500		160		2200				4000
Furnaces	B150						60				480						60	600
Ventilation	B175						20					5		10			10	200
Electrical	B200					10	5	20	25	25	140	5	2	2	1			225
Piping	B300					80	5	5	20	20	40	40	50	20	20			230
Steel	B400			20		200	200	200	200	200								900
Cranes	B500					50							400		50			500
Other	B999		5	25	5	10	20	20	50	5	5	10	5	10	5	2		177
CONSTRUCTION	C																	
Plant hire	C100			2	2	3	10	10	8	6	4	2	1	1				47
Roads	C200			10		20	40	80	60	5	5							220
External lighting	C250			5					40			5						50
Main building	C300																	
Labour	C310					10	30	100	150	200	400	100	50	40	20	20		1120
Materials	C320					2	10	30	100	200	220	200	100	100	10	5		977
Stores building	C400																	
Labour	C410						5	20	20	20	20	60	60	30	5	5		240
Materials	C420					2	2	5	15	5	5	15	30	15	10			107
CONTINGENCY SUM	Y999					10	20	25	30	30	30	35	35	45	45	50	50	400
ESCALATION	Z999					35	29	74	59	110	136	70	88	322	30	32	85	1070
TOTALS		14	30	104	102	715	519	1132	795	1338	1496	711	827	2802	206	128	619	11538

Figure 19.4   Cash outflow schedule for a construction project

| PROJECTS UNLIMITED LTD | | | | | Loxylene Chemical Plant for Lox Chemical Company | | | | | | | | | | | | Project number P21900 Issue date March 2008 | |

Quarterly periods — all figures £'000s

Cost item	2009				2010				2011				2012				2013	Total budget
	1	2	3	4	1	2	3	4	1	2	3	4	1	2	3	4	1	
INFLOWS																		
Agreed loans	50				150													200
Client's payments	10		50	100	200	500	1500	1000	1000	1750	1000	1000	1000	3000	1000	1000	1000	15110
Total inflows	60		50	100	350	500	1500	1000	1000	1750	1000	1000	1000	3000	1000	1000	1000	15310
OUTFLOWS																		
Engineering	14	25	59	80	85	63	43	23	12	11	9	6	7	10	14	14		475
Purchasing		5	45	5	550	310	745	295	750	665	215	457	2242	76	2	470		6832
Construction				17	35	97	245	393	436	654	382	241	186	45	30			2761
Contingency					10	20	25	25	30	30	35	35	45	45	50	50		400
Escalation					35	29	74	59	110	136	70	88	322	30	32	85		1070
Total outflows	14	30	104	102	715	519	1132	795	1338	1496	711	827	2802	206	128	619		11538
NET FLOWS																		
Periodic	46	(30)	(54)	(2)	(365)	(19)	368	205	(338)	254	289	173	(1802)	2794	872	381	1000	3772
Cumulative	46	16	(38)	(40)	(405)	(424)	(56)	149	(189)	65	354	527	(1275)	1519	2391	2772	3772	3772

Figure 19.5   Net cash flow schedule for a construction project

Although a positive cumulative balance of £3 772 000 (surplus or gross profit) is predicted at the end of the project, there will be some fairly substantial negative balances during the project life cycle (the figures placed in brackets along the bottom row in Figure 19.5). This does not necessarily mean bad news for the Loxylene project: but it does give the financial director fair warning of steps that he or she must take to make the funds available, or reach an prior agreement with the bank. Bear in mind, also, that these results are for the *project*, not for the *company* as a whole. In practice, the company might have other substantial reserves to take it through the lean periods.

USING PROJECT MANAGEMENT SOFTWARE TO SCHEDULE CASH OUTFLOWS

Cash is a replenishable project resource. As such, it can be scheduled by the same software, at the same time, and using the same basic methods as the project resource scheduling described in previous chapters. Computer systems with these capabilities have been in existence since the large mainframe machines of the 1960s and my colleagues and I were scheduling resources and cash outflows successfully for multiple projects in the latter half of that decade. However, cash flow scheduling using resource scheduling techniques requires considerable expertise, ingenuity and experience, not to mention a particular kind of aptitude. Willingness to resort to a few tricks and some manual intervention will usually be necessary, because the capability of critical path based resource scheduling will never stretch to cover every possible item of cash outflow. Inflows are even more difficult to accommodate.

All of this presupposes that the organization *is* carrying out project resource scheduling by computer. Unfortunately far too many do not. The subject is also covered very poorly in the literature, which accounts for the absence of any recommended further reading at the end of this chapter.

Scheduling labour costs

Project management computer programs usually allow a unit cost rate to be specified for each resource, and will also allow the planner the alternative option of stating an estimated cost for a whole activity (particularly useful for materials costs and other expenses). The resulting schedules are very valuable because they set out the predicted project costs (cash outflows) against the project timescale after all tasks have been scheduled as work-to lists, which will generally agree with the levels of each resource that are available for project work.

It is possible, in the best programs, to specify not only the standard cost rate, per hour or day, for each type of resource, but also to specify the higher rates payable for threshold resources. Threshold resources are those brought in from emergency availability levels (such as overtime or temporary agency staff) to carry out critical tasks that cannot be performed without overloading the resources normally available.

Suppose that a task has an estimated duration of 10 days (equivalent to 2 calendar weeks on the default calendar) and that its resource requirement is 1 engineer. Suppose, further, that the cost rate for this resource type (engineers) has been specified as £200 per day using normally available staff, and £250 per day for the threshold level. The computer will multiply the normal rate by the duration, giving £(10 X 200) = £2000 as the estimated or budget cost of the activity, and it will be able to produce a timed scheduled including all such labour costs for the project.

Should the total workload combined with the critical path cause the computer to call in resources from the threshold reserve to perform this task, it would assign the reserve resources, using the raised threshold rate of £250 in the cost calculation and schedule the task cost as £2500.

Costs for unspecified tasks

The computer schedule will include costs only for direct labour, and then only for the tasks that can be defined and entered in the network diagram. It will recognize neither any of the 'sludge' activities there were mentioned in Chapter 17 (tasks or absences that prevent staff from working on the project yet still cost money) nor the indirect (overhead) costs of the project. Manual intervention will usually be needed to add in correcting amounts (as a percentage) for these omissions. However, with skill, this procedure becomes entirely practicable. My own experiences in this field typically produced total project cost schedules that were within five per cent of those made by the cost estimating engineers, but with the important advantage that the costs were scheduled against time.

Scheduling costs for materials and other purchases

The estimated costs of materials and equipment can be scheduled by placing budget costs on the relevant purchasing activities on the network, and then allowing the computer to produce timed expenditure schedules. This will usually require the addition of activities to the network for the sole purpose of cost scheduling. Figure 19.6 is a network fragment that illustrates this method.

Each activity in Figure 19.6 represents a task connected with the purchase of an item of equipment or some project materials. Suppose that this purchase task is for a bulk load of granite blocks, to be shipped to the project site as one load at a total delivered cost of £5000. The planner can place this estimated cost on activity 1040, 'pay the supplier', to ensure that the computer will schedule this cost correctly as a cash outflow at the appropriate time. The duration of activity 1040 might be zero, in project terms, but some computers do not feel happy about assigning cost to activities with zero duration. So, in practice, the duration would probably be estimated as one day. Note that this is not the same as assigning a cost rate for a replenishable resource. Instead, it is a quite different process of assigning a cost to the whole activity.

Much later in the project, when work is actually taking place and orders for materials are being placed, the project manager will need to know the level of costs committed (rather than actually spent) at any given time as part of cost control. The same cost of £5000 for this load of granite could be added also on to activity 1025, which would then place the expenditure at the time of commitment rather than as an actual cash outflow.

Those among you who have followed this argument so far will now be asking, if this £5000 cost is shown on two different activities in the network, how can we prevent £5000 for the load of granite from being charged twice to the project in all the cost reports? The answer is to give all the commitment activities one department sort code, and give all the cash outflow activities a different sort code. Now the computer can be asked to filter and report costs against each of these different codes, thus producing one schedule for the forecast committed costs and another for the expected cash outflows.

These are just some of the ways in which project management software can be tweaked to report cash outflows and cost commitments. Anyone with sufficient ingenuity will soon learn to devise others.

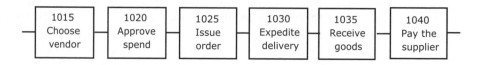

Figure 19.6 Network detail needed to schedule purchase commitments and cash outflows

USING THE COMPUTER TO SCHEDULE CASH INFLOWS

The procedure for scheduling cash inflows is very similar to that for scheduling the outflows associated with purchases.

The planner must first identify those tasks in the project that, when finished, will trigger revenue for the project. By far the most common of these are tasks that can be associated with the progress or stage payments specified in the project contract. The most important of these milestones will usually be the start activity of the network and the finish activity at the end of the project. However, in a typical project there will usually be several intermediate progress payments or other cash inflows.

The cash inflow scheduling process requires that there is a task in the network for every foreseeable case where a cash inflow should occur. Each of these tasks is then designated as a project milestone. It is best to create tasks especially for the purpose, rather that identify the completion of tasks with long durations as the trigger events. All this is easily achieved by inserting special milestone activities at the appropriate places in the network, each with a duration of one day, and each being given the relevant cash value.

All except really useless project management software can produce reports containing only milestones. Thus the computer can be arranged to schedule expected cash inflows.

CONCLUSION

When familiarity is gained with the use of a particular computer system, and with the allocation and use of filtering, sorting and reporting codes, the above methods can be combined to allow the preparation of schedules and graphs for both committed costs and cash outflows.

Planners who become familiar with a particular scheduling program will learn how to exploit its features to produce the schedules they need. They will, for instance, be able to solve the more complex problem of scheduling the expected timing of stage payments for capital equipment purchases and subcontracts so that these will be properly included in the total project cash outflow schedule. There must be at least one suitable activity in the network that can be identified with every case when a cash flow incident is expected to happen.

The capabilities and methods of use vary greatly between different computer systems, and there is usually more than one way to achieve a desired result even within one project management program. Even when a program appears not to possess the required capability, there are often 'tricks' that can be employed to produce the output needed. Scheduling *net* cash flows from project resource schedules is, however, a far more difficult problem, if not impossible, and manual intervention will probably be needed. But solving all these problems can be an enjoyable and creative pastime, far more productive and rewarding than solving crossword or Sudoku puzzles.

20 *Computer Applications*

The greatest contribution that computers can make to project management is in the processing, presentation and communication of management information. That includes the calculation of practicable project schedules and day-to-day departmental work-to lists from critical path network diagrams for even the largest projects. After describing procedures for choosing suitable software, this chapter journeys through a case example of resource scheduling for a small project. The progression to multi-project scheduling is explained in Chapter 28.

CHOOSING SUITABLE SOFTWARE

Early users of project management software were reluctant to grasp all the opportunities provided by the very few good systems that existed. Most people were content to run time analysis, print out the results, and attempt to run their projects using the earliest possible dates with little regard for resource constraints. In industries with great flexibility of resources, or where work is typically subcontracted to others who must provide and manage the resources, that disregard of detailed resource scheduling was (and remains) a sensible approach. In many companies, however, severe difficulties were experienced in trying to finish work on time when no easy way could be seen for allocating scarce resources among all the jobs clamouring for them.

Several programs became available in the 1960s that were advertised as being able to report costs and schedule resources. Only a two or three of these actually worked, notably various K & H Projects Systems' products and ICL's *PERT 1900*. The K & H technology survives in this market with 4c Systems Ltd, whose product *4c* is among the least known but probably the most versatile and powerful project management package available anywhere. Other programs that have since earned a high reputation are *Deltek Open Plan™ Professional* from Deltek and *Primavera*. *Artemis* is another name of repute.

All of the software so far mentioned is at the high end of the market, among the programs able to run very large networks and multiple projects, with many management features, and well deserving the adjective 'powerful'. These systems are relatively expensive to buy and they need special training before all their benefits can be enjoyed or even, in some cases, before they can even be started up.

Microsoft Project is by far the most widely known and used package, with millions of users. Early versions had their faults, but *Microsoft Project 98* and later versions have overcome those difficulties and this package returns good value for its reasonable price. As part of the *Microsoft Office* suite of programs it is user-friendly and its core features are easy to learn. It is ideal for the very many users whose projects do not require the extended capabilities of products from the higher end of the market, or who cannot justify the greater investment in cost and training that those more powerful systems demand.

Maintenance and support

The first year, at least, of hardware and software operation should be covered by guarantees. Thereafter, it is usual for suppliers to offer maintenance and support contracts that cost, typically, between 10 and 15 per cent per annum of the original purchase price. The user must be assured that the software provider will include free upgrades of the software and its documentation.

An important consideration is the availability of a hotline, which the user can telephone whenever difficulties arise. Some companies offer hotline services that fall short of perfection, perhaps because they are not accessible during all the hours when the user operates or because immediate answers to problems are not forthcoming. Some suppliers are merely agents for programs developed by other companies, and they might need to refer some queries back to source for answers. Others are not able to staff the hotline continuously, so that the user who calls with an urgent problem outside normal office hours could be frustrated by connection to a message answering service.

Need for caution

Some programs fail to live up to the claims of their suppliers' publicity. Even programs which receive good reviews in the independent computing journals are found to be flawed when they are put to the test by planning professionals. Unfortunately, price is no reliable guide. The most expensive system available, although undoubtedly very good, is not the best.

Much of the advertising needs to be read with critical awareness and circumspection. Wildly extravagant claims are sometimes made. The word 'powerful' is often misused to describe systems that, although valuable for small projects, do not bear comparison with the programs that can handle large volumes of data across big multi-project databases. This can all be very confusing to the project manager and it is easy to waste time and money on systems that fail to live up to their claims or the manager's expectations.

If a program fails to perform as expected, the results can be very costly. These costs include not only the price paid for the software, but also the investment in training and the time and effort wasted in pouring data into the useless system. There are two other serious disadvantages when a system fails, namely the loss of essential confidence and support from others in the project organization and the reduction in efficiency caused by the absence of the expected project work schedules.

Figure 20.1 outlines a procedure that I have found useful when advising a client on the purchase of high-end software.

User's specification and suppliers' questionnaire

The starting point in choosing any but the cheapest and simplest new software has to be a carefully reasoned specification of what the project manager's organization needs. The purchaser should approach the software houses with a firm set of objectives that, in effect, states 'This is what we need, what is your response?' This is far better than adopting the weak and more negative stance of pleading 'What do you offer and how do you think we might use it?'

Figure 20.2 lists some of the more significant factors to be considered when compiling the user's specification. This checklist will not suit every organization in every detail and some very advanced possibilities open to the expert have been excluded. Each organization is unique and will have its own special requirements. However, the checklist is a convenient starting point. Its most

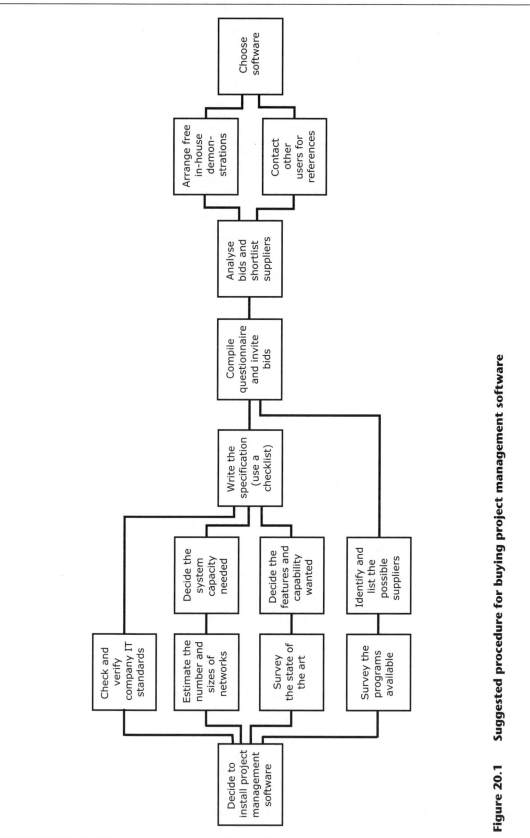

Figure 20.1   Suggested procedure for buying project management software

Item	Program characteristics
Environment	• Stand alone only? • Network? (details required)
Ease of use	• Are the drop-down menus helpful? • How good are the help screens? • How good is the documentation provided? • How fast is the expected processing time using: (a) our available hardware? (b) new hardware as recommended?
Activities	• Maximum number of activities possible in one project? • Maximum number of precedence links in one project? • Maximum number of activities possible altogether? • Maximum number of precedence links possible in system? • Maximum number of characters possible in activity ID code? • Can activity ID codes be alphanumeric? • Maximum number of characters in activity description? • Can activities be designated as splittable or non-splittable?
Calendars	• Total calendar time span? • How many different calendars can be specified? • What duration units are possible with these calendars?
Updating	• What progress reporting methods can be used? • Will activities reported as started be at risk of rescheduling?
Reports	• What standard report formats are provided? • What are the standard filtering and sorting facilities? • How good are the graphics? • How fast are the graphics printing speeds? • How easy is it to customize reports? • Will the system meet our needs for (say) the next five years
Error detection	• How effective are the error search routines? • Are error messages clear and in plain language? • Are loops effectively diagnosed or prevented?
Resources	• Can resource scheduling be performed? • How many different resource types can be specified? • How many characters may we use in each resource identifier code? • Can resources be assigned to groups or departments? • Can threshold resources be specified • Can alternative resources be specified? • Any special resource scheduling features?
Cost data	• Can the program assign an hourly or daily cost rate to each resource? • Can the program use both cost rates and charge-out rates? • Can different rates be specified for overtime or threshold resources? • Can an estimated cost be assigned to an activity? • What tabular cost reports are available? • Can cost/time graphs be produced? • Is there a staff timesheet facility?
Templating	• Does the program allow templating? • How easy is it to edit templates? • Can templates be merged automatically with interface links?
Projects	• How many projects can the system hold? • Maximum number of characters in a project identifier code? • Can project identifiers be alphanumeric? • Can the same activity ID numbers be used again in different projects? • Is multiproject scheduling possible? • Can projects be allocated to groups for multiproject scheduling? • Is what-if? scheduling available to test new project strategies etc?
Operational aspects	• What hardware is recommended? • Will the software run on our server? • Can the new software communicate with our main database? • Are there security safeguards against unauthorized access? • If so, how many levels of security are provided? • Can we customize these security levels?

Figure 20.2   Checklist for choosing project management software

Item	Program characteristics
System costs	• What is the basic price for a single PC user?
	• What is the basic price for 5 network users?
	• What is the basic price for 10 network users?
	• or, how much for our anticipated number of users?
	• Are any optional extras needed and, if so, at what cost?
	• How much training will be needed and at what cost?
	• If training is on our premises, do the training costs include travel, subsistence and accommodation expenses for the trainers?
	• If timesheet capability is to be used, what is the additional cost likely to be for all our timesheet users?
	• If we should need any customization, what is the likely scale of charges?
System support	• Is first-year support and maintenance free of charge?
	• What are the future support and maintenance charges expected?
	• Does system support include free software upgrades?
	• Is there a hotline service for advice and troubleshooting?
	• At what times is the hotline accessible:
	— Normal working hours?
	— Nights?
	— Weekends
	• Are we guaranteed immediate response and not an answering machine?
	• Was this software developed by the supplier or are they simply agents with less in-depth knowledge of the system?
	• How many systems have been sold?
	• How many of those users are in our country?
	• Is there a users' group?
	• Is the users' group supported by the software supplier?

Figure 20.2 *Concluded*

effective application is as the basis for compiling a questionnaire, to be sent to all potential software suppliers.

Without a certain amount of previous experience the intending user will probably not be competent to write a specification that accurately reflects the future needs of the organization. The specification writer must be a person who is thoroughly familiar with the use of critical path networks, principles of planning and resource scheduling, and the possibilities offered in general by project management software. A considerable amount of internal investigation will be needed to assess the size and nature of projects to be planned, so that parameters can be set for the various minimum capacities of the new software.

Once the user's specification has been written, a corresponding suppliers' questionnaire can be prepared. This simply lists all the requirements of the specification, but converts each statement into a question and leaves the quantities and required characteristics blank for the supplier to fill in and return.

Some skill is needed in setting the questions if the software capabilities are to be probed successfully. For instance, the question 'How many activities can be held in the system?' will often produce the answer 'The maximum number of activities depends only on the size of the available memory'. But answers to the supplementary questions 'How many characters can be assigned to an activity ID code?' and 'Can ID codes be alphanumeric' can be more revealing. For example, if the software can accept only three-digit numerical ID codes, there cannot be more than 999 activities in one network.

Investigating suppliers

Identifying possible suppliers

There are many potential suppliers and listing all of them might prove difficult. The more important software houses will usually exhibit at project management exhibitions. Other suppliers advertise in journals such as *Project Manager Today*. A useful start is to obtain brochures so that programs which are patently incapable of fulfilling the organization's needs can be eliminated painlessly at the start.

Initial correspondence

Once the questionnaire has been prepared it is safe to approach the would-be suppliers and invite them to quote. The imposition of a cut-off date for replies is highly advisable. Some companies will probably fail to reply, even after reminders. Others might reply to admit, with commendable honesty, that their product will not fulfil all the conditions suggested by the nature of the questions. However, it can be expected that a fair proportion of the questionnaires will be completed and returned.

Matrix chart and shortlisting

The returned questionnaires should be subjected to a formal and fair comparison, so that those products which fail to satisfy one or more vital conditions of the user's specification can be eliminated on a simple 'go' or 'no-go' basis. It is helpful to display all the answers on a matrix chart for this purpose, with each column of the chart allocated to one supplier's product and with the questions and answers spaced along the rows.

Demonstrations

A valuable approach is to invite the short-listed finalists to visit (separately) and demonstrate their systems. These should be live demonstrations on a computer (not simply audio-visual sales presentations). Such demonstrations can be very revealing, especially when the appropriate questions are asked and when particular tests are requested. The data for these demonstrations and witnessed tests should be provided by the intending purchaser, so that everything is as representative as possible of the projects that will eventually be scheduled. Excepting very cheap packages, most companies should be willing to carry out a demonstration free of charge.

The software purchaser has an obligation to complement the expense and effort asked of the suppliers by providing reasonable facilities for the demonstrator, and by ensuring that all those likely to be associated with the purchase decision process attend all the demonstrations.

Independent referees and other users

Contact with organizations which already use computer systems successfully for project planning and management can be useful: their people should be able to discuss and demonstrate their procedures and so make the intending user more aware of what can be done. The unbiased views of these independent users can also be important for revealing possible problems or limitations. However, many users do not make full use of their systems and fail to derive all the potential benefits, so that a false picture can be gained by consulting them. It might be necessary to employ a specialist independent consultant, at least in the early investigative days.

Making the final choice

It is probable that more than one supplier will be able to satisfy all the more important aspects of the user's specification. Under these circumstances, it is helpful to use a formal bid summary procedure, similar to that described in Chapter 23. Two bid summary tables might be needed, one to compare the technical capabilities and the other to compare prices and other commercial considerations. However, provided it has been designed with care, the matrix chart described above can be used for this purpose.

When making the final choice, it is best to start by considering only the most important requirements, so that the user is not overwhelmed by the all the features possible from a powerful project management package. However, the future must be borne in mind, so that the full potential of the user's specification can be realized as confidence and expertise are built up. It could well be advisable, therefore, to purchase a program which is sufficiently powerful and flexible to allow a small-scale start, whilst having the capabilities in reserve for more ambitious use later on.

SPECIAL NETWORK LOGIC REQUIREMENTS FOR COMPUTER APPLICATIONS

Project management software is designed to process precedence networks (often disguised as linked bar charts). There is no longer any system readily available that can process arrow networks. Thus the modern planner is forced either to use precedence logic or to convert early, hand-drawn arrow diagram sketches into precedence diagrams before the time comes to enter data.

Collecting start and finish nodes

In some early programs it was mandatory to have only one start node and one finish node for the whole network. Even with modern programs, this is a very desirable arrangement for the following reasons:

- A single start node provides a convenient place on which to hang a scheduled start date for the whole project.
- Similarly, a single finish node provides a place on which to hang a target end date for the project.
- Single start and finish nodes simplify the critical path calculations.
- Having one declared start node and one finish node is useful in analysing error reports. Any other reported starts and finishes can then be recognized as error dangles (see Figure 20.6).

Drawing and viewing network logic on a small screen

It is possible to draw the network diagram directly on the computer screen (either as a linked bar chart or as a precedence network). Precedence notation is ideal for this purpose and the process is usually rapid and easy, once the method for the particular program has been learned. However, only very tiny networks, or small portions of larger networks, can be displayed whole on a single screen at a zoom size large enough to display all the essential detail.

Although a large network can be viewed by scrolling the screen or by producing interim trial prints, this is not nearly as practicable as starting from a network drawn on a single sheet or roll of paper or film, where the network can be viewed as a whole, and all the logic constraints can be checked by running an inquisitive finger along the various paths. Nonetheless, the facility to be able to correct or update an existing network from the screen display will be found extremely useful, although it is always advisable to trace the logic through on a printout afterwards.

Fortunately, those working in or near engineering offices will have probably have access to a printer capable of printing on to A0 sheets or, better still, paper rolls. Then, provided that the software has good plotting capabilities and an adequate printer driver, one can produce a network diagram print that will allow detailed examination and checking.

PREPARING FOR THE FIRST COMPUTER SCHEDULE

Software varies considerably in its user-friendliness. Some programs (such as *Microsoft Project*) present a blank Gantt chart on the screen as soon as they are booted up and it is apparent to the user that task data can be typed in immediately.

Other products, such as *Deltek Open Plan™ Professional*, whilst being very powerful and capable systems, have an opening screen that needs some explanation and training before the planner can get started. This is often a price worth paying. The more capable the software and the more functions that it can perform, then the more complicated are likely to be the various toolbars and drop-down menus. Navigation of these menus in many project management software products requires good training and hands-on experience.

Two different approaches to the welcoming screen can be expected, depending on which software is chosen:

- On booting up the application, the user is presented with a blank Gantt chart on to which all the activity data can be entered. This can usually be changed to a network view according to the user's preference. When the data are complete, one uses the 'Save' or 'Save as' options from the 'File' menu to store the new project in the system.
- A screen appears with no prompts. It is necessary to go to the 'File' menu and click on 'New'. In some cases the user must then choose from a range of options in a browser, for which 'Project' would be the appropriate selection when entering a new project.

Most programs will allow the project to be saved as a 'baseline', which means that the initial version will stay unchanged in the memory to provide a base against which future updates can be compared to monitor actual performance and other properties against the original plan. Some users, no doubt, find this feature valuable.

Figure 20.3 outlines the principal steps that are typically necessary when attempting to use new software for the first time for project planning and resource scheduling. On-site training by the software house may be needed to achieve full capability.

Assuming that the program has been properly installed and tested, the first step in setting up the computer schedule for a new project is to prepare and enter all the data. The way in which this is done will depend on the requirements of the particular program, but modern systems are very easy to use in this respect, with screen prompts and help menus available at almost every step.

As users become more familiar with their systems they should find that data can be entered in a number of different ways; a straight listing of activity data, for example, is far quicker than entering the data as a series of responses to prompts. Some programs allow data entry straight into a screen plot of the network, so that links can be dragged into place with the mouse.

Whatever the method chosen for entering data, the information can usually be divided loosely into four main groups. These are:

- **project data** – which means the bundle of data that sets up the project file and contains the main details about the project;
- **calendar information** – from which one or more calendar files will be set up;

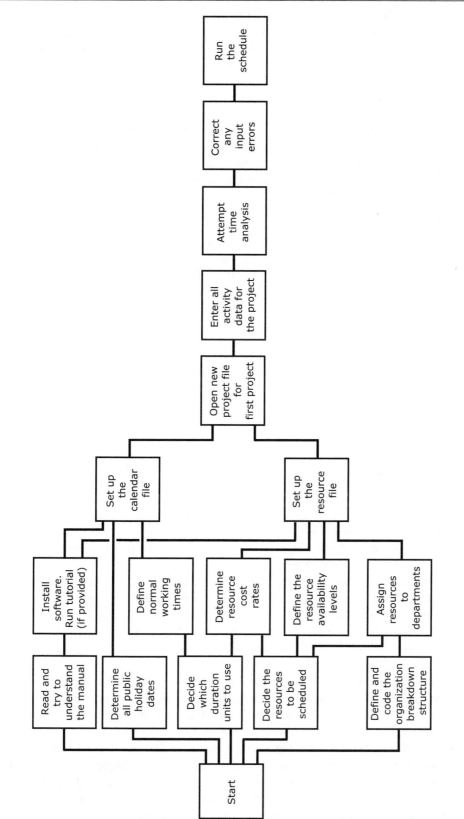

Figure 20.3 Suggested procedure for implementing new project management software

- **resource data** – this specifies the ID codes and descriptions of the resources to be scheduled, together with their cost rates and expected availability levels. For later filtering and reporting, an organization breakdown structure code should be assigned to each resource that signifies the departmental manager who will be need to resource schedules that are specific to their department;

- **activity records** – with one record for each activity (task) in the network, including its ID, description, estimated duration, activity type (for example is it a milestone activity, a project start or a project finish?), resource codes and numbers signifying the types and amounts of resources required, and so on. Crucial among these data is a list of IDs for *either* the activity's immediately preceding activities *or* its immediately successors – information that fixes the network logic in the computer's memory.

Project data

Basic project data mainly comprises information that has to be entered only once, when each new project file is created. It includes facts such as the project number and title, name of the project manager, perhaps the customer's name and so on. The planner might also want to set up codes for different departments or managers in the organization to facilitate the preparation of edited reports later.

Questions such as system security might also have to be answered at this stage, determining who shall have access to the system and at what level. For example, at the least senior access level (level 9, say), designated system users might be permitted to view project schedules on a screen but would not be allowed to change the data on file in any way. The computer technologist might, on the other hand, be given complete access to the system (at level 1) with authority to change fundamental parameters or to customize report formats.

Calendars

The subject of special calendars was introduced in Chapter 17 and, at the risk of some repetition, it will now be explained in greater detail.

Most, if not all, project management software allows more than one calendar to be set up and held as a calendar file. By far the most important of these is the default calendar, which will include all dates except those days on which work may not be scheduled (such as weekends). In many cases this default calendar will be the only one necessary. Most default calendars assume work over five weekdays, with Saturdays and Sundays removed. A task estimated to take 10 days will, therefore, occupy two weeks of the Gregorian calendar. Activities will be assigned to this calendar unless the planner gives different instructions when data for the activity record are entered.

Holidays will usually have to be taken out of the default calendar. Some systems adopt the alternative approach of allowing a separate holiday calendar file to be set up, in which only the holiday dates are specified. Holidays in this sense usually means public holidays or company holiday shutdowns when no project work can take place.

Care always has to be taken when writing or entering dates in numerical form, to ensure that confusion between the American and other conventions does not cause errors. For instance, 01-03-10 means 3 January 2010 to an American and 1 March 2010 to a British person. Most software allows the user to specify the date format.

It is necessary to decide and enter the units of duration that will be used throughout the networks, and to specify how these will relate to each calendar. For example, a standard unit of 1 might be chosen to represent 1 day, to work with a calendar of 5 working weekdays within each calendar week. If this were to be the main (default) calendar used throughout the system, then an estimated activity duration of one calendar week would be written as 5 on the network diagram and entered as 5 units in the computer. Most systems allow the user a very wide choice of units, ranging down to minutes in some cases.

Some project management programs allow hundreds of different calendars to be set up. Each separate calendar must be given its own identifying file number or name. When the computer calculates schedules, it will work with the main or default calendar unless one of the special calendars is allocated to an activity or a resource. Some examples follow to show why such special calendars might be needed, and how they might be defined. Methods vary from one program to another, and these examples are only a general guide.

Special calendar: Case 1

An organization works only on weekdays. All project work takes place within normal office hours. The project manager has decided that Saturday and Sunday working will never be required. The project manager would like to be able to schedule small jobs with estimated durations as short as one half day.

The solution for dealing with short duration units could be to specify the standard unit of duration as 0.5 day. Thus each working day will consist of 2 units (which can be taken as meaning one unit each for the morning and afternoon work periods). The computer will be told that the calendar comprises 10 units in 1 week, with only Monday through Friday as valid dates for scheduling. It is obvious that the same units must be written on the network diagram (so that an activity duration estimated at two Gregorian calendar weeks would have to be written as 20, for example).

The computer will count 2 units as a total calendar day for network time analysis. Work-to lists and all other reports from the system will then show only weekday dates, and Saturdays and Sundays will not be seen as permissible dates for scheduling.

Special calendar: Case 2

Most people in a company work only from Monday to Friday and they cannot be scheduled as working on Saturdays or Sundays. However, one department does work on Saturdays. The main (default) calendar in this case would be the common example that uses duration units of whole days, with only Monday to Friday as valid working days.

A special second calendar can then be defined, perhaps coded as 'Calendar 2', with 6 days available in the working week and with only Sundays excluded. Calendar 2 would be called into play whenever appropriate, usually by overriding the default calendar and specifying instead Calendar 2 when data are entered for each relevant activity or (if the software allows) by associating Calendar 2 with the type of labour resource affected.

Special calendar: Case 3

Activities for a project are to be carried out in two or more countries, some of which have different workday and public holiday arrangements. All the activities for the project are contained within one network diagram and it is not considered desirable or possible to draw a separate network for each country. The whole project is to be planned and progressed from project organization headquarters in London, England. The solution is to start by deciding where most of the activities will be carried out, and design the main (default) calendar to suit the work and holiday pattern of the relevant country.

A special calendar must be created for each country which has a different set of workday and holiday conditions. Activities would then be scheduled against the calendar relevant to the country in which they are planned to occur.

Special calendar: Case 4

A company has at least one department which operates more than one shift within each period of 24 hours. Some shifts operate continuously throughout weekdays and weekends.

A separate special calendar can be assigned for each different pattern of shiftworking. For example, 21 work periods would be specified as being equivalent to one calendar week if three shifts are to be worked for all days including weekends. The planner must determine how this will affect the duration estimates written on the network diagram (according to the requirements of the particular computer program).

Other methods for dealing with shiftwork require the use of tricks to obtain the desired results, such as retaining the default calendar but multiplying the number of resources needed for each shift on an activity by the number of shifts to be worked in each 24-hour period. Resource availability levels would have to be factored accordingly. Such tricks are always complicated to apply and are not generally recommended.

Special calendar: Case 5

Some passive activities will continue to progress over weekends and holidays, even when no effort or resources are expended on them. Examples are activities for the curing of concrete or the drying of paint. Allowing such tasks to be scheduled using the default calendar can create time analysis errors.

This problem can be solved, if considered necessary, by setting up a special calendar in which a week is seven working days, and in which no holidays are taken out of the days available for work.

Project start date

It is important to give the computer a datum point from which it will begin the project. This is usually done by imposing a start date on the first project activity or event.

Scheduled dates (target dates)

The planner might wish to impose fixed target dates on activities anywhere in the network. In some systems it is possible to specify:

- **an early ('not before') date** – the computer must not schedule the start of the activity before the imposed date. This facility might be used, for example, on the first site activity of a construction project where the date when the previous occupier must vacate the site is known;
- **a late date** – an imposed latest permissible date for the start or completion of an activity;
- **a fixed date** – some systems allow this by the imposition on the relevant activity of the same early and late dates.

Other options are usually possible, depending on the software used. Imposed scheduled dates will almost certainly conflict with the dates computed from time analysis, and so will affect float calculations. If an imposed date is logically impossible, negative float will be generated and reported, although programs differ considerably in their ability to indicate negative float clearly.

Resource data

The planner has to decide which resource types are to be scheduled. It is not necessary, and is indeed a mistake, to attempt scheduling every possible department or type of labour employed by the project organization. For example, it is not necessary to schedule canteen staff, cleaners, administrative office workers and so on. There are usually some direct workers who do not need to be included in the resource scheduling, because their work is provided as a service, or follows automatically on from the work of others who must be scheduled. These aspects were described more fully in Chapter 17.

Mandatory resource data

The following data must be entered for each type of resource deemed necessary for scheduling:

- **resource code** – an identifier code, which often comprises one, two or three characters. Examples might be ENG for engineers, BKL for bricklayers, FTR for fitters, TST for a test bay facility;
- **resource name** – the name of the resource type as it will appear in reports;
- **normal availability** – the number of resource units normally available to the program for allocation to simultaneous project activities and the start and finish dates of the period for which they are expected to be available. All competent software will allow for changes in resource levels during the project life cycle. This is achieved by specifying the relevant periods and their associated resource levels as described in Chapter 17.

It is generally not advisable to declare a total department strength as being available for scheduling. If in doubt, start with either 80 or 85 per cent of the total level. Reasons for this were explained in Chapter 17, under the section 'Specifying resource availability levels'. If a resource is being used with a special calendar for two- or three-shift working, the declared availability level must be reduced even further, to allow for the people to be distributed over the various shifts, and also to take account of their rest days.

Optional resource data

The following optional data can also be entered with most systems for each type or resource specified:

- **calendar** – the file name of any special calendar against which a particular resource is to be associated and scheduled. This might not be possible with some software. It is more usual to assign the special calendar to the relevant activities rather than to the resources;
- **cost rate** – the cost expected to be incurred by using one unit of the resource in normal circumstances for one network unit of duration: for example, 1 BKL = £180 per day;
- **threshold resources** – resources above the normal availability level, which the computer may call upon to be used if the project cannot be scheduled using only normal availability levels (see Figure 16.7): examples might be extra hours available by working overtime, or additional staff that could be taken on as temporary or subcontract workers;
- **threshold cost rate** – the cost rate expected when one unit of a threshold resource is used during one network duration period: for example, an overtime rate;
- **rate constancy** – the program may allow the user to declare each resource category as rate-constant or non rate-constant: in the normal case of rate-constant resources, scheduling takes place on the assumption that if two people are needed for an activity, they will be scheduled at the constant rate of two people throughout the activity duration. For non-

rate-constant resources a cyclical pattern of availability can be specified (for example, the resource is available for the first three days of every five-day period).

There are other classes of data associated with resources that depend very much on the software being used. At least one system allows a staff file to be set up, with the names of all project personnel and some of their career details to be entered in the common database.

Priority rules

If resource scheduling is wanted, certain priority rules will have to be defined, although the user might not be asked to make a decision until just before processing takes place. The main rules are:

- whether the schedule is to be time limited or resource limited (see Figure 16.7);
- the priority rule for allocating resources to competing activities (a useful choice is to give priority to activities with least remaining float).

Activity (task) records

Activity records comprise the bulk of the data to be entered before the initial run, and it is among these data that most input errors are likely to crop up. A sensible way of going about the task is to have a print of the network diagram sketch on hand, and tick off each activity and each logical link as it is entered into the computer. This will help to prevent errors of omission. It can also prevent duplication, although the software will probably not allow two or more activities bearing the same ID code to be entered.

Mandatory activity data

The following data must always be entered for every activity record, otherwise the computer will not even be able to carry out basic time analysis.

- the activity ID number;
- the ID numbers of all *either* immediately preceding activities *or* immediately succeeding activities;
- the type of precedence constraints, if default finish–start links do not apply. When complex constraints are used the time duration of the links must also be specified;
- the estimated activity duration, given in the units applicable to the project calendar.

Optional activity data

Activity descriptions   Although it is not mandatory to provide activity descriptions, resulting schedules would not be much use without them. Modern systems allow activity descriptions to contain many characters, although limited screen area will usually mean using greatly abbreviated descriptions in network diagram plots and tables. It will generally be found convenient to use sensibly abbreviated descriptions (containing perhaps about 30 characters).

Alternative duration estimates   Optimistic and pessimistic duration estimates can be added for use in PERT or risk analysis calculations. This application is relatively uncommon.

Editing and sorting codes   A departmental sort code can usually be specified so that reports only contain those activities which are of interest to each manager or department. Codes can also indicate the level of management, enabling summary reports to be prepared for senior managers. A few systems allow various sorting and editing sequences on different parts of the activity data. It might be possible, for example, to use part of the description field as a sort code (perhaps by including a job number or cost code at the start of the description for each activity).

Resource data   The code and average rate of resource usage estimated to be required for each resource type that the activity will use. This input can be used not only for resource scheduling but also for scheduling costs and cash outflows (provided that cost rates have been specified for the resources).

Cost   The estimated or budget cost of an activity. This method of entering cost data is used for activities that do not use human resources, but which nonetheless incur costs. The most common use is for equipment and materials costs.

Special constraint rules   Some advanced programs will allow special logic constraints to be defined for an activity. These include tied activities, in which two designated activities must follow each other without delay (for example, concrete pouring followed by curing time).

Splittable activities (applicable only to resource scheduling)   Activities may be declared as splittable if interruptions in their progress can be permitted. When this facility is chosen, the program is allowed to split an activity into two or more parts, interrupting the activity so that resources can be diverted for use elsewhere by another activity that has higher priority.

CASE EXAMPLE: THE GARAGE PROJECT

The project used for the case example throughout the remainder of this chapter is the same garage project that was introduced in Chapter 16. Its network diagram was originally given in Figure 16.1 in both arrow and precedence versions. The diagram is repeated in Figure 20.4 for convenience but, as modern software does not cater for arrow diagrams, only the precedence version is shown. The network logic and task duration estimates are unchanged from Figure 16.1, except for giving new ID codes to the start and finish activities (explained below).

There are a couple of logic errors in this network diagram that sharp eyes might pick out. However these were deliberate mistakes, forced by the limited number of activities that can clearly be shown on the page of a book. In practice, one would need to allow time for concrete to cure and for paint to dry. Correcting these omissions would add time to the project, but they can safely be ignored for the purposes of this case demonstration.

Remember that this is a project to build a detached garage for the owner of a private house. The project labour resources comprise a father and son team, who run their own construction business. The father is classified as skilled, and the son is a relatively unskilled labourer.

Data for the garage project

Project dates and calendar

The project start date is (or was, depending on when you read this) 10 May 2010. All the software products chosen for the examples in this chapter use a default calendar based on five weekdays and no special calendars have been introduced. Saturdays and Sundays are therefore removed from the schedule, no resources can be used on these days and no weekend dates will appear in any schedules. The network diagram in Figure 20.4 includes the estimated duration for each task in days.

Labour resources

The resources needed for each task are shown in Figure 20.4, with 1S representing one skilled person and 1L denoting one labourer. For this case study the specified resources will be scheduled using the

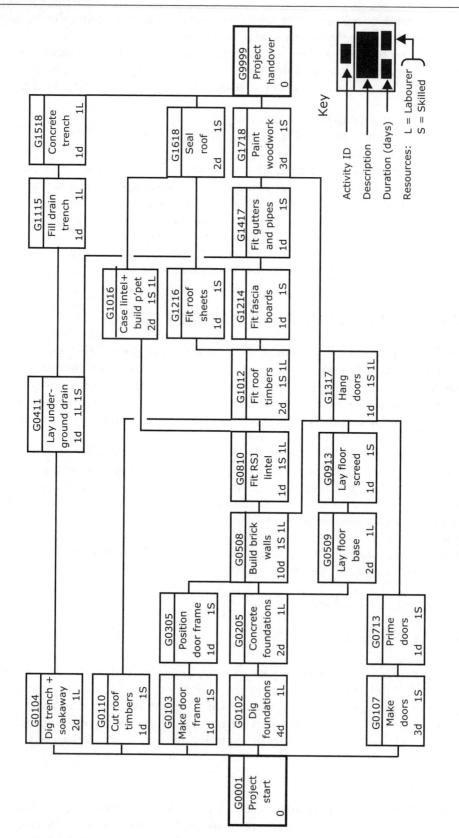

Figure 20.4   Garage project: precedence network diagram

usual convention that they will be used evenly throughout the duration of the task (rate-constant). The number of man-hours required for a task would, therefore, change in direct proportion to any change (estimated or actual) in the task duration. The quantities 2d 1L 1S on a network task would mean, for instance, a task estimated to last two weekdays, with one labourer and one skilled person working continuously on the task throughout those two days.

Splittable and non-splittable activities

Some resource scheduling software will allow tasks to be split (interrupted and then restarted at a later date) to achieve a smoother usage of resources and avoid overloads. For the garage project, however, the default non-splittable option has been chosen throughout. In most real project cases activity splitting is undesirable because of the disruption that it can cause at the workplace.

Labour costs

There are usually several ways available to the planner for specifying human resource costs. These include a fixed work content for the task, or arriving at a cost that is a product of the number of resource units multiplied by the task duration (which is my preferred method). For this garage project the labour rates chosen were as follows:

- **skilled worker** – £160 per day. Some software (including *Microsoft Project 2000*) has a default calendar based on an eight-hour day, so the cost for this resource becomes £20 per hour;
- **labourer** – £120 per day, or £15 per hour.

It has been assumed that no overtime will be worked. Thus there are no overtime premiums to consider.

Labour resources available

All software requires the dates and amounts of resources that are available for the project to be stated before resource scheduling can even be considered. For the garage project one unit (one person) of each resource type was specified as being available from 1 Jan 2010 to 31 Dec 2010. These dates were chosen far apart to ensure that they would cover the project period adequately.

A range of dates and numbers could have been entered to allow for any planned expansion or reduction of the workforce in future and for changes in the resource cost rates.

Cost of construction materials

Figure 20.5 shows the estimated costs of the more important materials for each task in the garage project. These are costs *per task* unlike the labour costs, which were costs *per labour unit per day*.

Consider, for example, the task to build the garage walls. The quantities of bricks and mortar needed can be estimated accurately, so that when the project starts these materials can be purchased and delivered to the site at a known, fixed cost. This contrasts with the time needed to build the walls, which might (depending on many uncontrollable factors) vary considerably from the original duration estimate. So, labour costs are more likely to vary with task duration than the materials used.

However, some software will allow materials usage and costs to be specified at a rate that *is* proportional to task duration for the comparatively uncommon cases when this is more appropriate

Activity ID	Activity description	Materials required	Estimated Cost £
G0001	Project start	No materials	
G0102	Dig foundations	No materials	
G0103	Make and prime door frame	Wood and primer	50
G0104	Dig soakaway and trench	No materials	
G0107	Make doors	Wood and sundries	300
G0110	Cut roof timbers	Wood	450
G0205	Concrete foundations	Concrete ingredients	150
G0305	Position door frame	No materials	
G0411	Lay underground drainpipe	Pipe	40
G0508	Build main brick walls	Bricks and mortar ingredients	650
G0509	Lay concrete floor base	Concrete ingredients	70
G0713	Prime the doors	Primer and sundries	20
G0810	Fit RSJ lintel over door frame	Rolled steel joist (RSJ)	40
G0913	Lay floor screed	Flooring compound	200
G1012	Fit roof timbers	No extra materials	
G1016	Case lintel and build parapets	Wood and concrete	60
G1115	Fill drain trench	No materials	
G1214	Fit fascia boards	Wood	30
G1216	Fit roof sheets	Sheets and fixings	360
G1317	Hang doors	Locks and hinges	80
G1417	Fit gutters and downpipes	Gutters, pipes, fixings	80
G1518	Concrete over drain trench	Concrete ingredients	20
G1618	Seal the roof	Sealant	30
G1718	Paint all woodwork	Paint and sundries	30
G9999	Project finish and handover	No materials	

Resource code	Resource name	Resource cost per day £
S	Skilled worker	160
L	Labourer	120

Figure 20.5 Garage project: cost estimates

than the fixed cost option. Examples include plant hire and (not relevant to this small garage project) site fuel costs and site office costs.

Task identifier codes

The task ID codes on the network diagram were originally designed to allow comparison between the arrow and precedence networks in Chapter 16 (Figure 16.1). So, G0103 in the precedence diagram, for example, is equivalent to activity 01–03 in the arrow diagram in Figure 16.1.

Now that this project is about to be processed by computer, the ID codes for the project start and finish activities have to be chosen sensibly. We could use simply 'start' and 'finish' (as in some earlier editions of this book). However, I have used instead G0001 and G9999 for the start and finish respectively, so that these start and finish tasks will print out first and last in reports during most sorting sequences.

In some of the illustrations that follow in this chapter, the activity ID numbers processed with *Microsoft Project 2000* are different from the network diagram in Figure 20.4 because that software assigns its own task ID numbers (according to the sequence in which tasks are entered).

Activity descriptions (task names)

The number of characters allowed by the software in the task name field is usually more than adequate. However, these descriptions or names frequently have to be abbreviated, owing to the limited space for showing them in some graphics reports such as network diagrams. Some software will simply truncate task names to show only the first few characters. Other packages will allow the user to specify an abbreviated name for every task.

Logic relationships

All relationships in this garage project are of the finish-start type. No new task can start until all its predecessors have been finished. This is the default assumed by all the software used here. Figure 14.13 showed the other options that can be used, whenever it is necessary to plan for more complex logical relationships.

DATA ENTRY ERRORS

Because there are so many ways in which undetectable mistakes can be made, it pays to be very careful during initial data entry. If a second person can be spared, good practice is to have one person keying in the data and the other assisting by ticking each item off on a copy of the network as it is entered.

After data entry, it can be very helpful to print a complete activity listing, so that all the data can be checked manually for errors and omissions. The most useful report for this purpose is a list of all activity records printed in ascending order of their ID codes, and with the links to preceding and succeeding activities and the activity durations included. Such a list is invaluable for checking that the logic input to the machine is free from mistakes that might otherwise go undetected.

If the software is incapable of printing such a list, a network plot is an acceptable alternative (see the section on network plotting, later in this chapter).

Error diagnostics

Whether the computer is to be used for time analysis only or for full resource and cost scheduling, once it has digested all the data its first processing job will be to attempt time analysis. For this it will make forward and backward passes through the network. It will recognize the network logic by means of the identification numbers of all the activities and their specified links. During these backward and forward passes, the program will identify all obvious errors.

All good project management software contains comprehensive error detection routines, designed to recognize particular types of mistakes and report them to the planner for correction (or for confirmation that the relevant data are correct as entered and that any apparent anomalies were intended). Errors might result from transpositions or other reading errors, keyboard mistakes, entering non-valid control data (for example a date which lies outside the main calendar), or some basic flaw in the network diagram logic itself.

If all the data have been entered correctly there is a possibility that the first attempt at time analysis will work when the appropriate command is given. In the absence of mistakes, the computer will complete the time analysis and write the results to its database. However, unless the network is really small, it can safely be assumed that something will go wrong, and that the computer will produce an unwelcome warning message.

Two categories of data errors

Data input errors can be divided into two categories:

1. Mistakes or apparent mistakes that the computer is able to recognize and report back as helpful error messages. Examples of these include the following:

   - invalid dates (such as 30 February or a target date that falls on a day specified in the calendar file as non-working);
   - duplicated activity records (most modern software will not allow duplicate ID codes to be entered);
   - dangles (explained below);
   - loops (explained below);
   - any other anomalies where the computer can recognize conflicting input data. For example, zero duration specified for an activity that also claims to need resources.

2. Mistakes that the computer cannot recognize, and which will remain undetected and lead to possible scheduling errors. Examples of these are as follows:

   - an incorrect activity duration;
   - an incorrect task name (for example where two names and ID codes are transposed);
   - the wrong type of constraint for an activity in a precedence network;
   - forgetting to specify the cost of materials for an activity;
   - entering the wrong resource or sort code for an activity.

Examples of data errors (with particular reference to the garage project case example)

It is not surprising that the most frequent source of input errors occurs in the activity records, since these represent by far the greatest amount of data to be entered. Putting such errors right for large networks can sometimes prove to be an interesting exercise in detection, with the computer reports merely providing clues. The three most common error types are as follows:

1. **Duplicate activities** – If two different activity records have been input with the same ID code number the computer will fail to distinguish between them and regard them as an error of duplication. It is almost certain that a modern system would report this type of mistake as soon as any attempt is made to enter the second activity record. Earlier systems made the unsuspecting planner wait until after the initial error run. The cause is likely to be one of the following:

   - a real attempt to input the same activity twice, which might happen (for instance) if the person entering the data happened to be interrupted, and forgot that the activity had already been entered;
   - a keyboard error in entering an identification number;
   - a numbering error on the original network diagram. (I am reminded here of an occasion when a colleague of mine was busily engaged in allocating activity ID numbers on a new network drawing that occupied a roll of paper over 5 metres long. There were well over 1000 activities in that project. The drawing was spread over and beyond a double A0 sized drawing board. Halfway through the activity numbering procedure, the planner was interrupted by a long telephone call. When he returned to his drawing board and picked up his pencil again he had lost his place, forgot the last number added and, as a result, duplicated over 50 activity numbers. The intimidating

pile of error warning pages from the computer listed many duplicated activities and several large loops. The disaster took a day and much of a night to put right.)

2. **Dangles** – Dangling activities occur whenever records have been created for activities that have no preceding activities (start dangles) or no succeeding activities (end or finish dangles). Clearly the first and last activities in a network will be seen as dangles. Unwanted dangles occur either because an activity has been omitted by mistake (leaving a gap in a network path) or because a link has been omitted or wrongly specified. In Figure 20.6 (a) two dangles have been created because the planner forgot to specify the finish-start link from activity G0509 to G0913. The computer will thus think that activity G0509 is a start activity and the G0913 is a finish activity. That will, of course, produce serious errors in time analysis and all resulting schedules.

3. **Loops** – A loop is a sequence of activities whose logical path forms a continuous loop. This kind of mistake can be caused by entering an incorrect activity number or precedence link, especially by placing a link in the wrong direction. A loop is impossible to time-analyse, and the computer becomes trapped in an endless cycle of activities from which there is no escape.

In Figure 20.6 (b) the planner has mistakenly entered the successor of activity G0810 as G0102 instead of G1012. This has created a loop containing activities G0102, G0205, G0508 and G0810.

The computer program should be capable of listing all the activities contained in a loop. Very early (DOS) versions of *Deltek Open Plan™* produced an error log which contained the words 'Loop detected', then listed the activities within the loop and ended with the chilling message 'Aborted: fatal error'. Now the modern version of that program, *Deltek Open Plan™ Professional*, in common with many other packages, checks the logic during data entry and will not allow the creation of a loop.

Other errors

All computer programs contain many more error-checking routines than those described in this chapter. Error reports will be generated, for example, if the planner has tried to enter a target project completion date which precedes the specified project start date (not a very clever thing to do, but easily done by mistake at the end of a tiring day).

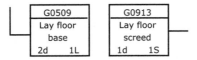

(a) Creation of two dangles

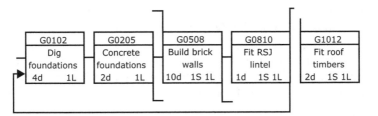

(b) Creation of a loop

Figure 20.6 Garage project: data errors

Other messages will arise if any of the program capacities are exceeded. This might happen, for example, if the network proved to be too large for the computer to handle. Another possibility is that the total project duration might be too long for the specified project calendar.

NETWORK PLOTTING

Network plots are necessary both as management control tools and for checking that the correct logic has been input to the computer. The ability to produce legible and useful plots varies considerably from one program to another. The best plots will position all the activities in the best possible pattern, showing in sufficient detail as many activity boxes on the screen as possible (and on paper prints). The rule that networks always flow from left to right should be observed, with all the links clearly shown (especially at crossover points).

Microsoft Project, especially in versions from *Microsoft Project 2000* onwards, is capable of producing very clear network plots with all the links shown without ambiguity. The disadvantage is that the standard network plot spreads over many A4 pages like an atlas. These have to be cut and pasted to form a logic diagram on one sheet. A printer with A0 sheet or paper roll capability is needed for best results. A very compact plot can, however, be obtained by choosing an alternative view, that shows only the IDs within activity boxes.

Software such as *Deltek Open Plan™ Professional* requires the user to carry out 'placements' from the 'Tools' menu before the program will draw the network on the screen in a sensible layout. These placements can either be performed automatically or manually. Manual placements enable the user to drag and drop activities and links on the screen to remove ambiguities where two or more links run along the same path and to make the plot more compact. Manual placements are, however, time consuming and inappropriate for larger networks. Other programs use different terms for placements, such as 'Refresh layout'.

The product *4c* produces near-perfect network plots that are clear, comprehensive and compact. The garage project, for example, plotted well, and even when rescaled to fit a single A4 sheet the links were shown clearly with no ambiguities. The result is not so clear when reduced to the size of a book page, but the summary plot is shown in Figure 20.7.

TIME ANALYSIS OF THE GARAGE PROJECT NETWORK

With no known remaining data errors, the computer can be commanded to carry out time analysis of the garage project. This involves forward and backward passes through the network to determine the amount of float, and the earliest possible and latest permissible times for the start and finish of every activity. Some software (such as *Microsoft Project 2000*) will carry out calculations and recalculations automatically as the network data are entered, without the need for separate commands.

A project management system will observe any constraints imposed by scheduled dates attached to activities anywhere in the network during time analysis and these will affect float and the route of the critical path.

Microsoft Project 2000 and *Primavera* both present a table of time analysis results on the left-hand side of the same display as a Gantt chart. Whenever a full tabular report is required after time analysis, the column headings can usually be customized to include the following data:

- activity ID
- activity description
- estimated duration
- earliest possible start date

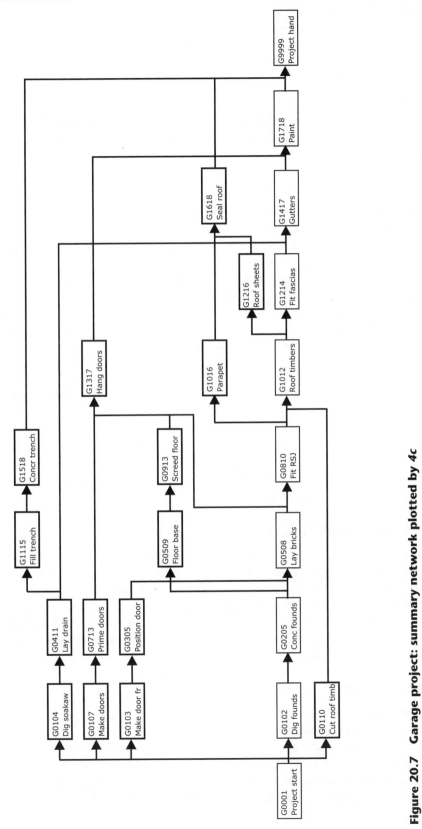

Figure 20.7 Garage project: summary network plotted by 4c

Task names had to be severely abbreviated to achieve this compact plot but this summary is ideal for checking that the network logic has been correctly entered into the computer.

- latest permissible start date
- earliest possible finish date
- latest permissible finish date
- free float (free slack)
- total float (total slack).

Competent software will allow the planner to choose many other data fields for the time analysis table. These include cost data, resource requirements, critical status and (once the project has started) progress information. *Microsoft Project 2000* produced the garage project time analysis data shown in Figure 20.8.

Usefulness of time analysis reports

If the project organization has access to unlimited and very flexible resources, or if human and other resource management are to be delegated to subcontractors, a time analysis report can be sufficient for planning and managing the project. Many projects are managed successfully on this basis, using the earliest possible dates as the schedule targets.

In any project where the project activities need people or other resources that are within the project manager's own organization, resource scheduling should always be considered.

Note that close of work time on one day and the beginning of work time on the next working day can, in some circumstances, be regarded as the same point in project time. The intervening hours simply do not exist in the project calendar and are therefore ignored.

RESOURCE SCHEDULING FOR THE GARAGE PROJECT

Remembering that the garage project company comprises only two workers, one skilled and one not, it is necessary to perform resource scheduling so that the available resources can be used as efficiently as possible. First, I shall outline the computer process and describe some basic rules under which schedules can be calculated. Both *Microsoft Project 2000* and *Primavera* were used to produce the garage project resource scheduling reports in this chapter.

Simple resource aggregation

Many early programs could not carry out resource scheduling, even if they claimed to be able to do so. They simply scheduled each activity at its earliest possible date, assigned the estimated number of resources for the period of the activity, and then repeated this for all other activities. No attempt was made to schedule any activity other than at its earliest possible time, and the resulting usage pattern for each type of resource was calculated by simple addition. Resource aggregation by early dates is clearly of very limited use because it produces unworkable schedules, mixing overloads with periods of comparative idleness.

Resource levelling or scheduling

Practically all modern programs, and certainly those used for this garage project case study are capable of true resource scheduling.

A typical program will attempt to schedule each activity at its earliest possible time, and will draw down the number of resource units for each relevant resource from the total amount specified as available in the project's resource definition file. When each activity ends, its resources are released and returned to the availability pool for reallocation to other activities as necessary.

ID	Task name	Duration	Early start	Early finish	Late start	Late finish	Free slack	Total slack
1	Project start	0 days	10 May '10	10 May '10	10 May '10	10 May '10	0 days	0 days
2	Dig trench and soakaway	2 days	10 May '10	11 May '10	02 Jun '10	03 Jun '10	0 days	17 days
3	Cut roof timbers	1 day	10 May '10	10 May '10	01 Jun '10	01 Jun '10	16 days	16 days
4	Make door frame	1 day	10 May '10	10 May '10	14 May '10	14 May '10	0 days	4 days
5	Dig foundations	4 days	10 May '10	13 May '10	10 May '10	13 May '10	0 days	0 days
6	Make doors	3 days	10 May '10	12 May '10	01 Jun '10	03 Jun '10	0 days	16 days
7	Position door frame	1 day	11 May '10	11 May '10	17 May '10	17 May '10	4 days	4 days
8	Concrete foundations	2 days	14 May '10	17 May '10	14 May '10	17 May '10	0 days	0 days
9	Prime doors	1 day	13 May '10	13 May '10	04 Jun '10	04 Jun '10	12 days	16 days
10	Build brick walls	10 days	18 May '10	31 May '10	18 May '10	31 May '10	0 days	0 days
11	Lay floor base	2 days	18 May '10	19 May '10	02 Jun '10	03 Jun '10	0 days	11 days
12	Fit RSJ lintel	1 day	01 Jun '10	01 Jun '10	01 Jun '10	01 Jun '10	0 days	0 days
13	Lay floor screed	1 day	20 May '10	20 May '10	04 Jun '10	04 Jun '10	7 days	11 days
14	Lay underground drain	1day	12 May '10	12 May '10	04 Jun '10	04 Jun '10	0 days	17 days
15	Fit roof timbers	2 days	02 Jun '10	03 Jun '10	02 Jun '10	03 Jun '10	0 days	0 days
16	Hang doors	1 day	01 Jun '10	01 Jun '10	07 Jun '10	07 Jun '10	4 days	4 days
17	Case lintel + build parapet	2 days	02 Jun '10	03 Jun '10	07 Jun '10	08 Jun '10	1 days	3 days
18	Fit roof sheets	1 day	04 Jun '10	04 Jun '10	08 Jun '10	08 Jun '10	0 days	2 days
19	Fit fascia boards	1 day	04 Jun '10	04 Jun '10	04 Jun '10	04 Jun '10	0 days	0 days
20	Fill drain trench	1 day	13 May '10	13 May '10	09 Jun '10	09 Jun '10	0 days	19 days
21	Fit gutters and pipes	1 day	07 Jun '10	07 Jun '10	07 Jun '10	07 Jun '10	0 days	0 days
22	Concrete trench	1 day	14 May '10	14 May '10	10 Jun '10	10 Jun '10	19 days	19 days
23	Seal roof	2 days	07 Jun '10	08 Jun '10	09 Jun '10	10 Jun '10	2 days	2 days
24	Paint woodwork	3 days	08 Jun '10	10 Jun '10	08 Jun '10	10 Jun '10	0 days	0 days
25	Project handover	0 days	10 Jun '10	10 Jun '10	10 Jun '10	10 Jun '10	0 days	0 days

Figure 20.8 Garage project: time analysis using *Microsoft Project 2000*

If insufficient resources remain in the pool for an activity to be started on its earliest date, the computer will make a decision based on priority rules set by the planner.

Priority rules

Influence of float

If the computer has to delay two or more activities as a result of a scarce resource, float is often used to decide which of these competing activities claims first priority for the resource. When the computer schedules an activity to take place later than its earliest possible date, it has obviously used up some of the total float originally possessed by the activity and its following activities. The amount of float left in each case is sometimes called the 'remaining float'. A very useful priority rule is to give priority to those activities that have least remaining float.

Time-limited scheduling

Perhaps the most important decision the planner must make regarding resource allocation priorities is to decide whether the schedule is to be resource-limited or time-limited. These rules were explained in Chapter 16 and illustrated in Figure 16.7.

If the time-limited rule is chosen, the computer will schedule all activities at dates necessary to ensure that the project is completed within the timescale specified. Any target dates imposed on the starts or finishes of individual activities within the network would also be given priority. If necessary, the computer will plan for resource usage levels higher than those which have been declared as available.

Resource-limited scheduling

If the computer is operating under the resource-limited rule, it is instructed never to schedule any activity at a date that would cause more resources of any particular type to be needed than the total quantity specified as being available for the project. This means that some activities might have to be delayed beyond their latest (critical) start dates, keeping them waiting until resources are released from other even more critical activities.

Thus, with resource-limited scheduling, the project might have to be extended beyond the earliest possible completion date shown to be possible by the length of the critical path. It might also mean that any target completion dates specified for key activities within the network would have to be ignored.

Effectiveness of resource levelling

It is recognized that resource scheduling by computer may not necessarily produce the smoothest possible pattern of resource usage. Even when a resource schedule is calculated which never exceeds the stated capacity, there can be peaks and troughs remaining that could be ironed out by further calculation.

Imagine that the computer is asked to schedule the usage of electricians on a project, and that a total of five electricians is available within the organization. If the computer is instructed never to schedule beyond the limit of five electricians, it will not do so and a schedule will be produced that never calls for more than five electricians. That much can be guaranteed. But usage throughout the project life cycle might vary from zero to all five electricians in an unacceptable series of peaks and troughs.

Provided that there was other work for the electricians in the organization, uneven scheduling for one project need not matter. But, suppose that the work on this project means establishing the electricians in overnight accommodation to work on a site away from the headquarters. Then the schedule needs to be optimized, so that the work of electricians is conveniently grouped to allow a level rate of usage and prevent unnecessary travel and wasteful use of accommodation.

Some programs attempt optimization by making more than one scheduling pass through the network. Generally speaking, the computer will produce smoother schedules when it is given the chance to handle a large number of activities and the resource requirements approach the numbers actually available.

Resource scheduling results for the garage project

Because the garage project workforce comprises a father and son business the schedule should obviously be resource-limited if possible because it is going to be very difficult, if not impossible, to augment this tiny labour force. However, I have run both time- and resource-limited schedules for comparison and to demonstrate the method. The *Primavera* reports were more compact than those produced by *Microsoft Project 2000*, and are therefore shown here.

From a given project start date of 10 May 2010, *Primavera* produced the time-limited report shown in Figure 20.9, which shows the project finishing on 10 June 2010 at the cost of serious resource overloads. Rescheduling under the resource-limited priority rule produced the perfect resource usage pattern shown in Figure 20.10, but the project finish date has been extended to 23 June 2010 as a result. The days when no resource usage is shown in both of these reports are obviously Saturdays and Sundays.

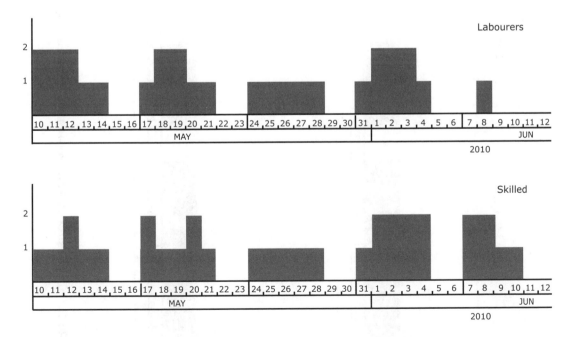

Figure 20.9   Garage project: time-limited resource histograms using *Primavera*

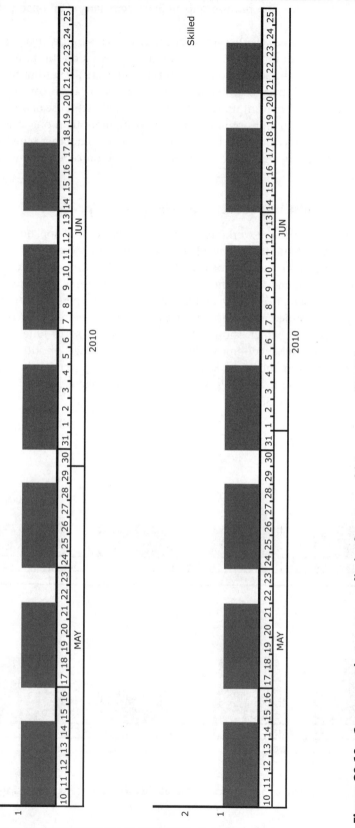

Figure 20.10 Garage project: resource-limited resource histograms using *Primavera*

Work-to list

One of the most useful types of report available from project management software is similar to the time analysis tabulation shown in Figure 20.8 but with additional columns giving the *scheduled* start and finish dates for each activity. These are the recommended start and finish dates for each activity after the resource scheduling process. The resulting schedule is often called a 'work-to list'. The report is not simply a list of work that has to be done. It is a recommendation to the relevant managers of the optimum sequence and timing of work to be done – a list to be worked to.

STANDARD AND CUSTOMIZED OUTPUT REPORTS

A taste of the output report possibilities has already been given, using the garage project data. It is likely that the system will give the user the option of choosing between either a range of standard output reports, or of reports that are adaptable or specially designed (customized) to suit the particular needs of the project organization. The commands to be entered for generating reports will depend on the program used.

Proprietary project management software usually contains a range of inbuilt report formats that can be used off the shelf, and many of those can be customized from simple drop-down menus. Some programs also give the project manager the option of creating new report formats to suit their own project needs, but those need some programming experience. One general word of advice can be given here, however, which is that the beginner would be well advised to start by using the standard formats provided by the system, and think about special report formats later, as confidence in using the system is gained.

Printers or larger plotters can produce network diagrams, Gantt charts and all manner of other graphical displays, enhanced by the use of colour. Work-to lists and scheduled resource requirements can be printed out showing great, day-by-day detail. Cost control data can be linked to the schedules, allowing budget cost curves, cost tables, and other presentations of planned and recorded expenditure to be printed. Figure 20.11, for example, is a graph from Primavera showing daily (line) and cumulative (bar) expenditure for the garage project after resource-limited scheduling.

All of these reports can be made available via an internal network or through the Internet or other electronic transmission methods to people inside or outside the project organization.

Filtering

After a big network has been processed, a very large volume of data is stored in the computer. The quantity of information usually far exceeds that needed for project management. Not only are there a lot of data, but also computers are capable of producing output in many different forms, even from a small selection of data. If all possible reports were to be produced, the result might be unmanageable, impressive for its bulk, but not for much else. It follows that the project manager must manage data carefully, ensuring that reports are concise, well presented and as effective as possible for their intended purpose.

The data content of every report must be carefully considered, to ensure that each recipient gets information that is particularly useful or relevant to them (preferably on a need-to-know basis). This is achieved by filtering (editing) the project data using one of the following options:

- assigning departmental or other report codes to all activity records;
- specifying milestones or key activities;
- reporting on selected resources;
- choosing some other activity parameters.

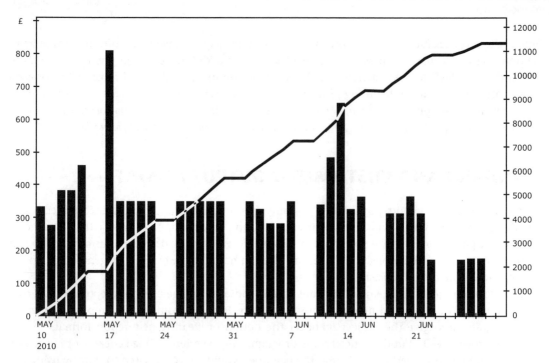

Figure 20.11   Garage project: cost report using *Primavera*

Most programs provide a menu from which filtering options can be selected.

If filtering is carefully designed and managed, each departmental manager can be given a work-to list containing only those tasks which they are expected to perform or manage. Thus, for example, the purchasing manager would receive information on all purchasing, expediting and materials handling activities.

All unwanted data should be excluded from reports. For example, the planner would probably filter out all activities that are already completed, so that they cease to appear in fresh work-to lists. Filtering can also be used to exclude information that is secret, confidential or otherwise restricted.

Sorting

Another important aspect of reports is the sequence in which data are presented. This is achieved by the process of sorting.

For example, the person with prime responsibility for planning would need an activity listing sorted according to the activity ID numbers as an aid to checking the input data for errors. A manager responsible for issuing work to a department needs a report that lists jobs in order of their earliest or scheduled start dates. A progress clerk or purchasing expeditor is best served by a report that lists jobs or materials deliveries in order of their planned completion dates.

Useful combined cost and resource table

Some expert customization might be needed before a report such as the combined cost and resource usage report for the garage project shown in Figure 20.12 can be produced, although one standard *Microsoft Project 2000* report comes very close. This figure, like all the other examples in his chapter, is actually a simulation, closely following the computer-produced originals but redrawn for clarity. The dates agree with the resource-limited version of the schedule.

GARAGE PROJECT SCHEDULED RESOURCE USAGE AND COST

Date	Resource LA: Labourer				Resource SK: Skilled				Task materials £	Cumulative project cost £
	Available	Used	Unused	Cost £	Available	Used	Unused	Cost £		
10 May 10	1	1		120	1	1		160	50	330
11 May 10	1	1		120	1	1		160		610
12 May 10	1	1		120	1	1		160	100	990
13 May 10	1	1		120	1	1		160	100	1 370
14 May 10	1	1		120	1	1		160	175	1 825
17 May 10	1	1		120	1	1		160	525	2 630
18 May 10	1	1		120	1	1		160	65	2 975
19 May 10	1	1		120	1	1		160	65	3 320
20 May 10	1	1		120	1	1		160	65	3 665
21 May 10	1	1		120	1	1		160	65	4 010
24 May 10	1	1		120	1	1		160	65	4 355
25 May 10	1	1		120	1	1		160	65	4 700
26 May 10	1	1		120	1	1		160	65	5 045
27 May 10	1	1		120	1	1		160	65	5 390
28 May 10	1	1		120	1	1		160	65	5 735
31 May 10	1	1		120	1	1		160	65	6 080
01 Jun 10	1	1		120	1	1		160	40	6 400
02 Jun 10	1	1		120	1	1		160		6 680
03 Jun 10	1	1		120	1	1		160		6 960
04 Jun 10	1	1		120	1	1		160	65	7 305
07 Jun 10	1	1		120	1	1		160	55	7 640
08 Jun 10	1	1		120	1	1		160	200	8 120
09 Jun 10	1	1		120	1	1		160	360	8 760
10 Jun 10	1	1		120	1	1		160	40	9 080
11 Jun 10	1	1		120	1	1		160	80	9 440
14 Jun 10	1	1		120	1	1		160	30	9 750
15 Jun 10	1	1		120	1	1		160	30	10 060
16 Jun 10	1	1		120	1	1		160	80	10 420
17 Jun 10	1	1		120	1	1		160	30	10 730
18 Jun 10	1		1		1	1		160	10	10 900
21 Jun 10	1		1		1	1		160	10	11 070
22 Jun 10	1		1		1	1		160	15	11 245
23 Jun 10	1		1		1	1		160	15	11 420
24 Jun 10	1		1		1		1			11 420
25 Jun 10	1		1		1		1			11 420
28 Jun 10	1		1		1		1			11 420
29 Jun 10	1		1		1		1			11 420
30 Jun 10	1		1		1		1			11 420
01 Jul 10	1		1		1		1			11 420
02 Jul 10	1		1		1		1			11 420

Figure 20.12   Garage project: useful cost and resource summary

This report shows, correctly, that the estimated total cost of the garage is £11 420. A glance down the table columns shows that the labourer should become free for other work on 18 June 2010, and the skilled person will be able to take up new work from 24 June 2010.

I have found reports of this type to be immensely useful for manpower planning and other purposes, especially when they showed all the company resources and were calculated for all current projects together (a process known as multi-project scheduling, which is described in Chapter 28).

Project summary reports

Most programs make provision for one-page project summary reports, intended as a management overview. If more than one project is contained in the system, some programs will allow summary reports to be printed out concisely for all projects in a type of report sometimes known as a project directory.

For those who like pretty colours, some versions show red, amber or green 'traffic light' signals against activities to show whether they are on course, at risk or behind schedule.

UPDATING THE SCHEDULES AND REPORTS

It is unlikely that any scheduling will live through the active life of a project without needing some change, either to accommodate changes in project scope or to reflect current progress. The updating of computer schedules, because it is part of progress management, is explained in Chapter 24.

21 *Managing Project Start-up*

O nce authorization has been received, the project ceases to be merely an object for planning and speculation and becomes instead a live entity and a commitment for the contractor or other organization responsible. Authorization procedures were discussed in Chapter 8, but now we are much farther on in the project lifecycle, with much of the planning already in place and with actual work and serious expenditure just about to begin. For the purposes of achieving all the project objectives, whether technical, budgetary or timescale, the appropriate project organization has to be set up, staffed and activated. All participants must be made fully aware of the particular roles they will be expected to play.

A common risk to projects is failure to start work on time. Very long delays can be caused by prevarication, legal or planning difficulties, shortage of information, lack of funds or other resources, and a host of other reasons. All of these factors can place a project manager in a difficult or impossible position. *A project that does not start on time is less likely to finish on time.*

PRELIMINARY ORGANIZATION OF THE PROJECT

Even when a clear technical specification has been prepared there are often many loose ends to be tied up before actual work can start. The extent and nature of these preliminary activities naturally depend on the type and size of project.

Getting the project manager started

One of the first tasks is to appoint the project manager. A desirable procedure in large projects with a high degree of complexity might be to seek out the person who spearheaded all the conceptual engineering studies during the proposal phase, and allow that person to take the actual project through to completion. In that way, what is eventually built should be what was actually sold or intended. However, that is not always practicable. Another way must be found to ensure that the project is handed over to the newly appointed project manager in such a way that there is no ambiguity about what has to be done, when and at what cost.

Different companies have their own ways of dealing with this requirement. In some cases a project identification document (PID) can define the project sufficiently. Other companies follow a project charter and project contract route, where the charter is either the business plan or a document closely related to it, and the contract is a subsequent document that creates a binding internal contract between the company and its newly designated project manager (even though there might be a separate, commercial and legally binding contract made between the company and an external customer).

Whatever the procedure used, the important element is a project specification that tells the project manager exactly what is required. In other words, using the popular jargon, the project specification defines the project deliverables.

Charting the organization

When the project manager has been named, an organization chart (organigram) should be drawn up and published to show all the key people and agencies concerned with the project. This chart must include senior members of all external groups who are to have any responsibility in the project. If the organization is large, the usual arrangement is to produce an overall summary chart and then draw a series of smaller charts that allow some of the groups to be shown in more detail. Depending, of course, on the actual arrangements, an overall project organization chart might have to show:

- key elements in the contractor's own organization, obviously including the project manager;
- management teams working away from the contractor's head office (especially site teams on construction projects);
- principal subcontractors;
- external purchasing agent (if employed) together with any outside groups responsible for expediting, equipment inspection and shipping arrangements;
- independent consultants, acting either for the customer or the contractor;
- representatives of government or local government departments (where relevant).

Allocating responsibilities: deciding who does what

People must know what is expected of them. One tool that can assist the project manager to allocate responsibilities is the *linear responsibility matrix*, an example of which is shown in Figure 21.1. The job titles of key members of the organization are listed above the matrix columns and various important task types are listed along the rows. Symbols are placed at the appropriate matrix intersections to show primary and secondary responsibility for each of the task types listed.

Some writers make the error of declaring that all project tasks should be listed on a responsibility matrix. With possible many thousands of tasks in a project, this is clearly asking too much, and inviting many wasted clerical hours and confuses the purpose of the responsibility matrix with the far more detailed work-to lists produced from computer scheduling. Instead, the responsibility matrix should be designed around task types or categories. For example, a matrix can show the person responsible for approving new designs in general, but it is not the place in which to list all the drawings that carry those designs (that function is performed by the drawings register or drawing schedule described in the final section of this chapter).

CORRESPONDENCE AND OTHER DOCUMENTS

The contractor will be well advised to take control procedures for project correspondence and document handling seriously. The contractor could be placed in a difficult position if vital letters or other documents were subsequently lost. It is necessary to ensure that positive steps are taken to deal with the routeing and control of documented information within the home office and with all external parts of the project organization.

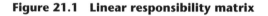

Task type:	The client	Project manager	Project engineer	Purchasing mngr	Drawing office	Construction mngr	Planning engineer	Cost engineer	Project accountant		and so on
Make designs		✚	●								
Approve designs	●	■	✚								
Purchase enquiries		■	✚	●							
Purchase orders	■	■	✚	●							
Planning	■	■	✚	✚	✚	✚	●	✚			
Cost control		●	✚			✚		✚			
Progress reports		●	✚	✚	✚	✚	✚				
Cost reports		●	✚			✚		✚	✚		

and so on

●   Principal responsibility (only one per task)

✚   Secondary responsibility

■   Must be consulted

Figure 21.1 Linear responsibility matrix

Documents: deciding who gets what

Most projects generate a great deal of paper. Once all the planning, control and administrative procedures have been decided, all the associated forms, expected reports and other types of documents can be listed. It is then possible to consider each of these document types in turn and decide who needs to receive copies as a matter of routine. This should usually be on a need-to-know rather than nice-to-have basis (except that all requests for documents from the customer must obviously be looked upon favourably unless these would give away information that the contractor wishes to remain confidential).

If the documents are to be made available in electronic form, accessible over a network, it might be necessary to impose different levels of access for security purposes, thus preventing unauthorized people from seeing or interfering with sensitive or confidential data.

Once the regular distribution or availability of documents has been agreed, the decision can be shown and communicated on a chart arranged as a matrix. This is, of course, secondary to the responsibility matrix shown in Figure 21.1. Each authorized recipient can be named and allocated a vertical column, and each category of documents can be allocated a horizontal row. A tick in the square at each grid intersection shows that access is permissible. Alternatively, a number written at the intersection shows how many hard copies of the relevant document each person should receive. Figure 21.2 illustrates the principle.

Document type:	Recipient:	The customer	General manager	Project manager	Project engineer	Works manager	Production control	Buyer	Quality manager	Accountant		and so on
Bought-out parts lists					1		1	2	1			
Material specifications					1			1	1			
Purchase requisitions					1			1*				
Purchase orders								1		1		
Shortage lists				1			1	1				
Committed cost reports			1	1	1			1		1		
Drawing list				1	1	1						
Drawings for approval		1			1*							

and so on.

1	Number of copies per recipient
*	Retains original signed document

Figure 21.2 Document distribution matrix

Internal routeing of hard copy documents

There is always a risk that documents received safely by a company will be lost or misrouted within the project organization. There is a useful discipline which can be imposed to help prevent this problem, and to ensure that every document reaches the person who should take appropriate action. This procedure is based on the concept of two levels of distribution, *primary* and *secondary*. The following description explains how this concept can be implemented. The case described here is for incoming project documents, but copies of outgoing correspondence can be distributed in similar fashion.

Primary distribution of incoming documents

Each original letter is date stamped on receipt and placed in central files. Sufficient copies are sent to the project manager, together with any enclosures from the original letter, to allow him or her to arrange for secondary distribution. The number of copies needed would be specified in a written procedure (such as a *project handbook* or *project manual*).

Secondary distribution

The project manager (or delegate) considers who should answer the incoming letter and take any necessary action. An action copy, with enclosures is passed to the chosen individual. One copy is placed in project office files (the project support office, if such exists) and the project manager may decide to direct copies to other managers or staff for information.

The copy intended for action must be clearly indicated as such, to ensure that action is neither neglected nor duplicated by the recipient of a 'for information only' copy.

Nominated addressees or contacts

It is good practice for each organization to nominate one of its senior members to act as a control point for receiving and sending all formal written communications and technical documents, however these are transmitted. Each nominated addressee then becomes responsible for seeing that the documents or the information contained in them is made known to all relevant people within their own organization.

Document transmission methods

International projects, where the contracting organization is overseas from the customer, construction site or other project groups, demand careful attention to the transmission routes of documents that must be sent as hard copy. If normal mail and airmail services are too slow or otherwise inadequate, a specialist express postal service or the use of an international courier company should be considered.

Airfreight can be used for bulky consignments of drawings or other heavy documents. When valuable documents have to be sent quickly to any overseas location, use of a regular air courier service means that the courier company can monitor or even accompany each consignment through all stages of its journey, with all movements and aircraft transfers under the surveillance of the agent's network. Such specialist services obviously reduce risk of losses and delays.

Good liaison between the company's travel department and the mailroom will ensure that travellers can be identified who might be persuaded to carry documents in their hand baggage, but this arrangement is often abused and individuals expecting to visit a site for a meeting or a short inspection can find themselves weighed down with an alarming heap of excess baggage.

At some overseas destinations the customs authorities can delay release of documents, and the contractor should always seek the professional advice of a carrier or courier familiar with the required route. Local industrial disputes can cause complete hold-ups or frustrating delays. In other cases customs authorities have been known to be awkward for no apparent reason – in one case known to me a consignment of drawings intended for a project site was held at a US airport while the customs authorities demanded payment of duty based not on the intrinsic value of the drawings but on the value of the whole project! The solution in that case was to abandon the drawings (they might still be gathering dust in the customs shed) and send a duplicate set through another route.

Many of these problems can be overcome by the electronic transmission of documents but some remote site offices may not have the high-volume, high-quality, large-size printers or plotters that are enjoyed by staff of the permanent home office, in which case the site staff will not appreciate receiving massive electronic files from which they are expected to print all their working specifications and drawings.

Serial numbering of correspondence documents

If a large amount of regular correspondence is expected, all the parties likely to correspond with each other can agree to use letter-reference serial numbers, prefixed with their own codes. Based on an actual case (but with the names changed) here is an example of how correspondence was numbered on one project from my experience. The project contractor was Alternative Engineering Limited

(AEL) and its overseas client was Quaint Smelters Inc. (QSI). All serial numbers build in a straight sequence from 0001.

	From AEL to QSI	*From QSI to AEL*
Letters	AQL 0001	QAL 0001
Faxes	AQF 0001	QAF 0001
Document transmittal forms	AQD 0001	QAD 0001

Apart from making consecutive filing and subsequent document retrieval easier, the use of a continuous series of numbers means that any gap in the sequence of numbers received at either end indicates a possible loss in transit that needs investigation.

The allocation of serial numbers requires some form of central register, to be administered by a suitable secretary or clerk (perhaps located in a project support office). Such formal procedures are really only suited to the despatch of documents that have particular contractual or technical significance, or for bulk consignments of documents such as drawings and specifications. E-mail correspondence, where many individuals on a single project can communicate immediately with others worldwide from their desks, does not lend itself to such formality and it is up to the senders to ensure that their messages have been properly received and understood.

Document transmittal letters

Consignments of drawings and other documents which are not accompanied by a serially numbered covering letter should be given consignment numbers, and this is best achieved by the use of standard 'document transmittal letter' forms. These are little more than packing lists, but each is given a serial number and copies are retained on file as a record of what was sent. In the case of the US customs problem mentioned above, for example, the file copy of the relevant document transmittal letter listed all the drawing prints in the impounded consignment, enabling a duplicate set of prints to be made and sent.

Correspondence progressing

Companies with a large volume of project correspondence arrange for a coordinator to ensure that every letter or other document that requires an answer is dealt with without undue delay. The same person will also follow up any possible losses in transit, apparent from gaps in the sequence of serial numbers received.

ENGINEERING STANDARDS AND PROCEDURES

Special design standards

The contractor will have to investigate whether or not the project calls for any special design standards, safety requirements, or compliance with government or other statutory regulations.

Drawing numbers and drawing format

It is often agreed that the drawings made for a project are the property of the customer, who will expect to be provided with a complete set of drawings at the end of the project and file them in their own system (the contractor would, of course, retain one set). In such a case the contractor will probably have to discuss and agree the drawing numbering system to be used for the project. Common practice is to number each drawing twice, using the customer's system and the contractor's normal standard, and then cross-reference these in the computer or drawing register.

Drawings may have to be laid out to the customer's own standard drawing format or drawing sheets, in which case the contractor must obtain supplies (or a digital template) before drawing can start. If the sheets are of a non-standard size this might also mean purchasing new equipment for filing hard copies.

Choice of project planning and control procedures

Companies accustomed to carrying out large projects may have at their disposal a considerable range of planning and control procedures. At the start of each new project these can be reviewed to determine which are appropriate for the particular project. Factors affecting this choice are the size and complexity of the project, the degree of difficulty and risk expected in meeting the end objectives, the number and locations of outside organizations and, last but never least, the wishes or directions of the customer.

Project manual or procedures manual

For some projects contractors will compile a project manual (otherwise known as a procedures manual or project handbook). This will list the particular procedures that will apply to the project. Listed below are just some of the items that a typical project manual might include:

- names and addresses of key organizations taking part in the project, not forgetting the customer;
- the names of key personnel in those organizations, particularly highlighting those who are the specific points of contact for various project matters;
- organization charts;
- drawing numbering system;
- project planning and scheduling system to be used;
- type and frequency of project cost and progress reports to be produced;
- linear responsibility matrix;
- document distribution matrix;
- incoming and outgoing correspondence prefix codes, if used.

PHYSICAL PREPARATIONS AND ORGANIZATION

Physical preparations must be made for any project that requires accommodation, plant, equipment, services such as gas, electric power, compressed air, water and so on. There is no typical case, because the requirements of every project depend very much on the nature of the project and the practices of its contractor. At one end of the scale is the project which will simply follow another in a factory, using the same staff, management and facilities. At the opposite extreme is the international project involving several large companies and a construction site in the middle of a desert with no communicating rail or road, and no other infrastructure. In the latter case, making physical preparation for the main project is, in itself, a collection of very large subprojects. Any discussion in this chapter must, therefore, be in general terms. None the less one or two important, general principles can be mentioned.

Importance of checklists

All project managers will know the feelings of frustration caused during the initial days and weeks when, keen to start, and with deadlines to meet, real work has to wait because there is no information, no staff and there is a general lack of other facilities. Lack of information is often the worst of these problems: not necessarily about the main objectives and features of the intended project but more likely about a hundred-and-one annoying details which have to be resolved before work can start.

The value of checklists is mentioned in several places in this book, and no apology is needed or made for giving additional space to this subject here. Standard checklists, applicable to all projects, present and future, can be used as questionnaires to pre-empt information requirements. The best checklists are developed and refined gradually through experience, so that lessons learned on one project are remembered, added to those already learned, and then put to use on projects which follow.

Construction site checklist example

An instance where a checklist is particularly useful is when a construction site organization has to be established, especially when this is to be overseas. Even for an experienced organization, that can be an enormous operation. All sorts of questions have to be asked, and answered. Some questions should already have been answered when the proposal was researched (see Chapter 3, Figure 3.2). When the project becomes real, the questions and answers are of a more definite and detailed nature. Some examples follow:

- How many people are going to be needed on site?
    - our own permanent staff, on overseas assignment?
    - our own fixed-term contract staff, hired for the purpose and duration only?
    - local recruits (will they need training?)
    - how many client's staff will be on site?
    - what about subcontractors and their staff?
- What accommodation will be required?
    - how much?
    - what standard?
    - who is responsible for providing it?
    - rent-free?
- What are the immigration rules?
    - passports and visas?
    - work permits?
    - any racial prejudices?
- Local employment laws and practices?
- What about expatriates' wives and families?
- Standard terms of employment?
- Pay and taxation arrangements?
- Insurances:
    - staff-related?
    - work-related?
- Staff medical, welfare and leisure facilities?
- Climate?
- Site access:
    - road?
    - rail?
    - air?
    - other?
- Vehicle fleet:
    - personnel carriers?

- – freight carriers?
- – how provided?
- – how managed and maintained?
- • Site plant:
  - – what is needed?
  - – when?
  - – how provided?
  - – how maintained?

... and so on for page after page, covering all aspects of the site and its legal, political and physical environment.

These questions need to be answered as completely and as early as possible. The better the checklist, the earlier and more completely the answers will be obtained.

GETTING WORK STARTED

The kick-off meeting

When the newly appointed project manager has collected his or her wits and absorbed the contents of the project specification (which will probably entail some late nights), the most urgent job is to mobilize all the project resources and tell the key participants what is expected of them.

This process takes place in different stages and by a variety of methods. The first executive action of the project manager is usually to call an initial meeting, often called the 'kick-off' meeting, which gives the project manager the opportunity to outline the main features of the project to managers whose departments will work on the project, and to the most senior design staff and other key people. If the project is organized as a team, the project manager will have the advantage of talking to people who are directly responsible to him or her. If the organization is a matrix, the task is more difficult – even getting people to attend the meeting becomes a question more of invitation and persuasion rather than issuing a direct summons.

Whatever the circumstances, the skilled project manager will make the best possible use of the initial meeting to get the project off to a good start. Everyone who attends the meeting should leave with a clear picture of the project's objectives, the part that they are expected to play in achieving them, and a sense of keenness and motivation to get on with the job.

Issuing initial planning information

Plans and schedules will do no good at all if they are merely hung on a wall and regarded thereafter as objects to be gazed at and admired. The project manager must make certain that the contents of these schedules are made known to every key person in the organization, preferably using well-targeted work-to lists.

Every contractor develops expertise according to the particular industry in which it operates. The contractor learns the sort of preliminary activities that must always be carried out to establish procedures and design standards before a typical project can start. A sensible contractor will write these into a standard checklist.

One company designed such a checklist in the form of a network diagram, a copy of which was used at the start of each new project. Figure 21.3 is based on that example. Time estimates and time analysis were never used on this standard network. It was used only as a checklist, but its value lay in the fact that it listed all likely preliminary activities in their logical sequence.

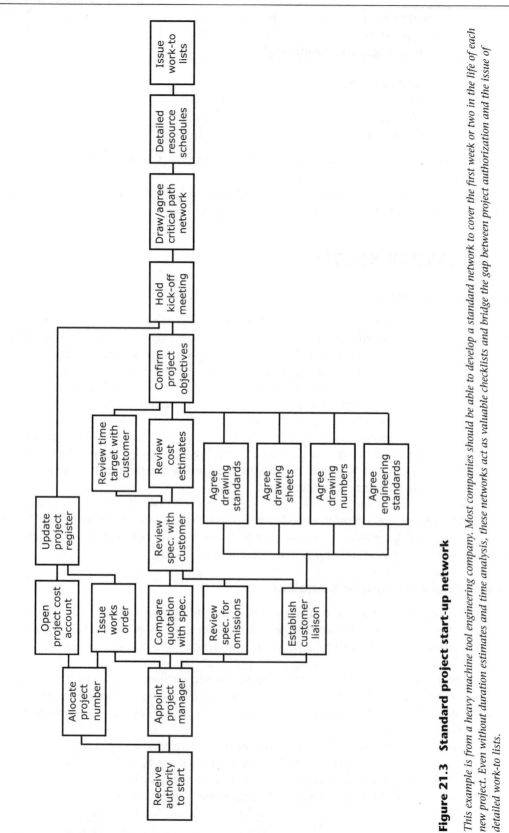

Figure 21.3 Standard project start-up network

This example is from a heavy machine tool engineering company. Most companies should be able to develop a standard network to cover the first week or two in the life of each new project. Even without duration estimates and time analysis, these networks act as valuable checklists and bridge the gap between project authorization and the issue of detailed work-to lists.

ISSUING DETAILED PLANNING AND WORK INSTRUCTIONS

Importance of personal agreement and commitment

Enough has already been written in earlier chapters about the methods available for producing plans and working schedules. If the project is of any significance at all in terms of its size, complexity or perceived importance, it must be taken for granted that detailed planning will be performed, and that this will involve input from at least one senior representative from every key project function. This involvement might mean full attendance at an intensive network brainstorming session, or it could mean instead asking these key representatives to view, review and approve a network produced automatically from templates or other standard library data (see Chapter 29).

Each key participant must, therefore, have some share in formulating and agreeing the detailed plan. This is just as it should be, because no plan can be imposed successfully in isolation. It must carry the acceptance and support of those who are to be bound by it.

As soon as detailed planning has been carried out, the computer can be instructed to analyse the network, carry out resource allocation (if required) and produce a work-to list for every project department.

Issuing work schedules: targeting action instructions

Dissemination of programme information must be made far more effective than the simple blanket distribution of common schedules to all and sundry. Instead each department should receive a work-to list showing only those tasks for which it is responsible. Instructions are often ignored when they are issued to too many people, instead of only to the person who is expected to arrange for action. If an instruction is issued in a document that goes to more than one department, each may do nothing and rely instead on the other to carry the instruction out. There is also a slighter risk that some tasks might be performed twice. Such risks exist when project networks or other schedules are distributed to a wide number of departments or people without any explanation or precise instructions for action. Properly filtered work-to lists, on the other hand, possess the advantage of being specific to their addressees, so that management responsibility for each item on each list is the clear responsibility of the recipient.

Work-to-lists usually need to be provided in detail to cover only a few weeks ahead, but longer-term summaries may have to be given to help departmental managers to recruit or reserve the necessary people. All of this is readily achievable with the filtering and sorting capabilities of project management software, and it is now that the benefits of coded work breakdown structures and organization breakdown structures described in Chapters 12 and 13 will begin to be realized.

Recognizing the authority of departmental managers

The instructions or reminders contained in work-to lists should in no way detract from the personal authority vested in each departmental manager. Although the source of each instruction is the project manager's office or the project support office, the information should derive from the detailed project plan that was first made, reviewed and agreed with the departmental managers themselves. The authority of these managers, far from being undermined, should actually be reinforced.

Each manager receives a list of the work required of his or her department, together with information about when the work should be performed, but is otherwise free to allocate the work to individuals within the department and to direct and control it. With work-to lists resulting from sensible resource scheduling, there should be no chronic departmental overloads (temporary overloads will always remain a risk). The departmental managers are in fact provided with very effective tools that should help them to control the project activities within their particular groups.

Work-to lists for manufacturing

Work-to lists for manufacturing will usually be sent to the production manager or production controller, who will issue internal works orders, job tickets, route cards or any other form of document demanded by the customary procedures used throughout the manufacturing organization.

The levels of detail shown in project networks (and, therefore, in the resulting work-to lists) are bound to be far coarser than those needed for the day-to-day (even minute-to-minute) planning and control of factory operations. Work-to lists will, for example, provide the expected start and required finish dates for each assembly and subassembly. It is highly unlikely that any work-to list derived from the project schedule will specify a greater degree of breakdown and will not include all the smallest components or parts needed for the project.

The manufacturing organization, will therefore, use its production engineering, planning and control facilities to interpret drawings, write instructions for numerically-controlled machines, identify the parts and materials required and carry out detail production scheduling. This must be done to satisfy the dates given on the work-to lists but, provided that project resource scheduling was carried out effectively, the overall rate of working implied by the work-to list should lie within the capacity of the manufacturing plant.

Engineering design

In engineering design departments, the work-to lists are more likely to be used for controlling day-to-day work without need for the multitude of additional documents and procedures that are always required in manufacturing departments.

However, networks are not always drawn with sufficient breakdown detail for the day-to-day allocation of work, and it might be necessary for design managers and supervisors to arrange for some manual task listing. For example, purchase and drawing schedules are usually needed to show a greater level of detail than is feasible on the project network diagram. A single network activity usually summarizes a group of drawings needed for a small work package or subassembly, and it is not usually desirable or possible to have a separate network activity for every individual project drawing.

Thus, in the same way that production department managers will be expected to regard the project work-to lists as a framework for their more detailed day-to-day jobs, so design managers must be expected to identify the daily chores and allocate jobs to individuals. They can, however, do this in the knowledge that the work-to lists feed work to their departments at a rate that should not cause overloads.

In most engineering design offices and other software groups, highly qualified staff can be found whose creative talents are beyond question. But, while their technical or scientific approach to project tasks might be well motivated and capable of producing excellent results, there is always a danger that these creative souls will not fully appreciate the importance of keeping within time and cost limits. The inclusion of estimated costs and target completion dates on work-to lists can help to make these specialists become more aware of their commercial responsibilities.

Purchase and drawing schedules

Purchase schedules, sometimes called purchase control schedules, list all the important items that have to be bought-in for a project. They usually list, for each significant purchase, the specification number, and subsequently the requisition and purchase order numbers. Once written manually in a very time-consuming chore, they will almost certainly be set up and maintained in a computer file. The subject of purchase schedules was introduced in the context of materials resource scheduling in Chapter 18, and a typical arrangement is shown in Figures 18.12 and 18.13.

Drawing schedule for Loxylene Plant (Huddersfield)		Page of pages			
Sub-schedule for storage tankhouse code LX 5150-459		Date			
Drawing number	Drawing title	Client approval (if req'd)		Issues	
		Date requested	Date approved	Date RFC*	Revision number

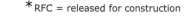

*RFC = released for construction

Figure 21.4   Possible column headings for a drawing schedule

Drawing schedules (or drawing control schedules) list all the drawings that will be needed for a project. They are very similar to a drawings register, and are indeed used for the allocation of drawing numbers. Figure 21.4 shows a possible arrangement for a drawings schedule sheet.

The central drawings register, where such exists, is a general company record, but drawing schedules are specific to each project. Many companies incorporate the project number in their drawing numbers, and go further by numbering and arranging the schedules in sets that correspond with higher levels of the WBS coding. Apart from being of immense value to the project workers and all who come after, numbering to incorporate these WBS codes will ensure that there is no duplication with a central company drawings register. WBS coding systems were described and illustrated in Chapter 12.

Establishing the drawings schedule for a project is usually carried out as a complementary function to setting up the purchase schedules. It is an essential part of the project start-up activities and, once again, the clerical chore of creating and updating them is made much easier using a computer.

A project support office can be the home for creating and maintaining purchase and drawing schedules. However, grouping these documents in sets structured on the WBS or the OBS higher-level codes will enable the task of creating them to be distributed over all the specialist design groups involved without fear of introducing the risk of errors of omission or duplication.

When the project is finished, the drawing and purchase control schedules have to be updated to show all the final drawing numbers with their correct revisions, and all the purchase specification numbers and their final revisions. When complete, these schedules then define the 'as built' condition of the project. They are similar to the build schedule documents that will be described in Chapter 30, the principal difference being that drawing and purchase schedules define a single project whereas build schedules are used for defining the content of manufactured products that are made in two or more different versions.

22 *Aspects of Commercial Management*

Many aspects of commercial management are highly specialized and, particularly for legal and insurance matters, these are areas where it can be dangerous for the layperson to venture without professional help. However, it is possible to outline some of the more important points. For study in greater depth there is a further reading list at the end of this chapter.

CONTRACTS

There might be many kinds of contracts made with or within a large project organization. For example, every employee should have a contract of employment. There will be a contract between a main contractor and the project owner, and more contracts between the main contractor and subcontractors. Every purchase involves a buyer–seller contract, usually embodied in a purchase order. For internal, or management change projects, a contract often exists between the company and the manager or other staff member who is assigned to manage the project.

This chapter is principally concerned with the contract made by the project owner with a main contractor, and with contracts for the purchase of project goods and services.

Essential elements of a contract

Although a legally binding contract can exist between two parties on the basis of a verbal agreement, for project management purposes it is assumed that the contract between the customer and the main contractor will be in writing. This applies also to all contracts made between the project contractor and the subcontractors and other suppliers of goods and services. Properly drafted written documents are likely to ensure that all aspects of each agreement are available for subsequent reference, both for routine administration of the contract and as evidence should any dispute require resolution.

The contract documentation might be a purchase order, an exchange of letters, a specially drafted contract or a standard form. It is assumed that any subsequent amendments to the contract will also be written on suitable documents.

Several conditions must be satisfied for a legally binding contract to exist. The following notes are a summary, and do not list the exceptions:

- **Intention** The parties must intend that the contract shall be legally binding. In project contracts this intention will be assumed unless the parties have specifically declared otherwise, in which case the contract becomes only a formal version of a 'gentleman's agreement'. Project managers are not likely to be concerned with this question of intention, except perhaps when problems arise with collective agreements between management and trade unions.

- **Offer and acceptance** The contractor (seller) must make a definite offer stating willingness to contract on specified terms, and the contract becomes legally binding on both parties when the customer (buyer) informs the contractor that the offer is accepted without qualification. The customer must communicate acceptance before the expiry of any offer time limit set by the contractor.

   It may happen that the picture becomes blurred as to what has been offered and what actually has been accepted. Therefore the offer must be defined by a specification that is as complete and up to date as possible, amended as necessary to take account of all changes agreed during negotiations.

- **Consideration** A contract must result in each party promising the other a valuable benefit. In projects, this usually means that one party promises to deliver certain goods, property or services by a specified date and the other promises to accept the goods, property or services and pay for them. Failure of one party to keep its promise can lead to action by the other for breach of contract.

- **Capacity** In general, if the offer made by a company falls outside the scope of its powers as set out in the objects clause of its memorandum of association, then the company has no power to make the offer and the contract is void (said to be *ultra vires*, or 'beyond the power').

Terms describing the parties to a project contract

In general this book refers to the two main parties in project contracts as the customer and the contractor, but many other terms are used in practice.

Terms describing the project purchaser

Some people use the term 'owner' to mean the customer, but this can be misleading because there are several possible circumstances where the customer will not have immediate legal title to the project. One example is where the project is being funded under a lease-purchase agreement, so that the finance house will be the initial legal owner. A few contractors adopt the confusing practice of calling their own project managers 'project owners', with the intention of stressing that the project managers 'own' responsibility for their projects until the completed work has been handed over to the purchasers (the real project owners).

   When a project is passed on by the customer to a third party, the expression 'end user' can be useful to describe the eventual recipient.

   The terms in most general use are 'customer', 'client', 'purchaser' or 'buyer' but the terms 'promoter' and 'employer' are occasionally seen. For simplicity, 'customer' is used in most cases throughout this book but 'client' is commonly preferred in projects involving construction or the supply of professional services.

Terms describing the project supplier

The organization carrying out the project may be described as the 'contractor', 'vendor', 'manufacturer', 'supplier' or 'seller'. The terms 'main contractor', 'managing contractor' and 'management contractor' are used to identify an organization employed by the project purchaser for help in managing and fulfilling a project. These terms are not strictly synonymous and the generally accepted distinctions between them are as follows:

- A 'main contractor' or 'managing contractor' is a person or (more likely) an organization that accepts commercial risk and responsibility on behalf of the customer and directly employs other contractors (subcontractors) to execute some or all of the work. A common arrangement is for the main contractor to carry out design work in its own offices and then engage and supervise subcontractors to supply specialist trades to perform some or all of the work.

- A 'management contractor' is a person or organization engaged by the project customer to provide professional assistance in planning, coordinating and supervising the work of other contractors.

Throughout this book I have used the term 'contractor' generally to mean the company or other organization that has entered into a contract to carry out all or most of the work required for a project.

However, for an in-house management change or IT project, the 'contractor' could be an internal department or senior member of the customer's own staff.

Independent consultants

Independent consultants often figure in large contracts, and may be appointed to safeguard the interests of one party or the other (usually the purchaser). In most cases the consultant is either a professional organization or a suitably qualified person, often referred to contractually as 'the engineer'. Refer, for example, to the role of the independent consulting engineer in a contract matrix, which is described briefly in Chapter 9 and illustrated in the organization chart of Figure 9.10.

Contract scope

The contract documents should specify, without ambiguity, the exact role that the contractor is required to perform. The purchaser and the contractor must both be clear on what is included in any quoted price or charging rate, and on what is excluded. At its lowest level, the contract scope might be limited to minor involvement by a company as a subcontractor. At the other extreme, a contractor could be completely in charge of a large project, with 'turnkey' responsibility for all the works (which means handing the project over to the customer only after completion and commissioning). Specifying the technical and commercial scope is part of the project definition process (see Chapter 3).

Abbreviations describing contract scope

Abbreviations are sometimes used as a succinct way to describe the scope expected of a contractor for a building or item of plant. These terms relate specifically to the expected role of the contractor in work such as the following:

- building the initial project;
- handing over the project ready for immediate use (turnkey);
- training the customer's staff to operate or use the project;
- operating the project for the customer initially;
- operating the project for the customer in the longer term;
- providing maintenance services.

The following are commonly used abbreviations:

BOOM	Build–own–operate–maintain
BOOT	Build–own–operate–transfer ownership
BOTO	Build–own–train–operate
OMT	Operate–maintain–train
TK	Turnkey

Contracts with model or standard terms and conditions

To avoid errors and omissions, and to promote the use of contracts that are likely to be most effective in use, many organizations use standard or model forms that either guide the process of drafting new contracts or remove the need altogether. The most common case of a standard form of contract intended to remove any need for drafting is the common purchase order.

Professional institutions (especially the engineering institutions), national bodies, trade associations and some large companies have developed model terms of contract that are relevant to their particular industries or specialized disciplines, and the New Engineering Contract (NEC) has gained prominence in recent years. All model contracts are subject to revision from time to time and intending users should always ensure that they have the latest edition, or that some new model has not been introduced. This is a vast subject area, well beyond the scope of this book, and it brings with it an equally vast amount of reading matter. The specialist UK publisher in this area is Thomas Telford and the website address of their online bookshop is http://www.thomastelford.com/books/.

PURCHASE ORDERS

Purchase orders are probably the most common type of contract that we encounter in our working lives. There are two main parts to a purchase order:

- a description of the goods or services to be purchased;
- a statement of the terms and conditions of contract, plus other commercial information such as the price, method of delivery and so on.

An example of a purchase order form is shown in Figure 22.1. This gives some idea of the information needed but limited space in the illustration has not allowed every possible item to be shown. A slightly more complete list of the information required on a purchase order is as follows:

- a purchase order number (for identification, filing and possible subsequent information retrieval);
- the name or description of the goods to be supplied;
- the quantity required;
- the agreed purchase price, as quoted by the supplier and accepted by the purchaser;
- if relevant, the reference number and date of the supplier's quotation document or catalogue item;
- the delivery date or schedule of deliveries required;
- the address to which the goods are to be delivered;
- the terms on which delivery are to be made (liability for transport, packing, insurance costs, and so on). See the section on Incoterms below;
- invoicing instructions;
- an authorizing signature.

Standard conditions of purchase

Purchase order forms usually have the purchaser's conditions of purchase attached or printed as a standard list on the reverse side. This is a form of standard contract, but it is only standard in the sense that it spells out the purchaser's usual expectations.

The set of conditions which follows is based on those used by one company and is fairly typical, but each firm must seek its own legal advice and draft its conditions of purchase according to its own experience, needs and current state of the law.

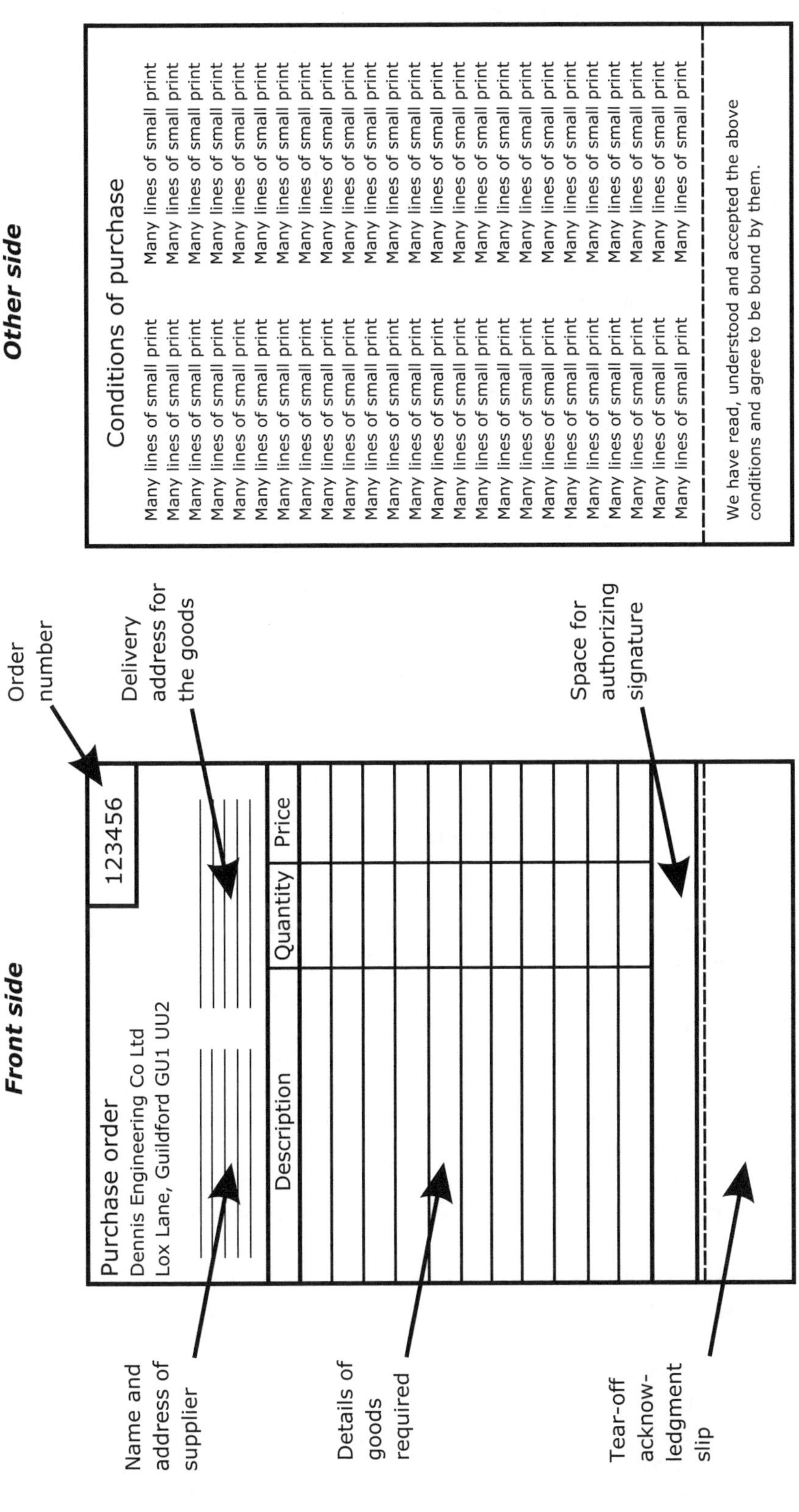

Front side

Name and address of supplier

Purchase order
Dennis Engineering Co Ltd
Lox Lane, Guildford GU1 UU2

Order number

123456

Delivery address for the goods

Description	Quantity	Price

Details of goods required

Space for authorizing signature

Tear-off acknow-ledgment slip

Other side

Conditions of purchase

Many lines of small print
Many lines of small print
Many lines of small print
Many lines of small print
Many lines of small print
Many lines of small print
Many lines of small print
Many lines of small print
Many lines of small print
Many lines of small print
Many lines of small print
Many lines of small print
Many lines of small print
Many lines of small print
Many lines of small print
Many lines of small print
Many lines of small print
Many lines of small print
Many lines of small print
Many lines of small print
Many lines of small print
Many lines of small print
Many lines of small print
Many lines of small print
Many lines of small print
Many lines of small print
Many lines of small print
Many lines of small print
Many lines of small print
Many lines of small print

We have read, understood and accepted the above conditions and agree to be bound by them.

Figure 22.1 Elements of a typical purchase order

1. **Definitions**

Company	means Lox Box Company Limited.
Seller	means the person, firm or company to whom the company's order is addressed.
Goods	means the supply and delivery of the goods, materials or equipment in accordance with the company's order together with any subsequent modifications specified by the company.
Contract	means the agreement between the company and the seller for the supply of goods.

2. **Payment** – Net cash against shipping documents or other proof of delivery unless otherwise agreed (subject to any deductions and retentions authorized in the terms of the order, and subject to the seller carrying out all his obligations).

3. **Prices** – All prices are fixed for the duration of the contract and, unless otherwise agreed, are not subject to escalation charges of any description.

4. **Quality and description** – The goods shall conform to description, be of sound materials and quality, and be equal in all respects to any specification given by the company to the seller.

5. **Indemnity** – The seller shall at his own expense make good by repair or replacement all defects attributable to faulty design and/or workmanship which appear in the goods within the period of 12 months from date of delivery. The seller shall also indemnify the company in respect of all damage or injury occurring before the above-mentioned period expires to any person or property and against all actions, suits, claims, demands, costs, charges or expenses arising in connection therewith to the extent that the same have been occasioned by the negligence of the seller, his servants or agents during such time as he or they were on, entering on to or departing from the company's premises for any purpose connected with this contract.

6. **Intellectual property** – The seller will indemnify the company against any claim for infringement of letters patent, trademark, registered design or copyright arising out of the use or sale of the goods and against all costs, charges and expenses occasioned thereby except in so far as such infringement is due to the seller having followed the design supplied by the company.

7. **Loss or damage** – All responsibility for any loss or damage, whether total or partial, direct or indirect from whatsoever cause, shall lie with the seller until full and complete delivery in terms of the order shall have been made by the seller. But it is agreed that the company will take all necessary steps to ensure that it does not in any way invalidate any claim which the seller may have against the carrier.

8. **Changes in the work** – No variations of, or extras to the order shall be carried out by the seller unless specifically authorized by the company on its official amendment form.

9. **Subsuppliers** – The seller shall provide a list of all subcontractors or subsuppliers when requested by the company.

10. **Expediting** – The company's expediting staff shall be given access at all reasonable times to the seller's works or offices or those of any subcontractor in order to view or discuss work in progress.

11. **Rejection** – The company may at any time, whether before or after delivery, reject (giving reasons therefore) any goods found to be inferior, damaged or if the seller commits any breach of the order. This condition shall apply notwithstanding that the goods may have been inspected or tested by the company.

12. **Arbitration** – Any dispute or difference arising from the contract shall, on the application of either the seller or the company, be submitted to arbitration of a single arbitrator who shall be agreed between the parties or who failing such agreement shall be appointed at the request of either party by the President for the time being of the Law Society.

13. **Time for completion** – The seller's promised delivery date must be firm, but if delivery is delayed through any cause beyond the control of the seller and immediately such cause arises the seller notifies the company in writing giving full particulars then a reasonable extension of time shall be granted. If delivery is not made within the time stipulated or within any extension of time the company shall be at liberty to cancel the contract without prejudice to any right or remedy which shall have accrued or which shall thereafter accrue to the company.

14. **Title to goods** – Title to the goods passes to the company on delivery to the specified place of delivery as requested by the company.

15. **Law of the contract** – Unless otherwise agreed the contract shall be subject to the laws of England.

Acceptance by the supplier

When the supplier has received the purchase order, complete with its set of conditions, the supplier is expected to acknowledge acceptance of the order. That then establishes a legal contract (offer and acceptance). The order form shown in Figure 22.1 carries a tear-off acknowledgment slip, which is a practice that is intended to encourage the supplier to accept the standard conditions and other requirements of the order. However, many suppliers ignore such arrangements. They acknowledge receipt of the order but instead supply their own set of standard conditions, which might differ from those of the purchaser.

It is possible for correspondence to develop, with each party to the contract continuing to send to the other the particular set of conditions that it prefers. In the event of a dispute it is then possible that the courts will regard the conditions contained in the last, delivered but unanswered piece of such correspondence as those which apply to the particular contract. The inference is that those conditions have not been rejected and have thus been accepted by default.

When purchases of goods or services are made online from a website that displays the supplier's standard list or catalogue, circumstances are quite different. The buyer has less chance of being able to argue about contract conditions and will probably be shown one or more pages between the 'basket' and the 'checkout' which make it clear that the transaction is being conducted on the supplier's own terms. Those terms will either be shown or, more probably, will be available on some hidden page that can be viewed on request. There might be two boxes before the 'confirm order' stage indicating either that the supplier's terms are accepted or that they are not. Ticking an 'I do not accept these conditions' box requires more courage than I have ever been able to find and would almost certainly put an instant stop to the proceedings.

TERMS OF TRADE USED IN INTERNATIONAL BUSINESS (INCOTERMS 2000)

A purchaser needs to know, and agree with the seller, exactly when responsibility transfers from one party to the other when goods are shipped. For local purchases this might have very little financial effect but international shipping is a different matter and it is important that the boundaries of responsibility for transportation are clearly defined in proposals, contracts and on purchase orders. Incoterms, defined and published by the International Chamber of Commerce, are accepted worldwide as the succinct and definitive method for setting out these boundaries (International Chamber of Commerce, 2000). The terms are listed below, in ascending order of the sender's scope of responsibility:

Group E Incoterms (departure)

- EXW   Ex works

Group F Incoterms (main carriage unpaid)

- FCA   Free carrier
- FAS   Free alongside ship
- FOB   Free on board

Group C Incoterms (main carriage paid)

- CFR   Cost and freight
- CIF   Cost, insurance and freight
- CIP   Carriage and insurance paid to

Group D Incoterms (arrival)

- DAF   Delivered at frontier
- DES   Delivered ex ship
- DEQ   Delivered ex quay
- DDU   Delivered duty unpaid
- DDP   Delivered duty paid

PRICING A CONTRACT PROPOSAL

It can be assumed that any company worth its salt will be equipped with a well-defined general pricing policy. Profit targets and the relationship between estimated costs and selling prices might be laid down very firmly. Pricing decisions for any significant project usually fall within the responsibility, not of the project manager, but of the company's higher management. Companies typically have procedures for authorizing quotations, and it is usual for new proposals to be discussed and agreed at senior management or board level meetings before the firm allows any commitment to be made to a potential customer.

One might imagine that a fixed selling price could always be obtained by taking a set of project estimates and marking up the cost at the specified level. Life, unfortunately, is seldom quite so straightforward. Even where a project is to be quoted on the basis of a schedule of rates or on some other cost-reimbursable basis, setting the level of charges can be a matter for expert judgement rather than simple accountancy.

Under certain conditions a firm may be forced to submit a tender or accept an order at a price so low that any possibility of making a fair profit is precluded right from the start. Consider, for example, a company that is temporarily short of work, but which can confidently foresee long-term continuity and expansion of its business. It may be that a period of market recession is seen to be coming to an end. Perhaps the start of one or more new projects is being delayed while customers arrange funding, or for other commercial, political or technical reasons (such delays are common with new projects).

The contractor might be faced with a real dilemma: the choice between dismissing idle staff as redundant or keeping them on the payroll for no return. Specialists and skilled people are difficult and expensive to recruit. Their training and acquired experience in a company's methods is an investment which represents a valuable part of the firm's invisible assets. Disbanding such a team can be compared to the cutting down of a mature tree. The act of chopping down and dismembering takes only a few hours, but to grow a replacement tree of similar size must take many years. No one can tell whether the new tree will turn out to be such a fine specimen as its predecessor. In addition, of course, trying to ensure the survival of workgroups can be argued (usually unsuccessfully) as a moral or social obligation of employers, especially in the larger industries where entire local communities may be dependent on one company for employment and local prosperity.

Contracts taken on to tide a firm over a lean period are sometimes termed 'bridging contracts' for obvious reasons. The profit motive becomes secondary in these circumstances, but there are, of course, risks to be considered and accepted in adopting such a policy. The impact of an estimating error or any other problem that causes a budget to be overspent is always greater without the cushioning effect of a planned profit margin. There is also some danger that customers who return with requests for projects in the future might be disappointed or aggrieved when they discover that prices for the new work are not quoted at comparable, artificially low rates. A more likely risk is that an underpriced project will materialize far later than expected (as many large projects have a way of doing), so that the workload no longer falls in the business trough but hits the contractor just when more profitable work is materializing. This could put the profitable work at risk: it might even prevent the contractor tendering for or accepting new profitable work until the underpriced project has been completed.

It might be expedient to submit a tender at an artificially low price in an attempt to gain entry into a market not previously exploited. There are, of course, other proven ways of achieving this end, not least of which is to acquire a firm that is already well established in the chosen market sector. Underpricing (offering loss-leaders) remains a common, less drastic alternative. It is hardly necessary to stress that any company which decides to adopt a deliberate policy of underpricing will soon suffer from badly burned fingers if it has not first done the essential marketing homework.

Market conditions generally dictate the price that can be charged for any commodity, service or project, although the exact relationship is not straightforward and can produce surprises. In certain cases sales can actually be increased by pricing high, contrary to normal expectations. Usually, however, the laws of supply and demand operate. Most project tenders stand a better chance of acceptance if they are kept low compared to competition. Even when a firm boasts a market monopoly, with competition entirely absent, the intensity of demand can influence the prices that can be charged; if a price is too high the potential customer might simply decide to do without the project altogether.

Local government authorities and other public bodies under strict obligations as trustees of public money may be compelled to accept the lowest tender for a given project. If such an organization wishes to place an order at anything other than the very lowest price possible, they must have an overriding reason which they are prepared to defend.

Orders can be unwelcome and possess nuisance value under some circumstances. Suppose, for example, that a firm has been asked to tender for a project at a time when the order book is already full to overflowing. This firm knows that either a very long delivery time must be quoted or, in the event of receiving the order, it will have to divert work that it would prefer to keep in-house out to subcontractors. Outsourcing conceptual engineering and design, for instance, might be a particularly unattractive option for a company that wishes to safeguard its hard-earned reputation for quality and reliability. Taking on too much work can give rise to overtrading and cash flow difficulties. Unless the company can foresee a continuing expansion of business, sufficient to justify raising new capital and increasing its permanent capacity, it may simply not want the order. In a case such as this the company can choose between quoting at a very high price or not quoting at all.

Accurate project definition and reliable cost estimates are essential to the pricing process. They provide the platform from which profits can be predicted relative to the price charged. Shaky estimates produce a tendency to increase contingency allowances and mark-up rate to cover the increased risk, possibly destroying any chance of gaining an order in a competitive market. Sound estimates are also vital as a basis for any subsequent price negotiations with the customer: the contractor must know as accurately as possible just how far it can be pushed into paring a price down before any hope of profit dwindles to useless proportions.

CONTRACT PAYMENT STRUCTURES

There are many ways in which contractors and their customers set up payment arrangements for project work. The payment terms will typically depend on the following factors:

- risk, uncertainty, and any other factor affecting the accuracy with which the project can be defined, estimated and budgeted;
- the customer's intention to set the contractor performance incentives – these incentives are usually aimed either at completion on time or at completion below budget, but they can also have a bearing on the standard of workmanship and quality. A penalty clause may be included in the contract as an attempt to limit failure in performance, the most common form being a penalty payment calculated according to the number of days, weeks or other stated periods by which the contractor is late in successfully completing the project.

Fixed-price (or firm-price) contracts

A fixed-price contract is the result of the familiar situation in which one or more contractors bid for work against a purchaser's clear specification, stating a total price for all the works. The purchaser understands that the contractor cannot, in normal circumstances, increase the price quoted. The offer to carry out a project for a fixed price demonstrates the contractor's confidence in being able to complete the specified project without spending more than its estimated costs.

In practice there are sometimes clauses, even in so-called fixed-price contracts, which allow limited price renegotiation or additional charges in the event of specified circumstances that may arise outside the contractor's control (national industry wage awards are a common cause).

Cost-reimbursable contracts

There are, of course, many types of contracts which do not start with the inclusion of a known total fixed price. Most of these are 'cost-reimbursable' contracts where the customer agrees to repay the contractor for work done against a prearranged scale of charges. These charges might be for certified quantities of work completed or for reimbursing the costs of labour time and materials used.

Fixed prices are usually avoided by contractors in cases where the final scope of a project cannot be predicted with sufficient accuracy when the contract is signed, or where the work is to be carried out under conditions of high risk. Projects for pure scientific research (where the amount of work needed and the possible results are completely unpredictable) would obviously be unsuitable for fixed-price quotations. Many construction contracts for major capital works or process plants are subject to high risk, owing to site conditions, the weather, or to political and economic factors outside the contractor's control.

Even in cost-reimbursable contracts, with no fixed prices to bid, managers have to decide the levels at which to set the various charging rates. It cannot be assumed that a contractor will charge all customers the same rates. Some customers will demand details of how the direct and overhead charges are built up, and will expect to negotiate the final rates before agreement can be reached.

In any contract where payment is related to agreed rates of working the customer will want to be assured of the veracity of the contractor's claims for payment. This might even entail access to the contractor's books of account by the customer or by auditors acting for the customer. In construction contracts based on payment by quantities, independent quantity surveyors can act for the customer by certifying the contractors' claims to verify that the work being billed has in fact been done.

Estimating accuracy might seem less important where there are no fixed prices operating but tenders for contracts with no fixed prices might have to contain advisory budgetary estimates of the total cost to the customer. If these are set too high, they can frighten a potential customer away, and the contractor stands to lose the contract to competitors. If the estimates are set too low, all kinds of problems could arise during the execution of the work, not least of which might be the customer running out of funds with which to pay the contractor. Any contractor wishing to retain a reputation for fair dealing will want to avoid the trap of setting budgetary estimates too low, especially where this is done deliberately in pursuit of an order. In any case, avoidable estimating inaccuracies must prejudice subsequent attempts at planning, scheduling, budgeting and management control.

Summary of contract types

Quoted prices or rates do not always fall entirely into the clear category of fixed price or cost reimbursable, often because one of the parties wishes to introduce an element of performance incentive or risk protection. Some contracts (compound contracts) incorporate a mix of these arrangements. Others (convertible contracts) allow for a change from a reimbursable contract to a fixed-price arrangement at some pre-agreed stage in the project when it becomes possible to define adequately the total scope of work and probable final costs.

Some well-known options are summarized below, and Figure 22.2 gives an idea of the relationships between risk and incentives.

Fixed price

A price is quoted by the contractor (seller) and accepted by the customer for the work specified in the contract. The price will only be varied if the customer varies the contract, or if the contract conditions allow for a price increase to be negotiated under particular circumstances (for example, a nationwide wage award in the particular industry). Thus the contractor accepts all the risks and, provided that the customer does not make changes to the scope or specification, the contractor must pay for any excess costs arising from underestimates, technical difficulties or other causes. Should the contractor realize, at some stage, that costs are rising well above budget, it can be argued that there might be a temptation to cut costs by skimping work and thus putting quality at risk.

Type of contract	Principal basis for payment	Degree of control and vigilance needed by the customer	Accuracy of project definition required	Contractor's risk compared to customer's risk	Contractor's incentive to meet the budget and timescale
Fixed price

Bill of quantities with scheduled rates

Target price

Reimbursement of costs plus fixed fee

Reimbursement of costs plus pro rata profit | Contractor's achievement ↑↓ Contractor's costs | Lowest ↑↓ Highest | Highest ↑↓ Lowest | Highest ↑↓ Lowest | Highest ↑↓ Lowest |

Figure 22.2 Relationship between payment terms and the control needed

Target price

Target-price contracts are similar to fixed-price contracts, but they are used where there is some justifiable uncertainty about the likely costs for carrying out project as it has been defined. The contract allows for price adjustment if the audited final project costs either exceed estimates or show a saving, so that the risks and benefits can be shared to some extent between the customer and the contractor.

Guaranteed maximum price

A guaranteed maximum price arrangement is a target-price contract in which, although cost savings can be shared, the contractor is limited in the extent to which excess costs may be added to the target price.

Simple reimbursable

A simple cost-reimbursable arrangement means that the contractor is reimbursed for costs and expenses, but makes no profit. This type of payment sometimes occurs when work is performed by a company for its parent company, or for another company which is wholly owned within the same group of companies. A formal contract might not be used in such cases.

Cost-plus

Cost-plus is a common form of reimbursable contract. As in simple reimbursable contracts, the contractor charges for materials used and for time recorded against the project on timesheets. But the charging rates agreed with the customer are set at levels which are intended not only to recover direct costs and overheads, but are marked up to yield profit.

Schedule of rates

Contracts with scheduled rates are reimbursable contracts (usually cost-plus), charged according to the number of work units performed. A specific work unit charging rate will be agreed with the customer beforehand for each trade or type of work involved.

Reimbursable plus management fee

This is a form of cost-reimbursable contract in which the contractor's profit element is charged as a fixed fee, instead of being built in as a 'plus' element in the agreed rates. Unlike cost-plus, the contractor's profit revenue does not increase with cost but instead decreases proportionally as total project costs rise, arguably providing an incentive for the contractor to keep costs low.

Bill of quantities with scheduled rates

A bill of quantities contract is reimbursable, operating with an agreed schedule of rates, but the total number of work units expected in each trade or type of work is estimated and quoted beforehand.

TIMING OF PAYMENTS

Timing of invoices for fixed-price contracts

Many large projects, spread out over timescales that might extend to several years, could involve the investment of large sums of the contractor's money. By the time the contract is completed and paid for, the resulting profit could be offset or nullified by the cost of capital employed. In other words, the contractor has had to bear the interest costs (real or notional) on all money tied up in stocks and work-in-progress. For these reasons, 'progress' or 'stage' payments are often agreed between the contractor and the customer. This enables the contractor to raise some invoices during the course of the project. The contractor is not called upon to carry the whole cost of the project until completion, when the final invoice can be issued.

The basis for making stage payment claims may be cut and dried contractually, being dependent upon completion of certain stages in the project or on the deliveries of specified items of equipment to the customer. Standard contract conditions for various trade organizations may define the stage payment requirements. The following example is remembered from a project that I once commissioned for the supply and installation of a passenger lift (elevator):

Percentage of the Total Contract Price	When Payable
10	On signing the contract (before the contractor actually starts work)
20	When the customer has approved the contractor's general design: this marks the point at which manufacture can start
30	Upon delivery of the main consignment of materials and components to the customer's premises
30	On handover of the new lift (elevator) to the customer for normal use
10	A final 'retention payment', to be withheld by the customer until the lift has given six months of satisfactory use or operation.
100	

In other cases, no such stages will be defined. Instead progress payments will be made at regular intervals, the amounts being decided according to a measurement of the actual work done (the amount of progress achieved). The customer will usually want to see evidence for claims, and these are typically provided by certificates signed by an independent professional person. It is obviously important that such work achievement can be accurately measured to ensure that invoicing is kept in step with real progress. The subject of relating achievement to costs is dealt with in Chapter 27.

Timing of invoices for cost-reimbursable projects

Payments for day works or casual work using temporary agency staff may be invoiced at weekly intervals but most contractors will invoice their customers at regular calendar monthly intervals, either against certificates of work done, timesheets, or other cost records that can be subjected to independent audit.

Cash flow implications

Most timing arrangements for payments are intended to protect the contractor's cash flow position, so that the contractor is not expected to invest large sums of money in work-in-progress over long periods for no return. Generally speaking, it is the purchaser's responsibility to make sure that there will be sufficient funds to pay for the project. Asking a contractor to commit large sums of money in work and purchases, but wait for payment until the project is finished and handed over, would effectively be expecting the contractor to assist the customer with project funding.

The project manager thus has a substantial role to play in protecting his or her organization's cash flow. Apart from managing the project itself to keep it on plan, the project manager must see that claims for payment are issued promptly. All invoices and other claims for payment from the customer must be correct, supported by contractually agreed certificates or other documentation. For international projects, all invoices and other export/import documentation must be completed properly, to avoid any reason for dispute. Claims for payment must be followed up with polite but prompt credit control action if payment becomes overdue.

FINANCIAL VIABILITY OF PARTICIPATING ORGANIZATIONS

A sensible contractor will take steps to try and investigate the financial viability of any important new customer. The contractor might start by asking for copies of the customer's audited annual accounts and reports for recent years. Wary customers often make similar enquiries of potential contractors and suppliers.

Complementary processes can exist, therefore, where on the one hand a contractor wants to be assured that the customer will be able to meet all proper claims for payment, while the customer takes steps to ensure that the contractor is not likely to get into financial difficulties or even go bankrupt before being able to complete the project.

There are several ways in which these investigations can be conducted. Some companies make discreet enquiries themselves, asking other companies who have used the organization under scrutiny to provide references. To preserve anonymity, a professional organization such as D&B (formerly Dun and Bradstreet) can usually research information on a company's financial performance and status on a confidential basis (http//www.dnb.com).

REFERENCES AND FURTHER READING

Duxbury, R. (2006), *Contract Law*, 7th Edition (London: Sweet & Maxwell); a good, affordable introduction in the 'Nutshell' series.

International Chamber of Commerce (2000), *Incoterms 2000*, ICC publication No. 560 (Paris: ICC Publishing SA).

Marsh, P. D. V. (2001), *Contract Negotiation Handbook*, 3rd Edition (Aldershot: Gower).

O'Reilly, M. (1999), *Civil Engineering Construction Contracts*, 2nd Edition (London: Thomas Telford).

Peel, E. (2007), *Treitel on the Law of Contract* (London: Sweet & Maxwell).

Trebes, B. and Mitchell, B. (2005), *NEC Managing Reality* (London: Thomas Telford); this five-manual set is just one example of the large range of titles on contract management available from this publisher.

Turner, J. R. (ed.) (2003), *Contracting for Project Management* (Aldershot: Gower).

Wright, D. (2004), *Law for Project Managers* (Aldershot: Gower).

23 *Managing Procurement*

Purchasing is a vital function of most projects. Purchasing is also a greedy function, because it consumes time and money in prodigious amounts. Purchased goods and services account for over half the total costs of most projects. Efficient purchasing and supply chain management are essential to avoid serious over-expenditure or delays through shortages and the acquisition of goods that are unfit for their intended purpose. Yet, with very few exceptions, project management writers either give the subject little prominence, or they ignore it altogether (Figure 23.1). Try an experiment. Visit your nearest technical library and look in the index of every available project management book for the word 'purchasing' or 'procurement'. In too many cases you will search in vain.

PURCHASING CYCLE

Contrary to popular belief, the role of the purchasing organization is not simply to despatch purchase orders. Activities for all significant project purchases start well before an order is placed and do not end until the materials have been delivered and put to use. Where international freight movements are needed, the purchasing department typically makes the arrangements, either directly or (more usually) by engaging a shipping or freight forwarding agent. Routine purchasing functions often include the establishment of preferred vendors lists, and the rating of vendors' performance.

The procedures for any purchasing event will depend to a very large extent on the value and importance of the goods. If the project desperately needs a sheet of plywood, the procedure can be as simple as sending someone to the nearest DIY store to buy it with petty cash, without even involving the purchasing department. But most project purchases need far more care and attention, to ensure that goods are bought at the right price, of the right quality, to be available at the right place and the right time.

The procedures described in this chapter are fairly comprehensive and would apply to a large range of project purchases, including items of capital equipment that have to be designed and manufactured specially for the project. Clearly not every procedure described here would apply to the routine purchases of goods from supplier's standard lists or catalogues.

The normal sequence of events for a significant project purchase is not unlike that of the project cycle shown earlier (see Figure 9.3). In fact, the purchase of a special or expensive piece of equipment or parcel of goods can be regarded as a mini-project in itself. The project manager is replaced in this analogy by the purchasing manager, purchasing agent or buyer. Activities in the purchasing cycle vary somewhat according to the type of goods or services involved (especially their cost or uniqueness) and the industry, but Figure 23.2 illustrates the principal steps in a typical process. After taking a glimpse

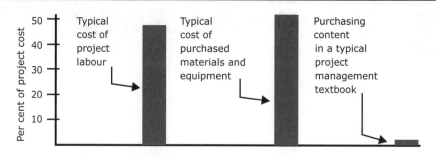

Figure 23.1   Value of purchasing in project management

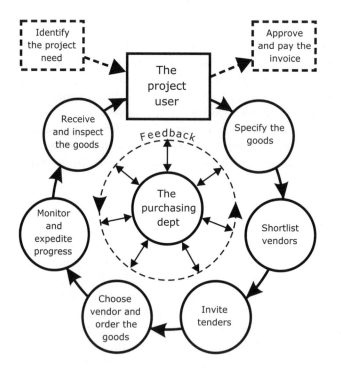

Figure 23.2   Purchasing cycle

at a purchasing organization for a large project, the remainder of this chapter is to a great extent modelled on this purchase life cycle, except that expediting and progress are discussed in Chapter 24, and aspects of purchase cost monitoring and control fit more comfortably in Chapter 26.

ROLES IN THE PURCHASING ORGANIZATION FOR A LARGE INTERNATIONAL PROJECT

Before embarking on a journey round the purchasing cycle it is necessary to understand how the purchasing and supply chain management functions might be organized. This chapter considers the larger, more complex case, which in this instance is the purchasing organization for an international project. 'International' in this sense means that the client, project manager, site of the project work and the suppliers are not all found within the same country. Figure 23.3 shows the key players who could be involved in a large international project. This cannot include all the possible organizational roles because, in practice, there are so many different arrangements; I must mention particularly the role of the architect in construction projects, where in practice an architect might perform many of the project engineering or project management functions described here. On the other hand, in many smaller projects some of the roles depicted in the chart of Figure 23.3 would not be needed.

The role with ultimate responsibility to the client is the *project manager* or *managing contractor*. Well-established contracting companies have their own purchasing departments, where the buyers effectively act as *purchasing agents* for all the contractor's projects (and all their project managers).

If there are to be a significant number of overseas purchases, a company will often appoint additional purchasing agents in the relevant countries, because those agents can act as local representatives. *Overseas purchasing agents* have the tremendous advantages of local knowledge and relative ease of access to the suppliers' premises. For example, they are often aware of local laws, regulations, standards and other factors of which the project manager would otherwise be unaware.

The person who directly bears the brunt of all the project's design and technical responsibility is often the *project engineer*. Among many other duties, the project engineer oversees the preparation of all the purchase specifications required for the project. He or she might be described as the project manager's right-hand person. The project engineer is employed within the project team, reports directly to the project manager, is engaged in the daily cut and thrust of project action, and is responsible principally for seeing that all the design and technical obligations are performed 'right first time'.

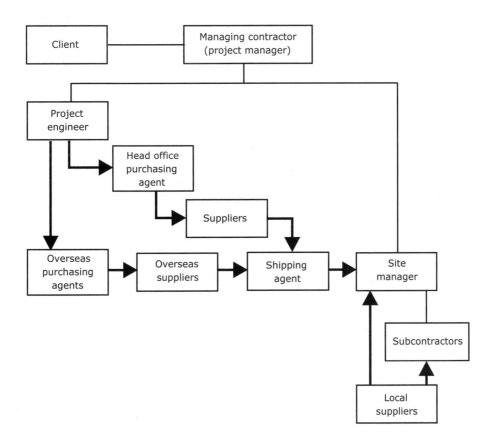

Figure 23.3 Elements of a purchasing organization for a large international project

The role of project engineer just described must not be confused with the role of 'engineer' in the contractual sense, because that contractual role describes a professional engineer (or company) who acts as an *independent* advisor to the client or project financing authority, who is *not* directly employed on the project team, and who most certainly does not report to the project manager.

If the project is for construction of any kind, at some stage a site organization must be established. Because of the long lines of communication involved, the *site manager* is usually given considerable independent power and must be able to operate autonomously in many respects. The site manager is responsible for the inspection of all goods received on site, and for their safe and secure storage until they are ready for use. A large site organization will have its own buyer or materials controller, who is empowered to purchase commonly used construction materials from local suppliers.

Last, but never least, is the *shipping agent* or *freight forwarder*. That role may not be as glamorous or powerful as some of the others described above, but it is so vital to international projects that it deserves its own special section here.

Shipping and freight forwarding agents

It is best to entrust arrangements for long-distance transport, shipping, airfreight, seaport and airport and international frontier formalities to a specialist organization. The purchasing agent (or agents) will undoubtedly have considerable experience and expertise, but the employment of a reputable freight forwarding agent will be invaluable to any project manager faced with all the commercial and strategic complexities of moving heavy project equipment and materials around the world.

Freight forwarding agents operate through their own worldwide organizations. They have staff or representatives stationed at most of the world's ports and airports and, through modern communication networks, are able to monitor the progress of every consignment through all stages from export packaging at the supplier's works to delivery at the project site.

Collaboration between the purchasing agent and a freight forwarding agent can achieve benefits from the economy of scale obtained when different consignments are consolidated to make up complete container loads.

The combined expertise of the purchasing agent and the freight forward agent can be a great comfort to project staff confronted for the first time with the need to deal with the formidable array of documents associated with the international movement of goods. Failure to get the documentation right first time can lead to delays, the impounding of goods and to financial penalties.

Local knowledge provided by the freight forwarding agent's contacts in the countries along the delivery route can yield important information about the type and capacity of port handling facilities, warning of any unusual congestion or industrial disputes (with suggestions for alternative routes), and details of inland road and rail systems (including size and weight restrictions). For example, one agent prevented a mistake in the shipment of some long structural steel sections by pointing out that a local railway company operated a particularly tight restriction on the maximum length of loads, because their route included tunnels with unusually sharp curves. In another case, the local agent's representative was able to warn about a peculiar security problem, where the local shantytown inhabitants were always on the lookout for fresh supplies of building timber. If such timber happened to exist in the shape of well-constructed packing crates protecting expensive project equipment standing on the dockside – well who could blame them?

Organizational roles and the purchasing cycle in greater detail

Now that we have some understanding of the purchasing cycle and the roles involved in a large purchasing organization it is possible to define the cycle and some of the role/responsibility relationships in greater detail. The results can be displayed to best advantage using a chart, such as a responsibility matrix. Figure 23.4, which approximates to the layout of a responsibility matrix, summarizes the role/responsibility relationships for a large international engineering project.

PURCHASE SPECIFICATION: DEFINING WHAT HAS TO BE BOUGHT

Once the need has been recognized for any significant purchase, action must be started by a request from the project design engineers to the organization's purchasing department or agent.

Buying standard goods from a catalogue without a project purchase specification

Bought-out parts, equipment and materials can often be specified by reference to a manufacturer's catalogue or part number. This would appear to be a sufficiently rigid description of the goods. It has to be remembered, however, that most manufacturers reserve the right to modify their designs. If goods are ordered through stockists or factors, then even the company of manufacture might be liable to change. Such a change could be slight and insignificant to most users of the item concerned, but it might render the product utterly useless in a particular case. An example of this would be where a manufacturer changed the material of a component: the catalogue description and illustration might be identical for both versions of the item but the strength, weight and other physical properties would change.

Some companies take no chances and produce their own drawings and specifications and allocate part numbers themselves. This practice costs a considerable amount of time from professional or technical staff, but has much to commend it. Apart from removing any ambiguity about what is being ordered, provision is thus made for a common part-numbering system, which simplifies procedures, eases the burden of the cost office and greatly assists subsequent information search and retrieval.

Case example

A manufacturing example will emphasize the pitfalls of inadequate purchase specifications and point to circumstances where the preparation of special drawings for bought-out components is justified.

A company manufacturing apparatus for hospital operating theatres had a product which had been in very low-volume production over a number of years without significant design change. This unit used three water taps of the elbow-lever action type; these enabled surgeons to operate the taps without contaminating their gloved hands. Each tap had a threaded hose outlet. The operating direction of the tap lever and its on and off positions were critical to the correct assembly and operation of the equipment.

No drawing of these taps existed, but for several years the small stock was replenished from the same reliable supplier, who manufactured them specially each time according to a mixture of written instructions on the order form and the manufacturer's memory of past orders.

A time came when orders for these taps had to be placed with a succession of different suppliers. A written description of the taps was given with each order, but there was still no drawing. Every conceivable error arose in the subsequent supply of these items. Taps arrived with the wrong hose connecting thread, or with no thread at all. Levers came as wrist action instead of elbow lever. Taps were discovered with the levers set at right angles to the required position and, on one occasion the

	1: List requirements	2: Prepare project plan	3: Prepare enquiry specifications	4: Enquiry request	5: Issue of enquiries (ITTs)	6: Suppliers' bidding
Project manager		Responsible to the client for scheduling, initiating and supervising all project activities and for successful completion of the project in all respects. Submits regular cost and progress reports to the client.				
		Draw critical path network and process by computer. Write dates to the purchase schedules				
Project engineer and design team	List all equipment requirements on PURCHASE SCHEDULES	Assist the project manager with planning the network logic and estimating task durations	Write a provisional purchase specification (ENQUIRY SPECIFI-CATION) for each item of equipment to be purchased	Send a REQUEST FOR ENQUIRY to the purchasing agent and recommend possible suppliers	Provide technical support to the purchase agent throughout the enquiry phase, including discussions with suppliers and assessment of suppliers' requests or proposals for amendments to the purchase specifications	
Purchase agent		Assist the project manager by providing estimated times for purchasing tasks and suppliers' delivery times		Maintain records of suppliers from which to augment the project engineers' suggested list of sources	Issue an invitation to tender (ITT) or PURCHASE ENQUIRY for each item. Send to jointly recommended suppliers	
Equip-ment suppliers						Prepare bids and submit them to the purchase agent on or before the relevant closing dates

Figure 23.4   Stages in the purchase of equipment for a large international project

	7: Evaluation of suppliers' bids	8: Approval and authorization	9: Purchase specification	10: Purchase requisition	11: Purchase order	12: Order fulfilment
The client		Study recommendations and approve and authorize major purchases				
Project manager	Responsible to the client for scheduling, initiating and supervising all project activities and for successful completion of the project in all respects. Submits regular cost and progress reports to the client.					
Project engineer and design team	Analyse and compare suppliers' bids. Discuss and jointly agree the most the most suitable supplier. For major items, recommend to the client and request authorization to purchase		Review changes to the enquiry specification and rewrite as the PURCHASE SPECIFICATION	Issue a PURCHASE REQUISITION to the purchase agent. Attach the purchase specification	Technical support to the purchase agent throughout the enquiry phase, including assisting, if required, during witnessed inspection and testing at the suppliers' premises	
Purchase agent					Issue a PURCHASE ORDER to the successful bidder. Attach the purchase specification. Ask for acknowledgment and acceptance	Arrange expediting and inspection. Monitor progress and verify any claims for stage or progress payments
Equipment suppliers					Acknowledge receipt of the purchase order and acceptance of its terms.	Proceed with supply. Provide facilities for the buyer's inspection and witnessed tests, if required

Figure 23.4 *Continued*

	13: Export preparation	14: Suppliers' documentation	15: Transport and shipping	16: Port and customs clearances	17: Site receipt and storage	18: Final payment
The client						Pay the supplier or subcontractor according to the contract terms
Project manager	Responsible to the client for supervising all project activities and for successful completion of the project in all respects.					
Project engineer	Technical support and liaison throughout, including asissting, as required, with final commissioning on site					
Purchase agent	Ensure suppliers observe packing, marking and documentation instructions. Liaise with freight forwarding agent. Report to the project manager regularly and on demand. Act to replace lost or damage materials.					Certify final payment
Equipment suppliers	Pack goods and mark crates in accordance with purchase order and specification.	Provide drawings, test certificates, and instructions for installation, operating and maintenance	If required by the purchase order, arrange for attendance on site during installation and commissioning and for training the client's personnel in the safe and efficient operation and maintenance of the equipment supplied.			
Freight forwarding agent	Arrange export and shipping documents. Book ship or aircraft.		Consolidate consignments. Monitor and progress the movement of goods through all stages of shipping, airfreight, road and rail transport, either directly with carriers or through associated overseas agents. Facilitate port and customs clearances. Advise the purchase agent immediately if problems arise.			
Site materials controller				Liaise with the freight forwarding agent or local representative to progress transit of goods from port of entry to project site	Arrange handling equipment and secure site storage. Examine goods on arrival. Certify safe receipt. Report shortages or damage.	

Figure 24.4 Concluded

taps had anticlockwise rotation instead of clockwise. Sometimes consignments were accepted into stores without the errors being discovered until the taps were withdrawn for use.

Eventually a drawing of an ideal tap was produced. This defined the outline dimensions, general shape, hose connection and the lever operating direction and positions. Thereafter, one copy of this drawing was sent with every purchase order, whilst a second copy was sent to the goods inwards inspectors to enable them to check each new consignment. Very few mistakes occurred subsequently and, when they did, the goods inwards inspectors were able to spot them immediately and have them rectified by the manufacturer. The improvement was dramatic, immediate and permanent. All the previous trouble could have been prevented if only the correct procedure to specify the goods had been followed all along.

Although this case example was on a small scale, it illustrates completely the need for the buyer to be in control when specifying exactly what is required for a project. Clearly the physical requirements for many project materials, components and equipment cannot be expressed on a single drawing. It is often necessary to prepare a full written specification, which might take many hours of a professional engineer's time to design and compile.

Preparation of purchase specifications

In many cases, purchase specifications start life in provisional form, and are developed as other design work proceeds. When potential suppliers are approached, they might make suggestions that could further influence the final content of some specifications.

It is therefore convenient to identify two stages in the preparation of a purchase specification. These are:

1. **Enquiry stage** – The purchase specification starts life as an enquiry specification. This is issued by the project engineering department to the purchasing agent under cover of a 'request for enquiry' or similar document. The purchasing agent sends the enquiry specification to potential suppliers along with a standard 'invitation to tender (ITT)', 'request for quotation' (RFQ) or 'enquiry letter'.
2. **Purchase order stage** – When a supplier has been chosen, the enquiry specification is reviewed and updated to include all changes resulting from discussions with the supplier. The enquiry specification has now become the purchase specification, which is re-issued to the purchasing agent by the project engineering department together with a purchase requisition. The purchasing agent then issues a purchase order to the chosen supplier, with the purchase specification attached.

There need be no difference in the method for preparing enquiry and purchase specifications, and the same format can be used for both. An example of a set of specification sheets is shown in Figures 23.5, 23.6 and 23.7 but in practice there are many different formats. Often the enquiry and purchase specifications are identical but if, during the course of pre-contract discussion with a supplier, amendments are made to the enquiry specification, the resulting purchase specification must contain all the agreed amendments.

Specification numbering and grouping by specialist functions

A common method for numbering purchase specifications in large projects is to allocate their serial numbers from purchasing schedules. The initial preparation of purchase schedules was mentioned at the end of Chapter 18 and Figure 18.12 showed the essential headings of a purchase schedule page. Figure 18.13 showed how these purchase schedules can be grouped in sets according to each specialist design group, which also allows each group to allocate its own serial numbers within the overall project numbering system.

SPECIFICATION

This specification comprises the sheets listed in the following table. At each revision only revised or additional sheets will be issued, together with a revision of this front sheet.

Sheet	Rev	Sheet	Rev	Sheet	Rev	Sheet	Rev	Sheet	Rev	Sheet	Rev

ATTACHMENTS

The following attached documents form part of this specification:

SUMMARY OF REVISIONS

Rev No	Date	Brief description of each revision

APPROVALS

Originated by:	Checked by:	Senior engineer:	Project engineer:

Client —
Project —
Plant
Discipline —
Title —
—

Spec. No:	Rev. No:	Sheet
		1

Figure 23.5   Purchase specification: front sheet

Example of a form used to head enquiry and purchase specifications.

SPECIFICATION

DRAWINGS AND OTHER DOCUMENTS

1 SCOPE OF SUPPLY. Complete engineering drawings, Installation instructions, operating/maintenance manuals, parts lists and recommended spares lists for all equipment and services covered by this specification.

2 QUANTITIES:

Drawings for approval – 3 prints
Final drawings   – 1 transparency or master in approved electronic format
Test certificates   – Original plus 5 copies, all signed
Other final documents – 6 copies

3 LANGUAGE: English

4 IDENTIFICATION: All documents shall bear the purchase order number under which this specification is issued, appropriate equipment and tag numbers as specified, and the purchaser's drawing numbers (when supplied).

5 REVISIONS: Any drawing revised after initial submission shall be resubmitted immediately, showing details of changes and the new revision number.

6 CERTIFICATION: Final drawings shall be certified as accurate.

7 AS-BUILT DRAWINGS: Where the specification includes installation and erection, as-built drawings reflecting any on-site changes shall be submitted as soon as possible after the work.

8 DATE OF SUBMISSION: All documents shall be submitted on or before the dates specified in the purchase order delivery schedule.

9 APPROVAL: All drawings for equipment specially designed to meet this specification shall be submitted for approval before manufacture unless otherwise agreed.

10 TEST CERTIFICATES: These shall show the British or other agreed national standard or code under which the tests were performed.

11 LUBRICATION REQUIREMENTS. Recommended lubricants and quantities sufficient for one year's operation shall be specified.

12 SPARES LISTS. Lists of recommended spares shall be given, suitable for one year's operation under the specified conditions. Each items shall include:

Identification, part or serial number
— Maker's name and reference
— Quantity recommended
— Current price and delivery

EQUIPMENT MARKING AND IDENTIFICATION

Each item shall be identified by its mark, equipment or tag number by the method indicated thus: ✓

☐ Painting   ☐ Wired-on stamped metal tags   ☐ Stamped nameplates

☐ Other, as specified later in this specification. See sheet number: _____

INSPECTION AND TESTING

Documented inspection and testing is required, as indicated in the following tables thus: ✓

Inspections by the purchaser	Required?	Testing required	Unwitnessed	Witnessed
During manufacture		Standard works		
Final inspection		No load running		
Of packing		Full load performance		
As specified later on sheet number		As specified later on sheet number		

Title		Spec. No:	Rev. No:	Sheet
				2

Figure 23.6 Purchase specification: second sheet

This lists various standard requirements and also acts as a checklist for the engineers. The main technical description follows on continuation sheets (Figure 23.7).

SPECIFICATION			
Title	Spec. No:	Rev. No:	Sheet

Figure 23.7   Purchase specification: continuation sheet

Since each final purchase specification is derived from (or may even be identical to) an initial enquiry specification, the serial number allocated to the enquiry specification should be used again for the corresponding purchase specification, if possible, so that the two documents can always be correlated. This seems logical and straightforward, but there are pitfalls for the unwary. These are mentioned later in this chapter.

Specification library

For equipment which is purchased often, such as pumps, valves, piping, motors and so on, an experienced project engineering organization will avoid the chores and risks associated with preparing a new specification for every occasion by developing a library of standard material and equipment specifications. The texts of these can be held on a computer file, to be extracted, adapted as necessary, and used to prepare the specification for each new requirement.

SUPPLIER SELECTION

The buyer's first responsibility is to identify a suitable source of supply. Occasionally only one supplier can be found, or one may be specified by the design engineers on the purchase requisition. Limitation of choice usually arises when goods are highly specialized but, even where there is only one possible manufacturer, there may be a choice between different stockists. There are, of course, occasions when urgency is the most important factor, so that there is simply no time in which to conduct a proper supplier selection procedure. In all other cases (except for low-cost purchases) the supplier should be chosen after the collection and perusal of several competitive quotations.

To start the enquiry process, the project engineers will send copies of the enquiry specification to the purchasing agent or buyer, asking the agent to issue a formal ITT or RFQ. The project engineers may have a good idea of which suppliers should be asked to bid and, indeed, they may already have discussed the project's requirements with some possible suppliers in advance. Provisional quotations might have been obtained from potential suppliers for some of the more expensive items when the project cost estimates were first prepared.

The project engineers can use a form similar to that shown in Figure 23.8 to convey their instructions and suggestions to the purchasing agent. Some of the information may be commercially confidential, not to be disclosed to bidders, and the purchasing agent will substitute their own official covering letter or standard form when sending out the enquiry specification to potential suppliers. The purchasing agent would usually be given complete freedom to add possible suppliers to any list put forward by the project engineers.

Enquiries should always be conducted in such a way that they encourage suppliers to submit their quotations according to a common format. Then all the bids can be compared on a like-for-like basis.

Distribution of purchase enquiry documents

In the relatively simple organizational arrangement where the purchasing agent is part of the main contractor or project engineering company, and where the purchasing and project engineering departments are located in the same building, there should be no problem with the distribution of enquiry instructions and in communicating quotations and subsequent progress. Circumstances become a little more difficult when the purchasing agent is part of an external organization, and more difficult still if that external organization happens to be located far away from the project engineers or overseas. Matters can become very complicated where a project requires more than one

---

REQUEST FOR PURCHASE ENQUIRY

To: (Purchasing agent)

Date:

Our reference:

Your reference:

Please obtain bids for the goods or services described in the attached specification.
Note the following requirements:

Vendors	Bids
☐ Only those listed below	☐ Forward bids as soon as received
☐ Those listed plus those of your choice	☐ Forward all bids after closing date
☐ Suitable vendors of your choice	☐ Supply a commercial bid summary

The closure date for receipt of bids should be:
Our required on-site delivery date is:
The recommended standard packing category is:
Your technical contact for this purchase is: Telephone:
Recommended vendors:

Notes and special requirements:

Project engineer

Client   —
Project   —
Plant   —
Discipline —

Title	Spec. No:	Rev. No:	Sheet

Figure 23.8   Purchase enquiry request

purchasing agent, perhaps with one in the client's country, one in the country of the main contractor, and others operating in other countries to provide local expediting and inspection services.

It is sometimes necessary to keep purchasing agents informed by sending them copies of enquiries and specifications that are intended for initial action by another purchasing agent in the project organization. Although each such enquiry (and any subsequent requisition) bears the name of the purchasing agent responsible for taking action, there could be a risk of another agent taking action as a result of receiving a copy that was only intended only to keep the agent informed. The project engineering company might wish to consider colour coding each batch of documents (by printing or photocopying them on coloured paper stock), with a different colour chosen to represent each of the purchasing agents. Then everyone on the project would know, for example, that a pink set of enquiry documents was for the action of the agent in Lagos, yellow sets were for the agent in Buenos Aires, while plain white sets were always intended for action by the purchasing department in the contractor's head office. This measure, especially when followed through to the documents used during the actual purchasing stage, can help to prevent unfortunate and expensive mix-ups where two different purchasing agents follow up the same enquiry and, in the worst case, place duplicate orders for the same goods.

Impact of the European Directives on Public Sector Purchasing

Readers working in the public sector should be aware of the requirements imposed by the following European public procurement directives:

- 93/36/EEG for the supply of products;
- 93/37/EEG for the design and construction of public works;
- 92/50/EEG for the provision of services;
- 92/38/EEG for suppliers, works and services in the utilities sectors.

These regulations apply to advertisements of contract tender opportunities where the contract value exceeds a specified threshold amount. These thresholds are revised from time to time.

The intention of these directives is to achieve fair competition and work opportunities throughout the EU. Opportunities for new contracts may not be advertised in the UK before a contract notice has been sent for publication in the *Official Journal of the European Union* (OJ). There are exceptions for contracts for secret work.

Guidance is necessary in deciding how to calculate the threshold values, in the relative timings between notifying the OJ and advertising in the UK and on methods for transmitting notices to the OJ. In the UK the Inland Revenue is a good source of information. A good place to start is their web page at www.inlandrevenue.gov.uk.

Formal bidding procedure

Figure 23.9 illustrates the principal stages in one form or bidding procedure. At frame 1, the purchasing agent sends all the possible suppliers a formal ITT, which sets out all the commercial and technical requirements and fixes a date by which all quotations must be presented.

Dealing with suppliers' queries during the bidding period

Some contractors' engineers become involved in discussions with suppliers during the bidding period, answering questions and perhaps listening to alternative proposals. It is necessary to preserve fairness, and allow all suppliers to compete on equal terms, with the same supply of information. To that end, if one supplier asks a question, a copy of the question and the answer is sent to all the competitors, as indicated in frames 2 and 3 of Figure 23.9. However, the purchasing agent should not reveal the source of any question.

To give an example, I was once on the receiving end of an ITT from a government department, and one condition of the contract was that the supplier (me) would take out professional indemnity insurance cover of £10 million. That seemed rather too high for my modest proposal, so I asked if cover could be reduced to £1 million. My request was allowed, and as a direct consequence, all the other bidders were informed of my question and of the reduction to £1 million.

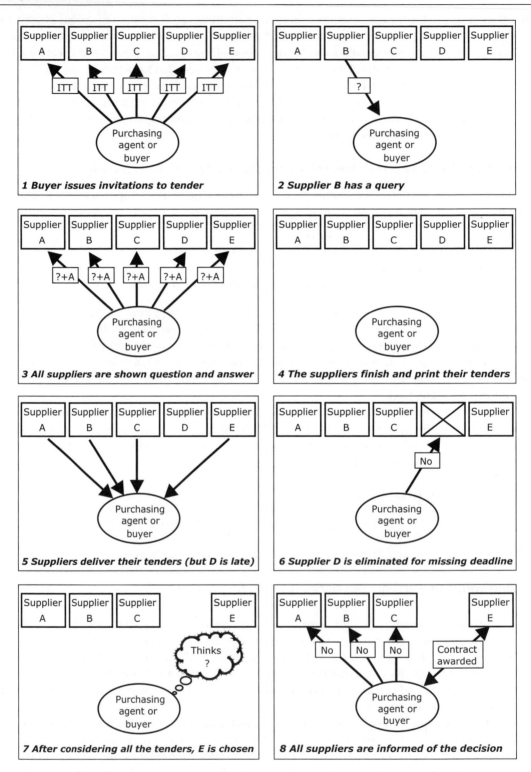

Figure 23.9 Common arrangement for inviting and considering bids

Late tenders

Any supplier who misses the deadline set for submission of the tender is automatically disqualified (frames 5 and 6 in Figure 23.9). This is a very reasonable and prudent step for a purchaser to take for three reasons:

- Proposals received late delay the process and disrupt the bid comparison procedure.
- It would be unfair to allow one supplier more time for preparation of the proposal than that granted to all the others.
- A supplier that is unable to submit a proposal on time will be more likely to run late in fulfilling the contract.

Bid evaluation

When all the bids are in, they have to be compared so the best option is selected. In a 'sealed bid procedure', each proposal is presented in two separate packages, one technical and the other commercial. The buyer opens all the technical bids first and rejects out of hand those that fail to meet the specification. Then the surviving commercial bids are compared.

The buyer would normally be expected to favour the lowest bidder, but this choice must be tempered by knowledge of the bidder's reputation for quality, delivery performance and commercial standing. It is usually undesirable and risky to allow the buyer to choose a supplier without the knowledge and agreement of the relevant project engineer. In some organizations vested interests or jealously guarded power means that this essential partnership between the purchasing agent and the project engineers is lacking. That is always unfortunate and should be corrected, if necessary by intervention of more senior management.

An essential part of bid comparisons requires that information received from bidders is tabulated on a summary form which allows direct comparison of quoted prices, promised delivery times and other critical factors. An example of a bid summary form is shown in Figure 23.10. This is a matrix that is intended to convert all bids into one common currency, and to include all required items that some bidders might quote as optional extras, so that the bottom lines of the bid summary allow the buyer to compare the cost delivered at the point of use. Thus estimated packing, carriage, insurance, port and customs costs arising from foreign bidders have to be included. These steps ensure that the total delivered costs are compared in every case on a like-for-like basis.

Similarly, delivery times are adjusted where necessary to include shipping and port delays, so that all quotations are compared according to the estimated delivery time at the point of use.

Technical evaluation of quotations must, of course, be a matter for the relevant project engineer. Sometimes this has to be done in collaboration with the client's own engineers. The bid summary form illustrated in Figure 23.10 is not suitable for making a detailed technical analysis (although it should be possible to expand it for that purpose). Once a technical preference has been identified, this can however be noted on the bid summary form, where it must count very heavily towards the final choice of supplier.

PURCHASE REQUISITION AND ORDER

Moving further round the purchasing cycle, when a supplier has been chosen, the enquiry specification is reviewed and updated to include all changes resulting from discussions with the supplier. The enquiry specification has now become the purchase specification, which is re-issued to the purchasing agent

BID SUMMARY							
SELLERS ⟶	A	B	C	D	E	F
Country of origin						
Bid reference						
Bid date						
Period of validity						
Bid currency						
Project exchange rate						

Item	Qty	Description	Price	Price	Price	Price	Price	Price

	A	B	C	D	E	F
Total quoted ex-works						
Discounts (if any)						
Packing and export prep cost						
Shipping cost						
Customs duty and tax						
Local transport cost						
Estimated total cost on site						
Delivery time ex-works						
Estimated total transport time						
Total delivery time to sit						

RECOMMENDED BY THE PURCHASING AGENT:

For purchasing agent

RECOMMENDED BY THE ENGINEER:

Project/ senior engineer

RECOMMENDATION TO THE CLIENT:

Project manager

Specification title:	Specification number:

Figure 23.10   Bid summary example

PURCHASE REQUISITION

To: (Purchasing agent)

Date:

Our reference:

Your reference:

☐ Please issue a purchase order

☐ Please also make all arrangements for transportation

☐ Please issue an amendment to the purchase order

for the equipment, materials or services detailed in the attached specification.

VENDOR (name and address)

Quotation reference and date

CONSIGNEE (name and address)

SPECIAL INSTRUCTIONS

Inspect in accordance with specification ☐

Recommended degree of expediting is: intense ☐   normal ☐   none ☐

Recommended standard packing category is ☐

Other (see continuation sheet attached)

PRICE		DELIVERY
Basis:		Original delivery promise:
Original budget		
Original quote		Current delivery promise:
Previous amendments		
This amendment		Required delivery to consignee:
TOTAL PRICE NOW		

APPROVALS

Originated by	Senior engineer	Project engineer	Project manager

Client —		Project number:
Project —		
Plant —		Specification number: / Revision
Discipline —		
Title:		Requisition number: / Amendment

Figure 23.11   Purchase requisition

by the project engineering department, attached to a purchase requisition. The purchase requisition (Figure 23.11) gives the purchasing agent formal permission to issue a purchase order.

Issuing the purchase order is the most routine and obvious job, usually consisting of typing and printing the order, checking it, signing it and the either popping it in the post or transmitting it to the supplier electronically along with a fresh copy of the purchase specification.

What has this short explanation of routine purchase order preparation got to do with project management? One answer is that it takes time. Several days or even weeks of valuable project time can be consumed by this mundane, relatively simple activity. Procurement lead-time estimates on the critical path network must always allow for such delays. In fact, unless emergency measures are contemplated, two weeks should often be regarded as a minimum estimate for purchase lead-times, even for items that can be obtained off the shelf from a local supplier's stock.

Purchase orders were described in Chapter 22, with a sample illustration in Figure 22.1.

EXPEDITING

Expediting is a follow-up process performed by the purchasing agent to check the progress of each order. It might require visits to suppliers' premises to verify progress claims and inspect for conformation with specification. This process is considered further in Chapter 24, which deals with managing all aspects of project progress.

SPECIAL TIMING OF ORDERS AND DELIVERIES

Early ordering of long-lead items

Engineers and others responsible for initiating project purchases have a duty to identify those items that are likely to have long lead-times and ensure that ordering instructions are passed to the purchasing department as soon as possible. This might mean issuing advance information on such things as special bearings, motors, castings and other bought-out components, at times when the relevant assembly drawings and final bills of material remain unfinished or even unstarted.

It is sometimes desirable to issue advance information even when the goods cannot be specified in exact detail, because this gives the purchasing department the chance to get started on obtaining provisional quotations and (in a really urgent case) on reserving capacity in a manufacturer's works by issuing a 'letter of intent'.

Any company with sufficient project experience will attempt to follow such practices as a matter of course. If a project has been planned using a critical path network any need to issue advance purchasing instructions will almost certainly be highlighted.

In some cases these urgent steps might preclude the possibility of operating a formal bid procedure, in which case the order will be given, wherever possible, to a supplier that has performed well in the past.

Just-in-time

The phrase 'just-in-time' (JIT) took on a specific meaning with the adoption by some companies of the Japanese approach to purchasing and manufacture which attempts to reduce stockholding to zero and, among other things, relies on suppliers to deliver direct to the workplace just-in-time .

This system relies heavily on establishing a great deal of trust, and the suppliers are expected to be fully responsible for delivering the supplies in the right quantities, at the right time and of the right quality without day-to-day supervision from the purchaser. But these ideals cannot be achieved overnight and cannot be expected to operate for project purchasing where regular use of suppliers and repeat orders are not the norm.

As a general rule, it is late or incorrect deliveries (and the shortages which they cause) that will always produce the biggest headaches for project managers, and any decision to delay the issue of a purchase order must be tempered with caution. Time must be allowed wherever possible for unforeseen contingencies. What would happen, for example, if an important consignment arrived just in time, only to be rejected as being damaged in transit or was otherwise unfit for project use?

Retarded deliveries and call-off orders

There are often reasons why deliveries of project materials should not be called for too early. Materials which are ordered so as to arrive long before they are needed will have to be paid for earlier than is necessary, inflating the amount of money tied up unprofitably in inventory and work-in-progress. Another problem is that storage difficulties can arise for items delivered prematurely. Some goods have a short shelf life and will deteriorate if kept too long in store.

Call-off orders

If an order is for a large quantity of parts, deliveries can be arranged to take place in batches, at an agreed rate over a specified period. Of course the suppliers must be willing to accept such arrangements, but the practice is common. The supplier can either store the balance of the order or manufacture to suit the schedule. This is known as a 'call-off' procedure, because the items are called off as they are needed for the project. It is older than, but not too far removed from, the just-in-time approach.

Although the deliveries of items in large, repeating quantities brings batch or mass production to mind, some single projects do consume large quantities of materials. For instance, one would hardly consider the building of a large office block as mass production, but enormous quantities of building supplies may be involved. There would be very obvious difficulties if all the supplies were to be delivered before work had begun on site clearance. Chaos would reign, with cement, sand, ballast, bricks and other supplies strewn all over the area. Access for site work would then be impossible, and those supplies which survived without being pilfered or ruined by exposure to the elements would have to be moved before work could start. By indicating the total quantities required for the project, the contractor can gain the benefits of quantity discounts, but the deliveries must be called off only when they are needed.

Now consider a manufacturing project requiring 10 000 small identical electro-mechanical components, costing £30 each, to be incorporated in subassemblies over a period of some two years. These components are small and present no storage problem. But they are not all needed at once, so why commit expenditure of £300 000 too early? Again, a call-off order is indicated, allowing the contractor to delay expenditure, keep inventory down and improve cash flow, whilst still reaping the benefits of the discount that can undoubtedly be negotiated because of the large quantity involved.

Common-sense timing

Once it is agreed that materials should be ordered to a project plan, there remain one or two questions regarding the common-sense application of that plan. Returning to the case of the 10 000 components costing £30 each, there is no question that the order for these items should be arranged on a call-off basis if possible. But what about the inexpensive items such as screws, nuts, washers, solder tags and so on? It would be nonsensical to attempt ordering these items to any plan. Rather, one would see to it that the whole quantity was ordered in advance, and with a generous supply to spare. Rigid control would not be necessary. The application of planning and control would probably cost more than the total value of the materials themselves, and might attract ridicule from the suppliers into the bargain.

PURCHASE QUANTITIES

Problems with orders for small quantities

Purchase orders for small quantities of materials or components are often a specific feature of projects where the work is non-repetitive and confined to the completion of only one end product. In these cases the purchasing department will be faced with appreciable handicaps when they attempt to achieve short-term deliveries and low costs. A single small component may be vital to the success of a project but, although this component assumes important dimensions in the eyes of the project manager, for the manufacturer it has only nuisance value, yielding small profit and disrupting work on larger orders for more-valued customers.

If the contractor is a large company, or part of a big group, there is always a possibility that the supplier may give good service in the fond hope of larger, follow-up orders. Although the supplier's optimism might be completely groundless, only a foolish project manager would set out deliberately to discourage it. Similar motives sometimes prompt suppliers to proffer free samples of their wares. Items obtained in this way not only cost nothing, but also can usually be obtained by return of post, or even out of a sales representative's briefcase. Small stocks are sometimes reserved by suppliers for this purpose, and if the paperwork and formal ordering formalities are circumvented in this way much valuable project time can be saved. Project managers would obviously be ill-advised to consider planning a project on the basis of materials supplied as free samples (although I knew a project site manager who added a church to a new mining township using only free hire-plant demonstrations and 'surplus' materials).

Items ordered in very small quantities will usually be priced higher than they would be if bought in larger, price-discounted amounts. Other penalties of small quantity orders include higher costs per unit for packing, transport, documentation and general handling. These are some of the factors which can induce suppliers to charge higher prices for very small purchases.

Attraction of quantity discounts

Quantity discounts or other inducements offered by suppliers have led purchasers to buy well beyond their immediate needs. Some reported cases have been spectacular. To take a modest example, based on an actual case, seven custom-built electronic instruments were required for a project. The manufacturer's quoted price was £20 000 for each unit, based on a total purchase quantity of seven instruments. However, someone on the project team decided to take advantage of a discounted unit price offer by the manufacturer, and 10 units were bought for 'only' £17 500 each. Thus the cost to the project was not the budgeted £140 000 but £175 000. The saving on unit cost was not worth the £35 000 additional cost. Three surplus units were left on the stores shelf at the end of the project, eventually to be disposed of as scrap.

The only possible justification for buying above the net requirement would be to offset expected breakages (in which case a budget must exist) or against a *certain* follow-up order from the customer for spares. Any unjustified inflation of order quantities must be vetoed by the project manager. Surplus stocks can accumulate with embarrassing speed if restraint is not exercised.

Materials purchased for use in continuous or batch production are also liable to become overstocked through the lure of quantity discounts. Overstocking leads to a reduction in the inventory turn ratio (annual sales value divided by the value of stock and work in progress), which increases the amount of investment required in the business compared to the profits generated.

Some suppliers offer personal inducements, perhaps in the form of free gifts, holidays or other services in return for orders. Managers must never allow themselves or their subordinates to be tempted by such offers into purchasing above the needs of the project. Strict protocols should be enforced across the project organization to make everyone aware of the risk, and of the penalties that they would personally face if they were sufficiently foolish and dishonest to disobey the rules.

PURCHASE ORDER AMENDMENTS

Should it become necessary to change any aspect of a purchase order after issue, the supplier's earliest agreement should be sought to determine the effect on price and delivery, and to ensure that the proposed change is within the supplier's capability. Once these facts have been successfully established, an amendment to the original purchase order must be issued.

Each purchase order amendment should bear the same reference number as the original purchase order, suffixed by a serial amendment number (amendment 1, 2, 3 and so on). Purchase order amendments should be prepared on a standard format and authorized in the same way as purchase orders. Amendments must be distributed so that they are received by all recipients of the original purchase order or its copies.

Amendment or new purchase order?

The amendment procedure is often used to add one or more items to an existing order. If, however, the introduction of a new item is likely to jeopardize the previously-agreed delivery date of any other item on the purchase order, the best policy is to issue a fresh order for the new item, so leaving the supplier to carry on unhindered and with no excuse for failing to meet the existing commitments.

The practice of adding a succession of new items to an existing order can result in a number of partial deliveries, none of which completes the order, so that administration becomes messy. The need to wade through a purchase order plus a pile of amendments in order to discover its total extent and the balance of deliveries and payments outstanding is time-consuming and irritating. Invoice control is likely to be made difficult and payment disputes can result. Issuing separate orders will prevent these difficulties.

CORRELATION BETWEEN SPECIFICATION, ENQUIRY, REQUISITION AND ORDER NUMBERS

The filing, retrieval and general handling of purchase documents would be a great deal simpler if the initial enquiry, the specification and the resulting purchase order could all have the same reference number.

Although it is often possible to use the specification number as the enquiry number, various events can intervene to prevent the same number being carried through to the purchase order. Not least of these is that each particular purchasing agent (and there could be more than one for the project) might wish to use their own standard order numbering system.

The supply of materials listed in several specifications might be consolidated into one purchase order. It might be advantageous, for example, to collect all the requirements for valves together and order them all from one supplier on a single purchase order. In that case several specifications would have to be attached to the purchase order, all with different numbers.

An even more difficult complication arises when it is decided to order materials defined in one specification as two separate orders, placed with different suppliers (which means that the original specification must be amended or split to suit the different suppliers, and will generate two requisitions as well as two purchase orders).

The authority responsible for project procedures must ensure that all these factors are considered and that, if a common numbering system is impossible, the system adopted allows all the related documents to be adequately cross-referenced. One organization used the following procedure:

1. Enquiry specifications were allocated serial numbers from the purchase control schedules in the manner indicated by Figure 18.13.
2. Purchase enquiries were given the same numbers as the specifications attached to them.
3. A completely different series of numbers was used for purchase requisitions, allocated from registers, and with a different series for each purchasing agent. These series were distinguished from one another by the use of a different letter prefix to denote the agent responsible. Every requisition also carried a cross-reference to the specification or specifications that accompanied it.
4. All the purchasing agents were persuaded to use the requisition numbers as his or her own purchase order numbers. This acceptance by the agents was made easier because each had been allocated their own continuous series of requisition numbers, which automatically meant that a purchase order system using the same numbers would have no awkward gaps left in the sequence of numbers issued. As with the requisitions, each purchase order also carried the number or numbers of all attached specifications.

Thus several different numbering systems were agreed and had to be accepted, all running together in the same organization and on the same projects. There was, however, full cross-referencing between all the vital documents.

PROJECT OR STOCK PURCHASING?

Projects supplied completely from stocked materials

Imagine a large factory, churning out a varied range of products in quantity, and suppose that this company does not operate just-in-time purchasing but holds comprehensive stocks of all possible materials requirements. If a special manufacturing project were to be handled in this environment it is just conceivable that it could be completed entirely from stock materials and components, with no need for any special project purchasing whatsoever. An unlikely possibility, certainly, but not absolutely impossible if the project happened to be in the firm's customary line of business.

This kind of stock purchasing attracts high inventory holding costs for the company but it provides local cost advantages from the point of view of a project manager. There is no need to buy any materials in small quantities, but rather one could order in economic batch sizes, so that the standard costs of materials charged to the project appear low. No special arrangements for materials storage need be contemplated, although the project manager would be well advised to see that the storekeepers reserve or pre-allocate any essential materials and components.

Projects supplied entirely from special purchases

Now consider a company which carries no stocks. Every time a new project appears on the scene each single item must be ordered, right down to the last nut, bolt and washer. This is an example of 'project purchasing' which for manufacturing projects might seem just as improbable as the stock purchasing case (although it is the norm for some other types of project).

There are definite advantages to be gained by adopting a project purchasing policy but, before moving on to discuss these, one or two of the disadvantages should be mentioned.

The most serious drawbacks of project purchasing in manufacturing projects occur when a company is running more than one project at a time in the same premises. With project purchasing in operation, any parts common to two or more of these contracts must be ordered and stored separately. Individual order quantities are therefore smaller, so that quantity discounts are forfeit or reduced. Such purchases increase the company's total inventory (and, therefore inventory holding costs) because safety stocks to allow for losses, breakages and scrap have to be held in more than one place (perhaps even as many places as there are projects). Two or more separate stores occupy more floor space than one combined store of the same total capacity. Administration costs (including security) must be higher. Why then should project purchasing ever be considered?

Of course the situation is completely different for construction and other companies whose projects are built on several sites remote from the company's premises, where materials have to be delivered to site by the suppliers. In these cases all materials handling and storage is specific to each project, and project purchasing is the obvious and usual method.

Several very good reasons exist for advocating project purchasing and storage for manufacturing projects wherever the size of the project and the nature of the operations allow this to be arranged conveniently. One of these is that it facilitates the physical pre-allocation of materials for a project.

Project purchasing as a condition of contract

Some projects where reliability and safety are paramount (for example, in the aerospace, defence and nuclear industries) demand that all items are purchased against certification of fitness for use. Even raw materials will be included, and samples may have to be tested in independent laboratories.

Another important quality aspect is 'traceability'. Suppose that a component fails in an aircraft in service. Good traceability will allow the original source and batch of the failed component to be traced. This, in turn will allow all other components from that batch to be traced so that they can be replaced to avoid problems in all the other aircraft that might be affected.

These conditions mean that the choice between stock purchasing and project purchasing has been taken out of the contractor's hands. Project buying has, in effect, become a condition of contract.

The additional inspection, documentation and storage measures required to satisfy these conditions will inflate the cost of project purchases and materials handling and should, if possible, be recovered in the contract price.

MARKING AND LABELLING GOODS BEFORE TRANSIT

The purchasing agent must ensure that every consignment is clearly marked before it leaves the supplier's premises. It is customary to include instructions for marking in the purchase specification or as a subset of conditions to the purchase order. Marking will usually involve suppliers stencilling easily recognizable markings on packing crates so that each item can be clearly identified through all stages of its journey and, not least, by the site personnel when it finally arrives. The purchase order number usually has to be included in all markings.

GOODS RECEIPT

Receipt of the goods is not the end of the purchasing story. The consignment must be examined at the project site or factory's receiving bay to check for possible lost items or damage caused in transit. There might also have been some mistake by the supplier, either in the quantity supplied or in the nature of the goods.

Goods inwards inspectors may wish to examine the goods more thoroughly to ensure that they comply with the purchase specification although, in recent years, the tendency has been to place more reliance on suppliers' own quality procedures.

If the goods are accepted, the goods inwards personnel will record the consignment, usually by preparing and distributing a goods inwards certificate or by copying the supplier's own despatch note (to act as a certificate). At least one copy of the certificate will go to the accounts department, who will need it before they can pay the supplier's invoice. Another copy will go to the buying department, to cut short any further expediting action and close off the file on that particular order. Routeing of other copies might include other departments such as the stores, but this depends on the nature of the company and the goods.

If the consignment is not received in satisfactory condition for any reason, it will be sent smartly back whence it came accompanied by a rejection note. Distribution of rejection notes generally follows the same pattern as acceptance certificates, but will produce opposite reactions from the various recipients. For example, the accounts department will not pay any associated invoice, and the purchasing department will redouble its expediting efforts.

When the correct goods have been received they will be passed into stores or placed with project stocks to await use.

STORES ADMINISTRATION

Most aspects of the physical storage of goods can be listed under a few well-defined categories:

- accommodation – requirements for floor space, racking and shelving, stockyards, and so on;
- labelling – marking the goods so that they can be identified later without ambiguity;
- location – recording the place where the goods have been stored so that they can be found when they are needed;
- preservation – paying attention to possible deterioration, limited shelf-life, cross-contamination between different materials and the storage environment generally;
- handling methods and equipment;
- health and safety – particularly associated with access, handling methods and hazardous materials;
- security – prevention of theft, wilful damage or misallocation;
- records and information systems.

Some of these items will now be discussed briefly.

Accommodation

With the exception of just-in-time systems or the receipt of goods to clear shortages, a decision usually has to be made about where incoming materials should be stored. The solution could be a very simple matter of placing a consignment of components in a bin on a vacant rack. On the other hand, the problem could be a large truck, taking up all the space in the goods inwards bay, and crammed to overflowing with bulky goods that cannot be unloaded because there is nowhere to put them. Problems of this type differ from purely mental worries. They possess a sickening and grotesque physical reality that can raise blood pressures and inflame human passions to dangerous levels. A truck driver who has travelled overnight on a long and tiring journey will not be disposed to offer any suggestions about where the goods can be put – at least none which might prove constructive.

Storage space problems are generally brought about by lack of foresight and inadequate planning. This is an area in which the project manager should be well-equipped to contribute. Space is just as much a project resource as labour. However, space is difficult to schedule because the problem is three dimensional and not suitable for the usual project management computer software. A simpler, effective, alternative is to give the materials manager a list of project purchasing tasks derived from the critical path network, sorted in ascending order of their expected delivery dates.

Labelling

Correct labelling of stored items is essential, otherwise mistakes in issuing are bound to happen. Stores staff cannot be expected to identify all the varied items needed for a project by their appearance alone. All parts must be given numbers so that ambiguities are not possible. A standard part numbering discipline, originating from the design office, is a necessary basis for a stock identification system. Each consignment will be marked with the correct part number on receipt into stores and, provided that the number and the goods do not become separated, identification is then made simple. Raw materials can be given the specification number as identification, in some cases backed up by dimensions. Commonly used raw materials, such as stock metals, can be painted with colour codes.

Location and retrieval

Location and retrieval of materials is a problem proportional to the size and layout of the stores. Valuable project materials have been known to vanish, causing urgent and expensive re-ordering, only to reappear at the back of a dusty shelf long after the project has been finished. The remedy is to give every rack, shelf, and bin an identifying 'address', which is usually a simple alphanumeric code. Stock records will show the stores address code (often called the bin number, even where no actual bin exists) against every item held. This is, of course, the common procedure in any well-run store or warehouse.

Physical pre-allocation of project materials

Pre-allocation is a stores procedure that usually entails placing a marker on the bin or the stock record to show that the particular item has been earmarked for use on a particular project. However, the only safe method for pre-allocating materials for use on forthcoming project work is to withdraw them from general stock and place them in a separate, securely locked project store. If this is not done it is certain that, pre-allocation or not, some of the stock will be used on other work, and so will be unavailable for the project when needed. Cheery assurances from the storekeeper that the deficient items are 'on order' or 'expected any day now' will not be well received. A project cannot be completed with empty promises.

Preservation

Any materials which are particularly susceptible to deterioration through mechanical shock, heat, cold or damp must be suitably protected. Some articles will deteriorate under any conditions, and must be used before their 'use-by' date. Certain raw materials are not suitable for storing in close proximity to each other because of the risk of damage through cross-contamination. For example, a prudent person would not store strongly scented soap alongside tea.

Security

Safe custody and security of stock demand that the storage area can be locked up outside normal working hours. At other times stores entry will usually be restricted to authorized stores personnel. Regulations such as these are designed not only to prevent theft, but also to minimize the possibility of irregular or unrecorded withdrawals. Construction site stores are particularly vulnerable and need special protection, which can include a full-time watchman, dogs, patrols, high fencing, alarms, closed-circuit television, security lighting and so on.

Irregular removals from stores are not all due to theft. They might arise from surreptitious attempts at making good losses, scrap or breakages on the site or workfloor. Over-zealous activity to clear shortages on one project could lead to unauthorized taking of stock pre-allocated for other projects.

Stores records and information systems

Information systems must be designed and implemented to provide accurate feedback of all material movements (arrivals and withdrawals) for stock control and cost accounting purposes.

Stores receipts are documented by goods inwards notes or, in the case of items manufactured within the premises, some form of completed job ticket, inspection ticket or stores receipt note. Serviceable items returned to stores for stock because they are no longer required for any reason must be similarly documented.

Issues from stores are usually authorized and documented by stores requisitions, bills of materials, stores issue schedules or parts lists. These withdrawals have to be reported against job numbers to the cost office or accounts department. Those responsible for stock control will rely on this information to maintain stock records as accurately as possible, and re-order items for general stock as appropriate.

VENDORS' DOCUMENTS

Provision must usually be made for the project engineers to receive and approve documents from the supplier for items manufactured specially for the project. The term 'vendors' documents' is often used, although the providers of the goods might also be referred to as manufacturers, sellers, suppliers or subcontractors.

The first step in ensuring the timely receipt of vendors' documents is to make certain that the obligations for providing them are always spelled out clearly on the purchase orders or their attached purchase specifications.

Foundation, capacity and installation drawings

In addition to general layout or assembly drawings, there is usually a requirement for the early availability of installation instructions. With heavy plant and machinery, for example, foundation drawings, power supply requirements and overall weights and dimensions are all vital information, the lack of which could hold up design work on the project. Obtaining such information and progressing any necessary approvals is all part of the expediting process (described in Chapter 24).

Other vendors' documents

When the equipment is delivered, a final set of drawings, certified test results, operating and maintenance manuals and a recommended spares holding list will probably be needed. In some cases, suppliers may be required to supply documents translated into a foreign language, according to the nationality of the project end user.

Serial numbering of vendors' documents

A great number of vendors' drawings and other documents can accumulate in a large project, and the project engineering company has to make certain that it will be able to find any of these quickly if the client reports operating difficulties or if the documents are needed again for any of the other reasons already listed. Thus copies of vendors' documents are usually serially numbered and recorded in registers before filing. To ensure that any of these documents can easily be found again in the future (location and retrieval are the buzzwords), the files must be arranged in some recognizable and logical sequence. This might be based on specification numbers, requisition numbers, purchase order numbers or the company's standard project work breakdown coding system.

Indexing

A cross-referenced index might have to be created so that, for example, a file can be found if only the equipment specification number or the supplier and approximate date of supply are known. If vendors' documents are kept in a secure file (for example, in an off-site vault) an index of those documents must be kept with them.

MATERIALS MANAGEMENT AS A SHARED OR COMMON SERVICE

Unless a project store has been set up specially within the project organization, project managers generally have no direct control over the materials management operation. The usual arrangement in a manufacturing company is for the purchasing and stores departments to operate as common services, often combined organizationally with other materials functions such as goods inwards and despatch under the command of a materials manager. The project manager is usually entirely dependent on the materials manager and the stores organization for all materials handling aspects of the project. The project manager may even be denied access to secure stores areas.

Reliance on common services can always cause problems for a project manager, where there might be a clash of priorities, and with any attempt at random independent checking regarded with suspicion – even hostility – by the common services manager, who regards the project manager's interest in the department's performance as unwarranted interference. In fact project managers might actually have less direct access and control over a common services department within the company than they have over an external supplier of goods and services where, at least, the purchase contract will probably give right of access for expediting and on-site inspection purposes.

Case example

This example illustrates how reliance on common services can let a project manager down. A company in the UK was carrying out a project to manufacture and install two prefabricated operating theatres in a Scandinavian country. The parts for these theatres were taken from stores, packed and shipped to the project site by the company's common services division. The highly experienced installation crew, which reported to the project manager, was flown out to the site as soon as all the materials had reached their destination.

The hospital authorities arranged for the initial erection of the main frames to be given full publicity, signifying the proud results of their new investment. Each operating theatre frame comprised eight legs, bolted to an octagonal welded top frame (so that each theatre skeleton resembled a large spider). Having marked out the floor accurately for the first theatre, members of the site team stood holding eight legs in position while, watched expectantly by the media and local dignitaries, the first top frame was lowered gently into position by a hoist. Of course, it did not fit: common services division had packed and despatched the wrong top frames.

If there is anything worse than being made to look foolish, it must be suffering that indignity under the bright lights of publicity. The acute embarrassment of the project manager and the company was the result of failure by a common services division over which the project manager had no direct control.

The immediate remedy in that case was for the common services division to airfreight two correct frames to site – an expensive operation because the large steel frames were heavy and bulky. The longer-term remedy in such cases is usually more difficult, but involves motivating common services to improve their service to the project through a mixture of education, persuasion and (if necessary) mobilizing support and action from the company's senior management.

REFERENCES AND FURTHER READING

Gattorna, J. L. (ed.) (2003), *Gower Handbook of Supply Chain Management*, 5th Edition (Aldershot: Gower).

Kerzner, H. (2006), *Project Management: A Systems Approach to Planning, Scheduling and Controlling*, 9th Edition (New York: Wiley).

Roylance, D. (2006), *Purchasing Performance: Measuring, Marketing and Selling the Purchasing Function* (Aldershot: Gower).

Ward, G. (2007), *Project Manager's Guide to Purchasing* (Aldershot: Gower).

24 *Managing Progress*

Figure 24.1 depicts a familiar roadside sign. It warns of forthcoming disruption and inconvenience to our journeys but promises better things ahead, when the road has been repaired and our travel has been made smoother and safer. But can we believe everything that it says? We can be reasonably certain about the last part of the statement: 'Delays possible'. It is likely, however, that the first day of July will come and go with no sign of activity. Perhaps by the middle of the month things might start to happen, with the arrival of machinery and the erection of temporary traffic signals and other impediments to the free flow of traffic. After that, the promised six weeks might drag out to eight, ten or even twelve weeks.

Road repair operations are usually relatively simple projects, yet delays are often apparent. Managing the progress of larger projects obviously poses greater difficulties, with far greater complexity in the

Figure 24.1 A familiar sign – but will this project start and finish on time?

organization, and with many more tasks to be performed. This chapter is about helping to prevent project delays. It must begin with the assumption that an effective schedule has been produced, and that all key project participants know, and have agreed to, what is expected of them.

PROGRESS MANAGEMENT AS A CLOSED-LOOP CONTROL SYSTEM

One prerequisite for any control system is a method for measuring the effect of any command given. The information so derived can then be fed back to the command source so that any errors can be corrected by modifying the original command.

An artillery commander watches the fall of his initial shots and uses the results as feedback signals to the gunners, so that they can correct the aim of the guns. In electronic amplifiers, well-established design practice is to arrange for some of the output signal to be fed back to the amplifier's input in opposite (cancelling) polarity. That process tends to correct any distortion of the signal created within the amplifying system.

Thus feedback signals are used to correct errors, whether these happen to be the aim of a cannon or distortion in an amplifier. If the feedback signal is disconnected, the system is said to operate as an open loop. When the feedback signals are applied to the input, the control loop is closed.

Effective project progress control is a form of closed-loop feedback system. For every instruction issued, progress is monitored, deviations from plan (errors) are detected and corrective feedback is applied. The competent project manager will ensure that these corrective actions do take place, so that the control loop is closed. This principle of *command – measure – feedback – correct* operates at the level of each individual task, at higher levels of the WBS, and for the whole project. Because of the close electronic analogy this process has been called 'cybernetic control'. The principle is shown in Figure 24.2.

'MANAGEMENT BY' STYLES

The development of management theory has one thing in common with the fashion industry, namely that *this* year's technique is *next* year's history. However, some of management theories do survive and become valuable in helping us either to understand management better or to apply the principles in practice. Over the past 60 years or so a number of different names have been associated with management styles that all begin with the words 'management by'. Five examples follow.

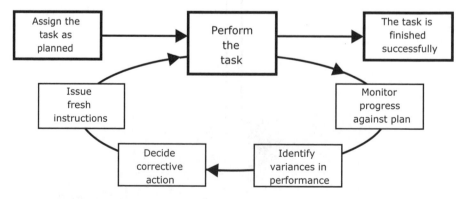

Figure 24.2   Control loop

Management by objectives

The technique of management by objectives (MbO), is based on setting each manager in an organization a set of quantifiable objectives, and then measuring how well or how badly each manager manages to achieve those objectives. Each objective must be quantifiable and measurable, and vague statements such as 'improve performance' are not acceptable.

At the most extreme level of MbO implementation, the organization must first be analysed and charted and then the role of every manager from the chief executive down to the lowliest supervisor is examined and specified in a job description. Then, quantified objectives are established at each level that, together, build to the objectives of the whole organization in a hierarchical pyramid. That concept is fine in theory and has much in common with the WBS for a project.

When MbO is applied formally to an organization the chances are that, by the time all the job descriptions have been written and the objectives have been set, the organization itself will have undergone fundamental change, thus wrecking the grand MbO design. However, when practised more informally, management by objectives has much to commend it. Managers and their subordinates set objectives at their local departmental or functional level, and review the results at three monthly intervals, setting new objectives at each review.

By now you might be asking, 'What has all this to do with project management?' The answer is clear. Project management is nothing less, nothing more, than management by objectives. Quantifiable objectives are set when the project is defined, they are distributed over a WBS and OBS, and then managers strive to achieve the set objectives by a predetermined date.

Management by the seat of the pants

This style of management derives its name from riding a horse or flying a plane. It refers to a kind of control that is based on instinctive feelings of whether or not things are going in the right direction. Although there are a few individuals who possess this ability in project management, most of us do not. Therefore we must rely on more scientific or practical methods, such as those described throughout this book.

Management by walking about

There was once an engineering director who sat in an office filled with beautiful antique furniture. He could only be approached through an outer office, also filled with beautiful antique furniture and a secretary (who was beautiful but not antique). Outside this small office complex was a vast floor occupied by many functional engineering managers, senior engineers and designers. The engineering director seldom emerged from his office, and only met his subordinates at meetings. The word went around the junior staff, as a joke with some substance, that the engineering director did not really exist, and there were only two offices and a secretary. That true story is the antithesis of management by walking about.

Managers who do 'walk about' will visit parts of the project to see for themselves the progress that is being made, and most important of all, to give motivating words of encouragement to everyone working on the project. If some of the activities are at a remote site, or overseas, the project manager should make occasional visits. People will respond well if they know that they and their work are appreciated. A small word of encouragement here and there costs little but the return on investment can be enormous.

Failure to perform this very simple function of walking about is a great demotivator. A project cannot be managed effectively by sitting all day behind a desk.

Management by surprise

Management by surprise has its origins in manufacturing, but it has universal application to any cybernetic control system where the loop is not closed. A manager puts work into the front end of a factory and is surprised when it doesn't come out at the other end.

Management by exception

With a cybernetic control system, error signals have greatest significance for control, because these are the factors that generate corrective action. In the management context, divergences from plans and budgets or any unexpected setbacks are called 'exceptions'. Cost and management accountants call their exceptions 'variances'. Exceptions and variances can apply to advantageous differences from plan but, for control purposes, it is the negative exceptions and potential failures that should crave attention.

Management by exception means concentrating management efforts on the bad variances or exceptions. If something is running five per cent below its budget, that's fine, leave it alone, don't tell me about it. But if another job is running five per cent over budget, concentrate on that and put it right.

Exception reporting

Exception reports are a product of management by exception. They might be accounts statements that show overspending or lists of jobs that are running late. At the other extreme, an exception report might be the frenzied beating on a senior manager's door by a distraught project manager who feels that her project and her world have suddenly fallen apart. A perfect personification of an exception report is the materials shortage list (Figure 24.3). Such lists are often used as a cry for help from the shop floor or construction site to the purchasing agent whenever progress is at risk from lack of supplies.

Before allowing any exception report to be passed up the organizational hierarchy to a more senior manager for action, the project manager must first be certain that some remedy within his or her own control cannot be found. However, once it has been established that events are likely to move out of control, the project manager has a clear duty to give senior management the facts without delay. All of this is, of course, following the management by exception principle that prevents senior managers being bombarded with large volumes of information that should be of concern only to junior managers and supervisors. The intention is to leave executive minds free to concentrate their efforts on higher corporate strategy, to the best advantage of the company.

SHORTAGE LIST				
Project:		Date issued::		
Department:		Issued by:		
To the purchasing manager. The items listed below have not been received. Please expedite and report.		Is work held up? Yes or No ➡		
Order No (if known)	Description of materials or equipment	Quantity needed	When needed	Reply from purchasing manager

Figure 24.3 Materials shortage list format

UPDATING SCHEDULES AND RECORDS

Drawing and purchase schedules

Drawing and purchase schedules contain much information that is liable to change as the project proceeds. Therefore they must be kept up to date. If everyone using the schedules has access to them over a computer network, the problems of issue and revision status are largely avoided. If, on the other hand, schedules are to be distributed as hard copy, they must be re-issued at regular intervals and subjected to rigid version control (by specifying the relevant revision number).

When the project is finished, the purchase control schedules, because they list all the purchase specifications, become part of the essential documentation that records the as-built state of the project. Similarly, the drawing schedules list all the drawings used on the project, together with their final revision status.

Updating the project schedule

Updating is the process of producing a fresh set of schedules and other reports to take account of one or more of the following:

- a change to the project parameters, such as an unexpected increase or decrease in the numbers of resources available, changed cost rates, or a newly imposed target date;
- a change in the network logic. This could arise, for example as a result of a serious technical problem and consequent change of design strategy. A change in the project scope requested by the customer is often another reason;
- a desire to produce new schedules that take into account progress made to date.

Some people like to save a baseline model of the project before making any changes so that they have a permanent record on file of the project as it was originally planned.

Updating frequency

If a schedule has been produced which proves to be practicable in all respects, and if everything goes according to plan, there is no need at all to return to the computer for a new schedule during the life of the project. This could very well be the case for a simple project, or for a schedule covering only a very short total time span. Even a more complex project has been known to run entirely according to its original plan, where the plan was well made and the project particularly well managed.

In most projects, however, too many unknown factors lurk. Just when things appear to be on plan, a key supplier fails to deliver vital materials, a design error is discovered that will take weeks to put right, the customer puts in a late modification, or a construction site supervisor is horrified to see the scaffolding and formwork for a bridge gradually settle into the shape of a graceful bow under the weight of much newly-poured and liberally reinforced concrete setting rapidly under a tropical sun (yes, it really did happen).

The integrity of a project schedule must be protected at all times. If anything happens that renders a schedule obsolete it must be updated as soon as possible; otherwise people will lose faith in the plans and disregard them. Updating frequency can be contemplated:

- on an occasional basis, which usually means that owing to a specific event or change the existing schedules have either become inconvenient to use or are actually wrong;

or

- on a regular basis (which often means monthly).

Regular updating may be needed if the project is very complex, with large volumes of progress data to be digested. For some projects, regularly updated schedules and their resulting reports provide an essential part of reporting to the project client.

For the day-to-day management of project work, it is the current schedule that counts. Updated schedules simply follow, to make certain that work yet to be done remains sensibly scheduled. If, for instance, only scrap is produced after six weeks of a manufacturing job, or if it is found that 100 metres of trench have been excavated along the wrong side of a road (another example from real life), the manager does not wait for an updated schedule, but takes immediate practical action. If the activity is critical or nearly so, it is obvious that all the stops need to be pulled out at once to put things right. Of course the schedule must be updated, but that is a consequential process that follows once steps have been taken to sort out the immediate problem.

COLLECTING PROGRESS INFORMATION

Whatever the method used to gather progress information, care must be taken to avoid either ambiguity or undue complication. The simpler the method, the more likely the chances of persuading all the managers involved to return data regularly on time. Even so, training all key participants to adopt the regular routine of progress reporting often provides project managers with a real test of their mettle. Many attempts at project control fail because this process cannot be established.

Using task lists or work-to lists as progress returns

Active projects depend on two-way communication between the project manager and every departmental manager. For every work instruction issued, information must be fed back on the resulting progress.

If the original commands are to be conveyed from the project manager to participants by way of work-to lists, why not use that procedure in reverse to feed back progress information. The only missing item is a document complementary to the work-to list for that purpose. This gap can be filled by:

- the use of specially designed progress return forms;

or

- direct input to the computer or server;

or

- line managers annotating copies of their work-to-lists.

Some project management software packages allow space for comments on their work-to lists. The example in Figure 24.4 is redrawn from a report that one version of Deltek's *Deltek Open Plan*™ includes in its standard range of reports. This example serves as a work-to list that can be annotated with progress information by all the departmental managers. Those managers will be expected to return their lists as progress reports to the project manager or project support office, who will replace them very shortly afterwards with fresh work-to lists.

For every task on the current work-to list, the project manager (or project support office) will need to be told about progress in one of the following ways:

- The task has not been started as planned, for reasons given.
- The task has just been started.
- The task is in progress, with an assessment of the percentage of the task completed.
- The task is in progress, with the latest best estimate of the duration remaining to completion.

Project: Garage

GARAGE PROJECT

Activity progress update questionnaire

Report date:

Page: 1

Task ID	Description	Orig dur	Scheduled start	Scheduled finish	Rem dur	Progress measured or estimated	
						% completed	Comment
1	Project start	0	13MAY13	13MAY13	0		
2	Make and prime door frame	1	13MAY13	13MAY13	1		
3	Dig foundations	4	13MAY13	16MAY13	4		
7	Position door frame	1	14MAY13	14MAY13	1		
4	Make doors	3	15MAY13	17MAY13	3		
8	Concrete foundations	2	17MAY13	20MAY13	2		
9	Prime doors	1	20MAY13	20MAY13	1		
11	Lay bricks for walls	10	21MAY13	03JUN13	10		
13	Fit RSJ lintel	1	04JUN13	04JUN13	1		
18	Case lintel, build parapets	2	05JUN13	06JUN13	2		
12	Lay floor base	2	07JUN13	10JUN13	2		
6	Cut roof timbers	1	07JUN13	07JUN13	1		
17	Screed floor	1	11JUN13	11JUN13	1		
21	Hang doors	1	12JUN13	12JUN13	1		

Figure 24.4   Combined work-to list and progress questionnaire

- The task is in progress, with the latest best estimate of the completion date.
- The task is completed.

Time-now date

All progress data should be collected with reference to the next 'time-now' date. 'Time now' is, paradoxically a date chosen in the future. It is the reference point from which time analysis and rescheduling will be calculated and from which the computer will reset all dates in work-to lists.

All people asked to provide progress information, whether directly from their keyboards or on paper, must be told the next time-now date. The planner will usually choose this time-now to be either the date on which rescheduling is to take place or a day or two later. Progress reporting against a time-now date therefore expects managers to forecast slightly ahead when assessing their results. With the rapid processing times of modern systems, it should not be necessary to place the time-now date more that a day or two into the future.

If the schedules have to be updated frequently, as a result of numerous changes or for any other reason, reprocessing might have to be arranged at regular intervals. If the intervals are regular, the time-now rescheduling dates can be announced and annotated on calendars for many months ahead.

Frequency of progress data collection

Progress feedback should be arranged at fairly frequent intervals, typically more often than the issue of revised work-to lists. Weekly intervals are suggested. If the intervals are too long, some problems might not come to light in sufficient time for corrective action to have any effect.

It is usually practicable for departmental managers and other senior staff to be given direct access to the computer from their own keyboards. These managers can then report progress continually by this direct method. The project manager will want to be assured that progress information fed directly to the computer in this way, without first being subjected to checking and critical examination, emanates only from reliable and reasonably senior staff. False statements could lead to subsequent errors in network analysis, future resource allocation and work-to lists.

If the computer system is holding a large, complex multi-project model, the group or person responsible for scheduling will always be wary of any input that could corrupt the files and cause many hours of restoration work, and a project support office is a good place from which to collect and check progress information.

Even with continuous input of progress information, work-to lists and other schedules will probably be revised and reissued only when the planner decides that data reprocessing is necessary. This decision must be made by the planner in advance, and the next time-now date must be announced as soon as it has been decided.

Questions of logic

If the progress information is being gathered on forms, rather than by direct input to the computer, there is another question that the perceptive project manager needs to ask for each task that is reported as done. That question is:

Can this task's immediate successor(s) be started now?

This is the acid test of whether or not an activity has truly been completed. If the network logic is correct, then a task cannot strictly be reported as complete if its immediately following dependent tasks cannot be started.

An alert project manager will recognize the danger behind a progress return which says that the percentage progress achieved is 100 per cent, but that the next activity cannot start. This could mean that the progress claimed has not in fact been made. This anomaly also occurs when a design engineer has completed a batch of drawings, but refuses to release them for issue through lack of confidence in the design, or because he or she feels that (given more time) the drawings could be improved.

Sometimes an activity *can* be started even though one or more of its predecessors is not finished. For example, a design activity, although not complete, could be sufficiently advanced to allow the release of procurement lists for long-lead items. A network diagram cannot indicate all such possibilities and opportunities for speeding progress might easily be missed it the right questions are not asked when progress data are collected.

Activities are sometimes reported as started before one or more predecessors have been reported as finished. This is in contradiction to the logic enshrined in the network so that, when it happens, it indicates that the network constraints were not absolute. Nevertheless, if that is the situation, it has to be accepted and reported to the computer accordingly. The computer will probably report such activities as being started 'out of sequence'.

STATISTICAL CHECKS

One very useful occasional check is to ask how many people in a department, or staff of a particular grade, are actually working on the project. The answer can then be compared with the manpower requirement scheduled for that date. Comparison of scheduled and actual cost curves can also be made, but the headcount is quicker, more positive and likely to produce the earlier warning of a potential problem.

Suppose that 35 design engineers are supposed to be working on scheduled activities on a given date. If only 18 people can be identified as working on the project, something is obviously very wrong somewhere. Although routine progress returns might indicate that everything is more or less on course, the headcount shows that work on the project in the design department is not taking place at the required rate. Closer investigation might reveal that the project design is held up for lack of information, that work for another project has been given priority or that the department is seriously under-staffed. The project manager must take action to set the right number of people to work.

Now suppose that the project manager has carried out two checks which indicate that both the use of manpower and the rate of expenditure appear to be on target. There used to be (perhaps there still are) people who would gladly accept such results as indicating that all was well with their projects, mistakenly believing that if the scheduled number of people are actually found to be working on a project (or if the costs *recorded* to date are in line with the costs *planned* to date) then progress must also be on course. Of course, no sensible modern project manager would make such an assumption because it is necessary also to assess the value earned from the expenditure. This argument will be developed further in Chapter 27.

MANAGING THE PROGRESS AND QUALITY OF BOUGHT-IN MATERIALS AND EQUIPMENT

Suppliers' procedures

A feature of project purchasing is that the buyer should take a detailed interest in the vendor's own project management and quality procedures. Several large companies and government departments insist that those who supply them with project equipment or carry out subcontracts at least use critical path analysis, and they will probably be expected to show that their quality policy and procedures satisfy the requirements of the international standard ISO 9000 series. It is not unknown for purchasers to offer advice to vendors in establishing their own internal systems.

Some UK Government purchasers might also wish to ensure that their suppliers are aware of, and implement, the PRINCE2 project management structure and principles (http//www.ogc.uk/prince).

Expediting

As far as the purchaser is concerned, the period following the issue of a purchase order will be one of waiting, and a great deal of reliance must be placed on the supplier. That is not to say that the purchaser can do nothing. This is the time when the expediters earn their money by keeping in touch with the supplier to investigate and spur progress. Expediting is not just a process of chasing up late deliveries. It requires communication (including possible visits) with the supplier during the waiting period. This either safeguards progress or provides an early warning system should the supplier experience any difficulty in meeting the order.

The expediter should react promptly and firmly whenever the reply to a routine expediting enquiry is unsatisfactory. The special efforts of the purchasing department should not stop until the supplier has either shown the necessary improvement or has actually delivered the goods.

Sometimes a new method of approach to the supplier can produce the desired result. An offer to arrange collection of the goods from the supplier's premises will, for instance, make the supplier aware that the purchaser is willing to participate constructively and that, on this occasion at least, there is genuine urgency.

Expediting and inspection visits to suppliers' premises

The purchaser might wish to arrange visits to a supplier's premises to check on progress, inspect the quality of workmanship or witness tests. Such visits are sometimes linked to the certification of suppliers' claims for stage payments.

There are several ways in which responsibility for carrying out inspection and expediting visits can be allocated or delegated. Where suitable engineers are available to the purchase agent concerned, it is often convenient for the agent to arrange visits which combine the inspection and expediting functions.

Where specialist engineering attendance is needed for inspection or to witness tests, the project engineering organization might send one or more of its own engineers to assist the purchasing agent. To avoid expensive overseas travel when foreign suppliers are involved, it is sometimes possible to engage a local professional engineering company to undertake the inspection and expediting visits.

Whatever the arrangement for staffing the inspection function, the project engineers must make arrangements (usually through the purchasing agent) for the inspectors to receive all necessary drawings and specifications, the purchase order, and all revisions to these documents. Some companies are also able to provide the inspecting engineers with checklists, to help ensure that no vital point is overlooked when they make their visits.

Inspection and expediting reports

The project manager (and sometimes the client) might want to see an inspection and expediting report from the relevant purchasing agent following every formal visit to a supplier. The inspecting engineer or expediter will probably be asked to use a convenient standard summary form for this purpose, an example of which is shown in Figure 24.5.

INSPECTION/EXPEDITING REPORT

Report number	Sheet 1 of	Date this visit	Date of last visit	Inspector/expediter

MAIN SUPPLIER DETAILS	Contract delivery date

MAIN SUPPLIER DETAILS

Name _____

Address _____

_____

Supplier's reference _____

Persons contacted _____

Equipment _____

_____

_____

_____

Contract delivery date

Current delivery estimate

Plans for next visit

Date _____

To expedite ☐

To continue inspection ☐

Final inspection ☐

To inspect packing ☐

SUB-SUPPLIER DETAILS

Main supplier's order number _____

Name _____

Address _____

_____

Sub-supplier's reference _____

Persons contacted _____

_____

Equipment _____

_____

_____

Agreed delivery to supplier

Current delivery estimate

Plans for next visit

Date _____

To expedite ☐

To continue inspection ☐

Final inspection ☐

To inspect packing ☐

ORDER STATUS SUMMARY (see attached sheets for details)

Assessed progress (by weeks)	Tests witnessed?	Complies with spec?	Released for packing?	Released for shipping?
Early ☐	Yes ☐	Yes ☐	Yes ☐	Yes ☐
Late ☐ _____	No ☐	No ☐	No ☐	No ☐

ACTION REQUIRED	ACTION BY

		Specification No	Revision
Title		Purchase order No	Amendment

Figure 24.5   Inspection and expediting report

Commitment and motivation of purchasing department and agents

The purchasing department will not usually be directing all their attention to one project, unless it is very big. Quite understandably, each purchasing order which passes through their hands could be regarded by the expediters as just another routine job.

Projects of sufficient size can justify the allocation of a buyer or even a group of buyers and expediters to the project. These staff should be seconded to the project from the purchasing department if possible but they might have to be recruited specially as temporary staff or contract staff. Special staffing should be particularly effective in a pure project team organization, because the reporting line is to the project manager rather than to the materials or purchasing manager. The buyer and expediter (they might be the same person), because they are part of the project team, should identify themselves more closely with the success or failure of the project and thus be more highly motivated.

Intervention by the project manager

If the supplier definitely cannot deliver on time, the project manager must be brought into the picture. He or she can then decide on just how important the delay is likely to be, and authorize emergency measures if these appear to be justified. In the last resort the project manager must feel free to intervene in the expediting process, even if this brings accusations of interference from the purchasing manager.

The project manager should be motivated by a sense of personal involvement with the success of the project. He or she will perhaps realize that their own career prospects can be closely linked to the success of the project. This realization should spur the project manager on to exercise initiative, perseverance, tact and (in the last resort) guile. For these reasons the project manager can sometimes be successful in preventing or clearing a materials shortage which has been accepted by others as inevitable. The effective project manager refuses to accept defeat and explores every avenue until a solution is found.

Alternative sourcing

When expediting appears to be failing, the design engineers might be able to suggest an alternative item that can be obtained more quickly. The solution might instead mean finding another source of supply. If the original order does have to be cancelled because the supplier failed to make the agreed delivery, there should be no penalty for the purchaser, because the supplier broke the contract by failing to fulfil the delivery conditions.

Purchase order status reports

The purchasing agent is usually required to keep the project manager informed of the progress status of all current purchase orders. This responsibility, in addition to the inspection and expediting reports already described, extends through all stages of the journey to the project site. This reporting can be done by means of regular order status reports, which list all purchase orders in progress, giving outline details of shipping and delivery dates, and highlighting any problems and corrective actions.

Efficient communications and dedicated, regular reporting by all the purchasing agents and freight forwarders involved on the project are essential if purchase order status reports are to be of any value.

It is also important to arrange the reports so that potential or real problems are highlighted, and not lost in the larger amount of detail reporting routine transactions that are proceeding according to plan.

MANAGING SUBCONTRACTORS AND AGENCY EMPLOYEES

Most companies use subcontractors. They can be used in a variety of ways, the most common of which include the following:

- to undertake tasks which require expertise or facilities that lie outside the main contractor's own capabilities (for example, heat treatment, plating and anodising, gear cutting, chemical analysis, certification testing) – this form of subcontracting is typically handled and progressed through the contractor's standard purchasing procedures;
- to provide additional temporary staff to work in the contractor's own premises to cover work overloads or to substitute for permanent staff who are absent for any reason;
- to undertake specified tasks externally, on the subcontractors' own premises, where the main contractor's accommodation, plant or workforce would otherwise be overloaded;
- to work on a construction site, carrying out the various trades or specialist services – a very brief account of construction site management is given later in this chapter.

Temporary staff working on the contractor's own premises

The supply of temporary staff for all kinds of duties has become accepted practice and many agencies exist, some specializing in particular trades or professional skills.

Some companies regard the employment of agency staff as a temporary expedient, to cover staff shortages caused by holidays, sickness or sudden work overloads. However, there are companies that plan always to keep a proportion of their total workforce as temporary staff, because that provides flexibility in the event of workload fluctuations and reduces the possibility of having to make permanent staff redundant when the order book is less than full.

Planning for the availability of temporary staff

Whenever agency staff have to be used, especially if the numbers are significant, the search for suitable agencies and ensuing negotiations should take place as early as possible so that manpower can be reserved at reasonable rates and with some guarantee of adequate performance. Project disasters excepted, the use of project resource scheduling techniques (such as those described in earlier chapters) should provide timely and sufficiently accurate forewarning. The project manager should ensure that the selected agencies are given enough time to mobilize or reserve their own resources. Care should be taken, however, to avoid long-term commitments and the payment of retaining fees – a request sometimes made by subcontractors on the grounds that they cannot otherwise guarantee to have people available when required. In my experience such retainers are unnecessary and I have never agreed to them.

Supervision

From the project control point of view, although the use of short-term agency staff may be unavoidable, there are risks of errors and inefficiency in all cases where tasks require a good understanding of the company's procedures and working practices. In those cases some time and money must be dedicated to providing initial or induction training. Longer-term temporary staff can often settle into an organization and acquit themselves well, becoming indistinguishable from the permanent employees until the fateful day arrives when there is no more work for them.

All temporary employees working on the contractor's own premises should normally come under the day-to-day supervision of the company's own departmental managers and work should be issued, progressed and measured according to the same project management procedures that govern permanent staff. The only additional feature is to ensure that invoices received from the various agencies claim for the hours actually worked, and at the agreed rates. Verification of hours worked is achieved using weekly timesheets.

Agencies will generally expect their staff to fill in the agency's own brand of timesheets and these will be used as the input documents for the resulting agency invoices. However, for detailed and accurate recording of task times worked against appropriate project cost codes, contractors will probably require agency staff also to record their time using the contractor's own internal timesheet procedures.

Temporary design staff working in outside offices

An extra dimension of risk is added when design tasks are entrusted to staff who cannot be accommodated within the contractor's own premises. In those cases, work allocation and day-to-day supervision is usually delegated to the subcontractor's own managers. The main contractor will want to take steps to ensure that design quality does not suffer, and that the hours claimed by the subcontractor equate to the hours actually worked. The outside offices may be situated at long distances from the main contractor's offices.

Subcontract liaison engineer

One way of overcoming these problems is to place a supervisor in the external office, which of course will require the agreement of the subcontractor. Another approach is to appoint one of the company's permanent engineering staff as 'subcontract liaison engineer'. The liaison engineer visits all the external offices at very frequent intervals to perform the following tasks:

- deliver new work;
- ensure that the main contractor's project design standards are known and followed;
- monitor and report back progress;
- answer technical queries on the spot;
- collect completed work.

Revealing task priorities and budgets to external agencies

Managers differ in their opinions regarding whether or not to give subcontractors information on the amount of float available for a task, or the cost budget that has been set aside for the work.

I prefer to tell subcontractors the amount of float available because that information conveys true priorities and is the main factor in deciding whether or not overtime working (and therefore overtime premium costs) are justified. The higher cost rates of overtime should usually be accepted for work on tasks that have little remaining float, are critical or are already running late.

Other companies will have different views. Some will argue that the only schedule information needed by the subcontractor is the scheduled start and finish date of each task, regardless of float.

If in doubt, a compromise can be suggested. Subcontractors should be told if any job has zero or negative float. For all other jobs, the subcontractor might be allowed to infer that float exists, but they will not be told how much – only that the work is expected to start and finish on the dates scheduled.

Budget data have to be treated differently. I take the view that if the total available budget is revealed on each subcontract order, then the subcontractor will be tempted to spend and claim costs up to that limit. If, on the other hand, the estimates are kept out of sight, progressing work within the scheduled dates should suffice to stop the work from overrunning its budgeted costs.

Effective costs: a paradox

When using about ten different subcontractors for an engineering company in the British Midlands, I reached the following conclusions:

- All the companies chosen performed well in respect of their work quality.
- The terms for recovering expenses and for charging travel time varied considerably.
- The hourly work rates quoted varied considerably from one company to another.
- The hours actually booked for equivalent jobs also varied from company to company – in inverse proportion to the hourly cost rates.

Those companies which quoted the higher hourly rates were thus not necessarily the most expensive to use, because they tended to claim fewer hours and expenses for the equivalent amount of work. In fact, there was little actual variation in the real costs of using all these subcontractors.

Special arrangements to protect standards and design quality

If significant design packages are subcontracted to external offices, there is a danger that the results might not properly match the project design concept, or that the solutions adopted would differ from those normally preferred by the company.

Most reputable companies would not allow new permanent staff to work unsupervised on their initial work, or before undergoing some basic training and induction into the company's preferred practices and standards. The same argument applies to external staff entrusted with design tasks.

This problem can be overcome to a large extent by nominating one or more members of a subcontractor's senior design staff as a 'key engineer'. Each key engineer can be invited to work in the contractor's main design office for a few weeks, working under competent guidance and absorbing the company's standards and practices.

A package of work is then selected for the external design office. The key engineer carries out the basic design and layout drawings for this work package in the contractor's main office. When this work has been checked and approved, the key engineer returns to the external office, where he or she supervises other subcontract staff in the detailing and checking of all the drawings needed to complete the work package.

As experience is gained, the main contractor will eventually allow some original design work to be carried out in the subcontractor's office, regarding the key engineer as a kind of agent or external supervisor.

ROUTINE PRIORITY ALLOCATION IN MANUFACTURING PROJECTS

Occasions will often arise when work cannot be carried out by manufacturing departments in a sequence that suits every project schedule. If the production control department were able to pick up all orders and load them sequentially, or according to their own machine and manpower schedules, no serious problem need arise. Sooner or later, however, an order is going to be placed which is wanted urgently, and the production controller will be asked to displace other orders in favour of the newcomer.

ABC system of priorities

Some organizations attempt to allocate order priorities, perhaps by labelling their works orders with the letters A, B or C (for example) to indicate the degree of urgency attaching to each order. A job carrying Priority A would be perceived as being more urgent than jobs at Priority B, leaving Priority C jobs as the poor relations. It is not difficult to imagine why such systems break down. Delayed C orders will eventually become wanted urgently but will continue to be labelled and treated as C orders. In the end, everyone will label their orders as A priority, so that everything is wanted at once and nothing in fact receives special attention. As W. S. Gilbert points out in *The Gondoliers* (1889), 'When everyone is somebodee, then no one's anybody.'

Wanted-by dates

A preferable arrangement is to schedule manufacturing orders by wanted-by dates. The production controller can then attempt to schedule to meet these dates, and inform those who are likely to be disappointed. If any project item is expected to be delayed beyond its critical date, the possibility of subcontracting the work can always be considered.

Resolving conflicting priorities

Special project work often has to take its place in the production organization alongside routine manufacturing work or jobs for other projects. Conflicts can arise between jobs with different priorities, and it is a brave person who attempts to intervene between two rival project managers who are fighting for the same production resources.

Critical path analysis and multi-project resource scheduling are the logical ways for deciding priorities but, unfortunately, some managers are not over impressed with logical reasoning when they see their project being delayed (taking advantage of available float) in favour of other work. If such problems cannot be resolved on the spot without bloodshed, a sensible approach is to refer the problem to a third-party arbitrator – preferably by a manager at a more senior level in the organization, capable of assessing the relative merits of the conflicting jobs.

WHEN THE NEWS IS BAD

How bad?

When jobs start to run late, the first thing to be considered is the effect that this is likely to have on:

- the current project
- projects or other work queuing in the pipeline
- last, but certainly not least, the customer.

On rare occasions, late running might be acceptable and require no action. Usually, however, some degree of corrective action is needed. The project manager must then assess the situation, decide the appropriate action and implement it.

Late jobs with free float

If the recalcitrant work has enough free float to absorb the total expected delay, then all that needs to be done is to ensure that the work is expedited and finished without further interruption, within the available free float time.

Late jobs with some total float

Total float that contains no free float has to be regarded more seriously because any total float used up by late working early in the programme will rob later tasks of their float. So, those jobs which possess total float but no free float should, wherever possible, be expedited to bring them back on schedule.

Remember that purchasing and manufacturing departments have always suffered at the hands of project managers by being expected to perform miracles when all the total float has been used up by late-running design tasks, long before work enters the purchasing and manufacturing phases.

Late jobs with zero or negative float

If critical tasks (tasks with zero or negative float) are late, then special measures must certainly be taken. It might be necessary to accept more expensive working methods to expedite these late jobs and bring them back on schedule.

If a task budgeted to cost £1000 is in danger of running several weeks late and jeopardizing the handover date of a project worth £1m, then obviously it would be worth spending £10 000 or even more on the problem task if that could rescue the project programme. The project manager must always view the costs of expediting individual activities against the potential effect on the whole project.

CORRECTIVE MEASURES

Orthodox measures

Corrective measures will only be successful if they are taken in time, which means that adequate warning of problems must be given. This will depend on monitoring progress regularly against a well-prepared schedule that is kept up to date.

Working overtime, perhaps over one or two weekends, can sometimes recover time. The project manager will be thankful, on such occasions, that overtime working was held back as a reserve and not built into the schedules as normal practice. Used occasionally, overtime can be an effective help in overcoming delays. Used regularly or too often, however, the law of diminishing returns will apply, with staff permanently tired and working under pressure, leaving inadequate reserves for coping with emergencies.

If problems are being caused by shortage of resources, perhaps these could be made available from external sources by subcontracting. Or, there might be additional capacity somewhere else in the contractor's own organization that could be mobilized.

The network logic should always be re-examined critically. Can some tasks can be overlapped, bypassed or even eliminated? Is there any task that could wait until after the main part of the project has been delivered?

If all else fails, try to find out what the customer's reaction would be to late delivery. If, for instance, the project is to supply and install new machinery in the customer's brand new manufacturing plant, it could be that the customer's own building programme is running late, so that a later delivery date can be negotiated with no one being inconvenienced.

Unorthodox measures

Special motivational measures, incentives or even unorthodox actions can sometimes give progress a much-needed boost, provided that these measures are legal, not repeated too often and used sensibly.

Case example 1

An export project for the central monitoring of hospital patients electronically, already many months late, was being subjected to further delays by the threat of engineering modifications. The project manager and chief engineer almost came to blows. The project manager booked space on a ship, challenged the assembly crew by placing a small bet with them that they could not meet the deadline, and told the chief engineer that any remaining essential modifications (such as cutting ventilation holes in panels) would have to be carried out on site. The assembly crew volunteered to work continuously for three days and nights. At triple rates the overtime payments were enormous but the consignment went on the ship as planned.

Case example 2

An operation for the routine maintenance and servicing of a large fleet of helicopters was causing trouble for an organization because too many aircraft were out of service at any time. Intensive progressing action by management cut the time for each aircraft's annual service from nine weeks to six weeks. The most successful ploy used was to offer the maintenance crews extra leave equivalent to the time saved.

Case example 3

A project manager had to rely on the manufacturing department in his company, over which he had no executive authority. Day after day he was distressed to see partly fabricated steel components for his project stacked in the factory with no sign of progress. Representations to management, first at junior and then at more senior level, had no effect.

During one lunch break, when the factory was deserted, this project manager took three strong colleagues into the factory, selected a large component weighing about 75 kilos, carried it into the works manager's office and laid it across his polished desk (which, unfortunately, was scratched in the process). The result was immediate, explosive, extremely unpleasant, but completely effective for that project and its successors.

In all of these examples, success was achieved through the project manager's determination and by motivating (in different ways) the key people.

IMMEDIATE ACTION ORDERS

One solution to the handling of really urgent priorities relies upon the use of special 'immediate action orders'. These are printed on highly distinctive card or paper, either brightly coloured or covered with vivid red or bright orange stripes, making them difficult to ignore. Fluorescent ink is ideal, the brighter the better. An example is illustrated in Figure 24.6.

Special measures are necessary to ensure that a proper degree of urgency and respect is always afforded to immediate action orders:

- Immediate action orders must be designed so that they stand out easily from all other documents, and cannot be ignored.
- Each order must be authorized at very senior level (for example, the managing director).
- Only one immediate action order may be in force at one time in the organization.

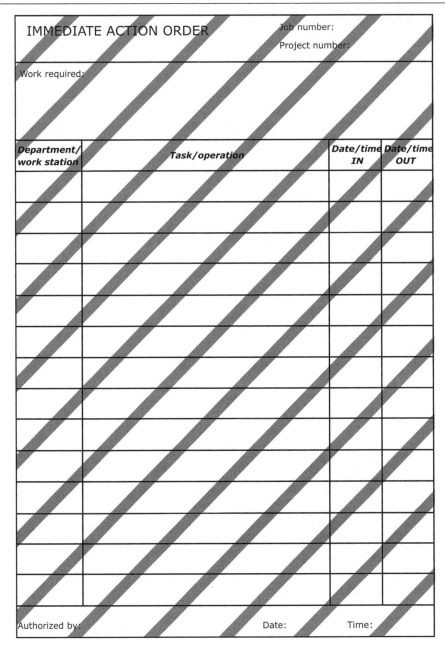

Figure 24.6   Immediate action order

- Immediate action orders must be hand-carried from department to department, and from workstation to workstation, with the date and time of entry and exit stamped against each operation.
- Every department named for action on an immediate action order must give the specified work absolute priority and interrupt other work if necessary – *immediately*.
- All possible means must be devoted to achieving the work, regardless of expense. For example, a vehicle or aircraft may have to be sent to collect vital components or materials from a supplier. Special prices might have to be paid to suppliers to compensate them for any urgent action.

Immediate action order case example

A project for a complex defence weapons system was under way, part of which was a rocket-borne radar unit. One of the components was a miniature 3000-volt transformer and, at the time of this incident, a single prototype was being made. The transformer was highly specialized, and required intricately machined parts, very careful winding, and awkward assembly. Because of its small size and high voltage, the transformer had to be encapsulated in epoxy resin before it could be used or even tested. This meant that, in the event of failure, none of the components could be reclaimed and used again.

The prototype transformer failed its insulation test. This left the project without a key component, and with an apparent transformer design problem. The prototype had taken six weeks to produce, with rigid inspection routines imposed throughout because of the requirements of HM Government. The idea of having to wait a further six weeks for a replacement, on top of the delay while the engineers sorted out the design problem, was simply out of the question.

The project manager prepared an immediate action order for design correction and manufacture of a new transformer. The order was authorized, but only after the project manager had convinced the company's general manager that the transformer really was critical, and desperately needed.

The first result of issuing the immediate action order was to preclude the possibility of any further immediate action orders being issued. Only one was allowed to be in force at any time.

A progress chaser was assigned full-time to the order, and he started by taking it to the chief engineer, placing it on his desk, and stamping the date and time of arrival against the 'investigate failure and modify design' operation. The investigation was put in hand immediately and the failure of the first unit was found to be due to air bubbles in the encapsulating resin. The engineers modified the design slightly to reduce the risk of air being trapped during the moulding process. The presence of an impatient progress chaser with a time-stamp in his hand, the general manager's signature, the vivid design of the order sheet, and the knowledge that a post-mortem examination would be carried out afterwards to look at all the in and out times caused such a flurry of activity that modified manufacturing drawings were ready and printed within about one hour of the immediate action order being signed.

When the order and the new drawings reached the manufacturing department, one operation required the use of a milling machine, but all machines were in use. Another job was therefore stopped and the workpiece was removed, half finished, from a milling machine to make way for the immediate action order. All the other components were made ready within a very short time, on the same day.

The quality management department had been warned in advance, and they inspected and passed the work without delay, but they did ensure that the required quality standards were maintained. The progress chaser stayed with the job, and continued time-stamping the order in and out of each department or workstation, through winding, assembly, resin encapsulation and final testing.

The new transformer passed all its performance tests. Without the impetus given by the immediate action order, this job would undoubtedly have taken at least six weeks. In fact it took only three days. Of course the cost was high, and might have been higher still had any special actions been needed to get materials. But the project programme was saved. In total terms, the cost of crashing all the transformer activities was easily compensated by the cost saving made in preventing a six-week slippage of the whole project.

The reasons why such dramatic success was achieved should be appreciated. In the first place, the order was rare and commanded immediate attention from all concerned. It was not 'just another high priority order' but was one of only about six issued by the company in a full year. Assigning a progress chaser to the job full-time meant that no component was left unattended on a rack at any time to await collection and transport to its next operation. Further, the high level of authorization, together with the sense of urgency created by time-stamping the arrival and departure times for each department, left absolutely no doubt in any mind regarding the genuine nature of the crash action request.

If special cases for priority are to be allowed, these must be strictly limited in number. But, once any job has been given top priority status, then all the force and weight of management must be used to back up that decision and ensure that the job is carried right through without interruption. There must be no half measures.

CONSTRUCTION SITE ORGANIZATION AND MANAGEMENT

The organization and management arrangements at a construction site obviously depend on the size and duration of the project and on the location of the site.

Coordination and planning

The need for planned coordination of construction activities is self-evident. Otherwise bricklayers might arrive to start building walls before the footings had been finished, electricians would turn up too early, the roofing contractor might arrive after the scaffolding had been removed, construction plant and building materials would be unavailable when wanted, or in places where they were not wanted, and so on.

Facilities

The main contractor will have to ensure that adequate site office provisions are made, with the usual facilities such as furniture and filing cabinets, telephones and other communications equipment, computers, stationery and a photocopier, all probably housed in a site hut or other temporary accommodation. Space or more detailed provision must also be made for site supervisors and others from the more important subcontractors. All of this is routine, established practice which no competent main contractor or site manager needs to be told.

However, the situation becomes far more complex when the project is very large and the site is remote. There may be no existing communications, power or water supplies. Setting up the site facilities and making all local arrangements then becomes a big project in itself, requiring very detailed planning well in advance. The main contractor might have to coordinate the provision of roads, temporary accommodation for site management and workers, secure stores, catering facilities, hospital, banking arrangements and much more. This is yet another case where the value of a checklist developed from previous experience is likely to be invaluable.

An organization for the site of a large construction project that has no special communications or location difficulties is shown in Figure 24.7.

Construction quality

Where the site is within the jurisdiction of a local authority, the local building inspector might be one of many who would be watching the quality of workmanship, materials and building methods. In addition to the main contractor's engineers, the subcontractors' own managers should be supervising their work. Architects, surveyors and even the client could be expected to take more than a passing interest. On some projects the client might appoint its own independent expert representative or consulting engineer to check on quality and progress.

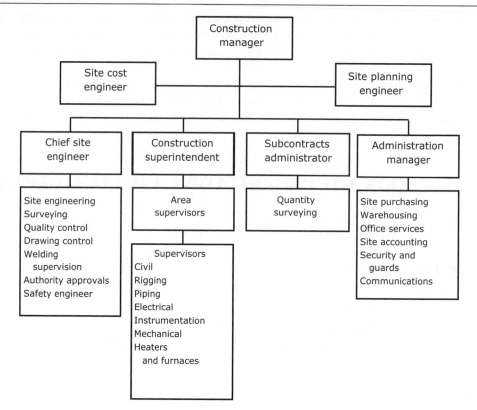

Figure 24.7 Construction site organization

With all these people bearing and sharing responsibility for quality, why should anything ever go wrong? When it does, some months after the building has been occupied, the main contractor might have quite a problem in deciding where to lay the blame and how to pass on the costs of rectification. Adequate records of all site meetings, subcontract documents, inspection reports, site incidents, photographs and so on should all be filed safely back at head office for subsequent retrieval.

Construction progress measurement

Progress monitoring and measurement has to be carried out not only to maintain the programme, but also to enable the subcontractors to generate claims for payment. These claims will have to be certified by an independent quantity surveyor. The main contractor, in turn, will probably be billing the client for progress payments on the total project, and these claims too must be supported by certificates.

PROJECT MEETINGS

Purpose of meetings

All who are concerned with engineering or projects will know that much time can be taken up by meetings. One client of mine seemed always to have its senior engineering staff locked in meetings and, when I complained of this to the engineering director I was told, 'Whenever we have a problem we kill it with meetings.' That was a successful company, so maybe he had a point. However, there are many reasons why meetings can be necessary. Meetings can be used to:

- inform
- collect and discuss data
- gather ideas through brainstorming
- consider proposed changes
- make rules and regulations
- hear grievances
- resolve disputes
- allow fruitful debate
- make collective decisions
- solicit action
- issue instructions and commands.

Perhaps it is not surprising that many organizations always seem to be plagued by having too many meetings. Different kinds of meetings encountered in projects include:

- pre-project sales meetings
- project kick-off meetings
- planning meetings
- cost estimating meetings
- technical design meetings
- ad hoc informal meetings
- site meetings
- change committee meetings
- meetings with suppliers
- meetings with subcontractors
- meetings with the client
- regular progress meetings
- irregular progress meetings (panic sessions)
- final handover meeting and celebration.

Administration of meetings

The chairperson bears responsibility for the conduct and arrangement of meetings. The project manager will often be in the chair. On manufacturing projects it is possible that some progress meetings will be chaired by a production manager. Architects often chair progress meetings for construction projects. There are many other possibilities.

Administrative arrangements should ensure, for example, that:

- a meeting room of suitable size has been reserved;
- appropriate visual aids are in place and functioning;
- there is adequate ventilation;
- visitors are met and conducted with courtesy to the meeting room;
- messages and incoming telephone calls are not allowed to interrupt the proceedings (a telephone able only to make outgoing calls can be a useful feature);
- refreshments are provided, if appropriate.

All those invited to the meeting should be given an agenda in advance, so that they have time to prepare their contributions, arguments or exhibits.

Overnight accommodation might have to be arranged for delegates travelling long distances. Otherwise, meetings should not be timed to start too early in the day if that would cause inconvenience to visiting delegates (especially those from the client).

Some argue that meetings should be scheduled for mid to late afternoon, so that there is an incentive to get proceedings over and done with as quickly as possible. On the other hand, people tend to be more alert early in the day, and more creative and collective brainpower is likely to be available then to deal with any knotty problems. The chairperson will have to decide which option is best for the particular occasion and the types of people expected to attend.

Resolving arguments or conflict

Arguments sometimes break out during meetings. These may not be altogether undesirable because meetings must be kept alive, with enthusiasm encouraged (provided always that any heat generated can be contained within extinguishable limits). However, arguments must be resolved within the meeting, so that agreement is reached before the members disperse. If that is not done, continuing friction can result, which is an entirely different condition from healthy enthusiasm and team cooperation.

In project work, responsibilities often fall between two or more departments, one of which can usually manage to lay blame at the other's door for any shortcomings or apparent negligence. Manufacturing problems or delays, for instance, might be blamed on poor design or on unreasonable rejections by inspectors. On some occasions these criticisms will have some foundation. At other times they will not. When such conflicts arise they must be resolved quickly. Unprofitable stalemate conditions must not be allowed to persist and disrupt team harmony.

The chairperson has a clear duty to discover the true facts which underlie any interdepartmental or interfunctional problems, not so much to apportion blame as to ensure the continued progress of the project for which they are responsible.

Sometimes an impasse is reached where two departmental managers give separate and conflicting accounts of the reasons for a common problem. There is only one way in which to overcome such arguments. The opposing individuals must be allowed to confront each in the presence of a responsible mediator, which in this case will usually be the chairperson. Each individual should now be more reluctant to make excuses that distort the exact truth, because they know that instant denial of any unjust criticism will be forthcoming from the opponent.

More constructively, the person-to-person discussion possible in meetings removes the communication delays that exist between impersonalized departments, often allowing solutions or compromises to common problems to be agreed on the spot.

Was the meeting successful?

When a meeting breaks up, it will have been successful only if all the members feel that they have achieved some real purpose and that actions have been agreed which will benefit the project. Demands made of members during the meeting must be achievable, so that promises extracted can be honoured.

Issuing the minutes

Publication of the minutes must be undertaken without delay in order that they do not become outdated by further events before distribution. Minutes should be clearly and concisely written, combining brevity with clarity, accuracy and careful layout, so that each action demanded can be seen to stand out from the page. Documents that are too bulky may not even be read by everyone. Short, pointed statements of fact are all that is required.

No ambiguity must be allowed after any statement as to who is directly responsible for taking action. Every person listed for taking action must receive a copy of the minutes (an obvious point that is sometimes overlooked). Times must be stated definitively. Expressions such as 'at the end of next week' or 'towards the end of the month' should be avoided in favour of actual dates.

Simple but effective meetings control procedure

Trevor Bentley (1976) described a simple form and set of rules which I have found effective for the management of meetings. The control form, an adaptation of Bentley's design, is shown in Figure 24.8.

MEETING ACTION SHEET	Meeting/project reference number	
Date, time and place		
Those to attend:		
Meeting called by (chairperson):		
Purpose of meeting and agenda:		
Decisions agreed:		
Actions agreed:	Action by whom?	Action by when?

Figure 24.8 Combined meeting agenda and action sheet

Source: After Trevor Bentley (1976), Information, Communications and the Paperwork Explosion (Maidenhead: McGraw-Hill)

The person calling the meeting (usually the chairperson) fills in the agenda on a form and lists all those invited to attend, after telephoning as many of them as possible to check that the proposed time and place will be convenient. Copies of the form are then distributed to all the members, preferably at least a week in advance of the meeting.

When the meeting takes place, the chairperson's copy of the form is used to record the proceedings. The first action is to tick or encircle the names of those who actually turn up. Decisions and actions agreed during the meeting are written on the chairperson's copy during the progress of the meeting.

Just before the meeting breaks up, the chairperson's copy of the form, now complete with all its annotations, is photocopied. Each member of the meeting is given a copy as he or she leaves. Thus instant issue of the minutes is achieved. All the decisions taken and actions are recorded exactly as they were agreed during the meeting, fresh in people's minds.

Bentley recommends that a copy of the control form, with its agreed actions, should be sent to the chairperson's immediate superior after each meeting. Then, if a meeting fails to result in any positive decision or action, the chairperson would be asked to explain why the meeting had been called and what purpose it had served.

Progress meetings

Any project manager worthy of the title will want to make certain that whenever possible his or her tactics are preventative rather than curative. If a special meeting can be successful in resolving problems, why not pre-empt trouble by having regular progress meetings, with senior representatives of all departments present?

Regular progress meetings provide a suitable forum where essential two-way communication can take place between planners, managers and other project participants. The main purposes of progress meetings emerge as a means of keeping a periodic check on the project progress, and the making of any consequential decisions to implement corrective action if programme slippages occur or appear likely to occur.

There are certain dangers associated with the mismanagement of progress meetings. For instance, it often happens that lengthy discussions arise between two specialists on technical issues that should be resolved outside the meeting. Such discussions can bore the other members of the meeting, waste their scarce and expensive time, and cause rapid loss of interest in the proceedings. Although it is never possible to divorce technical considerations from progress topics, design meetings and progress meetings are basically different functions which should be kept apart. Discussions should be kept to key progress topics, with irrelevancies swept aside.

The frequency with which meetings are held must depend to a large extent on the nature of the project, the size and geographical spread of its organization, and its overall timescale. On projects of short duration, and with much detail to be considered, there may be a good case for holding progress meetings frequently, say once a week, on an informal basis at supervisor level. For other projects, monthly meetings may be adequate. Meetings at relatively junior level can be backed up by less frequent meetings held at more senior level. Project review meetings, which can cover the financial prospects as well as simple progress, can also be arranged: the company's general manager may wish to attend such meetings and for some capital projects the customer might also wish to attend or be represented.

Meetings held more frequently than necessary create apathy or hostility. Supervisors and managers are usually busy people whose time should not be wasted.

Case example of progress meetings abandoned

The above account of progress meetings adheres to the conventional view that progress meetings are an accepted way of project life. Here is some food for less conventional thought.

A heavy engineering company had long been accustomed to holding progress meetings. Depending on the particular project manager, these were held either at regular intervals or randomly whenever things looked like going badly adrift (most readers will have encountered such firefighting meetings). Several projects were in progress at any one time, and the permanent engineering department of about 60 people was often augmented by as many as 80 subcontracted staff working either in-house or in external offices.

Meetings typically resulted in a set of excuses from participants as to why actions requested of them at previous meetings had been carried out late, ineffectually, or not at all. Each meeting would end with a new set of promises, ready to fuel a fresh collection of excuses at the next meeting. This is not to say that the company's overall record was particularly bad, but there was considerable room for improvement and too much time was being wasted at meetings.

Senior company management, recognizing the problem, supported a study which led to the introduction of critical path network planning for all projects, using a computer to schedule resources on a multi-project basis. The computer printed out detailed work-to lists, filtered and sorted for the attention of the relevant departmental managers using WBS and OBS codes.

Two progress engineers were engaged, one to follow up in-house work and the other to supervise outside subcontractors. Both engineers had the benefit of the work-to lists, which told them exactly which jobs should be in progress at any time, the scheduled start and finish dates for these jobs, how many people should be working on each of them, how many people should be working in total on each project at any time and the amount of remaining float available for every activity.

By following up activities on a day-by-day basis in accordance with the work-to lists, these two progress engineers succeeded in achieving a considerable improvement in progress and the smooth flow of work. If a critical or near-critical activity looked like running late, stops were pulled out to bring it back into line (by working overtime during evenings and weekends if necessary). Fortunately, all the staff were cooperative, grateful (in fact) for the new sense of order created in their working lives.

After several months under this new system it dawned on all the company managers that they were no longer being asked to attend progress meetings. Except for kick-off meetings at the introduction of new projects, progress meetings had been made redundant.

PROGRESS REPORTS

Internal progress reports to company management

Progress reports addressed to company management must set out the technical, fulfilment and financial status of the project and compare the company's performance in each of these respects with the scheduled requirements. For projects lasting more than a few months, such reports are usually issued at regular intervals, and they may be presented by the project manager during project review meetings.

Discussion of a report might trigger important management decisions that could lead to changes in contract policy or project organization. For this and many other reasons it is important that data relevant to the condition and management of the project are presented succinctly and factually, supported where necessary by explanations and forecasts.

Internal reports often contain detailed information of a proprietary nature. They might, therefore, have to be treated as confidential, with their distribution restricted.

Progress reports to the client or customer

The submission of formal progress reports to the client or customer could be one of the conditions of contract. If the customer does expect regular reports then, quite obviously, these can be derived from the same source that compiled all the data and explanations for the internal management reports. Some of the more detailed technical information in the internal reports may not be of interest to the customer or relevant to its needs. Customer progress reports, therefore, are often edited versions of internal management reports.

Whether or not financial reports accompany customers' progress reports will depend on the main contractor's role in each case. Under some circumstances cost and profitability predictions must be regarded as proprietary information, not to be disclosed outside the company. In other cases, the project manager may have to submit cost summaries or more detailed breakdowns and forecasts as part of an advisory service to the customer.

Although customer reports may have to be edited in order to improve clarity and remove proprietary information, they must never be allowed intentionally to mislead. It is always important to keep the customer informed of the true progress position, especially when slippages have occurred that cannot be contained within the available float. Any attempt to put off the evil day by placating a customer with optimistic forecasts or unfounded promises must eventually lead to unwelcome repercussions. Nobody likes to discover that they have been taken for a ride, and customers are no exception to this rule.

REFERENCES AND FURTHER READING

Burke, Rory (1999), *Project Management: Planning and Control*, 3rd Edition (Chichester: Wiley).

Devaux, S. A. (1999), *Total Project Control: a Manager's Guide to Integrated Planning, Measuring and Tracking* (New York: Wiley).

Gray, B., Gray, C. F. and Larson, E. W. (2005), *Project Management: the Managerial Process*, 3rd Edition (Singapore: McGraw-Hill).

Hartman, F. T. (2000), *Don't Park Your Brain Outside* (Newtown Square, PA: Project Management Institute); brimful of common sense for the more advanced reader.

Kerzner, H. (2006), *Project Management: A Systems Approach to Planning, Scheduling and Controlling*, 9th Edition (New York: Wiley); expensive but authoritative and encyclopaedic.

Lewis, J. P. (2001), *Project Planning Scheduling and Control: a Hands-on Guide to Bringing Projects in on Time and on Budget* (New York: McGraw-Hill).

Meredith, J. R. and Mantel, S. J. jnr (2003), *Project Management: a Managerial Approach*, 5th Edition (international edition) (New York: Wiley); good for its wealth of case studies.

Nicholas, J. M. (2004), *Project Management for Business and Engineering* (Elsevier).

Rosenau, M. D. jnr (2005), *Successful Project Management: a Step-by-Step Approach with Practical Examples*, 4th Edition (New York: Wiley).

25 *Managing Changes*

N o project of any significant size can be expected to run from start to finish without at least one change. The exception to this rule might exist as a project manager's dream of Utopia, but is unlikely to assume any more tangible form. My definition of a project change is:

a departure from the approved project scope or design as indicated by a change to any contract, drawing or specification after its approval and issue for action.

IMPACT OF CHANGES IN RELATION TO THE PROJECT LIFE CYCLE

Changes are usually unwelcome to a project manager at any stage, but changes that occur towards the end of a project have the potential to cause greater cost and disruption than those which are mooted before the project begins.

When a project is in its proposal or business plan stage, any proposed change in the scope or nature of the project may cause some annoyance and result in more investigations, revised financial appraisals and fresh planning. However, the same change when a project is nearing completion would be disastrous, meaning that much of the work in progress or completed would have to be scrapped and restarted.

Thus it is a general rule that the later the change happens, the greater the cost and disruption it will cause. This is illustrated in Figure 25.1.

ORIGIN AND CLASSIFICATION OF CHANGES

Changes can arise from a customer's request that changes the project scope or specification, a self-inflicted engineering design modification, or through some reason during work on the project that causes the finished result to differ in some respect from the issued drawings, specifications or other formal instructions. Changes (and therefore change management) can sometimes be needed even after the project has been finished and handed over to the customer. Figure 25.2 shows many routes through which changes can develop in, for example, a manufacturing project.

Classification of changes

Changes can usually be placed in one of two principal commercial categories namely:

- changes originating from within the contractor's own organization without any involvement from the customer or client;
- changes requested by the customer or client.

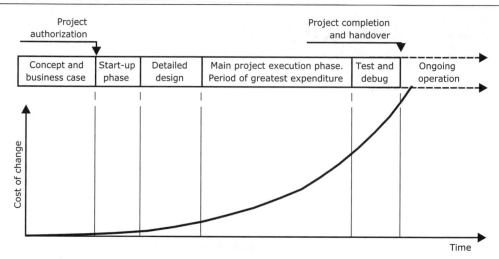

Figure 25.1 Cost of a given change in relation to project life cycle phases

There are, however, some borderline cases which cannot be put into either of these two classifications but which contain elements of both. A more useful way of classifying changes from the commercial point of view is to label them as 'funded or 'unfunded'. For a funded change the customer must take responsibility for the change and pay for it. For unfunded changes the contractor will have to absorb all the costs, with consequent risk to budget limits and expected profits. Whether or not a change is to be funded or unfunded will greatly influence how it is considered for authorization.

Funded changes

Changes to the specified project requested by the customer automatically imply a corresponding change to the contract, since the project specification should form part of the contract documentation. If, as usually happens, the modification results in an increase in the contractor's costs, a suitable change to the contract price must be negotiated. The delivery schedule may also be affected and any resulting delays must be predicted, discussed and agreed.

Customer-funded modifications may possess nuisance value and can disrupt the smooth flow of logically planned work, but they do nevertheless offer the prospect of compensation through an increase in price and possibly an increase in profit. When a customer asks for a change, the contractor is in a strong price-bargaining position because there is no competitor and the contractor has a monopoly.

Customer-funded changes are usually documented as purchase order amendments or contract variation orders (otherwise known as project variations).

Unfunded changes

If a contractor finds it necessary to introduce changes for reasons unconnected with the customer, it is hardly likely that the customer could be expected to pay (unless the changes are covered by some contingency for which provision was made in the contract). The contractor must be prepared to carry the additional costs, write off any scrapped work and answer to the customer for any resulting time delay. For these reasons, contractors have to be particularly wary about allowing unfunded (which really means contractor-funded) changes to proceed.

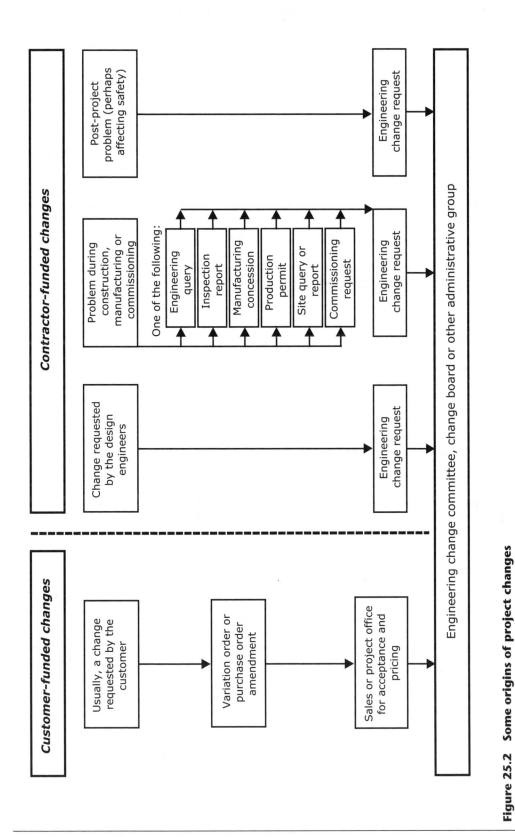

Figure 25.2 Some origins of project changes

The procedure for introducing an unfunded modification into an active project usually starts by raising a document called an engineering change request, engineering change order, modification request or some permutation of these terms. Some reasons for unfunded changes are shown in Figure 25.2 and the relevant documentation is described later in this chapter.

Permanent and temporary changes

Changes can be further classified as permanent or temporary:

- **Permanent changes** are carried out with the intention of leaving them permanently embodied in the design and execution of a project, and which will remain recorded in drawings and specifications to show the true as-built condition of the completed project.
- **Temporary changes** may be needed for expediency in getting a project finished, but they are carried out with the intention of either removing them or converting them to some alternative permanent change at a later, more convenient time.

AUTHORIZATION ARRANGEMENTS

The effects of any change, whether customer-requested or not, may be felt far beyond the confines of the project area that is most obviously and directly affected. This could be true of the technical, timescale or cost aspects. Most projects have to be regarded as a combination of technical and commercial systems, in which a change to one part can react adversely or beneficially with other parts of the system. Such reactions can bring about consequences that the change's originator may not have been able to foresee.

For these reasons alone it is prudent to ensure that every proposed change is considered and approved by selected key members of the project organization before it can be implemented. This precaution means that the overall effects can be predicted as reliably as possible. These selected referees form the 'change committee' or 'change board'. In some organizations, perhaps in larger companies, the change committee might be a properly constituted body that meets regularly in formal meetings. In small project organizations the arrangement is usually far less formal, but there must nevertheless be some means for change consideration and approval at senior level.

Change committee or change board

In many companies engaged on project work a regular panel of experts is appointed to consider changes and decide how they are to be handled.

Managers in or represented on the committee must include those who are able to answer for the safety, reliability, performance, cost and timescale consequences of changes, the effects on work-in-progress, on purchases, and on the feasibility or otherwise of introducing the change into manufacture or construction.

In projects involving the nuclear industry, aviation, defence or other cases where reliability, safety or performance assume great significance, two key members of the committee represent:

- the *design authority* – typically the chief engineer;
- the *inspecting authority* – a person such as a quality manager who should be independent and able to make assessments on the basis of quality alone, without commercial pressure.

Change committee meetings

Change committees for large projects often meet on a frequent, regular basis, dealing with change requests in batches. Others avoid meetings by circulating requests around the committee members, so that each member considers the effect of the proposed change on his or her own area of responsibility. Each method has its advantages and disadvantages. If formal committee meetings take place at monthly intervals, the wait for change decisions can hold up progress or result in the greater disruption to work that late changes cause. On the other hand, frequent committee meetings take up too much members' time. Informal committees, not meeting collectively but relying instead on the circulation of documents, suffer from a communication problem and can take longer to discuss and resolve misunderstandings or make decisions. Neither approach can be classified as right or wrong, but it will be assumed here that a formal procedure exists, with a change committee meeting at regular intervals (perhaps weekly).

Decision criteria

When each change request is considered for approval, the committee must weigh up all the possible consequences before making its decision. Points which need to be examined are listed below (not necessarily in order of importance):

- Is the change actually possible to make?
- Is it a customer-requested or a self-inflicted change?
- What is the estimated cost of the change?
- Will the customer pay? If so, what should be the price?
- If the change is not customer-requested, is it really necessary? Why?
- What will be the effect on the project time-scale?
- How will safety, reliability and performance be affected?
- If several identical sets of equipment are being produced, at what point in the production sequence should the change be introduced?
- Will scrap or redundant materials be created?
- Are any items to be changed retrospectively? Are these:
  - in progress?
  - in stock?
  - already delivered to the customer or otherwise built into the project?
- What drawings, specifications and other documents will have to be modified?

Figure 25.3 illustrates some of the steps in the change handling process.

Change committee's response

When the committee has considered all these questions, it has the following options:

- authorize the change as requested;
- give limited approval only, authorizing the change with specified limitations;
- refer the request back to the originator (or elsewhere), asking for clarification or for an alternative solution;
- reject the change, giving reasons.

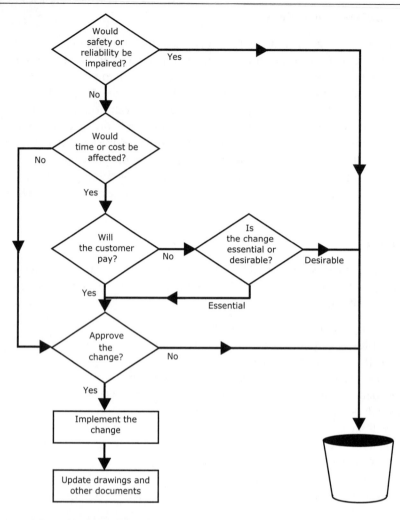

Figure 25.3　Decision tree for change requests

GENERAL ADMINISTRATION

Use of standard change request forms

Individuals who wish to request a change should always be asked to put their request in writing. This chapter is written on the assumption that all such requests will be addressed to a change committee. Where the organization does not operate a formal change committee, a suitably senior member of the organization, such as the chief engineer, should be designated as the person responsible for considering and authorizing changes.

To save the committee's time and to ensure that all requests are properly controlled and progressed, some kind of standard change request form must be used. This form should be designed in such a way that the originator is induced to answer in advance all the questions that the change committee will want to ask. In some projects, even the customer can be persuaded to submit change requests using the contractor's standard forms.

Because there are several routes along which changes can arise within any organization (see Figure 25.2) there are usually several different forms that can result in change requests. These forms are illustrated later in this chapter, in the section 'Forms and procedures'. However, the administration procedures described here are generally applicable to all of these different forms.

Change coordinator

In any project organization where changes are expected (which really means all project organizations) it is advisable to nominate a change coordinator. This is not usually a full-time role, and the person chosen will probably carry out other clerical or administrative duties for the project. The change coordinator may reside in a contracts office, the project manager's administration group, project support office, the engineering department or in some other department. His or her duties are likely to include:

- registering each change request and allocating serial numbers;
- distributing and filing copies of the change documents;
- following up to ensure that every request is considered by the change committee without avoidable delay;
- distributing and filing copies of the change documents after the committee's instructions have been given;
- following up to ensure that authorized changes are carried out and that all drawings and specifications affected by the change are updated and re-issued.

Numbering and registration

Upon receipt of any change request, the coordinator should enter brief details in a register. Apart from their initial use in allocating serial numbers, change registers are important for several other reasons, which include the following:

- to provide a base from which each change request can be progressed through all its stages, either to rejection or to approval and full documentation and implementation;
- to record changes in budgets and, if appropriate, prices so that the current valid budgets and prices will always be known;
- to provide a search base that allows tracking back ('traceability') so that the origins of all design and commercial changes can be found or verified, both during the life of the project and afterwards.

Change registers can be pages in a loose-leaf folder or, subject to safeguards against accidental erasure and loss, they can be held in a computer. Separate registers should be kept for project variations, engineering change requests, engineering queries, production permits and inspection reports. Usually a slightly different register format is used for each of these registers, but Figure 25.4 shows a fairly typical layout.

The change coordinator must allocate serial numbers from the appropriate register. The numbering systems should be kept simple, but must be designed so that no number is repeated on another project or in another register. The simple solution is to prefix each change with either the project number or a shorter code that is specific to the project, and to add one or two letters which denote the type of change. For example, if the project number is P123, engineering change request forms might be numbered in the series P123/ECR001, P123/ECR002, P123/ECR003 and so on. Concessions or production permits for the same project could be numbered in the series P123/PP001, P123/PP002, P123/PP003, and so on.

CHANGE REGISTER

Project number: Sheet number:

Serial number	Originator		Date requested	Brief details or title	Approved? (Yes or no)	Date of final distribution	Budget change (if any)
	Name	Dept.					

Figure 25.4   General-purpose change register

Distribution

The change coordinator's first duty after registering each change request is to arrange for its distribution. This process will be speeded up if the forms are stocked in multi-part sets or distributed via a network.

A typical distribution for any change request might be:

- engineering manager or chief engineer (who may wish to arrange further distribution within his or her department)
- change committee chairperson (the original 'top copy')
- other change committee members.

The originator should retain a copy, and the coordinator will keep another on a 'changes pending file', with a different file for each type of form in use.

Progressing

To prevent undue delays, or even the risk of forgotten requests, change registers should be designed to highlight all those requests that are 'active'. That means all requests which have yet to be approved or rejected. For example, a column can be provided on the register sheet headed 'final issue date' or something similar. The absence of a date in that column tells the coordinator that the change is still active and in need of monitoring and progressing.

Ideally, the coordinator should be able to use the registers to follow up the action after approval, to ensure that the relevant drawings and specifications are updated and re-issued.

ESTIMATING THE TRUE COST OF A CHANGE

Most changes will add to the cost of a project. Changes made late in a project often attract higher costs than those introduced earlier, because sunk costs are then higher and late changes can cause greater disruption to work in progress, causing scrap and rework.

It is not always appreciated that the total costs of an engineering modification can far exceed the straightforward estimate of costs directly attributable to the modification itself. A simple example will help to demonstrate some of the extra incidental costs which can be introduced when a change is made to a project.

Case example: competition car project

Suppose that a project is in hand to produce two competition cars within the main factory of AB Cars Ltd, (the ABC company) whose primary work is the quantity production of cars for sale to the general motoring public. The two special cars are being supplied to another company, Universal Wheeled Vehicles (UWV) Ltd. This is a normal commercial contract specified in UWV's purchase order to ABC. The two competition cars are identical. Although these cars are built from standard components, practically everything about them is special. The engines originally specified are standard production units from the works stores, but they will have to be stripped down, modified, rebuilt and bench-tested before they can be fitted.

During final assembly of the two cars the ABC company is informed that the two engines will not comply with the competition rules, a mistake which has arisen because UWV did not realize that its copy of the rules was out of date. UWV is, therefore, liable for any additional costs and has submitted an amendment to the original purchase order.

Suitable replacement engines are not available within ABC, but engines that will satisfy the competition rules can be purchased as modified stock engines from an outside company. These engines require different mountings, and some changes to the inlet and exhaust configuration.

When asked to forecast the cost of this change, ABC's cost estimator might produce a set of figures something like those shown in Figure 25.5.

In reality, however, it might take 12 weeks to get the new engines modified, prepared and delivered, during which time the project might have to be shelved temporarily. Even assuming that the fitters could be gainfully employed elsewhere in the works, it is unlikely that the total costs of the change would be limited to the basic £12 760 estimated. The cars, together with work benches, jigs, cradles, measuring equipment and special tools would probably occupy some 100 square metres of prime work space. Even when no work is taking place this accommodation still attracts costs in terms of rent, business rates, heating, maintenance, cleaning, insurance, security and so on. These costs might amount to £300 per square metre per annum.

Here is an example of overhead under-recovery. The cost of providing 100 square metres of idle factory floor space for 12 weeks would be nearly £7000, a sum not recovered in the selling price calculated in Figure 25.5.

Labour costs: £	£
Cost of removing old engines	
5 hours at £20 per hour	100
Cost of preparing two new engines	
60 hours at £20 per hour	1 200
Cost of modifying engine mountings	
10 hours at £20 per hour	200
Cost of fitting new engines	
20 hours at £20 per hour	400
Sundry other charges	
10 hours at £20 per hour	200
Testing and fine tuning	
30 hours at £20 per hour	600
Total direct labour cost	2 700
Overheads at 80 per cent	2 160
Materials:	
Two bought-out modified engines	6 000
New exhaust manifolds	600
New inlet manifolds	400
New fuel injection equipment	300
Total materials	7 900
Basic estimate	12 760
Contingency allowance (5 per cent)	638
Estimated total factory cost of modification	13 398
Mark up (40 per cent)	5 359
Additional project price for changing two engines	18 757

Figure 25.5　Car project: estimated modification cost

Other projects for which the space and facilities are needed could suffer a knock-on effect from the delay. Also, failure to meet the programme in the early part of a project can be reflected in increased activity later on, and this can cause problems and additional costs as a result of crash actions and overtime working.

Modifications often affect stocks of materials by making them redundant. It is not uncommon for items of quite high value to be forgotten completely, simply because they are out of sight in a store.

A direct result of the error in starting with the wrong engine might be that the cars are not ready in time for the competition, leading to damaged prestige and possible loss of prize money and other benefits.

If the error in choosing the wrong engines had been the fault of the ABC company, and not that of UWV Ltd, matters would have been far worse. The change would have to be classified as unfunded but essential, and the contractor would have to bear all the costs, both estimated and hidden. It would then have been quite likely that UWV would seek compensation from ABC for its losses by way of liquidated damages or by invoking a contract penalty clause for late delivery. The order might even be cancelled (with no possibility of redress, because ABC would have been judged to be at fault).

Assessing all the possible cost factors

Just as changes tend to cost more later in the project cycle, so they become more difficult to evaluate as project time passes. In an ideal world all individuals would include all possible costs of modifications in their estimates. Unfortunately the project manager must expect that some cost factors will be overlooked, whilst others might be impossible to evaluate. Checklists and searching questions can help to reset an estimator's train of thought:

- Is there to be no inspection and retesting on this job?
- Will existing stocks be affected?
- Will there be any purchase order cancellation costs?
- Will this change affect the prototype too?
- What about work-in-progress – how much of that will have to be scrapped and done again?
- How much will all the resulting delays cost?

Such questions must always be asked about the possible costs of changes, but the true answer will often be very difficult to establish.

Recording the actual cost of a change

Some of the difficulties to be expected in assessing the true costs of a change have now been outlined, and it is apparent that there are many factors which can easily be overlooked. Nevertheless, an estimate can be made in most cases, and this can be used to work out and justify any possible increase in price that the contractor feels able to demand.

Recording the actual costs of a modification can prove to be a far more difficult undertaking: it may even be impossible. Difficulties underlying the measurement and recording of actual modification costs may not always be appreciated by some managers and others who, quite reasonably, would like to know just how much their budgets are being affected by change.

Case example

Suppose that a modification is to be performed on a 'fuzzelbox', which is a complex piece of electronic equipment containing over 1 km of wire, thousands of electrical connections, piping and valves and many other components.

First, take the case where the fuzzelbox has already been assembled, inspected and fully tested. Here there need be no problem in identifying the cost of the change, because a fresh works order or job ticket can be issued for the modification work and materials, complete with a new cost code. All the subsequent work of stripping, changing, inspecting and retesting can be attributed directly to the change.

Now consider the different (but frequent) case in which drawings and specifications are modified during the course of manufacture. The fuzzelbox is in a semi-completed state, so that the modification will add new wires, delete others, re-route wires and pipes not yet installed and result in changed connections and components. How can anyone be expected to record accurately that part of the work which is directly attributable to the modification?

It is quite possible that many changes will occur on a job of this size before it is finished, so that the only apparent and measurable effect on costs will be an increase of expenditure compared with the initially estimated production costs. This situation has to be accepted and, if the modification costs are needed for any purpose, they will have to be estimated.

FORMS AND PROCEDURES

This section describes some of the routes through which changes can reach a project, together with their origins and associated forms (these routes were illustrated in Figure 25.2). The authorization and general administration procedures already described in this chapter will apply generally to all of these forms.

When is a formal change procedure necessary?

When a designer, in a fit of rage or despair, tears up a drawing or clears the computer screen and starts again, there is no need to invoke a formal change engineering procedure. Any new design might have to undergo many such interruptions and changes before it is committed to a fully-checked and issued drawing. This is all part of the normal, creative development process. Provided that the design intentions remain within the requirements of the design specification, any internal changes made before drawings are formally issued are not generally considered to be modifications or engineering changes, even though they might prove expensive.

Some companies circulate early, pre-issue drawings for discussion, advance information or approval. These issues are often distinguished from the fully released versions by labelling them as revision A, revision B and so on, changing the revision numbers to the series 0, 1, 2 and so on to denote official releases. A rule might, therefore, be suggested that formal engineering change procedures need only be applied to drawing revisions made after the first issue for manufacturing or construction. But such a rule can fall apart if preliminary issues are made for the manufacture of a prototype, in which changes must be properly controlled.

Another reason for invoking formal procedures is found whenever there is an intention to depart from the design specification, especially when the development work is being carried out for an external customer. This, again, is a case for using the formal change procedure before any drawing has been issued for manufacture or construction.

Some rule or criterion is needed that can determine at which point in the design process the formal change procedure should be introduced. The key question to be asked is 'Will the proposed change affect any instruction, specification, plan or budget that has already been agreed with other departments, the customer or other external organization?' If the answer to this question is 'Yes', the probability is that formal change committee approval will be needed.

Design freeze

Sometimes project organizations recognize that there is a point in the design and fulfilment of a project after which any change would be particularly irksome, inconvenient or potentially damaging. This leads to the announcement of a 'design freeze', after which the change committee will refuse to consider any change proposal unless there are compelling reasons, such as safety or a customer request. Ideally the customer should also agree to be bound by the design freeze. In some companies the design freeze stage is called 'stable design'.

Project variation orders

Changes requested by the customer which affect price, delivery or any other aspect of the original purchase order or contract require formal documentation. The request document should fulfil the following functions:

- It amends the purchase order or contract and describes the change.
- It authorizes the contractor to make the change.
- It promises payment.
- It records agreement to any associated timescale revision.

Where the original contract was in the form of a purchase order, the customer will usually request a change by issuing a purchase order amendment. In other cases, especially for projects involving construction, changes are recorded on project variation orders (sometimes called simply 'project variations' or 'contract variations'), an example of which is given in Figure 25.6. Similar changes arranged by a main contractor with site construction subcontractors are often known as site variation orders.

Quick procedure for simple, repetitive project variations

In projects where a considerable number of small changes are expected, it may be possible to streamline all the change procedures, perhaps with a prearranged scale of charges. Naturally such a procedure must be restricted to changes of a routine nature, where safety and reliability cannot be affected. Provided that the scope of a change can be defined adequately, and that the work can easily be identified separately from other project work, the costs of small changes can be recovered on some agreed time and materials basis or, for construction projects, against an agreed schedule of rates per units of measured work.

Case example

A contractor was engaged on a defence contract for designing and building automatic test equipment for the electronic systems installed in military aircraft. Each complete tester was housed in a trailer which could be towed out to an aircraft, connected by cables, and left to carry out a whole range of measurements, 'go' or 'no-go' checks and diagnostic fault-finding routines.

Every time the aircraft manufacturer (the customer) wanted to change any of the test parameters a small amount of software reprogramming was necessary in the test equipment. This happened many times during many months of prototype commissioning at an airfield. Some changes also required one, two or three wires to be re-routed as quick temporary fixes. Attempting to estimate the cost of each of these hundreds of changes and subjecting all of them to a formal change committee procedure was out of the question. Yet every change had to be recorded for incorporation into manufacturing drawings, and somehow the contractor had to recover the additional costs.

PROJECT VARIATION ORDER	PVO number:
	Project number:
Project title:	Issue date:

Summary of change (use continuation sheets if necessary):

Originator: Date:

Effect on project schedule:

Effect on costs and price: Cost estimate ref:

Customer's authorization details: Our authorization:

Distribution:

Figure 25.6   Project variation order

These difficulties were resolved by both companies agreeing to a set common price for all these trivial program changes. Simple, serially numbered, all-one-price, program change request forms were printed in triplicate on serially numbered no-carbon-required pads for use at the airfield. These documented the technical details of each change, were authorized by the signature of the customer's engineer, and accepted for on-the-spot action by the contractor's senior commissioning engineer. One copy of each change form was kept by the customer's engineer, and another was returned to the contractor's head office, where the relevant drawings and programming records were updated at regular intervals.

Weekly invoices were sent to the customer listing the serial numbers of all the changes in each batch. No technical details or descriptions were needed on the invoices, which were priced simply by multiplying the number of changes made each week by the standard price. The system was limited by mutual agreement to include only the simple changes to measurement parameters and test-point switching. Many hundreds of these changes were requested, actioned and billed using these very simple pre-priced request forms. That saved valuable time at the commissioning site, with the contractor collecting a satisfying level of revenue and the customer freed from the expense of preparing, negotiating and issuing a formal contract variation for every change.

Engineering change requests

The purpose of an engineering change request is to describe, document and seek formal permission for a permanent design change. The change may be unfunded, or it might be the result of a project variation order and, therefore, funded. Engineering change requests of the type shown in Figure 25.7 are used widely in engineering projects, although they may be known by different titles, invariably abbreviated to sets of initials. The following are among those which may be encountered:

- ECR – Engineering Change Request
- ECO – Engineering Change Order
- MR – Modification Request

There is no reason why any person, however junior, should not be allowed to originate an engineering change request because it can have no effect until it has been authorized by the change committee. The method for completing the form should be self-evident from Figure 25.7.

Concessions or production permits

Manufacturing departments, faced with the need to keep to a budget or to accomplish work within a scheduled timescale, sometimes find that they need to depart from the specific instructions contained in the manufacturing drawings to achieve their objective. Naturally, the quality control department will keep a wary eye open to ensure that no unauthorized shortcut or botching is allowed.

Suppose, however, that a drawing specifies the use of chromium-plated screws, but that these are simply not available when required. The purchasing department may be able to obtain alternative screws with a cadmium plate finish, or possibly some other thread size could be substituted. If the production team decided to make this substitution without reference to the design engineers, there would be a danger (remote in some companies) of an inspector noticing the difference and rejecting the work because it deviated from the drawing.

But would the use of these alternative screws really matter? It all depends, of course, on the actual circumstances and whether the screws are in a prominent position where they will be easily seen if they do not match adjacent chromium parts. Someone has to decide, and either authorize or reject the change.

Other requests for concessions might not be simply cosmetic. The use of alternative materials, different adhesives and acceptance of wider tolerances are all reasons for originating requests for concessions. These might represent a risk to performance, reliability, safety or interchangeability. As a general rule, therefore, concessions require the formal approval of the design authority.

Concessions (or production permits) usually fall into the classification of temporary changes. It is unlikely that the drawings will be updated to suit the change, it being assumed that the manufacturing department will either be able to adhere to the drawings in any future production, or will apply for a further concession.

Procedures for requesting concessions vary greatly from one company to another. They can range from the very informal 'Is it all right if we do it this way instead, George?' to a rigid discipline

ENGINEERING CHANGE REQUEST	ECR number:
Project title:	Project number:

Details of change requested (use continuation sheets if necessary):

Drawings and other documents affected:

Reason for request:

Originator: Date:

Emergency action requested (if any):

Effect on costs: Cost estimate ref:

Will customer pay,   yes ☐   no ☐   If yes, customer authorization ref:

Effect on project schedule?

COMMITTEE INSTRUCTIONS: CHANGE APPROVED ☐   NOT APPROVED ☐
Point of embodiment, stocks, work in progress, units in service, special restrictions etc:

Authorized by: Date:

Figure 25.7   Engineering change request

supervised by the quality control department. Rigid procedures can be expected in the defence, aerospace and nuclear industries, and in any other case where safety and quality rank high as objectives. Figure 25.8 shows a suitable form.

The reasons for instituting a formal concession discipline are fairly obvious, because any departure from the instructions contained in issued drawings or specifications must be either disallowed or treated with a great deal of caution. Concession records may have less significance than other project records once a project has been finished and handed over to the customer. Nevertheless, they can prove useful in the quality and reliability control function. Concession records are part of

```
┌─────────────────────────────────────────────────────────────────────┐
│ PRODUCTION PERMIT/CONCESSION                                          │
│                                                                       │
│ Drawing/spec. number:              Application number:                │
│                                                                       │
│ Revision number:                   Project or job number:             │
│ ┌───────────────────────────────────────────────────┬───────────────┤
│ │ Batch or product serial number(s) affected:        │ Is work held  │
│ │                                                     │ up?           │
│ │                                                     │   Yes: ☐      │
│ │                                                     │   No:  ☐      │
│ ├─────────────────────────────────────────────────────────────────── │
│ │ Application to allow non-compliance with the above drawing or       │
│ │ specification as follows:                                           │
│ │                                                                     │
│ │                                                                     │
│ │                                                                     │
│ │                                                                     │
│ ├─────────────────────────────────────────────────────────────────── │
│ │ Reason for this application:                                        │
│ │                                                                     │
│ │                                                                     │
│ │                                                                     │
│ │ Requested by:          Department:              Date:               │
│ ├─────────────────────────────────────────────────────────────────── │
│ │ Engineering assessment                                              │
│ │                                                                     │
│ │   Performance/reliability?                                          │
│ │                                                                     │
│ │   Health and safety?                                                │
│ │                                                                     │
│ │   Interchangeability?                                               │
│ │                                                                     │
│ │ For Engineering Department:                     Date:               │
│ ├─────────────────────────────────────────────────────────────────── │
│ │ Decision                                                            │
│ │   Granted: ☐    ─────────────────────   ──────────                  │
│ │                 For design authority         Date                   │
│ │   Refused: ☐    ─────────────────────   ──────────                  │
│ │                 For quality/inspecting authority   Date             │
└─────────────────────────────────────────────────────────────────────┘
```

Figure 25.8   Production permit or concession

the project records which a contractor needs to keep in order to trace the possible causes of poor performance, faults or failures in equipment after delivery. If one of a number of identical units should fail in service, it could be vital to trace all other units containing the same concession in order to prevent further failures.

The procedures associated with the granting of concessions can exist in a variety of permutations and combinations of the methods described in this chapter. Whichever method a company decides to adopt, the concession register will be complementary to the manufacturing drawings, modification records, inspection and test records, and build schedules in defining the exact composition of the completed project.

Engineering query notes

A feature of projects is that the manufacturing or construction drawings and specifications are usually completely new and untried. It is not surprising, therefore, that a higher incidence of problems in manufacture or construction is a characteristic of project work. These problems can range from design errors to difficulties in interpreting the drawing instructions. Design errors must, of course, be corrected by the re-issue of amended drawings, for which the full-scale engineering change procedure will usually be invoked. Simple problems associated with the interpretation of drawings can be resolved by an explanation on the spot from the appropriate engineer. Between these two extremes lies a no man's land of operational difficulties that are not a direct result of design errors, but which demand more than a simple explanation to get work on the move again.

In some firms any problems that cannot be resolved on the spot are channelled into a formalized 'engineering query' procedure, which relies on the use of forms similar to that shown in Figure 25.9. The general idea is that the works supervisor who comes up against a problem explains the difficulty on one of these forms and submits it to the engineering department for investigation and reply. Naturally, this system can only operate effectively and be accepted if each query is afforded reasonably urgent consideration. The advantages provided by adopting this routine are that all queries can be registered and progressed by the coordinating clerk to ensure that none is forgotten. Regrettably, one engineering director whom I knew preferred the formal system because it kept production personnel, together with their overalls, oil and grease, out of the nice clean engineering design offices.

Case example

Suppose that a specified adhesive, when used according to the appropriate process specification, failed to produce the specified bond strength, so that when the unfortunate worker removed the clamps his or her careful work disintegrated into its constituent parts. The supervisor would need to ask the engineers what to do, and that can be done using an engineering query note.

If this problem proved too difficult to sort out on the spot, the engineers might be forced to return the query note with a temporary solution suggested. The instruction might read: 'Clean off adhesive, and use six equally-spaced pop rivets instead. Drawings will be modified and re-issued.'

Conversion from engineering query to production permit

If, as in the above example, an engineering query note is returned to a production department with instructions that conflict with those given in the manufacturing drawings, the query note becomes a document that carries authority to deviate from drawings. It has therefore become a concession or production permit.

Because engineering query notes are often converted into concessions in this way, companies that use them should consider combining the concession and engineering query systems into one procedure, with a single common-purpose form designed to cope with both needs.

Inspection reports

Suppose that a block of extremely expensive raw material has been subjected to many hours of machining by highly skilled operators but, on final inspection, one of the measurements is found to be marginally outside the limits of tolerance. Too much material has been cut away; the error has resulted in the work being undersized and no rectification is possible. Any inspector would have to reject the job. In most companies the inspector would fill in an inspection report ticket or form, detailing the 'non-conformance'.

```
┌─────────────────────────────────────────────────────────────────────────────┐
│                                                                               │
│  ENGINEERING QUERY NOTE                                                       │
│                                                                               │
│  Drawing/spec. number:                      EQN number:                       │
│                                                                               │
│  Revision number:                   Project or job number:                    │
│                                                                ┌──────────────┤
│  Other relevant drawings or specifications:                    │Is work held up?│
│                                                                │              │
│                                                                │  Yes:  ☐     │
│                                                                │              │
│                                                                │  No:   ☐     │
├───────────────────────────────────────────────────────────────┴──────────────┤
│  Details of query or problem:                                                 │
│                                                                               │
│                                                                               │
│                                                                               │
│                                                                               │
│                                                                               │
│                                                                               │
│                                                                               │
│                                                                               │
│                                                                               │
│  Query raised by:              Department:              Date:                 │
├───────────────────────────────────────────────────────────────────────────────┤
│  Answer:                                                                      │
│                                                                               │
│                                                                               │
│                                                                               │
│                                                                               │
│                                                                               │
│                                                                               │
│                                                                               │
│                                                                               │
│                                                                               │
│  For Engineering Department:                            Date:                 │
├───────────────────────────────────────────────────────────────────────────────┤
│  Engineering follow-up action required (if any):                              │
│                                                                               │
│                                                                               │
│                                                                               │
│                                                                               │
└───────────────────────────────────────────────────────────────────────────────┘
```

Figure 25.9   Engineering query note

The relevant design engineers, if shown the inspection report, might decide that the error was too trivial to justify scrapping such an expensive workpiece. Perhaps it could still be used for the project or, alternatively, it might be possible to use it for a prototype assembly on the understanding that it must never be re-fitted into another assembly. A design engineer having the appropriate authority might feel able to annotate the inspection report accordingly, thus countermanding the inspector's rejection.

This is another method by which a job can be passed through an inspection stage, even though it does not conform to the issued drawings. The inspection report has been translated by the design authority into a concession or production permit.

Figure 25.10 shows an inspection report form which anticipates the possibility of subsequent conversion into a concession in appropriate cases.

VERSION CONTROL FOR MODIFIED DRAWINGS AND SPECIFICATIONS

It is necessary here to consider one or two pitfalls that can trap the unwary project engineering staff into issuing drawings or specifications that are not what their revision numbers would make them seem to be.

Issue of incorrect versions

Diazo prints and translucent 'reproducibles' or 'submasters' are easily recognizable as copies and are thus unlikely to be confused with original documents. With today's reprographic techniques and laser printers, however, copies of drawings are indistinguishable from their originals. Drawings produced from computer files can be printed at will on plain paper, so that more than one apparently original version of any drawing can easily exist.

Unless rigid safeguards are introduced, any designer can alter the design information in the computer and then cause a new 'original' to be produced without making the necessary change to the drawing or revision number. Unless there is a central drawings registry for the control and issue of drawings, there is no independent check to prevent such mistakes and measures must be devised to prevent the issue of drawings with incorrect revision numbers.

Case example

I once asked a design engineer to produce some layouts of a new design office. He began by measuring the accommodation area and producing an accurate drawing showing all the walls, doors, columns, windows and so on. He filed that drawing in his computer as a template, on which he overlaid all the subsequent electrical, lighting, partition and staff seating drawings. Every drawing that he produced still bore the original template number in its title box. Unfortunately that mistake was not realized until the local authority's planning inspector spotted it, to our acute embarrassment.

Interchangeability rule

The usual practice when a drawing is changed is to re-issue it with a new revision number. If, however, a change results in a manufactured component or assembly being made different from other items with which it was previously interchangeable, it is not sufficient merely to change the drawing revision number. The drawing number itself (and therefore the part number) must also be changed.

This is a golden rule to which no exception should ever be allowed, whether the item is a small component or a big assembly.

Case example

Suppose that a project requires the use of 1000 small spacers, and that after 500 had been produced in brass the design was cheapened to use mild steel. These spacers are truly interchangeable, and the part number need not be changed. But the drawing for the steel spacers would be given a new revision number.

```
┌─────────────────────────────────────────────────────────────────────────────┐
│  INSPECTION REPORT                          Report number:                    │
│                                                                               │
│  Project number:           Job number:            Report date:               │
├───────────────────────────────────────────────────────────────────────────────┤
│  Details of work inspected or tested:                                         │
│                                                                               │
│     Drawing number:                  Revision:                                │
│                                                                               │
│     Specification number:            Revision:                                │
│                                                                               │
│     Batch or serial number(s) affected:                                       │
├───────────────────────────────────────────────────────────────────────────────┤
│  Details of nonconformance:                                                   │
│                                                                               │
│                                                                               │
│                                                                               │
│                                                                               │
│                                                                               │
│                                                                               │
│                                                                               │
│                                                                               │
│                                                                               │
│                                                                               │
│                                              _____ Inspector/tester│
├───────────────────────────────────────────────────────────────────────────────┤
│  Application for concession (if required)                                     │
│         The above nonconformance will not affect reliability, safety or interchangeability│
│  Further comments                                                             │
│                                                                               │
│                                                                               │
│                                         ┌─────────┐                           │
│                                         │ Agreed  │                           │
│                                         ├─────────┤                           │
│  Requested by: _____ │ Refused │ _____ Design authority         │
│                                         └─────────┘                           │
├───────────────────────────────────────────────────────────────────────────────┤
│  Disposal instructions                                                        │
│                                                                               │
│            Scrap and remake:    ☐                                             │
│     Rectify and reinspect/retest: ☐                                           │
│          Concession granted:    ☐                                             │
│                                    _____               │
│                                    For inspecting authority/quality manager   │
└───────────────────────────────────────────────────────────────────────────────┘
```

Figure 25.10   Inspection report

Now suppose that the spacer design had been changed from metal to moulded nylon because on some later manufactured assemblies it became necessary for the spacers to be electrically insulating. The old metal spacers can no longer be used on all assemblies. The metal and nylon spacers are not interchangeable. The drawing for the nylon version of these spacers must therefore be given a new drawing number.

EMERGENCY MODIFICATIONS

We live in an impatient age, and project time can usually be regarded as a scarce commodity. If the need for an essential modification is discovered during the active production phase of a programme, there may simply be no time available in which to issue suitably changed drawings. There are right and wrong ways of dealing with this situation and the following case is an example of the latter.

Case example – the Kosy-Kwik Company

Project setting

Kosy-Kwik was a company which specialized in the design, supply and installation of heating and air-conditioning systems. In 1990 it was awarded a contract, as subcontractors to a large building group, to plan and install all the heating and ventilation arrangements in a new multi-storey office block commissioned by the Coverite Insurance Company Ltd, who wished to use it for their headquarters. Two engineers, Clarke and Jackson, were assigned to the project. Whilst Clarke was given overall design responsibility, Jackson was detailed off to plan the central control panel and its associated controls and instrumentation.

Early difficulties

We join the project near the end of the preparation period in the Kosy-Kwik factory. By this time most deliveries of plant and equipment had been made to the Coverite premises, except for the control panel, which was still being fabricated, later than scheduled.

Jackson was a conscientious engineer who took a great interest in his jobs as they passed through the factory. He was in the habit of making periodical tours (management by walking about) to keep a check on progress and the results of his design. During one of these tours the sheet metal shop foreman pointed out to Jackson that the almost-completed control panel was decidedly weak and wobbly.

Jackson could only agree with the foreman. The front panel was indeed decidedly flimsy, as a result of a glaring design error in specifying a gauge of steel that was far too thin. Delivery of this panel to site was already late, and threatened to delay the whole project. There was simply no time available in which to start building a new control panel. In any case, the extra cost would have been unwelcome. A simpler solution had to be found – a rescue package in fact.

Marked-up drawings

The engineer asked the foreman to weld some suitably chunky pieces of channel iron to the rear face of the panel in order to stiffen it. The foreman agreed, but was worried about getting the job past the inspection stage with the changes. 'No problem!' said Jackson, who took a pen from his pocket, marked up the foreman's copy of the drawing with the channel iron additions, and signed it to authorize the alteration.

The modification was successful. Everyone concerned was very relieved, not least Jackson, whose reputation had been likely to suffer. Only a few hours were lost, and the panel was duly delivered. The remainder of the project went ahead without further mishap, and the Coverite Insurance Company Ltd joined the long list of Kosy-Kwik's satisfied customers.

Follow-up project

In the summer of 2000 Kosy-Kwik were awarded a follow-up contract by the Coverite Insurance Company. Their offices were to be extended, with a new wing to house computer services and staff. Coverite were working to a well-planned but tight schedule, which demanded that the new wing should be opened on the first working day of 2001. Because of the rigid timescale restrictions, several contract conditions were imposed on Kosy-Kwik. In particular, the only complete shut-down period allowed for the existing heating and ventilating plant (for connecting and testing the additional circuits and controls) was to be during the December 2000 Christmas break. Otherwise the Coverite Company would suffer loss of work by their office staff. There was also to be a penalty payment of £500 for every week or part of a week by which Kosy-Kwik failed to meet the scheduled end-date.

During the ten years which separated these two projects several changes had occurred in the Kosy-Kwik organization. Clarke received well-deserved promotion to a remote branch office, where he became area manager. Jackson retired to enjoy his pension. The engineering department expanded, and attracted several new recruits. Among these was Stevens, an experienced contract engineer. He had no means of contact with Clarke or Jackson, and would never meet either of them.

Preparation for the new project

Stevens was appointed as engineer in charge of the new Coverite project. He knew that the best policy would be to prefabricate as many parts of the project as possible in the factory. This would reduce the amount of work to be done on site, and ensure that the final link-up and testing could be accomplished during the Christmas break. Stevens found a roll of drawings labelled 'Coverite Project' in a dead file drawer, dusted them off and set to work.

Most of the system was found to be straightforward, and the final tying-in with the existing installation was to be achieved by providing the installation engineers with a bolt-on package that could be fitted to the original control panel. This package was duly designed, manufactured and delivered to site along with all the other essential materials. By the time Christmas arrived, all equipment, pipes and ducts were in place in the new part of the building. All that remained was for the final installation team to arrive, shut down the plant, modify the control panel with the kit provided, and then test and set-up the whole system.

Installation attempt

Early on Christmas Eve, two Kosy-Kwik fitters were sent to shut down the plant and start work on the control panel. Their first job was to cut a large rectangular hole in an unused part of the original panel in order to fit the new package. A template had been provided for this purpose, which they now placed in position. When they started cutting, the engineers met unexpected resistance in the shape of several large channel iron ribs welded to the rear face of the panel. The engineers had come prepared only to tackle the thin sheet shown on the old drawings. It took them over two hours and many saw blades before the hole was finished. Then they found that the connections to the new control package were fouled by what remained of the channel iron. Worse still, the panel was now weak and wobbly again.

The two engineers were experienced and trained as skilled installation fitters, but were equipped neither materially nor mentally to deal with problems of this magnitude without help. They suffered an acute sense of frustration and isolation, although they found different (much shorter) words with which to express their feelings.

A cry for help was indicated. Unfortunately, however, the response to their impassioned telephone call to Kosy-Kwik headquarters was less than satisfactory. Against the background noise of a lively office party they learned that all the senior engineering and management staff had already left to begin their Christmas holidays. The telephone operator wished the fitters a 'Merry Christmas' and suggested that they 'Have a nice day'. The two engineers interpreted these greetings as good advice, gave up and went home to start their unexpected holidays.

The extra cost

There is no real need to dwell at length on the consequences of this case, or to describe the scenes of anguish and recriminations back at headquarters in the New Year. A short summary of the additional cost items follows:

		£
1	Design and manufacture new control panel modification kit	3500
2	Cost of time wasted time during first visit of the two fitters	500
3	Cost of repairing weakened panel, on site	180
4	Contract penalty clause, 4 weeks at £400 per week	2000
	Total additional costs, directly attributable	6180

Post mortem

A retrospective glance at the circumstances leading to the disastrous consequences of the Coverite project provides a useful basis for describing a more reliable method of dealing with very urgent modifications.

In this example, all troubles can be traced back to the use of a marked-up drawing on the sheet metal shop floor, the details of which were not incorporated in the filed project drawings. The use of marked-up drawings is generally to be deplored, but we have to be realistic and accept that there will be occasions when they are unavoidable, when there is simply no time in which to update the master drawings or computer file and issue new copies of the drawing. Under these circumstances, some sort of temporary documentation must suffice, but only where safeguards are in place to ensure that the original drawings do get changed to show the true 'as-built' condition of the project.

Safeguards

One way in which the updating of final drawings can be safeguarded in the event of emergency changes relies on a streamlined version of the formal modification procedure, which does not bypass any of the essential control points.

The originator of an emergency modification must write out an engineering change request in the usual way and get it registered by the change coordinator. After seeking the immediate approval of the chief engineer (or the nominated deputy), the originator must pass one copy to the design office in order that the change will eventually be incorporated in the drawings. Another copy of the change request is kept by the coordinating clerk, who must make certain that it is seen at the next change committee meeting.

The original change request form is passed to the production department for action, where it becomes part of the issued manufacturing instructions, so that there is no need to wait for the official issue of revised drawings.

If a working copy of a drawing does have to be marked up, which may be inevitable if there is insufficient space to show all the details on the change request form, an *identical* marked up copy must be deposited in the design office, together with their copy of the change request. The original change request must accompany the job right through all its production stages, particularly until it reaches final inspection and testing.

26 *Managing Project Costs*

Many things can happen during the life of a project to distort the expected rate and magnitude of expenditure or to delay expected revenues. The direction of change is usually disadvantageous. Some of the reasons may be unavoidable or unforeseen but, in many cases, the fault will lie somewhere within the project organization. The principal purpose of cost control is to ensure that no preventable wastage of money or unauthorized increase in expenditure is allowed to happen.

Strictly, cost management means far more than the control of expenditure. It also includes the control of revenue, making sure that all possible and justifiable income is recovered from the customer or other possible sources. Cost management involves ensuring not only that the amounts of money spent and received are in accordance with budgets, but also that the timing of each transaction is appropriate and in line with the scheduled cash flows.

Cost management is not a separate function of project management. While it is true that some people specialize in the cost aspects of project management, possibly holding titles such as 'cost and planning engineer' or even the more specialized 'cost engineer', their roles are part of a far wider framework of project cost control, which must involve many people working throughout the project organization.

A common misconception is to confuse cost reporting with cost control. Accurate and timely cost reporting is essential but cost *reporting* is not the same as cost *control*. By the time overspending has been measured and reported, damage has already been done. Cost accountants (although they might be called cost and management accountants) spend most of their time in measuring, analysing and reporting costs, revenues and trends, but not in actually controlling expenditure.

This chapter begins with a section on cost (expenditure) control principles, but much of what follows here and in Chapter 27 is necessarily concerned more with methods for measuring, analysing and reporting project costs.

PRINCIPLES OF COST CONTROL

Understanding the main elements of project costs

Cost control methods depend to a very large extent on the nature of the costs, so it is first necessary that project managers understand the different categories of costs they will have to deal with. Some of these issues were discussed in Chapter 4, in the context of cost estimating, and the definitions given in the beginning of Chapter 4 are also relevant here. It is convenient to repeat some of these definitions in the following paragraphs.

Figure 26.1 illustrates the main cost elements that make up the costs of a typical project. These split into two main groups, as follows:

- **Variable costs** – costs that are incurred at a rate which is proportional to the rate of working on the project: these are generally the same as the *direct* costs. 'Direct' means that these costs can be measured and associated directly with, and only with, a particular job or project.
- **Fixed costs** – costs that with few exceptions constitute the company's overhead or *indirect* costs. 'Indirect' means that these are costs incurred generally in running the business, so that they cannot be directly associated with any one of several projects that might be in progress. The only exception to this rule is where the company has been specially created to conduct only one project, in which case of course all the company's costs can be directly associated with that project.

Figure 26.1 shows that the variable costs split into two additional subcategories, namely:

- the costs of purchasing direct materials, services and hired tools, plant and equipment;
- the direct labour costs (wages, salaries and related employer's expenses).

CONTROLLING VARIABLE COSTS

Materials and expenses

Materials and expenses often constitute more than half the costs of a project, and controlling their costs is thus particularly important. Cost control is exercised by following sensible purchasing procedures, as described in Chapter 23. By far the most important act of cost control is exercised at the point of commitment, which means when the purchase order is issued or a contract is signed.

Once a contract has been made with a supplier, the buyer's competitive advantage has gone and the seller has a one-to-one monopoly when fixing the price of subsequent order amendments or cancellation costs. It is generally important to avoid purchase order amendments as far as possible, because these can push costs over budget.

The hire of plant and machinery is a special case, because the costs of these items depends not only on the initial contract terms, but also upon the length of time for which the hire continues. To some extent these hirings combine the characteristics of both variable and fixed costs. Thus progress

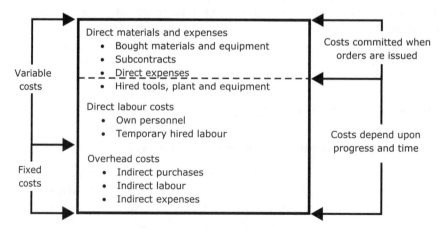

Figure 26.1   Project cost elements in the context of cost control

management is a principal factor in controlling hire costs. For example, the costs of scaffolding on a construction site can be significant. If a construction site is left unattended through bad weather or whilst the workforce is redeployed elsewhere, the hire charges for scaffolding will continue to accrue to the project.

Direct labour costs

A job that finishes on time will generally incur only the budgeted labour costs, which should be derived from the original cost estimate. Obviously that depends on using only the amount of labour resources (people) intended and listed in the project resource schedules or work-to lists. Conversely, jobs that run late tend also to overrun their budgets.

The exception here would be a job into which extra resources and overtime have been injected to accelerate a critical task to prevent it from running late. Although this job might then finish on time, it will incur additional costs as a direct result of the additional resources used. However, those additional costs will usually be more than compensated by the time (and therefore costs) saved for the whole project.

Thus good motivation of people and the control of progress are very important factors in controlling direct labour costs.

CONTROLLING FIXED COSTS AND OVERHEAD COST RECOVERY

Whatever the industry, management must always strive to keep the fixed (indirect or overhead) costs as low as possible in relation to the variable (direct) costs, because high overheads can kill a company's chances of being competitive in the marketplace.

Project manager's control of fixed costs

Most project managers work in premises or environments where they can have no substantive influence on the organization's fixed costs. The project manager is not usually responsible for the periodic costs of accommodation, heat and light, sales and marketing, accounting, communications or the salaries and other expenses of general management.

However, as Figure 26.2 indicates, these fixed (overhead) costs are incurred by the organization every day, without fail, whether or not any work takes place on the project. A feature of fixed costs is that they continue to accrue, in the background, for as long as the project is active, taking up space, and using the company's infrastructure services. Thus, if a project runs late, it will most likely use more indirect costs than expected or budgeted. Figure 26.2 illustrates this condition.

Thus the principal control that the project manager can exercise over fixed costs is to make sure that the project will be finished in time.

Cases where the project manager can exercise limited control over the rate of overhead expenditure

The boundary between fixed costs and variable costs is not always precise. For example, overhead costs, although they are predominately fixed, often contain a variable element. Communications, printing and photocopying are all activities which are often regarded as indirect or overheads, because they are costs incurred in running the business that cannot easily be identified with particular jobs. But these are variable costs, because they will increase or decrease with the level of business activity.

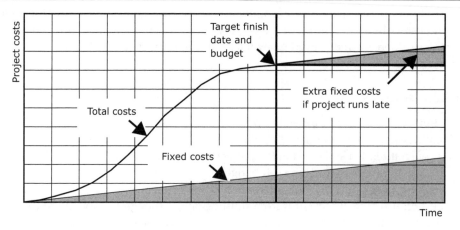

Figure 26.2 Typical project cost/time patterns and the impact of fixed costs

It is in this variable portion of the overhead costs where the easiest and quickest savings can be made by the project manager.

Some contracts allow the contractor to claim reimbursement of sundry expenses such as telephone calls, printing, photocopying and some clerical tasks, provided that these can be identified directly with the project. This is sometimes the case with companies in the mining and petrochemical industries, and for some professional organizations such as architects and legal partnerships.

In organizations carrying out several projects simultaneously it can be awkward to isolate the costs associated with one client or one project but the effort should be made if possible. Although it is unlikely that the sums involved will be large compared with mainstream project activities, they are usually significant and worth recovering. Every expense that can be charged directly against a project should be so charged. Otherwise these expenses will simply inflate the general overhead costs, which must always be kept as low as possible if the contractor is to remain competitive in the market.

Suggested collection methods include:

*   the use of a simple requisition system for all bulk photocopying and other reprographics services, with mandatory use of client or cost codes;
*   mandatory use of cost codes on petty cash vouchers and all expense claims forms;
*   the installation and proper day-to-day management of an automatic call logging system covering all telephone, and facsimile lines.

In one case from my experience this last measure reduced a company's total annual communications bill from £100 000 to £50 000 by preventing fraudulent use. Also, £25 000 of these legitimate £50 000 costs were identified, allocated to their projects, and recovered from clients. So, £75 000 was removed from the company's overhead account for very little expense and effort.

Recovering overhead costs

Most project costing systems work on the basis of charging direct labour costs (including the labour burden) as time recorded on the job multiplied by the standard hourly cost applicable to the grade. An amount is then added to this labour cost (usually as a rate per cent) to recover a part of the company's indirect, overhead costs.

This method of recovering overheads as a levy on direct labour costs is called 'absorption costing'. Setting the percentage overhead rate is a task demanding perception and skill from the organization's cost and management accountants. Getting the answer right depends on accurate workload forecasts and effective overhead cost estimating, budgeting and control.

The overhead rate charged will vary enormously from one company to another, and even from one project to another (because customers sometimes wish to negotiate the amount of a company's fixed costs that they are prepared to fund). Companies with a high level of research and development to fund will probably have very high overhead costs, which might be charged at well over 200 per cent. In labour-intensive industries, with little research and development and no high-grade premises, the overhead rate might be 50 per cent or even less. It is not possible to indicate norms, because the circumstances of companies vary considerably from one to another (even where they are carrying out similar work).

The company which manages to keep its indirect costs (and overhead rate) to a minimum enjoys a competitive cost and pricing advantage.

Clients for large capital projects wield considerable power, and can be very critical of proposed overhead rates chargeable to their projects. They might ask for detailed explanations of what the overhead costs are intended to include. The overhead rate used for a large project might have to be negotiated with the client before a contract can be made.

Overhead under-recovery

If the planned direct workload should fail to materialize for any reason (perhaps through cancelled orders or over-optimistic sales forecasts), the amount of direct labour costs that can be allocated to jobs and charged out in invoices will be less than the forecast. Because overheads have been estimated as a fixed percentage of the direct labour costs, the amount of revenue received to pay for the overheads will also fall below plan. This condition is called overhead under-recovery. The principal remedies to consider include the following:

- increasing the overhead rate (thus increasing prices, which might reduce the quantity of products or project work sold);
- increasing sales by a marketing drive to sell more products or project work;
- persuading each new project client to agree to pay for some jobs previously regarded as indirect. This will depend on being able to identify those jobs and record their costs in a way that would satisfy subsequent audit. Examples of such costs are special printing and copying of project drawings and other documents, telephone calls, travel expenses and so on;
- making economies to reduce the overhead costs. That can lead to painful actions, even to the extent of dismissing administrative staff and managers.

Overhead over-recovery

Overhead over-recovery will occur if workload and direct labour billings exceed expectations, so that the per cent rate set proves to be too high. Although this can increase profitability in the short term, it may not be desirable because it can imply that the company's pricing is not sufficiently competitive, with damaging consequences for future order prospects.

ADDITIONAL COST CONTROL FACTORS

Adherence to cost budgets

Taking the narrowest view, a project contractor should be concerned (for many obvious reasons) that the project is completed successfully without exceeding the planned costs (authorized budgets). In many cases, this is the only cost objective set for the project manager. Most of the conventional cost reporting and control procedures, including those described in this and the following chapter, aim to achieve that objective.

In some cases (for example in internal management change and IT projects) budgets are the only cost consideration. There is no external customer and no profit to be safeguarded: simply the need to contain spending within the amounts previously authorized by the organization's senior management against the business plan.

Where there is a profit objective, it has to be remembered that profits are fragile and easily destroyed by overspending. When a company is operating in a highly competitive market, margins might have to be kept low. If the project is very keenly priced, say for a 10 per cent profit, a budget overspend of only 5 per will halve that profit.

Contractor's responsibility to the customer or project owner

The contractor usually has some degree of responsibility for ensuring that the customer's cost objectives are also satisfied. The most obvious manifestation of this is the firm price contract, in which the contractor's firm *price* is the customer's firm *cost*. Unless the customer rocks the boat by asking for changes, or the contractor goes bankrupt or is otherwise unable to finish the project successfully, the customer can plan capital expenditure with confidence against a fixed budget.

In cost-plus projects, where the contractor is able to mark up costs and pass them on to the client with no fixed price limit, there is less incentive for the contractor to limit costs. In fact, the converse can be true: the greater the amount spent, the greater will be the 'plus' or profit. A long-running cost-plus service contract or an ill-defined reimbursable-cost project can be regarded as a gravy train. Then the contractor has an ethical, but difficult, duty to ensure that:

- only legitimate costs are claimed;
- work is carried out as efficiently as if the contractor were spending its own money.

Where large capital investments are involved, the managing contractor's project manager can have a specific cost management duty to the client, which broadens the cost objective further. The project cost management function then extends to predicting and reporting costs to the client, working with the client to help schedule and control expenditure and marshal the necessary funds.

TOTAL COST APPROACH

The 'total cost' approach is a way of regarding costs holistically, solving logistical problems or otherwise planning to achieve the lowest overall cost. This approach can be used in a wide variety of situations. It has been used, for example, in distribution logistics where decisions have to be made about the location of warehouses and designation of transport methods so as to achieve the lowest possible total distribution costs of retail goods.

Total costs in project management

In the context of project management, total cost considerations mean that managers in the project organization work together, each considering unselfishly how the work contribution of their department is likely to affect the costs incurred by other departments. One example is where a suggested change in design approach, although resulting in greater design difficulties and costs, might save considerable time and money in the resulting production or construction methods. The total cost approach can, therefore, mean increasing the planned expenditure in one department in order to generate greater cost savings in the rest of the organization.

Example

I was once privileged, in the role of planning consultant, to witness a convincing demonstration of the total cost approach in action. The scene was a project-planning meeting in the engineering director's office of a company in the USA. The company was about to start three new projects, each for the design and manufacture of special purpose heavy machining equipment for external customers. The engineering director was in the chair. Also present at the meeting were the chief engineer and other senior engineers, and (significantly) the manufacturing manager and his senior production engineers.

Various design proposals were passed back and forwards between the design engineers and the production people and, one by one, design approaches were agreed that would lead to the lowest total company cost, while maintaining high quality standards. A high level of enthusiasm, motivation and cooperation was generated from the start.

The three projects, planned with multi-project resource allocation and given effective project management, were all subsequently completed on or before time and well below their originally budgeted costs (that is, below the total cost levels previously experienced by the company for comparable projects).

Involving the customer

The true total cost approach should extend to include the costs to be incurred by the customer after the project has been handed over. These are the costs of operating and maintaining the installed equipment or plant. The customer might have to be convinced of the contractor's good intentions, because a higher initial cost might be needed as a justifiable investment in reducing the total life cost.

Example

This principle is well known to the US company mentioned above, who widened their total cost approach to involve their customers in continuous design, quality and cost discussions.

The special purpose machines are sold to customers for machining components in the customers' plants (typically performing all the operations needed to convert rough castings into finished components). Many of these components are complex, such as gear cases, cylinder heads or cylinder blocks for the automotive industry.

In a typical project development, the concept and design of the machines to be supplied, the design and development of the customer's components and the planned methods for operating and maintaining the machines all form part of continuing discussion and cooperation between the supplier's engineers and the customer's engineers.

This process is variously called integrated engineering, simultaneous engineering and (most commonly) concurrent engineering. It strives to achieve the customer's performance and quality requirements at lowest total cost, resulting in a deal that benefits both companies.

CHECKLIST OF COST MANAGEMENT FACTORS

1	Cost awareness by those responsible for design and engineering, preferably involving a 'total cost' approach
2	Cost awareness by all other project participants throughout the life of the project
3	A project work breakdown which yields work packages of manageable size
4	A code of accounts system which can be aligned with the work breakdown structure
5	Cost budgets, divided so that each work package is given its own share of the total budget
6	A cost accounting system that can collect and analyse costs as they are incurred and allocate them with minimum delay to their relevant cost codes
7	A practicable work schedule
8	Effective management of well-motivated staff, to ensure that progress meets or beats the work schedule
9	A method for comparing expenditure with that planned for the work actually done
10	Effective supervision and quality control of all activities to aim at getting things right first time
11	Proper drafting of specifications and contracts
12	Discreet investigation to ensure that the customer is of sound financial standing, with sufficient funds available to make all contracted payments
13	Similar investigation, not necessarily so discreet, of all significant suppliers and subcontractors new to the contractor's experience
14	Effective use of competitive tendering for all purchases and subcontractors to ensure the lowest costs commensurate with quality and to avoid committing costs that would exceed budgets
15	Appropriate consideration and control of modifications and contract variations, including the passing of justifiable claims for price increases on to the customer
16	Avoidance, where possible, of unbudgeted dayworks on construction contracts
17	Where dayworks are unavoidable, proper authorization and retention of dayworks sheets
18	Strict control of payments to suppliers and subcontractors, to ensure that all invoices and claims for progress payments are neither overpaid nor paid too soon
19	Recovery from the customer of all incidental expenses allowed for in the contract charging structure (for example, telephone calls, printing, travel and accommodation)
20	Proper invoicing to the customer, especially ensuring that claims for progress payments or cost reimbursement are made at the appropriate times and at the correct levels, so that disputes do not justify the customer delaying payments
21	Effective credit control, to expedite overdue payments from the customer
22	Occasional internal security audits, to prevent losses through theft or fraud
23	Effective and regular cost/progress reports to senior management, highlighting potential schedule or budget overruns in time for corrective action to be taken.

SETTING AND RESETTING COST BUDGETS

Plainly the initial project cost budgets should be derived from the cost estimates used when the commercial tender or internal business plan was prepared. That means the budgets before the addition of below-the-line allowances and indirect costs. If the target financial benefits are not to be eroded, these budgets must become the maximum authorized levels of expenditure.

The work, organization and cost breakdown structures (WBS, OBS and CBS) described in earlier chapters will allow this control budget to be distributed among the various departmental and functional managers responsible for carrying out all the project tasks.

It is not only the top budget limits that are important, but also the rate at which expenditure is scheduled to take place. That aspect, which was dealt with (in the context of cash flow scheduling) in Chapter 19 will be revisited in Chapter 27 for the purpose of assessing work achieved measured costs.

Labour budgets

Use of man-hours

It is often said, with good reason, that managers and supervisors should be given their work budgets in terms of man-hours rather than as the resulting costs of wages and overheads. The argument is that a manager should never be held accountable for meeting targets where he or she has no authority to control the causal factors. Project managers are rarely responsible for wage and salary levels, increases in wages and salaries, and company overhead expenses. They are, however, responsible for progress and (through supervision) the time taken to complete each work package.

In these chapters, therefore, it is assumed that each manager with budget responsibility will be given, and will be expected to observe, the man-hour budget for every work package under his or her control.

Resetting budgets to cope with project changes

Budgets on most projects are not static. They increase each time a contract variation order results in an agreed increase in the project price. At any time it should be possible for the budget to be stated in terms of its initial amount, additions subsequently approved by the client and, therefore, the total current budget. If possible, these changes to the budgets should be made at work package level so that all parts of the budget remain up to date and valid.

Taking authorized budget changes into account, as time proceeds the typical project budget graph should resemble an *S* curve on to which a stepped rise has been grafted for every significant addition to the budget.

Budget adjustments for below-the-line allowances

If the project spreads over more than a few months, cost escalation and (for international projects) foreign exchange-rate fluctuations will probably have to be taken into account. Any relevant below-the-line provisions for such changes made in the original project estimate, provided they have been built into the pricing or charging structure, can be regarded as 'reserve budgets'. Appropriate sums can be drawn down from these reserves from time to time as necessary to augment the active control budget.

Currency units for foreign transactions

The currency units used in cost estimates, budgets, cost reports and in other project documents are obviously important. For projects conducted entirely within the borders of one country there should be no problem, and the national currency is the natural choice for all budgeting and reporting purposes. If the project is to use imported services or materials, the logical method for expressing both the budget and the expenditure is to convert all sums into the home currency, being careful to state the exchange rate used in each case.

When a project involves working for a foreign client, the contractor may be obliged by the terms of the contract or the agreed project procedures to prepare budgets and report all expenditure in the currency of the client's country, or in some other international currency (such as Euros or US dollars). The currency chosen may then have to become the control currency for the project.

COST COLLECTION METHODS

It can be assumed that every established company will have procedures in place for collecting, analysing and recording project costs. It is important that this analysis and reporting, of both incurred and committed costs, is carried out promptly. If the figures are a month or more old when they reach the project manager, what chance does he or she have of taking action in time to reverse any bad trend?

Most of the procedures for collecting costs and allocating them to the project cost codes are the responsibility of the company's cost accountants but cooperation from the project manager and other operational managers is usually essential to prevent delays and mistakes.

Collecting the costs of bought-in materials and equipment

It can be assumed that the organization's purchasing, accounting and stores procedures will ensure that the costs of materials and bought-in equipment are always collected and recorded. The routine cost accounting systems would normally cover costs associated with the payment of invoices, and the later job costs when materials are issued from stores for manufacturing jobs. The three options are as follows:

- the dates when orders are placed (the committed costs). This is the earliest possible time for monitoring the costs of materials and the most useful for assessing performance against budget;
- the dates when invoices from the suppliers of goods and services are due to be paid (the actual costs);
- particularly for manufacturing projects, job costing that depends on the evaluation of stores requisitions (when the materials are withdrawn from stores for use on the project). That can often be after the suppliers' invoices have been paid.

Figure 26.3 is a graphical representation of these three different methods, each of which has its own advantages and disadvantages. All the curves have one thing in common. Each has been drawn by adding together the materials expenditure on a month-by-month basis as soon as the data are known. The main difference between these curves is the information route through which the cost data have been obtained.

Cost data from committed purchase costs

Whenever the project is of the kind where equipment, materials or subcontracts are ordered specifically for use on the project, the project manager should be concerned particularly to see that

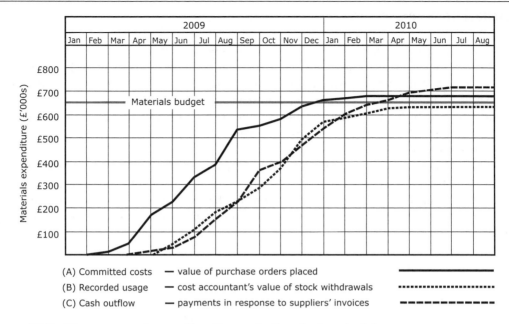

Figure 26.3   Three ways of recording the cost of project materials

a system is in place for recording and tabulating the values of purchase orders as they are placed. This information, at the time of commitment, will give the earliest possible indication of cost trends against the budget (see curve (A) of Figure 26.3). It is unlikely that the purchasing organization or the company's cost accounting procedures will be set up to record committed costs in this way, and cooperation between the project manager and the purchasing organization is essential if this form of communication is to be established and maintained.

Any items already available from general stocks, and which are not to be ordered specially for the project, must of course be allowed for and included in the total commitment. This is easily accomplished: all that is necessary is to withdraw these stocks from general stock and pre-allocate them by transfer into the project stores. The requisitions used to withdraw these materials from production stores can be costed at their standard cost, and the costs added to the total project commitment.

Cost data from stores issues

Curve (B) in Figure 26.3 is the only graph which could be derived in all circumstances, whether stock or project purchasing had been adopted. In this case, the materials costs have been found by valuing all the items listed on stores requisitions or similar paperwork (usually at standard cost) as the items have been withdrawn from stores for use on the project. This method is particularly applicable to manufacturing projects.

Errors can arise owing to discrepancies between the amounts listed and the amounts actually issued or used. Valuations can also be inaccurate if outdated standard costs have been applied. These errors ought not to be significant, however, unless there are serious shortcomings in the stores or costing administration. The real disadvantage of this most usual form of costing only becomes apparent when the results are compared with those obtained from alternative methods. It is not called 'historic costing' for nothing. The project manager would have to wait until after the materials had actually been used before any under- or over-spending trend became apparent. Thus the data obtained from this method will be of no help in controlling project costs.

Cost data from suppliers' invoices

Payments made against suppliers' invoices provide the most accurate account of purchased materials costs for a contract. Project purchasing is an essential condition, otherwise all invoices cannot easily be related to the project being costed. Curve (C) in Figure 26.3 shows how this kind of cost information might build up as the project progresses.

Note that Curve (C) lags behind both the other two curves by an appreciable period. Most invoices will be paid only after the goods have been received or, in many cases, after they have actually been built into the project.

The significant fact which emerges here is that information derived from suppliers' invoices is far too late to be of any use whatsoever in budgetary control. By the time the facts are known, the money has long since been committed and nothing can be done. This emphasizes the importance of measuring and controlling project purchase costs at the point of commitment, which means when the purchase orders are issued.

Comparative accuracy

Before leaving Figure 26.3, observe that all three curves attain different final levels. In this example the differences have been exaggerated deliberately, and in practice no more than about 5 per cent of the total material costs should separate the highest and lowest asymptotes.

The curve of committed costs (Curve (A)), did not quite reach the true final cost value (Curve (C)) owing to slight differences between suppliers' quotations (the amounts shown on the purchase orders and used to compile Curve A) and the final prices actually invoiced. These extra costs arose because one or two purchase orders were placed after the suppliers' quotations were time-expired, and because of incidental expenses, such as freight, packing, insurance, and port and customs duties that were not originally taken into account.

Curve (B) (materials actually withdrawn from project stores) also fell slightly short of the real total as shown by Curve (C). This could imply that some over-ordering took place (leaving some goods in stock at the end of the project). Changes to the scope or specification of the project during its execution might also have led to materials being left unused in stores. When surpluses are accumulated in this way these should really be written off as a charge against project profits, unless they can be returned to the suppliers for full credit or used elsewhere on other projects. Otherwise the surplus materials will only have to be written off at a later date.

Collecting labour costs

General timesheets

A common method for recording and collecting the time spent on projects by professional and other direct office staff on projects is to ask each individual to complete timesheets at regular intervals. Timesheets are usually compiled weekly and require each person to enter the time spent against each relevant cost code or job number, probably expressed to the nearest half-hour. An example of a weekly timesheet is shown in Figure 26.4.

An important part of the timesheet procedure is that the person's supervisor should check and verify the entries before adding an approval signature.

Whatever the method used for collecting labour costs, the time records should be as accurate as possible. If the project is organized as a team, so that everyone works on the project all the time, the only errors to be expected would be in allocations to subcodes within the project. If, however, the organization is a matrix, people might be working on more that one project during a week, or

Job number	Sat'day	Sunday	Monday		Tuesday		Wednesday		Thursday		Friday	
			Normal	O'time	Normal	O'time	Normal	O'time	Normal	O'time	Normal	O'time
	.	.	.	.	.	.	.	.	.	.	.	.
	.	.	.	.	.	.	.	.	.	.	.	.
	.	.	.	.	.	.	.	.	.	.	.	.
	.	.	.	.	.	.	.	.	.	.	.	.
	.	.	.	.	.	.	.	.	.	.	.	.
	.	.	.	.	.	.	.	.	.	.	.	.
	.	.	.	.	.	.	.	.	.	.	.	.
	.	.	.	.	.	.	.	.	.	.	.	.
	.	.	.	.	.	.	.	.	.	.	.	.
	.	.	.	.	.	.	.	.	.	.	.	.

TIMESHEET

Name: _____   Staff number: _____

Department: For week ending:

For accounts department use only

Enter times to nearest half-hour. For holidays use 0096 sickness 0097; special leave 0098; waiting time 0099

Signature: _____   Approved: _____

Figure 26.4   Weekly timesheet

even on the same day, and the apportionment of time between projects becomes more subjective and open to error or abuse.

Staff often have times when they work less efficiently or actually waste time, and there is always a risk that such time will be booked wrongly to the most convenient number available. People should be encouraged to fill in the entries on their timesheets every day. If this chore is left until collection of timesheets at the end of the week, mistakes will inevitably be made as individuals strive in vain to remember what they were doing earlier in the week.

Timesheet errors on firm price contracts can throw up false profit and loss assessments and reduce the value of historical cost records for future analysis and comparative cost estimating. In cost-plus contracts, timesheet mistakes will result in billing errors to the customer, which could be at best unethical and, at worst, fraudulent.

Timesheets should, therefore, only be signed as approved by those nominated as being authorized to do so. It may be necessary introduce a higher-level check by arranging for a suitable independent person to carry out an occasional timesheet audit. In cost-plus contracts the customers will probably insist on some such safeguard.

Timesheets for agency staff

Staff supplied by external agencies to work in the contractor's offices will be provided with their own agency timesheets, which the project contractor is expected to sign to show that the company agrees with the hours for which the temporary employee will be paid by the agency, and which will eventually appear on the agencies' invoices. These timesheets are rarely suitable as project cost records, and it will probably be necessary to ask the agency staff also to fill in the contractor's own timesheets (which can be colour coded if required to distinguish them from the timesheets used by permanent staff).

The time spent by agency staff working in agency offices will usually be charged for weekly, supported by detailed timesheets from the agency. The contractor may wish to specify and supply the timesheets that are to be used. Checking and correct authorization are obviously important, and the contractor may decide to arrange random, unannounced inspection visits to the external office as a precaution against fraud.

Direct input of timesheet data to the computer

Some of the more powerful project management software systems, when networked, allow staff to key in their timesheet data directly. This procedure can save considerable time but the following must be borne in mind:

- Checking, auditing and approval are more difficult to arrange and errors can be expected.
- The system will not work unless everyone is clear about the cost codes to be used, and how these compare with the task information on file.
- There will be additional system costs, which can be considerable and might even be a multiple of the number of staff who will enter data.

Dayworks sheets for casual work from subcontractors

A common method for dealing with miscellaneous work carried out by subcontractors depends on the use of dayworks sheets. Some such subcontractors submit their bills infrequently, or only after very long delays. It can prove very difficult trying to reconcile invoices received six months or even longer after the work has been done, especially since dayworks sheets tend to be scrappy tear-offs from duplicate pads. Even longer delays between the work dates and receipt of final invoices have been known.

One instance I remember concerned a project for various external and internal improvements to an office building in central London. In addition to the work specified in the original fixed price contract, there were numerous incidental costs, such as miscellaneous plant rentals, the provision of rubbish skips, rental charges for a site hut, sundry materials and many other small additional tasks carried out at the request of the office occupier. All of these extra costs were recorded as they were incurred on hundreds of dayworks sheets, each signed by the office manager. The total project costs exceeded £100 000, much of which was attributable to the dayworks. The project lasted many months and the construction company, well known and respected in the City of London, submitted its invoice almost a year late. There was no dishonesty, but the lapse of time made the invoice extremely difficult to check and approve. The services of an independent quantity surveyor were required, at extra cost, before the invoice could be reconciled and passed for payment.

It is important that any company employing contractors or subcontractors checks, approves and retains copies of all dayworks sheets until the relevant invoices have been received and cleared for payment.

AUDITS AND FRAUD PREVENTION MEASURES

The need for timesheet entries to be checked and approved by managers and supervisors has already been mentioned. This is, in effect, a form of auditing. It helps to protect the client of a cost-plus project from being overcharged. Incidentally, it also helps to ensure that archived records of fixed price projects will be relatively free from errors, and therefore of more use when making comparative estimates for future projects.

Any company must always be aware of the possible risks when any manager or other member of staff has authority to commit expenditure or authorize payments on its behalf. Even where complete trust exists between senior management and their subordinates, the procedures should be audited and, where necessary amended, to reduce the possibility of fraud.

A company should set financial limits above which any manager must seek superior approval before authorizing any particular item of expenditure (for example a purchase requisition).

Payment of suppliers' invoices should be authorized by a responsible person who is not the same person who signed the associated purchase orders. That will provide an independent check and reduce any temptation for a buyer to order goods or services for their own use.

Rules should be laid down as to the levels of hospitality or gifts that those with purchasing authority may accept from suppliers and subcontractors. These should be drafted carefully so that they do not destroy normal goodwill and accepted moderate practices, but instead deter managers from receiving pecuniary benefits that might tend to corrupt, distort judgement or generate feelings of obligation to one source of supply.

Petty cash vouchers are open to misuse. I remember a case where a highly regarded member of the purchasing department regularly made small purchases of sundry stationery items, claiming reimbursement against petty vouchers. All would have been well if she had not made a common practice of adding considerable amounts to each petty cash claim voucher for fictitious purchases that were not on the original requisitions. Thousands of pounds could have been saved if a procedures audit had been carried out.

COMPARING ACTUAL COSTS AGAINST PLANNED COSTS

This chapter has described some of the measures needed to establish a project budgeting and cost recording system, as a preliminary step towards implementing effective cost management. The next step is to decide how to make use of cost measurements, and how to analyse and compare these against the work schedules and budgets in order to effect cost control. That will be discussed in the following chapter.

REFERENCES AND FURTHER READING

Goldsmith, L. (2005), *Project Management Accounting: Budgeting, Tracking, and Reporting Costs and Profitability* (Chichester: Wiley).

Stenzel, C. and Stenzel, J. (2002), *Essentials of Cost Management* (New York: Wiley).

27 Earned-Value Analysis and Cost Reporting

The previous chapter outlined principles and practices for the establishment of project budgets and the collection of cost data. This chapter continues the subject of cost management by describing techniques that can evaluate performance against budgets, analyse trends and attempt to predict the total final project costs. The tools described are important ingredients of cost management because they can provide information in time for corrective action to be taken.

MILESTONE ANALYSIS

Milestone analysis is one of the simpler methods which managers can use throughout the project life cycle to compare the actual costs and progress experienced with the costs and progress planned. The method is less effective and less detailed than others described later in this chapter, but it has the merit of needing a relatively modest amount of management effort to set up and maintain. It also requires less sophisticated cost accounting than other methods and can be used when project schedules are not particularly detailed.

Perhaps the best way to demonstrate the benefits of milestone analysis would be to begin by considering what happens when actual costs are compared against cost budgets when there are no milestones or other relevant information about the progress achieved.

Cost monitoring without milestones

Figure 27.1 shows the kinds of curves that might result if total project costs are recorded regularly and plotted on a graph against time and the budget.

The practice depends on first plotting a graph of expected costs against time. Such graphs are sometimes known as time-scaled budgets. The time-scaled budget in Figure 27.1 is represented by the dotted curve. This curve was plotted by combining information from the cost estimates and the project plan, so that the estimated costs for all work packages are included in the curve at their scheduled times. The project manager should, therefore, be able to consult the graph at any time during the execution of the project to find the amount of total project costs that should have been reached if all is going to plan.

In the absence of a suitable work breakdown with budgets it would not, of course, be possible to draw a time-scaled budget curve. In that case, the best that could be done would be to draw the budget as a straight line joining two points, starting from zero cost at the graph's origin and reaching the total estimated cost at the planned completion date. That approach can be dismissed as being of no use whatever.

The actual cumulative project costs can be plotted at suitable intervals on the same axes as the time-scaled budget. If the costing system is at all reasonable, it will be possible to plot these costs fairly accurately. This has been done in Figure 27.1, where it can be seen that actual costs have been recorded up to the end of week 28.

Interpreting the result where there are no milestones

Graphs that attempt to compare actual costs with the time-scaled budget, even when they are plotted with great care, are of very limited management use as they stand. The missing piece of information in Figure 27.1 is the corresponding progress or achievement.

At one extreme, if no money is being spent at all, then it is a fair assumption that no progress is being made either. It is also true and easily understood that a significantly low rate of expenditure usually indicates an inadequate rate of progress and achievement. Unfortunately, some managers then proceed to make the less acceptable assumption that if expenditure is being incurred at the planned rate, then progress and achievement must also be either on plan or 'about right'. This is a very rough and ready guide that can lead to dangerously wrong conclusions.

Suppose that the project illustrated in Figure 27.1 has been running for 32 weeks, when the planned expenditure should then be £500 000. There are people who would be well satisfied on being told that the reported expenditure is at or just below £500 000. But those people fail to ask all the vital questions which should be considered by any project manager, namely:

- How much have we spent to date?
- What should we have spent to date?
- What have we achieved so far?
- What should we have achieved by this time?
- What are the final cost and delivery prospects for the project if our performance continues at the current level?

Milestone monitoring can help to answer these questions.

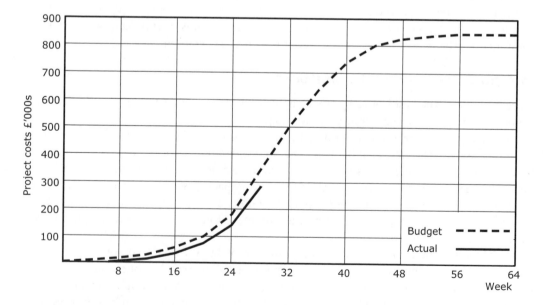

Figure 27.1 Comparison of actual costs against a time-scaled budget

Explanation of the milestone method

Identifying milestones

The first requirement in milestone analysis is to understand what is meant by a milestone. A milestone denotes a particular, easily identifiable stage in the progress of a project towards completion. It might be acceptance by the customer of a final design concept or layout drawing, the issue of a package of drawings for work to begin, the day when a building is made watertight so that internal trades can start, the date when electrical power is first switched on to a new installation, or any other such occasion.

All good project management software allows the user to designate appropriate activities as milestones. Each milestone is then achieved when the relevant milestone activity is reported as finished. This becomes a little complicated when a true project milestone depends on completion of more than one parallel activity. Precedence notation, however, is very adaptable and it is easy to solve this problem by creating milestone events artificially. All that is necessary is to insert milestone activities with zero or unit duration at the appropriate network intersections. This is rather similar to the creation of artificial dummies that was shown earlier, in Figure 14.14.

Milestone analysis starts, therefore, by choosing and naming the achievements that can most effectively be used as project milestones. Ideally, milestones should coincide with the completion of packages from the work breakdown structure. That approach will be assumed here.

Plotting the budget/milestone plan

For each milestone, two pieces of data are required. These are:

- the date on which the milestone is scheduled to be achieved;
- the estimated cost or budget for the associated work package (that is, the expected cost of all the work needed to achieve the milestone).

When all milestone data are available the milestone/budget curve can be plotted. This process starts by sketching the time-scaled budget curve. The position of each point is determined by matching the cumulative cost estimates for the project work packages against the planned achievement dates for those work packages. It might be necessary to use all the constituent tasks, rather than complete work packages, to produce sufficient points on the graph. Care must be taken to ensure that no estimated costs are left out, so that the budget curve will reach the cost estimated for the project. So far this is similar to the process used to produce the time-scaled budget curve in Figure 27.1.

To complete the budget/milestone graph, symbols must be added to the budget curve to represent all the milestones. Each milestone must be positioned on the budget curve at the date scheduled for its completion.

Plotting the graph of actual expenditure and milestone achievement

To be able to plot the graph of actual expenditure for comparison against the plan, two further items of information must be collected:

- the date on which each milestone was actually achieved;
- the project costs actually incurred (including committed costs of purchased items) at the end of each cost monitoring period.

It must therefore be assumed that a procedure exists for recording the total costs actually incurred and committed for the project at suitable intervals. These intervals might be weekly or monthly, and will depend to some extent on the life cycle time for the project.

The actual costs can be plotted as a graph on the same axes as the time-scaled budget. Points on the graph should be highlighted by symbols that indicate the actual completion date for each milestone. To be able to compare the planned and actual graphs sensibly, it helps enormously if all the milestones can be given simple numbers. If the milestones marked on the budget curve are, for example, numbered 1, 2, 3 and so on, the corresponding points on the actual cost graph can carry the same numbers to make comparison easy.

Milestone analysis example

A construction project lasting just over one year is the basis for this example and Figure 27.2 displays the relevant graphs.

The dotted curve in Figure 27.2 shows the time-scaled budget for the project, drawn by combining data from the project schedule and the authorized cost estimates. Thirteen milestones have been identified for the project, and the schedule and cost data for these are tabulated in Figure 27.3.

Each milestone has been indicated on the planned curve by placing a circle at the time when it should be achieved. The numbers within the circles identify the particular milestones.

Monitoring method

Actual cost and progress data have been gathered up to the end of week 30 for this project and these are included in the tabulated data shown in Figure 27.3. The results have been plotted, at two-weekly intervals, as the solid line curve in Figure 27.2. Any milestone passed during each two-weekly period has been indicated on the actual cost curve by means of a diamond containing the milestone's identification number.

Interpreting the results of milestone analysis

Of course, if all is going exactly according to plan, the budget and actual graphs should lie together on the same path and the milestone points should coincide. When they do not, investigation should give some indication of the project cost and achievement performance to date.

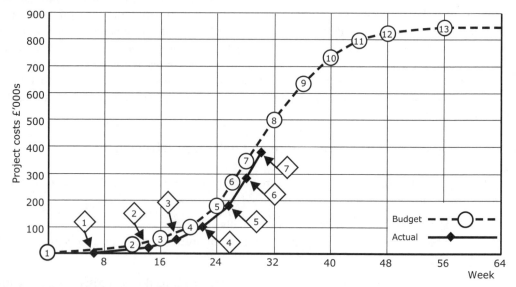

Figure 27.2 Project cost and achievement comparison using milestones

Milestone description	Schedule (week number)		Cumulative cost £(1000s)	
	Plan	Actual	Budget	Actual
1 Project start authorized	0	6	0	0
2 Design approved	12	14	25	20
3 Drawings issued for building	16	18	60	55
4 Foundations completed	20	22	100	100
5 Drawings issued for services	24	26	180	180
6 All equipment for services ordered	26	28	275	290
7 Walls built to eaves	28	30	345	385
8 Windows and doors finished	32		500	
9 Roof on, building watertight	36		630	
10 Wiring and plumbing finished	40		730	
11 Services installed and tested	44		795	
12 Internal finishes completed	48		825	
13 Site and building handover	56		845	

Figure 27.3   Data for a milestone chart

Imagine that you are the general manager of the construction company responsible for this project and that it has been running for just over 8 weeks. If you look at week 8 on Figure 27.2 you will see that milestone 1, project start, has been achieved six weeks late, as indicated by the position of the diamond compared with the circle. The very low costs recorded at week 8 indicate that little or no activity is taking place. So, you can easily see that the project has started late and that more effort is needed urgently if progress is to catch up with the plan.

When you receive your updated milestone chart at the end of week 14 it tells you that milestone 2 has been reached. It should have happened at week 12, but the project has now been pulled up from being 6 weeks late to only 2 weeks late. Costs recorded up to week 14 are £20 000. These costs compare against a budget of £25 000 for achieving milestone 2.

Expenditure at week 14 should have reached about £45 000 (the dotted curve). So you conclude that the project is still running slightly late and that the rate of expenditure is lower than plan, so extra effort is needed. You are, however, getting value for the money spent because milestone 2 was achieved for £5000 less than its estimated cost.

If you continue to observe the chart at consecutive two-weekly intervals, you can see how it depicts the changing trend. In particular, the cost performance gradually deteriorates. One significant report from the project manager is the milestone chart updated to the end of week 28. The graphs indicate that milestone 6 should have been achieved at week 26 for a project cost of £275 000. You can see from the graphs, however, that milestone 6 has only just been reached at week 28 at a cost of £290 000. So the project is not only still running 2 weeks late but is now also £15 000 over budget.

By week 30, it is apparent that the project programme, as indicated by milestone 7, continues to run 2 weeks late, and the costs at £385 000 have risen to £40 000 over the corresponding budget for milestone 7.

Without the milestones as measuring points, none of this analysis would have been possible.

Need for replotting

If a change in project scope or any other reason causes rescheduling of work or costs, then the data for future milestones will obviously change too. The curve of predicted expenditure and milestones will have to be amended at each significant authorized change so that it remains up to date and a true basis for comparison of actual costs against plan.

Disadvantages of the milestone method

The milestone method suffers from a few disadvantages. These include the following:

- The information that can be extracted for management use in controlling the project is often obtained after the damage has been done, and certainly much later than the predictions possible with more detailed earned-value analysis (described below).
- If programme slippages are going to occur very often, the curves may have to be redrawn frequently, unless a computer can be used or some very flexible charting method is devised.
- The method takes only an approximate account of work-in-progress (work packages which have been started, but where the milestones have yet to be achieved).
- The method only shows coarse trends rather than the more detailed measurements obtainable with earned-value analysis.
- It is not easy to use the results of milestone analysis to predict the probable final outcome for the project.

However, the method involves comparatively little effort, is a considerable improvement on simple cost versus budget comparison, and may therefore commend itself to the busy project manager.

EARNED-VALUE ANALYSIS

Earned-value analysis can be regarded as the missing link between cost reporting and cost control. It depends on the existence of a sound framework of planning and control, including the following:

- a detailed work breakdown structure;
- a correspondingly detailed cost coding system;
- timely and accurate collection and reporting of cost data;
- a method for monitoring and quantifying the amount of work done, including work-in-progress.

The earned-value process aims to compare the costs incurred for an accurately identified amount of work with the costs budgeted for that same work. It can be applied at the level of individual tasks or complete work packages and the data are usually rolled up for the whole project. The procedure uses the results to produce a cost performance index. If everything is going exactly according to plan the cost performance index will be 1.0. An index less than 1.0 indicates that the value earned for the money being spent is less than that expected.

Importance of work breakdown structure

The first stage in establishing an effective procedure for assessing achievement is to decide which work elements are to be subjected to measurement, analysis and reporting. In fact, this choice should be clear; the work packages from the project work breakdown, together with their cost estimates or budgets must provide the framework. It is important to carry this breakdown through to the level of activities performed by individual departments or work groups, so that each responsible manager or supervisor can be given quantified objectives that can be monitored by the earned-value process.

Earned-value nomenclature and definitions

The following are a few of the names and abbreviations used in earned-value analysis. The list is not complete but includes the most commonly used quantities.

Abbreviation	What it means
ACWP	Actual Cost of the Work Performed at the measurement date
BCWP	Budgeted Cost of Work Performed – this is the amount of money or labour time that the amount of work actually performed at the measurement date should have cost to be in line with the budget or cost estimate. It is usually necessary to take into account work that is in progress in addition to tasks actually completed.
BCWS	Budgeted Cost of Work Scheduled – this is the budget or cost estimate for work scheduled to be complete at the measurement date. It corresponds with the time-scaled budget.
CPI	Cost Performance Index – this factor that indicates the measure of success in achieving results against budget. Anything less than unity indicates that the value earned from money spent is less than that intended.
SPI	Schedule Performance Index – this can be used as a measure of progress performance against plan, but is less commonly used than the CPI. Anything less than unity shows progress slower than that planned.

These quantities can be used in the following expressions:

$$CPI = BCWP / ACWP$$

$$SPI = BCWP / BCWS$$

Brick wall project: a simple example of earned-value analysis

For this example of earned-value analysis I have chosen a project comprising one main activity for which progress can be measured quantitatively without difficulty or ambiguity.

Imagine a bricklayer and a labourer engaged in building a new boundary wall enclosing a small country estate. If the amount of progress made had to be assessed at any time, work achieved could be measured in terms of the area of wall built or, more simply here, by the length of wall finished.

The scope, budget and schedule for this project have been defined by the following data:

- total length of wall to be built = 1000 m
- estimated total project cost = £40 000
- planned duration for the project = 10 weeks (with 5 working days in each week = 50 days)
- rate of progress is expected to be uniform and linear

When the above data are considered, the following additional facts emerge:

- budget cost per day = £800
- planned rate of building = 20 m of wall per day
- budget cost for each metre of wall finished = £40

At the end of day 20 the project manager has been asked to carry out an earned-value analysis. The actual and planned data for the end of day 20 are as follows:

- work performed: 360 m of wall have been competed
- ACWP: £18 000 (total project cost at the end of day 20)
- BCWS: 20 days at £800 per day = £16 000
- BCWP: 360 m of wall should have cost £40 per metre or £14 400

Cost implications

The cost implications of these data can be analysed using earned-value analysis as follows:

$$CPI = BCWP / ACWP = 14\ 400 / 18\ 000 = 0.8$$

The implication of this for final project cost can be viewed in at least two ways.

- We could divide the original estimate of £40 000 by the cost performance index and say that the predicted total project cost has risen to £50 000, which gives a forecast cost variance of £10 000 for the project at completion.
- Alternatively, we can say that £18 000 has been spent to date, and then work out the likely remaining cost. The 360 m of wall built so far have actually cost £18 000, which is a rate of £50 per metre. The amount of work remaining is 640 m of wall and, if this should also cost £50 per metre, that will mean a further £32 000 predicted cost remaining to completion. So, adding costs measured to date and remaining costs predicted to completion again gives an estimated total cost at project completion of £50 000.

Schedule implications

Earned-value data can be used to predict the likely completion date for an activity or a project, although a straightforward comparison of progress against the plan is probably an easier and more effective method. If the earned-value method is used, the first step is to calculate the schedule performance index. For the wall project at day 20 the SPI is found by:

$$SPI = BCWP / BCWS = 14\ 400 / 16\ 000 = 0.9$$

The original estimate for the duration of this project was 50 working days. Dividing by the SPI gives a revised total project duration of about 56 days.

Methods for assessing progress

Most earned-value analysis must be performed not just on one activity, as in the brick wall project just described, but on many project activities. At any given measurement time in a large project, three stages of progress can apply to all the activities. These stages are as follows:

- activity not started – earned value is therefore zero;
- activity completed – earned value is therefore equal to the activity's cost budget;
- activity in progress or interrupted. For construction projects, as in the case of the brick wall project, earned value for work in progress can often be assessed by measuring actual quantities of work done. For other, less tangible tasks, it is necessary to estimate the proportion or percentage of work done, and then take the same proportion of the current authorized cost estimate as the actual value of work performed.

Earned-value assessment for an engineering design department

When reviewing the progress of all engineering design activities in a project, one approach is to determine how many drawings and specifications are to be produced, and then divide this number by the number of drawings actually issued, multiply the answer by 100 and declare this as the percentage of design completed. Although some companies do use this method, it is really too crude because it fails to take into account all the conceptual design work needed, and assumes that the work involved in producing one drawing is equivalent to the amount of work needed to produce any other drawing. The method can however be used in limited cases, such as for a department which is producing a large number of similar drawings, like electrical wiring or piping diagrams.

In most design jobs the only way to assess progress is to ask the engineer, or the engineer's superior, for an estimate. 'What percentage of this task do you consider has been achieved?' might be asked or, perhaps more provocatively, 'How much longer is this job going to take? This process must be carried through all activities in the project.

In the case of the bricklayers in the wall project the answers obtained were objective, accurate and proof against fear of contradiction. Many other jobs on a project, especially the software activities, are far less straightforward and much more difficult to assess quantitatively in terms of progress achieved. The engineer may be guilty of unwarranted optimism or poor judgement when giving a progress report. This is the penalty that must be paid when changing from an objective to subjective assessment of progress. Nevertheless, there is no need to abandon the quest. At least an answer of sorts can be extracted and, although by no means perfect, surely this is better than having no answer at all.

Work-in-progress assessments will inevitably be less accurate than the data for completed activities. However, because work-in-progress should account for only a small proportion of the total work, assessment errors should be diluted by the larger, more reliable, estimates for jobs that are definitely finished. This will, or course, be less true for short-term projects, or at the start of any project, where the proportion of work-in-progress to completed work may be higher. If the individual activities are large, owing to insufficient work breakdown, then again the work-in-progress could rank high because it will take correspondingly longer to cross off the completed activities.

Example

An earned-value calculation in an engineering design department is demonstrated in Figure 27.4 using a manual method. In this example an engineering project is well under way. The total department estimate (the total potential earned value) is seen to be 2975 man-hours.

An analysis of the work completed or in progress reveals that the BCWP (budget cost of work performed) is 1389 man-hours. This is the project earned value at the measurement date.

Against this achievement, the ACWP is seen to be 1142 man-hours. This figure represents all the hours actually booked to these jobs on timesheets. Although 46.7 per cent of the work has been done, only 38.4 per cent of the budget has been spent. This is a good result, and indicates that work generally is costing less than the budget.

Dividing the BCWP by the ACWP for this project gives a cost performance index or CPI of 1.22. If things are allowed to go on in the same way, the project budget of 2975 hours is likely to be underspent. Dividing by the CPI predicts a final engineering design department expenditure of only 2438 man-hours. The accountants would call this a positive variance of 537 man-hours.

Earned-value analysis for manufacturing

Production departments, at first sight, might seem to be a very different proposition from the engineering design department just considered, being concerned with hardware rather than software and far removed from the abstract world of design and development. However, there is no practical reason preventing the use of similar methods to cover all production activities. In fact, the process is made easier, since one is dealing not with theories and subjective assessments but with the tangible fruits of productive labour.

Choice of manufacturing cost centres for analysis

Production activities often employ a wide range of different labour grades drawn from several departments. Which of these should be subjected to achievement analysis must depend to some extent on the degree of control considered necessary.

EARNED VALUE ANALYSIS

Department: Engineering   Date: May 2008

Project: Sensor and servo control unit   Sheet: 1   of: 1

Activity		Budget man-hours	Per cent achieved	Earned value BCWP	Actual cost ACWP
0001	System design	350	100	350	255
0002	Write system specification	35	100	35	35
0003	Design +25v power supply	105	100	105	140
0004	Breadboard stage	70	100	70	35
0005	Package	70	100	70	40
0006	Prove prototype	35			
0007	Write test specification	35			
0008	Design +10v power supply	105	100	105	65
0009	Breadboard stage	70	100	70	50
0010	Package	70	50	35	25
0011	Prove prototype	35			
0012	Write test specification	35			
0013	Design -15v power supply	105			
0014	Breadboard stage	70			
0015	Package	70			
0016	Prove prototype	35			
0017	Write test specification	35			
0018	Design sensor circuit	350	100	350	288
0019	Breadboard stage	105	100	105	124
0020	Package	105	40	42	50
0021	Prove prototype	70			
0022	Write test specification	35			
0023	Design servo and controls	175	20	35	15
0024	Breadboard stage	140			
0025	Package	70			
0026	Prove prototype	105			
0027	Write test specification	35			
0028	Design main frame	70	25	17	20
0029	System testing	70			
0030	Environmental tests	70			
0031	Write production test spec.	140			
0032	Write operating manual	105			
	Departmental totals	2975	46.7	1389	1142

Figure 27.4   Earned-value analysis for an engineering department

It is probably unwise to attempt a detailed analysis for every conceivable cost centre. Over-ambition in this direction, leading to a multiplicity of facts, figures and prediction curves, could involve so much effort for so little return that disillusionment with the whole process of earned-value measurement would soon set in.

Probably the best course is to analyse the performance of departments, rather than individual labour grades or machines and other facilities. In this way, each departmental manager can be provided with a feedback of departmental performance against budgets. Each chosen cost centre must be analysed regularly and given its separate place in the achievement measurements, so that effective cost versus budget comparisons can be made.

Cost accounting

Steps must be taken to ensure that the collection of cost data from production aligns with the project work breakdown. This is achieved using a structured cost coding system, and by paying particular attention to the allocation of job numbers. The time booked to every production operation will then be recorded against a number which incorporates an identifier code, enabling the work and its costs to be related to the correct project task. This system and the cost coding methods will become clearer by reference back to Chapter 12.

Level of detail for manufacturing earned-value analysis

The basis for allocating work values to each production activity derives from the project work breakdown, together with its associated estimates. For the purposes of earned-value analysis it is not necessary or desirable for the project manager to consider production task breakdowns in any greater detail than the tasks identified in the work breakdown and overall project schedule.

Earned-value analysis for subcontracts

Earned-value measurement may have to include subcontracted activities. However, if the subcontracted work is being obtained on a fixed-price basis, the subcontractor carries the financial risk and earned-value measurements for internal control are then the prime responsibility of the subcontractor.

The project manager will have to pay close attention to the measurement techniques used by subcontractors whenever they submit claims for progress payments. Such payment claims must be made against the achievement of recognizable events or be supported by certificated measurement. It is those results or other reports from the subcontractors that the project manager must include in the earned-value picture for the whole project

EARNED-VALUE ANALYSIS PREDICTION RELIABILITY AND IMPLICATIONS

Early predictions of final costs always tend to be unreliable. There are at least four principal reasons for this:

- Estimates of progress, or of work remaining to completion are only judgements, and people usually err on the side of optimism.
- During the first few weeks or even months of a large project, the sample of work analysed in earned-value calculations is too small to produce valid indications of later trends.

- There is no guarantee that the performance levels early in a project, even when they have been accurately assessed, will remain at those same levels throughout the remainder of the project.
- Although many activities, especially in design, might be declared as 100 per cent completed, it is inevitable that further work will be needed when questions arise as drawings and specifications are put to use in manufacturing or construction. It is quite likely that some drawings will have to be reissued with corrections or modifications. Unless due allowance has been made elsewhere for this 'after issue' work, the project budget might eventually be exceeded.

What if the prediction is bad?

Suppose the actual hours recorded in the example shown in Figure 27.4 had significantly exceeded the earned value, so that the resulting prediction indicated final costs well in excess of the budget. The first thing to be noted is that the project manager should be grateful to this method for producing the earliest possible warning. Escape may be possible even from an apparently hopeless situation, provided that suitable action can be taken in time.

Stricter control of modifications should help to curb unnecessary expenditure and conserve budgets. While changes requested by a customer will be paid for, and so should augment the budget, all other requests for changes must be thoroughly scrutinized before authorization. Only essential unfunded changes should be allowed. Change control, a very important aspect of project management, was described in Chapter 25.

In the face of vanishing budgets, the demands made on individuals will have to be more stringent, but this can only be achieved through good communications, by letting all the participants know what the position is, what is expected of them, and why. It is important to gain their full cooperation. The project manager will find this easiest to achieve within a project team organization. If a matrix organization exists, the project manager must work through all the departmental managers involved to achieve good communications and motivation.

The performance of individuals can often be improved considerably by setting short- and medium-term goals or objectives. These must always be quantifiable, so that the results can be measured objectively, removing any question of favouritism or bias in performance assessment, and helping the individual to monitor their own performance.

In the project context, these personal objectives must be equated (by means of the work breakdown structure) with the objectives of time, cost and performance for the project as a whole. The three objectives go hand-in-hand and, if work is done on time, the cost objective should be met. Although all the objectives should have been set at the start of a project, they can be reviewed if things are going wrong and budgets appear to be at risk. However, care must be taken not to set objectives that cannot possibly be met.

If, in spite of all efforts, a serious overspend still threatens, there remains the possibility of replenishing the project coffers from their original source – the customer. This feat can sometimes be accomplished by re-opening the fixed-price negotiation whenever a suitable opportunity presents itself. An excuse to renegotiate may be provided, for example, if the customer should ask for a substantial change, or as a result of economic factors that are beyond the contractor's control. Failing this step, smaller modifications or project spares can be priced generously to offset the areas of loss or low profitability. Care must also be taken to ensure that every item that the contract allows to be charged as an expense to the customer is so charged.

Remember that without earned-value analysis, forewarning of possible overspending may not be received in time to allow any corrective action at all. The project manager must always be examining cost trends, rather than simple historical cost reports. When the predictions are bad, despair is the wrong philosophy. It is far better to carry out a careful reappraisal of the remaining project activities and explore all possible avenues that might lead to a restoration of the original financial targets.

EVALUATING COST PERFORMANCE FOR MATERIALS AND BOUGHT-IN EQUIPMENT

Measurement of purchasing achievement, in terms of the cost of materials, components and equipment against their estimates, differs considerably from the measurement and consideration of labour costs. If a person is asked to work on a particular job, the hours and associated labour costs are incurred then and there. If ten hours are worked, ten hours should be booked against the appropriate job number and ten hours will appear in the records as the cost of the job. Purchase orders, on the other hand, are usually originated well in advance of the time when the goods will be received and invoiced, and there may be a further delay before they are actually used. The costs are committed irrevocably some time before the day of reckoning arrives.

It must be stressed, therefore, that purchasing cost control is exercised when each order is placed. Once an order has been issued which, for any reason, is priced higher than the budget, then it is too late to avoid spending over budget.

The procedures which follow can only contribute to cost control in the sense that they will indicate adverse trends as early as possible. If poor purchasing performance has been experienced early in the project, the best that can be done is to ensure that an improvement takes place when the remaining orders are committed.

Graphs of cumulative expenditure on purchases

A curve can be plotted to show the cumulative value of purchase orders as they are placed. This is a curve of committed expenditure which can be compared with the original budget. An example was given in Figure 26.3.

Any curve showing materials commitments will be far more useful if a budget comparison curve is first plotted on the graph, like a track along which the committed expenditure is expected to run as the points are plotted. The points for plotting the time-scaled budget for materials must be calculated by adding together the materials cost estimates for each task, and timing them according to the dates when the orders are scheduled to be issued, not forgetting to include the value of common stock items. Inclusion of milestones on the graph (as described earlier in this chapter) will enhance the value of this method.

Allowance for materials issued from common stock

If a curve of material commitments is to be drawn, care must be taken to allow for any materials that do not have to be ordered specifically for the project, but which will be issued from stores or other common stocks. The quantities of these stock items must be estimated, and their costs have to be added to the cumulative totals in the curve so that the predicted cost shown reflects the total materials cost for the project.

Tabulations for material purchase costs

Another, more accurate, approach to monitoring purchasing cost performance is to tabulate actual costs against the corresponding estimates whenever a new purchase order is issued. If this is done at regular intervals a pattern will emerge which shows, for all the orders committed to date, whether any trend towards over- or under-spending is emerging. The experience gained can be used in carrying out regular reviews of the cost estimates for all goods yet to be ordered. This will allow regular predictions to be made of the total materials expenditure, so that these can be compared with the authorized budgets to help in updating the forecast project profitability.

Where it is intended to use this method, four sets of data have to be gathered. These are:

- the total value of all orders already placed;
- the total estimated value of all purchase orders yet to be placed (using the task list or purchase control schedule as a check);
- the cost of any materials already issued from general stock;
- the estimated cost of any materials still to be used from general stock.

Surplus materials

When the final reckoning of project material costs is made, the total cannot be restricted only to those materials that have actually been used, scrapped or wasted. Any items which have become surplus to requirements must be included in the total. Such surpluses may have resulted from over-ordering, design modifications and other causes. The only surplus stocks that need not be taken into account are those which can be returned to the supplier for full credit, or which can be used profitably on a known alternative project for which a firm order exists.

There is often an understandable reluctance to write off materials left over at the end of a project. Individuals are sometimes tempted to take these items into general stock in the hope that one day, possibly, they may eventually become useful. It is surprising how quickly a storage area can become completely cluttered with such stock. Not only can large volumes of storage space be taken up, but also the value to be written off can eventually accumulate to embarrassing proportions if it is allowed to mount up unchecked. The day of reckoning has to come, and it is better to recognize stock as redundant at the time when it first deserves that description.

EFFECT OF PROJECT CHANGES ON EARNED-VALUE ANALYSIS

Every change introduced into a project can be expected to have some effect on the level of achievement attained by the departments involved. Before this effect can be measured, one significant question must always be answered: Can the customer be held liable for any additional costs, or must the additional work be paid for out of the existing budget (and, therefore, out of the potential profits)?

Control of project changes was dealt with in the Chapter 25. It can be assumed that, long before any modification reaches the stage of implementation, the change committee or other designated authority will have ensured that every approved change is clearly defined as 'customer funded' or 'unfunded'.

Unfunded changes

Each unfunded change will affect the total workload remaining, usually with no corresponding change to the authorized budgets. In most cases changes increase the remaining workload, so that the proportion of earned value achieved is depressed in all the departments affected.

It should be possible to make an appropriate correction to the achievement measurement for each department to allow for unfunded changes. Each modification would have to be added to the task list, along with a cost estimate for the additional work needed. Change costs are, however, often extremely difficult to estimate and record, because of the way in which the work is intermingled with the original task affected.

There can, of course, be no corresponding increase in the authorized budget. But for practical purposes, such adjustments are unnecessary, and unfunded modifications can be ignored provided that:

- They are not too numerous or horrendous.
- They do not cancel out work already reported as achieved.

Work on unfunded modifications will therefore show up as apparent overspending – which is of course just what it is. Earned-value predictions will be self-correcting as these overspends are picked up, even if they are not immediately identifiable as being expressly due to unfunded modifications.

Completed work rendered void by unfunded changes

Unfunded changes that nullify work already carried out must always be taken into account by erasure of the relevant earned-value elements from the records. This should be done for every department affected, and either whole tasks or parts of them may have to be reinstated into the remaining workload. In this way, the earned-value calculations can be kept on a true course.

Suppose, for example, that in the case illustrated by Figure 27.4 there arose a modification which demanded a complete restart of activities 0018, 0019 and 0020 (the sensor circuit design). Earned value for this item would have to revert to zero, which would mean subtracting 497 man-hours from the column total of earned value. This would cut the earned value for the project back from 1389 to 892 man-hours. The CPI has been cut from 1.22 to 0.78 and the predicted cost at completion becomes 3809 man-hours.

Customer-funded changes

Funded changes can be considered as new tasks, for addition both to the task list and its authorized budgets. The customer should be asked to pay for any work which is scrapped as a result of the change, in which case that work can be considered as having been sold and, therefore, achieved. It need not be subtracted from the achievement tally.

PROJECT LEDGER CONCEPT

A picture has now been built up of a collection of methods by which data can be displayed on graphs or in tables to show the predicted and measured performance of each department against plans and budgets. Successful budgetary control and cost prediction obviously require a certain amount of accurate book-keeping, not only within the boundaries of the accounts department, but also under the administration of the project manager.

The dossier of progress assessments and budgets, all collated with respect to the project task list, can be regarded as a project ledger, with two sets of balancing entries.

- The ledger account is credited with the initial cost budgets plus any authorized additions, such as those arising from customer-requested changes and contract variation orders.
- The earned values achieved are debited from the ledger as they are reported.

At any time it should be possible to consult the ledger in order to recalculate the cost performance index for the project or parts of it, and to predict the costs remaining to completion.

The ledger will most probably be set up in a computer, either in a management information system or using one of the more powerful project management packages.

PREDICTING PROFITABILITY FOR A WHOLE PROJECT

Once a basis has been established for the collection of earned-value statistics from all parts of the project organization, it is a logical and progressive step to put all these results together into a composite prediction of total project costs.

Of course, the first such prediction is that made before the start of the project, when the initial cost estimates and budgets are prepared and when progress can confidently be declared as zero.

Subsequent analysis and cost predictions can be regarded as a continuous process by which the original estimate is steadily refined. As more work is completed, the total estimate to completion contains an increasing proportion of actual cost data, so that the predictions should become more accurate.

For cost-control purposes, it is necessary that these data are presented in a way that shows unwanted trends as early as possible, before it becomes too late for anything to be done.

Graphical prediction method

Cost predictions can be plotted on a graph against project time for direct comparison with the budget, so that any upward or downward trends can be seen clearly and early.

Before the cost data for all the various departments or groups can be brought together and combined with the cost of purchased equipment and materials, they must all be expressed in terms of one common denominator, which must be the control currency for the project. The man-hour units that were appropriate for scheduling and supervisory control must now be converted into costs, using the appropriate rate for each labour grade. The man-hour records must, however, be kept because these will provide the stable and reliable yardsticks (unaffected by cost inflation) when comparative cost estimates for future projects are made.

Cost monitoring and prediction are aimed primarily at containing costs within budgets but, when a project has been sold commercially for profit, the profit becomes the end objective. Accordingly, the final prediction graphs should relate the cost and budget levels to the effective net selling price. Both the targeted and predicted gross margins will be displayed so that, as time passes, a wary eye can be kept on the likely outcome. The budget and price levels will have to be readjusted whenever a variation order or other change is introduced that affects the contract price.

Figure 27.5 shows the type of curves that can result from the regular plotting of cost predictions for the whole project. This contains the following two curves:

- a curve of cumulative recorded expenditure for the whole project, plotted at four-weekly intervals. The materials and bought-out equipment costs have been included at the time of commitment, and not at the time of invoice payment (which would be too late for control purposes);
- a curve showing the final cost prediction from earned-value analysis calculations made at four-weekly intervals.

In this example, the project has been finished. It is possible to recapture some of the sense of occasion that would have existed during the active stages of the project by placing a piece of card over the diagram and moving it from left to right to expose the graphs in four-weekly steps.

The first point plotted on the prediction graph, taken at zero project time, is the initial prediction for project expenditure before it has been influenced by actual experience. In other words, this is the original estimate and budget taken straight from the total task list and work breakdown.

The next three or four points on the prediction graph display rather startling variations because they are based, in statistical parlance, on samples that are too small. These early results also contain a high proportion of assessed progress rather than activities that have definitely been completed. As time proceeds and the tally of completed work begins to mount up it is not very long before a more consistent trend shows so that, after a few months, the results carry sufficient weight to be taken seriously in determining any need for corrective action.

At about the 24th week, a fairly consistent overspending condition begins to show. Any manager faced with the prospect of overrunning budgets must take some action, and a degree of success in

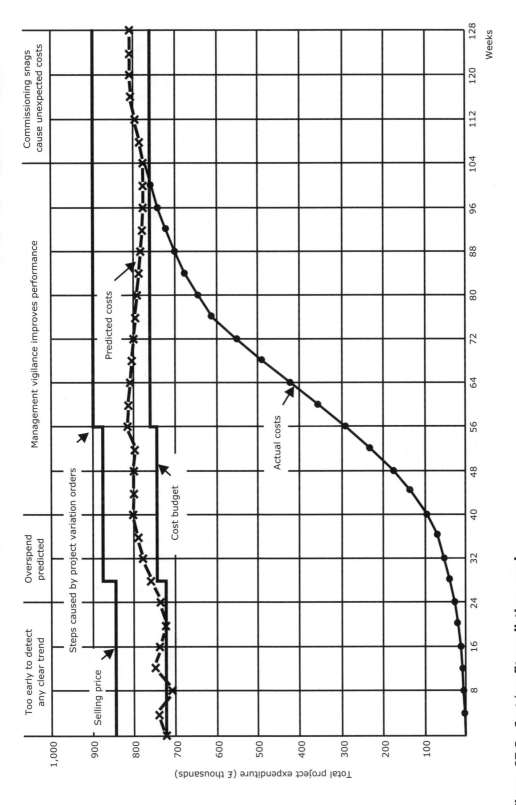

Figure 27.5   Cost/profit prediction graph

holding down the rate of expenditure was obviously gained in this case. The rate of overspending is seen to decline, to be followed by a long period in which the cost performance steadily improves.

In most projects a danger exists that expenditure will not be cut off immediately when the last scheduled task has been finished. Clean-up operations, on-site activities, drawing corrections and commissioning problems are all possible causes of last-minute additions to costs. Sometimes feverish activity takes place during the final phases of a project in order to get it finished on time, and this too can give rise to unexpected expenditure. Something of this nature has obviously happened over the last weeks of the project in Figure 27.5.

Now compare the graph showing predicted expenditure with that drawn to record actual costs. The curve of actual costs is cumulative, showing the total build-up of costs rather than just the costs incurred during each period of measurement. Notice how much more information can be gleaned from one glance at the prediction curve than can be derived from the cumulative cost curve, especially during the early and middle parts of the project. The overspending danger is simply not shown up at all by the actual cost curve until very late in the project, at which time it is far too late to take any corrective action.

Spreadsheet presentation

Project cost summaries and predictions are commonly presented in tabular or spreadsheet form. Figure 27.6 shows a widely used arrangement, suitable for preparation from purely clerical methods or from computer systems. Tables such as this are typically bound into regular cost and progress reports, often produced at monthly intervals. A description of this format on a column-by-column basis will serve to round off this chapter with a reiteration of the principles embodied in the interpretation of cost and progress data. The spreadsheet columns have been labelled A, B, C and so on, for ease of reference.

The report form is headed with the project title and project number information. The report date is important, being the effective common reference date for all measurements and progress assessments.

The time lag between the effective report date and the actual report issue date depends on the size and complexity of the project to a great extent: it obviously takes more time to collect results from a project spread over a large, geographically scattered organization than it would where the whole project is conducted within one office or factory. Nevertheless, all possible steps must be taken to produce these reports before they become outdated and too late to provoke constructive management response.

Column A lists the main work packages from the project work breakdown. This list must include all cost items, including software tasks and summarized miscellaneous items. If more detail is required, this can be provided on back-up sheets.

Column B gives the cost code for every item. This makes it easier to refer back to the original estimates and budgets and to audit the data presented.

In column C the original budgets for the work packages are shown, and these add up to the total original project budget at the foot of the column. This is the cost budget originally authorized and approved, which should be equal to the original cost estimates. Consideration must be given to the inclusion or otherwise of escalation and other below-the-line estimates, and it may be necessary to add explanatory notes in the accompanying report text.

As the project proceeds, it can be expected that a number of variations or modifications will arise that are agreed with the client, and for which the client will pay. These must obviously increase both the project revenue and the budget. Budget increments from this cause are listed in column D. These, when added to the original budget for each project section give the current revised authorized budgets, in column E (the current budget).

In any project of significant size there are usually variations under consideration or awaiting approval that could ultimately affect the budget (and progress assessment). Until such variations

PROJECT COST REPORT SUMMARY

Project title:

Project number:

Page   of

Report date:

A Item	B Cost code	C Original budget	D Authorized budget changes	E Authorized current budget	F ACWP	G BCWP (assessed)	H CPI	J Forecast costs remaining (E-G)/H	K Forecast costs at completion F+J	L Forecast variance at completion E-K

Figure 27.6 Tabulated project cost report

have been agreed with the client it is obviously not possible to take the additional revenue for granted. It may, nevertheless, be of considerable interest to know the value of any such proposals which happen to be 'in the pipeline' at the report date. Although not shown in the example of Figure 27.6, a column can be included in the report layout, if desired, to give this advance information.

Column F lists the costs actually recorded as at the report date. These comprise the Actual Cost of Work Performed (ACWP) and include the following:

- all labour hours booked to the project (on timesheets or job tickets) converted at standard cost or other appropriate rates into the project control currency;
- overheads and administrative costs;
- payments for directly relevant insurance premiums, licences, legal fees and consultants' fees;
- payments made to, or legitimately claimed by, subcontractors;
- the cost of all materials committed, which includes the cost of all materials and equipment already used or delivered, plus the value of all other materials and equipment for which orders have been placed at the report date. In all cases freight, packing, insurance, agents' fees and duties paid or committed must be included;
- any other costs incurred or committed up to the report date that can be directly attributed to the project.

Column G is obtained as a result of earned-value analysis using the methods described earlier in this chapter. It shows the assessed earned value of all project work performed at the report date.

In column H the cost performance index has been calculated from the data in columns F and G. If the CPI is shown on an item-by-item basis, as here, any variation between the different work packages might be useful management information.

Column J forecasts the costs remaining to completion, obtained by factoring estimates for work remaining by the cost performance index.

Column K indicates the best prediction possible of the final, total project costs at completion. As time passes, the forecast element of this figure will become less, the proportion of actual costs will become greater, and the final prediction will grow more accurate.

The final column, L, highlights any variances between the authorized budgets and the predicted final costs.

POST MORTEM

When the project is finished and the final costs become known an investigation can be conducted to compare the actual expenditure with the original estimates. Such post-mortem examinations are obviously far too late to be of benefit to the completed project, but they can be helpful in pointing out mistakes to be avoided when estimating or conducting future projects.

REFERENCES AND FURTHER READING

APM Earned Value Specific Interest Group (2002), *Earned Value Management: APM Guide for the UK* (High Wycombe: APM).

Fleming, Q. W. and Koppelman, J. M. (2000), *Earned Value Project Management*, 2nd Edition (Newtown Square, PA: Project Management Institute).

Webb, A. (2003), *Using earned Value: a Project Manager's Guide* (Aldershot: Gower).

28 *Managing Multiple Projects, Programmes and Portfolios*

This chapter looks above and beyond the individual project and considers how a company's resources might be employed across a wide mix of projects that together constitute a programme of projects. Thus we are here taking a step up from project management into the wider world of programme management.

PROJECT MANAGEMENT OR PROGRAMME MANAGEMENT?

The project management principles and practices described throughout this book focus almost exclusively on the execution of a single project. We know that a project might be very small or incredibly big. We also know that a project can be a venture carried out for an external client or customer, or that it could be an internal management change or IT project that has no external customer but is self-contained within the business. One certain thing that all these projects have in common is that each will need effective project management to bring it to a successful conclusion. There is, however, a fundamental difference between external and internal projects:

- Commercial projects carried out for external customers are usually expected to generate revenue that includes profit. Further, that profit should be realized during or immediately after project completion and handover. 'Profit' is money earned directly that can be distributed to the shareholders and other investors in the company or added to capital reserves (after allowing for taxation).
- Internal management change and IT projects are funded from investors and capital reserves, not from external customers. These projects do not generate profits directly but they are usually intended to increase profitability. 'Profitability' here means the organization's ability to make profits from its future commercial operations. Thus these internal projects can be regarded as enabling projects, because if they are successful they should enable an organization to operate more efficiently and thus realize greater benefits in the future.

The mix between commercial and internal projects is indicated, somewhat simplistically, in Figure 28.1. This particular illustration represents a contracting company that routinely carries out commercial projects for paying customers. Whilst the company strives to gain business for as many commercial projects as it can, the senior management is often faced with the need to refuse applications from well-meaning managers who foresee real or imaginary benefits from their own ideas for new internal management change and IT projects.

Another quite different arrangement would be for a company in a service industry. Thousands of companies operate in the services industries which include, among others, banking, financial

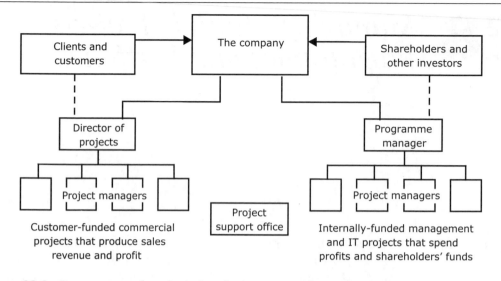

Figure 28.1   Programme of projects in a large contracting company

and legal services, hotels and catering, cleaning, healthcare and insurance. Such companies rarely, if ever, conduct projects for profit but they might have several management change and IT projects running simultaneously. If Figure 28.1 were to be redrawn for one of those companies, the commercial projects in the left-hand side of the figure would be replaced by routine operations, but the right-hand side would still show a number of internal projects, some of which might be extremely expensive – anything from introducing a new brand or corporate logo, to acquisitions and mergers with other companies.

MANAGING A PORTFOLIO OF MANAGEMENT CHANGE AND IT PROJECTS

Business change and IT projects can involve enormous expense and cause considerable disruption throughout an organization. The consequences of failure can be devastating; hindering or even stopping the organization's daily business and operations, damaging tangible and intangible assets, wrecking market reputation and causing distress or even despair among the staff (the most important asset of all). It is thus particularly important that senior management are given a business plan to study for every new project proposal, and that only projects which have acceptably low risk and that promise to contribute to the corporate objectives are allowed to proceed.

The number of business change and IT projects that fail greatly exceeds those that achieve success and there are always several in the public eye that seem to cost several times their original budgets without delivering the promised benefits. Any manager faced with a proposal to authorize a new internally-funded project must always bear this risk in mind. In a company of any significant size, it is probable that senior management will be faced at any given time with more than one proposal for a new internal project, and in a group of companies the problem will undoubtedly be greater.

The first action needed is to establish a procedure to ensure that any person who submits an idea for a new management change or internal IT project prepares a business plan. Further, every business plan should be presented to a common format, so that senior management are more easily able to compare one with another on a like-for-like basis. This principle is not dissimilar to the bid summary proposal used for purchases, but now the stakes are far higher. An initial screening process can also be put in place that should identify on sight projects that could be of no practical benefit to the organization.

There are managers who propose grandiose schemes that might boost their own egos but would be of absolutely no benefit to the company. I remember one such example of a proposal where a company's training manager lobbied senior management to invest in an expensive new corporate training centre, to be housed in new purpose-built premises, complete with its own machine shop. That was made as a serious proposal, to be pursued as an 'act of faith' at a time when the company was on a steep downward path to bankruptcy with a bank overdraft of such proportions that it was having to withhold payments to the suppliers of essential goods and services.

There is a finite limit to the resources available even to the largest group of companies. Even if all the new business plan proposals were rock-solid, cast-iron, guarantees of success, it is most probable that many would have to be rejected through lack of resources. Resources in this sense means not only cash reserves, but also the highly-skilled people needed to manage and drive through these projects to successful implementation.

Portfolio management is an active process needing decisive and incisive actions to ensure that:

- priorities for new proposals are based on the amount and timing of the expected benefits (expressed as cash values), the inherent risks, the amount of resources needed and the availability of those resources;
- no investment is committed on any project unless it has been expressly authorized by senior management, who must always bear in mind that they will be committing investors' and shareholders' funds that might otherwise have been available for distribution as dividends;
- only the most expert people available are assigned, so that the risk of mistakes through incompetence or inexperience are minimized;
- every active project is regularly monitored with the understanding that the plug can be pulled to stop further funds being sunk into any venture that shows early signs of failure.

An organization that directs its effort wrongly in these respects could be investing (or rather, wasting) tens of millions, or even hundreds of millions, of pounds in inappropriate projects. Even billions of pounds have been wasted in a few public sector IT projects (for example in the UK's National Health Service). In an ideal world, a company's shareholders should be able to see how each and every project adds value to the shares in their pockets.

MULTI-PROJECT RESOURCE SCHEDULING

Case for multi-project scheduling

Many companies choose to do without network-based multi-project scheduling or even without resource scheduling at all. In some instances this may not be serious. For instance, construction companies that rely mainly on subcontractors for their site work will be able to leave most manpower resource scheduling to the external firms. Only head office design and supervision staff will have to be scheduled, and relatively primitive scheduling methods can often be used satisfactorily for that limited purpose.

It is in those organizations which employ their own permanent direct labour force for a number of simultaneous projects where multi-project scheduling is more likely to be essential. A multi-project schedule has benefits for an organization beyond the planning and control of existing work. The schedule, if properly prepared, is a model of a company's total workload. As such, it becomes a powerful aid to manpower and corporate planning. It is possible to run what-if trial schedules, testing possible new projects in the multi-project model to see what effect these might have on the company's future workload and capacity requirements.

The remainder of this chapter assumes that portfolio management priority difficulties have been sorted out, so that the only problem remaining is knowing how to marry the individual project plans and resource needs to the resources available in the company. I have to make one or two assumptions before I can conclude this chapter. These are:

- that the principles of resource scheduling explained in Chapters 16 and 17 have been absorbed and understood, particularly with regard to scheduling people with specialist skills;
- that every project in the resource-scheduling mix has been subjected to at least WBS and OBS breakdowns, without which work-instructions cannot be targeted to the relevant managers and supervisors;
- that a critical path network diagram has been drawn with sufficient detail and care for every project;
- that the project management software has been chosen to ensure that it will be able to cope with the volume and complexity of data in the multi-project model.

All of this can still present an apparently difficult problem. The system has to digest a vast amount of data, priority conflicts must be resolved and all logical task interdependencies need to be observed. In addition, the result has to be dynamic and responsive to changes, such as design modifications, technical problems, work cancellations, the introduction of new projects or fluctuations in total resource capacities.

In the past such planning had to be carried out mentally, using adjustable bar charts, which severely restricted the capability and flexibility of the system. However, as in the case of single-project scheduling, computer systems are available to everyone for this process.

Projects and subprojects

In multi-project scheduling there is an important difference of scale from single project scheduling. The organization's total workload can be regarded as 'the project'. Each of the former individual projects becomes, effectively, a 'subproject' within the new total project.

Terminology varies from one software system to another. *Deltek Open Plan™* and *4C*, for instance, both refer to the total workload as the 'group of projects', with each separate network called a 'project' in the normal way. In other multi-project systems (and often in this chapter) the term 'subproject' is used to mean each separate whole project within the total multi-project model.

Network task identifiers

There is a probability that the same task identifying code numbers will crop up on different subproject networks. This will be true particularly if the tasks for each subproject are numbered in a simple numeric series.

With some software this can be disastrous. When presented with two or more subprojects containing duplicated numbers, the computer sees the whole conglomeration of data as one huge error-laden network. The confusion and number of errors generated can be imagined, with all sorts of complex constraints and paths being created across all the subprojects by mistake. There are several possible solutions to this problem, which depend largely on the capabilities of the software chosen.

One solution is to ensure that duplicate numbers can never arise between different subnetworks. A good way to prevent duplication is to prefix all the task ID codes within each subproject with a unique string of characters. The length of this string will obviously depend on the number of subprojects to be managed, but it is unlikely to be more than two or three characters. Some software can add such prefixes automatically across all the tasks in a subproject network. Project numbers, or parts of them, can provide useful and logical prefixes. It is, however, easy to build up very long task ID codes. These are best avoided if possible because long numbers increase work and the risk of human errors. Some of the cheaper systems can only accept ID codes containing perhaps four or six characters in total, which does not allow much space for a prefix.

Fortunately, most software packages do not demand that every number in the overall multi-project model is unique. It is only necessary to make certain that every identifier is unique within its own subproject network diagram. The vital point then becomes that each subproject *must* be given its own identifying subproject code.

Managing the multi-project model

The multi-project model can be expected to have a continuous but constantly changing existence. It will comprise a variable number of subprojects, each with its own different finite life. At regular or irregular intervals, new projects must be added, completed projects removed, and progress information or other changes injected for current projects. Managing such a model can be a formidable (but worthwhile) task. Even though individual project networks might be of manageable size, perhaps containing only one or two hundred tasks, the total multi-project model for a medium-sized company can easily contain many thousands of tasks.

Strict attention to data preparation, system security and updating disciplines must be observed if the whole model is to be maintained in a useful state. This usually means that access levels to the system must be carefully controlled, through entry passwords. Certainly the data should be accessible for all authorized people to view, but only those with the necessary training and skills should be allowed to enter data or commands that could materially affect the project files and the resulting schedules. Access that can change the system parameters must be even more jealously guarded. Figure 28.2 shows the arrangement that I favour for maintaining the integrity of the multi-project model, while still allowing adequate access for the system users.

The coordination function need not be expensive. It can often be performed by one skilled, appropriately trained person. Training and hands-on experience must, however, be given to at least one deputy. In larger organizations the ideal home for administering the multi-project model is the project support office.

Data preparation for the multi-project model

Preparation for multi-project scheduling is very similar to that required for single project scheduling. Anyone who has mastered the problems associated with single-project resource scheduling will find the step up into multi-project modelling very easy.

A separate network must be drawn for every significant, definable subproject in the organization. Estimates for durations, costs and resources are made in the normal way and prepared for input to the computer. All of this follows the methods explained in previous chapters.

Calendars and holiday files will normally be the same as those used for carrying out single project scheduling in the organization.

Resource definition file

When the resource definition file is established, it will have to be structured for the whole model rather than for any individual subproject. This means that the total availability level of each resource will be the total amount of that resource which is available for allocation to all subprojects. That, fortunately, is an easier process than attempting to specify the resource availability for individual subprojects.

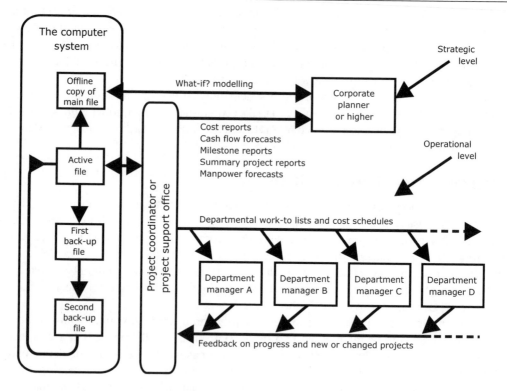

Figure 28.2 Managing a multi-project model

The use of resources on non-project work must be taken into account when the total multi-project schedule is calculated. Such requirements might include the manufacture of customer spares items for stock, or the setting aside of staff to provide a general inquiry, consultancy or other commitment under a service contract with a major customer. There are two ways in which this problem can be approached:

- The total level for each resource in the organization that is declared as being available for projects can be reduced by an amount equivalent to the miscellaneous work and staff absences, which means using the sludge factor described in Chapter 17.
- The non-project work can be introduced into the scheduling calculations as if it were one continuous project. This would require a network (which might need only one task) having a duration spanning not less than the life of the whole multi-project schedule, and carrying the forecast non-project usage level for each category of resource in the model.

The second of these approaches is over-complicated and less satisfactory, but is likely to be more accurate if the organization wishes to use the results of multi-project scheduling in corporate manpower planning (for recruitments or downsizing).

Allocation of priorities between subprojects

Planners are always able to choose from a number of priority rules for allocating resources to tasks within each subproject, just as in single project scheduling. In the multi-project case, however, there is a further level of priorities to be decided, namely the allocation of resources between different subprojects.

The ideal solution is very simple and it works well. First, it is necessary to specify target start and completion dates for every subproject. These dates should obviously be the contractual dates committed and agreed with the various customers and they should already exist in the filed data. The computer will carry out time analysis for all subprojects independently and calculate float from these imposed target dates. After that, priority claims for scarce resources during multi-project processing can be decided automatically according to the amount of float possessed by each task.

Senior management, sales managers and individual project managers will undoubtedly have views on priority differences between all the subprojects in the model. There are occasions, for example, when one customer might be regarded as being more important than another. There is then a risk of interference with the scheduling process, with a desire to force the progress of one or two projects at the expense of others. If the project planner cannot overcome these undesirable external influences, the favoured subproject will have to be given some form of higher priority by artificial means. This can be achieved by placing an artificially early target completion date on the relevant subproject.

Some software will allow specific priority levels to be imposed for different subprojects. The planner will need to ask the relevant software company how the particular system deals with this aspect. However, all such artificial allocation of priorities must be resisted wherever possible. When a successful multi-project scheduling operation has been established, it should earn the benefit of management trust and be left to deal with priorities in its own logical and equitable fashion. Allocation of resources according only to remaining float is an elegant solution that is easy to apply.

Interface tasks (activities) in multi-project scheduling

There may be a few instances where it is necessary for one or more subproject networks to share the same task or have a linking constraint. In such cases the common tasks must bear the same identifier, and be designated as interface tasks. Interfaces are highlighted on network diagrams by enclosing the task box with a double-ruled border.

The incidence of interfaces in multi-project scheduling should be rare. It is not good practice, for example, to use them in an attempt to force priorities between different subprojects (where reliance on remaining float relative to scheduled target dates is the more sensible option). There are, however, exceptions. One example is in the allocation of final factory assembly space for large items of plant or machinery, where one subproject cannot be assembled until another has cleared the area. Assembly space for large engineering projects is very difficult, if not impossible, to specify and allocate as a resource using project management programs because it involves area shapes and can even mean considering headspace and overhangs. In such cases the sequence in which projects arrive in the assembly bay will have to be decided by the planners in conjunction with factory management. Then, these decisions can be forced into the computer schedules by the use of interface tasks or by the insertion of constraints between subprojects.

It is safer to create special interface tasks (with zero duration) rather than designate existing tasks representing real work as interfaces. Two or more common interfaces must be given the same ID number. Some software will accept interface links but will ignore or corrupt such data as the task description, duration and resource requirements (because these data are effectively being entered more than once when two or more subnetworks bearing the interfaces are entered and processed together).

Updating intervals for multi-project schedules

The increased amount of stored data, and the far higher probability of frequent changes, mean that regular updating of the multi-project model will probably be mandatory. Updating in this sense means the declaration of a new time-now and complete reprocessing of all time analysis, resource schedules and cost calculations throughout the model. The frequency of updating will depend on the amount of data and rate of change in the system, but will probably have to be every two or four weeks or calendar monthly.

Organization breakdown structure and information filtering

With the increased amount of data stored in the multi-project model, even more careful thought has to be given to the organization breakdown structure as it is arranged within the computer. This is essential for ensuring that data can be properly filtered to give each departmental manager reports that contain only information that is personally relevant, interesting and useful to him or her.

Output reports can be sorted for each subproject, so that (sub)project managers will not be inconvenienced by receiving data for subprojects being handled by other managers in the organization. All project managers' reports should be similar to those that they might expect to receive from a computer system handling only their own project. Now, however, each manager can have added confidence that the resources needed to meet the schedule are more likely to be available on time, because the organization's total needs have been taken into account.

Tasks which are the joint responsibility of two of more managers

Allocation of departmental codes, working group codes, resource codes and task level codes can all be used to facilitate editing and filtering. A difficulty that sometimes arises concerns tasks which cross boundaries and require resources simultaneously from more than one department. One example is from an engineering company where prototype manufactured assemblies are subjected to testing that has to be performed by one department and witnessed by another. How can the system be made to produce a report containing the same prototype test tasks for each of the two managers concerned without including non-relevant tasks?

One answer in this particular case is to filter the reports according to the resource codes. Tasks using two or more resource types would simply appear in the corresponding number of reports. Where tasks involve two separate departments but use no significant resources, there is a simple trick. Artificial resources can be created, to allow sorting on their codes. These artificial resources can be given a cost rate of zero and be stated as being available in numbers that cannot possible constrain resource scheduling. *4c* software makes this subterfuge easier, because it allows specified resources to be deselected for the scheduling process.

Processing time

Whereas the schedule for a small project can usually be calculated in a matter of microseconds, multi-project schedules can take considerably longer. More significant is the time taken to print out reports. If this process is likely to take more than one or two hours, consideration should be given to leaving the equipment to perform the operation overnight or at weekends.

What-if testing

Once a multi-project model has been established it is likely to be viewed as fertile ground in which to plant trial projects for what-if testing.

When a new project opportunity arises, the planner can create a simple summary network to represent the new project and inject it into the multi-project model, carry out complete processing, and report back to senior management on the results. There is no need to draw a *detailed* network for each trial subproject, but there must be sufficient summary tasks on which to load the estimated resources and to produce an approximate timescale if the organization's total capacity is to be tested realistically. Such testing can be invaluable for influencing strategic management decisions.

System security safeguards must be designed when what-if calculations are anticipated. All what-if trials must be carried out on a copy of the main model, not on the working file, so that working schedules and the database cannot be corrupted. Some software will allow what-if testing to be performed with adequate safety. Others will use the main model so that, when the what-if test ends, the planner has to delete the trial subproject, reprocess the multi-project model and hope that the database, the schedules and the work-to lists will all be restored to their pre-test state.

Less centralized multi-project option

Most of the discussion in this chapter assumes that the organization's project management scheduling will be carried out centrally by people with special skills and training. In some companies, however, the preferred method is to rely on individual managers using their own computers, each running relatively simple and user-friendly software. At one time this approach denied the organization any possibility of multi-project resource scheduling and reporting.

One approach allows a multi-project database to be set up on a server, but with individual project managers encouraged to carry out their own scheduling using their accustomed software (usually a version of *Microsoft Project*) on network-linked desktops. Innate Management Systems developed software dedicated to this approach, claiming interface capability with a database at the server and with other company systems such as accounting, payroll and procurement. *Artemis Views* is another of the project management software systems available that can coordinate data from individual managers who use *Microsoft Project*.

These are interesting developments but, with several users of different planning skill levels entering project files and progress data, it still needs (perhaps more than ever) one or more experts to oversee the core functions to prevent corruption of the central model.

PROJECT RESOURCE SCHEDULING IN THE CORPORATE CONTEXT

In any organization, planning has to be carried out at several levels. These range from overall, strategic corporate long-range plans to the day-to-day allocation of tasks to individual people and machines. Project scheduling generally lies between these extremes, and can serve several purposes in the general planning context.

Project schedules (combined with sales forecasts of possible work to come) provide the data from which manpower, financial and other long-range corporate plans can be formulated. These data are not needed in great depth of detail. They should instead be summarized in quantities that will suit the broad corporate plans that they feed. This is the 'upward looking' purpose of project schedules, for which they should predict departmental manpower and facilities needed, the types of skills required, cash flows and the like. If the organization is a joint venture or other company set up to handle a single large project, there is one level of planning less for the company to do, because the overall project schedule doubles as the corporate plan.

The principal 'downward looking' purpose of project schedules is to list the jobs that all departments will have to carry out. These are sometimes known as 'work-to' lists. The purpose of these lists is to feed work to all the departments in correct sequence, timed to fit in with project needs. Effective resource scheduling, leading to the issue of work-to lists that are sorted and filtered for the attention of individual managers, should ensure that work is fed to departments at rates that will not cause overloads.

It should then be the job of the departmental managers to arrange the lowest layer of scheduling (the last of the 'seven steps'), which is the day-to-day allocation of jobs to individual people according to their availability or particular aptitudes.

REFERENCES AND FURTHER READING

Bartlett, J. (2000), *Managing Programmes of Business Change*, 3rd Edition (Hook, Hampshire: Project Manager Today).

Bradley, G. (2006), *Benefit Realisation Management: A Practical Guide to Achieving Benefits Through Change* (Aldershot: Gower).

Fowler, A. and Lock, D. (2006), *Accelerating Business and IT Change: Transforming Project Delivery* (Aldershot: Gower).

Kor, R. and Wijnen, G. (2000), *50 Checklists for Project and Programme Managers*, (Aldershot: Gower).

Loftus, J. (ed.) (1999), *Project Management of Multiple Projects and Contracts* (London: Thomas Telford).

Reiss, G. (1996), *Programme Management Demystified: Managing Multiple Projects Successfully* (London: Spon).

29 *More Advanced or Less Frequently Used Techniques*

This chapter explains some project management methods that are less frequently used than those described in earlier chapters or that some people might consider to be advanced.

LINE OF BALANCE CHARTS IN CONSTRUCTION PROJECTS

One line of balance method, a forerunner of MRP II (material requirements planning), can be used for parts and materials scheduling in manufacturing projects. That process was described at some length (in the context of a project to manufacture a small number of filing cabinets) in Chapter 18.

There is, however, another, quite different line of balance method. This is suitable for projects in which a number of similar or identical buildings have to be erected in a planned sequence. A good example is for a construction project where a number of similar houses have to be erected for a new housing estate. The method has two variants, depending upon the number of units to be built. Both will now be described here.

Line of balance for a five-house construction project

Figure 29.1 is a simple bar chart for the construction of five similar houses on a new estate. The same pattern of tasks is repeated for each house but the starts of houses 2, 3, 4 and 5 have been progressively delayed to allow for the various trade groups to progress from one house to the next. A vertical date cursor placed on the current date allows a rough and ready idea of progress to be formed. Everything to the left of the cursor should have been finished.

Line of balance is a refinement of the date cursor method that gives a more accurate picture of planned and actual progress on the day of measurement. A line of balance chart can be drawn for this small construction project by rearranging the bar chart from Figure 29.1 to the pattern shown in Figure 29.2 Notice that there are vertical arrows showing the logical links between consecutive tasks. These are constraints arising from the use of shared resources. They mean that each task requiring a particular trade must be finished before the corresponding task can be started on the next house. Brickwork is the longest task, for which two separate teams (Teams *A* and *B*) have been planned to speed up the whole project.

Anyone attempting to draw such a chart will soon notice a slight scheduling problem, caused because not all tasks have the same duration. The trades engaged on the shortest tasks might have to stand by and suffer idle periods while their busier colleagues catch up. However, as shown in Figure 29.2, buffers can be introduced as a solution to that difficulty.

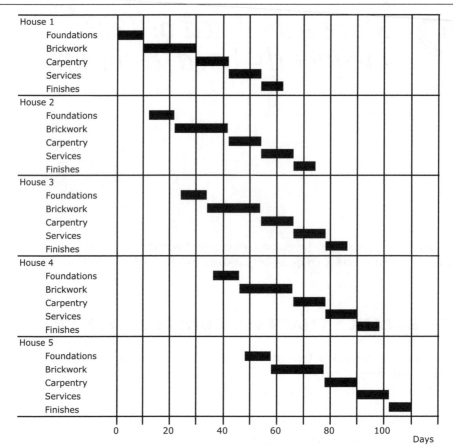

Figure 29.1   Five-house project: Gantt chart

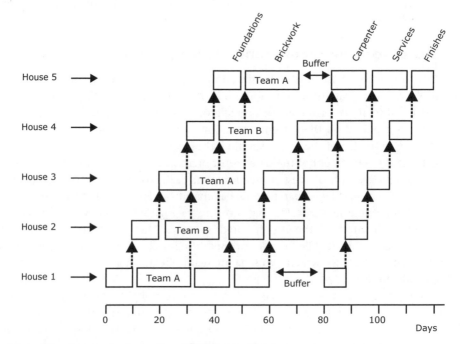

Figure 29.2   Five-house project: line of balance chart

Line of balance for an eighty-house construction project

Figure 29.3 is another line of balance chart, again displaying a plan for building houses, but this project is for 80 houses. There are 15 separate tasks in the plan for each house (only five tasks per house were planned for the five-house project in Figures 29.1 and 29.2). Although this chart looks very different from the charts used in the five-house project, it uses a similar method. The principal difference is that, rather than endure the tedium of drawing a bar chart showing in stepped sequence the 1200 separate tasks needed to construct all 80 houses, the drawing has been coarsened. Every set of 80 identical stepped and linked tasks is represented in Figure 29.3 by a single sloping line. The thickness of each line is proportional to the duration of the task at each house. The slope of each line depends on the time allowed by the planner for completion of all 80 identical tasks. The bent line for glazing tasks introduces a time buffer.

When a vertical 'today's day' cursor is placed on the chart, it will intersect each bar to show the number of houses for which the various tasks should have been completed on that day. The scale should be chosen so that the bars slope at the least possible angle from the horizontal. Then the angle between the cursor and the bars will be greater, allowing greater accuracy when reading off the figures.

DEALING WITH NETWORK PLANS FOR LARGE PROJECTS

Rolling wave planning

One method for dealing sensibly with the problem of planning projects that stretch into the distant future has been called rolling wave planning. The idea is illustrated in Figure 29.4. The planner compiles the project network with as much detail as is sensible and possible, given the information available at the start of the project. It should be possible to plan at least the first few months of work

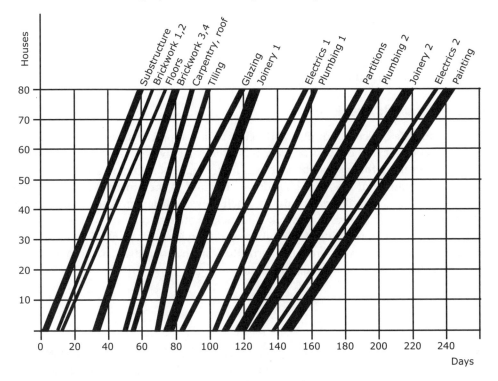

Figure 29.3 Eighty-house project: line of balance chart

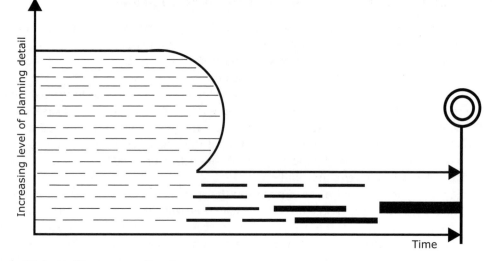

Figure 29.4   Rolling wave planning

in adequate detail and with some confidence. Beyond a certain time, however, the information presented to the planner might be vague or non-existent. Activities towards the end of the project may have to be shown on the network as representing relatively large items of work, perhaps even with single activities representing whole work packages.

So, the network for a project lasting many years could contain many small activities and detailed logic near the project start, but with the level of detail having to decrease as the plan moves into the future. The later stages would show relatively few, but correspondingly larger activities as the final completion activity is approached.

When the time arrives for each network update, the planner must review the information available on later activities and, if possible, introduce more detail into those stages of the network. Thus a picture emerges of the planner gradually pushing the level of detail in the network forward, like a rolling wave, as work on the project proceeds.

Hierarchical network breakdown

Big network diagrams are difficult to display and follow on a computer screen. Prints are better but unwieldy. It is possible to avoid networks having thousands of activities, yet still plan in sufficient depth of detail, by breaking the main network down into a series of subnetworks. A logical way of attempting this is to start from the work breakdown structure of the project. Each work package can be planned separately, with its own relatively small network diagram. A summary network is necessary that interfaces with all the subnetworks and makes coherent time analysis possible. Figure 29.5 illustrates this approach, with just a few subnetworks depicted for clarity. Special skills must be learned to make this process work properly, particularly in the coordination of input from work package managers and in the use of interface activities.

PERT

PERT (programme evaluation and review technique) is a form of critical path network analysis that can be used whenever a planner is particularly doubtful about the accuracy of all the task duration estimates.

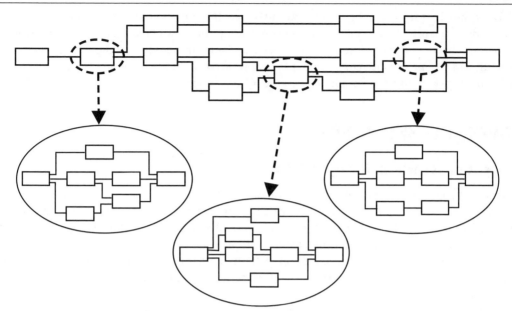

Figure 29.5   Breaking down a large project plan into subnetworks

For PERT, three time estimates are required for every activity:

t_o = *the most optimistic duration that could be foreseen*

t_m = *the most likely duration*

t_p = *the most pessimistic duration*

From these quantities an expected (or probable) duration is calculated for each activity, on a statistical basis, assuming that the errors will fall within a normal distribution curve when all the project activities are taken as the sample:

$$t_e = (t_o + 4t_m + t_p) / 6$$

where t_e is the expected duration

This calculation is repeated on all activities in the network and used to predict the probability of completing the project within the scheduled time. A computer removes the drudgery from these calculations and enables the results to be made available in time for appropriate action to be taken.

Some authorities do not accept that a normal distribution curve is suitable for predicting the spread of estimating errors. Estimates are frequently too optimistic rather than too pessimistic. Allowance for this tendency can be made by skewing the distribution curve deliberately. As an example, the following variation of the formula has been used:

$$t_e = (t_o + 3t_m + 2t_p) / 6$$

Whichever statistical basis is chosen, PERT will produce a critical path in the same way as any other network analysis method. The emphasis has changed slightly, however, from cost-time analysis and concentration on the critical path to a more statistical approach, predicting the probability of completing the project by a given date.

When suitable project management software is used, the computer can carry out many iterations of the critical path calculation, substituting pessimistic, optimistic and most likely duration estimates at random. This is a form of Monte Carlo analysis, and after hundreds or thousands of reiterations the result will be a probability curve similar to that shown earlier, in Figure 6.7. The method can be used to predict costs (as in the example of Figure 6.7) or project duration.

STANDARD NETWORKS

Concept of standard library networks

When a company looks over the plans of its past and current projects, a broad common pattern of working can often be found. It is likely that those project plans will contain common elements – identical work patterns or subplans that occur at various stages in most of the company's projects. By analysing past project plans and by carefully considering current working methods it is often possible to identify and use these common patterns as templates, either to produce complete standard network diagrams, or to isolate standard network elements for use as building blocks in larger networks.

It might be argued that the concept of 'standard' networks is a contradiction in terms. Networking is, after all, supposed to inspire logical thought. It was never intended to regiment planning into a stereotyped routine, devoid of creative thought or constructive imagination. Nevertheless, standard networks have proved their worth. When the time allowed for planning is short, standard networks can sometimes prove to be such timesavers that they will be used when the networking process might otherwise have been ignored altogether.

Standard networks developed during brainstorming sessions by a company's most competent staff should represent the ideal sequence for performing project work. As experience is gained, the standards can be gradually improved so that they capture knowledge and ensure that lessons learned in the past are not forgotten.

Some companies fight shy of standard networks and network modules, and either continue to draw a completely new Gantt chart or network for each fresh project or skimp the planning process. The excuse most often heard is: 'We are a special case. It can't be done here because we are different from other companies and all our projects are different too.' Of course these standardization techniques cannot be applied to *all* projects. Failing even to consider them, however, might deny the firm substantial cost and time benefits.

Standard networks in practice

The easiest type of standard network to envisage is the whole-project template. This is a complete network plan that can be applied directly to two or more identical projects, with no need to change any part of the logic or data. Not surprisingly, this condition seldom arises in real life. There are, however, many cases where a standard master network can be devised that will at least act as a general pattern for planning similar projects.

The technique is carried out by first drawing a master network covering all activities required for a project which is judged to be typical of a range of projects carried out by the organization. It is valuable if as many suitably experienced people as possible are consulted or, better, are actually on hand in a brainstorming session when the master network is sketched. The aim must be to produce (within reason) the most comprehensive collection of tasks likely to be encountered and to plan them in the most efficient and practicable work sequence that can be devised. It is quite likely that this process will reveal some inefficiencies or deficiencies in current working methods and lead to immediate cost-effective changes.

Many companies sell projects that can be designed and built with a range of options. In these cases the standard network should be drawn to include all the options, or at least all the more common options. If, for example, the network is produced for a range of houses to be built with or without a garage, the standard version should include the garage. It is a simple matter for the project manager to strike out the activities not needed for houses ordered without garages.

The master standard network can be kept as hard copy or it can be stored in the computer files. When each new project materializes, the master network is discussed with the project manager or other responsible person, who then takes the following steps:

- Delete activities relating to options that the customer has not ordered or are otherwise not required.
- Delete or modify design activities in the light of any available retained engineering (designs from earlier projects that can be used directly or adapted for the new project).
- Add any special constraints or new activities needed for the particular project (for example, A must be designed before B).
- Review the standard estimated duration, resource and cost data for all activities according to project complexity.

The modified or edited standard network is then adopted as the network plan for the new project. The original standard network remains on file, unchanged, for reuse. (The standard might be changed if, in the light of much experience, some of its standard estimates or logic should be changed permanently.)

House construction example

A number of identical or very similar detached houses are to be built by a construction company on different sites and at different times. Here is an obvious case where a network diagram drawn for the erection of the first house must have relevance to all subsequent houses of the same design. The network for the first house could, therefore, be drawn and filed as a library standard, to be used whenever a house of the same or similar design is to be built. However, although the network configuration (logic) may be identical throughout, it might be necessary to review all the duration estimates for each house according to its particular environment and ground conditions.

Engineering company example

A company making special-purpose heavy machine tools to individual customer orders used the same standard project network templates very successfully in its engineering plants on both sides of the Atlantic. The simplest of these was used solely as a logic diagram, without time estimates. It served as a sequenced checklist for the start-up activities needed every time a new order for a machining system was received. A slightly simplified view of this network was shown in Figure 21.3.

The same company made full use of project standard networks for its range of adjustable rail milling machines (also known as plano-mills) and scalpers. Machines varied greatly in size, but a typical machine weighed hundreds of tonnes and was built on a bed about 20 metres in length. In spite of big differences in the size and power of these machines, all had similar configurations. Although each of these projects could last up to 18 months and might be valued at several million pounds, the use of a universal standard network kept the network planning cost down to only a few hundred pounds.

When a new order was received, it was only necessary for the chief engineer or project manager to spend an hour or so in marking up a copy of the master network template with appropriate estimates and logic changes. The result in each case was a network whose logic embodied all the lessons learned on similar previous projects, yet was fully customized for the particular project in hand.

TEMPLATES (STANDARD NETWORK MODULES)

A search through networks from past projects should reveal several small repeating network elements, perhaps occurring more than once within each network and common throughout all the projects. Two examples follow that show how these can be used as templates to create networks for new projects.

Templating example using paper-based modules

The machine tool company mentioned above reviewed its network diagrams for several special transfer line machine projects. As a result, it was able to break down those networks into areas that could be represented by small, standardized modules or templates. Summarized briefly, this company's breakdown approach was first to divide the main project network into three consecutive subnetworks:

1. engineering design and drawing
2. procurement and machining
3. assembly.

Within each of these three main areas, small network modules were identified which could be used for every subassembly and main assembly. Examples of these modules are illustrated in Figures 29.6 and 29.7 (arrow notation was in use at the time).

Taken from the design subnetwork template library, Figure 29.6 shows the module used for the design and drawing of any machine along the transfer line that required manufactured (as opposed to purchased) machining heads.

The module used for machining all the components needed for any mechanical subassembly is shown in Figure 29.7. This would be linked into the network by interface events or dummies so that it fitted in between its relevant design engineering and assembly activities (from the preceding and succeeding subnetwork modules).

The whole system only needed about 12 different module designs. All of these were printed in suitable quantities on transparent, self-adhesive film and kept as a library for use in the small planning department. Whenever a new project had to be planned, the network was constructed by sticking the appropriate modules on a large piece of polyester film or translucent paper.

This process could be carried out by junior staff, using the sales engineer's block schematic drawing of the transfer line machine as the guide. Standard start and finish modules were available for sticking at the front and back ends of the network, respectively. The project manager was called in to spend an hour or so in modifying, editing and approving the network before computer scheduling.

Event numbers were partly preprinted on the modules, the planner simply having to complete each number by prefixing two digits from each module's relevant work breakdown (cost) code. This procedure made it impossible to duplicate event numbers by mistake.

Using the company's well-documented past cost records, standard tables were later developed for the duration, resource and materials cost estimates, based on a few simple rules about machine size and complexity.

The network data produced by these methods were fed into the computer to produce work-to lists, resource and cost schedules. The system was fully multi-project across the whole company. The resulting resource schedules and work-to lists were very effective and resulted in a considerable

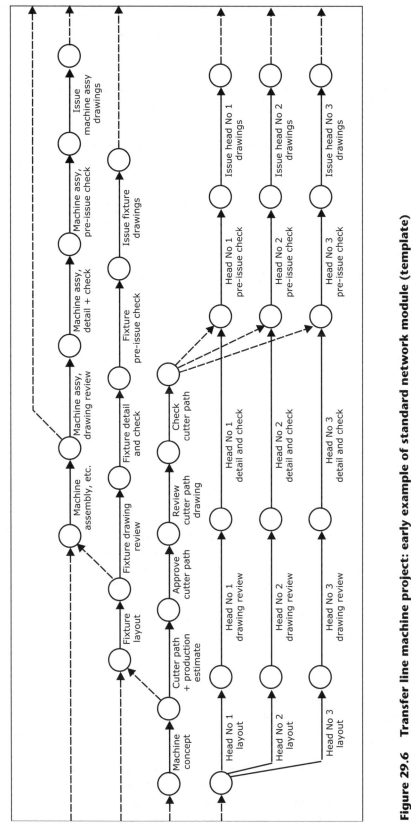

Figure 29.6   Transfer line machine project: early example of standard network module (template)

When fewer than three heads are required, the unwanted activities are simply crossed out and ignored. A different module caters for machines with bought-out heads. One stand-ard start-up module precedes all these design modules. Each design module feeds into subassembly modules for purchasing and manufacturing (see Figure 29.7).

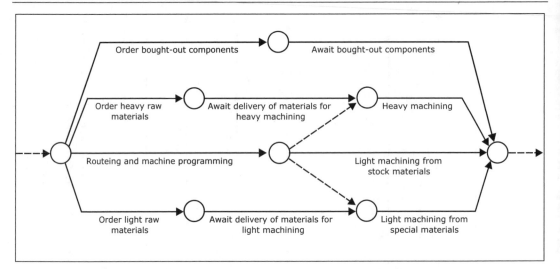

Figure 29.7   Transfer line machine project: procurement and machining template

This standard network module contains the activities needed to provide the components for one subassembly from the design module illustrated in Figure 29.6. These subassembly modules feed a final assembly and test module to complete the project network.

improvement in 'cost and time performance. Cost estimates generated from the system were within ± 5 per cent overall of those calculated separately by the company's cost estimating department.

Templating case example using computer-generated networks

The templating example demonstrated in this section was processed using *4c* (now available from 4c Systems Limited). The project was given the file name 'Templa' and the title 'Templating Case Study Project'. The project start date was specified as 13 May 2002.

The project

The project for this case study is based on a templating application actually used by a manufacturing company within my consulting experience. I have, however, changed the nature of the product to protect the company's proprietary information. The network templates and full diagrams used here are slightly simpler than their real counterparts so that they can be kept clear and legible within the confines of a book page.

For every new customer order, the company has to adapt or redesign a number of electronic or electrical subassemblies, for each generic type of which there is a subnetwork template to cover its design and manufacture. The number and choice of these sub-assemblies varies from one project to the next, and all are finally assembled in a cabinet or frame to produce one complete project unit. The cabinet design will depend on the nature and number of subassemblies needed for the project. The assembled project unit has to be subjected to final inspection and testing before it can be packed and shipped to the customer. Figure 29.8 illustrates the range of templates held in the template library in the computer and indicates how the appropriate templates are selected to suit a particular project.

All projects in this company start with a range of similar start-up tasks that can easily be fitted into one standard master project start template network diagram, shown as the upper template in Figure 29.9. This start template is joined to all the following selected subassembly network templates by means of interface activity AA9.

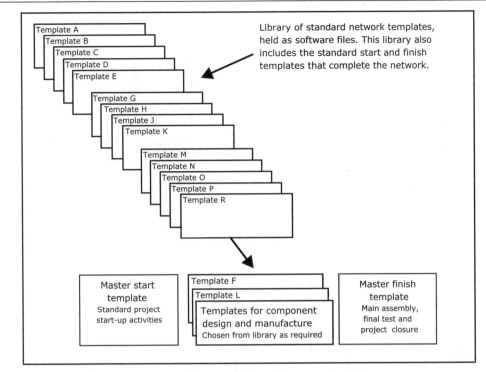

Figure 29.8 Templating case example: template library principle

The lower half of Figure 29.9 depicts template B, one of the standard subassembly templates chosen for this project. Another, template D, is shown as the upper half of Figure 29.10. This project, therefore, has only two subassemblies, designated by the code letters *B* and *D*.

Whichever subassembly templates are chosen for any project, they all feed (via interface FF1) to the standard finish template shown in the lower half of Figure 29.10.

To summarize, Project Templa uses four standard templates from the total number contained in the template library. The chosen templates are as follows:

- start template, coded TCSAA (mandatory for all similar projects)
- subassembly template type B
- subassembly template type D
- finish template, coded TCSFF (mandatory for all similar projects).

Creating the project network

Once the new project had been opened as a project file using the *4c* software, the project templating mode was selected. The screen then displayed the contents of the template library (Figure 29.11 shows a screen detail).

The new project network was created quickly and simply by selecting templates TCSAA, B, D and TCSFF (shown highlighted in Figure 29.11). The software then merged all four templates in one quick operation. Figure 29.12 depicts another screen capture from *4c*, showing the complete network in outline. Figure 29.13 is a zoomed-in view showing how the links surrounding one of the interfaces (AA9) have been observed correctly by the software.

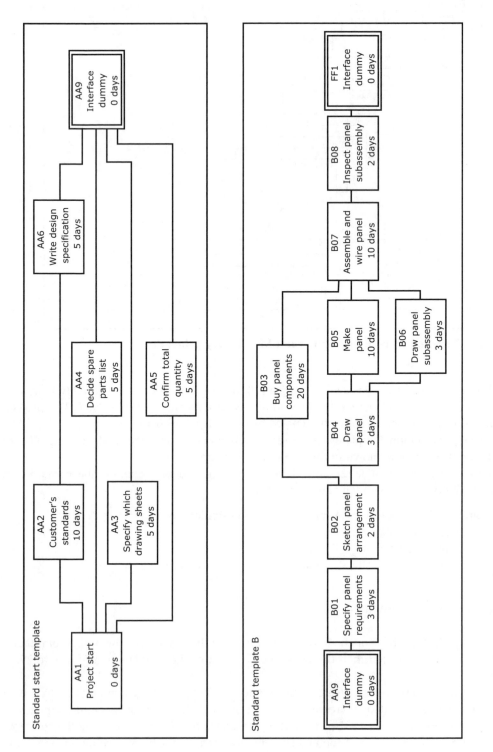

Figure 29.9 Templating case example: standard start template TCSAA and template B

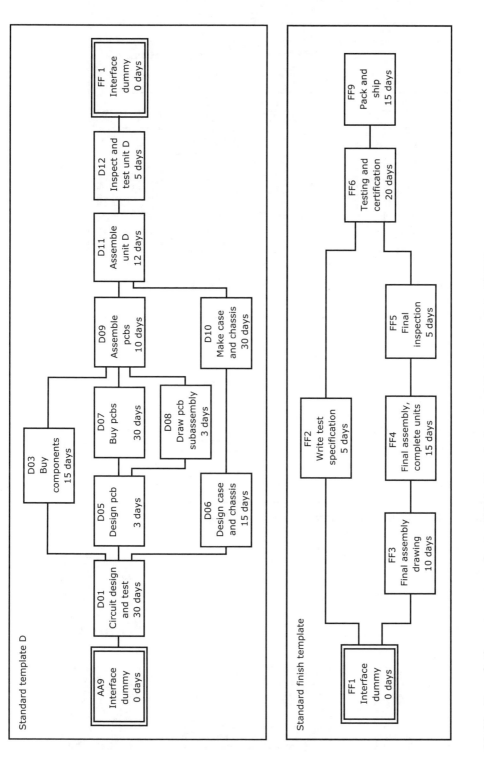

Figure 29.10 Templating case example: template D and standard finish template TCSFF

Template Reference	Description
A	Master link 1 (prototype)
TCSAA	Template case study start template
B	Master link 2 (permanent equipment)
TCSB	Template B for case study
C	Bearing unit
TCSD	Template D for case study
E	Turbine housing design
F	Turbine housing prototype
TCSFF	Template case study finish template
G	Turbine housing (permanent equipment)
Garage1	Standard garage network
H	Turbine wheel design
J	Turbine wheel prototype
K	Turbine wheel (permanent equipment)

Figure 29.11   Templating case example: template library browser

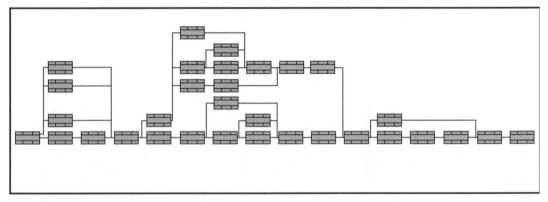

Figure 29.12   Templating case example: network diagram

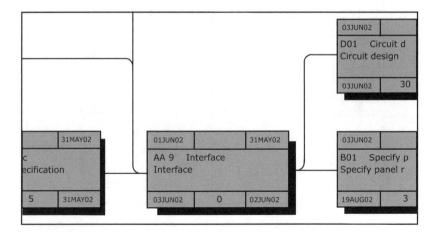

Figure 29.13   Templating case example: network fragment

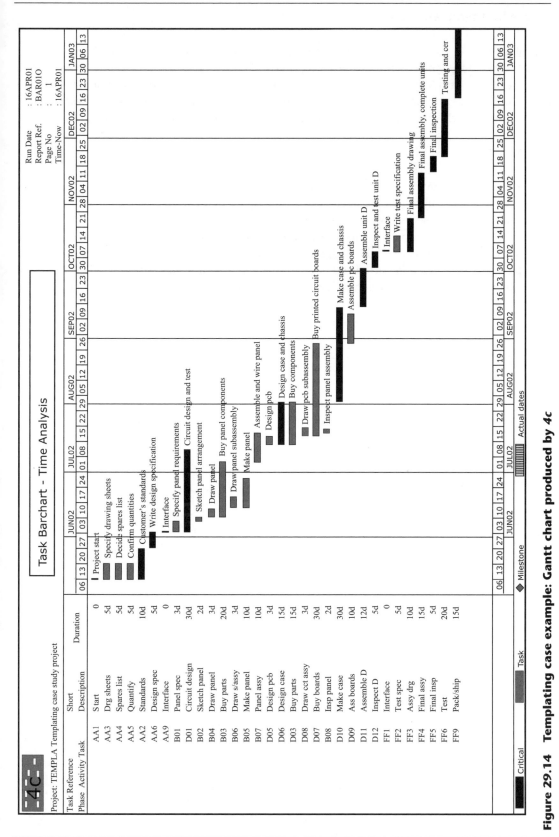

Figure 29.14 Templating case example: Gantt chart produced by 4c

Note about template interfaces

One problem with templating is the treatment of inter-template links or interfaces. Most programs capable of merging templates into whole project networks do not possess the capability of *4c* and will not observe the links between interface activities on the different templates. The planner will then have to enter these links separately after the merging process. This might be a small inconvenience in some cases, but a checklist of such links will always be necessary to prevent errors and omissions.

Processing

Once the templates have been merged, the project network exists in the computer files as a normal project, available for all processing in the usual way. Figure 29.14 shows the Gantt chart produced by *4c* for this templating case example project, based on early dates from time analysis.

In the real-life case on which this case example is based, the number of activities in an actual template varies between 15 and 100. A typical project could comprise some 10 templates altogether, perhaps containing about 350 activities. Full resource and cost information is included. With well over 100 projects in the multi-project model at any time, templating saves this company a great deal of time and effort.

30 *Managing Project Closure*

Project management activities do not usually end abruptly when all the tasks on the plan have been performed successfully. A number of loose but important ends need to be tied up in a process which some (with inadequate respect for the English language) call 'closeout'.

REASONS FOR CLOSING A PROJECT

Projects do not always end successfully and there are a number of reasons why projects are occasionally closed before their intended finish date. Here are a few of the many possible reasons for stopping work on a project:

- The project has been completed and handed over to the project owner, with or without complete success.
- The project contractor has run out of funds, leaving the owner to find a new contractor.
- The project owner has permanently run out of funds, killing the project.
- The project owner wishes to make fundamental changes, causing the project to be scrapped and restarted.
- Changed economic or political conditions mean that the project will no longer be financially viable for the owner in the foreseeable future (for example, a fall in the price or demand for a commodity that removes financial justification for building new plant to increase production capacity).
- The customer asks for the project to be 'put on hold' (delayed indefinitely) pending a possible improvement in market conditions or to await the results of a reappraisal.
- Government policy changes (possible for many reasons) resulting in termination of some government contracts. Defence contracts for weapons systems, ships and aircraft are always subject to such risks.
- An Act of God (flood, tempest and so on) has intervened, causing further work on the project to be suspended or abandoned.
- Hostile activities have broken out in an internal or international conflict, making work on the project impossible.

Premature project closure can affect the closure procedures required but all sections in this chapter (except for final as-built definition) assume successful completion and handover to the project owner.

FORMAL PROJECT CLOSURE

Just as it was necessary to issue a formal document of authority to open a project and allow expenditure to begin, so the end of a project or its indefinite interruption must be marked by a formal announcement that stops further expenditure and sets the closure procedures in motion.

Cost cut-off

The most significant reason for issuing a formal project closure statement is to forbid further expenditure against the main project cost accounts. This is particularly important if hard-won profits are not to be eroded by an insidious continuation of timesheet bookings to the project simply because the account still happens to be open. It is well known that the recording of hours on timesheets is open to abuse; there is always a tendency for the less scrupulous staff to try and 'lose' unaccountable or wasted time by booking it to large projects where, it is hoped, it will go unnoticed. Good supervision will minimize this risk, but an instruction to the computer to reject all further timesheet entries against the project number is more effective.

Company accountants may wish to hold a project account open for their own use beyond the official project closure date to collect a few tail-end costs. Although further man-hour time bookings are banned after the closure date, there are usually items such as late invoices from suppliers and subcontractors to be accounted for. On a large project these can continue to arrive for several months after project completion. They can represent considerable sums, but they should not affect the calculated profit significantly because (unless there has been loose control of subcontracts and dayworks) these costs should have been known and accrued in the accounts when they were committed (that is, when the purchase orders or subcontracts were issued).

Project closure document

The formal closure notice need only be a very simple form, but it should contain the following information:

- project title
- project number
- effective closure date
- reason for closure
- any special instructions
- signature authorizing the closure
- distribution, which should at least include all those who received the authorization notice when the project was opened.

An example of a fairly comprehensive closure notice is given in Figure 30.1.

Authorizing post-project expenditure

Although a guillotine must be imposed on time bookings at project closure, it must be recognized that large projects often leave a backwash of documentation work in their wake. Some of these activities are summarized in this chapter. They may require considerable effort, although much of this can be assigned to clerical and fairly junior engineering staff. Just how well such tasks are performed depends to a large extent upon how much money the contractor is prepared to spend on them. Best practice is to keep all documentation as up to date as possible during the active course of the project, so that updating and filing or archiving at the end of the project requires as little effort as possible.

NOTICE OF PROJECT CLOSURE

The following project will be closed to time bookings and all expenses with effect from the date given below

Client: **Lox Chemicals Limited**   Project number: **LX 5150**

Project title: **Loxylene Plant (Huddersfield)**   Closure date: **20 Apr 04**

The following budgets are hereby authorized for the closedown activities marked in the checklist below

Department	hours by standard cost staff grade						£
	1	**2**	**3**	**4**	**5**	**6**	
Project engineering	10			20	40		960
Planning				10			140
Purchasing			15				240
Installation and commissioning							
Construction management	5						100
Computing				1			14
Records and archives			10		200		2560
TOTALS	15		25	31	240		4014

Special ins tructions:

   Take special care with filing. A follow-up project is expected.
   All files to be destroyed after five years unless otherwise
   directed below.

CHECKLIST OF PROJECT CLOSURE ACTIVITIES

Project case history	PM to write, keep it brief
Project specification	Has been kept up to date but needs checking
Project variations	List and check that the file is complete
Drawing schedules	Keep 10 years in engineering files
Design calculations	Keep indefinitely in engineering files
Our drawings	Check they are as-built and keep indefinitely
Client's drawings	Return to client
Purchase control schedules	Keep 10 years in engineering files
Vendors' drawings	Keep 10 years
Purchase orders	
Expediting/inspection reports	
Test certificates	Keep 10 years
Operating/maintenance instructions	Keep 15 years
Spares lists	
Maintenance contracts	
Subcontract documents	Keep 10 years
Correspondence files	
Final cost records	Keep 10 years in general reference files
Photographs	Edit. Discuss with publicity dept and client
Critical path networks	Destroy after 1 year and erase computer files
Management information system	Delete project from MIS at year end

Prepared by: **A.Scribe**   Project manager: **I.Diddit**   Authorized by: *B. I. G. Whitechief*

Figure 30.1   Project closure notice with checklist

In some firms, final documentation will be treated as an overhead expense, while others may be more fortunate in having budgets and funding contractually agreed with their clients for this purpose.

Whether treated as an overhead cost or as a directly recoverable expense, post-project work should be regarded as a work package, separately identifiable from the main project, which should be allocated its own, separate, strictly budgeted account number. This work, all in-house and under local supervision, should be relatively easy to monitor and control. It is often prudent to limit authorization to a few named individuals, so that only timesheets bearing the staff or roll numbers of these people will be accepted by the computer for bookings against the closure account.

The form illustrated in Figure 30.1 not only announces project closure but also acts as an authorization document for a limited amount of expenditure on the post-project work package. By no means typical, this example would obviously need modification in practice to suit each contractor's own project circumstances and management systems. It does, however, demonstrate a method that can help to ensure the orderly closedown of a project. The version in Figure 30.1 states the budgets allowed. It also includes a checklist of all the final project activities, together with some management directives regarding the disposal of documents.

FINAL PROJECT COST RECORDS

Final cost accounting information provides an important databank from which comparative cost estimates can be made for future projects. This is especially true of the man-hour records. Costs for materials and purchased equipment, and the monetary conversion of man-hours into wages plus overheads, are not quite so useful because these records become invalidated by cost inflation as time passes. Those needing to retrieve information from any of these records will find their task made immeasurably easier if all the data have been filed under a logical and standard cost-coding system which has been rigidly applied across all projects.

DISPOSAL OF SURPLUS MATERIAL STOCKS

Surplus materials and components often remain upon completion of a project. Sensible consideration must be given to the most cost effective method of their disposal.

Some specialized components may be saleable to the customer as part of a recommended holding of spare parts. Other items may be returned to common stock, sold or (if necessary) scrapped.

Redundant stocks must not be allowed to accumulate because they represent a useless investment in money and space. It might be argued that quantities of very tiny, low-cost items take up little space and represent insignificant investment ('worth keeping because they might come in useful one day') but even these can cost time and money to store, and to count at each annual stocktaking.

If project materials and components are never going to be used, their value can be expected to dwindle steadily towards zero as they deteriorate or become obsolete. Get rid of them.

FINAL PROJECT DEFINITION: THE END OF A CONTINUOUS PROCESS

Chapter 3 described the project definition process, and Figure 3.1 showed how this process can develop throughout the life cycle of a project. In any substantial project, definition does not end until after the project has been finished, when the last document has been updated, registered and filed or archived.

Formal project variation, modification and concession procedures are all part of this process (see Chapter 25). The project manager or engineers must ensure that any deviations from drawings are fed back for incorporation. This can be a particularly significant problem where work has taken place at a site remote from the contractor's home office.

The remainder of this chapter is concerned with documenting the as-built project and with the safe retention of documents.

AS-BUILT CONDITION OF A MANUFACTURING OR CAPITAL ENGINEERING PROJECT

Whether a project is for manufactured equipment or for a mining, civil engineering, petrochemical or other capital project, it is important that the as-built condition on completion is adequately recorded. This is vital if the contractor is to be able to fulfil post-contract obligations to the client. In theory, all that is necessary is to list every drawing, specification, and other document describing the project design, configuration and content (not forgetting to include the serial and correct revision numbers of all these documents). All engineering changes should have been incorporated, so that every document is in its final condition.

Records should also include spare copies of operating and maintenance instructions, including those written by the contractor for the whole project as well as those received from the suppliers of bought-out equipment built into the project.

Provided that all this material is stored in a properly indexed, secure system, there should be no serious information problems in store for people concerned with operating, maintaining, repairing or modifying the project in the future.

Engineering design records

For engineering design records the first need is to keep a set of project drawings. Sometimes clients will, having paid for the engineering design of a project, consider all project drawings to be their own property. The client's own drawing sheets may even have been used. The contractor will still want to keep a set of drawings on file (almost certainly in digital form).

The key to indexing and defining all the drawings at the end of a project is either the central drawing register or, preferably, specific project drawing schedules (described in Chapter 21 and illustrated in Figure 21.4). For manufacturing projects, bills of materials or parts lists will identify all the project drawings.

The final set of drawing schedules should list every drawing used in the project and give its drawing number and correct revision number.

Documenting purchased equipment

For the purposes of illustration, suppose that a client has formally accepted the handover of a complex manufacturing plant, the result of a very large turnkey project. Everything has been managed for the client, including the construction of the buildings, purchasing and installation of all the plant, cranes and other equipment, and final commissioning. Quite obviously, the contractor retains a follow-up responsibility to the client for arranging service under guarantee, assisting with operating problems, and in being able (if required) to carry out future modifications or extensions to the plant.

To provide such a post-project service, the contractor needs adequate technical records of the equipment that was purchased from external suppliers. These records have to be obtained from the vendors during the course of the project in the form of layout drawings, technical specifications, operating and maintenance instructions, lists of recommended spares, lubrication charts, test certificates and so on.

In most cases at least one copy of all such documents would be sent to the client but every prudent contractor will retain a set. While it should theoretically always be possible to go back to the relevant vendor for information in the event of a subsequent problem, vendor companies have a distressing habit of going out of business, or of losing their former identities in mergers and take-overs.

There may also be a considerable benefit to the contractor in keeping detailed records of equipment purchases, because these can often be of use to engineers when specifying equipment for future, non-related projects.

Purchase schedules

On large capital projects the purchase schedules are the main index of purchasing documentation. The relevant purchase specification numbers (with their correct revision status), supplier and purchase order details should all be traceable through this route. Purchase schedules were described in Chapter 18 and are illustrated in Figures 18.12 and 18.13.

Other documentation

Design calculations

Design calculations are a vital part of project records. It is essential that these are numbered, indexed and stored with at least as much care as that given to the main drawing files. They may be called for in the unfortunate event of subsequent malfunction or structural failure, especially if personal injury results.

Change documents and inspection certificates

All contract variations, modifications, engineering change requests, concessions, production permits, final inspection reports, test certificates and similar documents that help to define the final design status and quality of the project should be filed and indexed.

Correspondence

Letters to and from vendors can be filed with the relevant purchase order files, where they form part of the technical and contractual record. Other correspondence, not least that with the client, can be filed by date order.

An embarrassing problem sometimes arises because files have been built up in at least two places, in the central filing registry and in the project engineering department. One way of turning this difficulty into an advantage is to have all the important project correspondence filed twice, in two different ways. Files held in the project engineering department can be filed by subject according to the project work breakdown structure codes. Provided that these project files are properly managed, they can be added to the central files when the project ends. The central registry files can be kept in simple date order. This dual archiving approach ensures that any document should be retrievable if either its subject or its date is known.

Internal correspondence between departments is usually of less importance, but can be kept along with the relevant subject files if required.

E-mails can present a big end-of-project problem because of their numbers and often trivial nature. Most can probably be deleted from the files. One solution might be to earmark significant messages at the time of receipt or transmission and place them in secure project files. Then, all the other more ephemeral messages can be deleted by clearing out all personal e-mail files whenever they become too cluttered.

Case history or project diary

If sufficient time and money can be spared for the purpose, it is sometimes useful for the project manager to write a brief case history or diary of the project. This document does not have to be a literary masterpiece, but it should record every significant event, and list all serious problems together with their solutions. When filed with the project specification, minutes of meetings and other key documents, a case history become a valuable asset in the future if legal or other questions arise about the project. Reference to past case histories may also help when formulating the strategy for new projects, and reading about past mistakes can help new managers to avoid repeating them in the future. 'Lessons learned' should, therefore, feature as a main heading.

This, in particular, is a document that can be written in diary fashion as the project journeys through its life cycle.

AS-BUILT CONDITION OF A MULTIPLE MANUFACTURING PROJECT

Many manufacturing ventures, although starting from one initial design project, result in the manufacture of more than one final product. Although these final products all start from the same initial design, if they are not all made in one identical batch it is highly possible that modifications will be introduced between batches. It is even possible for changes to be allowed during the production of one batch. Similar problems exist when the final product is made in continuous manufacture and assembly.

The individual build state of every part of the project or every product must be known for reasons of maintenance, interchangeability of parts and to allow recall or investigation in the event of any failure in service. A familiar example is the automobile manufacturer, who will introduce modifications throughout the production life of a vehicle. When any owner takes a model of that vehicle for repair or servicing, the garage will need to know the actual build status of that particular car. That is achieved by reference to the year of manufacture, more particularly, the chassis or engine serial number. The manufacturer will provide a comprehensive set of build schedules that the service engineer can access from a computer to tell him or her exactly which components have been built into the vehicle.

Identifying individual units

The first requirement is that each unit built should be identifiable by some mark or number which distinguishes it from its fellows. This objective is usually achieved by the allocation of batch or serial numbers. These, together with a type or part number, enable any unit to be identified positively, with no possible fear of misinterpretation.

A diesel-engined a.c. generator type 10256, serial number 1023, leaves no room for doubt. If this unit is received back at the factory for servicing, repair or modification, there is no question regarding its origin, and its design status and build content should be known. It should be possible to look at the general assembly drawing and parts list or bills of material for the generator and so discover the numbers of all the drawings and process specifications that went into its making.

Document revision numbers

Document serial numbers, by themselves, are not a sufficient description. It must always be possible to find out the relevant revision numbers and modification status of drawings and specifications that relate to a particular serial numbered unit or production batch.

Suppose that several diesel a.c. generators of the type just described have been supplied for a large project at different times. All are called a.c. generator type 10256, but they are *not* all identical. A number of modifications have been introduced over the period, so that different production batches contain small but significant design differences. How now can anyone tell exactly what went into the making of one of these generators, knowing only its type number and serial number?

The most common method of circumventing this problem is to compile a build schedule for each batch. This is tedious but possibly unavoidable.

Build schedules

A build schedule comprises a list of all the drawings and specifications used in the manufacture of every unit, with the correct revision number of every drawing shown. If there is any drawing which has more than one sheet, the revision number of every sheet must be given. A separate build schedule must be compiled for every project item that is made and assembled as a single unit, but one build schedule can be used to cover a number of items where these are made as an identical batch.

Formats such as that shown in Figure 30.2 allow all the essential details to be recorded. Build schedules might be single-page affairs or, for larger projects, many pages. Build schedule data were originally compiled on paper sheets, then microfiche or microfilm became popular, but build schedules are now ideally suited to computer-based systems. Build schedules are in many ways to manufacturing projects what purchase and drawing schedules are to capital construction projects.

Note that there is little point in maintaining build schedules of units with differing build standards if all the drawing information cannot be retrieved. It follows that reference files must be kept of all relevant revisions of each drawing in such cases.

Also, the comfortable premise that the latest issue of a drawing must be the correct issue is destroyed. Indeed it can happen that different revisions of the same drawing are in use at the same time when a factory is dealing with assemblies or batches of different modification status.

Product labelling

The build schedule procedure should be supported by labelling the actual products or project hardware components. Each label should be durable and show the part number and the batch or serial number. Small engraved or stamped metal plates are often used. Some companies also provide spaces on the labels to allow modification numbers to be added as each modification is carried out (which includes modifications made in the field).

AS-BUILT CONDITION OF A PROJECT THAT IS INTERRUPTED BEFORE COMPLETION

This chapter started by listing a few reasons why a project might be closed or put on hold before its successful completion. An as-built record will be particularly important, yet most difficult to achieve, if there is any expectation that the customer will resurrect a cancelled project at a later date. Interrupted projects pose great difficulties, especially if work-in-progress has reached the stage when materials have been bought or some components are in various stages of manufacture.

BUILD SCHEDULE			Product number:		
Product or assembly:			Issue date:		
Batch/serial numbers covered:			Sheet of sheets		

Drawing or spec. number	Sheet	Rev	Drawing or spec. number	Sheet	Rev

The following modification numbers are incorporated in this build schedule issue									

HONEYCOMBE PRODUCTS LIMITED   LUTON   BEDFORDSHIRE

Figure 30.2   Build schedule sheet

I remember one large project for a copper mine expansion that was suspended late in its engineering design phase because of a fall in the price and sales of copper. Closing and archiving the project took many months. Although the actual costs of recording the as-built condition of this project were recovered from the customer on a cost-plus basis, the contractor incurred considerable subsequent cost and space problems in storing the vast quantities of drawings and other engineering data. That project was never restarted.

Project interruptions usually prove very expensive for the contractor. Even if all the sunk costs are recovered from the customer, it is not easy to estimate the considerable costs of mothballing the project against the day when it might be restarted. Questions might arise about where responsibility lies for storage of partially completed drawings and hardware. Some very difficult contractual negotiations might be needed before a solution is found that is fair to both parties.

MANAGING FILES AND ARCHIVES

The amount of work needed at the end of a project to close down all the files and store the information safely will be indirectly proportional to the care and attention given to files during the active life of the project. A contractor that has been careless in document control during project execution will pay a higher price for this neglect at the end of the project when the time comes to put adequate records in storage in a form from which any items can easily be retrieved on demand.

Storage

It is very easy to build up substantial files in a very short space of time. These can occupy large areas of expensive office floor. I used to assert that no company could hope to have an infinite life, because as time tends to infinity the company will choke to death on its own files. In recent years various technologies have helped to overcome this problem, first through the use of microfilm and, later, through digital storage on a range of media. It seems, however, that paper will never be absent from the office.

If bulky documents are a problem, the following options can be considered:

- Hire off-site space for the storage of non-active files, possibly in a secure repository managed by one of the specialist archive companies. This method has the drawback that the files can easily be forgotten, the only reminder of their existence being the regular monthly invoices for space rental.
- Label each file prominently with a review date, at which time the file must be considered for microfilming or scanning before being destroyed.
- Invest in space-saving filing equipment. Lateral filing cabinets use less space than drawer-type filing cabinets. Motorized rotary files can be purchased which extend upwards into ceiling voids. Anyone who has ridden in a paternoster form of elevator will recognize the principle.

If any method other than hard copy is used (which really means either microfilm or digital storage) adequate safeguards need to be taken to ensure compatibility with existing and future equipment.

Indexing and retrieval

Finding any document in a large file repository, regardless of the storage medium used, demands that all records are carefully indexed. It should be possible, for instance, to be able to search for an individual letter from a client either by reference to its subject, or by its date, or by both of these. If the storage medium is digital, searching to retrieve information should be easier using keywords.

Security

Records are usually at risk from fire, flood, accidental erasure or other loss and it is always good sense to consider maintaining a security copy (on the basis that tragedy is unlikely to strike in two places simultaneously). If, however, there should be a fire which consumes the original files, the back-up copy will be of less practical use without an index of its contents. An up-to-date copy of the index for the main files must therefore form part of the security files.

The security of computer files is obviously important, but this is a subject that should be familiar to any competent person responsible for computing activities in a company. That person will ensure that regular back-up copies are made and held off-line in data safes or other secure areas.

Information held in computer files has to be remembered at project closure time. Unwanted files should be erased. While a few unwanted items left on disks may not present a problem, a forgotten set of project management files held on a hard disk (possibly including a large network analysis exercise, drawing schedules and purchase schedules) is a needless waste of disk space. Any such files that are not required as part of an online database should be erased or transferred to some more suitable offline storage as part of the project closure procedure.

Bibliography

Andersen, E. S., Grude, K. V. and Haug, T. (1998), *Goal Directed Project Management: Effective Techniques and Strategies*, 2nd Edition (London: Kogan Page).

APM Earned Value Specific Interest Group (2002), *Earned Value Management: APM Guide for the UK* (High Wycombe: APM).

APM (2004), *Project Risk Analysis & Management (PRAM) Guide*, 2nd Edition (High Wycombe: Association for Project Management).

APM (2006), *APM Body of Knowledge*, 5th Edition (High Wycombe: Association for Project Management).

Backhouse, C. J. and Brookes, N. J. (eds) (1996), *Concurrent Engineering* (Aldershot: Gower); in association with The Design Council.

Baguley, P. (1999), *Project Management* (London: Teach Yourself Books).

Bartlett, J. (2000), *Managing Programmes of Business Change*, 3rd Edition (Hook, Hampshire: Project Manager Today).

Belbin, R. M. (2003), *Management Teams: Why They Succeed or Fail*, 2nd Edition (Oxford: Elsevier Butterworth-Heinemann).

Bradley, G. (2006), *Benefit Realisation Management: A Practical Guide to Achieving Benefits Through Change* (Aldershot: Gower).

Buchanan, D. A. and Huczyinski, A. (2003), *Organizational Behaviour: An Introductory Text*, 5th Edition (Hemel Hempstead: FT Prentice-Hall).

Burke, R. (1999), *Project Management: Planning and Control*, 3rd Edition (Chichester: Wiley).

Buttrick, R. (2005), *The Project Workout*, 3rd Edition (London: FT Prentice Hall).

Capon, C. and Didsbury, A. (2003), *Understanding Organisational Context: Inside and Outside Organisations*, 2nd Edition (London: Financial Times Management).

Carroll, T. (2006), *Project Delivery in Business-as-Usual Organizations* (Aldershot: Gower).

Chapman, C. B., Cooper, D. F. and Page, M. J. (1987), *Management for Engineers* (Chichester: Wiley).

Chapman, C. B. and Ward, S. A. (2002), *Project Risk Management: Processes, Techniques and Insights* (Chichester: Wiley).

Churchhouse, C. (1999), *Managing Projects: A Gower Workbook* (Aldershot: Gower).

Cleland, D. I. (ed.) (1998), *Field Guide to Project Management* (New York: Van Nostrand Reinhold).

Cleland, D. I., and King, W. R. (1998), *Project Management Handbook* (New York: Van Nostrand Reinhold).

Crosby, P. B. (1979), *Quality is Free: the Art of Making Quality Certain* (New York: McGraw-Hill).

Dayananda, D., Irons, R., Harrison, S., Herbohn, J. and Rowland, P. (2002), *Capital Budgeting: Financial Appraisal of Investment Projects* (Cambridge: Cambridge University Press).

Devaux, S. A. (1999), *Total Project Control: a Manager's Guide to Integrated Planning, Measuring and Tracking* (New York: Wiley).

Fleming, Q. W. and Koppelman, J .M. (2000), *Earned Value Project Management*, 2nd Edition (Newtown Square, PA, Project Management Institute).

Fowler, A. and Lock, D. (2006), *Accelerating Business and IT Change: Transforming Project Delivery* (Aldershot: Gower).

Frigenti, E. and Comninos, D. (2002), *The Practice of Project Management: A Guide to the Business-Focused Approach* (London: Kogan Page).

Gattorna, J. L. (ed.) (2003), *Gower Handbook of Supply Chain Management*, 5th Edition (Aldershot: Gower).

Goldsmith, L. (2005), *Project Management Accounting: Budgeting, Tracking, and Reporting Costs and Profitability* (Chichester: Wiley).

Gordon, J. and Lockyer, K. (2005), *Project Management and Project Planning*, 7th Edition (London: FT Prentice-Hall).

Gray, B., Gray, C. F. and Larson, E. W. (2005), *Project Management: the Managerial Process*, 3rd Edition (Singapore: McGraw-Hill).

Kor, R. and Wijnen, G. (2000), *50 Checklists for Project and Programme Managers* (Aldershot: Gower).

Hamilton, A. (1997), *Management by Projects* (London: Thomas Telford.

Harrison, F. and Lock, D. (2004), *Advanced Project Management: A Structured Approach*, 4th Edition (Aldershot: Gower).

Hartman, F. T. (2000), *Don't Park Your Brain Outside* (Newtown Square, PA: Project Management Institute).

Healey, P. L. (1997), *Project Management: Getting the Job Done on Time and in Budget* (Oxford: Butterworth-Heinemann).

Holroyd, T. (1999), *Site Management for Engineers* (London: Thomas Telford).

International Chamber of Commerce (2000), *Incoterms 2000*, ICC publication No 560 (Paris: ICC Publishing SA).

Juran, J. and Godfrey, A.B. (eds) (1999), *Juran's Quality Handbook*, 5th Edition (New York: McGraw-Hill).

Kerzner, H. (2000), *Applied Project Management: Best Practices on Implementation* (New York: Wiley).

Kerzner, H. (2006), *Project Management: A Systems Approach to Planning, Scheduling and Controlling*, 9th Edition (New York: Wiley).

Kliem, R. L. and Ludin, I. S. (1992), *The People Side of Project Management* (Gower: Aldershot).

Lester, A. (2006), *Project Planning and Control*, 5th Edition (Oxford: Butterworth-Heinemann).

Lewis, J. P. (2001), *Project Planning Scheduling and Control: a Hands-on Guide to Bringing Projects in on Time and on Budget* (New York: McGraw-Hill).

Lock, D. (ed.), (1993), *Handbook of Engineering Management*, 2nd Edition (Oxford: Butterworth-Heinemann).

Lock, D. (2004), *Project Management in Construction* (Aldershot: Gower).

Lock, D. (2007), *The Essentials of Project Management*, 3rd Edition (Aldershot: Gower).

Loftus, J. (ed.) (1999), *Project Management of Multiple Projects and Contracts* (London: Thomas Telford).

Mantel, S. J., Meredith, J. R., Shafer, S. M. and Sutton, M. M. (2001), *Project Management in Practice* (New York: Wiley).

Maylor, H. (2002), *Project Management*, 3rd Edition (London: Financial Times/Pitman).

Meredith, J. R. and Mantel, S. J. jnr (2003), *Project Management: a Managerial Approach*, 5th Edition (New York: Wiley).

Morris, P. (1994), *The Management of Projects* (London: Thomas Telford).

Nicholas, J. M. (2004), *Project Management for Business and Engineering*, 2nd Edition (Burlington, MA: Elsevier Butterworth-Heinemann).

Office of Government Commerce (2005), *Managing Successful Projects with PRINCE2* (London: OGC).

Olson, D. (2003), *Introduction to Project Management: A Systems Approach* (Maidenhead: McGraw-Hill).

O'Neill, J. J. (1989), *Management of Industrial Construction Projects* (Oxford: Heinemann Newnes).

PMI (2004), *A Guide to the Project Management Body of Knowledge (PMBOK® Guide)*, 3rd Edition (Newtown Square, PA: Project Management Institute).

Reiss, G. (1995), *Project Management Demystified: Today's Tools and Techniques*, 2nd Edition (London: Spon).

Reiss, G. (1996), *Programme Management Demystified: Managing Multiple Projects Successfully* (London: Spon).

Rosenau, M. D. jnr (2005), *Successful Project Management: a Step-by-Step Approach with Practical Examples*, 4th Edition (New York: Wiley).

Shtub, A. and Bard, J. F. (1994), *Project Management: Engineering, Technology and Implementation* (Englewood Cliffs: Prentice Hall).

Slack, N., Chambers, S. and Johnston, R. (2003), *Operations Management*, 4th Edition, (London: FT Prentice-Hall).

Stevens, M. (ed.) (2002), *Project Management Pathways* (High Wycombe: Association for Project Management).

Teale, D. (2001), *Project Risk Assessment* (London: Hodder & Stoughton).

Turner, J. R. (1998), *Handbook of Project-based Management: Improving the Process for Achieving Strategic Objectives*, 2nd Edition (Maidenhead: McGraw-Hill).

Turner, J. R. and Simister, S. J. (eds) (2000), *Gower Handbook of Project Management*, 3rd Edition (Aldershot: Gower).

Turner, J. R. (ed.) (2003), *Contracting for Project Management* (Aldershot: Gower).

Ward, G. (forthcoming), *Project Manager's Guide to Purchasing* (Aldershot: Gower).

Watson, M. (1998), *Managing Smaller Projects* (Hook, Hampshire: Project Manager Today).

Wearne, S. H. (1989), *Control of Engineering Projects* (London: Thomas Telford).

Webb, A. (2000), *Project Management for Successful Product Innovation* (Aldershot: Gower).

Webb, A. (2003), *The Project Manager's Guide to Handling Risk* (Aldershot: Gower).

Webb, A. (2003), *Using Earned Value: A Project Manager's Guide* (Aldershot: Gower).

Webster, G. (1999), *Managing Projects at Work* (Aldershot: Gower).

Woodward, J. F. (1997), *Construction Project Management: Getting it Right First Time* (London: Thomas Telford).

Wren, A. (2003), *The Project Management A-Z: A Compendium of Project Management Techniques and How to Use Them* (Aldershot: Gower).

Contents Comparison Between the Eighth and Ninth Editions

Previous Eighth Edition	Equivalent or Replacement in this Ninth Edition (Chapter)
1 The nature and purpose of project management	Introduction to project management (1)
Projects	Different types of projects (1)
The primary project objectives	Success or failure factors in relation to the initial project definition (2)
Balancing the primary objectives	The triangle of objectives and trade-offs between cost, performance and time (2)
Perceptions of project success or failure beyond the three primary objectives	Perceptions of project success or failure beyond the three primary objectives (2)
Customers, clients and end-users	Customers, contractors, clients and end-users (1)
Project life cycle	Project life cycles and life histories (1)
Associations representing the profession of project management	Organizations representing the profession of project management (1)
2 Project management organization	Project organization structures (9)
Effective organization and communications	Effective organization and communications (9)
The emergence of project management in a developing company	The emergence of project management in a developing company (9)
Project matrix organizations	Project matrix organizations (9)
Project teams and task forces	Project teams and task forces (9)
Organization of central administrative functions	Organization of central administrative functions (9)
Which type of organization is best?	Which type of project organization is best (9)
The project manager	The project manager (11)
Project services groups	Project support office (11)
Organizations with more than one project manager	Organizations with more than one project manager (9)
3 Defining the project	Defining the project task (3)
Projects which are difficult or impossible to define	Projects which are difficult or impossible to define (3)
Feasibility studies to improve early project definitions	Feasibility studies to improve early project definition (3)
Checklists	Checklists (3)
Defining a project for financial approval	Defining the project scope (3)
Customer enquiries	Enquiries and proposals for new projects (3)
The contractor's specification and questions of strategy	The contractor's strategy and design specification (3)
Specifications for product development projects	Specifications for internally funded projects (3)
Developing and documenting the project specification	Developing and documenting the project specification (3)
4 Cost estimates, Part 1: Definitions and principles	Estimating the project costs (4)
Cost definitions and principles	Introduction to cost estimating (4); Classification of costs as direct or indirect (4)
Estimating accuracy	Estimating accuracy (4)
Classification of estimates according to confidence	Classification of estimates according to confidence (4)
Estimating accuracy in relation to prices and profits	Estimating accuracy in relation to prices and profits (4)
Version control of project cost estimates	Version control of project cost estimates (4)
Work Breakdown Structure	Work Breakdown Structure (12)
Cost Coding Systems	Coding systems (12)
Benefits of a logical coding system	Benefits of a logical coding system (12)
Choosing a coding system	Choosing a coding system (12)
What happens when the customer says '... use my coding system!'?	What happens when the customer says '...use my coding system!'? (12)
5 Cost estimates, Part 2: Estimating in practice	Estimating the project costs (4)
Top-down or bottom-up?	Top-down or bottom-up? (4)
Compiling the task list	Compiling the task list (4)
Level of detail in project cost estimating	Level of detail in project cost estimating (4)
Estimating formats	Estimating formats (4)
Estimating manufacturing costs	Estimating manufacturing costs (4)
Collecting estimates for labour times	Estimating project labour costs (4)
Personal estimating characteristics	Personal estimating characteristics (4)
Estimates for material and equipment costs	Estimates for material and equipment costs (4)
Below-the-line costs	Introduction to cost estimating (4)
Reviewing the cost estimates	Reviewing the estimates (4)
6 Commercial management	Aspects of commercial management (22)
Project feasibility analysis	Project feasibility analysis (6)
Financial project appraisal	Introduction to project financial appraisal methods (6)
Sensitivity analysis	How much confidence can we place in the data (6)
Project funding	Project funding (6)
Contracts	Contracts (22)
Contract payment structures	Contract payment structures (22)
7 An introduction to planning and scheduling	First steps in planning the timescale (5)
The planning and scheduling environment	A general introduction to project planning (5)
Distinction between planning and scheduling	Distinction between planning and scheduling (5)
The planning time frame	A general introduction to project planning (5)
Matrix charts	Deleted
Simple tabular planning (timetables)	The museum project: a case example (5)
Bar charts (Gantt charts)	The museum project: a case example (5) Gantt charts: their advantages and limitations (14)
Line of balance charts (manufacturing projects)	Line of balance (18)
Line of balance charts (construction projects)	Line of balance charts in construction projects (29)
8 Network analysis: Logic diagrams and the critical path	Detailed planning: an introduction to critical path networks (14)
Background	Background to critical path network analysis (14)
The different network notation systems	The different network notation systems (14)
Critical path analysis using arrow diagrams	Critical path analysis using arrow diagrams (14)
Critical path analysis using precedence notation	Critical path analysis using precedence notation (14)

Previous Eighth Edition	*Equivalent or Replacement Section in this Ninth Edition (Chapter)*
Case study: furniture project	Case example: furniture project (14)
Case study: gantry project	Case example: the museum project (15)
PERT	PERT (29)
More complex network notation	More complex notation (14)
9 Network analysis in practice	Detailed planning: critical path networks in practice (15)
Developing network logic	Developing network logic (15)
Level of detail in network planning	Level of detail in network planning (15)
Interface events and activities	Interface events and activities (15)
Milestones	Miestones (15)
Estimating activity durations	Estimating task durations (15)
Is the timescale shown too long?	Is the predicted timescale too long (15)
A case for drawing networks from right to left	A case for drawing networks from right to left (15)
Network analysis as a management tool	Network analysis as a management tool (15)
10 Scheduling resources, Part 1: Principles	Principles of resource scheduling (16)
What are resources and which of them can be scheduled?	What are resources and which of them can be scheduled? (16)
The role of network analysis in resource scheduling	The role of network analysis in resource scheduling (16)
Case study: Garage project	A resource scheduling case example: the garage project (16)
Float	Float or slack (16)
Two fundamental priority rules for resource scheduling	Two fundamental priority rules for resource scheduling (16)
Summary: the elements of a practicable schedule	Summary: the elements of a practicable schedule (16)
11 Scheduling resources, Part 2: In practice	Now three chapters: Scheduling people (and other re-usable resources) (17); Scheduling materials (18) and Scheduling cash flows (19)
Choice of labour resources to be scheduled	Choosing which resources to schedule (17)
Choice of resource units	Choice of resource units (17)
Rate constant and non-rate constant use of resources	Rate constant and non-rate constant use of resources
Specifying resource availability levels	Specifying resource availability levels
Using different calendars for resource scheduling	Using different calendars for resource scheduling
Scheduling labour costs	Using project management software to schedule cash outflows (19)
Scheduling costs for materials and other purchases	Using project management software to schedule cash outflows (19)
Scheduling cash flow	Scheduling cash flows (19)
The seven steps or resource scheduling	The seven steps of resource scheduling (17)
Project scheduling in the corporate context	Project scheduling in the corporate context (28)
12 Project management computer systems, Part 1: Preparation	Computer applications (20)
Scheduling with or without a computer	Deleted
Facilities required	Deleted
System requirements	Deleted
Choosing a suitable computer program	Choosing a suitable computer program (20)
Special network logic requirements for computer applications	Deleted
Preparing for the first computer schedule	Preparing for the first computer schedule (20)
13 Project management computer systems: Part 2, Typical applications	Computer applications (20)
The welcoming screen	In Preparing for the first computer schedule (20)
Case study project	Case example: the garage project (20)
Data entry errors	Data entry errors (20)
Network plotting	Network plotting (20)
Time analysis of the garage project network	Time analysis of the garage project (20)
Resource scheduling: The general process	Resource scheduling for the garage project (20)
Resource scheduling for the garage project	Resource scheduling for the garage project (20)
Output reports	Standard and customized output reports (20)
Updating	Updating the schedules and reports (20)
14 Project management computer systems, Part 3: Specialized applications	More advanced or less frequently used techniques (29)
Dealing with large networks	Dealing with network plans for larger projects (29)
Multi-project resource scheduling	Multi-project resource scheduling (28)
Standard networks	Standard networks (29)
Templates (standard network modules)	Templates (standard network modules) (29)
Programs for probability and risk analysis	How much confidence can we place in the data? (6)
Software sources	Deleted
15 Scheduling parts for manufacturing projects	Scheduling materials (18)
Parts scheduling compared with project scheduling	Parts scheduling compared with project scheduling (18)
Identifying and quantifying common parts	Identifying and quantifying common parts for manufacturing projects (18)
Filing cabinet project	Case example: a filing cabinet project (18)
Line of balance	Line of balance (18)
Computer solutions	Computer solutions for scheduling materials (18)
16 Purchasing, Part 1: Principles and initial ordering	Managing procurement (23)
The importance of purchasing and materials control	Opening paragraph (23)
The purchasing cycle	The purchasing cycle (23)
The purchase order	Purchase orders (22)
Commercial conditions of purchase	Purchase orders (22)
Terms of trade used in international business (Incoterms 2000)	Terms of trade used in international business (Incoterms) (22)
Specifying the goods	Purchase specification: defining what has to be bought (23)
Timing of orders and deliveries	Special timing of orders and deliveries (23)
Purchase quantities	Purchase quantities (23)
17 Purchasing, Part 2: Post-order activities and wider aspects of materials control	Managing procurement (23)

Previous Eighth Edition	Equivalent or Replacement Section in this Ninth Edition (Chapter)
Purchase order amendments	Purchase order amendments (23)
Expediting	Expediting (23)
Shortages	'Management by' styles (24) Managing the quality and progress of bought-in materials and equipment (24)
The Pareto principle and stock management	Deleted
Project or stock purchasing?	Project or stock purchasing? (23)
Project purchasing as a condition of contract	Project or stock purchasing? (23)
Stores administration	Stores administration (23)
Materials management as a shared or common service	Materials management as a shared or common service (23)
18 Purchasing, Part 3: Procedures for capital projects	Managing procurement (23)
The purchasing organization	Roles in the purchasing organization for a large international project (23)
Purchase control schedules	Using purchase control schedules to schedule equipment for capital projects (18)
Purchase specifications	Purchase specification: defining what has to be bought (23)
Purchase enquiries	Supplier selection (23)
Bid evaluation	Supplier selection (23)
Purchase requisitions and orders	Purchase requisition and order (23)
Correlation between specification, enquiry and order numbers	Correlation between specification, enquiry and order numbers (23)
Assuring quality and progress	Managing the quality and progress of bought-in materials and equipment (24)
Vendors' documents	Vendors' documents (23)
Shipping, port and customs formalities	Freight forwarding agents Roles in the purchasing organization for a large international project (23)
Purchase order status reports	Managing the quality and progress of bought-in materials and equipment (24)
19 Managing project start-up	Project start-up (21)
Project authorization	Project authorization (8)
Authorizing work without a contract or customer's order	Authorizing work without a contract or customer's order (8)
Preliminary organization of the project	Preliminary organization of the project (21)
Correspondence and other documents	Correspondence and other documents (21)
Project engineering standards and procedures	Engineering standards and procedures (21)
Physical preparations and organization	Physical preparations and organization (21)
Getting work started	Getting work started (21)
Issuing detailed planning and work instructions	Issuing detailed planning and work instructions (21)
20 Managing progress	Managing progress (24)
Project progressing as a closed-loop control system	Progress management as a closed-loop control system (24)
Routine collection of progress data	Collecting progress information (24)
The non-routine approach to progressing	'Management by' styles (24) Statistical checks (24)
Managing subcontractors and agency employees	Managing subcontractors and agency employees (24)
Routine priority allocation in manufacturing projects	Routine priority allocation in manufacturing projects (24)
When the news is bad	When the news is bad (24)
Corrective measures	Corrective measures (24)
Immediate action orders	Immediate action orders (24)
Haste versus good management	Deleted
Construction site organization and management	Construction site organization and management (24)
Conduct of progress meetings	Project meetings (24)
Progress meetings	Project meetings (24)
Progress meetings abandoned	Project meetings (24)
Project progress reports	Progress reports (24)
21 Managing costs	Managing project costs (26)
Objectives of project cost management	Introductory paragraphs to Chapter 26
A checklist of cost management factors	Principles of cost control (26)
The total cost approach	The total cost approach (26)
Budgets	Setting and resetting cost budgets (26)
Cost-collection methods	Cost collection methods (26)
Audits	Audits and fraud prevention measures (26)
Comparing actual costs with planned costs	Comparing actual costs against planned costs (26)
22 Earned-value analysis	Earned-value analysis and cost reporting (27)
Milestone analysis	Milestone analysis (27)
Earned-value analysis	Earned-value analysis (27)
Earned-value analysis prediction reliability and implications	Earned-value analysis prediction reliability and implications (27)
Evaluating cost performance for materials and bought-out equipment	Evaluating cost performance for materials and bought-in equipment (27)
Effect of project changes on earned-value analysis	Effect of project changes on earned-value analysis (27)
The project ledger concept	The project ledger concept (27)
Predicting profitability for the whole project	Predicting profitability for the whole project (27)
Post mortem	Post mortem (27)
23 Managing project changes	Managing changes (25)
Classification of changes	Origin and classification of changes (25)
Authorization arrangements	Authorization arrangements (25)
General administration	General administration (25)
Estimating the true cost of a change	Estimating the true cost of a change (25)
Forms and procedures	Forms and procedures (25)
Version control for modified drawings and specifications	Version control for modified drawings and specifications (25)
Emergency modifications	Emergency modifications (25)

Previous Eighth Edition	Equivalent or Replacement Section in this Ninth Edition (Chapter)
24 Managing project risk	Risk (7)
Identifying and assessing risks	Identifying the possible risks (7)
Methods for dealing with risks	Methods for dealing with risks (7)
Insurance	Insurance (7)
Planning for a crisis	Planning for a crisis (7)
25 Managing project closure	Managing project closure (30)
Reasons for closing a project	Reasons for closing a project (30)
Formal project closure	Formal project closure (30)
Final project cost records	Final project cost records (30)
Disposal of surplus material stocks	Disposal of surplus material stocks (30)
Final project definition: the end of a continuous process	Final project definition: the end of a continuous process (30)
As-built condition of a manufacturing or capital engineering project	As-built condition of a manufacturing or capital engineering project (30)
As-built condition of a multiple manufacturing project	As-built condition of a multiple manufacturing project (30)
As-built condition of a project that is interrupted before completion	As-built condition of a project that is interrupted before completion (30)
Managing files and archives	Managing files and archives (30)

Index

ABC production priorities 412
Absorption costing 49, 71
Accurate estimators 67, 73
Achievement analysis *see* Earned value analysis
Action learning 160
Activity *see* Task
Activity lists *see* Task lists; Work-to lists
Activity-on-arrow (AoA) *see* Network analysis
Activity-on-node (AoN) *see* Network analysis
ACWP (actual cost of work performed)
        see Earned value analysis
ADM (arrow diagram) *see* Network analysis
After-issue work 69
Agency employees *see* Subcontractors
All Cars case example 411–14
Alternative resources 246–7
APM (Association for Project Management) 14
Archives *see* Document filing and archives
Artemis 285
As-built condition and records 29–30, 491, 495–9
    see also Document filing and archives;
        Project definition
Association for Project Management (APM) 14
Authorizing work without a customer's
        order 123–5

Balanced matrix 137
Ballpark estimates 52
Bar charts 3–4, 44, 78, 187, 233, 237–41, 468
Barnes, Dr Martin 21–2
Below-the-line costs 49–50, 437, 462
Benefits realization 18, 26–7
    different viewing platforms for the investor
        and the contractor 84–6
Best, enemy of the good 44
BCWP (budget cost of work performed)
        see Earned value analysis
BCWS (budget cost of work scheduled)
        see Earned value analysis
Bid evaluation (bid summary) 291, 358, 361–2

Brainstorming 218, 226, 228, 257, 327, 397, 480
Bridging contracts 339
Brick wall project (earned value example) 451–2
Brunel, Isambard Kingdom 2
Budgets and cost breakdowns 7–8, 17–20, 22–3,
        31, 33, 38–41, 49, 51–4, 56–8, 64, 66, 68,
        72–3, 75, 77
    breakdown 185–6
    currency units 438, 460
    labour 437
    purchases and subcontracts 60
    use of man-hours 437
    see also Below-the-line costs; Cash flow; Cost
        management; Earned value analysis
Build schedules 329, 419, 497–9
Business plan 10, 18, 27, 30, 36, 49, 71, 77–8,
        81, 95, 115, 117–19, 149–52

Calendar dates 203, 216, 233, 254, 264
Calendars (in planning and scheduling) 294–5,
        299
Case examples
    All Cars Ltd 411–14
    Bikes 'n Skates project 41–4
    boiler replacement project 87–91
    brick wall project 451–2
    Coverite plc office relocation 150–4
    filing cabinet project 261–71
    furniture project 199–203
    garage project 231–43, 299–306
    immediate action order 394–5
    IT management information services
        project 45–6
    Kozy-Kwik emergency modification 424–5
    lawnmower project 180–6
    luxury service apartments project 84–6
    medical trade exhibition project 226–7
    museum project 75–82, 218–26
    Street Components Ltd organization
        development 129–31

tollbridge project 91–2
tree project 191–3, 197–8
Case history of a project at closure 497
Cash flow and cash flow scheduling 17–24,
    86,88, 96, 214, 230, 275–83, 344, 365,
    429, 437, 470 473
    see also Discounted cash flow
Certification of project managers 14
Certification of payments 14
Changes and modifications 44, 69
    administration procedures 408, 414
    authorization 406–8
    change committee (change board) 44, 405–9,
        411, 414–15, 417, 426, 458
    classification 403–6
    contract variations 415–17
    coordinator 409
    decision criteria 407
    design freeze 415
    emergency modifications 424–5
    engineering change requests 417
    engineering query notes 420
    estimating the true cost 411–14
    interchangeability rule 422–3
    Kosy-Kwik case history 424–5
    numbering and registration 409–10
    relation to project life cycle 403
    progressing 411
    project variation orders 415–7
    resetting budgets 437
    stable design 415
    see also Concessions; Production permits;
        Purchase order amendments; Version
        control
Claims for payment and invoices 147, 275, 340,
    344, 396
Client *see* Customer
Closed loop control system 376
Closeout *see* Project closure
Coding and numbering systems
    benefits of logical system 173–4
    choosing a system 175–6
    code of accounts and cost accounting 450,
        455, 494
    functions of code 171
    heavy engineering example 174
    mining engineering example 175
    need for simplicity 176
    radiocommunications example 172–3
    use of customer's own system 176–7
    WBS coding 329, 373
Commissioning 461–2
Committed purchase costs 282–3, 438–40, 447
Common parts and materials collation 260
Communications 127, 132–3
Comparative cost estimates 52–3

Computers *see* Project Management Software;
    Scheduling by computer
Concessions or production permits 417–9
    see also Changes, Engineering change
        requests; Engineering queries;
Concurrent engineering and working 74–5,
    224, 435
Conduct of meetings 397–9
Configuration *see* As-built records
Construction site management 273, 387, 395
Construction specification 41
    see also Project specification
Contingencies 4, 31, 49, 53, 55, 61, 85, 112–13,
    217, 233, 339, 365, 404
Contract matrix 146, 159, 333
Contract variations *see* Project variations
Contractor, definition of 12
Contractor's strategy and design specification 39
    see also Project specification
Contracts
    bill of quantities 341, 343
    bridging 339
    capacity 332
    consideration 332
    cost-plus 45, 342, 434, 441–2, 499
    cost reimbursable 338, 340–43
    essential elements 331
    fixed or firm price 31, 340–3, 434, 442, 455–6
    guaranteed maximum price 342
    intention 331
    model forms 334
    offer and acceptance 332, 337
    payment structures and terms 340–4
    penalty clauses 24, 340, 413, 426
    reimbursable 338, 340–3
    reimbursable plus management fee 342
    schedule of rates 338, 342–3, 415
    scope 379, 403, 415, 440, 449
    standard conditions 334, 337
    target price 341–2
    terms describing the parties 332–3
    variations 41, 404, 409, 415–17, 436–7,
        459–62, 496
Corporate strategy 72–3, 400
Correction factors for estimates 67
Correspondence 51, 147, 318, 320–3, 496
    see also Document filing and archives
Cost accounting terms 49–51
Cost analysis *see* Budgets; Cost management;
    Earned value analysis
Cost and profit predictions *see* Earned value
    analysis
Cost budgets *see* Budgets
Cost coding *see* Coding and numbering
    systems
Cost collection *see* Cost management

Cost control *see* Budgets; Cash flow; Cost management
Cost curves *see* Cost/time graphs
Cost cut-off at project closure 492
Cost definitions 49–51
Cost escalation 49, 437
Cost estimates 49–69
    accuracy 51–2
    accuracy relative to prices and profits 53–4
    after-issue work 69
    ballpark 52
    below-the-line allowances 49–50
    bottom-up 55
    checklists 56
    comparative 52–3
    contingency allowances 49, 53, 55, 61
    correction factors 67
    definitive 53
    escalation 49
    feasibility 53
    forgotten tasks 56–7
    formats and forms 57–61
    labour costs 53–6
    level of detail 57
    manufacturing costs (with drawings) 61
    manufacturing costs (without drawings) 62–3
    materials and equipment 60, 67–8
    personal estimating characteristics 66–7
    provisional sums 31
    reviewing 68–9
    software tasks 56
    top-down 55
    version control 54–5
Cost management
    audits 433, 441–3
    below-the-line allowances 49–50, 437, 462
    checklist of factors 436
    committed costs for purchases 282–3, 438–40, 447
    comparing actual costs against planned costs 443, 445–50
    cost breakdown structure 185–6
    cost cut-off at project closure 492
    credit control 96, 344, 436
    currency units 438
    dayworks sheets 436, 442, 492
    incidental expenses 57, 411, 436, 440, 442
    timesheets 442, 453, 464, 492, 494
    total cost approach 434–6
    see also Budgets; Cash flow; Cost definitions; Earned value analysis; Purchasing; Subcontractors
Cost objective 19–20, 433–4, 456
Cost of sales 49
Cost penalties 24, 340, 413, 426

Cost performance index (CPI) *see* Earned value analysis
Cost-plus contracts 45, 342, 434, 441–2, 499
Cost/time graphs (S-curves) 33, 460–2
Cost/time optimization 221, 223
Cost variance 54, 452
Costs of financing 23
    see also Funding
CPA (Critical path analysis) *see* Network analysis
CPI (cost performance index) *see* Earned value analysis
CPM (Critical path method) *see* Network analysis
Crashing (time) 75, 221–6, 394–5, 413
    see also Fast-tracking
Credit control 96, 344, 436
    see also Cash flow
Creeping improvement sickness (scope creep) 41
Crisis planning and management 112–13
Critical path analysis *see* Network analysis
Customer, definition of 12
Customer enquiries 36
    screening and action plan 34, 36–8, 52
Customers' changes *see* Changes
Customers' numbering systems 176
Customer's project specification 37
    see also Project specification
Customer training 6, 39, 57
Customs formalities 321–2, 361, 440
Cybernetic control 376, 378

Dangles 305
Data errors 305–6
Dayworks 436, 442, 492
Defining the project *see* Project definition
Definitive cost estimates 53
Deltek Open Plan™ 285, 292, 305–6, 380, 468
Design achievement analysis *see* Earned value analysis
Design authority 406, 417, 421
Design calculations 106, 496
Design freeze 415
Design specification 39, 62, 66, 414
    see also Project specification
Detailed planning *see* Network analysis
Devaux, Stephen 165, 205
Diary planning method 77–8
Direct costs 49, 430–31
Discounted cash flow *see* Financial appraisal
Discount factors 89–92
Document distribution 320, 323
Document filing and archives 52, 63, 121, 500–1
Document transmittal letters 322
Documentation *see* As-built records; Correspondence; Document filing and archives: Project definition

Drawing numbers 120, 322–3, 329, 422–3, 496
Drawing schedules 329, 379, 495, 498, 501
Drawing sheets 323, 495
Dun and Bradstreet 344
Du Pont 3

Earned value analysis (EVA) 445–64
    actual cost of work performed (ACWP) 451,
      453, 464
    brick wall project 451–2
    budget cost of work performed (BCWP)
      451–4, 463
    budget cost of work scheduled (BCWS) 451–2
    cost performance index (CPI) 451–3, 459, 464
    effect of changes 458–9
    schedule performance index (SPI) 451–2
ECGD (Export Credits Guarantee Department)
    111, 147
Eighty-house construction project 477
Emergency changes (modifications) 424–7
End user, definition of 12–13
Engineering change requests 417
Engineering query notes 420–21, 469
Engineering standards and procedures 47, 322
Estimates *see* Cost estimates
Estimators' personal characteristics 66–7
European public procurement directives 77, 359
Eurotunnel 5, 98
Exception reports 378
Expediting *see* Purchasing
Expenditure versus achievement *see* Earned
    value analysis
Export Credits Guarantee Department (ECGD)
    111, 147

Failure mode and effect analysis (FMEA) 101–2
Failure mode effect criticality analysis (FMECA)
    103–4
Fast-tracking 221, 224
Fault-tree risk analysis 100–1
Feasibility analysis and studies 31–2, 83–4
Feasibility cost estimates 53
Filing cabinet case example 261–71
Financial appraisal 83–96
    confidence or uncertainty in the data 92–5
    discount factors and rates 89
    discounted cash flow 89–93
    introduction to methods 86–7
Monte Carlo analysis 93–4
    net present value (NPV) 89–93, 117
    rate of return on investment 90–1
    relevance to the investor 86
    sensitivity analysis 93
    simple payback 87–8
    tollbridge project 91–2

Financial viability of organizations 96, 344
Financing costs 23
Fiscal measures 87
Fixed costs 49, 430–33
Fixed price contracts 31, 340–43, 434, 442, 455–6
Five-house construction project 475–6
Float
    free 242–3
    independent 242–3
    negative 244, 296, 388, 391
    total 244, 308, 310, 391
    remaining 240, 244, 298, 310, 388, 401, 471
FMEA (Failure mode and effect analysis) 101–2
FMECA (Failure mode effect criticality analysis)
    103–4
Ford, Henry 3
Foreign currencies and exchange rates 52, 111,
    437
Free float 242–3, 308, 390–1
Freight forwarding agents 213, 345, 348, 386
Functional matrix 134–6, 140
Funding 95–6
Furniture project 199–203

Gantt charts *see* Bar charts
Gantt, Henry 3, 187
Garage project case example 231–43, 299–306
General and administrative costs 49
Goes-into chart *see* Work breakdown structure
Guaranteed maximum price contracts 342

Haydn's *Farewell Symphony* 142
Health and Safety at Work Act (1974) 109
Holidays 50, 69, 203, 216, 218, 233, 253, 255–6,
    294, 296, 366, 387, 441
Hybrid organization 144–5

ICC (International Chamber of Commerce)
    337–8
IJ networks *see* Network analysis (arrow
    diagrams)
Immediate action orders 392–4
Inconsistent estimators 67
Incoterms 337–8
Independent float 242–3
Indirect costs (overheads) 23, 49–51, 249, 282,
    430–3, 437
In-house projects *see* Management change and
    IT projects
Inspecting authority 406, 419
Inspection and expediting 384–6
Inspection certificates 109, 496
Inspection reports 420–3, 496
Insurance 107–12
    accident and sickness 110–11

contractors' all risks 110
contractual requirements 109–10
decennial (latent defects) 110
export credit 111
key person 111
legal liabilities 109–10
obligatory 108–11
pecuniary 111
professional liability 110
statutory requirements 108–10
Integrated engineering see Concurrent
    engineering
Interchangeability rule 422–3
Interface activities and events 215
International Project Management Association
    (IPMA) 13–14
International Chamber of Commerce (ICC) 337–8
Invitation to tender (ITT) 213, 353, 357–8
Invoices see Claims for payment
Ishikawa fishbone 100–1
ISO 9000 series quality standard 20
Isochron Limited 27, 34–6, 94
Joint venture 6, 96, 106, 147, 473
Just-in-time (JIT) 364–5, 368, 370

K&H Project Systems 285
Kick-off meeting 42, 45, 325, 397, 401
Kosy-Kwik case history 424–5

Labour burden (cost) 50
Labour costs 50–51, 59, 63–4, 185, 281, 301,
    430–3, 462, 479
Ladder activities 205
Lawnmower project 180–86
Library modules and networks see Templates
Line and function organization 128, 131–2,
    150, 180
Linear responsibility matrix 318–9, 323
Line of balance
    in construction projects 475–7
    in manufacturing projects 261–71
Linked bar charts 291
Logic diagram see Network analysis
Loop error detection 304–5

Main contractor 331–2, 357–8, 387–9, 395–6, 402
Management by exception 51, 269, 378
Management by objectives 377
Management by surprise 378
Management by the seat of the pants 377
Management by walking about 157, 377
Management change and IT projects 333, 434,
    465–6
    authorization 117–20
    special characteristics 6–7, 149–54

Management communications
    see Communications
Management contractor see Main contractor
Management pressure (unreasonable) 73, 471
Management support 136, 158
Managing changes see Changes
Managing contractor 145–6, 332, 347, 434
Managing costs see Cost management
Managing progress see Progress management
Managing risk see Risk management
Manufacturing projects 6, 403, 438–9, 475, 495,
    497–8
Manufacturing Requirements Planning (MRPII)
    260, 272, 475
Marked-up drawings 424, 426
Master record index see Build schedules
Materials burden (cost) 50
Materials costs 60, 68, 174, 281, 299, 439–40,
    457, 482
Materials management see Purchasing;
    Scheduling parts and materials for
    manufacturing projects; Shortages; Stores
    administration; Surplus materials
Mayo, Elton 3
Meetings administration 397–99
Microsoft Project 306, 308–9, 311, 314, 473
Milestones 7, 10, 24, 27, 44, 115–16, 212–13,
    215–16, 277, 283, 294, 313, 445–50, 457,
    470, 489
Mining and quarrying 8
Minutes of meetings 398–400, 497
Model conditions of contract 334
Modifications see Changes
Modular networks see Templates
Monte Carlo simulation 93–5, 100, 480
Motivation 18–19, 22, 31, 84, 86, 127, 136–7,
    140, 142, 156, 158, 162, 229, 325, 328,
    374, 377, 386, 391–2, 451, 435–6, 456
MPM (method of potentials) 189
MRPII (manufacturing requirements planning)
    294, 260, 272, 475
Multi-project resource scheduling 390, 435,
    467–73
Museum project case example 75–81, 218–26

Negative float 244, 296, 388, 391
Net present value (NPV) 89–93, 117
Network analysis
    activity-on-arrow (AoA) 190–5
    activity-on-node (AoN) 196–9
    arrow diagram (ADM) 190–5
    as a management tool 227
    background and origins 188
    brainstorming 209–11
    choice of notation system 189–90

complex constraints 203–7
crash actions 75, 221–6, 394–5, 413
critical path 194
different notation systems 188–90
duration estimates 216–17
duration units 216
errors in logic 305
furniture project 199–203
interfaces 215
large networks 214–15
level of detail 212–14
milestones 215–16
museum project 218–26
precedence diagrams (PDM) 196–9
presentation of times on arrow networks 194–5
time analysis 193–4, 198–9
see also Fast-tracking, Float; Optimized time/cost crash action, Scheduling by computer; Templates
Not invented here 39
Numbering and coding systems see Coding and numbering systems

Objectives see Project objectives
OBS see Organization breakdown structure
Offer and acceptance (contracts) 332, 337
Optimistic estimators 66
Optimized time/cost crash action 221, 223–4
Organigram 318
Organization
   balanced matrix 137
   best choice 140–42
   central administration functions 139
   charts (organigrams) 127–9, 318
   construction site 133
   contract matrix 145–7
   coordination matrix 133–4, 162, 180
   different matrix strengths 135–7
   functional matrix 133–5
   hybrid 144–5
   joint venture 147
   management change and IT projects 150–3
   more than one project manager 144–8
   overlay matrix 137
   project matrix 137
   project services groups (project support office) 321–2, 327, 329, 380, 382, 409, 466, 469–70
   purchasing and supply chain 145–6, 345–6
   secondment matrix 137
   Street Components Ltd case example 129–31
   strong matrix 137
   task force 138–9, 152–3
   team 137–9, 141–2, 456
   weak matrix 136
   see also Communications
Organization breakdown structure (OBS) 180–6, 329, 377, 401, 437, 468
Organization charts 127–9, 318
Outsourcing see Purchasing; Subcontractors
Overhead costs see Indirect costs
Overhead rate 50–51, 56, 432–3
Overhead recovery 432–3
Overlapping activities (tasks) 189, 196–7, 203–5, 221, 224, 391
Overlay matrix 137
Overtime 64, 110, 130, 217, 221, 233, 254, 281, 297, 388, 391–2, 431

Parkinson's Law 75
Payback 86–90, 92
Payment structures see Contracts
PDM (precedence diagram) 196–9
Penalty clauses 24, 340, 413, 426
Performance objective 20
PERT (Program Evaluation and Review Technique) 478–9
Pessimistic estimators 66–7
Planning
   agreement and commitment 327
   as different from scheduling 81
   bottom-up 74, 79
   corporate strategy 73
   diary method 77–8, 80, 247
   first steps 71–81
   for a crisis 112–13
   how-not-to case example 247
   target-led 74–5
   time frame 74–5
   top-down 74–5
   see also Bar charts; Network analysis; Resource scheduling; Scheduling by computer
Planning environment 72
PMI (Project Management Institute) 14–15
Pre-allocation of materials 369, 371
Precedence networks (PDM) 196–9
Primavera 285, 306, 308, 311–14
Prime cost 51
Prince 2™ 140, 154, 384
Priority (objectives) 21
Priority (risk management) 101–4
Priority (work schedules) 73, 118, 136–7, 153, 188–9, 194, 231, 244–6, 298–9, 310–11, 388–90, 382–5, 467–8, 470–1
Probability analysis see Monte Carlo analysis; PERT
Procedures manual 323
Product development specification 44

Production method definition and specification 40–1

Production permits 417–19

Professional liability insurance 110

Programme support office *see* Project support office

Progress management
closed loop control system 376
construction site 395–6
corrective measures 391–2
collection of progress data 380–3
exception reports 378
expediting purchases 384–6, 391, 493
immediate action orders 392–5
'management-by' styles 376–8
meetings 153, 396–401
statistical checks 383
updating schedules 379–80
when the news is bad 390–1
see also Earned value analysis; Motivation; Priority (work schedules); Subcontractors

Progress payments 84–6, 96, 160, 216, 277–8, 283, 343, 384,396, 436, 455

Progress reports 380, 382, 401–2, 453, 462

Project appraisal *see* Financial appraisal

Project authorization
authorization without a contract or order 123–5
charter and contract 118–19
criteria for the project owner or investor 116–18
internal authorization document 118–20
management and IT projects 117–20
minor works 116–17
purpose of 115–16

Project categories or classification 5–7

Project closure
closure document 492–3
cost cut-off 492
disposal of surplus material 494
final cost records 494
formal notice 492–3
post-project expenditure 492
project diary 491
reasons for closure 491
see also As-built records; Document filing and archives; Project definition

Project communications 127, 132–3

Project control *see* Cost management; Progress management

Project definition 10, 17–19, 29–48, 52, 55–7
see also As-built records; Feasibility studies; Project scope; Project specification

Project diary 497

Project engineer 159–60

Project engineering standards and procedures 47, 322

Project enquiries 34–7

Project feasibility *see* Feasibility analysis and studies

Project funding
contractor's viewpoint 96
owner's (investor's) viewpoint 95–6

Project ledger concept 459
see also Earned value analysis

Project life cycle and life history 7–12

Project management history 1–5

Project management associations 13–15

Project management software
choosing 285–91
checklist 288–9
see also Artemis; Microsoft Project; Deltek Open Plan™; Primavera; 4c

Project manager
certification 14
current awareness 157
need for 132–3
perceptiveness 157
personality 156
role in the organization 156
seniority and status 156
support for 158–9
training 158–9
women 159

Project Management Institute (PMI) 14–15

Project managers in customer/supplier chains 145–6

Project numbers 171, 294, 329, 353, 469, 492

Project objectives 7, 21, 29–30, 37, 156, 317

Project organization *see* Organization

Project proposals 34–7

Project or stock purchasing? 368–9

Project procedures manual 323

Project registration 120–21, 161–2

Project scheduling *see* Resource scheduling

Project scope 17, 31, 37–9, 54–5

Project specification
construction 41
contractor's 39
customer's 37
developing and documenting 46–7
internally funded projects 41–6
product development 43–4
see also Project definition

Project strategy 17, 19, 83–4, 218

Project support office 321–2, 327, 329, 380, 382, 409, 466–70

Project variation orders 415–17

Project war room 137

Projects difficult to define 29–31

Provisional cost items (provisional sums) 31–49

Purchase control schedules 272
Purchase enquiries (invitations to tender or ITT) 213, 353, 357–8
Purchase order amendments 42, 367, 404
Purchase orders 42, 53, 67–8, 121, 132, 146, 213–14, 251–2, 260, 266, 276, 331, 334–7, 345, 353, 355, 364–9, 372–3, 384
Purchase requisitions 357, 361, 363, 368, 443
Purchase schedules *see* Purchase control schedules
Purchase specifications 357, 361, 364, 369, 372, 379, 496
Purchasing
   agents 368–9, 378, 384, 386
   bid summary and choice of supplier 291, 358, 361–2
   call-off quantities 365
   committed costs 438–40, 447, 457, 464, 492
   cycle 345–6, 348
   discounts 365–6, 368
   early ordering of long–lead items 204–5, 383
   expediting 384–6, 391, 493
   inspection and expediting visits 384–6
   intervention by the project manager 386
   just-in-time (JIT) 364–5, 368, 370
   letter of intent 121, 364
   level of detail in networks 214
   organization 346
   quantity discounts 365–6, 368
   sealed bids 361
   shipping formalities 348–9
   shortages 23, 217, 269, 272, 365, 372
   small quantities 366
   supplier selection 291, 358, 361–2
   terms of trade in international business (Incoterms) 337–8
   vendors' documents 372–3
   see also Incoterms; Materials; Materials management; Project or stock purchasing; Purchase orders
Pure project team *see* Project team

Quality
   as a performance objective 20–23
   construction 395–6
   ISO 9000 20
   purchased equipment 369, 383–4
   subcontractors 388–9
Quality/cost relationship 22–3
Quantity discounts 365–6, 368

Remaining float 240, 244, 298, 310, 388, 401, 471
Research projects 7, 30–31
Resource allocation *see* Resource scheduling
Resource scheduling
   alternative resources 246–7

definition of resources 229–31
elements of a practical schedule 247–8
how not to schedule 247
influence of float 240–44
priority rules 245–7
resource aggregation 233, 308
resource-limited 310–14
role of network analysis 231
seven steps 279, 474
shiftworking 296
splittable activities 301
time-limited 238, 241, 245–7, 310–11
weekend working 294, 296, 299, 391, 401, 472
   see also Garage project case example; Float; Multi-project resource scheduling; Resources; Scheduling by computer; Scheduling costs
Resources
   alternative 246–7
   availability levels 231–2, 246–7, 252–6, 281, 294, 296–8, 387, 467, 469
   exhaustible 230
   rate-constant 252–3, 297–8, 301
   replenishable 230
   reusable 230–31
   threshold 297
   see also Resource scheduling; Scheduling by computer
Responsibility matrix 318–9, 323
Return on investment 17, 85, 89–91, 100, 115, 117, 377
Reviewing cost estimates 68–9
Risk (and uncertainty) management 99–113
   classification matrices 101–4
   contingency planning 112–13
   fault trees 100–4
   identifying and assessing risk 100–4
   insurance 107–12
   introduction 99
   methods for dealing with risk 105–13
   Monte Carlo analysis and PERT 93–5, 100, 478–80
   qualitative analysis 100–3
   quantitative analysis 103–4
   register or log 104–5
   sensitivity analysis 93
   tabletop exercises 113
Rolling wave planning 477–8
Roy method 189

Sales enquiries *see* Customer enquiries
Schedule performance index (SPI) *see* Earned value analysis
Scheduling, as different from planning 81

Scheduling by computer
   Artemis 285
   choosing software 285–91
   data errors 303–6
   Deltek Open Plan™ 285, 292, 305–6, 380, 468
   garage project case example 299–306
   getting started 292–9
   Microsoft Project 306, 308–9, 311, 314, 473
   Monte Carlo analysis 93–5, 100, 480
   network plotting 306
   multi-project scheduling 390, 435, 467–73
   Primavera 285, 306, 308, 311–14
   priority rules 310–11
   reports 313–6
   resource data 297–8
   software checklist 288–9
   special calendars 294–6
   special network logic requirements 291–2
   task (activity) data 298–9
   time-now date 79, 382, 472
   what-if? modelling and testing 468, 470, 472–3
   4c software 484–5, 489–99
   see also Cash flow; Float; Network analysis, Project management software; Resource scheduling; Work-to lists
Scheduling cash flow 275–83
Scheduling parts and materials for manufacturing projects *see* Filing cabinet project case example; Manufacturing requirements planning (MRPII)
Scheduling resources *see* Resource scheduling; Scheduling by computer
Scientific research projects 7, 30–1
Scope creep *see* Creeping improvement sickness
Sealed bids 361
Secondment matrix 137
Sensitivity analysis 93
Seven steps of project scheduling 279, 474
Shiftworking 296
Shipping formalities 337–8, 345, 348, 369
Shortage lists 378
Simple payback 86–92
Simultaneous engineering 435
Site organization 133
Slack *see* Float
Software *see* Project management software
Software tasks 56, 131
Solution engineering 47
SPI (schedule performance index) *see* Earned value anlaysis
Stable design (design freeze) 415
Stage-gate control 7, 30, 107
Stage payments *see* Progress payments
Stakeholders 1, 9, 17–18, 24–7, 115–25
Stakeholders matrix 26

Standard conditions of purchase 334–7
Standard costing 51, 59, 63–4, 173, 368, 439, 494
Standard networks 325–6, 480–5
Standard sub-network modules *see* Templates
Starting work without a contract or customer's order 123–5
Stock pre-allocation 369, 371
Stock records 371–2
Street Components Limited organization case example 129–31
Strong matrix 137
Subcontractors 19, 24, 109, 116, 130, 144–6
Success or failure factors 17–27
Surplus materials 366,440, 458, 494

Target-led planning 74–5
Task force 137–9, 149, 152–4
Task lists 55–8 , 74, 77, 165, 200, 236, 380, 458–60
   see also Work-to lists
Taylor, Frederick Winslow 3
Team organization 137–9, 141–2, 456
Telford, Thomas 2
Templates (standard network modules) 215, 327, 480–90
Temporary staff *see* Subcontractors
Terms of trade in international business (Incoterms) 337–8
Threshold resources 297
Time is money 23, 43, 74
Time/cost optimization 221, 223
Time/cost relationship 23–4
Time-limited resource scheduling *see* Resource Scheduling
Time-now date 79, 382, 472
Time objective 20–21
Timesheets 388, 440–2, 453, 464, 492, 494
Tollbridge project case example 91–2
Total cost approach 434–6
Total quality management (TWM) 20, 22
Total float 244, 308, 310, 391
Traceability 369, 409
Training
   of customers' personnel 6, 39, 57
   of in-house staff 106, 139, 154, 162, 210, 228, 255, 275–6, 292, 338, 380, 387, 389, 491
   of the project manager 158–9
Tree project 191–3, 197–8
Triangle of objectives 21–2
Turnkey operation 39, 333–5

Unreasonable management pressure 73, 471

Variable costs 49–50, 430–1
Variances 51, 54, 378, 452–3, 463–4
Vendors' documents 372–3

Version control 54–5, 379, 422

War room 137
WBS *see* Work breakdown structure
Weak matrix 136–7, 143, 158
Weekend working 221, 255, 294–6
What-if? modelling and testing 468, 470, 472–3
Work breakdown structure (WBS) 57–9, 165–170
    charity project 166–7
    mining project 167–8
    railway project 168–9
    wedding project 169–70
    see also Coding and numbering systems
Working without an order 123–5
Works order 122
Work-to lists 121, 247, 250–1, 255, 273, 275, 281, 285, 313–14, 318, 325–8, 380–2, 401, 431, 473
Wren, Sir Christopher 2

4c software 484–5, 489–99

Project Management
Ninth Edition

Dennis Lock

Is available as a *Student's Edition* in paperback (978-0-566-08772-1) and as a *Tutor's Edition* in hardback with CD ROM (978-0-566-08769-1)

In addition to the text, the *Tutor's Edition* includes a CD ROM containing 25 PowerPoint presentations (over 650 slides with animation and sound) that are designed to help support lecturers and presenters who are using the book to teach or train project management techniques.

See overleaf for contents of the CD ROM.

For further information on *Project Management, Tutor's Edition* visit our online catalogue:

www.gowerpub.com/online.htm

All online orders receive a discount

GOWER

Contents of CD ROM
for *Project Management, Tutor's Edition*

Presentation	Book Chapter	Title	Number of Slides
1	1	Introduction to Project Management	32
2	2	Factors for Project Success or Failure	23
3	3	Defining the Project Task	31
4	4	Costing Estimating and Budgeting	34
5	5	First Steps in Timescale Planning	34
6	6	Financial Appraisal	29
7	7	Managing Project Risk	36
8a	9	Project Organization Part 1: Organigrams and Matrix Structures	30
8b	9, 10 and 11	Project Organization Part 2: Project Teams and the Project Manager	24
8c	9	Project Organization Part 3: Contract Matrix Organizations	16
9	12 and 13	Work Breakdown Structure and Coding	39
10a	14 and 15	Critical Path Methods Part 1: Introduction and Arrow Diagrams	28
10b	14 and 15	Critical Path Methods Part 2: Precedence Diagrams	32
11a	16, 17 and 18	Scheduling Resources for a Single Project	28
11b	28	Multi-Project Resource Scheduling	25
12	19	Scheduling Cash Flows	17
13	8, 21 and 24	Project Start-up and Progressing	48
14	22	Aspects of Commercial Management	17
15	23	Procurement and the Supply Chain	24
16	25	Managing Project Changes	17
17	26 and 27	Managing Project Costs	42
18	28	Managing Project Portfolios and Programmes	16
19	29	More Advanced (or Less Frequently Used) Techniques	34
20	30	Managing Project Closure	10

GOWER